TCP/IP Tutorial and Technical Overview

7th Edition

ADOLFO RODRIGUEZ ■ **JOHN GATRELL**
JOHN KARAS ■ **ROLAND PESCHKE**

PRENTICE HALL PTR
UPPER SADDLE RIVER, NEW JERSEY 07458
www.phptr.com

ISBN 0-13-067610-1

90000

9 790130 676107

Comments may be addressed to:

IBM Corporation, International Technical Support Organization
Dept. HZ8 Building 678
P.O. Box 12195
Research Triangle Park, NC 27709-2195

When you send information to IBM, you grant IBM a non-exclusive right to use or distribute the information in any way it believes appropriate without incurring any obligation to you.

Published by Prentice Hall PTR
Prentice-Hall, Inc.
Upper Saddle River, NJ 07458

Prentice Hall books are widely used by corporations and government agencies for training, marketing, and resale.
The publisher offers discounts on this book when ordered in bulk quantities. For more information, contact Corporate Sales Department, Phone 800-382-3419; FAX: 201-236-7141;
E-mail (Internet): corpsales@prenhall.com
Or write: Prentice Hall PTR, Corporate Sales Department, One Lake Street, Upper Saddle River, NJ 07458.

> **Take Note!**
> Before using this information and the product it supports, be sure to read the general information in Appendix B, "Special Notices," on page 913.

Printed in the United States of America
10 9 8 7 6 5 4 3 2 1

ISBN   0-13-067610-1

Pearson Education LTD.
Pearson Education Australia PTY, Limited
Pearson Education Singapore, Pte. Ltd.
Pearson Education North Asia Ltd.
Pearson Education Canada, Ltd.
Pearson Educación de Mexico, S.A. de C.V.
Pearson Education—Japan
Pearson Education Malaysia, Pte. Ltd.

Contents

Preface xix
The team that wrote this redbook xix
Comments welcome xxi

Part 1. Core TCP/IP protocols 1

Chapter 1. Architecture, history, standards, and trends 3
1.1 TCP/IP architectural model 3
    1.1.1 Internetworking 3
    1.1.2 The TCP/IP protocol layers 5
    1.1.3 TCP/IP applications 8
    1.1.4 Bridges, routers, and gateways 10
1.2 The roots of the Internet 11
    1.2.1 ARPANET 13
    1.2.2 NSFNET 14
    1.2.3 Commercial use of the Internet 16
    1.2.4 Internet2 17
    1.2.5 The Open Systems Interconnection (OSI) Reference Model 19
1.3 TCP/IP standards 21
    1.3.1 Request For Comments (RFC) 22
    1.3.2 Internet standards 24
1.4 Future of the Internet 26
    1.4.1 Multimedia applications 26
    1.4.2 Commercial use 26
    1.4.3 The wireless Internet 27

Chapter 2. Network interfaces 29
2.1 Ethernet and IEEE 802.x Local Area Networks (LANs) 29
2.2 Fiber Distributed Data Interface (FDDI) 32
2.3 Serial Line IP (SLIP) 33
2.4 Point-to-Point Protocol (PPP) 34
    2.4.1 Point-to-Point encapsulation 35
2.5 Integrated Services Digital Network (ISDN) 36
2.6 X.25 38
2.7 Frame relay 40
    2.7.1 Frame format 40
    2.7.2 Interconnect issues 41
    2.7.3 Data link layer parameter negotiation 41
    2.7.4 IP over frame relay 42
2.8 PPP over SONET and SDH circuits 43

2.8.1 Physical layer 43
2.9 Multi-Path Channel+ (MPC+) 44
2.10 Asynchronous Transfer Mode (ATM) 44
   2.10.1 Address resolution (ATMARP and InATMARP) 45
   2.10.2 Classical IP over ATM 48
   2.10.3 ATM LAN emulation 54
   2.10.4 Classical IP over ATM versus LAN emulation 57
2.11 Multiprotocol over ATM (MPOA) 58
   2.11.1 Benefits of MPOA 58
   2.11.2 MPOA logical components 59
   2.11.3 MPOA functional components 59
   2.11.4 MPOA operation 62
2.12 References 63

Chapter 3. Internetworking protocols 65
3.1 Internet Protocol (IP) 65
   3.1.1 IP addressing 65
   3.1.2 IP subnets 69
   3.1.3 IP routing 74
   3.1.4 Methods of delivery - unicast, broadcast, multicast, and anycast 80
   3.1.5 The IP address exhaustion problem 83
   3.1.6 Intranets - private IP addresses 86
   3.1.7 Classless Inter-Domain Routing (CIDR) 86
   3.1.8 IP datagram 90
3.2 Internet Control Message Protocol (ICMP) 102
   3.2.1 ICMP messages 103
   3.2.2 ICMP applications 112
3.3 Internet Group Management Protocol (IGMP) 113
3.4 Address Resolution Protocol (ARP) 114
   3.4.1 ARP overview 114
   3.4.2 ARP detailed concept 115
   3.4.3 ARP and subnets 118
   3.4.4 Proxy-ARP or transparent subnetting 118
3.5 Reverse Address Resolution Protocol (RARP) 120
   3.5.1 RARP concept 120
3.6 Bootstrap protocol (BOOTP) 121
   3.6.1 BOOTP forwarding 125
   3.6.2 BOOTP considerations 126
3.7 Dynamic Host Configuration Protocol (DHCP) 126
   3.7.1 The DHCP message format 127
   3.7.2 DHCP message types 129
   3.7.3 Allocating a new network address 130
   3.7.4 DHCP lease renewal process 133

3.7.5 Reusing a previously allocated network address. 134
3.7.6 Configuration parameters repository. 135
3.7.7 DHCP considerations 135
3.7.8 BOOTP and DHCP interoperability 136

Chapter 4. Routing protocols 137
4.1 Autonomous systems 138
4.2 Types of IP routing and IP routing algorithms. 140
4.2.1 Static routing 140
4.2.2 Distance vector routing. 142
4.2.3 Link state routing 143
4.2.4 Hybrid routing. 144
4.3 Routing Information Protocol (RIP). 145
4.3.1 RIP packet types 145
4.3.2 RIP packet format. 146
4.3.3 RIP modes of operation 146
4.3.4 Calculating distance vectors. 147
4.3.5 Convergence and counting to infinity 148
4.3.6 RIP limitations 152
4.4 Routing Information Protocol Version 2 (RIP-2) 152
4.4.1 RIP-2 packet format 153
4.4.2 RIP-2 limitations 155
4.5 RIPng for IPv6 155
4.5.1 Differences between RIPng and RIP-2 155
4.5.2 RIPng packet format. 156
4.6 Open Shortest Path First (OSPF). 158
4.6.1 OSPF terminology 159
4.6.2 OSPF packet types. 165
4.6.3 Neighbor communication 166
4.6.4 OSPF neighbor state machine 168
4.6.5 OSPF virtual links and transit areas 169
4.6.6 OSPF route redistribution 170
4.6.7 OSPF stub areas 172
4.6.8 OSPF route summarization. 173
4.7 Enhanced Interior Gateway Routing Protocol (EIGRP). 174
4.7.1 Features of EIGRP. 174
4.7.2 Terminology 175
4.7.3 Neighbor discovery and recovery 177
4.7.4 The DUAL algorithm 177
4.7.5 EIGRP packet types 179
4.8 Exterior Gateway Protocol (EGP). 180
4.9 Border Gateway Protocol (BGP). 180
4.9.1 BGP concepts and terminology. 181

4.9.2 IBGP and EBGP communication. 183
4.9.3 Protocol description 185
4.9.4 Path selection. 188
4.9.5 BGP synchronization 191
4.9.6 BGP aggregation 193
4.9.7 BGP confederations 194
4.9.8 BGP route reflectors. 196
4.10 Routing protocol selection 197
4.11 Additional functions performed by the router 198
4.12 Routing processes in UNIX-based systems 199

Chapter 5. Transport layer protocols 201
5.1 Ports and sockets. 201
5.1.1 Ports. 201
5.1.2 Sockets 202
5.2 User Datagram Protocol (UDP) 204
5.2.1 UDP datagram format. 205
5.2.2 UDP application programming interface 206
5.3 Transmission Control Protocol (TCP) 206
5.3.1 TCP concept. 207
5.3.2 TCP application programming interface 220
5.3.3 TCP congestion control algorithms 221

Chapter 6. IP multicast. 229
6.1 Multicast addressing. 229
6.1.1 Multicasting on a single physical network 230
6.1.2 Multicasting between network segments. 231
6.2 Internet Group Management Protocol (IGMP). 232
6.2.1 IGMP messages. 233
6.2.2 IGMP operation 234
6.3 Multicast delivery tree 235
6.4 Multicast forwarding algorithms 236
6.4.1 Reverse path forwarding algorithm 236
6.4.2 Center-based tree algorithm. 237
6.4.3 Multicast routing protocols 238
6.5 Distance Vector Multicast Routing Protocol (DVMRP) 238
6.5.1 Protocol overview. 239
6.5.2 Building and maintaining multicast delivery trees 240
6.5.3 DVMRP tunnels 242
6.6 Multicast OSPF (MOSPF). 242
6.6.1 Protocol overview. 243
6.6.2 MOSPF and multiple OSPF areas 244
6.6.3 MOSPF and multiple autonomous systems. 245

6.6.4 MOSPF interoperability. 245
6.7 Protocol Independent Multicast (PIM). 245
6.7.1 PIM dense mode 246
6.7.2 PIM sparse mode 247
6.8 Interconnecting multicast domains 251
6.8.1 Multicast Source Discovery Protocol (MSDP) 251
6.8.2 Border Gateway Multicast Protocol. 253
6.9 The multicast backbone 254
6.9.1 MBONE routing 254
6.9.2 Multicast applications 256

Part 2. TCP/IP application protocols 259

Chapter 7. Application structure and programming interfaces 261
7.1 Characteristics of applications 261
7.1.1 Client/server model. 261
7.2 Application programming interfaces (APIs). 262
7.2.1 The socket API. 262
7.2.2 Remote Procedure Call (RPC) 266
7.2.3 Windows Sockets Version 2 (Winsock V2.0). 271
7.2.4 SNMP Distributed Programming Interface (SNMP DPI) 273
7.2.5 FTP API 276
7.2.6 CICS socket interface. 277
7.2.7 IMS socket interface. 277
7.2.8 Sockets Extended. 277
7.2.9 REXX sockets 278

Chapter 8. Directory and naming protocols 279
8.1 Domain Name System (DNS). 279
8.1.1 The hierarchical namespace. 280
8.1.2 Fully Qualified Domain Names (FQDNs). 281
8.1.3 Generic domains 281
8.1.4 Country domains 282
8.1.5 Mapping domain names to IP addresses 282
8.1.6 Mapping IP addresses to domain names – pointer queries. . . . 282
8.1.7 The distributed name space 283
8.1.8 Domain name resolution. 284
8.1.9 Domain Name System resource records. 288
8.1.10 Domain Name System messages 290
8.1.11 A simple scenario. 294
8.1.12 Extended scenario 297
8.1.13 Transport 298
8.1.14 DNS applications 299

8.1.15 References 299
8.2 Dynamic Domain Name System 300
    8.2.1 The UPDATE DNS message format 301
    8.2.2 The IBM implementation of DDNS 304
    8.2.3 Proxy A Record update (ProxyArec) 313
8.3 Network Information System (NIS) 315
8.4 Lightweight Directory Access Protocol (LDAP) 316
    8.4.1 LDAP - iightweight access to X.500 317
    8.4.2 The LDAP directory server 319
    8.4.3 Overview of LDAP architecture 320
    8.4.4 LDAP models 321
    8.4.5 LDAP security 329
    8.4.6 LDAP URLs 331
    8.4.7 LDAP and DCE 332
    8.4.8 The directory-enabled networks initiative (DEN) 334
    8.4.9 Web-Based Enterprise Management (WBEM) 335
    8.4.10 References 335

Chapter 9. Remote execution and distributed computing 337
9.1 TELNET 337
    9.1.1 TELNET operation 337
    9.1.2 Terminal emulation (Telnet 3270) 344
    9.1.3 TN3270 enhancements (TN3270E) 345
    9.1.4 References 347
9.2 Remote Execution Command protocol (REXEC and RSH) 347
    9.2.1 Principle of operation 348
9.3 Introduction to the Distributed Computing Environment (DCE) 348
    9.3.1 DCE directory service 350
    9.3.2 DCE security service 352
    9.3.3 DCE threads 357
    9.3.4 DCE remote procedure call 358
    9.3.5 Distributed time service 359
    9.3.6 Distributed file service (DFS) 361
    9.3.7 References 363

Chapter 10. File related protocols 365
10.1 File Transfer Protocol (FTP) 365
    10.1.1 Overview of FTP 365
    10.1.2 FTP operations 366
    10.1.3 Reply codes 369
    10.1.4 FTP scenario 370
    10.1.5 A sample FTP session 371
    10.1.6 Anonymous FTP 371

10.1.7 Remote job entry using FTP 371
10.2 Trivial File Transfer Protocol (TFTP) 371
   10.2.1 TFTP usage 372
   10.2.2 Protocol description 372
   10.2.3 TFTP multicast option 375
   10.2.4 Security issues 375
10.3 Network File System (NFS) 375
   10.3.1 NFS concept 376
   10.3.2 NFS Version 4 381
   10.3.3 WebNFS 382
   10.3.4 References 383
10.4 The Andrew File System (AFS) 383

Chapter 11. Mail applications 387
11.1 Simple Mail Transfer Protocol (SMTP) 387
   11.1.1 How SMTP works 389
   11.1.2 SMTP and the Domain Name System 396
   11.1.3 References 398
11.2 Multipurpose Internet Mail Extensions (MIME) 399
   11.2.1 How MIME works 402
   11.2.2 The Content-Type field 403
   11.2.3 The Content-Transfer-Encoding field 410
   11.2.4 Using non-ASCII characters in message headers 416
   11.2.5 References 418
11.3 Post Office Protocol (POP) 418
   11.3.1 POP3 commands and responses 419
   11.3.2 References 420
11.4 Internet Message Access Protocol Version 4 (IMAP4) 420
   11.4.1 IMAP4 underlying electronic mail models 421
   11.4.2 IMAP4 commands and responses 421
   11.4.3 Message numbers 422
   11.4.4 IMAP4 states 423
   11.4.5 Client commands 425
   11.4.6 References 426

Chapter 12. The World Wide Web 427
12.1 Web browsers 427
12.2 Web servers 429
12.3 Hypertext Transfer Protocol (HTTP) 429
   12.3.1 Overview of HTTP 430
   12.3.2 HTTP operation 431
12.4 Content 440
   12.4.1 Static content 441

12.4.2 Client-side dynamic content 441
12.4.3 Server-side dynamic content 442
12.4.4 Objects 443
12.4.5 Developing content with IBM Web Application Servers 446
12.5 References 447

Chapter 13. Multimedia protocols 449
13.1 Real-Time Protocols: RTP and RTCP 449
13.1.1 The Real-Time Transport Protocol (RTP) 450
13.1.2 The Real-Time Control Protocol 455
13.1.3 RTCP packet format 457
13.1.4 RTP translators and mixers 459
13.1.5 Real-time applications 462
13.2 IP telephony 463
13.2.1 Introduction 463
13.2.2 The IP telephony protocol stack 464
13.2.3 ITU-T recommendation H.323 465
13.2.4 Session Initiation Protocol (SIP) 470
13.2.5 Media Gateway Control Protocol (MGCP) 472
13.2.6 Media Gateway Controller (Megaco) 473
13.2.7 Signaling protocol functional comparison 474
13.2.8 Voice encoding and compression 476

Chapter 14. Wireless Application Protocol (WAP) 479
14.1 The WAP environment 479
14.2 Key elements of the WAP specifications 480
14.2.1 Overview of the WAP programming model 480
14.2.2 WAP network configurations 483
14.3 Wireless Markup Language (WML) and WMLScript 486
14.3.1 WML 486
14.3.2 WMLScript 488
14.4 Push architecture 489
14.4.1 Push framework 490
14.4.2 Push proxy gateway (PPG) 491
14.4.3 Push access control protocol (PAP) 492
14.4.4 Service indication 493
14.4.5 Push over-the-air protocol (OTA) 494
14.4.6 Client-side infrastructure 494
14.4.7 Security 494
14.5 Overview of the WAP protocol stack 495
14.5.1 Wireless application environment (WAE) 496
14.5.2 Wireless Telephony Application (WTA) 498
14.5.3 Wireless Session Protocol (WSP) 498

14.5.4 Wireless Transaction Protocol (WTP) 511
14.5.5 Wireless Transport Layer Security (WTLS) 514
14.5.6 Wireless Datagram Protocol (WDP) 519
14.6 Protocol summary 521

Chapter 15. Network management 525
15.1 Simple Network Management Protocol and MIB overview 525
15.2 Structure and identification of management information (SMI) 526
15.3 Management Information Base (MIB) 528
15.3.1 IBM-specific MIB part 531
15.4 Simple Network Management Protocol (SNMP) 532
15.5 Simple Network Management Protocol Version 2 (SNMPv2) 535
15.5.1 SNMPv2 entity 536
15.5.2 SNMPv2 party 536
15.5.3 GetBulkRequest 537
15.5.4 InformRequest 539
15.6 MIB for SNMPv2 539
15.7 The new administrative model 540
15.8 Simple Network Management Protocol Version 3 (SNMPv3) 542
15.8.1 Single authentication and privacy protocol 543
15.9 References 544

Chapter 16. Utilities 547
16.1 Remote printing (LPR and LPD) 547
16.2 X Window system 547
16.2.1 Functional concept 548
16.2.2 Protocol 553
16.3 Network News Transfer Protocol (NNTP) 553
16.4 Finger protocol 554
16.5 Netstat 554

Part 3. Advanced concepts and new technologies 557

Chapter 17. IP Version 6 559
17.1 IPv6 overview 560
17.2 The IPv6 header format 561
17.2.1 Packet sizes 564
17.2.2 Extension headers 565
17.2.3 IPv6 addressing 572
17.2.4 Traffic class 578
17.2.5 Flow labels 579
17.3 Internet Control Message Protocol Version 6 (ICMPv6) 579
17.3.1 Neighbor discovery 581

17.3.2 Stateless address autoconfiguration 590
17.3.3 Multicast Listener Discovery (MLD) 592
17.4 DNS in IPv6 595
17.4.1 Format of IPv6 resource records 595
17.5 DHCP in IPv6 598
17.5.1 Differences between DHCPv6 and DHCPv4 599
17.5.2 DHCPv6 messages 599
17.6 Mobility support in IPv6 600
17.7 Internet transition - Migrating from IPv4 to IPv6 601
17.7.1 Dual IP stack implementation - the IPv6/IPv4 node 601
17.7.2 Tunneling 603
17.7.3 Header translation 610
17.7.4 Interoperability summary 610
17.8 The drive towards IPv6 611
17.9 References 612

Chapter 18. Multiprotocol Label Switching (MPLS) 613
18.1 MPLS overview 613
18.1.1 Conventional routing model 613
18.1.2 MPLS forwarding model 613
18.1.3 Additional benefits 614
18.2 Components of an MPLS network 615
18.2.1 Terminology 616
18.2.2 Label swapping 618
18.2.3 Label switched path (LSP) 620
18.2.4 Label stack and label hierarchies 620
18.2.5 MPLS stacks in a BGP environment 622
18.3 Label distribution protocols 624
18.3.1 Types of label distribution protocols 624
18.3.2 Label distribution methods 625
18.4 Stream merge 625
18.4.1 Merging in a frame-based environment 625
18.4.2 Merging in an ATM environment 626
18.5 Multiprotocol Lambda Switching 627

Chapter 19. Mobile IP 629
19.1 Mobile IP overview 629
19.2 Mobile IP operation 630
19.3 Mobility agent advertisement extensions 632
19.4 Mobile IP registration process 634
19.5 Tunneling 637
19.6 Broadcast datagrams 638
19.7 Move detection 638

19.7.1 Returning home 639
19.8 ARP considerations 639
19.9 Mobile IP security considerations 639

Chapter 20. Integrating other protocols with TCP/IP 641
20.1 Enterprise Extender 641
20.1.1 Performance and recovery 642
20.2 Data Link Switching 642
20.2.1 Introduction 642
20.2.2 Functional description 643
20.3 Multiprotocol Transport Network (MPTN) 645
20.3.1 Requirements for mixed-protocol networking 645
20.3.2 MPTN architecture 646
20.3.3 MPTN methodology 646
20.3.4 MPTN major components 647
20.4 NetBIOS over TCP/IP 649
20.4.1 NetBIOS Name Server (NBNS) implementations 652

Chapter 21. TCP/IP security 655
21.1 Security exposures and solutions 655
21.1.1 Common attacks against security 655
21.1.2 Solutions to network security problems 656
21.1.3 Implementations of security solutions 657
21.1.4 Network security policy 659
21.2 A short introduction to cryptography 660
21.2.1 Terminology 660
21.2.2 Symmetric or secret-key algorithms 663
21.2.3 Asymmetric or public-key algorithms 664
21.2.4 Hash functions 669
21.2.5 Digital certificates and certification authorities 675
21.2.6 Random-number generators 676
21.2.7 Export/import restrictions on cryptography 677
21.3 Firewalls 678
21.3.1 Firewall concept 679
21.3.2 Components of a firewall system 680
21.3.3 Packet-filtering router 680
21.3.4 Application level gateway (proxy) 682
21.3.5 Circuit level gateway 687
21.3.6 Types of firewall 689
21.4 Network Address Translation (NAT) 694
21.4.1 NAT concept 694
21.4.2 Translation mechanism 695
21.4.3 NAT limitations 697

21.5 The IP security architecture (IPsec) 698
    21.5.1 Concepts 698
    21.5.2 Authentication Header (AH) 702
    21.5.3 Encapsulating Security Payload (ESP) 708
    21.5.4 Combining IPsec protocols 715
    21.5.5 The Internet Key Exchange protocol (IKE) 721
21.6 SOCKS 739
    21.6.1 SOCKS Version 5 (SOCKSv5) 741
21.7 Secure Shell (I) 746
    21.7.1 SSH overview 747
21.8 Secure Sockets Layer (SSL) 747
    21.8.1 SSL overview 747
    21.8.2 SSL protocol 749
21.9 Transport Layer Security (TLS) 755
21.10 Secure Multipurpose Internet Mail Extension (S-MIME) 755
21.11 Virtual private networks (VPN) overview 755
    21.11.1 VPN Introduction and benefits 755
21.12 Kerberos authentication and authorization system 757
    21.12.1 Assumptions 758
    21.12.2 Naming 758
    21.12.3 Kerberos authentication process 759
    21.12.4 Kerberos database management 763
    21.12.5 Kerberos Authorization Model 764
    21.12.6 Kerberos Version 5 enhancements 764
21.13 Remote access authentication protocols 765
21.14 Layer 2 Tunneling Protocol (L2TP) 768
    21.14.1 Terminology 768
    21.14.2 Protocol overview 769
    21.14.3 L2TP security issues 772
21.15 Secure electronic transactions (SET) 773
    21.15.1 SET roles 773
    21.15.2 SET transactions 774
    21.15.3 The SET certificate scheme 777
21.16 References 778

Chapter 22. Quality of Service 781
22.1 Why QoS? 781
22.2 Integrated Services 782
    22.2.1 Service classes 786
    22.2.2 The Resource Reservation Protocol (RSVP) 790
    22.2.3 Integrated Services outlook 803
22.3 Differentiated Services 804
    22.3.1 Differentiated Services architecture 806

22.3.2 Integrated Services (Intserv) over Diffserv networks 815
22.3.3 Configuration and administration of DS with LDAP 818
22.3.4 Using Differentiated Services with IPSec 819
22.4 References. 820

Chapter 23. Availability, scalability, and load balancing 823
23.1 Availability 823
23.2 Scalability. 825
23.3 Load balancing. 825
23.4 Terms used in this chapter 826
    23.4.1 Sysplex. 826
    23.4.2 Workload Manager (WLM) 826
    23.4.3 Virtual IP-address (VIPA) 827
    23.4.4 Dynamic XCF 828
    23.4.5 Dynamic IP addressing in a sysplex 828
    23.4.6 Takeover/takeback of DVIPA addresses. 830
23.5 Introduction of available solutions. 832
23.6 Network Dispatcher 833
    23.6.1 Network Dispatcher components 833
    23.6.2 Load balancing with weights. 837
    23.6.3 High availability 838
    23.6.4 Server affinity 840
    23.6.5 Rules-based balancing 840
    23.6.6 Wide Area Network Dispatcher. 841
    23.6.7 Combining ISS and Dispatcher. 842
    23.6.8 Advisors and custom advisors 843
    23.6.9 SNMP support 843
    23.6.10 Co-location option. 843
    23.6.11 ISP configuration 844
    23.6.12 OS/390 Parallel Sysplex support 845
23.7 Cisco LocalDirector 847
    23.7.1 Overview 847
    23.7.2 Connection and datagram flow 848
23.8 IBM Sysplex Distributor 849
    23.8.1 Sysplex Distributor elements 849
    23.8.2 Sysplex Distributor initialization and takeover/takeback 850
    23.8.3 Sysplex Distributor load balancing rules 851
    23.8.4 Handling connection requests. 851
    23.8.5 Data path after connection establishment 851
    23.8.6 Takeover/takeback 852
    23.8.7 Attaining availability, scalability, and load balancing 853
23.9 Cisco MultiNode Load Balancing (MNLB) 854
    23.9.1 Overview of the MultiNode Load Balancing functions 855

23.9.2 Connection establishment and subsequent data flow 856
23.9.3 Client-server connection restart 859
23.9.4 Attaining availability, scalability, and load balancing 859
23.10 IBM Sysplex Distributor and Cisco MNLB 861
23.10.1 What does this mean? 862
23.10.2 Overview of IBM Sysplex Distributor with Service Manager . 863
23.10.3 Cisco Forwarding Agent: overview and functions 864
23.10.4 Cisco Workload Agent 864
23.10.5 Connection establishment process 864
23.10.6 Stack, Server, or LPAR failure 867
23.10.7 Failure of the Sysplex Distributor 867
23.10.8 Routing packets 867
23.10.9 Additional tasks of the MNLB components 868
23.11 OS/390 DNS/WLM 870
23.11.1 DNS in a sysplex environment 870
23.11.2 DNS/WLM with remote name server 874
23.12 Virtual Router Redundancy Protocol (VRRP) 875
23.12.1 Introduction 876
23.12.2 VRRP Definitions 877
23.12.3 VRRP overview 877
23.12.4 Sample configuration 879
23.12.5 VRRP packet format 880
23.13 Round-robin DNS 883
23.14 Alternative solutions to load balancing 884
23.14.1 Network address translation 884
23.14.2 Encapsulation 887

Appendix A. Platform implementations 889
A.1 IBM Communications Server for OS/390 V2R10 889
A.1.1 Supported connectivity protocols and devices 889
A.1.2 Supported routing applications 892
A.1.3 Enterprise Extender 893
A.1.4 Virtual IP Addressing (VIPA) 893
A.1.5 Sysplex Distributor 894
A.1.6 Quality of Service (QoS) 896
A.2 IBM OS/400 V5R1 897
A.2.1 GUI configuration support 897
A.2.2 TCP/IP Connectivity Utilities for IBM @server iSeries 898
A.2.3 Dynamic IP routing (RIP and RIP2) 898
A.2.4 Advanced functions 899
A.2.5 Proxy Address Resolution Protocol (Proxy ARP) 900
A.2.6 Point-to-Point Protocol (PPP) 901
A.2.7 Security features 901

A.2.8 Virtual IP Addressing (VIPA). 903
A.2.9 Application programming interfaces (APIs) 903
A.2.10 Supported applications 905
A.3 Linux 909
A.3.1 Linux firewall 909
A.4 The network computer 910

Appendix B. Special notices 913

Appendix C. Related publications 917
C.1 IBM Redbooks 917
C.2 IBM Redbooks collections 918
C.3 Other resources 918
C.4 Referenced Web sites 920

How to get IBM Redbooks 921
IBM Redbooks fax order form 922

Abbreviations and acronyms 923

Index 931

IBM Redbooks review 957

Preface

The TCP/IP protocol suite has become the *de facto* standard for computer communications in today's networked world. The ubiquitous implementation of a specific networking standard has led to an incredible dependence on the applications enabled by it. Today, we use the TCP/IP protocols and the Internet not only for entertainment and information, but to conduct our business by performing transactions, buying and selling products, and delivering services to customers. We are continually extending the set of applications that leverage TCP/IP, thereby driving the need for further infrastructural support.

In TCP/IP Tutorial and Technical Overview, we take an in-depth look into the TCP/IP protocol suite. In Part I, we introduce TCP/IP, providing a basic understanding of the underlying concepts essential to the protocols. We continue our discussion in Part II with a survey of today's most popular TCP/IP application protocols, including emerging wireless and multimedia applications.

Finally, in Part III, we cover advanced concepts and the latest infrastructural trends in networking, including IPv6, security, Quality of Service, IP mobility, and MPLS. We address the challenges that TCP/IP is currently facing and the technology being developed to overcome them.

The team that wrote this redbook

This redbook was produced by a team of specialists from around the world working at the International Technical Support Organization Raleigh Center.

Adolfo Rodriguez is an Advisory I/T Specialist at the International Technical Support Organization, Raleigh Center. He writes extensively and teaches IBM classes worldwide on all areas of TCP/IP. Before joining the ITSO, Adolfo worked in the design and development of Communications Server for OS/390, in RTP, NC. He holds a B.A. degree in Mathematics and B.S. and M.S. degrees in Computer Science from Duke University, Durham, NC. He is currently pursuing a Ph.D. degree in Computer Science at Duke University, with a concentration on Networking Systems.

John Gatrell works for IBM in the UK. He has 15 years experience in communications customer support, and a further seven years in programming. He holds a B.A. Honours degree in Physics from Oxford University. His specialized areas include UNIX and communications.

John Karas is a network architect in IBM Global Services in the United States. He has 14 years of experience in the data networking field. He holds a Masters of Science degree in Telecommunications from Pace University. His areas of expertise include IP routing algorithms, complex network design, capacity planning, and application performance testing. He has written extensively on supporting OSPF and BGP networks, as well as performance monitoring in SAP environments.

Roland Peschke is a Senior IT Networking Specialist working for IBM customers requesting consulting and education services for the OS/390 TCP/IP and SNA environment. His comprehensive experiences in these areas come from working at IBM Germany and ITSO Raleigh for more than three decades. He worked intensively on several SNA- and TCP/IP Redbooks.

Thanks to the following people for their invaluable contributions to this project:

International Technical Support Organization, Raleigh Center
Gail Christensen, Margaret Ticknor, Jeanne Tucker, David Watts, Juan Rodriguez, Byron Braswell, Thomas Barlen, Linda Robinson

International Technical Support Organization, Austin Center
Wade Wallace and Matthew Parente

IBM Communication Server for OS/390 Development
Jeff Haggar, Bebe Isrel, Dinakaran Joseph

Cisco Systems, Inc.
Rick Williams and Edward Mazurek

BOPS, Inc.
Ricardo Rodriguez

North Carolina State University
Karina Rodriguez

FIrst Edition authors
Peter Frick, Gerard Bourbigot, Frank Vandewiele

Second Edition authors
Peter Frick, Lesia Cox, Ricardo Haragutchi

Third Edition authors
Philippe Beaupied and Frederic Debulois

Fourth Edition authors

Philippe Beaupied and Francis Li

Fifth Edition authors

Eamon Murphy, Matthias Enders, Steve Hayes

Sixth Edition authors

Martin Murhammer, Orcun Atakan, Stefan Bretz, Larry Pugh, Kazunari Suzuki, David Wood

Comments welcome

Your comments are important to us!

We want our Redbooks to be as helpful as possible. Please send us your comments about this or other Redbooks in one of the following ways:

- Fax the evaluation form found in "IBM Redbooks review" on page 957 to the fax number shown on the form.
- Use the online evaluation form found at ibm.com/redbooks
- Send your comments in an Internet note to redbook@us.ibm.com

Part 1. Core TCP/IP protocols

Chapter 1. Architecture, history, standards, and trends

Today, the Internet and World Wide Web (WWW) are familiar terms to millions of people all over the world. Many people depend on applications enabled by the Internet, such as electronic mail and Web access. In addition, the increase in popularity of business applications places additional emphasis on the Internet. The Transmission Control Protocol/Internet Protocol (TCP/IP) protocol suite is the engine for the Internet and networks worldwide. Its simplicity and power has lead to its becoming the single network protocol of choice in the world today. In this chapter, we give an overview of the TCP/IP protocol suite. We discuss how the Internet was formed, how it developed and how it is likely to develop in the future.

1.1 TCP/IP architectural model

The TCP/IP protocol suite is so named for two of its most important protocols: Transmission Control Protocol (TCP) and Internet Protocol (IP). A less used name for it is the Internet Protocol Suite, which is the phrase used in official Internet standards documents. We use the more common, shorter term, TCP/IP, to refer to the entire protocol suite in this book.

1.1.1 Internetworking

The main design goal of TCP/IP was to build an interconnection of networks, referred to as an *internetwork*, or *internet,* that provided universal communication services over heterogeneous physical networks. The clear benefit of such an internetwork is the enabling of communication between hosts on different networks, perhaps separated by a large geographical area.

The words internetwork and internet is simply a contraction of the phrase *interconnected network*. However, when written with a capital "I", the Internet refers to the worldwide set of interconnected networks. Hence, the Internet is an internet, but the reverse does not apply. The Internet is sometimes called the *connected Internet*.

The Internet consists of the following groups of networks:

- Backbones: Large networks that exist primarily to interconnect other networks. Currently the backbones are NSFNET in the US, EBONE in Europe, and large commercial backbones.

- Regional networks connecting, for example, universities and colleges.

- Commercial networks providing access to the backbones to subscribers, and networks owned by commercial organizations for internal use that also have connections to the Internet.
- Local networks, such as campus-wide university networks.

In most cases, networks are limited in size by the number of users that can belong to the network, by the maximum geographical distance that the network can span, or by the applicability of the network to certain environments. For example, an Ethernet network is inherently limited in terms of geographical size. Hence, the ability to interconnect a large number of networks in some hierarchical and organized fashion enables the communication of any two hosts belonging to this internetwork. Figure 1 shows two examples of internets. Each is comprised of two or more physical networks.

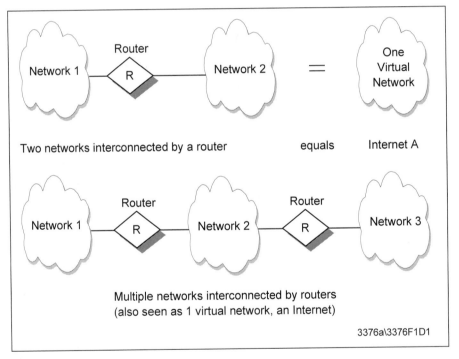

Figure 1. Internet examples - Two interconnected sets of networks, each seen as one logical network

Another important aspect of TCP/IP internetworking is the creation of a standardized abstraction of the communication mechanisms provided by each type of network. Each physical network has its own technology-dependent communication interface, in the form of a programming interface that provides basic communication functions (primitives). TCP/IP provides communication services that run between the programming interface of a physical network and user applications. It enables a common interface for these applications, independent of the underlying physical network. The architecture of the physical network is therefore hidden from the user and from the developer of the application. The application need only code to the standardized communication abstraction to be able to function under any type of physical network and operating platform.

As is evident in Figure 1, to be able to interconnect two networks, we need a computer that is attached to both networks and can forward data packets from one network to the other; such a machine is called a *router*. The term *IP router* is also used because the routing function is part of the Internet Protocol portion of the TCP/IP protocol suite (see 1.1.2, "The TCP/IP protocol layers" on page 5).

To be able to identify a host within the internetwork, each host is assigned an address, called the *IP address*. When a host has multiple network adapters (interfaces), such as with a router, each interface has a unique IP address. The IP address consists of two parts:

```
IP address = <network number><host number>
```

The *network number* part of the IP address identifies the network within the internet and is assigned by a central authority and is unique throughout the internet. The authority for assigning the *host number* part of the IP address resides with the organization that controls the network identified by the network number. The addressing scheme is described in detail in 3.1.1, "IP addressing" on page 65.

1.1.2 The TCP/IP protocol layers

Like most networking software, TCP/IP is modeled in *layers*. This layered representation leads to the term *protocol stack*, which refers to the stack of layers in the protocol suite. It can be used for positioning (but *not* for functionally comparing) the TCP/IP protocol suite against others, such as Systems Network Architecture (SNA) and the Open System Interconnection (OSI) model. Functional comparisons cannot easily be extracted from this, as there are basic differences in the layered models used by the different protocol suites.

By dividing the communication software into layers, the protocol stack allows for division of labor, ease of implementation and code testing, and the ability to develop alternative layer implementations. Layers communicate with those above and below via concise interfaces. In this regard, a layer provides a service for the layer directly above it and makes use of services provided by the layer directly below it. For example, the IP layer provides the ability to transfer data from one host to another without any guarantee to reliable delivery or duplicate suppression. Transport protocols such as TCP make use of this service to provide applications with reliable, in-order, data stream delivery. Figure 2 shows how the TCP/IP protocols are modeled in four layers.

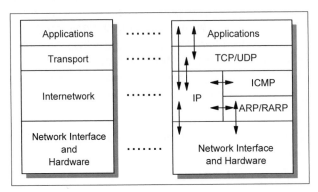

Figure 2. The TCP/IP protocol stack - Each layer represents a package of functions

These layers include:

Application layer
The application layer is provided by the program that uses TCP/IP for communication. An application is a user process cooperating with another process usually on a different host (there is also a benefit to application communication within a single host). Examples of applications include Telnet and the File Transfer Protocol (FTP). The interface between the application and transport layers is defined by port numbers and sockets, which is described in more detail in 5.1, "Ports and sockets" on page 201.

Transport layer
The transport layer provides the end-to-end data transfer by delivering data from an application to its remote peer. Multiple applications can be supported simultaneously. The most-used transport layer protocol is the Transmission Control Protocol (TCP), which provides connection-oriented reliable data delivery, duplicate data suppression, congestion control, and flow control. It is discussed in more detail in

5.3, "Transmission Control Protocol (TCP)" on page 206.

Another transport layer protocol is the User Datagram Protocol (UDP, discussed in 5.2, "User Datagram Protocol (UDP)" on page 204). It provides connectionless, unreliable, best-effort service. As a result, applications using UDP as the transport protocol have to provide their own end-to-end integrity, flow control, and congestion control, if it is so desired. Usually, UDP is used by applications that need a fast transport mechanism and can tolerate the loss of some data.

Internetwork layer   The internetwork layer, also called the *internet layer* or the *network layer*, provides the "virtual network" image of an internet (this layer shields the higher levels from the physical network architecture below it). Internet Protocol (IP) is the most important protocol in this layer. It is a connectionless protocol that doesn't assume reliability from lower layers. IP does *not* provide reliability, flow control, or error recovery. These functions must be provided at a higher level.

IP provides a routing function that attempts to deliver transmitted messages to their destination. IP is discussed in detail in 3.1, "Internet Protocol (IP)" on page 65. A message unit in an IP network is called an *IP datagram*. This is the basic unit of information transmitted across TCP/IP networks. Other internetwork layer protocols are IP, ICMP, IGMP, ARP and RARP.

Network interface layer   The network interface layer, also called the *link layer* or the *data-link layer*, is the interface to the actual network hardware. This interface may or may not provide reliable delivery, and may be packet or stream oriented. In fact, TCP/IP does not specify any protocol here, but can use almost any network interface available, which illustrates the flexibility of the IP layer. Examples are IEEE 802.2, X.25 (which is reliable in itself), ATM, FDDI, and even SNA. Some physical networks and interfaces are discussed in Chapter 2, "Network interfaces" on page 29.

TCP/IP specifications do not describe or standardize any network layer protocols per se; they only standardize ways of accessing those protocols from the internetwork layer.

A more detailed layering model is included in Figure 3.

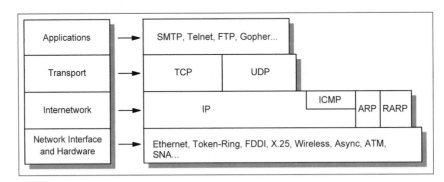

Figure 3. Detailed architectural model

1.1.3 TCP/IP applications

The highest-level protocols within the TCP/IP protocol stack are application protocols. They communicate with applications on other internet hosts and are the user-visible interface to the TCP/IP protocol suite.

All application protocols have some characteristics in common:

- They can be user-written applications or applications standardized and shipped with the TCP/IP product. Indeed, the TCP/IP protocol suite includes application protocols such as:
  - TELNET for interactive terminal access to remote internet hosts.
  - FTP (file transfer protocol) for high-speed disk-to-disk file transfers.
  - SMTP (simple mail transfer protocol) as an internet mailing system.

  These are some of the most widely implemented application protocols, but many others exist. Each particular TCP/IP implementation will include a lesser or greater set of application protocols.

- They use either UDP or TCP as a transport mechanism. Remember that UDP is unreliable and offers no flow-control, so in this case, the application has to provide its own error recovery, flow control, and congestion control functionality. It is often easier to build applications on top of TCP because it is a reliable stream, connection-oriented, congestion-friendly, flow control enabled protocol. As a result, most application protocols will use TCP, but there are applications built on UDP to achieve better performance through reduced protocol overhead.

- Most applications use the client/server model of interaction.

1.1.3.1 The client/server model

TCP is a peer-to-peer, connection-oriented protocol. There are no master/slave relationships. The applications, however, typically use a client/server model for communications.

A *server* is an application that offers a service to internet users; a *client* is a requester of a service. An application consists of both a server and a client part, which can run on the same or on different systems. Users usually invoke the client part of the application, which builds a *request* for a particular service and sends it to the server part of the application using TCP/IP as a transport vehicle.

The server is a program that receives a request, performs the required service and sends back the results in a *reply*. A server can usually deal with multiple requests and multiple requesting clients at the same time.

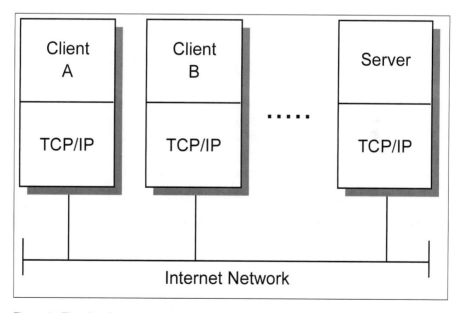

Figure 4. The client/server model of applications

Most servers wait for requests at a *well-known port* so that their clients know which port (and in turn, which application) they must direct their requests. The client typically uses an arbitrary port called an *ephemeral port* for its communication. Clients that wish to communicate with a server that does not use a well-known port must have another mechanism for learning to which port they must address their requests. This mechanism might employ a registration service such as portmap, which does use a well-known port.

For detailed information on TCP/IP application protocols, please refer to Part 2, "TCP/IP application protocols" on page 259.

1.1.4 Bridges, routers, and gateways

There are many ways to provide access to other networks. In an internetwork, this done with *routers*. In this section, we distinguish between a router, a bridge and a gateway for allowing remote network access.

Bridge   Interconnects LAN segments at the network interface layer level and forwards frames between them. A bridge performs the function of a MAC relay, and is independent of any higher layer protocol (including the logical link protocol). It provides MAC layer protocol conversion, if required.

A bridge is said to be *transparent* to IP. That is, when an IP host sends an IP datagram to another host on a network connected by a bridge, it sends the datagram directly to the host and the datagram "crosses" the bridge without the sending IP host being aware of it.

Router   Interconnects networks at the internetwork layer level and routes packets between them. The router must understand the addressing structure associated with the networking protocols it supports and take decisions on whether, or how, to forward packets. Routers are able to select the best transmission paths and optimal packet sizes. The basic routing function is implemented in the IP layer of the TCP/IP protocol stack, so any host or workstation running TCP/IP over more than one interface could, in theory and also with most of today's TCP/IP implementations, forward IP datagrams. However, dedicated routers provide much more sophisticated routing than the minimum functions implemented by IP.

Because IP provides this basic routing function, the term "IP router," is often used. Other, older terms for router are "IP gateway," "Internet gateway," and "gateway." The term *gateway* is now normally used for connections at a higher layer than the internetwork layer.

A router is said to be *visible* to IP. That is, when a host sends an IP datagram to another host on a network connected by a router, it sends the datagram to the router so that it can forward it to the target host.

Gateway Interconnects networks at higher layers than bridges and routers. A gateway usually supports address mapping from one network to another, and may also provide transformation of the data between the environments to support end-to-end application connectivity. Gateways typically limit the interconnectivity of two networks to a subset of the application protocols supported on either one. For example, a VM host running TCP/IP may be used as an SMTP/RSCS mail gateway.

> **Note**
>
> The term "gateway," when used in this sense, is *not* synonymous with "IP gateway."

A gateway is said to be *opaque* to IP. That is, a host cannot send an IP datagram through a gateway; it can only send it *to* a gateway. The higher-level protocol information carried by the datagrams is then passed on by the gateway using whatever networking architecture is used on the other side of the gateway.

Closely related to routers and gateways is the concept of a *firewall*, or *firewall gateway*, which is used to restrict access from the Internet or some untrusted network to a network or group of networks controlled by an organization for security reasons. See 21.3, "Firewalls" on page 678 for more information on firewalls.

1.2 The roots of the Internet

Networks have become a fundamental, if not the most important, part of today's information systems. They form the backbone for information sharing in enterprises, governmental and scientific groups. That information can take several forms. It can be notes and documents, data to be processed by another computer, files sent to colleagues, and multimedia data streams.

A number of networks were installed in the late 60s and 70s, when network design was the "state of the art" topic of computer research and sophisticated implementers. It resulted in multiple networking models such as packet-switching technology, collision-detection local area networks, hierarchical networks, and many other excellent communications technologies.

The result of all this great know-how was that any group of users could find a physical network and an architectural model suitable for their specific needs. This ranges from inexpensive asynchronous lines with no other error recovery than a bit-per-bit parity function, through full-function wide area networks (public or private) with reliable protocols such as public packet-switching networks or private SNA networks, to high-speed but limited-distance local area networks.

The down side of the development of such heterogeneous protocol suites is the rather painful situation where one group of users wishes to extend its information system to another group of users who have implemented a different network technology and different networking protocols. As a result, even if they could agree on some network technology to physically interconnect the two environments, their applications (such as mailing systems) would still not be able to communicate with each other because of different application protocols and interfaces.

This situation was recognized in the early 70s by a group of U.S. researchers funded by the *Defense Advanced Research Projects Agency* (DARPA). Their work addressed *internetworking*, or the interconnection of networks. Other official organizations became involved in this area, such as ITU-T (formerly CCITT) and ISO. The main goal was to define a set of protocols, detailed in a well-defined suite, so that applications would be able to communicate with other applications, regardless of the underlying network technology or the operating systems where those applications run.

The official organization of these researchers was the ARPANET Network Working Group, which had its last general meeting in October 1971. DARPA continued its research for an internetworking protocol suite, from the early *Network Control Program* (NCP) host-to-host protocol to the TCP/IP protocol suite, which took its current form around 1978. At that time, DARPA was well known for its pioneering of packet-switching over radio networks and satellite channels. The first real implementations of the *Internet* were found around 1980 when DARPA started converting the machines of its research network (ARPANET) to use the new TCP/IP protocols. In 1983, the transition was completed and DARPA demanded that *all* computers willing to connect to its ARPANET use TCP/IP.

DARPA also contracted Bolt, Beranek, and Newman (BBN) to develop an implementation of the TCP/IP protocols for Berkeley UNIX on the VAX and funded the University of California at Berkeley to distribute the code free of charge with their UNIX operating system. The first release of the *Berkeley Software Distribution* (BSD) to include the TCP/IP protocol set was made available in 1983 (4.2BSD). From that point on, TCP/IP spread rapidly among universities and research centers and has become the standard communications subsystem for all UNIX connectivity. The second release (4.3BSD) was distributed in 1986, with updates in 1988 (4.3BSD Tahoe) and 1990 (4.3BSD Reno). 4.4BSD was released in 1993. Due to funding constraints, 4.4BSD was the last release of the BSD by the Computer Systems Research Group of the University of California at Berkeley.

As TCP/IP internetworking spread rapidly, new wide area networks were created in the U.S. and connected to ARPANET. In turn, other networks in the rest of the world, not necessarily based on the TCP/IP protocols, were added to the set of interconnected networks. The result is what is described as *The Internet*. Some examples of the different networks that have played key roles in this development are described in the next sections.

1.2.1 ARPANET

Sometimes referred to as the "grand-daddy of packet networks," the ARPANET was built by DARPA (which was called ARPA at that time) in the late 60s to accommodate research equipment on packet-switching technology and to allow resource sharing for the Department of Defense's contractors. The network interconnected research centers, some military bases and government locations. It soon became popular with researchers for collaboration through electronic mail and other services. It was developed into a research utility run by the Defense Communications Agency (DCA) by the end of 1975 and split in 1983 into MILNET for interconnection of military sites and ARPANET for interconnection of research sites. This formed the beginning of the "capital I" Internet.

In 1974, the ARPANET was based on 56 Kbps leased lines that interconnected *packet-switching nodes* (PSN) scattered across the continental U.S. and western Europe. These were minicomputers running a protocol known as *1822* (after the number of a report describing it) and dedicated to the packet-switching task. Each PSN had at least two connections to other PSNs (to allow alternate routing in case of circuit failure) and up to 22 ports for user computer (*host*) connections. These 1822 systems offered reliable, flow-controlled delivery of a packet to a destination node. This is the reason why the original NCP protocol was a rather simple protocol. It was replaced by the TCP/IP protocols, which do not assume reliability of the underlying network hardware and can be used on other-than-1822 networks. This 1822 protocol did not become an industry standard, so DARPA decided later to replace the 1822 packet switching technology with the *CCITT X.25* standard.

Data traffic rapidly exceeded the capacity of the 56 Kbps lines that made up the network, which were no longer able to support the necessary throughput. Today the ARPANET has been replaced by new technologies in its role of backbone on the research side of the connected Internet (see NSFNET later in this chapter), whereas MILNET continues to form the backbone of the military side.

1.2.2 NSFNET

NSFNET, the National Science Foundation (NSF) Network, is a three-level internetwork in the United States consisting of:

- The backbone: A network that connects separately administered and operated mid-level networks and NSF-funded supercomputer centers. The backbone also has transcontinental links to other networks such as EBONE, the European IP backbone network.
- Mid-level networks: Three kinds (regional, discipline-based, and supercomputer consortium networks).
- Campus networks: Whether academic or commercial, connected to the mid-level networks.

Over the years, the NSF upgraded its backbone to meet the increasing demands of its clients:

First backbone   Originally established by the NSF as a communications network for researchers and scientists to access the NSF supercomputers, the first NSFNET backbone used six DEC LSI/11 microcomputers as packet switches, interconnected by 56 Kbps leased lines. A primary interconnection between the NSFNET backbone and the ARPANET existed at Carnegie Mellon, which allowed routing of datagrams between users connected to each of those networks.

Second backbone   The need for a new backbone appeared in 1987, when the first one became overloaded within a few months (estimated growth at that time was 100 percent per year). The NSF and MERIT, Inc., a computer network consortium of eight state-supported universities in Michigan, agreed to develop and manage a new, higher-speed backbone with greater transmission and switching capacities. To manage it, they defined the *Information Services* (IS), which is comprised of an Information Center and a Technical Support Group. The Information Center is responsible for information dissemination, information resource management, and electronic communication. The Technical Support Group provides support directly to the field. The purpose of this is to provide an integrated information system with easy-to-use-and-manage interfaces accessible from any point in the network supported by a full set of training services.

Merit and NSF conducted this project in partnership with IBM and MCI. IBM provided the software, packet-switching and network-management equipment, while MCI provided the long-distance transport facilities. Installed in 1988, the new network initially used 448 Kbps leased circuits to interconnect 13 *nodal switching systems* (NSS), supplied by IBM. Each NSS was composed of nine IBM RISC systems (running an IBM version of 4.3BSD UNIX) loosely coupled via two IBM Token-Ring Networks (for redundancy). One Integrated Digital Network Exchange (IDNX) supplied by IBM was installed at each of the 13 locations, to provide:

- Dynamic alternate routing
- Dynamic bandwidth allocation

Third backbone   In 1989, the NSFNET backbone circuits topology was reconfigured after traffic measurements and the speed of the leased lines increased to T1 (1.544 Mbps) using primarily fiber optics.

Due to the constantly increasing need for improved packet switching and transmission capacities, three NSSs were added to the backbone and the link speed was upgraded. The migration of the NSFNET backbone from T1 to T3 (45Mbps) was completed in late 1992. The subsequent migration to gigabit levels has already started and is continuing today.

In April 1995, the US government discontinued its funding of NSFNET. This was, in part, a reaction to growing commercial use of the network. About the same time, NSFNET gradually migrated the main backbone traffic in the U.S. to commercial network service providers, and NSFNET reverted to being a network for the research community. The main backbone network is now run in cooperation with MCI and is known as the vBNS (very high speed Backbone Network Service).

NSFNET has played a key role in the development of the Internet. However, many other networks have also played their part and/or also make up a part of the Internet today.

1.2.3 Commercial use of the Internet

In recent years the Internet has grown in size and range at a greater rate than anyone could have predicted. A number of key factors have influenced this growth. Some of the most significant milestones have been the free distribution of Gopher in 1991, the first posting, also in 1991, of the specification for hypertext and, in 1993, the release of Mosaic, the first graphics-based browser. Today the vast majority of the hosts now connected to the Internet are of a commercial nature. This is an area of potential and actual conflict with the initial aims of the Internet, which were to foster open communications between academic and research institutions. However, the continued growth in commercial use of the Internet is inevitable, so it will be helpful to explain how this evolution is taking place.

One important initiative to consider is that of the *Acceptable Use Policy* (AUP). The first of these policies was introduced in 1992 and applies to the use of NSFNET. At the heart of this AUP is a commitment "to support open research and education." Under "Unacceptable Uses" is a prohibition of "use for for-profit activities," unless covered by the General Principle or as a specifically acceptable use. However, in spite of this apparently restrictive stance, the NSFNET was increasingly used for a broad range of activities, including many of a commercial nature, before reverting to its original objectives in 1995.

The provision of an AUP is now commonplace among Internet service providers, although the AUP has generally evolved to be more suitable for commercial use. Some networks still provide services free of any AUP.

Let us now focus on the Internet service providers who have been most active in introducing commercial uses to the Internet. Two worth mentioning are PSINet and UUNET, which began in the late 80s to offer Internet access to both businesses and individuals. The California-based CERFnet provided services free of any AUP. An organization to interconnect PSINet, UUNET and CERFnet was formed soon after, called the Commercial Internet Exchange (CIX), based on the understanding that the traffic of any member of one network may flow without restriction over the networks of the other members. As of July 1997, CIX had grown to more than 146 members from all over the world, connecting member internets. At about the same time that CIX was formed, a non-profit company, Advance Network and Services (ANS), was formed by IBM, MCI and Merit, Inc. to operate T1 (subsequently T3) backbone connections for NSFNET. This group was active in increasing the commercial presence on the Internet.

ANS formed a commercially oriented subsidiary called ANS CO+RE to provide linkage between commercial customers and the research and education domains. ANS CO+RE provides access to NSFNET as well as being linked to CIX. In 1995 ANS was acquired by America Online.

In 1995, as the NSFNET was reverting to its previous academic role, the architecture of the Internet changed from having a single dominant backbone in the U.S. to having a number of commercially operated backbones. In order for the different backbones to be able to exchange data, the NSF set up four Network Access Points (NAPs) to serve as data interchange points between the backbone service providers.

Another type of interchange is the Metropolitan Area Ethernet (MAE). Several MAEs have been set up by Metropolitan Fiber Systems (MFS), who also have their own backbone network. NAPs and MAEs are also referred to as public exchange points (IXPs). Internet service providers (ISPs) typically will have connections to a number of IXPs for performance and backup. For a current listing of IXPs, consult the Exchange Point at:

`http://www.ep.net`

Similar to CIX in the United States, European Internet providers formed the RIPE (Réseaux IP Européens) organization to ensure technical and administrative coordination. RIPE was formed in 1989 to provide a uniform IP service to users throughout Europe. Today, the largest Internet backbones run at OC48 (2.4 Gbps) or OC192 (96 Gbps).

1.2.4 Internet2

The success of the Internet and the subsequent frequent congestion of the NSFNET and its commercial replacement led to some frustration among the research community who had previously enjoyed exclusive use of the Internet. The university community, therefore, together with government and industry partners, and encouraged by the funding component of the Next Generation Internet (NGI) initiative, have formed the *Internet2* project.

The NGI initiative is a federal research program that is developing advanced networking technologies, introducing revolutionary applications that require advanced networking technologies and demonstrating these technological capabilities on high-speed testbeds.

1.2.4.1 Mission

The Internet2 mission is to facilitate and coordinate the development, operation, and technology transfer of advanced, network-based applications and network services to further U.S. leadership in research and higher education and accelerate the availability of new services and applications on the Internet.

The goals of Internet2 are the following:

- Demonstrate new applications that can dramatically enhance researchers' ability to collaborate and conduct experiments.

- Demonstrate enhanced delivery of education and other services (for instance, health care, environmental monitoring, etc.) by taking advantage of *virtual proximity* created by an advanced communications infrastructure.

- Support development and adoption of advanced applications by providing middleware and development tools.

- Facilitate development, deployment, and operation of an affordable communications infrastructure, capable of supporting differentiated Quality of Service (QoS) based on applications requirements of the research and education community.

- Promote experimentation with the next generation of communications technologies.

- Coordinate adoption of agreed working standards and common practices among participating institutions to ensure end-to-end quality of service and interoperability.

- Catalyze partnerships with governmental and private sector organizations.

- Encourage transfer of technology from Internet2 to the rest of the Internet.

- Study the impact of new infrastructure, services, and applications on higher education and the Internet community in general.

1.2.4.2 Internet2 participants

Internet2 has 180 participating universities across the United States. Affiliate organizations provide the project with valuable input. All participants in the

Internet2 project are members of the University Corporation for Advanced Internet Development (UCAID).

In most respects, the partnership and funding arrangements for Internet2 will parallel those of previous joint networking efforts of academia and government, of which the NSFnet project is a very successful example. The United States government will participate in Internet2 through the NGI initiative and related programs.

Internet2 also joins with corporate leaders to create the advanced network services necessary to meet the requirements of broadband, networked applications. Industry partners work primarily with campus-based and regional university teams to provide the services and products needed to implement the applications developed by the project. Major corporations currently participating in Internet2 include Alcatel, Cisco Systems, IBM, Nortel Networks, Sprint and Sun Microsystems. Additional support for Internet2 comes from collaboration with non-profit organizations working in research and educational networking. Affiliate organizations committed to the project include MCNC, Merit, National Institutes of Health (NIH), and the State University System of Florida.

For more information on Internet2, see their Web page at:

http://www.internet2.edu

1.2.5 The Open Systems Interconnection (OSI) Reference Model

The OSI (Open Systems Interconnect) Reference Model (ISO 7498) defines a seven-layer model of data communication with physical transport at the lower layer and application protocols at the upper layers. This model, shown in Figure 5, is widely accepted as a basis for the understanding of how a network protocol stack should operate and as a reference tool for comparing network stack implementation.

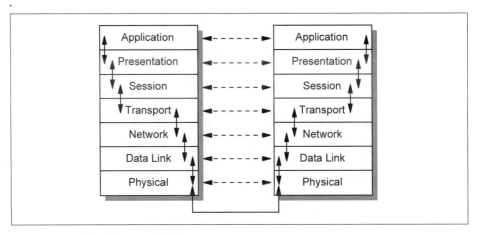

Figure 5. The OSI Reference Model

Each layer provides a set of functions to the layer above and, in turn, relies on the functions provided by the layer below. Although messages can only pass vertically through the stack from layer to layer, from a logical point of view, each layer communicates directly with its peer layer on other nodes.

The seven layers are:

Application   Network applications such as terminal emulation and file transfer

Presentation Formatting of data and encryption

Session   Establishment and maintenance of sessions

Transport   Provision of reliable and unreliable end-to-end delivery

Network   Packet delivery, including routing

Data Link   Framing of units of information and error checking

Physical   Transmission of bits on the physical hardware

In contrast to TCP/IP, the OSI approach started from a clean slate and defined standards, adhering tightly to their own model, using a formal committee process without requiring implementations. Internet protocols use a less formal engineering approach, where anybody can propose and comment on RFCs, and implementations are required to verify feasibility. The OSI protocols developed slowly, and because running the full protocol stack is resource intensive, they have not been widely deployed, especially in the desktop and small computer market. In the meantime, TCP/IP and the

Internet were developing rapidly, with deployment occurring at a very high rate.

1.3 TCP/IP standards

TCP/IP has been popular with developers and users alike because of its inherent openness and perpetual renewal. The same holds true for the Internet as an open communications network. On the other hand, this openness could easily turn into a sword with two edges if it were not controlled in some way. Although there is no overall governing body to issue directives and regulations for the Internet – control is mostly based on mutual cooperation – the Internet Society (ISOC) serves as the standardizing body for the Internet community. It is organized and managed by the Internet Architecture Board (IAB).

The IAB itself relies on the Internet Engineering Task Force (IETF) for issuing new standards, and on the Internet Assigned Numbers Authority (IANA) for coordinating values shared among multiple protocols. The RFC Editor is responsible for reviewing and publishing new standards documents.

The IETF itself is governed by the Internet Engineering Steering Group (IESG) and is further organized in the form of Areas and Working Groups where new specifications are discussed and new standards are propsoed.

The Internet Standards Process, described in RFC 2026 – The Internet Standards Process - Revision 3, is concerned with all protocols, procedures, and conventions that are used in or by the Internet, whether or not they are part of the TCP/IP protocol suite.

The overall goals of the Internet Standards Process are:

- Technical excellence
- Prior implementation and testing
- Clear, concise, and easily understood documentation
- Openness and fairness
- Timeliness

The process of standardization is summarized below:

- In order to have a new specification approved as a standard, applicants have to submit that specification to the IESG where it will be discussed and reviewed for technical merit and feasibility and also published as an

Internet draft document. This should take no shorter than two weeks and no longer than six months.

- Once the IESG reaches a positive conclusion, it issues a last-call notification to allow the specification to be reviewed by the whole Internet community.

- After the final approval by the IESG, an Internet draft is recommended to the Internet Engineering Taskforce (IETF), another subsidiary of the IAB, for inclusion into the standards track and for publication as a Request for Comment (see 1.3.1, "Request For Comments (RFC)" on page 22).

- Once published as an RFC, a contribution may advance in status as described in 1.3.2, "Internet standards" on page 24. It may also be revised over time or phased out when better solutions are found.

- If the IESG does not approve of a new specification after, of if a document has remained unchanged within, six months of submission, it will be removed from the Internet drafts directory.

1.3.1 Request For Comments (RFC)

The Internet protocol suite is still evolving through the mechanism of *Request For Comments* (RFC). New protocols (mostly application protocols) are being designed and implemented by researchers, and are brought to the attention of the Internet community in the form of an Internet draft (ID).[1] The largest source of IDs is the Internet Engineering Task Force (IETF) which is a subsidiary of the IAB. However, anyone may submit a memo proposed as an ID to the RFC Editor. There are a set of rules which RFC/ID authors must follow in order for an RFC to be accepted. These rules are themselves described in an RFC (RFC 2223) which also indicates how to submit a proposal for an RFC.

Once an RFC has been published, all revisions and replacements are published as new RFCs. A new RFC which revises or replaces an existing RFC is said to "update" or to "obsolete" that RFC. The existing RFC is said to be "updated by" or "obsoleted by" the new one. For example RFC 1542, which describes the BOOTP protocol, is a "second edition," being a revision of RFC 1532 and an amendment to RFC 951. RFC 1542 is therefore labelled like this: "Obsoletes RFC 1532; Updates RFC 951." Consequently, there is never any confusion over whether two people are referring to different versions of an RFC, since there is never more than one current version.

---

[1] Some of these protocols, particularly those dated April 1, can be described as impractical at best. For instance, RFC 1149 (dated 1990 April 1) describes the transmission of IP datagrams by carrier pigeon and RFC 1437 (dated 1993 April 1) describes the transmission of people by electronic mail.

Some RFCs are described as *information documents* while others describe Internet protocols. The Internet Architecture Board (IAB) maintains a list of the RFCs that describe the protocol suite. Each of these is assigned a *state* and a *status*.

An Internet protocol can have one of the following states:

Standard   The IAB has established this as an official protocol for the Internet. These are separated into two groups:

1. IP protocol and above, protocols that apply to the whole Internet.
2. Network-specific protocols, generally specifications of how to do IP on particular types of networks.

Draft standard   The IAB is actively considering this protocol as a possible standard protocol. Substantial and widespread testing and comments are desired. Comments and test results should be submitted to the IAB. There is a possibility that changes will be made in a draft protocol before it becomes a standard.

Proposed standard   These are protocol proposals that may be considered by the IAB for standardization in the future. Implementations and testing by several groups are desirable. Revision of the protocol is likely.

Experimental   A system should not implement an experimental protocol unless it is participating in the experiment and has coordinated its use of the protocol with the developer of the protocol.

Informational   Protocols developed by other standard organizations, or vendors, or that are for other reasons outside the purview of the IAB may be published as RFCs for the convenience of the Internet community as informational protocols. Such protocols may, in some cases, also be recommended for use on the Internet by the IAB.

Historic   These are protocols that are unlikely to ever become standards in the Internet either because they have been superseded by later developments or due to lack of interest.

Protocol status can be any of the following:

Required   A system must implement the required protocols.

Recommended   A system should implement the recommended protocol.

Elective   A system may or may not implement an elective protocol. The general notion is that if you are going to do something like this, you must do exactly this.

Limited use   These protocols are for use in limited circumstances. This may be because of their experimental state, specialized nature, limited functionality, or historic state.

Not recommended These protocols are not recommended for general use. This may be because of their limited functionality, specialized nature, or experimental or historic state.

1.3.2 Internet standards

Proposed standard, draft standard, and standard protocols are described as being on the *Internet Standards Track*. When a protocol reaches the standard state, it is assigned a standard number (STD). The purpose of STD numbers is to clearly indicate which RFCs describe Internet standards. STD numbers reference multiple RFCs when the specification of a standard is spread across multiple documents. Unlike RFCs, where the number refers to a specific document, STD numbers do not change when a standard is updated. STD numbers do not, however, have version numbers since all updates are made via RFCs and the RFC numbers are unique. Thus to clearly specify which version of a standard one is referring to, the standard number and all of the RFCs which it includes should be stated. For instance, the Domain Name System (DNS) is STD 13 and is described in RFCs 1034 and 1035. To reference the standard, a form like "STD-13/RFC1034/RFC1035" should be used.

For some standards track RFCs, the status category does not always contain enough information to be useful. It is therefore supplemented, notably for routing protocols, by an *applicability statement* which is given either in STD 1 or in a separate RFC.

References to the RFCs and to STD numbers will be made throughout this book, since they form the basis of all TCP/IP protocol implementations.

The following Internet standards are of particular importance:

- STD 1 - Internet Official Protocol Standards

  This standard gives the state and status of each Internet protocol or standard and defines the meanings attributed to each state or status. It is issued by the IAB approximately quarterly. At the time of writing this standard is in RFC 2800.

- STD 2 – Assigned Internet Numbers

  This standard lists currently assigned numbers and other protocol parameters in the Internet protocol suite. It is issued by the Internet Assigned Numbers Authority (IANA). The current edition at the time of writing is RFC1700.

- STD 3 – Host Requirements

  This standard defines the requirements for Internet host software (often by reference to the relevant RFCs). The standard comes in three parts: RFC1122 – Requirements for Internet hosts – communications layer, RFC1123 – Requirements for Internet hosts – application and support, and RFC 2181 – Clarifications to the DNS Specification.

- STD 4 – Router Requirements

  This standard defines the requirements for IPv4 Internet gateway (router) software. It is defined in RFC 1812 – Requirements for IPv4 Routers.

1.3.2.1 For Your Information (FYI)

A number of RFCs that are intended to be of wide interest to Internet users are classified as *For Your Information* (FYI) documents. They frequently contain introductory or other helpful information. Like STD numbers, an FYI number is not changed when a revised RFC is issued. Unlike STDs, FYIs correspond to a single RFC document. For example, FYI 4 - FYI on Questions and Answers - Answers to Commonly asked "New Internet User" Questions, is currently in its fifth edition. The RFC numbers are 1177, 1206, 1325 and 1594, and 2664.

1.3.2.2 Obtaining RFCs

RFC and ID documents are available publicly and online and may be best obtained from the IETF Web site:

`http://www.ietf.org`

A complete list of current Internet Standards can be found in RFC 2800 – Internet Official Protocol Standards.

1.4 Future of the Internet

Trying to predict the future of the Internet is not an easy task. Few would have imagined, even five years ago, the extent to which the Internet has now become a part of everyday life in business, homes and schools. There are a number of things, however, about which we can be fairly certain.

1.4.1 Multimedia applications

Bandwidth requirements will continue to increase at massive rates; not only is the number of Internet users growing rapidly, but the applications being used are becoming more advanced and therefore consume more bandwidth. New technologies such as Dense Wave Division Multiplexing (DWDM) are emerging to meet these high bandwidth demands being placed on the Internet.

Much of this increasing demand is attributable to the increased use of multimedia applications. One example is that of Voice over IP technology. As this technology matures, we are almost certain to see a sharing of bandwidth between voice and data across the Internet. This raises some interesting questions for phone companies. The cost to a user of an Internet connection between Raleigh, NC and Lima, Peru is the same as a connection within Raleigh - not so for a traditional phone connection. Inevitably, voice conversations will become video conversations as phone calls become video conferences.

Today, it is possible to hear radio stations from almost any part of the globe via the Internet with FM quality. We can watch television channels from all around the world leading to the clear potential of using the Internet as the vehicle for delivering movies and all sorts of video signals to consumers everywhere. It all comes at a price, however, as the infrastructure of the Internet must adapt to such high bandwidth demands.

1.4.2 Commercial use

The Internet has been through an explosion in terms of commercial use. Today, almost all large business depend on the Internet, whether for marketing, sales, customer service, or employee access. These trends are expected to continue. Electronic stores will continue to flourish by providing convenience to customers that do not have time to make their way to traditional stores.

Businesses will rely more and more on the Internet as a means for communicating branches across the globe. With the popularity of Virtual

Private Networks (VPNs), businesses can securely conduct their internal business over a wide area using the Internet; employees can work from home offices yielding a *virtual office* environment. Virtual meetings probably will be common occurrences.

1.4.3 The wireless Internet

Perhaps the most widespread growth in the use of the Internet, however, is that of wireless applications. Recently, there has been an incredible focus on the enablement of wireless and pervasive computing. This focus has been largely motivated by the convenience of wireless connectivity. For example, it is impractical to physically connect a mobile workstation, which by definition, is free to roam. Constraining such a workstation to some physical geography simply defeats the purpose. In other cases, wired connectivity simply is not feasible. Examples would include the ruins of Macchu Picchu or offices in the Sistine Chapel. In these circumstances, fixed workstations would also benefit from otherwise unavailable network access.

Protocols such as Bluetooth, IEEE 802.11, and Wireless Application Protocol (WAP) are paving the way towards a wireless Internet. While the personal benefits of such access are quite advantageous, even more appealing are the business applications that are facilitated by such technology. Every business, from factories to hospitals, could enhance their respective services. Wireless devices will become standard equipment in vehicles, not only for the personal enjoyment of the driver, but also for the flow of maintenance information to your favorite automobile mechanic. The applications are limitless.

Chapter 2. Network interfaces

This chapter provides an overview of the protocols and interfaces that allow TCP/IP traffic to flow over various kinds of physical networks. TCP/IP, as an internetwork protocol suite, can operate over a vast number of physical networks. The most common and widely used of these protocols is, of course, Ethernet. The number of network protocols that have provisions for natively supporting IP is clearly beyond the scope of this redbook. However, we provide a summary of some of the different networks most commonly used with TCP/IP.

2.1 Ethernet and IEEE 802.x Local Area Networks (LANs)

Two frame formats can be used on the Ethernet coaxial cable:

1. The standard issued in 1978 by Xerox Corporation, Intel Corporation and Digital Equipment Corporation, usually called *Ethernet* (or *DIX* Ethernet).

2. The international IEEE 802.3 standard, a more recently defined standard.

See Figure 6 for more details.

The difference between the two standards is in the use of one of the header fields, which contains a protocol-type number for Ethernet and the length of the data in the frame for IEEE 802.3.

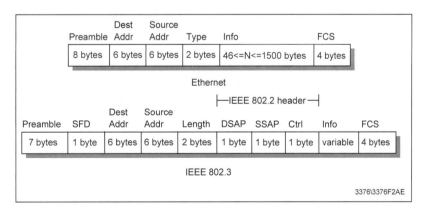

Figure 6. ARP - Frame formats for Ethernet and IEEE 802.3

- The type field in Ethernet is used to distinguish between different protocols running on the coaxial cable, and allows their coexistence on the same physical cable.

- The maximum length of an Ethernet frame is 1526 bytes. This means a data field length of up to 1500 bytes. The length of the 802.3 data field is also limited to 1500 bytes for 10 Mbps networks, but is different for other transmission speeds.

- In the 802.3 MAC frame, the length of the data field is indicated in the 802.3 header. The type of protocol it carries is then indicated in the 802.2 header (higher protocol level; see Figure 6). In practice, however, both frame formats can coexist on the same physical coax. This is done by using protocol type numbers (type field) greater than 1500 in the Ethernet frame. However, different device drivers are needed to handle each of these formats.

Thus, for all practical purposes, the Ethernet physical layer and the IEEE 802.3 physical layer are compatible. However, the Ethernet data link layer and the IEEE 802.3/802.2 data link layer are incompatible.

The 802.2 Logical Link Control (LLC) layer above IEEE 802.3 uses a concept known as *link service access point* (LSAP), which uses a 3-byte header, where DSAP and SSAP stand for destination and source service Access Point respectively. Numbers for these fields are assigned by an IEEE committee (see Figure 7).

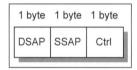

Figure 7. ARP - IEEE 802.2 LSAP header

Due to a growing number of applications using IEEE 802 as lower protocol layers, an extension was made to the IEEE 802.2 protocol in the form of the Sub-Network Access Protocol (SNAP) (see Figure 8). It is an extension to the LSAP header in Figure 7, and its use is indicated by the value 170 in both the SSAP and DSAP fields of the LSAP frame Figure 7.

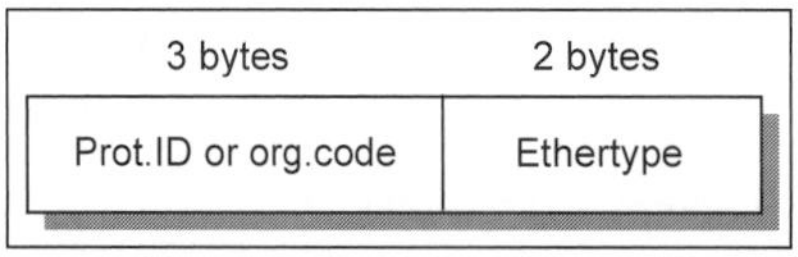

3 bytes	2 bytes
Prot.ID or org.code	Ethertype

Figure 8. ARP - IEEE 802.2 SNAP header

In the evolution of TCP/IP, three standards were established that describe the encapsulation of IP and ARP frames on these networks:

1. Introduced in 1984, RFC 894 – Standard for the Transmission of IP Datagrams over Ethernet Networks specifies only the use of Ethernet type of networks. The values assigned to the type field are:

   a. 2048 (hex 0800), for IP datagrams

   b. 2054 (hex 0806), for ARP datagrams

2. Introduced in 1985, RFC 948 – Two Methods for the Transmission of IP Datagrams over IEEE 802.3 Networks specifies two possibilities:

   a. The Ethernet compatible method: The frames are sent on a real IEEE 802.3 network in the same fashion as on an Ethernet network, that is, using the IEEE 802.3 data-length field as the Ethernet type field, thereby violating the IEEE 802.3 rules, but compatible with an Ethernet network.

   b. IEEE 802.2/802.3 LLC type 1 format: Using 802.2 LSAP header with IP using the value 6 for the SSAP and DSAP fields.

   The RFC indicates clearly that the IEEE 802.2/802.3 method is the preferred method, that is, that all future IP implementations on IEEE 802.3 networks are supposed to use the second method.

3. Introduced in 1987, RFC 1010 – Assigned Numbers (now obsoleted by RFC 1700, dated 1994) notes that as a result of IEEE 802.2 evolution and the need for more Internet protocol numbers, a new approach was developed based on practical experiences exchanged during the August 1986 TCP Vendors Workshop. It states, in an almost completely overlooked part of this RFC, that all IEEE 802.3, 802.4, and 802.5 implementations should use the Sub-Network Access Protocol (SNAP) form of the IEEE 802.2 LLC, with the DSAP and SSAP fields set to 170 (indicating the use of SNAP), with SNAP assigned as follows:

   a. 0 (zero) as organization code.

   b. EtherType field:

      1. 2048 (hex 0800), for IP datagrams

      2. 2054 (hex 0806), for ARP datagrams

      3. 32821 (hex 8035), for RARP datagrams

   These are the same values used in the Ethernet type field.

4. In 1988, RFC 1042 – Standard for the Transmission of IP Datagrams over IEEE 802 Networks was introduced. As this new approach (very important for implementations) passed almost unnoticed in a little note of an unrelated RFC, it became quite confusing, and finally, in February 1988, it was repeated in an RFC on its own: RFC 1042, which obsoletes RFC 948.

The relevant IBM TCP/IP products implement RFC 894 for DIX Ethernet and RFC 1700 for IEEE 802.3 networks.

However, in practical situations, there are still TCP/IP implementations that use the older LSAP method (RFC 948 or 1042). Such implementations will not communicate with the more recent implementations (such as IBM's).

Also note that the last method covers not only the IEEE 802.3 networks, but also the IEEE 802.4 and 802.5 networks, such as the IBM Token-Ring LAN.

2.2 Fiber Distributed Data Interface (FDDI)

The FDDI specifications define a family of standards for 100 Mbps fiber optic LANs that provides the physical layer and media access control sublayer of the data link layer, as defined by the ISO/OSI Model.

IP-FDDI is a draft-standard protocol. Its status is elective. It defines the encapsulating of IP datagrams and ARP requests and replies in FDDI frames. Figure 9 shows the related protocol layers.

It is defined in RFC 1188 – A Proposed Standard for the Transmission of IP Datagrams over FDDI Networks for single MAC stations. Operation on dual MAC stations will be described in a forthcoming RFC.

RFC 1188 states that all frames are transmitted in standard IEEE 802.2 LLC Type 1 Unnumbered Information format, with the DSAP and SSAP fields of the 802.2 header set to the assigned global SAP value for SNAP (decimal 170). The 24-bit Organization Code in the SNAP header is set to zero, and the remaining 16 bits are the EtherType from Assigned Numbers (see RFC 1700), that is:

- 2048 for IP
- 2054 for ARP

The mapping of 32-bit Internet addresses to 48-bit FDDI addresses is done via the ARP dynamic discovery procedure. The broadcast Internet addresses (whose <host address> is set to all ones) are mapped to the broadcast FDDI address (all ones).

IP datagrams are transmitted as series of 8-bit bytes using the usual TCP/IP transmission order called *big-endian* or *network byte order*.

The FDDI MAC specification (ISO 9314-2 - ISO, Fiber Distributed Data Interface - Media Access Control) defines a maximum frame size of 4500 bytes for all frame fields. After taking the LLC/SNAP header into account, and to allow future extensions to the MAC header and frame status fields, the MTU of FDDI networks is set to 4352 bytes.

Please refer to *LAN Concepts and Products,* SG24-4753 for more details on the FDDI architecture.

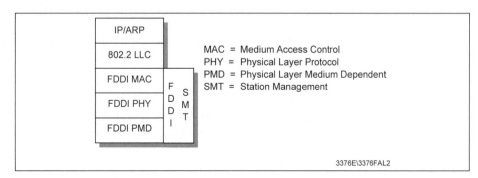

MAC = Medium Access Control
PHY = Physical Layer Protocol
PMD = Physical Layer Medium Dependent
SMT = Station Management

3376E\3376FAL2

Figure 9. IP and ARP over FDDI

2.3 Serial Line IP (SLIP)

The TCP/IP protocol family runs over a variety of network media: IEEE 802.3 and 802.5 LANs, X.25 lines, satellite links, and serial lines. Standards for the encapsulation of IP packets have been defined for many of these networks, but there is no standard for serial lines. SLIP is currently a *de facto* standard, commonly used for point-to-point serial connections running TCP/IP. Even though SLIP is not an Internet standard, it is documented by RFC 1055.

SLIP is just a very simple protocol designed quite a long time ago and is merely a packet framing protocol. It defines a sequence of characters that frame IP packets on a serial line, and nothing more. It does not provide any of the following:

- Addressing: Both computers on a SLIP link need to know each other's IP address for routing purposes. SLIP defines only the encapsulation protocol, not any form of handshaking or link control. Links are manually connected and configured, including the specification of the IP address.

- Packet type identification: SLIP cannot support multiple protocols across a single link; thus, only one protocol can be run over a SLIP connection.

- Error detection/correction: SLIP does no form of frame error detection. The higher level protocols should detect corrupted packets caused by errors on noisy lines. (IP header and UDP/TCP checksums should be sufficient.) Because it takes so long to retransmit a packet that was altered, it would be efficient if SLIP could provide some sort of simple error correction mechanism of its own.

- Compression: SLIP provides no mechanism for compressing frequently used IP header fields. Many applications over slow serial links tend to be single-user interactive TCP traffic, such as TELNET. This frequently involves small packet sizes and a relatively large overhead in TCP and IP headers that does not change much between datagrams, but which can have a noticeably detrimental effect on interactive response times.

  However, many SLIP implementations now use *Van Jacobsen Header Compression*. This is used to reduce the size of the combined IP and TCP headers from 40 bytes to 8 bytes by recording the states of a set of TCP connections at each end of the link and replacing the full headers with encoded updates for the normal case, where many of the fields are unchanged or are incremented by small amounts between successive IP datagrams for a session. This compression is described in RFC 1144.

The SLIP protocol has been essentially replaced by the Point-to-Point Protocol (PPP). Please see 2.4, "Point-to-Point Protocol (PPP)" on page 34.

2.4 Point-to-Point Protocol (PPP)

PPP is a network-specific standard protocol with STD number 51. Its status is elective. It is described in RFC 1661 and RFC 1662.

There are a large number of *proposed standard protocols*, which specify the operation of PPP over different kinds of point-to-point link. Each has a status of elective. The reader is advised to consult STD 1 – Internet Official Protocol Standards for a list of PPP-related RFCs which are on the Standards Track.

Point-to-point circuits in the form of asynchronous and synchronous lines have long been the mainstay for data communications. In the TCP/IP world, the de facto standard SLIP protocol has served admirably in this area, and is still in widespread use for dial-up TCP/IP connections. However, SLIP has a number of drawbacks that are addressed by the point-to-point protocol.

PPP has three main components:

1. A method for encapsulating datagrams over serial links.

2. A *Link Control Protocol (LCP)* for establishing, configuring, and testing the data-link connection.

3. A family of *Network Control Protocols* (NCPs) for establishing and configuring different network-layer protocols. PPP is designed to allow the simultaneous use of multiple network-layer protocols.

Before a link is considered to be ready for use by network-layer protocols, a specific sequence of events must happen. The LCP provides a method of establishing, configuring, maintaining, and terminating the connection. LCP goes through the following phases:

1. Link establishment and configuration negotiation: In this phase, link control packets are exchanged and link configuration options are negotiated. Once options are agreed upon, the link is *open*, but not necessarily *ready* for network-layer protocols to be started.

2. Link quality determination: This phase is optional. PPP does not specify the policy for determining quality, but does provide low-level tools, such as echo request and reply.

3. Authentication: This phase is optional. Each end of the link authenticates itself with the remote end using authentication methods agreed to during phase 1.

4. Network-layer protocol configuration negotiation: Once LCP has finished the previous phase, network-layer protocols may be separately configured by the appropriate NCP.

5. Link termination: LCP may terminate the link at any time. This will usually be done at the request of a human user, but may happen because of a physical event.

2.4.1 Point-to-Point encapsulation

A summary of the PPP encapsulation is shown in Figure 10.

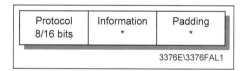

Figure 10. PPP encapsulation frame

Where:

- Protocol Field: The protocol field is one or two octets, and its value identifies the datagram encapsulated in the Information field of the packet. Up-to-date values of the Protocol field are specified in RFC 1700 – Assigned Numbers.

- Information Field: The Information field is zero or more octets. The Information field contains the datagram for the protocol specified in the Protocol field. The maximum length for the information field, including padding, but not including the Protocol field, is termed the Maximum Receive Unit (MRU), which defaults to 1500 octets. By negotiation, other values can be used for the MRU.

- Padding: On transmission, the information field may be padded with an arbitrary number of octets up to the MRU. It is the responsibility of each protocol to distinguish padding octets from real information.

The *IP Control Protocol (IPCP)* is the NCP for IP and is responsible for configuring, enabling, and disabling the IP protocol on both ends of the point-to-point link. The IPCP options negotiation sequence is the same as for LCP, thus allowing the possibility of reusing the code.

One important option used with IPCP is Van Jacobson Header Compression, which is used to reduce the size of the combined IP and TCP headers from 40 bytes to approximately 4 by recording the states of a set of TCP connections at each end of the link and replacing the full headers with encoded updates for the normal case, where many of the fields are unchanged or are incremented by small amounts between successive IP datagrams for a session. This compression is described in RFC 1144.

2.5 Integrated Services Digital Network (ISDN)

This section describes how to use the PPP encapsulation over ISDN point-to-point links. PPP over ISDN is documented by RFC 1618. Its status is elective. Since the ISDN B-channel is by definition a point-to-point circuit, PPP is well suited for use over these links.

The ISDN Basic Rate Interface (BRI) usually supports two B-channels with a capacity of 64 kbps each, and a 16 kbps D-channel for control information. B-channels can be used for voice or data or just for data in a combined way.

The ISDN Primary Rate Interface (PRI) may support many concurrent B-channel links (usually 30) and one 64 Kbps D-channel. The PPP LCP and NCP mechanisms are particularly useful in this situation in reducing or eliminating manual configuration, and facilitating ease of communication between diverse implementations. The ISDN D-channel can also be used for sending PPP packets when suitably framed, but is limited in bandwidth and often restricts communication links to a local switch.

PPP treats ISDN channels as bit or octet-oriented synchronous links. These links must be full-duplex, but may be either dedicated or circuit-switched. PPP presents an octet interface to the physical layer. There is no provision for sub-octets to be supplied or accepted. PPP does not impose any restrictions regarding transmission rate other than that of the particular ISDN channel interface. PPP does not require the use of control signals. When available, using such signals can allow greater functionality and performance.

The definition of various encodings and scrambling is the responsibility of the DTE/DCE equipment in use. While PPP will operate without regard to the underlying representation of the bit stream, lack of standards for transmission will hinder interoperability as surely as lack of data link standards. The D-channel interface requires NRZ encoding. Therefore, it is recommended that NRZ be used over the B-channel interface. This will allow frames to be easily exchanged between the B and D channels. However, when configuration of the encoding is allowed, NRZI is recommended as an alternative in order to ensure a minimum ones density where required over the clear B-channel. Implementations that want to interoperate with multiple encodings may choose to detect those encodings automatically. Automatic encoding detection is particularly important for primary rate interfaces, to avoid extensive pre-configuration.

Terminal adapters conforming to V.120[1] can be used as a simple interface to workstations. The terminal adapter provides asynchronous-to-synchronous conversion. Multiple B-channels can be used in parallel. V.120 is not interoperable with bit-synchronous links, since V.120 does not provide octet stuffing to bit stuffing conversion. Despite the fact that HDLC, LAPB, LAPD, and LAPF are nominally distinguishable, multiple methods of framing should not be used concurrently on the same ISDN channel. There is no requirement that PPP recognize alternative framing techniques, or switch between framing techniques without specific configuration. Experience has shown that the LLC Information Element is not reliably transmitted end to end. Therefore, transmission of the LLC-IE should not be relied upon for framing or encoding determination. No LLC-IE values that pertain to PPP have been assigned. Any other values that are received are not valid for PPP links, and can be ignored for PPP service. The LCP recommended sync configuration options apply to ISDN links. The standard LCP sync configuration defaults apply to ISDN links. The typical network connected to the link is likely to have an MRU size of either 1500 or 2048 bytes or greater. To avoid fragmentation, the maximum transmission unit (MTU) at the network layer should not exceed 1500, unless a peer MRU of 2048 or greater is specifically negotiated.

[1] CCITT Recommendations I.465 and V.120, "Data Terminal Equipment Communications over the Telephone Network with Provision for Statistical Multiplexing", CCITT Blue Book, Volume VIII, Fascicle VIII.1, 1988.

2.6 X.25

This topic describes the encapsulation of IP over X.25 networks, in accordance with ISO/IEC and CCITT standards. IP over X.25 networks is documented by RFC 1356 which obsoletes RFC 877. RFC 1356 is a Draft Standard with a status of elective. The substantive change to the IP encapsulation over X.25 is an increase in the IP datagram MTU size, the X.25 maximum data packet size, the virtual circuit management, and the interoperable encapsulation over X.25 of protocols other than IP between multiprotocol routers and bridges.

One or more X.25 virtual circuits are opened on demand when datagrams arrive at the network interface for transmission. Protocol data units (PDUs) are sent as X.25 *complete packet sequences*. That is, PDUs begin on X.25 data packet boundaries and the M bit (more data) is used to fragment PDUs that are larger than one X.25 data packet in length. In the IP encapsulation, the PDU is the IP datagram. The first octet in the call user data (CUD) field (the first data octet in the Call Request packet) is used for protocol demultiplexing, in accordance with the Subsequent Protocol Identifier (SPI) in ISO/IEC TR 9577. This field contains a one octet Network Layer Protocol Identifier (NLPID), which identifies the network layer protocol encapsulated over the X.25 virtual circuit. For the Internet community, the NLPID has four relevant values:

1. The value hex CC (binary 11001100, decimal 204) is IP.

2. The value hex 81 (binary 10000001, decimal 129) identifies ISO/IEC 8473 (CLNP).

3. The value hex 82 (binary 10000010, decimal 130) is used specifically for ISO/IEC 9542 (ES-IS). If there is already a circuit open to carry CLNP, then it is not necessary to open a second circuit to carry ES-IS.

4. The value hex 80 (binary 10000000, decimal 128) identifies the use of the IEEE Subnetwork Access Protocol (SNAP) to further encapsulate and identify a single network-layer protocol. The SNAP-encapsulated protocol is identified by including a five-octet SNAP header in the Call Request CUD field immediately following the hex 80 octet. SNAP headers are not included in the subsequent X.25 data packets. Only one SNAP-encapsulated protocol can be carried over a virtual circuit opened using this encoding.

The value hex 00 identifies the null encapsulation used to multiplex multiple network layer protocols over the same circuit. RFC 1700 contains one other non-CCITT and non-ISO/IEC value that has been used for Internet X.25 encapsulation identification, namely hex C5 (binary 11000101, decimal 197) for Blacker X.25. This value may continue to be used, but only by prior preconfiguration of the sending and receiving X.25 interfaces to support this value. The hex CD (binary 11001101, decimal 205), listed in RFC 1700 for ISO-IP, is also used by Blacker and can only be used by prior preconfiguration of the sending and receiving X.25 interfaces.

Each system must only accept calls for protocols it can process. Every Internet system must be able to accept the CC encapsulation for IP datagrams. Systems that support NLPIDs other than hex CC (for IP) should allow their use to be configured on a per-peer address basis. The Null encapsulation, identified by a NLPID encoding of hex 00, is used in order to multiplex multiple network layer protocols over one circuit. When the Null encapsulation is used, each X.25 complete packet sequence sent on the circuit begins with a one-octet NLPID, which identifies the network layer protocol data unit contained only in that particular complete packet sequence. Further, if the SNAP NLPID (hex 80) is used, then the NLPID octet is immediately followed by the five-octet SNAP header, which is then immediately followed by the encapsulated PDU. The encapsulated network layer protocol may differ from one complete packet sequence to the next over the same circuit.

Use of the single network layer protocol circuits is more efficient in terms of bandwidth if only a limited number of protocols are supported by a system. It also allows each system to determine exactly which protocols are supported by its communicating partner. Other advantages include being able to use X.25 accounting to detail each protocol and different quality of service or flow control windows for different protocols. The Null encapsulation, for multiplexing, is useful when a system, for any reason (such as implementation restrictions or network cost considerations), may only open a limited number of virtual circuits simultaneously. This is the method most likely to be used by a multiprotocol router to avoid using an unreasonable number of virtual circuits. If performing IEEE 802.1d bridging across X.25 is required, then the Null encapsulation must be used.

IP datagrams must, by default, be encapsulated on a virtual circuit opened with the CC CUD. Implementations may also support up to three other possible encapsulations of IP:

- IP datagrams may be contained in multiplexed data packets on a circuit using the Null encapsulation. Such data packets are identified by a NLPID of hex CC.

- IP may be encapsulated within the SNAP encapsulation on a circuit. This encapsulation is identified by containing, in the 5-octet SNAP header, an

Organizationally Unique Identifier (OUI) of hex 00-00-00 and Protocol Identifier (PID) of hex 08-00.

- On a circuit using the Null encapsulation, IP may be contained within the SNAP encapsulation of IP in multiplexed data packets.

2.7 Frame relay

The frame relay network provides a number of virtual circuits that form the basis for connections between stations attached to the same frame relay network. The resulting set of interconnected devices forms a private frame relay group, which may be either fully interconnected with a complete *mesh* of virtual circuits, or only partially interconnected. In either case, each virtual circuit is uniquely identified at each frame relay interface by a data link connection identifier (DLCI). In most circumstances, DLCIs have strictly local significance at each frame relay interface. Frame relay is documented in RFC 2427.

2.7.1 Frame format

All protocols must encapsulate their packets within a Q.922 Annex A frame{1}. Additionally, frames contain the necessary information to identify the protocol carried within the protocol data unit (PDU), thus allowing the receiver to properly process the incoming packet (refer to Figure 11). The format will be as follows:

- The control field is the Q.922 control field. The UI (0x03) value is used unless it is negotiated otherwise. The use of XID (0xAF or 0xBF) is permitted.

- The pad field is used to align the data portion (beyond the encapsulation header) of the frame to a two octet boundary. If present, the pad is a single octet and must have a value of zero.

- The Network Level Protocol ID (NLPID) field is administered by ISO and the ITU. It contains values for many different protocols, including IP, CLNP, and IEEE Subnetwork Access Protocol (SNAP). This field tells the receiver what encapsulation or what protocol follows. Values for this field are defined in ISO/IEC TR 9577 {2}. An NLPID value of 0x00 is defined within ISO/IEC TR 9577 as the null network layer or inactive set. Since it cannot be distinguished from a pad field, and because it has no significance within the context of this encapsulation scheme, an NLPID value of 0x00 is invalid under the frame relay encapsulation.

There is no commonly implemented minimum or maximum frame size for frame relay. A network must, however, support at least a 262-octet maximum.

Generally, the maximum will be greater than or equal to 1600 octets, but each frame relay provider will specify an appropriate value for its network. A frame relay data terminal equipment (DTE) must allow the maximum acceptable frame size to be configurable.

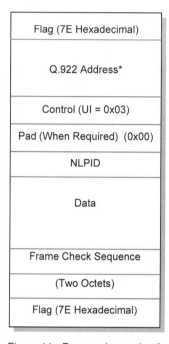

Figure 11. Frame relay packet format

2.7.2 Interconnect issues

There are two basic types of data packets that travel within the frame relay network: routed packets and bridged packets. These packets have distinct formats and must contain an indicator that the destination can use to correctly interpret the contents of the frame. This indicator is embedded within the NLPID and SNAP header information.

2.7.3 Data link layer parameter negotiation

Frame relay stations may choose to support the Exchange Identification (XID) specified in Appendix III of Q.922 {1}. This XID exchange allows the following parameters to be negotiated at the initialization of a frame relay circuit: maximum frame size, retransmission timer, and the maximum number of outstanding information (I) frames.

If this exchange is not used, these values must be statically configured by mutual agreement of data link connection (DLC) endpoints, or must be defaulted to the values specified in Section 5.9 of Q.922 {1}.

There are situations in which a frame relay station may wish to dynamically resolve a protocol address over permanent virtual circuits (PVCs). This may be accomplished using the standard Address Resolution Protocol (ARP) encapsulated within a SNAP-encoded frame relay packet.

Because of the inefficiencies of emulating broadcasting in a frame relay environment, a new address resolution variation was developed. It is called Inverse ARP, and describes a method for resolving a protocol address when the hardware address is already known. In a frame relay network, the known hardware address is the DLCI. Support for Inverse ARP is not required to implement this specification, but it has proven useful for frame relay interface autoconfiguration.

Stations must be able to map more than one IP address in the same IP subnet to a particular DLCI on a frame relay interface. This need arises from applications such as remote access, where servers must act as ARP proxies for many dial-in clients, each assigned a unique IP address while sharing bandwidth on the same DLC. The dynamic nature of such applications results in frequent address association changes with no effect on the DLC's status.

As with any other interface that utilizes ARP, stations may learn the associations between IP addresses and DLCIs by processing unsolicited (*gratuitous*) ARP requests that arrive on the DLC. If one station wishes to inform its peer station on the other end of a frame relay DLC of a new association between an IP address and that PVC, it should send an unsolicited ARP request with the source IP address equal to the destination IP address, and both set to the new IP address being used on the DLC. This allows a station to "announce" new client connections on a particular DLCI. The receiving station must store the new association, and remove any old existing association, if necessary, from any other DLCI on the interface.

2.7.4 IP over frame relay

Internet Protocol (IP) datagrams sent over a frame relay network conform to the encapsulation described previously. Within this context, IP could be encapsulated in two different ways: NLPID value, indicating IP, or NLPID value, indicating SNAP.

Although both of these encapsulations are supported under the given definitions, it is advantageous to select only one method as the appropriate mechanism for encapsulating IP data. Therefore, IP data should be encapsulated using the NLPID value of 0xcc, indicating an IP packet. This option is more efficient, because it transmits 48 fewer bits without the SNAP header and is consistent with the encapsulation of IP in an X.25 network.

2.8 PPP over SONET and SDH circuits

This discussion describes the use of the PPP encapsulation over Synchronous Optical Network (SONET) and Synchronous Digital Hierarchy (SDH) links, which is documented by RFC 1619. Since SONET and SDH are by definition point-to-point circuits, PPP is well suited to use over these links. SONET is an octet-synchronous multiplex scheme that defines a family of standard rates and formats. Despite the name, it is not limited to optical links. Electrical specifications have been defined for single-mode fiber, multimode fiber, and CATV 75 ohm coaxial cable. The transmission rates are integral multiples of 51.840 Mbps, which may be used to carry T3/E3 bit-synchronous signals. The allowed multiples are currently specified as:

Table 1. SONET Speed Hierarchy

Kind	Length	Meaning
0	-	End of option list
1	-	No-Operation
2	4	Maximum segment size
3	3	Window scale
4	2	Sack-Permitted
5	X	Sack
8	10	Timestamps

The CCITT Synchronous Digital Hierarchy defines a subset of SONET transmission rates beginning at 155.52 Mbps, as shown in Table 1.

2.8.1 Physical layer

PPP presents an octet interface to the physical layer. There is no provision for sub-octets to be supplied or accepted. SONET and SDH links are full-duplex by definition. The octet stream is mapped into the SONET/SDH Synchronous Payload Envelope (SPE) with the octet boundaries aligned with the SPE octet boundaries. No scrambling is needed during insertion into the SPE. The path signal label is intended to indicate the contents of the SPE.

The experimental value of 207 (hex CF) is used to indicate PPP. The multiframe indicator is currently unused and must be zero.

The basic rate for PPP over SONET/SDH is that of STS-3c/STM-1 at 155.52 Mbps. The available information bandwidth is 149.76 Mbps, which is the STS-3c/STM-1 SPE with section, line, and path overhead removed. This is the same upper layer mapping that is used for ATM and FDDI. Lower signal rates must use the Virtual Tributary (VT) mechanism of SONET/SDH. This maps existing signals up to T3/E3 rates asynchronously into the SPE or uses available clocks for bit-synchronous and byte-synchronous mapping. Higher signal rates should conform to the SDH STM series rather than the SONET STS series as equipment becomes available. The STM series progresses in powers of 4 instead of 3 and employs fewer steps, which is likely to simplify multiplexing and integration.

2.9 Multi-Path Channel+ (MPC+)

The MPC support is a protocol layer that allows multiple read and write subchannels to be treated as a single transmission group between the host and channel-attached devices. One level of MPC support, high performance data transfer (HPDT), also referred to as MPC+, provides more efficient transfer of data than non-HPDT MPC connections. Multi-Path Channel+ (MPC+) connections allow you to define a single transmission group (TG) that uses multiple write-direction and read-direction subchannels. Because each subchannel operates in only one direction, the half-duplex turnaround time that occurs with other channel-to-channel connections is reduced.

If at least one read and one write path is allocated successfully, the MPC+ channel connection is activated. Additional paths (defined but not online) in an MPC+ group can later be dynamically added to the active group using the MVS VARY device ONLINE command.

For example, if there is a need for an increase in capacity to allow for extra traffic over a channel, additional paths can be added to the active group without disruption. Similarly, paths can be deleted from the active group when no longer needed using the MVS VARY device OFFLINE command.

2.10 Asynchronous Transfer Mode (ATM)

ATM-based networks are of increasing interest for both local and wide area applications. There are already some products available to build your physical ATM network. The ATM architecture is new and therefore different from the standard LAN architectures. For this reason, changes are required so that traditional LAN products will work in the ATM environment. In the case of TCP/IP, the main change required is in the network interface (to provide support for ATM).

There are several approaches already available, two of which are important to the transport of TCP/IP traffic. They are described in 2.10.2, "Classical IP over ATM" on page 48 and 2.10.3, "ATM LAN emulation" on page 54. They are also compared in 2.10.4, "Classical IP over ATM versus LAN emulation" on page 57.

2.10.1 Address resolution (ATMARP and InATMARP)

The address resolution in an ATM logical IP subnet is done by the ATM Address Resolution Protocol (ATMARP), based on RFC 826, and the Inverse ATM Address Resolution Protocol (InATMARP), based on RFC 1293 (which is updated in RFC 2390). ATMARP is the same protocol as the ARP protocol, with extensions needed to support ARP in a unicast server ATM environment. InATMARP is the same protocol as the original InARP protocol, but applied to ATM networks. Use of these protocols differs depending on whether permanent virtual connections (PVCs) or switched virtual connections (SVCs) are used.

Both ATMARP and InATMARP are defined in RFC 2225 (updating RFC 1577), which is a proposed standard with a state of elective.

The encapsulation of ATMARP and InATMARP requests/replies is described in 2.10.2, "Classical IP over ATM" on page 48.

2.10.1.1 InATMARP

The ARP protocol is used to resolve a host's hardware address for a known IP address. The InATMARP protocol is used to resolve a host's IP address for a known hardware address. In a switched environment, you first establish a virtual connection (VC) of either a permanent virtual connection (PVC) or switched virtual connection (SVC) in order to communicate with another station. Therefore, you know the exact hardware address of the partner by administration, but the IP address is unknown. InATMARP provides dynamic address resolution. InARP uses the same frame format as the standard ARP, but defines two new operation codes:

- InARP request=8
- InARP reply=9

Please see 3.4.2.1, "ARP packet generation" on page 115 for more details.

Basic InATMARP operates essentially the same as ARP, with the exception that InATMARP does not broadcast requests. This is because the hardware address of the destination station is already known. A requesting station simply formats a request by inserting its source hardware and IP address and the known target hardware address. It then zero fills the target protocol address field and sends it directly to the target station. For every InATMARP request, the receiving station formats a reply using the source address from the request as the target address of the reply. Both sides update their ARP tables. The hardware type value for ATM is 19 decimal and the EtherType field is set to 0x806, which indicates ARP, according to RFC 1700.

2.10.1.2 Address resolution in a PVC environment

In a PVC environment, each station uses the InATMARP protocol to determine the IP addresses of all other connected stations. The resolution is done for those PVCs that are configured for LLC/SNAP encapsulation. It is the responsibility of each IP station supporting PVCs to revalidate ARP table entries as part of the aging process.

2.10.1.3 Address resolution in an SVC environment

SVCs require support for ATMARP in the non-broadcast environment of ATM. To meet this need, a single ATMARP server must be located within the Logical IP Subnetwork (LIS) (see 2.10.2.1, "The Logical IP Subnetwork (LIS)" on page 51). This server has authoritative responsibility for resolving the ATMARP requests of all IP members within the LIS. For an explanation of ATM terms, please refer to 2.10.2, "Classical IP over ATM" on page 48.

The server itself does not actively establish connections. It depends on the clients in the LIS to initiate the ATMARP registration procedure. An individual client connects to the ATMARP server using a point-to-point VC. The server, upon the completion of an ATM call/connection of a new VC specifying LLC/SNAP encapsulation, will transmit an InATMARP request to determine the IP address of the client. The InATMARP reply from the client contains the information necessary for the ATMARP server to build its ATMARP table cache. This table consists of:

- IP address
- ATM address
- Timestamp
- Associated VC

This information is used to generate replies to the ATMARP requests it receives.

> **Note**
>
> The ATMARP server mechanism requires that each client be administratively configured with the ATM address of the ATMARP server.

ARP table add/update algorithm
Consider the following:

- If the ATMARP server receives a new IP address in an InATMARP reply, the IP address is added to the ATMARP table.

- If the InATMARP IP address duplicates a table entry IP address and the InATMARP ATM address does not match the table entry ATM address, and there is an open VC associated with that table entry, the InATMARP information is discarded and no modifications to the table are made.

- When the server receives an ATMARP request over a VC, where the source IP and ATM address match the association already in the ATMARP table and the ATM address matches that associated with the VC, the server updates the timeout on the source ATMARP table entry. For example, if the client is sending ATMARP requests to the server over the same VC that it used to register its ATMARP entry, the server notes that the client is still "alive" and updates the timeout on the client's ATMARP table entry.

- When the server receives an ARP_REQUEST over a VC, it examines the source information. If there is no IP address associated with the VC over which the ATMARP request was received and if the source IP address is not associated with any other connection, then the server adds this station to its ATMARP table. This is not the normal way because, as mentioned above, it is the responsibility of the client to register at the ATMARP server.

ATMARP table aging
ATMARP table entries are valid:

- In clients for a maximum time of 15 minutes
- In servers for a minimum time of 20 minutes

Prior to aging an ATMARP table entry, the ATMARP server generates an InARP_REQUEST on any open VC associated with that entry and decides what to do according to the following rules:

- If an InARP_REPLY is received, that table entry is updated and not deleted.

- If there is no open VC associated with the table entry, the entry is deleted.

Therefore, if the client does not maintain an open VC to the server, the client must refresh its ATMARP information with the server at least once every 20 minutes. This is done by opening a VC to the server and exchanging the initial InATMARP packets.

The client handles the table updates according to the following:

- When an ATMARP table entry ages, the ATMARP client invalidates this table entry.
- If there is no open VC associated with the invalidated entry, that entry is deleted.
- In the case of an invalidated entry and an open VC, the ATMARP client revalidates the entry prior to transmitting any non-address resolution traffic on that VC. There are two possibilities:
  - In the case of a PVC, the client validates the entry by transmitting an InARP_REQUEST and updating the entry on receipt of an InARP_REPLY.
  - In the case of an SVC, the client validates the entry by transmitting an ARP_REQUEST to the ATMARP server and updating the entry on receipt of an ARP_REPLY.
- If a VC with an associated invalidated ATMARP table entry is closed, that table entry is removed.

As mentioned above, every ATM IP client that uses SVCs must know its ATMARP server's ATM address for the particular LIS. This address must be named at every client during customization. There is at present no well-known ATMARP server address defined.

2.10.2 Classical IP over ATM

The definitions for implementations of classical IP over Asynchronous Transfer Mode (ATM) are described in RFC 2225, which is a proposed standard with a status of elective according to RFC 2400 (STD 1). This RFC considers only the application of ATM as a direct replacement for the "wires," local LAN segments connecting IP endstations (members) and routers operating in the classical LAN-based paradigm. Issues raised by MAC level bridging and LAN emulation are not covered.

For ATM Forum's method of providing ATM migration, please see 2.10.3, "ATM LAN emulation" on page 54.

Initial deployment of ATM provides a LAN segment replacement for:

- Ethernets, token-rings, or FDDI networks
- Local area backbones between existing (non-ATM) LANs
- Dedicated circuits of frame relay PVCs between IP routers

This RFC also describes extensions to the ARP protocol (RFC 826) in order to work over ATM. This is discussed separately in 2.10.1, "Address resolution (ATMARP and InATMARP)" on page 45.

First some ATM basics:

Cells

All information (voice, image, video, data, and so on) is transported through the network in very short (48 data bytes plus a 5-byte header) blocks called *cells*.

Routing

Information flow is along paths (called *virtual channels*) set up as a series of pointers through the network. The cell header contains an identifier that links the cell to the correct path that it will take towards its destination.

Cells on a particular virtual channel always follow the same path through the network and are delivered to the destination in the same order in which they were received.

Hardware-based switching

ATM is designed so that simple hardware-based logic elements may be employed at each node to perform the switching. On a link of 1 Gbps, a new cell arrives and a cell is transmitted every .43 microseconds. There is not a lot of time to decide what to do with an arriving packet.

Virtual Connection (VC)

ATM provides a virtual connection switched environment. VC setup can be done on either a permanent virtual connection (PVC) or a dynamic switched virtual connection (SVC) basis. SVC call management is performed via implementations of the Q.93B protocol.

End-user interface

The only way for a higher layer protocol to communicate across an ATM network is over the ATM Adaptation Layer (AAL). The function of this layer is to perform the mapping of protocol data units (PDUs) into the information field of the ATM cell and vice versa. There are four different AAL types defined: AAL1, AAL2, AAL3/4, and AAL5. These AALs offer different services for higher layer protocols. Here are the characteristics of AAL5, which is used for TCP/IP:

- Message mode and streaming mode
- Assured delivery
- Non-assured delivery (used by TCP/IP)
- Blocking and segmentation of data
- Multipoint operation

AAL5 provides the same functions as a LAN at the Medium Access Control (MAC) layer. The AAL type is known by the VC endpoints via the cell setup mechanism and is not carried in the ATM cell header. For PVCs, the AAL type is administratively configured at the endpoints when the connection (circuit) is set up. For SVCs, the AAL type is communicated along the VC path via Q.93B as part of call setup establishment and the endpoints use the signaled information for configuration. ATM switches generally do not care about the AAL type of VCs. The AAL5 format specifies a packet format with a maximum size of 64KB - 1 byte of user data. The *primitives*, which the higher layer protocol has to use in order to interface with the AAL layer (at the AAL service access point - SAP), are rigorously defined. When a high-layer protocol sends data, that data is processed first by the adaptation layer, then by the ATM layer, and then the physical layer takes over to send the data to the ATM network. The cells are transported by the network and then received on the other side first by the physical layer, then processed by the ATM layer, and then by the receiving AAL. When all this is complete, the information (data) is passed to the receiving higher layer protocol. The total function performed by the ATM network has been the non-assured transport (it might have lost some) of information from one side to the other. Looked at from a traditional data processing viewpoint, all the ATM network has done is to replace a physical link connection with another kind of physical connection. All the higher layer network functions must still be performed (for example, IEEE 802.2).

Addressing

An ATM Forum endpoint address is either encoded as a 20-byte OSI NSAP-based address (used for private network addressing, three formats possible) or is an E.164 Public UNI address (telephone number style address used for public ATM networks).[2]

Broadcast, Multicast

There are currently no broadcast functions similar to LANs provided. But there is a multicast function available. The ATM term for multicast is *point-to-multipoint connection.*

2.10.2.1 The Logical IP Subnetwork (LIS)

The term LIS was introduced to map the logical IP structure to the ATM network. In the LIS scenario, each separate administrative entity configures its hosts and routers within a closed logical IP subnetwork (same IP network/subnet number and address mask). Each LIS operates and communicates independently of other LISs on the same ATM network. Hosts that are connected to an ATM network communicate directly to other hosts within the same LIS. This implies that all members of a LIS are able to communicate via ATM with all other members in the same LIS. (VC topology is fully meshed.) Communication to hosts outside of the local LIS is provided via an IP router. This router is an ATM endpoint attached to the ATM network that is configured as a member of one or more LISs. This configuration may result in a number of separate LISs operating over the same ATM network. Hosts of differing IP subnets must communicate via an intermediate IP router, even though it may be possible to open a direct VC between the two IP members over the ATM network.

---

[2] The ATM Forum is a worldwide organization, aimed at promoting ATM within the industry and the end-user community. The membership includes more than 500 companies representing all sectors of the communications and computer industries, as well as a number of government agencies, research organizations, and users.

2.10.2.2 Multiprotocol encapsulation

If you want to use more than one type of network protocol (IP, IPX, and so on) concurrently over a physical network, you need a method of multiplexing the different protocols. This can be done in the case of ATM either by VC-based multiplexing or LLC encapsulation. If you choose VC-based multiplexing, you have to have a VC for each different protocol between the two hosts. The LLC encapsulation provides the multiplexing function at the LLC layer and therefore needs only one VC. TCP/IP uses, according to RFC 2225 and 1483, the second method, because this kind of multiplexing was already defined in RFC 1042 for all other LAN types, such as Ethernet, token-ring, and FDDI. With this definition, IP uses ATM simply as a LAN replacement. All the other benefits ATM has to offer, such as transportation of isochronous traffic, and so on, are not used. There is an IETF working group with the mission of improving the IP implementation and to interface with the ATM Forum in order to represent the interests of the Internet community for future standards.

To be exact, the TCP/IP PDU is encapsulated in an IEEE 802.2 LLC header followed by an IEEE 802.1a SubNetwork Attachment Point (SNAP) header and carried within the payload field of an AAL5 CPCS-PDU (Common Part Convergence Sublayer). The AAL5 CPCS-PDU format is shown in Figure 12.

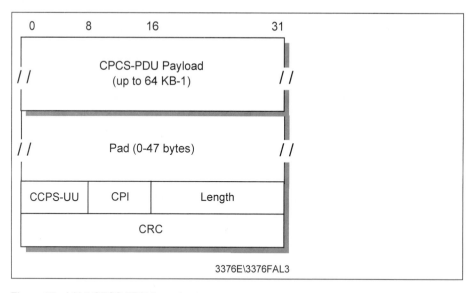

Figure 12. AAL5 CPCS-PDU format

Where:

CPCS-PDU Payload The CPCS-PDU payload is shown in Figure 13.

Pad The Pad field pads out the CDCS-PDU to fit exactly into the ATM cells.

CPCS-UU The CPCS-UU (User-to-User identification) field is used to transparently transfer CPCS user-to-user information. This field has no function for the encapsulation and can be set to any value.

CPI The Common Part Indicator (CPI) field aligns the CPCS-PDU trailer with 64 bits.

Length The Length field indicates the length, in bytes, of the payload field. The maximum value is 65535, which is 64KB - 1.

CRC The CRC field protects the entire CPCS-PDU, except the CRC field itself.

The payload format for routed IP PDUs is shown in Figure 13.

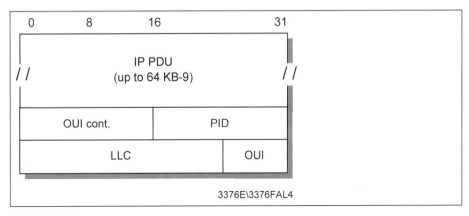

Figure 13. CPCS-PDU payload format for IP PDUs

Where:

IP PDU Normal IP datagram, starting with the IP header.

LLC 3-byte LLC header with the format DSAP-SSAP-Ctrl. For IP data it is set to 0xAA-AA-03 to indicate the presence of a SNAP header. The Ctrl field always has the value 0x03, specifying Unnumbered Information Command PDU.

OUI   The 3-byte Organizationally Unique Identifier (OUI) identifies an organization that administers the meaning of the following 2-byte Protocol Identifier (PID). To specify an EtherType in PID, the OUI has to be set to 0x00-00-00.

PID   The Protocol Identifier (PID) field specifies the protocol type of the following PDU. For IP datagrams, the assigned EtherType or PID is 0x08-00.

The default MTU size for IP members in an ATM network is discussed in RFC 1626 and defined to be 9180 bytes. The LLC/SNAP header is 8 bytes; therefore, the default ATM AAL5 PDU size is 9188 bytes. The possible values can be between zero and 65535. You are allowed to change the MTU size but then all members of a LIS must be changed as well in order to have the same value. RFC 1755 recommends that all implementations should support MTU sizes up to and including 64 KB.

The address resolution in an ATM network is defined as an extension of the ARP protocol and is described in 2.10.1, "Address resolution (ATMARP and InATMARP)" on page 45.

There is no mapping from IP broadcast or multicast addresses to ATM *broadcast* or multicast addresses available. But there are no restrictions for transmitting or receiving IP datagrams specifying any of the four standard IP broadcast address forms as described in RFC 1122. Members, upon receiving an IP broadcast or IP subnet broadcast for their LIS, must process the packet as if addressed to that station.

2.10.3 ATM LAN emulation

Another approach to provide a migration path to a native ATM network is ATM LAN emulation. ATM LAN emulation is still under construction by ATM Forum working groups. For the IETF approach, please see 2.10.2, "Classical IP over ATM" on page 48. There is no ATM Forum implementation agreement available covering virtual LANs over ATM, but there are some basic agreements on the different proposals made to the ATM Forum. The descriptions below are based on the IBM proposals.

The concept of ATM LAN emulation is to construct a system such that the workstation application software "thinks" it is a member of a real shared medium LAN, such as a token-ring. This method maximizes the reuse of existing LAN software and significantly reduces the cost of migration to ATM. In PC LAN environments, for example, the LAN emulation layer could be implemented under the NDIS/ODI-type interface. With such an implementation, all the higher layer protocols, such as IP, IPX, NetBIOS, and SNA, could be run over ATM networks without any change.

Refer to Figure 14 for the implementation of token-ring and Ethernet.

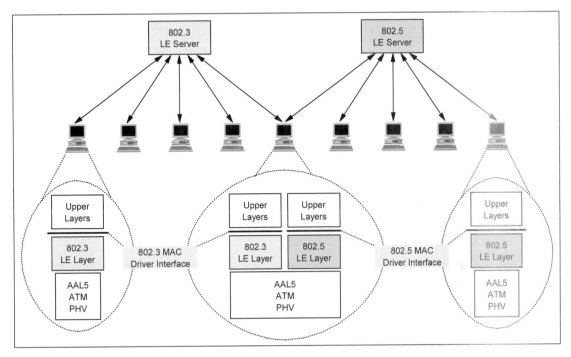

Figure 14. Ethernet and token-ring LAN emulation

2.10.3.1 LAN emulation layer (workstation software)

Each workstation that performs the LE function needs to have software to provide the LE service. This software is called the LAN emulation layer (LE layer). It provides the interface to existing protocol support (such as IP, IPX, IEEE 802.2 LLC, NetBIOS, and so on) and emulates the functions of a real shared medium LAN. This means that no changes are needed to existing LAN application software to use ATM services. The LE layer interfaces to the ATM network through a hardware ATM adapter.

The primary function of the LE layer is to transfer encapsulated LAN frames (arriving from higher layers) to their destination either directly (over a direct VC) or through the LE server. This is done by using AAL5 services provided by ATM.

Each LE layer has one or more LAN addresses as well as an ATM address.

A separate instance (logical copy or LE client) of the LE layer is needed in each workstation for each different LAN or type of LAN to be supported. For example, if both token-ring and Ethernet LAN types are to be emulated, then you need two LE layers. In fact, they will probably just be different threads within the same copy of the same code, but they are logically separate LE layers. Separate LE layers would also be used if one workstation needed to be part of two different emulated token-ring LANs. Each separate LE layer needs a different MAC address, but can share the same physical ATM connection (adapter).

2.10.3.2 LAN emulation server

The basic function of the LE server is to provide directory, multicast, and address resolution services to the LE layers in the workstations. It also provides a connectionless data transfer service to the LE layers in the workstations, if needed.

Each emulated LAN must have an LE server. It would be possible to have multiple LE servers sharing the same hardware and code (via multithreading), but the LE servers are logically separate entities. As for the LE layers, an emulated token-ring LAN cannot have members that are emulating an Ethernet LAN. Thus, an instance of an LE server is dedicated to a single type of LAN emulation. The LE server can be physically internal to the ATM network or provided in an external device, but logically it is always an external function that simply uses the services provided by ATM to do its job.

2.10.3.3 Default VCs

A default VC is a connection between an LE layer in a workstation and the LE server. These connections can be permanent or switched.

All LE control messages are carried between the LE layer and the LE server on the default VC. Encapsulated data frames can also be sent on the default VC.

The presence of the LE server and the default VCs is necessary for the LE function to be performed.

2.10.3.4 Direct VCs

Direct VCs are connections between LE layers in the end systems. They are always switched and set up on demand. If the ATM network does not support switched connections, then you cannot have direct VCs, and all the data must be sent through the LE server on default VCs. If there is no direct VC available for any reason, then data transfer must take place through the LE server. (There is no other way.)

Direct VCs are set up on request by an LE layer. (The server cannot set them up, as there is no third party call setup function in ATM.) The ATM address of a destination LE layer is provided to a requesting LE layer by the LE server. Direct VCs stay in place until one of the partner LE layers decides to end the connection (because there is no more data).

2.10.3.5 Initialization

During initialization, the LE layer (workstation) establishes the default VC with the LE server. It also discovers its own ATM address, which is needed if it is to later set up direct VCs.

2.10.3.6 Registration

In this phase, the LE layer (workstation) registers its MAC addresses with the LE server. Other things, such as filtering requirements (optional), may be provided.

2.10.3.7 Management and resolution

This is the method used by ATM endstations to set up direct VCs with other endstations (LE layers). This function includes mechanisms for learning the ATM address of a target station, mapping the MAC address to an ATM address, storing the mapping in a table, and managing the table.

For the server, this function provides the means for supporting the use of direct VCs by endstations. This includes a mechanism for mapping the MAC address of an end system to its ATM address, storing the information and providing it to a requesting endstation.

This structure maintains full LAN function and can support most higher layer LAN protocols. Reliance on the server for data transfer is minimized by using switched VCs for the transport of most bulk data.

2.10.4 Classical IP over ATM versus LAN emulation

These two approaches to providing an easier way to migrate to ATM were made with different goals in mind.

Classical IP over ATM defines an encapsulation and address resolution method. The definitions are made for IP only and not for use with other protocols. So if you have applications requiring other protocol stacks (such as IPX or SNA), then IP over ATM will not provide a complete solution. On the other hand, if you only have TCP or UDP-based applications, then this might be the better solution, since this specialized adaptation of the IP protocol to the ATM architecture is likely to produce less overhead than a more global solution, and therefore be more efficient. Another advantage of this implementation is the use of some ATM-specific functions, such as large MTU sizes, and so on.

The major goal of the ATM Forum's approach is to run layer 3 and higher protocols unchanged over the ATM network. This means that existing protocols, for example, TCP/IP, IPX, NetBIOS and SNA, and their applications can use the benefits of the fast ATM network without any changes. The mapping for all protocols is already defined. The LAN emulation layer provides all the services of a classic LAN; thus, the upper layer does not know of the existence of ATM. This is both an advantage and a disadvantage, because the knowledge of the underlying network could be used to provide a more effective implementation.

In the near future, both approaches will be used depending on the particular requirements. Over time, when the mapping of applications to ATM is fully defined and implemented, the scheme of a dedicated ATM implementation may be used.

2.11 Multiprotocol over ATM (MPOA)

The objectives of MPOA are to:

- Provide end-to-end layer 3 internetworking connectivity across an ATM network. This is for hosts that are attached either:

    - Directly to the ATM network

    - Indirectly to the ATM network on a legacy LAN

- Support the distribution of the internetwork layer (for example, an IP subnet) across legacy and ATM-attached devices. Removes the port to layer 3 network restriction of routers to enable the building of protocol-based virtual LANs (VLANs).

- Ensure interoperability among the distributed routing components while allowing flexibility in implementations.

- Address how internetwork layer protocols use the services of an ATM network.

Although the name is multiprotocol over ATM, the actual work being done at the moment in the MPOA subworking group is entirely focused on IP.

2.11.1 Benefits of MPOA

MPOA represents the transition from LAN emulation to direct exploitation of ATM by the internetwork layer protocols. The advantages are:

- Protocols would see ATM as more than just another link. Hence, we are able to exploit the facilities of ATM.

- Eliminates the need for the overhead of the legacy LAN frame structure.

The MPOA solution has the following benefits over both Classical IP (RFC 1577) and LAN emulation solutions:

- Lower latency by allowing direct connectivity between end systems that can cut across subnet boundaries. This is achieved by minimizing the need for multiple hops through ATM routers for communication between end systems on different virtual LANs.

- Higher aggregate layer 3 forwarding capacity by distributing processing functions to the edge of the network.

- Allows mapping of specific flows to specific QOS characteristics.

- Allows a layer 3 subnet to be distributed across a physical network.

2.11.2 MPOA logical components

The MPOA solution consists of a number of logical components and information flows between those components. The logical components are of two kinds:

MPOA server   MPOA servers maintain *complete* knowledge of the MAC and internetworking layer topologies for the IASGs they serve. To accomplish this, they exchange information among themselves and with MPOA clients.

MPOA client   MPOA clients maintain local caches of mappings (from packet prefix to ATM information). These caches are populated by requesting the information from the appropriate MPOA server on an as-needed basis.

The layer 3 addresses associated with an MPOA client would represent either the layer 3 address of the client itself, or the layer 3 addresses reachable through the client. (The client has an edge device or router.)

An MPOA client will connect to its MPOA server to register the client's ATM address and the layer 3 addresses reachable via the client.

2.11.3 MPOA functional components

Figure 15 shows the mapping between the logical and physical components, which are split between the following layers:

- MPOA Functional Group Layer

- LAN Emulation Layer

- Physical Layer

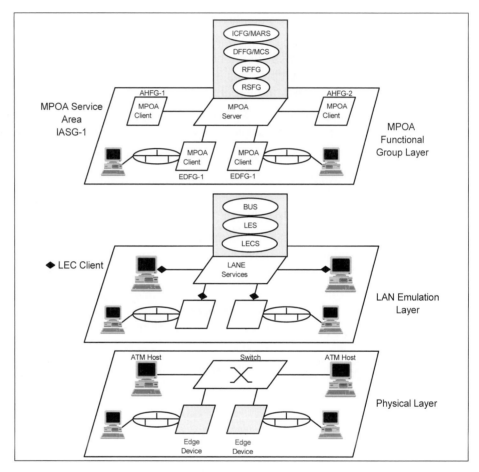

Figure 15. MPOA functional components

The MPOA solution will be implemented into various functional groups that include:

- Internetwork Address Sub-Group (IASG): A range of internetwork layer addresses (for example, an IPv4 subnet). Hence, if a host operates two internetwork layer protocols, it will be a member of, at least, two IASGs.

- Edge Device Functional Group (EDFG): EDFG is the group of functions performed by a device that provides internetworking level connections between a legacy subnetwork and ATM.

- An EDFG implements layer 3 packet forwarding, but does not execute any routing protocols (executed in the RSFG).

- Two types of EDFG are allowed: *simple* and *smart*.

  • Smart EDFGs request resolution of internetwork addresses (that is, it will send a query ARP type frame if it does not have an entry for the destination).

  • Simple EDFGs will send a frame via a default class to a default destination if no entry exists.

- A coresident proxy LEC function is required.

• ATM-Attached Host Functional Group (AHFG): AHFG is the group of functions performed by an ATM-attached host that is participating in the MPOA network.

A coresident proxy LEC function is optional.

Within an IASG, LAN emulation is used as a transport mechanism to either legacy devices or LAN emulation devices, in which case access to a LEC is required. If the AHFG will not be communicating with LANE or legacy devices, then a co-resident LEC is not required.

• IASG Coordination Functional Group (ICFG): ICFG is the group of functions performed to coordinate the distribution of a single IASG across multiple legacy LAN ports on one or more EDFG and/or ATM device. The ICFG tracks the location of the functional components so that it is able to respond to queries for layer 3 addresses.

• Default Forwarder Function Group (DFFG): In the absence of direct client-to-client connectivity, the DFFG provides default forwarding for traffic destined either within or outside the IASG.

- Provides internetwork layer multicast forwarding in an IASG; that is, the DFFG acts as the multicast server (MCS) in an MPOA-based MARS implementation.

- Provides *proxy* LAN emulation function for AHFGs (that is, for AHFGs that do not have a LANE client) to enable AHFGs to send/receive traffic with legacy-attached systems.

• Route Server Functional Group (RSFG): RSFG performs internetworking level functions in an MPOA network. This includes:

- Running conventional internetworking routing protocols (for example, OSPF, RIP, and BGP)

- Providing address resolution between IASGs, handling requests, and building responses

- Remote Forwarder Functional Group (RFFG): RFFG is the group of functions performed in association with forwarding traffic from a source to a destination, where these can be either an IASG or an MPOA client. An RFFG is synonymous with the *default router* function of a typical IPv4 subnet.

> **Note**
>
> One or more of these functional groups may co-reside in the same physical entity. MPOA allows arbitrary physical locations of these groups.

2.11.4 MPOA operation

The MPOA system operates as a set of functional groups that exchange information in order to exhibit the desired behavior. To provide an overview of the MPOA system, the behavior of the components is described in a sequence order by *significant events*:

Configuration	Ensures that all functional groups have the appropriate set of administrative information.
Registration and discovery	Includes the functional groups informing each other of their existence and of the identities of attached devices and EDFGs informing the ICFG of legacy devices.
Destination resolution	The action of determining the route description given a destination internetwork layer address and possibly other information (for example, QOS). This is the part of the MPOA system that allows it to perform cut-through (with respect to IASG boundaries).
Data transfer	To get internetworking layer data from one MPOA client to another.
Intra-IASG coordination	The function that enables IASGs to be spread across multiple physical interfaces.
Routing protocol support	Enables the MPOA system to interact with traditional internetworks.
Spanning tree support	Enables the MPOA system to interact with existing extended LANs.

Replication Support   Provides for replication of key components for reasons of capacity or resilience.

2.12 References

The following RFCs provide detailed information on the connection protocols and architectures presented throughout this chapter:

- RFC 826 – Ethernet Address Resolution Protocol
- RFC 894 – Standard for the Transmission of IP Datagrams over Ethernet Networks
- RFC 1042 – Standard for the Transmission of IP Datagrams over IEEE 802 Networks
- RFC 1055 – Nonstandard for Transmission of IP Datagrams over Serial Lines: SLIP
- RFC 1144 – Compressing TCP/IP Headers for Low-Speed Serial Links
- RFC 1188 – Proposed Standard for the Transmission of IP Datagrams over FDDI Networks
- RFC 1356 – Multiprotocol Interconnect on X.25 and ISDN in the Packet Mode
- RFC 1483 – Multiprotocol Encapsulation over ATM Adaptation Layer 5
- RFC 1618 – PPP over ISDN
- RFC 1619 – PPP over SONET/SDH
- RFC 1661 – The Point-to-Point Protocol (PPP)
- RFC 1662 – PPP in HDLC-Like Framing
- RFC 1700 – Assigned Numbers
- RFC 1755 – ATM Signaling Support for IP over ATM
- RFC 1795 – Data Link Switching: Switch-to-Switch Protocol AIW DLSw RIG: DLSw Closed Pages, DLSw Standard Version 1
- RFC 2225 – Classical IP and ARP over ATM
- RFC 2390 – Inverse Address Resolution Protocol
- RFC 2400 – Internet Official Protocol Standards
- RFC 2427 – Multiprotocol Interconnect over Frame Relay

Chapter 3. Internetworking protocols

This chapter provides an overview of the most important and common protocols associated with the TCP/IP internetwork layer. These include:

- Internet Protocol (IP)
- Internet Control Message Protocol (ICMP)
- Address Resolution Protocol (ARP)
- Reverse Address Resolution Protocol (RARP)
- Bootstrap Protocol (BOOTP)
- Dynamic Host Configuration Protocol (DHCP)

These protocols perform datagram addressing, routing and delivery, dynamic address configuration, and resolve between the internetwork layer addresses and the network interface layer addresses.

3.1 Internet Protocol (IP)

IP is a standard protocol with STD number 5. The standard also includes ICMP (see 3.2, "Internet Control Message Protocol (ICMP)" on page 102) and IGMP (see 6.2, "Internet Group Management Protocol (IGMP)" on page 232). IP has a status of required.

The current IP specification can be found in RFCs 791, 950, 919 and 922, with updates in RFC 2474.

IP is the protocol that hides the underlying physical network by creating a *virtual network* view. It is an unreliable, best-effort, and connectionless packet delivery protocol. Note that best-effort means that the packets sent by IP may be lost, arrive out of order, or even be duplicated. IP assumes higher layer protocols will address these anomalies.

One of the reasons for using a connectionless network protocol was to minimize the dependency on specific computing centers that used hierarchical connection-oriented networks. The United States Department of Defense intended to deploy a network that would still be operational if parts of the country were destroyed. This has been proven to be true for the Internet.

3.1.1 IP addressing

IP addresses are represented by a 32-bit unsigned binary value. It is usually expressed in a dotted decimal format. For example, 9.167.5.8 is a valid IP address. The numeric form is used by IP software. The mapping between the IP address and an easier-to-read symbolic name, for example myhost.ibm.com, is done by the *Domain Name System (DNS)* discussed in 8.1, "Domain Name System (DNS)" on page 279.

3.1.1.1 The IP address

IP addressing standards are described in RFC 1166 – Internet Numbers. To identify a host on the Internet, each host is assigned an address, the *IP address*, or in some cases, the *Internet address*. When the host is attached to more than one network, it is called *multi-homed* and has one IP address for each network interface. The IP address consists of a pair of numbers:

```
IP address = <network number><host number>
```

The *network number* portion of the IP address is administered by one of three Regional Internet Registries (RIR):

- American Registry for Internet Numbers (ARIN): This registry is responsible for the administration and registration of Internet Protocol (IP) numbers for North America, South America, the Caribbean and sub-Saharan Africa.

- Reseaux IP Europeens (RIPE): This registry is responsible for the administration and registration of Internet Protocol (IP) numbers for Europe, Middle East, parts of Africa.

- Asia Pacific Network Information Centre (APNIC): This registry is responsible for the administration and registration of Internet Protocol (IP) numbers within the Asia Pacific region.

IP addresses are 32-bit numbers represented in a *dotted decimal* form (as the decimal representation of four 8-bit values concatenated with dots). For example, 128.2.7.9 is an IP address with 128.2 being the network number and 7.9 being the host number. The rules used to divide an IP address into its network and host parts are explained below.

The binary format of the IP address 128.2.7.9 is:

```
10000000 00000010 00000111 00001001
```

IP addresses are used by the IP protocol to uniquely identify a host on the Internet (or more generally, any internet). Strictly speaking, an IP address identifies an interface that is capable of sending and receiving IP datagrams. One system can have multiple such interfaces. However, both hosts and routers must have at least one IP address, so this simplified definition is acceptable. IP datagrams (the basic data packets exchanged between hosts) are transmitted by a physical network attached to the host. Each IP datagram contains a *source IP address* and a *destination IP address*. To send a datagram to a certain IP destination, the target IP address must be translated or mapped to a physical address. This may require transmissions on the network to find out the destination's physical network address. (For example, on LANs, the Address Resolution Protocol, discussed in 3.4, "Address Resolution Protocol (ARP)" on page 114, is used to translate IP addresses to physical MAC addresses.)

3.1.1.2 Class-based IP addresses
The first bits of the IP address specify how the rest of the address should be separated into its network and host part. The terms *network address* and *netID* are sometimes used instead of network number, but the formal term, used in RFC 1166, is network number. Similarly, the terms *host address* and *hostID* are sometimes used instead of host number.

There are five classes of IP addresses. They are shown in Figure 16.

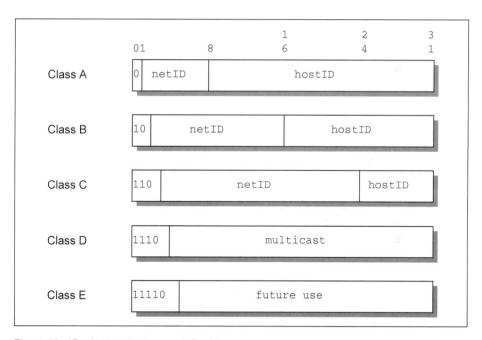

Figure 16. IP - Assigned classes of IP addresses

Where:

- Class A addresses: These addresses use 7 bits for the <network> and 24 bits for the <host> portion of the IP address. This allows for 2^7-2 (126) networks each with 2^{24}-2 (16777214) hosts; a total of over 2 billion addresses.

- Class B addresses: These addresses use 14 bits for the <network> and 16 bits for the <host> portion of the IP address. This allows for 2^{14}-2 (16382) networks each with 2^{16}-2 (65534) hosts; a total of over 1 billion addresses.

- Class C addresses: These addresses use 21 bits for the <network> and 8 bits for the <host> portion of the IP address. That allows for 2^{21}-2 (2097150) networks each with 2^{8}-2 (254) hosts; a total of over half a billion addresses.

- Class D addresses: These addresses are reserved for multicasting (a sort of broadcasting, but in a limited area, and only to hosts using the same class D address).

- Class E addresses: These addresses are reserved for future use.

A Class A address is suitable for networks with an extremely large number of hosts. Class C addresses are suitable for networks with a small number of hosts. This means that medium-sized networks (those with more than 254 hosts or where there is an expectation of more than 254 hosts) must use Class B addresses. However, the number of small- to medium-sized networks has been growing very rapidly. It was feared that if this growth had been allowed to continue unabated, all of the available Class B network addresses would have been used by the mid-1990s. This was termed the IP address exhaustion problem (refer to 3.1.5, "The IP address exhaustion problem" on page 83).

The division of an IP address into two parts also separates the responsibility for selecting the complete IP address. The network number portion of the address is assigned by the RIRs. The host number portion is assigned by the authority controlling the network. As shown in the next section, the host number can be further subdivided: this division is controlled by the authority which manages the network. It is not controlled by the RIRs.

3.1.1.3 Reserved IP addresses

A component of an IP address with a value *all bits 0* or *all bits 1* has a special meaning:

- All bits 0: An address with all bits zero in the host number portion is interpreted as *this* host (IP address with <host address>=0). All bits zero in the network number portion is *this* network (IP address with <network address>=0). When a host wants to communicate over a network, but does not yet know the network IP address, it may send packets with <network address>=0. Other hosts on the network interpret the address as meaning *this* network. Their replies contain the fully qualified network address, which the sender records for future use.

- All bits 1: An address with all bits one is interpreted as *all* networks or *all* hosts. For example, the following means all hosts on network 128.2 (class B address):

  `128.2.255.255`

  This is called a directed broadcast address because it contains both a valid <network address> and a broadcast <host address>.

- Loopback: The class A network 127.0.0.0 is defined as the loopback network. Addresses from that network are assigned to interfaces that process data within the local system. These loopback interfaces do not access a physical network.

3.1.2 IP subnets

Due to the explosive growth of the Internet, the principle of assigned IP addresses became too inflexible to allow easy changes to local network configurations. Those changes might occur when:

- A new type of physical network is installed at a location.
- Growth of the number of hosts requires splitting the local network into two or more separate networks.
- Growing distances require splitting a network into smaller networks, with gateways between them.

To avoid having to request additional IP network addresses, the concept of IP subnetting was introduced. The assignment of subnets is done locally. The entire network still appears as one IP network to the outside world.

The host number part of the IP address is subdivided into a second network number and a host number. This second network is termed a *subnetwork* or *subnet*. The main network now consists of a number of subnets. The IP address is interpreted as:

`<network number><subnet number><host number>`

The combination of subnet number and host number is often termed the *local address* or the *local portion* of the IP address. *Subnetting* is implemented in a way that is transparent to remote networks. A host within a network that has subnets is aware of the subnetting structure. A host in a different network is not. This remote host still regards the local part of the IP address as a host number.

The division of the local part of the IP address into a subnet number and host number is chosen by the local administrator. Any bits in the local portion can be used to form the subnet. The division is done using a 32-bit *subnet mask*. Bits with a value of zero bits in the subnet mask indicate positions ascribed to the host number. Bits with a value of one indicate positions ascribed to the subnet number. The bit positions in the subnet mask belonging to the original network number are set to ones but are not used (in some platform configurations, this value was actually specified with zeros instead of ones, but either way it is not used). Like IP addresses, subnet masks are usually written in dotted decimal form.

The special treatment of all bits zero and all bits one applies to each of the three parts of a subnetted IP address just as it does to both parts of an IP address that has not been subnetted (see 3.1.1.3, "Reserved IP addresses" on page 68). For example, subnetting a Class B network could use one of the following schemes:

- The first octet is the subnet number; the second octet is the host number. This gives 2^8-2 (254) possible subnets, each having up to 2^8-2 (254) hosts. Recall that we subtract two from the possibilities to account for the all ones and all zeros cases. The subnet mask is 255.255.255.0.

- The first 12 bits are used for the subnet number and the last four for the host number. This gives 2^{12}-2 (4094) possible subnets but only 2^4-2 (14) hosts per subnet. The subnet mask is 255.255.255.240.

In this example, there are several other possibilities for assigning the subnet and host portions of the address. The number of subnets and hosts and any future requirements should be considered before defining this structure. In the last example, the subnetted Class B network has 16 bits to be divided between the subnet number and the host number fields. The network administrator defines either a larger number of subnets each with a small number of hosts, or a smaller number of subnets each with many hosts.

When assigning the subnet part of the local address, the objective is to assign a *number* of bits to the subnet number and the remainder to the local address. Therefore, it is normal to use a contiguous block of bits at the beginning of the local address part for the subnet number. This makes the addresses more readable. (This is particularly true when the subnet occupies 8 or 16 bits.) With this approach, either of the subnet masks above are "acceptable" masks. Masks such as 255.255.252.252 and 255.255.255.15 are "unacceptable." In fact, most TCP/IP implementations do not support non-contiguous subnet masks. Their use is universally discouraged.

3.1.2.1 Types of subnetting

There are two types of subnetting: static and variable length. Variable length subnetting is more flexible than static. Native IP routing and RIP Version 1 support only static subnetting. However, RIP Version 2 supports variable length subnetting (refer to Chapter 4, "Routing protocols" on page 137).

Static subnetting

Static subnetting implies that all subnets obtained from the same network use the same subnet mask. While this is simple to implement and easy to maintain, it may waste address space in small networks. Consider a network of four hosts using a subnet mask of 255.255.255.0. This allocation wastes 250 IP addresses. All hosts and routers are required to support static subnetting.

Variable length subnetting

When variable length subnetting is used, allocated subnets within the same network can use different subnet masks. A small subnet with only a few hosts can use a mask that accommodates this need. A subnet with many hosts requires a different subnet mask. The ability to assign subnet masks according to the needs of the individual subnets helps conserve network addresses. Variable length subnetting divides the network so that each subnet contains sufficient addresses to support the required number of hosts.

An existing subnet can be split into two parts by adding another bit to the subnet portion of the subnet mask. Other subnets in the network are unaffected by the change.

Mixing static and variable length subnetting

Not every IP device includes support for variable length subnetting. Initially, it would appear that the presence of a host that only supports static subnetting prevents the use of variable length subnetting. This is not the case. Routers interconnecting the subnets are used to hide the different masks from hosts. Hosts continue to use basic IP routing. This offloads subnetting complexities to dedicated routers.

3.1.2.2 Static subnetting example

Consider the class A network shown in Figure 17.

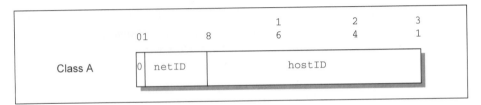

Figure 17. IP - Class A address without subnets

Using the following IP address:

```
00001001 01000011 00100110 00000001      a 32-bit address
    9       67       38       1          decimal notation (9.67.38.1)


        9.67.38.1                     is an IP address  (class A)  having


        9                             as the <network  address>
              67.38.1                 as the <host address>
```

The network administrator may wish to choose the bits from 8 to 25 to indicate the subnet address. In that case, the bits from 26 to 31 indicate the actual host addresses. Figure 18 shows the subnetted address derived from the original class A address.

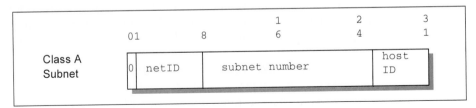

Figure 18. IP - Class A address with subnet mask and subnet address

A bit mask, known as the subnet mask, is used to identify which bits of the original host address field indicate the subnet number. In the above example, the subnet mask is 255.255.255.192 (or 11111111 11111111 11111111 11000000 in bit notation). Note that, by convention, the <network address> is included in the mask as well.

Because of the all bits 0 and all bits 1 restrictions, this defines 2^{18}-2 (from 1 to 262143) valid subnets. This split provides 262142 subnets each with a maximum of 2^6-2 (62) hosts.

The value applied to the subnet number takes the value of the full octet with non-significant bits set to zero. For example, the hexadecimal value 01 in this subnet mask assumes an 8-bit value 01000000. This provides a subnet value of 64.

Applying the 255.255.255.192 to the sample class A address 9.67.38.1 provides the following information:

```
00001001 01000011 00100110 00000001 = 9.67.38.1 (class A address)
11111111 11111111 11111111 11------   255.255.255.192 (subnet mask)
===================================== logical_AND
00001001 01000011 00100110 00------ = 9.67.38.0(subnet base address)
```

This leaves a host address of:

```
-------- -------- -------- --000001 = 1        (host address)
```

IP will recognize all host addresses as being on the local network for which the logical_AND operation described above produces the same result. This is important for routing IP datagrams in subnet environments (refer to 3.1.3, "IP routing" on page 74).

The actual subnet number is:

```
-------- 01000011 00100110 00------ = 68760    (subnet number)
```

This subnet number is a relative number. That is, it is the 68760th subnet of network 9 with the given subnet mask. This number bears no resemblance to the actual IP address that this host has been assigned (9.67.38.1). It has no meaning in terms of IP routing.

The division of the original <host address> into <subnet><host> is chosen by the network administrator. The values of all zeroes and all ones in the <subnet> field are reserved.

> **Note:**
>
> Because the range of available IP addresses is decreasing rapidly, many routers now support the use of all zeroes and all ones in the <subnet> field. This is not consistent with the defined standards.

3.1.2.3 Variable length subnetting example

Consider a corporation that has been assigned the Class C network 165.214.32.0. The corporation has the requirement to split this address range into five separate networks each with the following number of hosts:

- Subnet #1: 50 hosts

- Subnet #2: 50 hosts
- Subnet #3: 50 hosts
- Subnet #4: 30 hosts
- Subnet #5: 30 hosts

This cannot be achieved with static subnetting. For this example, static subnetting divides the network into four subnets each with 64 hosts or eight subnets each with 32 hosts. This subnet allocation does not meet the stated requirements.

To divide the network into five subnets, multiple masks should be defined. Using a mask of 255.255.255.192, the network can be divided into four subnets each with 64 hosts. The fourth subnet can be further divided into two subnets each with 32 hosts by using a mask of 255.255.255.224. There will be three subnets each with 64 hosts and two subnets each with 32 hosts. This satisfies the stated requirements.

3.1.2.4 Determining the subnet mask

Usually, hosts will store the subnet mask in a configuration file. However, sometimes this cannot be done, for example, as in the case of a diskless workstation. The ICMP protocol includes two messages: address mask request and address mask reply. These allow hosts to obtain the correct subnet mask from a server (refer to 3.2.1.10, "Address Mask Request (17) and Address Mask Reply (18)" on page 111).

3.1.2.5 Addressing routers and multi-homed hosts

Whenever a host has a physical connection to multiple networks or subnets, it is described as being *multi-homed*. By default, all routers are multi-homed since their purpose is to join networks or subnets. A multi-homed host has different IP addresses associated with each network adapter. Each adapter connects to a different subnet or network.

3.1.3 IP routing

An important function of the IP layer is *IP routing*. This provides the basic mechanism for routers to interconnect different physical networks. A device can simultaneously function as both a normal host and a router.

A router of this type is referred to as a router with partial routing information. The router only has information about four kinds of destinations:

- Hosts that are directly attached to one of the physical networks to which the router is attached.

- Hosts or networks for which the router has been given explicit definitions.

- Hosts or networks for which the router has received an ICMP redirect message.

- A default for all other destinations.

Additional protocols are needed to implement a full-function router. These types of routers are essential in most networks, because they can exchange information with other routers in the environment. The protocols used by these routers are reviewed in Chapter 4, "Routing protocols" on page 137.

There are two types of IP routing: direct and indirect.

3.1.3.1 Direct routing
If the destination host is attached to the same physical network as the source host, IP datagrams can be directly exchanged. This is done by encapsulating the IP datagram in the physical network frame. This is called direct delivery and is referred to as direct routing.

3.1.3.2 Indirect routing
Indirect routing occurs when the destination host is not connected to a network directly attached to the source host. The only way to reach the destination is via one or more IP gateways. (Note that in TCP/IP terminology, the terms gateway and router are used interchangeably. This describes a system that performs the duties of a router.) The address of the first gateway (the first hop) is called an indirect route in the IP routing algorithm. The address of the first gateway is the only information needed by the source host to send a packet to the destination host.

In some cases, there may be multiple subnets defined on the same physical network. If the source and destination hosts connect to the same physical network but are defined in different subnets, indirect routing is used to communicate between the pair of devices. A router is needed to forward traffic between subnets.

Figure 19 shows an example of direct and indirect routes.

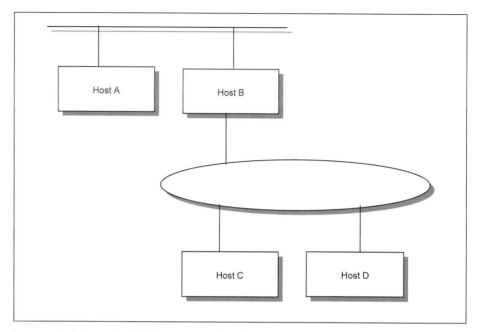

Figure 19. IP - Direct and indirect routes - Host C has a direct route to hosts B and D, and an indirect route to host A via gateway B

3.1.3.3 IP routing table

The determination of direct routes is derived from the list of local interfaces. It is automatically composed by the IP routing process at initialization. In addition, a list of networks and associated gateways (indirect routes) may be configured. This list is used to facilitate IP routing. Each host keeps the set of mappings between the following:

- Destination IP network address(es)
- Route(s) to next gateway(s)

This information is stored in a table called the IP routing table. Three types of mappings are found in this table:

1. The direct routes describing locally attached networks.

2. The indirect routes describing networks reachable via one or more gateways.

3. The default route which contains the (direct or indirect) route used when the destination IP network is not found in the mappings of type 1 and 2 above.

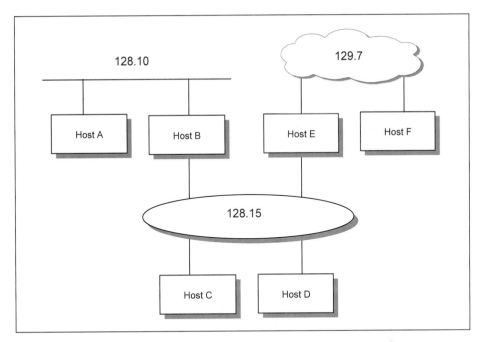

Figure 20. IP - Routing table scenario

Figure 20 presents a sample network. The routing table of host D might contain the following (symbolic) entries:

```
destination      router     interface

    129.7.0.0    E          lan0
    128.15.0.0   D          lan0
    128.10.0.0   B          lan0
    default      B          lan0
    127.0.0.1    loopback   lo
```

Since D is directly attached to network 128.15.0.0, it maintains a direct route for this network. To reach networks 129.7.0.0 and 128.10.0.0, however, it must have an indirect route through E and B, respectively, since these networks are not directly attached to it.

The routing table of host F might contain the following (symbolic) entries:

```
destination       router    interface

  129.7.0.0       F         wan0
  default         E         wan0
  127.0.0.1       loopback  lo
```

Because every host not on the 129.7.0.0 network must be reached via host E, F simply maintains a default route through E.

3.1.3.4 IP routing algorithm

IP uses a unique algorithm to route datagrams as illustrated in Figure 21.

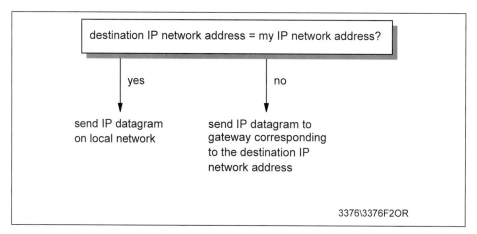

Figure 21. IP - Routing without subnets

To differentiate between subnets, the IP routing algorithm is updated as shown in Figure 22.

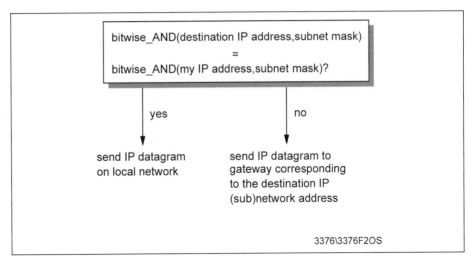

Figure 22. IP - Routing with subnets

Some implications of this change include:

- This algorithm represents a change to the general IP algorithm. Therefore, to be able to operate this way, the particular gateway must contain the new algorithm. Some implementations may still use the general algorithm, and will not function within a subnetted network, although they can still communicate with hosts in other networks that are subnetted.

- As IP routing is used in all of the hosts (and not just the routers), all of the hosts in the subnet must have:

  - An IP routing algorithm that supports subnetting.

  - The same subnet mask (unless subnets are formed within the subnet).

- If the IP implementation on any of the hosts does not support subnetting, that host will be able to communicate with any host in its own subnet but not with any machine on another subnet within the same network. This is because the host sees only one IP network and its routing cannot differentiate between an IP datagram directed to a host on the local subnet and a datagram that should be sent via a router to a different subnet.

In case one or more hosts do not support subnetting, an alternative way to achieve the same goal exists in the form of *proxy-ARP*. This does not require any changes to the IP routing algorithm for single-homed hosts. It does require changes on routers between subnets in the network (refer to 3.4.4, "Proxy-ARP or transparent subnetting" on page 118).

The entire IP routing algorithm is illustrated in Figure 23.

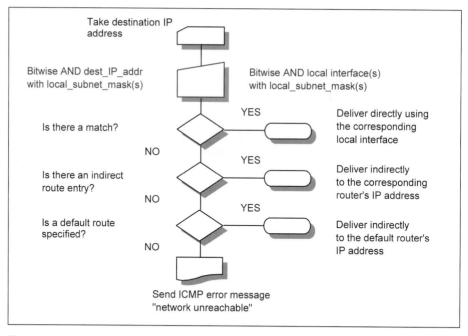

Figure 23. IP - Routing algorithm (with subnets)

Notes

1. This is an iterative process. It is applied by every host handling a datagram, except for the destination host.

2. Routing tables and the routing algorithm are local to any host in an IP network. In order to be able to forward IP datagrams, routers usually exchange their routing table information with other routers in the network. This is done using special routing protocols (refer to Chapter 4, "Routing protocols" on page 137).

3.1.4 Methods of delivery - unicast, broadcast, multicast, and anycast

The majority of IP addresses refer to a single recipient, this is called a *unicast* address. Unicast connections specify a one-to-one relationship between a single source and a single destination. Additionally, there are three special types of IP addresses used for addressing multiple recipients: broadcast addresses, multicast addresses, and anycast addresses. Their operation is shown in Figure 24.

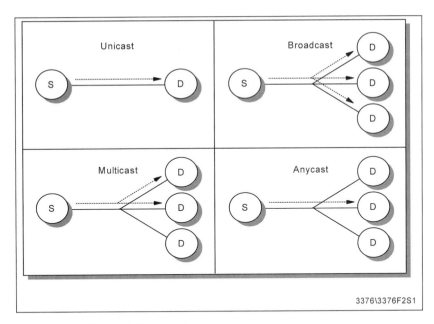

Figure 24. IP - Packet delivery modes

A *connectionless* protocol can send unicast, broadcast, multicast or anycast messages. A *connection-oriented* protocol can only use unicast addresses (a connection must exist between a specific pair of hosts).

3.1.4.1 Broadcasting

Broadcast addresses are never valid as a source address. They must specify the destination address. The different types of broadcast addresses include:

- Limited broadcast address: This uses the address 255.255.255.255 (all bits 1 in all parts of the IP address). It refers to all hosts on the local subnet. This is recognized by every host. The hosts do not need any IP configuration information. Routers do not forward this packet.

  One exception to this rule is called *BOOTP forwarding*. The BOOTP protocol uses the limited broadcast address to allow a diskless workstation to contact a boot server. BOOTP forwarding is a configuration option available on some routers. Without this facility, a separate BOOTP server is required on each subnet (refer to 3.6, "Bootstrap protocol (BOOTP)" on page 121).

- Network-directed broadcast address: This is used in an unsubnetted environment. The network number is a valid network number and the host number is all ones (for example, 128.2.255.255). This address refers to all hosts on the specified network. Routers should forward these broadcast messages. This is used in ARP requests (refer to 3.4, "Address Resolution Protocol (ARP)" on page 114) on unsubnetted networks.

- Subnet-directed broadcast address: If the network number is a valid network number, the subnet number is a valid subnet number and the host number is all ones, then the address refers to all hosts on the specified subnet. Since the sender's subnet and the target subnet may have different subnet mask, the sender must somehow find out the subnet mask in use at the target. The actual broadcast is performed by the router that receives the datagram into the subnet.

- All-subnets-directed broadcast address: If the network number is a valid network number, the network is subnetted and the local part is all ones (for example, 128.2.255.255), then the address refers to all hosts on all subnets in the specified network. In principle routers may propagate broadcasts for all subnets but are not required to do so. In practice, they do not. There are very few circumstances where such a broadcast is desirable. If misconfigured, it can lead to problems. Consider the misconfigured host 9.180.214.114 in a subnetted Class A network. If the device was configured with the address 9.255.255.255 as a local broadcast address instead of 9.180.214.255, all of the routers in the network will forward the request to all clients.

If routers do respect all-subnets-directed broadcast address, they use an algorithm called *reverse path forwarding* to prevent the broadcast messages from multiplying out of control. See RFC 922 for more details on this algorithm.

3.1.4.2 Multicasting

If an IP datagram is broadcast to a subnet, it is received by every host on the subnet. Each host processes the packet to determine if the target protocol is active. If it is not active, the IP datagram is discarded. Multicasting avoids this overhead by selecting destination groups.

Each group is represented by a Class D IP address. For each multicast address, a set of zero or more hosts are listening for packets addressed to the address. This set of hosts is called the *host group*. Packets sent to a multicast address are forwarded only to the members of the corresponding host group. Multicast enables one-to-many connections (refer to Chapter 6, "IP multicast" on page 229).

3.1.4.3 Anycasting

Sometimes, the same IP services are provided by different hosts. For example, a user wants to download a file via FTP and the file is available on multiple FTP servers. Hosts that implement the same service provide an anycast address to other hosts that require the service. Connections are made to the first host in the anycast address group to respond. This process is used to guarantee the service is provided by the host with the best connection to the receiver.

The anycast service is included in IPV6 (refer to 17.2.3, "IPv6 addressing" on page 572).

3.1.5 The IP address exhaustion problem

The number of networks on the Internet has been approximately doubling annually for a number of years. However, the usage of the Class A, B, and C networks differs greatly. Nearly all of the new networks assigned in the late 1980s were Class B, and in 1990 it became apparent that if this trend continued, the last Class B network number would be assigned during 1994. On the other hand, Class C networks were hardly being used.

The reason for this trend was that most potential users found a Class B network to be large enough for their anticipated needs, since it accommodates up to 65534 hosts, whereas a class C network, with a maximum of 254 hosts, severely restricts the potential growth of even a small initial network. Furthermore, most of the class B networks being assigned were small ones. There are relatively few networks that would need as many as 65,534 host addresses, but very few for which 254 hosts would be an adequate limit. In summary, although the Class A, Class B, and Class C divisions of the IP address are logical and easy-to-use (because they occur on byte boundaries), with hindsight, they are not the most practical because Class C networks are too small to be useful for most organizations, while Class B networks are too large to be densely populated by any but the largest organizations.

In May 1996, all Class A addresses were either allocated or assigned, as well as 61.95 percent of Class B and 36.44 percent of Class C IP network addresses. The terms assigned and allocated in this context have the following meanings:

- Assigned: The number of network numbers in use. The Class C figures are somewhat inaccurate, because the figures do not include many class C networks in Europe, which were allocated to RIPE and subsequently assigned but which are still recorded as allocated.

- Allocated: This includes all of the assigned networks and additionally, those networks that have either been reserved by IANA (for example, the 63 class A networks are all reserved by IANA) or have been allocated to regional registries by IANA and will subsequently be assigned by those registries.

Another way to look at these numbers is to examine the proportion of the address space that has been used. The figures in the table do not show, for example, that the Class A address space is as big as the rest combined, or that a single Class A network can theoretically have as many hosts as 66,000 Class C networks.

Since 1990, the number of assigned Class B networks has been increasing at a much lower rate than the total number of assigned networks and the anticipated exhaustion of the Class B network numbers has not yet occurred. The reason for this is that the policies on network number allocation were changed in late 1990 to preserve the existing address space, in particular to avert the exhaustion of the Class B address space. The new policies can be summarized as follows.

- The upper half of the Class A address space (network numbers 64 to 127) is reserved indefinitely to allow for the possibility of using it for transition to a new numbering scheme.

- Class B networks are only assigned to organizations that can clearly demonstrate a need for them. The same is, of course, true for Class A networks. The requirements for Class B networks are that the requesting organization:

  - Has a subnetting plan that documents more than 32 subnets within its organizational network

  - Has more than 4096 hosts

  Any requirements for a Class A network would be handled on an individual case basis.

- Organizations that do not fulfill the requirements for a Class B network are assigned a consecutively numbered block of Class C network numbers.

- The lower half of the Class C address space (network numbers 192.0.0 through 207.255.255) is divided into eight blocks, which are allocated to regional authorities as follows:

  192.0.0 - 193.255.255 Multi-regional

  194.0.0 - 195.255.255 Europe

  196.0.0 - 197.255.255 Others

  198.0.0 - 199.255.255 North America

  200.0.0 - 201.255.255 Central and South America

202.0.0 - 203.255.255 Pacific Rim

204.0.0 - 205.255.255 Others

206.0.0 - 207.255.255 Others

The ranges defined as Others are to be where flexibility outside the constraints of regional boundaries is required. The range defined as multi-regional includes the Class C networks that were assigned before this new scheme was adopted. The 192 networks were assigned by the InterNIC and the 193 networks were previously allocated to RIPE in Europe.

The upper half of the Class C address space (208.0.0 to 223.255.255) remains unassigned and unallocated.

- Where an organization has a range of class C network numbers, the range provided is assigned as a *bit-wise contiguous* range of network numbers, and the number of networks in the range is a power of 2. That is, all IP addresses in the range have a common prefix, and every address with that prefix is within the range. For example, a European organization requiring 1500 IP addresses would be assigned eight Class C network numbers (2048 IP addresses) from the number space reserved for European networks (194.0.0 through 195.255.255) and the first of these network numbers would be divisible by eight. A range of addresses satisfying these rules would be 194.32.136 through 194.32.143, in which case the range would consist of all of the IP addresses with the 21-bit prefix 194.32.136, or B '110000100010000010001'.

The maximum number of network numbers assigned contiguously is 64, corresponding to a prefix of 18 bits. An organization requiring more than 4096 addresses but less than 16,384 addresses can request either a Class B or a range of Class C addresses. In general, the number of Class C networks assigned is the minimum required to provide the necessary number of IP addresses for the organization on the basis of a two-year outlook. However, in some cases, an organization can request multiple networks to be treated separately. For example, an organization with 600 hosts would normally be assigned four class C networks. However, if those hosts were distributed across 10 token-ring LANs with between 50 and 70 hosts per LAN, such an allocation would cause serious problems, since the organization would have to find 10 subnets within a 10-bit local address range. This would mean at least some of the LANs having a subnet mask of 255.255.255.192 which allows only 62 hosts per LAN. The intent of the rules is not to force the organization into complex subnetting of small networks, and the organization should request 10 different Class C numbers, one for each LAN.

The current rules are to be found in RFC 2050 – Internet Registry IP Allocation Guidelines, which updates RFC 1466. The reasons for the rules for the allocation of Class C network numbers will become apparent in the following sections. The use of Class C network numbers in this way has averted the exhaustion of the Class B address space, but it is not a permanent solution to the overall address space constraints that are fundamental to IP. A long-term solution is discussed in Chapter 17, "IP Version 6" on page 559.

3.1.6 Intranets - private IP addresses

Another approach to conserve the IP address space is described in RFC 1918 – Address Allocation for Private Internets. This RFC relaxes the rule that IP addresses must be globally unique. It reserves part of the global address space for use in networks that do not require connectivity to the Internet. Typically these networks are administered by a single organization. Three ranges of addresses have been reserved for this purpose:

- 10.0.0.0: A single Class A network

- 172.16.0.0 through 172.31.0.0: 16 contiguous Class B networks

- 192.168.0.0 through 192.168.255.0: 256 contiguous Class C networks

Any organization can use any address in these ranges. However, because these addresses are not globally unique, they are not defined to any external routers. Routers in networks not using private addresses, particularly those operated by Internet service providers, are expected to quietly discard all routing information regarding these addresses. Routers in an organization using private addresses are expected to limit all references to private addresses to internal links. They should neither externally advertise routes to private addresses nor forward IP datagrams containing private addresses to external routers.

Hosts having only a private IP address do not have direct IP layer connectivity to the Internet. All connectivity to external Internet hosts must be provided with application gateways (refer to 21.3.4, "Application level gateway (proxy)" on page 682), SOCKS (refer to 21.6, "SOCKS" on page 739), or Network Address Translation (NAT) (refer to 21.4, "Network Address Translation (NAT)" on page 694).

3.1.7 Classless Inter-Domain Routing (CIDR)

Standard IP routing understands only class A, B, and C network addresses. Within each of these networks, subnetting can be used to provide better granularity, however there is no way to specify that multiple Class C networks are related. The result of this is termed the *routing table explosion* problem: A Class B network of 3000 hosts requires one routing table entry at each backbone router. The same environment, if addressed as a range of Class C networks, requires 16 entries.

The solution to this problem is called Classless Inter-Domain Routing (CIDR). CIDR is described in RFCs 1518 to 1520. CIDR does not route according to the class of the network number (hence the term classless). It is based solely on the high order bits of the IP address. These bits are termed the IP prefix.

Each CIDR routing table entry contains a 32-bit IP address and a 32-bit network mask, which together give the length and value of the IP prefix. This is represented as the tuple <IP_address network_mask>. For example, to address a block of eight Class C addresses with one single routing table entry, the following representation suffices: <192.32.136.0 255.255.248.0>. This would, from a backbone point of view, refer to the Class C network range from 192.32.136.0 to 192.32.143.0 as one single network. This is illustrated in Figure 25:

```
    11000000 00100000 10001000 00000000 = 192.32.136.0 (class C
address)
      11111111 11111111 11111--- -------- = 255.255.248.0 (network mask)
      ==================================== logical_AND
      11000000 00100000 10001--- -------- = 192.32.136  (IP prefix)

    11000000 00100000 10001111 00000000 = 192.32.143.0 (class C
address)
      11111111 11111111 11111--- -------- = 255.255.248.0 (network mask)
      ==================================== logical_AND
      11000000 00100000 10001--- -------- = 192.32.136  (same IP prefix)
```

Figure 25. Classless Inter-Domain Routing - IP supernetting example

This process of combining multiple networks into a single entry is referred to as *supernetting*. Routing is based on network masks that are shorter than the natural network mask of an IP address. This contrasts subnetting (see 3.1.2, "IP subnets" on page 69) where the subnet masks are longer than the natural network mask.

The current Internet address allocation policies and the assumptions on which those policies were based, are described in RFC 1518 – An

Architecture for IP Address Allocation with CIDR. They can be summarized as follows:

- IP address assignment reflects the physical topology of the network and not the organizational topology. Wherever organizational and administrative boundaries do not match the network topology, they should *not* be used for the assignment of IP addresses.

- In general, network topology will closely follow continental and national boundaries. Therefore IP addresses should be assigned on this basis.

- There will be a relatively small set of networks that carry a large amount of traffic between routing domains. These networks will be interconnected in a non-hierarchical way that crosses national boundaries. These networks are referred to as *transit routing domains (TRDs)*. Each TRD will have a unique IP prefix. TRDs will not be organized in a hierarchical way when there is no appropriate hierarchy. However, whenever a TRD is wholly within a continental boundary, its IP prefix should be an extension of the continental IP prefix.

- There will be many organizations that have attachments to other organizations that are for the private use of those two organizations. The attachments do not carry traffic intended for other domains (transit traffic). Such private connections do not have a significant effect on the routing topology and can be ignored.

- The great majority of routing domains will be single-homed. That is, they will be attached to a single TRD. They should be assigned addresses that begin with that TRD's IP prefix. All of the addresses for all single-homed domains attached to a TRD can therefore be aggregated into a single routing table entry for all domains outside that TRD.

> **Note:**
>
> This implies that if an organization changes its Internet service provider, it should change all of its IP addresses. This is not the current practice, but the widespread implementation of CIDR is likely to make it much more common.

- There are a number of address assignment schemes that can be used for multi-homed domains. These include:

  - The use of a single IP prefix for the domain. External routers must have an entry for the organization that lies partly or wholly outside the normal hierarchy. Where a domain is multi-homed, but all of the attached TRDs themselves are topologically nearby, it would be appropriate for the domain's IP prefix to include those bits common to all of the attached TRDs. For example, if all of the TRDs were wholly within the United States, an IP prefix implying an exclusively North American domain would be appropriate.

- The use of one IP prefix for each attached TRD with hosts in the domain having IP addresses containing the IP prefix of the most appropriate TRD. The organization appears to be a set of routing domains.

- Assigning an IP prefix from one of the attached TRDs. This TRD becomes a default TRD for the domain but other domains can explicitly route by one of the alternative TRDs.

- The use of IP prefixes to refer to sets of multi-homed domains having the TRD attachments. For example, there may be an IP prefix to refer to single-homed domains attached to network A, one to refer to single-homed domains attached to network B, and one to refer to dual-homed domains attached to networks A and B.

Each of these has various advantages, disadvantages and side effects. For example, the first approach tends to result in inbound traffic entering the target domain closer to the sending host than the second approach. Therefore, a larger proportion of the network costs are incurred by the receiving organization.

Because multi-homed domains vary greatly in character. None of the above schemes is suitable for every domain. There is no single policy that is best. RFC 1518 does not specify any rules for choosing between them.

3.1.7.1 CIDR implementation
The implementation of CIDR in the Internet is primarily based on Border Gateway Protocol Version 4 (see 4.9, "Border Gateway Protocol (BGP)" on page 180). The implementation strategy, described in RFC 1520 – Exchanging Routing Information Across Provider Boundaries in the CIDR Environment, involves a staged process through the routing hierarchy beginning with backbone routers. Network service providers are divided into four types:

• Type 1: Those providers that cannot employ any default inter-domain routing.

• Type 2: Those providers that use default inter-domain routing but require explicit routes for a substantial proportion of the assigned IP network numbers.

• Type 3: Those providers that use default inter-domain routing and supplement it with a small number of explicit routes.

- Type 4: Those providers that perform inter-domain routing using only default routes.

The CIDR implementation began with the Type 1 network providers, then the Type 2, and finally the Type 3 providers.

3.1.8 IP datagram

The unit of transfer in an IP network is called an IP datagram. It consists of an IP header and data relevant to higher level protocols. See Figure 26 for details.

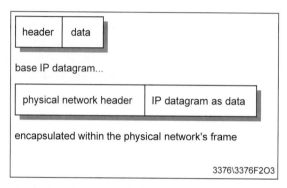

Figure 26. IP - Format of a base IP datagram

IP can provide fragmentation and re-assembly of datagrams. The maximum length of an IP datagram is 65,535 octets. All IP hosts must support 576 octets datagrams without fragmentation.

Fragments of a datagram each have a header. The header is copied from the original datagram. A fragment is treated as a normal IP datagrams while being transported to their destination. However, if one of the fragments gets lost, the complete datagram is considered lost. Since IP does not provide any acknowledgment mechanism, the remaining fragments are discarded by the destination host.

3.1.8.1 IP datagram format

The IP datagram header has a minimum length of 20 octets:

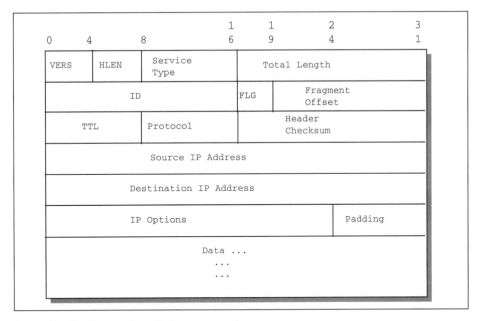

Figure 27. IP - Format of an IP datagram header

Where:

- **VERS**: The field contains the IP protocol version. The current version is 4. 5 is an experimental version. 6 is the version for IPv6 (see 17.2, "The IPv6 header format" on page 561).

- **HLEN**: The length of the IP header counted in 32-bit quantities. This does not include the data field.

- **Service Type**: The service type is an indication of the quality of service requested for this IP datagram. This field contains the following information:

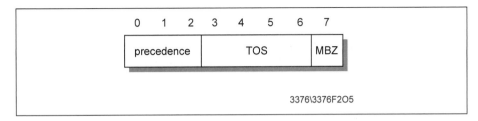

Figure 28. IP - Service type

Where:

- Precedence: This field specifies the nature and priority of the datagram:

  - 000: Routine
  - 001: Priority
  - 010: Immediate
  - 011: Flash
  - 100: Flash override
  - 101: Critical
  - 110: Internetwork control
  - 111: Network control

- TOS: Specifies the type of service value:

  - 1000: Minimize delay
  - 0100: Maximize throughput
  - 0010: Maximize reliability
  - 0001: Minimize monetary cost
  - 0000: Normal service

  A detailed description of the type of service can be found in the RFC 1349 (refer to 22.1, "Why QoS?" on page 781).

- MBZ: Reserved for future use.

- Total Length: The total length of the datagram, header and data.

- Identification: A unique number assigned by the sender to aid in reassembling a fragmented datagram. Each fragment of a datagram has the same identification number.

- Flags: This field contains control flags:

Figure 29. IP - Flags

Where:

- 0: Reserved, must be zero.

- DF (Do not Fragment): 0 means allow fragmentation; 1 means do not allow fragmentation.

- MF (More Fragments): 0 means that this is the last fragment of the datagram; 1 means that additional fragments will follow.

- Fragment Offset: This is used to aid the reassembly of the full datagram. The value in this field contains the number of 64-bit segments (header bytes are not counted) contained in earlier fragments. If this is the first (or only) fragment, this field contains a value of zero.

- Time to Live: This field specifies the time (in seconds) the datagram is allowed to travel. Theoretically, each router processing this datagram is supposed to subtract its processing time from this field. In practise, a router processes the datagram in less than 1 second. Thus the router subtracts one from the value in this field. The TTL becomes a hop-count metric rather than a time metric. When the value reaches zero, it is assumed that this datagram has been traveling in a closed loop and is discarded. The initial value should be set by the higher level protocol that creates the datagram.

- Protocol Number: This field indicates the higher level protocol to which IP should deliver the data in this datagram. These include:
  - 0: Reserved
  - 1: Internet Control Message Protocol (ICMP)
  - 2: Internet Group Management Protocol (IGMP)
  - 3: Gateway-to-Gateway Protocol (GGP)
  - 4: IP (IP encapsulation)
  - 5: Stream
  - 6: Transmission Control Protocol (TCP)
  - 8: Exterior Gateway Protocol (EGP)
  - 9: Private Interior Routing Protocol
  - 17: User Datagram Protocol (UDP)
  - 41: IP Version 6 (IPv6)
  - 50: Encap Security Payload for IPv6 (ESP)
  - 51: Authentication Header for IPv6 (AH)
  - 89: Open Shortest Path First

  The complete list is detailed in STD 2 – Assigned Internet Numbers.

- Header Checksum: This field is a checksum for the information contained in the header. If the header checksum does not match the contents, the datagram is discarded.

- Source IP Address: The 32-bit IP address of the host sending this datagram.

- Destination IP Address: The 32-bit IP address of the destination host for this datagram.

- Options: An IP implementation is not required to be capable of generating options in a datagram. However, all IP implementations are required to be able to process datagrams containing options. The Options field is variable in length (there may be zero or more options). There are two option formats; the format for each is dependent on the value of the option number found in the first octet:

  - A type octet alone:

Figure 30. IP - A type byte

  - A type octet, a length octet and one or more option data octets:

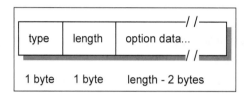

Figure 31. IP - A type byte, a length byte, and one or more option data bytes

The type byte has the same structure in both cases:

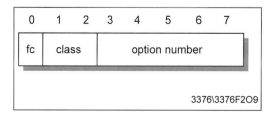

Figure 32. IP - The type byte structure

Where:

  - fc (Flag copy): This field indicates whether (1) or not (0) the option field is copied when the datagram is fragmented.

  - class: The option class is a 2-bit unsigned integer:

    - 0: control
    - 1: reserved

- 2: debugging and measurement
- 3: reserved

- option number: The option number is a 5-bit unsigned integer.

  - 0: End of option list. It has a class of 0, the fc bit is set to zero, and it has no length byte or data. That is, the option list is terminated by a X'00' byte. It is only required if the IP header length (which is a multiple of 4 bytes) does not match the actual length of the options.

  - 1: No operation. It has a class of 0, the fc bit is not set and there is no length byte or data. That is, a X'01' byte is a NOP. It may be used to align fields in the datagram.

  - 2: Security. It has a class of 0, the fc bit is set and there is a length byte with a value of 11 and 8 bytes of data). It is used for security information needed by U.S. Department of Defense requirements.

  - 3: Loose source routing. It has a class of 0, the fc bit is set and there is a variable length data field. This option is discussed in more detail below.

  - 4: Internet timestamp. It has a class of 2, the fc bit is not set and there is a variable length data field. The total length may be up to 40 bytes. This option is discussed in more detail below.

  - 7: Record route. It has a class of 0, the fc bit is not set and there is a variable length data field. This option is discussed in more detail below.

  - 8: Stream ID. It has a class of 0, the fc bit is set and there is a length byte with a value of 4 and one data byte. It is used with the SATNET system.

  - 9: Strict source routing. It has a class of 0, the fc bit is set and there is a variable length data field. This option is discussed in more detail below.

- length: This field counts the length (in octets) of the option, including the type and length fields.

- option data: Contains data relevant to the specific option.

- Padding: If an option is used, the datagram is padded with all-zero octets up to the next 32-bit boundary.

- Data: The data contained in the datagram. It is passed to the higher level protocol specified in the protocol field.

3.1.8.2 Fragmentation

When an IP datagram travels from one host to another, it may pass through different physical networks. Each physical network has a maximum frame size. This is called the *maximum transmission unit* (MTU). It limits the length of a datagram that can be placed in one physical frame.

IP implements a process to fragment datagrams exceeding the MTU. The process creates a set of datagrams within the maximum size. The receiving host reassembles the original datagram. IP requires that each link support a minimum MTU of 68 octets. This is the sum of the maximum IP header length (60 octets) and the minimum possible length of data in a non-final fragment (8 octets). If any network provides a lower value than this, fragmentation and re-assembly must be implemented in the network interface layer. This must be transparent to IP. IP implementations are not required to handle unfragmented datagrams larger than 576 bytes. In practice, most implementations will accommodate larger values.

An unfragmented datagram has an all-zero fragmentation information field. That is, the more fragments flag bit is zero and the fragment offset is zero. The following steps are performed to fragment the datagram:

- The DF flag bit is checked to see if fragmentation is allowed. If the bit is set, the datagram will be discarded and an ICMP error returned to the originator.

- Based on the MTU value, the data field is split into two or more parts. All newly created data portions must have a length that is a multiple of 8 octets, with the exception of the last data portion.

- Each data portion is placed in an IP datagram. The headers of these datagrams are minor modifications of the original:

  - The more fragments flag bit is set in all fragments except the last.

  - The fragment offset field in each is set to the location this data portion occupied in the original datagram, relative to the beginning of the original unfragmented datagram. The offset is measured in 8-octet units.

  - If options were included in the original datagram, the high order bit of the option type byte determines if this information is copied to all fragment datagrams or only the first datagram. For example, source route options are copied in all fragments.

  - The header length field of the new datagram is set.

  - The total length field of the new datagram is set.

  - The header checksum field is re-calculated.

- Each of these fragmented datagrams is now forwarded as a normal IP datagram. IP handles each fragment independently. The fragments can traverse different routers to the intended destination. They can be subject to further fragmentation if they pass through networks specifying a smaller MTU.

At the destination host, the data is reassembled into the original datagram. The identification field set by the sending host is used together with the source and destination IP addresses in the datagram. Fragmentation does not alter this field.

In order to reassemble the fragments, the receiving host allocates a storage buffer when the first fragment arrives. The host also starts a timer. When subsequent fragments of the datagram arrive, the data is copied into the buffer storage at the location indicated by the fragment offset field. When all fragments have arrived, the complete original unfragmented datagram is restored. Processing continues as for unfragmented datagrams.

If the timer is exceeded and fragments remain outstanding, the datagram is discarded. The initial value of this timer is called the IP datagram time to live (TTL) value. It is implementation-dependent. Some implementations allow it to be configured. The `netstat` command can be used on some IP hosts to list the details of fragmentation. An example of this is the `netstat -i` command in TCP/IP for OS/2.

3.1.8.3 IP datagram routing options
The IP datagram Options field provides two methods for the originator of an IP datagram to explicitly provide routing information. It also provides a method for an IP datagram to determine the route that it travels.

Loose source routing
The loose source routing option, also called the loose source and record route (LSRR) option, provides a means for the source of an IP datagram to supply explicit routing information. This information is used by the routers when forwarding the datagram to the destination. It is also used to record the route:

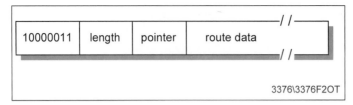

Figure 33. IP - Loose source routing option

The fields of this header include:

- 1000011(decimal 131): is the value of the option type octet for loose source routing.

- length: Contains the length of this option field, including the type and length fields.

- pointer: Points to the option data at the next IP address to be processed. It is counted relative to the beginning of the option, so its minimum value is four. If the pointer is greater than the length of the option, the end of the source route is reached and further routing is to be based on the destination IP address (as for datagrams without this option).

- route data: This field contains a series of 32-bit IP addresses.

When a datagram arrives at its destination and the source route is not empty (pointer < length) the receiving host:

- Takes the next IP address in the route data field (the one indicated by the pointer field) and puts it in the destination IP address field of the datagram.

- Puts the local IP address in the source list at the location pointed to by the pointer field. The IP address for this is the local IP address corresponding to the network on which the datagram will be forwarded. (Routers are attached to multiple physical networks and thus have multiple IP addresses.)

- Increments the pointer by 4.

- Transmits the datagram to the new destination IP address.

This procedure ensures that the return route is recorded in the route data (in reverse order) so that the final recipient uses this data to construct a loose source route in the reverse direction. This is a *loose* source route because the forwarding router is allowed to use any route and any number of intermediate routers to reach the next address in the route.

> **Note:**
>
> The originating host puts the IP address of the first intermediate router in the destination address field and the IP addresses of the remaining routers in the path, including the target destination are placed in the source route option. The recorded route in the datagram when it arrives at the target contains the IP addresses of each of the routers that forwarded the datagram. Each router has moved one place in the source route, and normally a different IP address will be used, since the routers record the IP address of the outbound interface but the source route originally contained the IP address of the inbound interface.

Strict source routing

The strict source routing option, also called the strict source and record route (SSRR) option, uses the same principle as loose source routing except the intermediate router *must* send the datagram to the next IP address in the source route via a directly connected network. It cannot use an intermediate router. If this cannot be done, ICMP Destination Unreachable error message is issued. Figure 34 gives an over of the SSRR option.

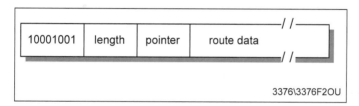

Figure 34. IP - Strict source routing option

Where:

- 1001001 (Decimal 137): The value of the option type byte for strict source routing.

- length: This information is described in the loose source routing section.

- pointer: This information is described in the loose source routing section.

- route data: A series of 32-bit IP addresses.

Record route

This option provides a means to record the route traversed by an IP datagram. It functions similarly to the source routing option. However, this option provides an empty routing data field. This field is filled in as the datagram traverses the network. Sufficient space for this routing information must be provided by the source host. If the data field is filled before the datagram reaches its destination, the datagram is forwarded with no further recording of the route. Figure 35 gives an overview of the record route option.

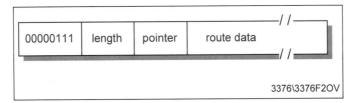

Figure 35. IP - Record route option

Where:

- 0000111 (Decimal 7): The value of the option type byte for record route
- length: This information is described in the loose source routing section.
- pointer: This information is described in the loose source routing section.
- route data: A series of 32-bit IP addresses.

3.1.8.4 Internet timestamp

A timestamp is an option forcing some (or all) of the routers along the route to the destination to put a timestamp in the option data. The timestamps are measured in seconds and can be used for debugging purposes. They cannot be used for performance measurement for two reasons:

- Because most IP datagrams are forwarded in less than one second, the timestamps are not precise.
- Because IP routers are not required to have synchronized clocks, they may not be accurate.

Figure 36 gives an overview of the Internet timestamp option.

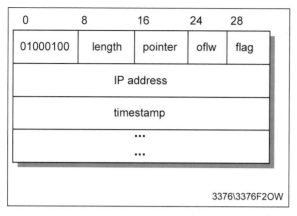

Figure 36. IP - Internet timestamp option

Where:

- 01000100 (Decimal 68): is the value of the option type for the internet time stamp option.

- length: Contains the total length of this option, including the type and length fields.

- pointer: Points to the next timestamp to be processed (first free time stamp).

- oflw (overflow): This field contains the number of devices that cannot register timestamps due to a lack of space in the data field.

- flag: Is a 4-bit value which indicates how timestamps are to be registered:
    - 0: Timestamps only, stored in consecutive 32-bit words.
    - 1: Each timestamp is preceded by the IP address of the registering device.
    - 2 The IP address fields are pre-specified, an IP device only registers when it finds its own address in the list.

- Timestamp: A 32-bit timestamp recorded in milliseconds since midnight UT (GMT).

The originating host must compose this option with sufficient data area to hold all the timestamps. If the timestamp area becomes full, no further time stamps are added.

3.2 Internet Control Message Protocol (ICMP)

ICMP is a standard protocol with STD number 5. That standard also includes IP (see 3.1, "Internet Protocol (IP)" on page 65) and IGMP (see 6.2, "Internet Group Management Protocol (IGMP)" on page 232). Its status is required. It is described in RFC 792 with updates in RFC 950.

Path MTU Discovery is a draft standard protocol with a status of elective. It is described in RFC 1191.

ICMP Router Discovery is a proposed standard protocol with a status of elective. It is described in RFC 1256.

When a router or a destination host must inform the source host about errors in datagram processing, it uses the Internet Control Message Protocol (ICMP). ICMP can be characterized as follows:

- ICMP uses IP as if ICMP were a higher level protocol (that is, ICMP messages are encapsulated in IP datagrams). However, ICMP is an integral part of IP and must be implemented by every IP module.

- ICMP is used to report errors, *not* to make IP reliable. Datagrams may still be undelivered without any report on their loss. Reliability must be implemented by the higher-level protocols using IP services.

- ICMP cannot be used to report errors with ICMP messages. This avoids infinite repetitions.ICMP responses are sent in response to ICMP query messages (ICMP types 0, 8, 9, 10 and 13 through 18).

- For fragmented datagrams, ICMP messages are only sent about errors with the first fragment. That is, ICMP messages never refer to an IP datagram with a non-zero fragment offset field.

- ICMP messages are never sent in response to datagrams with a broadcast or a multicast destination address.

- ICMP messages are never sent in response to a datagram that does not have a source IP address representing a unique host. That is, the source address cannot be zero, a loopback address, a broadcast address or a multicast address.

- RFC 792 states that ICMP messages *can* be generated to report IP datagram processing errors. However, this is not required. In practice, routers will almost always generate ICMP messages for errors. For destination hosts, ICMP message generation is implementation dependent.

3.2.1 ICMP messages

ICMP messages are described in RFC 792 and RFC 950, belong to STD 5 and are mandatory.

ICMP messages are sent in IP datagrams. The IP header has a Protocol number of 1 (ICMP) and a type of service of zero (routine). The IP data field contains the ICMP message shown in Figure 37.

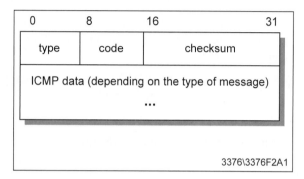

Figure 37. ICMP - Message format

The message contains the following components:

- Type: Specifies the type of the message:
    - 0: Echo reply
    - 3: Destination unreachable
    - 4: Source quench
    - 5: Redirect
    - 8: Echo
    - 9: Router advertisement
    - 10: Router solicitation
    - 11: Time exceeded
    - 12: Parameter problem
    - 13: Timestamp request
    - 14: Timestamp reply
    - 15: Information request (obsolete)
    - 16: Information reply (obsolete)
    - 17: Address mask request
    - 18: Address mask reply
    - 30: Traceroute
    - 31: Datagram conversion error
    - 32: Mobile host redirect
    - 33: IPv6 Where-Are-You
    - 34: IPv6 I-Am-Here

- 35: Mobile registration request
- 36: Mobile registration reply
- 37: Domain name request
- 38: Domain name reply
- 39: SKIP
- 40: Photuris

- Code: Contains the error code for the datagram reported by this ICMP message. The interpretation is dependent upon the message type.

- Checksum: Contains the checksum for the ICMP message starting with the ICMP Type field. If the checksum does not match the contents, the datagram is discarded.

- Data: Contains information for this ICMP message. Typically it will contain the portion of the original IP message for which this ICMP message was generated.

Each of the ICMP messages is described individually.

3.2.1.1 Echo (8) and Echo Reply (0)

Echo is used to detect if another host is active on the network. It is used by the Ping command (refer to 3.2.2.1, "Ping" on page 112).The sender initializes the identifier, sequence number, and data field. The datagram is then sent to the destination host. The recipient changes the type to Echo Reply and returns the datagram to the sender. See Figure 38 for more details.

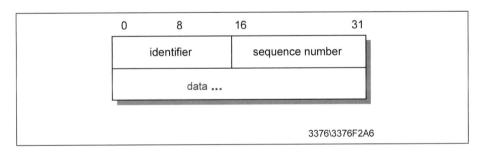

Figure 38. Echo and Echo Reply

3.2.1.2 Destination Unreachable (3)

If this message is received from an intermediate router, it means that the router regards the destination IP address as unreachable.

If this message is received from the destination host, it means that either the protocol specified in the protocol number field of the original datagram is not active or the specified port is inactive. (Refer to 5.2, "User Datagram Protocol (UDP)" on page 204 for additional information regarding ports.) See Figure 39 for more details.

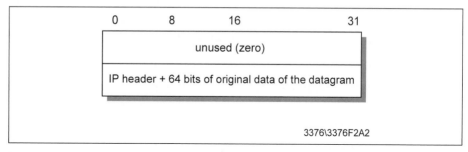

0   8   16   31

unused (zero)

IP header + 64 bits of original data of the datagram

3376\3376F2A2

Figure 39. ICMP - Destination Unreachable

The ICMP header code field contains one of the following values:

- 0: Network unreachable
- 1: Host unreachable
- 2: Protocol unreachable
- 3: Port unreachable
- 4: Fragmentation needed but the Do Not Fragment bit was set
- 5: Source route failed
- 6: Destination network unknown
- 7: Destination host unknown
- 8: Source host isolated (obsolete)
- 9: Destination network administratively prohibited
- 10: Destination host administratively prohibited
- 11: Network unreachable for this type of service
- 12: Host unreachable for this type of service
- 13: Communication administratively prohibited by filtering
- 14: Host precedence violation
- 15: Precedence cutoff in effect

If a router implements the Path MTU Discovery protocol, the format of the destination unreachable message is changed for code 4. This includes the MTU of the link that did not accept the datagram. See Figure 40 for more information.

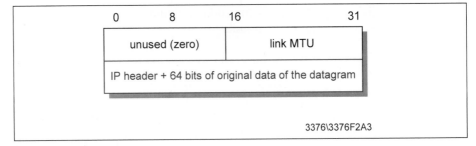

Figure 40. ICMP - Fragmentation required with link MTU

3.2.1.3 Source Quench (4)

If this message is received from an intermediate router, it means that the router did not have the buffer space needed to queue the datagram.

If this message is received from the destination host, it means that the incoming datagrams are arriving too quickly to be processed.

The ICMP header code field is always zero.

See Figure 41 for more details.

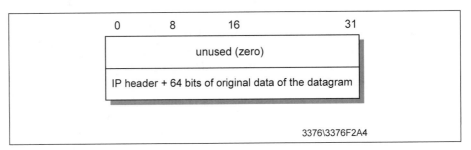

Figure 41. ICMP - Source Quench

3.2.1.4 Redirect (5)

If this message is received from an intermediate router, it means that the host should send future datagrams for the network to the router whose IP address is specified in the ICMP message. This preferred router will always be on the same subnet as the host that sent the datagram and the router that returned the IP datagram. The router forwards the datagram to its next hop destination. This message will not be sent if the IP datagram contains a source route.

The ICMP header code field will have one of the following values:

- 0: Network redirect
- 1: Host redirect
- 2: Network redirect for this type of service
- 3: Host redirect for this type of service

See Figure 42 for more details.

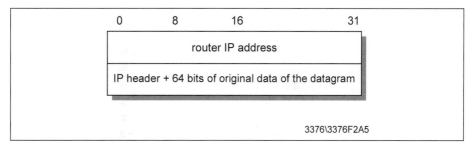

Figure 42. ICMP - Redirect

3.2.1.5 Router Advertisement (9) and Router Solicitation (10)

ICMP messages 9 and 10 are optional. They are described in RFC 1256, which is elective. See Figure 43 and Figure 44 for details.

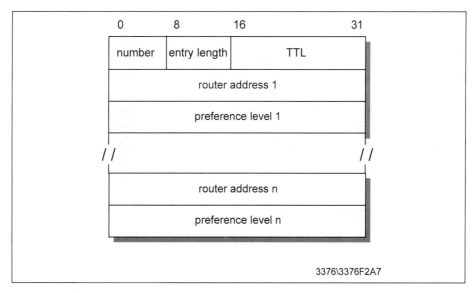

Figure 43. ICMP - Router Advertisement

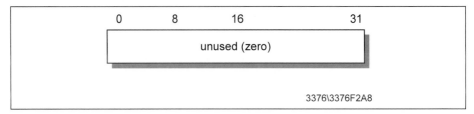

0	8	16	31

unused (zero)

3376\3376F2A8

Figure 44. ICMP - Router Solicitation

Where:

- number: The number of entries in the message.

- entry length: The length of an entry in 32-bit units. This is 2 (32 bits for the IP address and 32 bits for the preference value).

- TTL: The number of seconds that an entry will be considered valid.

- router address: One of the sender's IP addresses.

- preference level: A signed 32-bit level indicating the preference to be assigned to this address when selecting a default router. Each router on a subnet is responsible for advertising its own preference level. Larger values imply higher preference; smaller values imply lower. The default is zero, which is in the middle of the possible range. A value of X'80000000' (-231) indicates the router should never be used as a default router.

The ICMP header code field is zero for both of these messages.

These two messages are used if a host or a router supports the router discovery protocol. Routers periodically advertise their IP addresses on those subnets where they are configured to do so. Advertisements are made on the all-systems multicast address (224.0.0.1) or the limited broadcast address (255.255.255.255). The default behavior is to send advertisements every 10 minutes with a TTL value of 1800 (30 minutes). Routers also reply to solicitation messages they receive. They may reply directly to the soliciting host, or they may wait a short random interval and reply with a multicast.

Hosts may send solicitation messages. Solicitation messages are sent to the all-routers multicast address (224.0.0.2) or the limited broadcast address (255.255.255.255). Typically, three solicitation messages are sent at 3-second intervals. Alternatively a host may wait for periodic advertisements. Each time a host receives an advertisement with a higher preference value, it updates its default router. The host also sets the TTL timer for the new entry to match the value in the advertisement. When the host receives a new advertisement for its current default router, it resets the TTL value to that in the new advertisement.

This process also provides a mechanism for routers to declare themselves unavailable. They send an advertisement with a TTL value of zero.

3.2.1.6 Time Exceeded (11)

If this message is received from an intermediate router, it means that the time to live field of an IP datagram has expired.

If this message is received from the destination host, it means that the IP fragment reassembly time to live timer has expired while the host is waiting for a fragment of the datagram. The ICMP header code field may have the one of the following values:

- *0:* transit TTL exceeded
- *1:* reassembly TTL exceeded

See Figure 45 for more details.

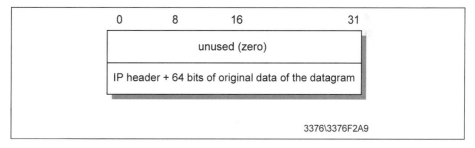

Figure 45. ICMP - Time Exceeded

3.2.1.7 Parameter Problem (12)

This message indicates that a problem was encountered during processing of the IP header parameters. The pointer field indicates the octet in the original IP datagram where the problem was encountered. The ICMP header code field may have the one of the following values:

- 0: unspecified error
- 1: required option missing

See Figure 46 for more details.

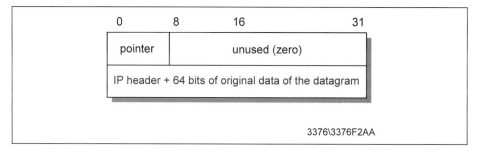

Figure 46. ICMP - Parameter Problem

3.2.1.8 Timestamp Request (13) and Timestamp Reply (14)

These two messages are for debugging and performance measurements. They are not used for clock synchronization.

The sender initializes the identifier and sequence number (which is used if multiple timestamp requests are sent), sets the originate timestamp and sends the datagram to the recipient. The receiving host fills in the receive and transmit timestamps, changes the type to timestamp reply and returns it to the original sender. The datagram has two timestamps if there is a perceptible time difference between the receipt and transmit times. In practice, most implementations perform the two (receipt and reply) in one operation. This sets the two timestamps to the same value. Timestamps are the number of milliseconds elapsed since midnight UT (GMT).

See Figure 47 for details.

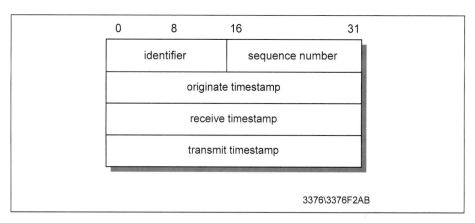

Figure 47. ICMP - Timestamp Request and Timestamp Reply

3.2.1.9 Information Request (15) and Information Reply (16)

An information request is issued by a host to obtain an IP address for an attached network. The sender fills in the request with the destination IP address in the IP header set to zero (meaning this network) and waits for a reply from a server authorized to assign IP addresses to other hosts. The ICMP header code field is zero. The reply contains IP network addresses in both the source and destination fields of the IP header. This mechanism is now obsolete (see also 3.5, "Reverse Address Resolution Protocol (RARP)" on page 120).

See Figure 48 for more details.

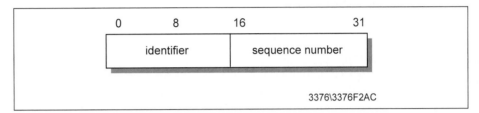

Figure 48. ICMP - Information Request and Information Reply

3.2.1.10 Address Mask Request (17) and Address Mask Reply (18)

An address mask request is used by a host to determine the subnet mask used on an attached network. Most hosts are configured with their subnet mask(s). However some, such as diskless workstations, must obtain this information from a server. A host uses RARP (see 3.5, "Reverse Address Resolution Protocol (RARP)" on page 120) to obtain its IP address. To obtain a subnet mask, the host broadcasts an address mask request. Any host on the network that has been configured to send address mask replies will fill in the subnet mask, convert the packet to an address mask reply and return it to the sender. The ICMP header code field is zero.

See Figure 49 for more details.

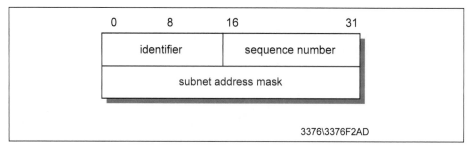

Figure 49. ICMP - Address Mask Request and Reply

3.2.2 ICMP applications

There are two simple and widely used applications based on ICMP: Ping and Traceroute. Ping uses the ICMP Echo and Echo Reply messages to determine whether a host is reachable. Traceroute sends IP datagrams with low TTL values so that they expire en route to a destination. It uses the resulting ICMP Time Exceeded messages to determine where in the internet the datagrams expired and pieces together a view of the route to a host. These applications are discussed in the following sections.

3.2.2.1 Ping

Ping is the simplest of all TCP/IP applications. It sends IP datagrams to a specified destination host and measures the round trip time to receive a response. The word *ping*, which is used as a noun and a verb, is taken from the sonar operation to locate an underwater object. It is also an abbreviation for *Packet InterNet Groper*.

Traditionally, if you could successfully ping a host, other applications such as Telnet or FTP could reach that host. With the advent of security measures on the Internet, particularly firewalls (see 21.3, "Firewalls" on page 678), which control access to networks by application protocol and/or port number, this is no longer necessarily true. Nonetheless, the first test of reachability for a host is still to attempt to ping it.

The syntax that is used in different implementations of ping varies from platform to platform. The syntax here is for the OS/2 implementation:

```
ping [-switches] host [size [packets]]
```

Where:

- switches: Switches to enable various ping options
- host: The destination, either a symbolic name or an IP address
- size: The size of the data portion of the packet

- packets: The number of packets to send

Ping uses the ICMP Echo and Echo Reply messages (refer to 3.2.1.1, "Echo (8) and Echo Reply (0)" on page 104). Since ICMP is required in every TCP/IP implementation, hosts do not require a separate server to respond to ping requests.

Ping is useful for verifying an IP installation. The following variations of the command each require the operation of an different portion of an IP installation:

- ping loopback: Verifies the operation of the base TCP/IP software.
- ping my-IP-address: Verifies whether the physical network device can be addressed.
- ping a-remote-IP-address: Verifies whether the network can be accessed.
- ping a-remote-host-name: Verifies the operation of the name server (or the flat namespace resolver, depending on the installation).

Ping is implemented in all IBM TCP/IP products.

3.2.2.2 Traceroute

The Traceroute program is used to determine the route IP datagrams follow through the network.

Traceroute is based upon ICMP and UDP. It sends an IP datagram with a TTL of 1 to the destination host. The first router decrements the TTL to 0, discards the datagram and returns an ICMP Time Exceeded message to the source. In this way, the first router in the path is identified. This process is repeated with successively larger TTL values to identify the exact series of routers in the path to the destination host.

Traceroute sends UDP datagrams to the destination host. These datagrams reference a port number outside the standard range. When an ICMP Port Unreachable message is received, the source determines the destination host has been reached.

Traceroute is implemented in all IBM TCP/IP products.

3.3 Internet Group Management Protocol (IGMP)

IGMP is a standard protocol with STD number 5. That standard also includes IP (see 3.1, "Internet Protocol (IP)" on page 65) and ICMP (see 3.2, "Internet Control Message Protocol (ICMP)" on page 102). Its status is recommended. It is described in RFC 1112 with updates in RFC 2236.

Similar to ICMP, the Internet Group Management Protocol (IGMP) is also an integral part of IP. It allows hosts to participate in IP multicasts. IGMP further provides routers with the capability to check if any hosts on a local subnet are interested in a particular multicast.

Refer to 6.2, "Internet Group Management Protocol (IGMP)" on page 232 for a detailed review of IGMP.

3.4 Address Resolution Protocol (ARP)

The ARP protocol is a network-specific standard protocol. The address resolution protocol is responsible for converting the higher level protocol addresses (IP addresses) to physical network addresses. It is described in RFC 826.

3.4.1 ARP overview

On a single physical network, individual hosts are known on the network by their physical hardware address. Higher level protocols address destination hosts in the form of a symbolic address (IP address in this case). When such a protocol wants to send a datagram to destination IP address w.x.y.z, the device driver does not understand this address.

Therefore, a module (ARP) is provided that will translate the IP address to the physical address of the destination host. It uses a lookup table (sometimes referred to as the *ARP cache*) to perform this translation.

When the address is not found in the ARP cache, a broadcast is sent out on the network, with a special format called the *ARP request*. If one of the machines on the network recognizes its own IP address in the request, it will send an *ARP reply* back to the requesting host. The reply will contain the physical hardware address of the host and source route information (if the packet has crossed bridges on its path). Both this address and the source route information are stored in the ARP cache of the requesting host. All subsequent datagrams to this destination IP address can now be translated to a physical address, which is used by the device driver to send out the datagram on the network.

An exception to the rule constitutes the Asynchronous Transfer Mode (ATM) technology where ARP cannot be implemented in the physical layer as described previously. Therefore, every host, upon initialization, must register with an ARP serve in order to be able to resolve IP addresses to hardware addresses (please also see 2.10, "Asynchronous Transfer Mode (ATM)" on page 44).

ARP was designed to be used on networks that support hardware broadcast. This means, for example, that ARP will not work on an X.25 network.

3.4.2 ARP detailed concept

ARP is used on IEEE 802 networks as well as on the older DIX Ethernet networks to map IP addresses to physical hardware addresses see 2.1, "Ethernet and IEEE 802.x Local Area Networks (LANs)" on page 29). To do this, it is closely related to the device driver for that network. In fact, the ARP specifications in RFC 826 only describe its functionality, not its implementation. The implementation depends to a large extent on the device driver for a network type and they are usually coded together in the *adapter microcode*.

3.4.2.1 ARP packet generation

If an application wishes to send data to a certain IP destination address, the IP routing mechanism first determines the IP address of the next hop of the packet (it can be the destination host itself, or a router) and the hardware device on which it should be sent. If it is an IEEE 802.3/4/5 network, the ARP module must be consulted to map the <protocol type, target protocol address> to a physical address.

The ARP module tries to find the address in this ARP cache. If it finds the matching pair, it gives the corresponding 48-bit physical address back to the caller (the device driver), which then transmits the packet. If it doesn't find the pair in its table, it *discards the packet* (assumption is that a higher level protocol will retransmit) and generates a network *broadcast* of an ARP request. See Figure 50 for more details.

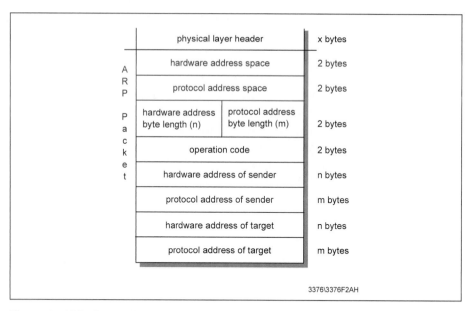

Figure 50. ARP - Request/reply packet

Where:

- Hardware address space: Specifies the type of hardware; examples are Ethernet or Packet Radio Net.

- Protocol address space: Specifies the type of protocol, same as the EtherType field in the IEEE 802 header (IP or ARP).

- Hardware address length: Specifies the length (in bytes) of the hardware addresses in this packet. For IEEE 802.3 and IEEE 802.5 this will be 6.

- Protocol address length: Specifies the length (in bytes) of the protocol addresses in this packet. For IP this will be 4.

- Operation code: Specifies whether this is an ARP request (1) or reply (2).

- Source/target hardware address: Contains the physical network hardware addresses. For IEEE 802.3 these are 48-bit addresses.

- Source/target protocol address: Contains the protocol addresses. For TCP/IP these are the 32-bit IP addresses.

For the ARP request packet, the target hardware address is the only undefined field in the packet.

3.4.2.2 ARP packet reception

When a host receives an ARP packet (either a broadcast request or a point-to-point reply), the receiving device driver passes the packet to the ARP module, which treats it as shown in Figure 51.

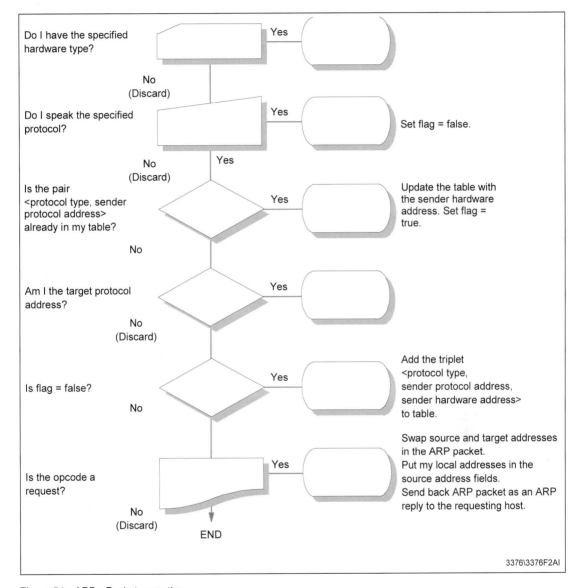

Figure 51. ARP - Packet reception

The requesting host will receive this ARP reply, and will follow the same algorithm to treat it. As a result of this, the triplet <protocol type, protocol address, hardware address> for the desired host will be added to its lookup table (ARP cache). The next time a higher level protocol wants to send a packet to that host, the ARP module will find the target hardware address and the packet will be sent to that host.

Note that because the original ARP request was a broadcast on the network, all hosts on that network will have updated the sender's hardware address in their table (only if it was already in the table).

3.4.3 ARP and subnets

The ARP protocol remains unchanged in the presence of subnets. Remember that each IP datagram first goes through the IP routing algorithm. This algorithm selects the hardware device driver that should send out the packet. Only then, the ARP module associated with that device driver is consulted.

3.4.4 Proxy-ARP or transparent subnetting

Proxy-ARP is described in RFC 1027 – Using ARP to Implement Transparent Subnet Gateways, which is in fact a subset of the method proposed in RFC 925 – Multi-LAN Address Resolution. It is another method to construct local subnets, without the need for a modification to the IP routing algorithm, but with modifications to the routers that interconnect the subnets.

3.4.4.1 Proxy-ARP concept

Consider one IP network that is divided into subnets and interconnected by routers. We use the "old" IP routing algorithm, which means that no host knows about the existence of multiple physical networks. Consider hosts A and B, which are on different physical networks within the same IP network, and a router R between the two subnetworks:

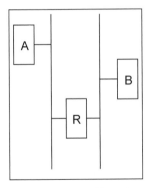

Figure 52. ARP - Hosts interconnected by a router

When host A wants to send an IP datagram to host B, it first has to determine the physical network address of host B through the use of the ARP protocol.

As host A cannot differentiate between the physical networks, its IP routing algorithm thinks that host B is on the local physical network and sends out a broadcast ARP request. Host B doesn't receive this broadcast, but router R does. Router R understands subnets, that is, it runs the subnet version of the IP routing algorithm and it will be able to see that the destination of the ARP request (from the target protocol address field) is on another physical network. If router R's routing tables specify that the next hop to that other network is through a different physical device, it will reply to the ARP as if it were host B, saying that the network address of host B is that of the router R itself.

Host A receives this ARP reply, puts it in its cache, and will send future IP packets for host B to the router R. The router will forward such packets to the correct subnet.

The result is transparent subnetting:

- Normal hosts (such as A and B) don't know about subnetting, so they use the "old" IP routing algorithm.
- The routers between subnets have to:
    - Use the subnet IP routing algorithm.
    - Use a modified ARP module, which can reply on behalf of other hosts.

See Figure 53 for more details.

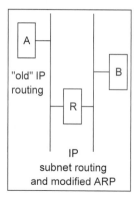

Figure 53. ARP - Proxy-ARP router

3.5 Reverse Address Resolution Protocol (RARP)

The RARP protocol is a network-specific standard protocol. It is described in RFC 903.

Some network hosts, such as diskless workstations, do not know their own IP address when they are booted. To determine their own IP address, they use a mechanism similar to ARP, but now the hardware address of the host is the known parameter, and the IP address the queried parameter. It differs more fundamentally from ARP in the fact that a RARP server must exist on the network that maintains that a database of mappings from hardware address to protocol address must be pre-configured.

3.5.1 RARP concept

The reverse address resolution is performed the same way as the ARP address resolution. The same packet format (see Figure 50) is used as for ARP.

An exception is the operation code field that now takes the following values:

- 3: For the RARP request
- 4: For the RARP reply

And of course, the physical header of the frame will now indicate RARP as the higher-level protocol (8035 hex) instead of ARP (0806 hex) or IP (0800 hex) in the EtherType field.

Some differences arise from the concept of RARP itself:

- ARP only assumes that every host knows the mapping between its own hardware address and protocol address. RARP requires one or more server hosts on the network to maintain a database of mappings between hardware addresses and protocol addresses so that they will be able to reply to requests from client hosts.

- Due to the size this database can take, part of the server function is usually implemented outside the adapter's microcode, with optionally a small cache in the microcode. The microcode part is then only responsible for reception and transmission of the RARP frames, the RARP mapping itself being taken care of by server software running as a normal process in the host machine.

- The nature of this database also requires some software to create and update the database manually.

- In case there are multiple RARP servers on the network, the RARP requester only uses the first RARP reply received on its broadcast RARP request, and discards the others.

3.6 Bootstrap protocol (BOOTP)

The bootstrap protocol (BOOTP) enables a client workstation to initialize with a minimal IP stack and request it's IP address, a gateway address, and the address of a name server from a BOOTP server. If BOOTP is to be used in your network, then the server and client are usually on the same physical LAN segment. BOOTP can only be used across bridged segments when source-routing bridges are being used, or across subnets, if you have a router capable of BOOTP forwarding.

BOOTP is a draft standard protocol. Its status is recommended. The BOOTP specifications can be found in RFC 951 – Bootstrap Protocol.

There are also updates to BOOTP, some relating to interoperability with DHCP (see 3.7, "Dynamic Host Configuration Protocol (DHCP)" on page 126), described in RFC 1542 – Clarifications and Extensions for the Bootstrap Protocol, which updates RFC 951 and RFC 2132 – DHCP Options and BOOTP Vendor Extensions. The updates to BOOTP are draft standards with a status of elective and recommended respectively.

The BOOTP protocol was originally developed as a mechanism to enable diskless hosts to be remotely booted over a network as workstations, routers, terminal concentrators, and so on. It allows a minimum IP protocol stack with no configuration information to obtain enough information to begin the process of downloading the necessary boot code. BOOTP does not define how the downloading is done, but this process typically uses TFTP (see also 10.2, "Trivial File Transfer Protocol (TFTP)" on page 371) as described in RFC 906 – Bootstrap Loading Using TFTP. Although still widely used for this purpose by diskless hosts, BOOTP is also commonly used solely as a mechanism to deliver configuration information to a client that has not been manually configured.

The BOOTP process involves the following steps:

1. The client determines its own hardware address; this is normally in a ROM on the hardware.

2. A BOOTP client sends its hardware address in a UDP datagram to the server. The full contents of this datagram are shown in Figure 54. If the client knows its IP address and/or the address of the server, it should use them, but in general BOOTP clients have no IP configuration data at all. If the client does not know its own IP address, it uses 0.0.0.0. If the client does not know the server's IP address, it uses the limited broadcast address (255.255.255.255). The UDP port number is 67.

3. The server receives the datagram and looks up the hardware address of the client in its configuration file, which contains the client's IP address. The server fills in the remaining fields in the UDP datagram and returns it to the client using UDP port 68. One of three methods may be used to do this:

    a. If the client knows its own IP address (it was included in the BOOTP request), then the server returns the datagram directly to this address. It is likely that the ARP cache in the server's protocol stack will not know the hardware address matching the IP address. ARP will be used to determine it as normal.

    b. If the client does not know its own IP address (it was 0.0.0.0 in the BOOTP request), then the server must concern itself with its own ARP cache.

    c. ARP on the server cannot be used to find the hardware address of the client because the client does not know its IP address and so cannot reply to an ARP request. This is called the "chicken and egg" problem. There are two possible solutions:

        1. If the server has a mechanism for directly updating its own ARP cache without using ARP itself, it does so and then sends the datagram directly.

        2. If the server cannot update its own ARP cache, it must send a broadcast reply.

4. When it receives the reply, the BOOTP client will record its own IP address (allowing it to respond to ARP requests) and begin the bootstrap process.

Figure 54 gives an overview of the BOOTP message format.

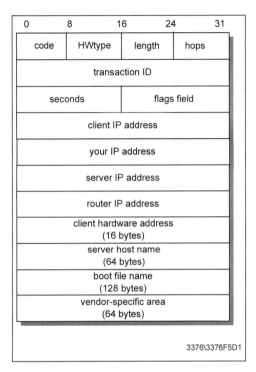

Figure 54. BOOTP message format

Where:

- code: Indicates a request or a reply.
  - 1: Request
  - 2: Reply
- HWtype: The type of hardware, for example:
  - 1: Ethernet
  - 6: IEEE 802 Networks:

  Refer to STD 2 – Assigned Internet Numbers for a complete list.
- length: Hardware address length in bytes. Ethernet and token-ring both use 6, for example.
- hops: The client sets this to 0.

It is incremented by a router that relays the request to another server and is used to identify loops. RFC 951 suggests that a value of 3 indicates a loop.

- Transaction ID: A random number used to match this boot request with the response it generates.

- Seconds: Set by the client. It is the elapsed time in seconds since the client started its boot process.

- Flags field: The most significant bit of the flags field is used as a broadcast flag. All other bits must be set to zero; they are reserved for future use. Normally, BOOTP servers attempt to deliver BOOTREPLY messages directly to a client using unicast delivery. The destination address in the IP header is set to the BOOTP *your IP address* and the MAC address is set to the BOOTP *client hardware address*. If a host is unable to receive a unicast IP datagram until it knows its IP address, then this broadcast bit must be set to indicate to the server that the BOOTREPLY must be sent as an IP and MAC broadcast. Otherwise this bit must be set to zero.

- Client IP address: Set by the client, either to its known IP address or 0.0.0.0.

- Your IP address: Set by the server if the client IP address field was 0.0.0.0.

- Server IP address: Set by the server.

- Router IP address: This is the address of a BOOTP relay agent, *not* a general IP router to be used by the client. It is set by the forwarding agent when BOOTP forwarding is being used (see 3.6.1, "BOOTP forwarding" on page 125).

- Client hardware address: Set by the client and used by the server to identify which registered client is booting.

- Server host name: Optional server host name terminated by X'00'.

- Boot file name: The client either leaves this null or specifies a generic name, such as router indicating the type of boot file to be used. The server returns the fully qualified file name of a boot file suitable for the client. The value is terminated by X'00'.

- Vendor-specific area: Optional vendor-specific area. It is recommended that clients always fill the first four bytes with a "magic cookie." If a vendor-specific magic cookie is not used the client should use 99.130.83.99 followed by an end tag (255) and set the remaining bytes to zero. The vendor-specific area can also contain *BOOTP Vendor extensions*. These are options that can be passed to the client at boot time along with its IP address. For example, the client could also receive the address of a default router, the address of a domain name server and a subnet mask. BOOTP shares the same options as DHCP, with the exception of several DHCP-specific options. Please see RFC 2132 for full details.

Once the BOOTP client has processed the reply, it may proceed with the transfer of the boot file and execute the full boot process. See RFC 906 for the specification of how this is done with TFTP. In the case of a diskless host, the full boot process will normally replace the minimal IP protocol stack, loaded from ROM, and used by BOOTP and TFTP, with a normal IP protocol stack transferred as part of the boot file and containing the correct customization for the client.

3.6.1 BOOTP forwarding

The BOOTP client uses the limited broadcast address for BOOTP requests, which requires the BOOTP server to be on the same subnet as the client. BOOTP forwarding is a mechanism for routers to forward BOOTP requests across subnets. It is a configuration option available on most routers. The router configured to forward BOOTP requests is known as a *BOOTP relay agent*.

A router will normally discard any datagrams containing illegal source addresses, such as 0.0.0.0, which is used by a BOOTP client. A router will also generally discard datagrams with the limited broadcast destination address. However, a BOOTP relay agent will accept such datagrams from BOOTP clients on port 67. The process carried out by a BOOTP relay agent on receiving a BOOTPREQUEST is as follows:

1. When the BOOTP relay agent receives a BOOTPREQUEST, it first checks the hops field to check the number of hops already completed, in order to decide whether to forward the request. The threshold for the allowable number of hops is normally configurable.

2. If the relay agent decides to relay the request, it checks the contents of the router IP address field. If this field is zero, it fills this field with the IP address of the interface on which the BOOTPREQUEST was received. If this field already has an IP address of another relay agent, it is not touched.

3. The value of the hops field is incremented.

4. The relay agent then forwards the BOOTPREQUEST to one or more BOOTP servers. The address of the BOOTP server(s) is preconfigured at the relay agent. The BOOTPREQUEST is normally forwarded as a unicast frame, although some implementations use broadcast forwarding.

5. When the BOOTP server receives the BOOTPREQUEST with the non-zero router IP address field, it sends an IP unicast BOOTREPLY to the BOOTP relay agent at the address in this field on port 67.

6. When the BOOTP relay agent receives the BOOTREPLY, the HWtype, length and client hardware address fields in the message supply sufficient link-layer information to return the reply to the client. The relay agent checks the broadcast flag. If this flag is set, the agent forwards the BOOTPREPLY to the client as a broadcast. If the broadcast flag is not set, the relay agent sends a reply as a unicast to the address specified in your IP address.

When a router is configured as a BOOTP relay agent, the BOOTP forwarding task is considerably different to the task of switching datagrams between subnets normally carried out by a router. Forwarding of BOOTP messages can be considered to be receiving BOOTP messages as a final destination, then generating new BOOTP messages to be forwarded to another destination.

3.6.2 BOOTP considerations

The use of BOOTP allows centralized configuration of multiple clients. However, it requires a static table to be maintained with an IP address preallocated for every client that is likely to attach to the BOOTP server, even if the client is seldom active. This means that there is no relief on the number of IP addresses required. There is a measure of security in an environment utilizing BOOTP, because a client will only be allocated an IP address by the server if it has a valid MAC address.

3.7 Dynamic Host Configuration Protocol (DHCP)

DHCP is a draft standard protocol. Its status is elective. The current DHCP specifications can be found in RFC 2131 – Dynamic Host Configuration Protocol and RFC 2132 – DHCP Options and BOOTP Vendor Extensions.

The Dynamic Host Configuration Protocol (DHCP) provides a framework for passing configuration information to hosts on a TCP/IP network. DHCP is based on the BOOTP protocol, adding the capability of automatic allocation of reusable network addresses and additional configuration options. For information regarding BOOTP, please refer to 3.6, "Bootstrap protocol (BOOTP)" on page 121. DHCP messages use UDP port 67, the BOOTP server's well-known port and UDP port 68, the BOOTP client's well-known port. DHCP participants can interoperate with BOOTP participants. See 3.7.8, "BOOTP and DHCP interoperability" on page 136 for further details.

DHCP consists of two components:

1. A protocol that delivers host-specific configuration parameters from a DHCP server to a host.

2. A mechanism for the allocation of temporary or permanent network addresses to hosts.

IP requires the setting of many parameters within the protocol implementation software. Because IP can be used on many dissimilar kinds of network hardware, values for those parameters cannot be guessed at or assumed to have correct defaults. The use of a distributed address allocation scheme based on a polling/defense mechanism, for discovery of network addresses already in use, cannot guarantee unique network addresses because hosts may not always be able to defend their network addresses.

DHCP supports three mechanisms for IP address allocation:

1. Automatic allocation

   DHCP assigns a permanent IP address to the host.

2. Dynamic allocation

   DHCP assigns an IP address for a limited period of time. Such a network address is called a *lease*. This is the only mechanism that allows automatic reuse of addresses that are no longer needed by the host to which it was assigned.

3. Manual allocation

   The host's address is assigned by a network administrator.

3.7.1 The DHCP message format

The format of a DHCP message is shown in Figure 55.

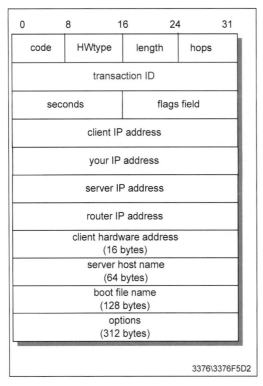

0	8	16	24	31
code	HWtype	length	hops	
transaction ID				
seconds		flags field		
client IP address				
your IP address				
server IP address				
router IP address				
client hardware address (16 bytes)				
server host name (64 bytes)				
boot file name (128 bytes)				
options (312 bytes)				

3376\3376F5D2

Figure 55. DHCP message format

Where:

- code: Indicates a request or a reply

  - 1 Request
  - 2 Reply

- HWtype: The type of hardware, for example:

  - 1 Ethernet
  - 6 IEEE 802 Networks

  Refer to STD 2 – Assigned Internet Numbers for a complete list.

- length: Hardware address length in bytes. Ethernet and token-ring both use 6, for example.

- hops: The client sets this to 0. It is incremented by a router that relays the request to another server and is used to identify loops. RFC 951 suggests that a value of 3 indicates a loop.

- Transaction ID: A random number used to match this boot request with the response it generates.
- Seconds: Set by the client. It is the elapsed time in seconds since the client started its boot process.
- Flags field: The most significant bit of the flags field is used as a broadcast flag. All other bits must be set to zero, and are reserved for future use. Normally, DHCP servers attempt to deliver DHCP messages directly to a client using unicast delivery. The destination address in the IP header is set to the DHCP *your IP address* and the MAC address is set to the DHCP *client hardware address*. If a host is unable to receive a unicast IP datagram until it knows its IP address, then this broadcast bit must be set to indicate to the server that the DHCP reply must be sent as an IP and MAC broadcast. Otherwise this bit must be set to zero.
- Client IP address: Set by the client. Either its known IP address, or 0.0.0.0.
- Your IP address: Set by the server if the client IP address field was 0.0.0.0.
- Server IP address: Set by the server.
- Router IP address: This is the address of a BOOTP relay agent, *not* a general IP router to be used by the client. It is set by the forwarding agent when BOOTP forwarding is being used (see 3.6.1, "BOOTP forwarding" on page 125).
- Client hardware address: Set by the client. DHCP defines a client identifier option that is used for client identification. If this option is not used the client is identified by its MAC address.
- Server host name: Optional server host name terminated by X'00'.
- Boot file name: The client either leaves this null or specifies a generic name, such as router, indicating the type of boot file to be used. In a DHCPDISCOVER request this is set to null. The server returns a fully qualified directory path name in a DHCPOFFER request. The value is terminated by X'00'.
- Options: The first four bytes of the options field of the DHCP message contain the magic cookie (99.130.83.99). The remainder of the options field consists of tagged parameters that are called *options*. Please see RFC 2132 for details.

3.7.2 DHCP message types

DHCP messages fall into one of the following categories:

- DHCPDISCOVER: Broadcast by a client to find available DHCP servers.

- DHCPOFFER: Response from a server to a DHCPDISCOVER and offering IP address and other parameters.

- DHCPREQUEST: Message from a client to servers that does one of the following:

    - Requests the parameters offered by one of the servers and declines all other offers.

    - Verifies a previously allocated address after a system or network change (a reboot for example).

    - Requests the extension of a lease on a particular address.

- DHCPACK: Acknowledgement from server to client with parameters, including IP address.

- DHCPNACK: Negative acknowledgement from server to client, indicating that the client's lease has expired or that a requested IP address is incorrect.

- DHCPDECLINE: Message from client to server indicating that the offered address is already in use.

- DHCPRELEASE: Message from client to server cancelling remainder of a lease and relinquishing network address.

- DHCPINFORM: Message from a client that already has an IP address (manually configured for example), requesting further configuration parameters from the DHCP server.

3.7.3 Allocating a new network address

This section describes the client/server interaction if the client does not know its network address. Assume that the DHCP server has a block of network addresses from which it can satisfy requests for new addresses. Each server also maintains a database of allocated addresses and leases in permanent local storage.

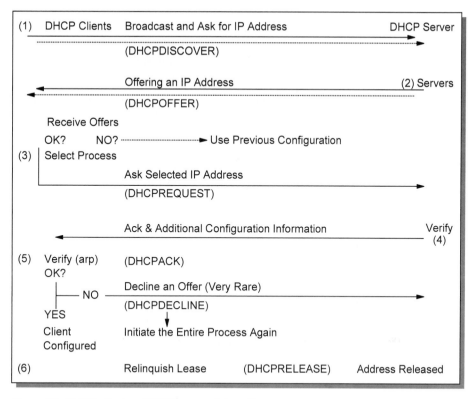

(1) DHCP Clients   Broadcast and Ask for IP Address   DHCP Server

          (DHCPDISCOVER)

                      Offering an IP Address   (2) Servers

          (DHCPOFFER)

      Receive Offers

      OK?   NO? ──────────────► Use Previous Configuration
(3)   Select Process

                      Ask Selected IP Address

          (DHCPREQUEST)

                      Ack & Additional Configuration Information   Verify
                                                                          (4)
(5)   Verify (arp)   (DHCPACK)
      OK?
                      Decline an Offer (Very Rare)
       ├─── NO ────────────────────────────────────
      YES   (DHCPDECLINE)

      Client   Initiate the Entire Process Again
      Configured

(6)   Relinquish Lease   (DHCPRELEASE)   Address Released

Figure 56. DHCP client and DHCP server interaction

The following is a description of the DHCP client/server interaction steps illustrated in Figure 56:

1. The client broadcasts a DHCPDISCOVER message on its local physical subnet. At this point, the client is in the INIT state. The DHCPDISCOVER message may include some options such as network address suggestion or lease duration.

2. Each server may respond with a DHCPOFFER message that includes an available network address (your IP address) and other configuration options. The servers may record the address as offered to the client to prevent the same address being offered to other clients in the event of further DHCPDISCOVER messages being received before the first client has completed its configuration.

3. The client receives one or more DHCPOFFER messages from one or more servers. The client chooses one based on the configuration parameters offered and broadcasts a DHCPREQUEST message that includes the server identifier option to indicate which message it has

selected and the requested IP address option, taken from your IP address in the selected offer.

In the event that no offers are received, if the client has knowledge of a previous network address, the client may reuse that address if its lease is still valid, until the lease expires.

4. The servers receive the DHCPREQUEST broadcast from the client. Those servers not selected by the DHCPREQUEST message use the message as notification that the client has declined that server's offer. The server selected in the DHCPREQUEST message commits the binding for the client to persistent storage and responds with a DHCPACK message containing the configuration parameters for the requesting client. The combination of client hardware and assigned network address constitute a unique identifier for the client's lease and are used by both the client and server to identify a lease referred to in any DHCP messages. The your IP address field in the DHCPACK messages is filled in with the selected network address.

5. The client receives the DHCPACK message with configuration parameters. The client performs a final check on the parameters, for example with ARP for allocated network address, and notes the duration of the lease and the lease identification cookie specified in the DHCPACK message. At this point, the client is configured.

   If the client detects a problem with the parameters in the DHCPACK message (the address is already in use on the network, for example), the client sends a DHCPDECLINE message to the server and restarts the configuration process. The client should wait a minimum of ten seconds before restarting the configuration process to avoid excessive network traffic in case of looping. On receipt of a DHCPDECLINE, the server must mark the offered address as unavailable (and possibly inform the system administrator that there is a configuration problem).

   If the client receives a DHCPNAK message, the client restarts the configuration process.

6. The client may choose to relinquish its lease on a network address by sending a DHCPRELEASE message to the server. The client identifies the lease to be released by including its network address and its hardware address.

> **Note:**
>
> Responses from the DHCP server to the DHCP client may be broadcast or unicast, depending on whether the client is able to receive a unicast message before the TCP/IP stack is fully configured; this varies between implementations. (See Flags field on page 129.)

3.7.4 DHCP lease renewal process

This section describes the interaction between DHCP servers and clients that have already been configured and the process that ensures lease expiration and renewal.

1. When a server sends the DHCPACK to a client with IP address and configuration parameters, it also registers the start of the lease time for that address. This lease time is passed to the client as one of the options in the DHCPACK message, together with two timer values, T1 and T2. The client is rightfully entitled to use the given address for the duration of the lease time. On applying the received configuration, the client also starts the timers T1 and T2. At this time, the client is in the BOUND state. Times T1 and T2 are options configurable by the server but T1 must be less than T2, and T2 must be less than the lease time. According to RFC 2132, T1 defaults to (0.5 * lease time) and T2 defaults to (0.875 * lease time).

2. When timer T1 expires, the client will send a DHCPREQUEST (unicast) to the server that offered the address, asking to extend the lease for the given configuration. The client is now in the RENEWING state. The server would usually respond with a DHCPACK message indicating the new lease time, and timers T1 and T2 are reset at the client accordingly. The server also resets its record of the lease time. In normal circumstances, an active client would continually renew its lease in this way indefinitely, without the lease ever expiring.

3. If no DHCPACK is received until timer T2 expires, the client enters the REBINDING state. It now broadcasts a DHCPREQUEST message to extend its lease. This request can be confirmed by a DHCPACK message from any DHCP server on the network.

4. If the client does not receive a DHCPACK message after its lease has expired, it has to stop using its current TCP/IP configuration. The client may then return to the INIT state, issuing a DHCPDISCOVER broadcast to try and obtain any valid address.

Figure 57 shows the DHCP process and changing client state during that process.

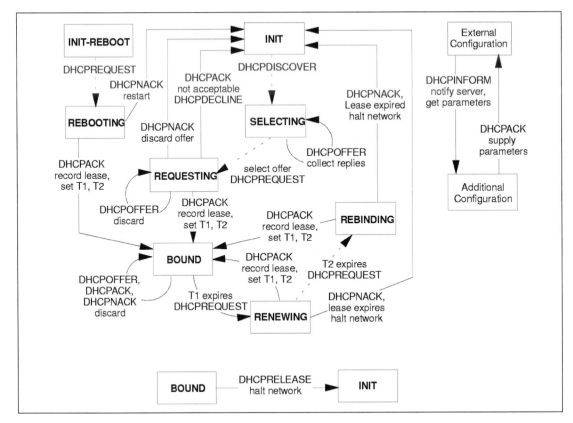

Figure 57. DHCP client state and DHCP process

3.7.5 Reusing a previously allocated network address

If the client remembers and wishes to reuse a previously allocated network address, then the following steps are carried out:

1. The client broadcasts a DHCPREQUEST message on its local subnet. The DHCPREQUEST message includes the client's network address.

2. A server with knowledge of the client's configuration parameters responds with a DHCPACK message to the client (provided the lease is still current), renewing the lease at the same time.

   If the client's lease has expired, the server with knowledge of the client responds with DHCPNACK.

3. The client receives the DHCPACK message with configuration parameters. The client performs a final check on the parameters and notes the duration of the lease and the lease identification cookie

specified in the DHCPACK message. At this point, the client is configured and its T1 and T2 timers are reset.

If the client detects a problem with the parameters in the DHCPACK message, the client sends a DHCPDECLINE message to the server and restarts the configuration process by requesting a new network address. If the client receives a DHCPNAK message, it cannot reuse its remembered network address. It must instead request a new address by restarting the configuration process as described in 3.7.3, "Allocating a new network address" on page 130.

Note

A host should use DHCP to reacquire or verify its IP address and network parameters whenever the local network parameters have changed, for example, at system boot time or after a disconnection from the local network, as the local network configuration may change without the host's or user's knowledge. If a client has multiple IP interfaces, each of them must be configured by DHCP separately.

For further information, please refer to the above-mentioned RFCs.

3.7.6 Configuration parameters repository

DHCP provides persistent storage of network parameters for network clients. A DHCP server stores a key-value entry for each client, the key being some unique identifier, for example an IP subnet number and a unique identifier within the subnet (normally a hardware address), and the value contains the configuration parameters last allocated to this particular client.

One effect of this is that a DHCP client will tend to always be allocated to the same IP address by the server, provided the pool of addresses is not over-subscribed and the previous address has not already been allocated to another client.

3.7.7 DHCP considerations

DHCP dynamic allocation of IP addresses and configuration parameters relieves the network administrator of a great deal of manual configuration work. The ability for a device to be moved from network to network and to automatically obtain valid configuration parameters for the current network can be of great benefit to mobile users. Also, because IP addresses are only allocated when clients are actually active, it is possible, by the use of reasonably short lease times and the fact that mobile clients do not need to be allocated more than one address, to reduce the total number of addresses in use in an organization. However, the following should be considered when DHCP is being implemented:

- DHCP is built on UDP, which is inherently insecure. In normal operation, an unauthorized client could connect to a network and obtain a valid IP address and configuration. To prevent this, it is possible to preallocate IP addresses to particular MAC addresses (similar to BOOTP), but this increases the administration workload and removes the benefit of recycling of addresses. Unauthorized DHCP servers could also be set up, sending false and potentially disruptive information to clients.

- In a DHCP environment where automatic or dynamic address allocation is used, it is generally not possible to predetermine the IP address of a client at any particular point in time. In this case, if static DNS servers are also used, the DNS servers will not likely contain valid host name to IP address mappings for the clients. If having client entries in the DNS is important for the network, one may use DHCP to manually assign IP addresses to those clients and then administer the client mappings in the DNS accordingly.

3.7.8 BOOTP and DHCP interoperability

The format of DHCP messages is based on the format of BOOTP messages, which enables BOOTP and DHCP clients to interoperate in certain circumstances. Every DHCP message contains a DHCP message type (51) option. Any message without this option is assumed to be from a BOOTP client.

Support for BOOTP clients at a DHCP server must be configured by a system administrator, if required. The DHCP Server responds to BOOTPREQUEST messages with BOOTPREPLY, rather than DHCPOFFER. Any DHCP server that is not configured in this way will discard any BOOTPREQUEST frames sent to it. A DHCP server may offer static addresses, or automatic addresses (from its pool of unassigned addresses) to a BOOTP client (although not all BOOTP implementations will understand automatic addresses). If an automatic address *is* offered to a BOOTP client, then that address must have an infinite lease time, as the client will not understand the DHCP lease mechanism.

DHCP messages may be forwarded by routers configured as BOOTP relay agents.

Chapter 4. Routing protocols

One of the basic functions provided by the IP protocol is the ability to form connections between different physical networks. A system that performs this function is termed an *IP router*. This type of device attaches to two or more physical networks and forwards datagrams between the networks.

When sending data to a remote destination, a host passes datagrams to a local router. The router forwards the datagrams towards the final destination. They travel from one router to another until they reach a router connected to the destination's LAN segment. Each router along the end-to-end path selects the *next hop* device used to reach the destination. The next hop represents the next device along the path to reach the destination. It is located on a physical network connected to this intermediate system. Since this physical network differs from the one on which the system originally received the datagram, the intermediate host has *forwarded* (that is, routed) the IP datagram from one physical network to another.

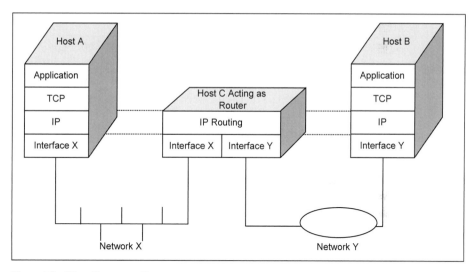

Figure 58. IP routing operations

Figure 58 shows an environment where Host C is positioned to forward packets between Network X and Network Y.

The IP routing table in each device is used to forward packets between network segments. The basic table contains information about a router's locally connected networks. The configuration of the device can be extended to contain information detailing remote networks. This information provides a more complete view of the overall environment.

A robust routing protocol provides the ability to dynamically build and manage the information in the IP routing table. As network topology changes occur, the routing tables are updated with minimal or no manual intervention. This chapter details several IP routing protocols and how each protocol manages this information.

Note

In other sections of this book, the position of each protocol within the layered model of the OSI protocol stack is shown. The routing function is included as part of the internetwork layer. However, the primary function of a routing protocol is to exchange routing information with other routers. In this respect, routing protocols behave more like an application protocol. Therefore, this chapter makes no attempt to represent the position of these protocols within the overall protocol stack.

Note

Early IP routing documentation often referred to an IP router as an *IP gateway.*

4.1 Autonomous systems

The definition of an autonomous system (AS) is integral to understanding the function and scope of a routing protocol. An AS is defined as a logical portion of a larger IP network. An AS is normally comprised of an internetwork within an organization. It is administered by a single management authority. As shown in Figure 59, an AS may connect to other autonomous systems managed by the same organization. Alternatively, it may connect to other public or private networks.

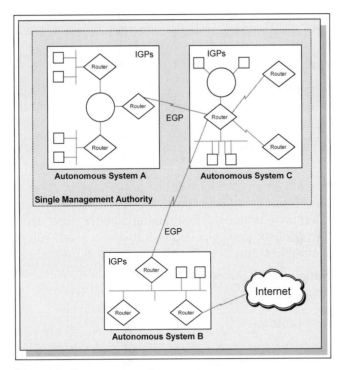

Figure 59. Autonomous systems

Some routing protocols are used to determine routing paths within an AS. Others are used to interconnect a set of autonomous systems:

- Interior Gateway Protocols (IGPs): Interior gateway protocols allow routers to exchange information within an AS. Examples of these protocols are Open Short Path First (OSPF) and Routing Information Protocol (RIP).

- Exterior Gateway Protocols (EGPs): Exterior gateway protocols allow the exchange of summary information between autonomous systems. An example of this type of routing protocol is Border Gateway Protocol (BGP).

Figure 59 depicts the interaction between interior and exterior protocols. It shows the interior protocols used to maintain routing information within each AS. The figure also shows the exterior protocols maintaining the routing information between autonomous systems.

Within an AS, multiple interior routing processes may be used. When this occurs, the AS must appear to other autonomous systems as having a single, coherent interior routing plan. The AS must present a consistent view of the internal destinations

4.2 Types of IP routing and IP routing algorithms

Routing algorithms are used to build and maintain the IP routing table on a device. There are two primary methods used to build the routing table:

- Static routing: Static routing use preprogrammed definitions representing paths through the network.

- Dynamic routing: Dynamic routing algorithms allow routers to automatically discover and maintain awareness of the paths through the network. This automatic discovery can use a number of currently available dynamic routing protocols. The difference between these protocols is the way they discover and calculate new routes to destination networks. They can be classified into three broad categories:

  - Distance vector protocols

  - Link state protocols

  - Hybrid protocols

The remainder of this section details the operation of each algorithm.

There are several reasons for the multiplicity of protocols:

- Routing within a network and routing between networks typically have different requirements for security, stability, and scalability. Different routing protocols have been developed to address these requirements.

- New protocols have been developed to address the observed deficiencies in established protocols.

- Different-sized networks can use different routing algorithms. Small to medium-sized networks often use routing protocols that reflect the simplicity of the environment. However, these protocols do not scale to support large, interconnected networks. More complex routing algorithms are required to support these environments.

4.2.1 Static routing

Static routing is manually performed by the network administrator. The administrator is responsible for discovering and propagating routes through the network. These definitions are manually programmed in every routing device in the environment.

Once a device has been configured, it simply forwards packets out the predetermined ports. There is no communication between routers regarding the current topology of the network.

In small networks with minimal redundancy, this process is relatively simple to administer. However, there are several disadvantages to this approach for maintaining IP routing tables:

- Static routes require a considerable amount of coordination and maintenance in non-trivial network environments.

- Static routes cannot dynamically adapt to the current operational state of the network. If a destination subnetwork becomes unreachable, the static routes pointing to that network remain in the routing table. Traffic continues to be forwarded toward that destination. Unless the network administrator updates the static routes to reflect the new topology, traffic is unable to use any alternate paths that may exist.

Normally, static routes are used only in simple network topologies. However, there are additional circumstances when static routing can be attractive. For example, static routes can be used:

- To manually define a default route. This route is used to forward traffic when the routing table does not contain a more specific route to the destination.

- To define a route that is not automatically advertised within a network.

- When utilization or line tariffs make it undesirable to send routing advertisement traffic through lower-capacity WAN connections.

- When complex routing policies are required. For example, static routes can be used to guarantee that traffic destined for a specific host traverses a designated network path.

- To provide a more secure network environment. The administrator is aware of all subnetworks defined in the environment. The administrator specifically authorizes all communication permitted between these subnetworks.

- To provide more efficient resource utilization. This method of routing table management requires no network bandwidth to advertise routes between neighboring devices. It also uses less processor memory and CPU cycles to calculate network paths.

4.2.2 Distance vector routing

Distance vector algorithms are examples of dynamic routing protocols. These algorithms allow each device in the network to automatically build and maintain a local IP routing table.

The principle behind distance vector routing is simple. Each router in the internetwork maintains the *distance* or *cost* from itself to every known destination. This value represents the overall desirability of the path. Paths associated with a smaller cost value are more attractive to use than paths associated with a larger value. The path represented by the smallest cost becomes the preferred path to reach the destination.

This information is maintained in a *distance vector table*. The table is periodically advertised to each neighboring router. Each router processes these advertisements to determine the best paths through the network.

The main advantage of distance vector algorithms is that they are typically easy to implement and debug. They are very useful in small networks with limited redundancy. However, there are several disadvantages with this type of protocol:

- During an adverse condition, the length of time for every device in the network to produce an accurate routing table is called the *convergence time*. In large, complex internetworks using distance vector algorithms, this time can be excessive. While the routing tables are converging, networks are susceptible to inconsistent routing behavior. This can cause routing loops or other types of unstable packet forwarding.

- To reduce convergence time, a limit is often placed on the maximum number of hops contained in a single route. Valid paths exceeding this limit are not usable in distance vector networks.

- Distance vector routing tables are periodically transmitted to neighboring devices. They are sent even if no changes have been made to the contents of the table. This may cause noticeable periods of increased utilization in reduced capacity environments.

Enhancements to the basic distance vector algorithm have been developed to reduce the convergence and instability exposures. These enhancements are described in 4.3.5, "Convergence and counting to infinity" on page 148.

RIP and BGP are two popular examples of distance vector routing protocols.

4.2.3 Link state routing

The growth in the size and complexity of networks in recent years has necessitated the development of more robust routing algorithms. These algorithms address the shortcoming observed in distance vector protocols.

These algorithms use the principle of a *link state* to determine network topology. A link state is the description of an interface on a router (for example, IP address, subnet mask, type of network) and its relationship to neighboring routers. The collection of these link states forms a link state database.

The process used by link state algorithms to determine network topology is straightforward:

- Each router identifies all other routing devices on the directly connected networks.

- Each router advertises a list of all directly connected network links and the associated cost of each link. This is performed through the exchange of link state advertisements (LSAs) with other routers in the network.

- Using these advertisements, each router creates a database detailing the current network topology. The topology database in each router is identical.

- Each router uses the information in the topology database to compute the most desirable routes to each destination network. This information is used to update the IP routing table.

4.2.3.1 Shortest-Path First (SPF) algorithm

The SPF algorithm is used to process the information in the topology database. It provides a tree-representation of the network. The device running the SPF algorithm is the root of the tree. The output of the algorithm is the list of shortest-paths to each destination network. Figure 60 provides an example of the shortest-path algorithm executed on router A.

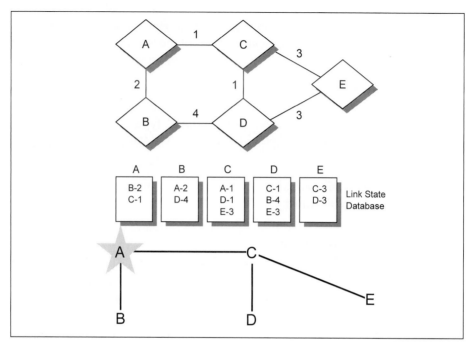

Figure 60. Shortest-Path First (SPF) example

Because each router is processing the same set of LSAs, each router creates an identical link state database. However, because each device occupies a different place in the network topology, application of the SPF algorithm produces a different tree for each router.

The OSPF protocol is a popular example of a link state routing protocol.

4.2.4 Hybrid routing

The last category of routing protocols is hybrid protocols. These protocols attempt to combine the positive attributes of both distance vector and link state protocols. Like distance vector, hybrid protocols use metrics to assign a preference to a route. However, the metrics are more accurate than conventional distance vector protocols. Like link state algorithms, routing updates in hybrid protocols are event driven rather than periodic. Networks using hybrid protocols tend to converge more quickly than networks using distance vector protocols. Finally, these protocols potentially reduce the overhead of link state updates and distance vector advertisements.

Although open hybrid protocols exist, this category is almost exclusively associated with the proprietary EIGRP algorithm. EIGRP was developed by Cisco Systems, Inc.

4.3 Routing Information Protocol (RIP)

RIP is an example of an interior gateway protocol designed for use within small autonomous systems. RIP is based on the Xerox XNS routing protocol. Early implementations of RIP were readily accepted because the code was incorporated in the Berkeley Software Distribution (BSD) UNIX-based operating system. RIP is a distance vector protocol.

In mid-1988, the IETF issued RFC 1058, which describes the standard operations of a RIP system. However, the RFC was issued after many RIP implementations had been completed. For this reason, some RIP systems do not support the entire set of enhancements to the basic distance vector algorithm (for example, poison reverse and triggered updates).

4.3.1 RIP packet types

The RIP protocol specifies two packet types. These packets may be sent by any device running the RIP protocol:

- Request packets: A request packet queries neighboring RIP devices to obtain their distance vector table. The request indicates if the neighbor should return either a specific subset or the entire contents of the table.

- Response packets: A response packet is sent by a device to advertise the information maintained in its local distance vector table. The table is sent during the following situations:

  - The table is automatically sent every 30 seconds.
  - The table is sent as a response to a request packet generated by another RIP node.
  - If triggered updates are supported, the table is sent when there is a change to the local distance vector table. Triggered updates are presented in 4.3.5.3, "Triggered updates" on page 152.

When a response packet is received by a device, the information contained in the update is compared against the local distance vector table. If the update contains a lower cost route to a destination, the table is updated to reflect the new path.

4.3.2 RIP packet format

RIP uses a specific packet format to share information about the distances to known network destinations. RIP packets are transmitted using UDP datagrams. RIP sends and receives datagrams using UDP port 520.

RIP datagrams have a maximum size of 512 octets. Updates larger than this size must be advertised in multiple datagrams. In LAN environments, RIP datagrams are sent using the MAC all-stations broadcast address and an IP network broadcast address. In point-to-point or non-broadcast environments, datagrams are specifically addressed to the destination device.

The RIP packet format is shown in Figure 61.

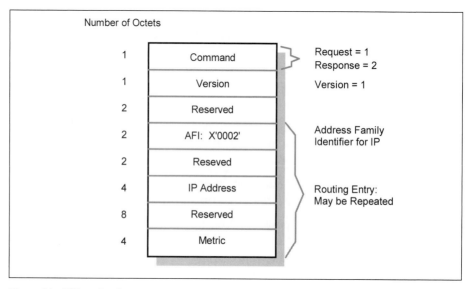

Figure 61. RIP packet format

A 512 byte packet size allows a maximum of 25 routing entries to be included in a single RIP advertisement.

4.3.3 RIP modes of operation

RIP hosts have two modes of operation:

- Active mode: Devices operating in active mode advertise their distance vector table and also receive routing updates from neighboring RIP hosts. Routing devices are typically configured to operate in active mode.

- Passive (or silent) mode: Devices operating in this mode simply receive routing updates from neighboring RIP devices. They do not advertise their distance vector table. End stations are typically configured to operate in passive mode.

4.3.4 Calculating distance vectors

The distance vector table describes each destination network. The entries in this table contain the following information:

- The destination network (vector) described by this entry in the table.

- The associated cost (distance) of the most attractive path to reach this destination. This provides the ability to differentiate between multiple paths to a destination. In this context, the terms distance and cost can be misleading. They have no direct relationship to physical distance or monetary cost.

- The IP address of the next-hop device used to reach the destination network.

Each time a routing table advertisement is received by a device, it is processed to determine if any destination can be reached via a lower cost path. This is done using the RIP distance vector algorithm. The algorithm can be summarized as:

- At router initialization, each device contains a distance vector table listing each directly attached networks and configured cost. Typically, each network is assigned a cost of 1. This represents a single hop through the network. The total number of hops in a route is equal to the total cost of the route. However, cost can be changed to reflect other measurements such as utilization, speed, or reliability.

- Each router periodically (typically every 30 seconds) transmits its distance vector table to each of its neighbors. The router may also transmit the table when a topology change occurs.

- Each router uses this information to update its local distance vector table:

  - The total cost to each destination is calculated by adding the cost reported in a neighbor's distance vector table to the cost of the link to that neighbor. The path with the least cost is stored in the distance vector table.

  - All updates automatically supersede the previous information in the distance vector table. This allows RIP to maintain the integrity of the routes in the routing table.

- The IP routing table is updated to reflect the least-cost path to each destination.

Figure 62 illustrates the distance vector tables for three routers within a simple internetwork.

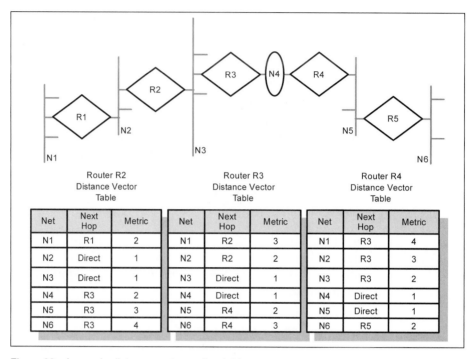

Net	Next Hop	Metric	Net	Next Hop	Metric	Net	Next Hop	Metric
N1	R1	2	N1	R2	3	N1	R3	4
N2	Direct	1	N2	R2	2	N2	R3	3
N3	Direct	1	N3	Direct	1	N3	R3	2
N4	R3	2	N4	Direct	1	N4	Direct	1
N5	R3	3	N5	R4	2	N5	Direct	1
N6	R3	4	N6	R4	3	N6	R5	2

Figure 62. A sample distance vector routing table

4.3.5 Convergence and counting to infinity

Given sufficient time, this algorithm will correctly calculate the distance vector table on each device. However, during this convergence time, erroneous routes may propagate through the network. This problem is shown in Figure 63.

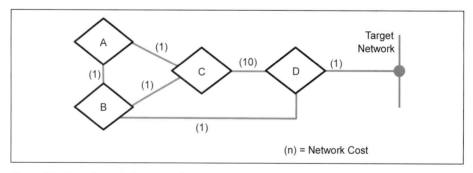

Figure 63. Counting to infinity sample network

This network contains four interconnected routers. Each link has a cost of 1, except for the link connecting router C and router D; this link has a cost of 10. The costs have been defined so that forwarding packets on the link connecting router C and router D is undesirable.

Once the network has converged, each device has routing information describing all networks. For example, to reach the target network, the routers have the following information:

- Router D to the target network: Directly connected network. Metric 1.
- Router B to the target network: Next hop is router D. Metric is 2.
- Router C to the target network: Next hop is router B. Metric is 3.
- Router A to the target network: Next hop is router B. Metric is 3.

Consider an adverse condition where the link connecting router B and router D fails. Once the network has reconverged, all routes use the link connecting router C and router D to reach the target network. However, this reconvergence time can be considerable. Figure 64 illustrates how the routes to the target network are updated throughout the reconvergence period. For simplicity, this figure assumes all routers send updates at the same time.

Time	⇒		⇒									
D:	Direct	1	Direct	1	Direct	1	Direct	1	....	Direct	1	Direct	1
B:	Unreachable		C	4	C	5	C	6		C	11	C	12
C:	B	3	A	4	A	5	A	6		A	11	D	11
A:	B	3	C	4	C	5	C	6	....	C	11	C	12

Figure 64. Network convergence sequence

Reconvergence begins when router B notices that the route to router D is unavailable. Router B is able to immediately remove the failed route because the link has timed-out. However, a considerable amount of time passes before the other routers remove their references to the failed route. This is described in the sequence of updates shown in Figure 64:

1. Prior to the adverse condition occurring, router A and router C have a route to the target network via router B.

2. The adverse condition occurs when the link connecting router D and router B fails. Router B recognizes that its preferred path to the target network is now invalid.

3. Router A and router C continue to send updates reflecting the route via router B. This route is actually invalid since the link connecting router D and router B has failed.

4. Router B receives the updates from router A and router C. Router B believes it should now route traffic to the target network through either router A or router C. In reality, this is not a valid route, since the routes in router A and router C are vestiges of the previous route through router B.

5. Using the routing advertisement sent by router B, router A and router C are able to determine that the route via router B has failed. However, router A and router C now believe the preferred route exists via the partner.

Network convergence continues as router A and router C engage in an extended period of mutual deception. Each device claims to be able to reach the target network via the partner device. The path to reach the target network now contains a routing loop.

The manner in which the costs in the distance vector table increment gives rise to the term *counting to infinity*. The costs continues to increment, theoretically to infinity. To minimize this exposure, whenever a network is unavailable, the incrementing of metrics through routing updates must be halted as soon as it is practical to do so. In a RIP environment, costs continue to increment until they reach a maximum value of 16. This limit is defined in the RFC.

A side effect of the metric limit is that it also limits the number of hops a packet can traverse from source network to destination network. In a RIP environment, any path exceeding 15 hops is considered invalid. The routing algorithm will discard these paths.

There are two enhancements to the basic distance vector algorithm that can minimize the counting to infinity problem:

- Split horizon with poison reverse
- Triggered updates

These enhancements do not impact the maximum metric limit.

4.3.5.1 Split horizon
The excessive convergence time caused by counting to infinity may be reduced with the use of split horizon. This rule dictates that routing information is prevented from exiting the router on an interface through which the information was received.

The basic split horizon rule is not supported in RFC 1058. Instead, the standard specifies the enhanced split horizon with poison reverse algorithm. The basic rule is presented here for background and completeness. The enhanced algorithm is reviewed in the next section.

The incorporation of split horizon modifies the sequence of routing updates shown in Figure 64. The new sequence is shown in Figure 65. The tables show that convergence occurs considerably faster using the split horizon rule.

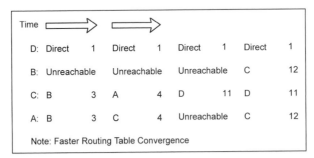

Figure 65. Network convergence with split horizon

The limitation to this rule is that each node must wait for the route to the unreachable destination to time out before the route is removed from the distance vector table. In RIP environments, this timeout is at least three minutes after the initial outage. During that time, the device continues to provide erroneous information to other nodes about the unreachable destination. This propagates routing loops and other routing anomalies.

4.3.5.2 Split horizon with poison reverse

Poison reverse is an enhancement to the standard split horizon implementation. It is supported in RFC 1058. With poison reverse, all known networks are advertised in each routing update. However, those networks learned through a specific interface are advertised as unreachable in the routing announcements sent out to that interface.

This drastically improves convergence time in complex, highly-redundant environments. With poison reverse, when a routing update indicates that a network is unreachable, routes are immediately removed from the routing table. This breaks erroneous, looping routes before they can propagate through the network. This approach differs from the basic split horizon rule where routes are eliminated through timeouts.

Poison reverse has no benefit in networks with no redundancy (single path networks).

One disadvantage to poison reverse is that it may significantly increase the size of routing annoucements exchanged between neighbors. This is because all routes in the distance vector table are included in each announcement. While this is generally not an issue on local area networks, it can cause periods of increased utilization on lower-capacity WAN connections.

4.3.5.3 Triggered updates
Like split horizon with poison reverse, algorithms implementing triggered updates are designed to reduce network convergence time. With triggered updates, whenever a router changes the cost of a route, it immediately sends the modified distance vector table to neighboring devices. This mechanism ensures that topology change notifications are propagated quickly, rather than at the normal periodic interval.

Triggered updates are supported in RFC 1058.

4.3.6 RIP limitations

There are a number of limitations observed in RIP environments:

- Path cost limits: The resolution to the counting to infinity problem enforces a maximum cost for a network path. This places an upper limit on the maximum network diameter. Networks requiring paths greater than 15 hops must use an alternate routing protocol.

- Network-intensive table updates: Periodic broadcasting of the distance vector table can result in increased utilization of network resources. This can be a concern in reduced-capacity segments.

- Relatively slow convergence: RIP, like other distance vector protocols, is relatively slow to converge. The algorithms rely on timers to initiate routing table advertisements.

- No support for variable length subnet masking: Route advertisements in a RIP environment do not include subnet masking information. This makes it impossible for RIP networks to deploy variable length subnet masks.

4.4 Routing Information Protocol Version 2 (RIP-2)

The IETF recognizes two versions of RIP:

- RIP Version 1 (RIP-1): This protocol is described in RFC 1058.

- RIP Version 2 (RIP-2): RIP-2 is also a distance vector protocol designed for use within an AS. It was developed to address the limitations observed in RIP-1. RIP-2 is described in RFC 1723. The standard was published in late 1994.

In practice, the term RIP refers to RIP-1. Whenever the reader encounters the term RIP in TCP/IP literature, it is safe to assume the reference is to RIP Version 1 unless otherwise stated. This same convention is used in this document. However, when the two versions are being compared, the term RIP-1 is used to avoid confusion.

RIP-2 is similar to RIP-1. It was developed to extend RIP-1 functionality in small networks. RIP-2 provides these additional benefits not available in RIP-1:

- Support for CIDR and VLSM: RIP-2 supports supernetting (that is, CIDR) and variable-length subnet masking. This support was the major reason the new standard was developed. This enhancement positions the standard to accommodate a degree of addressing complexity not supported in RIP-1.

- Support for multicasting: RIP-2 supports the use of multicasting rather than simple broadcasting of routing annoucements. This reduces the processing load on hosts not listening for RIP-2 messages. To ensure interoperability with RIP-1 environments, this option is configured on each network interface.

- Support for authentication: RIP-2 supports authentication of any node transmitting route advertisements. This prevents fraudulent sources from corrupting the routing table.

- Support for RIP-1: RIP-2 is fully interoperable with RIP-1. This provides backward-compatibility between the two standards.

As noted in the RIP-1 section, one notable shortcoming in the RIP-1 standard is the implementation of the metric field. RIP-1 specifies the metric as a value between 0 and 16. To ensure compatibility with RIP-1 networks, RIP-2 preserves this definition. In both standards, networks paths with a hop-count greater than 15 are interpreted as unreachable.

4.4.1 RIP-2 packet format

The original RIP-1 specification was designed to support future enhancements. The RIP-2 standard was able to capitalize on this feature. RIP-2 developers noted that a RIP-1 packet already contains a version field and that 50 percent of the octets are unused.

Figure 66 illustrates the contents of a RIP-2 packet. The packet is shown with authentication information. The first entry in the update contains either a routing entry or an authentication entry. If the first entry is an authentication entry, 24 additional routing entries can be included in the message. If there is no authentication information, 25 routing entries can be provided.

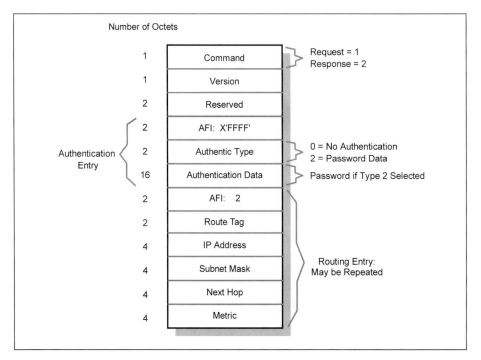

Figure 66. RIP-2 packet format

The use of the command field, IP address field, and metric field in a RIP-2 message is identical to the use in a RIP-1 message. Otherwise, the changes implemented in a RIP-2 packets include:

- Version: The value contained in this field must be two. This instructs RIP-1 routers to ignore any information contained in the previously unused fields.

- AFI (Address Family): A value of x'0002' indicates the address contained in the network address field is an IP address. An value of x'FFFF' indicates an authentication entry.

- Authentication Type: This field defines the remaining 16 bytes of the authentication entry. A value of 0 indicates *no* authentication. A value of two indicates the authentication data field contains password data.

- Authentication Data: This field contains a 16-byte password.

- Route Tag: This field is intended to differentiate between internal and external routes. Internal routes are learned via RIP-2 within the same network or AS.

- Subnet Mask: This field contains the subnet mask of the referenced network.

- Next Hop: This field contains a recommendation about the next hop the router should use when sending datagrams to the referenced network.

4.4.2 RIP-2 limitations

RIP-2 was developed to address many of the limitations observed in RIP-1. However, the path cost limits and slow convergence inherent in RIP-1 networks are also concerns in RIP-2 environments.

In addition to these concerns, there are limitations to the RIP-2 authentication process. The RIP-2 standard does not encrypt the authentication password. It is transmitted in clear text. This makes the network vulnerable to attack by anyone with direct physical access to the environment.

4.5 RIPng for IPv6

RIPng was developed to allow routers within an IPv6-based network to exchange information used to compute routes. It is documented in RFC 2080. Additional information regarding IPv6 is presented in Chapter 17, "IP Version 6" on page 559.

Like the other protocols in the RIP family, RIPng is a distance vector protocol designed for use within a small autonomous system. RIPng uses the same algorithms, timers, and logic used in RIP-2.

RIPng has many of the same limitations inherent in other distance vector protocols. Path cost restrictions and convergence time remain a concern in RIPng networks.

4.5.1 Differences between RIPng and RIP-2

There are two important distinctions between RIP-2 and RIPng:

- Support for authentication: The RIP-2 standard includes support for authenticating a node transmitting routing information. RIPng does not include any native authentication support. Rather, RIPng uses the security features inherent in IPv6. In addition to authentication, these security features provide the ability to encrypt each RIPng packet. This can control the set of devices that receive the routing information.

One consequence of using IPv6 security features is that the AFI field within the RIPng packet is eliminated. There is no longer a need to distinguish between authentication entries and routing entries within an advertisement.

- Support for IPv6 addressing formats: The fields contained in RIPng packets were updated to support the longer IPv6 address format.

4.5.2 RIPng packet format

RIPng packets are transmitted using UDP datagrams. RIPng sends and receives datagrams using UDP port number 521.

The format of a RIPng packet is similar to the RIP-2 format. Specifically both packets contain a 4 octet command header followed by a set of 20 octet route entries. The RIPng packet format is shown in Figure 67.

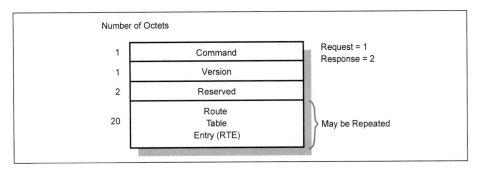

Figure 67. RIPng packet format

The use of the command field and the version field is identical to the use in a RIP-2 packet. However, the fields containing routing information have been updated to accommodate the 16 octet IPv6 address. These fields are used differently than the corresponding fields in a RIP-1 or RIP-2 packet. The format of the RTE is shown in Figure 68.

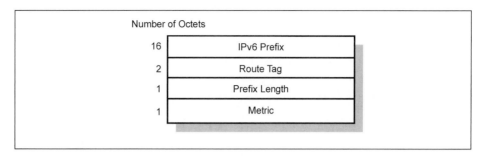

Figure 68. Route Table Entry (RTE)

In RIPng, the combination of the IP prefix and the prefix length identifies the route to be advertised. The metric remains encoded in a 1 octet field. This length is sufficient since RIPng uses a maximum hop-count of 16.

Another difference between RIPng and RIP-2 is the process used to determine the next hop. In RIP-2, each route table entry contains a next hop field. In RIPng, including this information in each RTE would have doubled the size of the advertisement. Therefore, in RIPng, the next hop is included in a special type of RTE. The specified next hop applies to each subsequent routing table entry in the advertisement. The format of an RTE used to specify the next hop is shown in Figure 69.

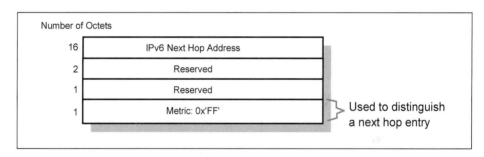

Figure 69. Next Hop Route Table Entry (RTE)

The next hop RTE is identified by a value of 0x'FF' in the metric field. This reserved value is outside the valid range of metrics.

The use of RTEs and next hop RTEs is shown in Figure 70.

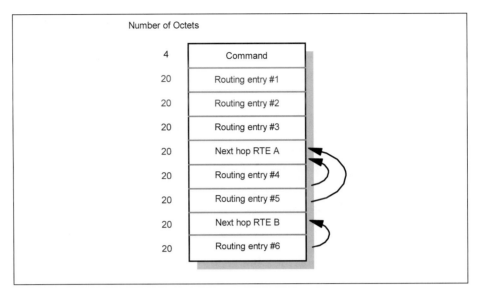

Figure 70. Using the RIPng RTE

In this example, the first three routing entries do not have a corresponding next hop RTE. The address prefixes specified by these entries will be routed through the advertising router. The prefixes included in routing entries 4 and 5 will route through the next hop address specified in the next hop RTE A. The prefix included in routing entry 6 will route through the next hop address specified in the next hop RTE B.

4.6 Open Shortest Path First (OSPF)

The Open Shortest Path First (OSPF) protocol is another example of an interior gateway protocol. It was developed as a non-proprietary routing alternative to address the limitations of RIP. Initial development started in 1988 and was finalized in 1991. Subsequent updates to the protocol continue to be published. The current version of the standard is documented in RFC 2328.

OSPF provides a number of features not found in distance vector protocols. Support for these features has made OSPF a widely-deployed routing protocol in large networking environments. In fact, RFC 1812 – Requirements for IPv4 Routers, lists OSPF as the only required dynamic routing protocol. The following features contribute to the continued acceptance of the OSPF standard:

- Equal cost load balancing: The simultaneous use of multiple paths may provide more efficient utilization of network resources.

- Logical partitioning of the network: This reduces the propagation of outage information during adverse conditions. It also provides the ability to aggregate routing announcements that limit the advertisement of unnecessary subnet information.

- Support for authentication: OSPF supports the authentication of any node transmitting route advertisements. This prevents fraudulent sources from corrupting the routing tables.

- Faster convergence time: OSPF provides instantaneous propagation of routing changes. This expedites the convergence time required to update network topologies.

- Support for CIDR and VLSM: This allows the network administrator to efficiently allocate IP address resources.

OSPF is a link state protocol. As with other link state protocols, each OSPF router executes the SPF algorithm (refer to 4.2.3.1, "Shortest-Path First (SPF) algorithm" on page 143) to process the information stored in the link state database. The algorithm produces a shortest-path tree detailing the preferred routes to each destination network.

4.6.1 OSPF terminology

OSPF uses specific terminology to describe the operation of the protocol.

4.6.1.1 OSPF areas

OSPF networks are divided into a collection of *areas*. An area consists of a logical grouping of networks and routers. The area may coincide with geographic or administrative boundaries. Each area is assigned a 32-bit *area ID*.

Subdividing the network provides the following benefits:

- Within an area, every router maintains an identical topology database describing the routing devices and links within the area. These routers have no knowledge of topologies outside the area. They are only aware of routes to these external destinations. This reduces the size of the topology database maintained by each router.

- Areas limit the potentially explosive growth in the number of link state updates. Most LSAs are distributed only within an area.

- Areas reduce the CPU processing required to maintain the topology database. The SPF algorithm is limited to managing changes within the area.

Backbone area and area 0

All OSPF networks contain at least one area. This area is known as area 0 or the backbone area. Additional areas may be created based on network topology or other design requirements.

In networks containing multiple areas, the backbone physically connects to all other areas. OSPF expects all areas to announce routing information directly into the backbone. The backbone then announces this information into other areas.

Figure 71 depicts a network with a backbone area and 4 additional areas.

4.6.1.2 Intra-area, area border and AS boundary routers

There are three classifications of routers in an OSPF network. Figure 71 illustrates the interaction of these devices.

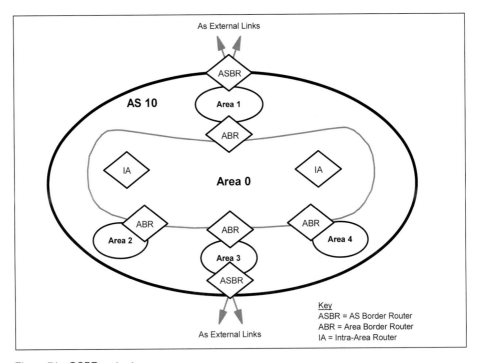

Figure 71. OSPF router types

Where:

- Intra-Area Routers: This class of router is logically located entirely within an OSPF area. Intra-area routers maintain a topology database for their local area.

- Area Border Routers (ABR): This class of router is logically connected to two or more areas. One area must be the backbone area. An ABR is used to interconnect areas. They maintain a separate topology database for each attached area. ABRs also execute separate instances of the SPF algorithm for each area.

- AS Boundary Routers (ASBR): This class of router is located at the periphery of an OSPF internetwork. It functions as a gateway exchanging reachability between the OSPF network and other routing environments. ASBRs are responsible for announcing AS external link advertisements through the AS. External link advertisements are further detailed in 4.6.6, "OSPF route redistribution" on page 170.

Each router is assigned a 32-bit *router ID (RID)*. The RID uniquely identifies the device. One popular implementation assigns the RID from the lowest-numbered IP address configured on the router.

4.6.1.3 Physical network types

OSPF categorizes network segments into three types. The frequency and types of communication occurring between OSPF devices connected to these networks is impacted by the network type:

- Point-to-point: Point-to-point networks directly link two routers.

- Multi-access: Multi-access networks support the attachment of more than two routers. They are further subdivided into two types:

  - Broadcast networks have the capability of simultaneously directing a packet to all attached routers. This capability uses an address that is recognized by all devices. Ethernet and token-ring LANs are examples of OSPF broadcast multi-access networks.

  - Non-broadcast networks do not have broadcasting capabilities. Each packet must be specifically addressed to every router in the network. X.25 and frame relay networks are examples of OSPF non-broadcast multi-access networks.

- Point-to-Multipoint: Point-to-multipoint networks are a special case of multi-access, non-broadcast networks. In a point-to-multipoint network, a device is not required to have a direct connection to every other device. This is known as a partially meshed environment.

4.6.1.4 Neighbor routers and adjacencies

Routers that share a common network segment establish a neighbor relationship on the segment. Routers must agree on the following information to become neighbors:

- Area-id: The routers must belong to the same OSPF area.
- Authentication: If authentication is defined, the routers must specify the same password.
- Hello and dead intervals: The routers must specify the same timer intervals used in the Hello protocol. This protocol is further described in 4.6.2, "OSPF packet types" on page 165.
- Stub area flag: The routers must agree that the area is configured as a stub area. Stub areas are further described in 4.6.7, "OSPF stub areas" on page 172.

Once two routers have become neighbors, an adjacency relationship can be formed between the devices. Neighboring routers are considered adjacent when they have synchronized their topology databases. This occurs through the exchange of link state information.

4.6.1.5 Designated and backup designated router

The exchange of link state information between neighbors can create significant quantities of network traffic. To reduce the total bandwidth required to synchronize databases and advertise link state information, a router does not necessarily develop adjacencies with every neighboring device:

- Multi-access networks: Adjacencies are formed between an individual router and the (backup) designated router.
- Point-to-point networks: An adjacency is formed between both devices.

Each multi-access network elects a designated router (DR) and backup designated router (BDR). The DR performs two key functions on the network segment:

- It forms adjacencies with all routers on the multi-access network. This causes the DR to become the focal point for forwarding LSAs.
- It generates network link advertisements listing each router connected to the multi-access network. Additional information regarding network link advertisements is contained in 4.6.1.7, "Link state advertisements and flooding" on page 163.

The BDR forms the same adjacencies as the designated router. It assumes DR functionality when the DR fails.

Each router is assigned an 8-bit priority, indicating its ability to be selected as the DR or BDR. A router priority of zero indicates that the router is not eligible to be selected. The priority is configured on each interface in the router.

Figure 72 illustrates the relationship between neighbors. No adjacencies are formed between routers that are not selected to be the DR or BDR.

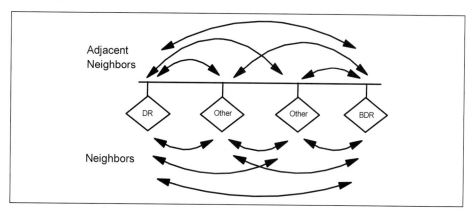

Figure 72. Relationship between adjacencies and neighbors

4.6.1.6 Link state database

The link state database is also called the *topology database*. It contains the set of link state advertisements describing the OSPF network and any external connections. Each router within the area maintains an identical copy of the link state database.

> **Note:**
>
> RFC 2328 uses the term link state database in preference to topology database. The former term has the advantage in that it describes the contents of the database. The latter term is more descriptive of the purpose of the database. This book has previously used the term topology database for this reason. However for the remainder of the OSPF section, we refer to it as the link state database.

4.6.1.7 Link state advertisements and flooding

The contents of an LSA describes an individual network component (that is, router, segment, or external destination). LSAs are exchanged between adjacent OSPF routers. This is done to synchronize the link state database on each device.

When a router generates or modifies an LSA, it must communicate this change throughout the network. The router starts this process by forwarding the LSA to each adjacent device. Upon receipt of the LSA, these neighbors store the information in their link state database and communicate the LSA to their neighbors. This store and forward activity continues until all devices receive the update. This process is called *reliable flooding*. Two steps are taken to ensure this flooding effectively transmits changes without overloading the network with excessive quantities of LSA traffic:

- Each router stores the LSA for a period of time before propagating the information to its neighbors. If, during that time, a new copy of the LSA arrives, the router replaces the stored version. However, if the new copy is outdated, it is discarded.

- To ensure reliability, each link state advertisement must be acknowledged. Multiple acknowledgements can be grouped together into a single acknowledgement packet. If an acknowledgement is not received, the original link state update packet is retransmitted.

Link state advertisements contain five types of information. Together these advertisements provide the necessary information needed to describe the entire OSPF network and any external environments:

- Router LSAs: This type of advertisement describes the state of the router's interfaces (links) within the area. They are generated by every OSPF router. The advertisements are flooded throughout the area.

- Network LSAs: This type of advertisement lists the routers connected to a multi-access network. They are generated by the DR on a multi-access segment. The advertisements are flooded throughout the area.

- Summary LSAs (Type-3 and Type-4): This type of advertisement is generated by an ABR. There are two types of summary link advertisements:

    - Type-3 summary LSAs describe routes to destinations in other areas within the OSPF network (inter-area destinations).
    - Type-4 summary LSAs describe routes to ASBRs.

  Summary LSAs are used to exchange reachability information between areas. Normally, information is announced into the backbone area. The backbone then injects this information into other areas.

- AS external LSAs: This type of advertisement describes routes to destinations external to the OSPF network. They are generated by an ASBR. The advertisements are flooded throughout all areas in the OSPF network.

Figure 73 illustrates the different types of link state advertisements.

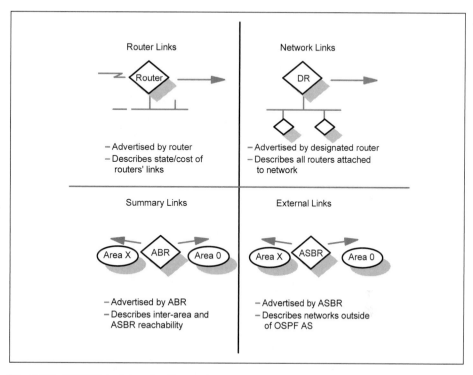

Figure 73. OSPF link state advertisements

4.6.2 OSPF packet types

OSPF packets are transmitted in IP datagrams. They are not encapsulated within TCP or UDP packets. The IP header uses protocol identifier 89. OSPF packets are sent with an IP ToS of 0 and an IP precedence of internetwork control. This is used to obtain preferential processing for the packets. Further discussion of ToS and IP precedence is located in 22.2, "Integrated Services" on page 782

Wherever possible, OSPF uses multicast facilities to communicate with neighboring devices. In broadcast and point-to-point environments, packets are sent to the reserved multicast address 224.0.0.5. RFC 2328 refers to this as the AllSPFRouters address. In non-broadcast environments, packets are addressed to the neighbor's specific IP address.

All OSPF packets share the common header shown in Figure 74. The header provides general information including area identifier, RID, checksum, and authentication information.

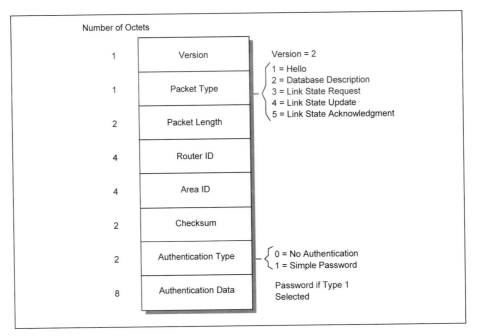

Figure 74. OSPF common header

The type field identifies the OSPF packet as one of five possible types:

- Hello: This packet type is used to discover and maintain neighbor relationships.
- Database description: This packet type describes the set of LSAs contained in the router's link state database
- Link state request: This packet type is used to request a more current instance of an LSA from a neighbor.
- Link state update: This packet type is used to provide a more current instance of an LSA to a neighbor.
- Link state acknowledgement: This packet type is used to acknowledge receipt of a newly received LSA.

The use of these packets is presented in the next section.

4.6.3 Neighbor communication

OSPF is responsible for determining the optimum set of paths through a network. To accomplish this, each router exchanges LSAs with other routers in the network. The OSPF protocol defines a number of activities to accomplish this information exchange:

- Discovering neighbors

- Electing a designated router
- Establishing adjacencies and synchronizing databases

The five OSPF packet types are used to support these information exchanges.

4.6.3.1 Discovering neighbors - the OSPF Hello protocol

The Hello protocol discovers and maintains relationships with neighboring routers. Hello packets are periodically sent out to each router interface. The packet contains the RID of other routers whose hello packets have already been received over the interface.

When a device sees its own RID in the hello packet generated by another router, these devices establish a neighbor relationship.

The hello packet also contains the router priority, DR identifier, and BDR identifier. These parameters are used to elect the DR on multi-access networks.

4.6.3.2 Electing a designated router

All multi-access networks must have a DR. A BDR may also be selected. The backup ensures there is no extended loss of routing capability if the DR fails.

The DR and BDR are selected using information contained in hello packets. The device with the highest OSPF router priority on a segment becomes the DR for that segment. The same process is repeated to select the BDR. In case of a tie, the router with the highest RID is selected. A router declared the DR is ineligible to become the BDR.

Once elected, the DR and BDR proceed to establish adjacencies with all routers on the multi-access segment.

4.6.3.3 Establishing adjacencies and synchronizing databases

Neighboring routers are considered adjacent when they have synchronized their link state databases. A router does not develop an adjacency with every neighboring device. On multi-access networks, adjacencies are formed only with the DR and BDR. This is a two step process:

Step 1: Database exchange process

The first phase of database synchronization is the database exchange process. This occurs immediately after two neighbors attempt to establish an adjacency. The process consists of an exchange of database description packets. The packets contain a list of the LSAs stored in the local database.

During the database exchange process, the routers form a master/slave relationship. The master is the first to transmit. Each packet is identified by a sequence number. Using this sequence number, the slave acknowledges each database description packet from the master. The slave also includes its own set of link state headers in the acknowledgements.

Step 2: Database loading
During the database exchange process, each router notes the link state headers for which the neighbor has a more current instance (all advertisements are time stamped). Once the process is complete, each router requests the more current information from the neighbor. This request is made with a link state request packet.

When a router receives a link state request, it must reply with a set of link state update packets providing the requested LSA. Each transmitted LSA is acknowledged by the receiver. This process is similar to the reliable flooding procedure used to transmit topology changes throughout the network.

Every LSA contains an age field indicating the time in seconds since the origin of the advertisement. The age continues to increase after the LSA is installed in the topology database. It also increases during each hop of the flooding process. When the maximum age is reached, the LSA is no longer used to determining routing information and is discarded from the link state database. This age is also used to distinguish between two otherwise identical copies of an advertisement.

4.6.4 OSPF neighbor state machine
The OSPF specification defines a set of neighbor states and the events that can cause a neighbor to transition from one state to another. A state machine is used to describe these transitions:

- Down: This is the initial state. It indicates that no recent information has been received from any device on the segment.

- Attempt: This state is used on non-broadcast networks. It indicates that a neighbor appears to be inactive. Attempts continue to reestablish contact.

- Init: Communication with the neighbor has started, but bidirectional communication has not been established. Specifically, a hello packet was received from the neighbor, but the local router was not listed in the neighbor's hello packet.

- 2-way: Bidirectional communication between the two routers has been established. Adjacencies can be formed. Neighbors are eligible to be elected as designated routers.

- ExStart: The neighbors are starting to form an adjacency.

- Exchange: The two neighbors are exchanging their topology databases.

- Loading: The two neighbors are synchronizing their topology databases.

- Full: The two neighbors are fully adjacent and their databases are synchronized.

Network events cause a neighbor's OSPF state to change. For example, when a router receives a hello packet from a neighboring device, the OSPF neighbor state changes from Down to Init. When bidirectional communication has been established, the neighbor state changes from Init to 2-Way. RFC 2328 contains a complete description of the events causing a state change.

4.6.5 OSPF virtual links and transit areas

Virtual links are used when a network does not support the standard OSPF network topology. This topology defines a backbone area that directly connects to each additional OSPF area. The virtual link addresses two conditions:

- It may logically connect the backbone area when it is not contiguous.

- It may connect an area to the backbone when a direct connection does not exist.

A virtual link is established between two ABRs sharing a common non-backbone area. The link is treated as a point-to-point link. The common area is known as a *transit area*. Figure 75 illustrates the interaction between virtual links and transit areas when used to connect an area to the backbone.

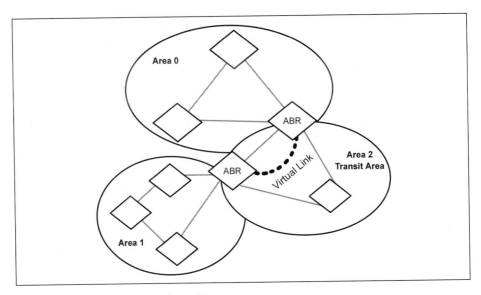

Figure 75. OSPF virtual link and transit areas

This diagram shows that area 1 does not have a direct connection to the backbone. Area 2 can be used as a transit area to provide this connection. A virtual link is established between the two ABRs located in area 2. Establishing this virtual link logically extends the backbone area to connect to area 1.

A virtual link is used only to transmit routing information. It does not carry regular traffic between the remote area and the backbone. This traffic, in addition to the virtual link traffic, is routed using the standard intra-area routing within the transit area.

4.6.6 OSPF route redistribution

Route redistribution is the process of introducing external routes into an OSPF network. These routes may be either static routes or routes learned via another routing protocol. They are advertised into the OSPF network by an ASBR. These routes become OSPF external routes. The ASBR advertises these routes by flooding OSPF AS external LSAs throughout the entire OSPF network.

The routes describe an end to end path consisting of two portions:

- External portion: This is the portion of the path external to the OSPF network. When these routes are distributed into OSPF, the ASBR assigns an initial cost. This cost represents the *external cost* associated with traversing the external portion of the path.

- Internal portion: This is the portion of the path internal to the OSPF network. Costs for this portion of the network are calculated using standard OSPF algorithms.

OSPF differentiates between two types of external routes. They differ in the way the cost of the route is calculated. The ASBR is configured to redistribute the route as:

- External type 1: The total cost of the route is the sum of the external cost and any internal OSPF costs.

- External type 2: The total cost of the route is always the external cost. This ignores any internal OSPF costs required to reach the ASBR.

Figure 76 illustrates an example of the types of OSPF external routes.

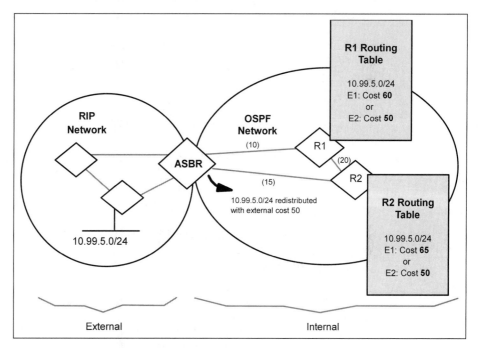

Figure 76. OSPF route redistribution

In this example, the ASBR is redistributing the 10.99.5.0/24 route into the OSPF network. This subnet is located within the RIP network. The route is announced into OSPF with an external cost of 50. This represents the cost for the portion of the path traversing the RIP network.

- If the ASBR redistributed the route as an E1 route, R1 will contain an external route to this subnet with a cost of 60 (50 + 10). R2 will have an external route with a cost of 65 (50 + 15).

- If the ASBR redistributed the route as an E2 route, both R1 and R2 will contain an external route to this subnet with a cost of 50. Any costs associated with traversing segments within the OSPF network are not included in the total cost to reach the destination.

4.6.7 OSPF stub areas

OSPF allows certain areas to be defined as a stub area. A stub area is created when the ABR connecting to a stub area excludes AS external LSAs from being flooded into the area. This is done to reduce the size of the link state database maintained within the stub area routers. Since there are no specific routes to external networks, routing to these destinations is based on a default route generated by the ABR. The link state databases maintained within the stub area contain only the default route and the routes from within the OSPF environment (for example, intra-area and inter-area routes).

Since a stub area does not allow external LSAs, a stub area cannot contain an ASBR. No external routes can be generated from within the stub area.

Stub areas can be deployed when there is a single exit point connecting the area to the backbone. An area with multiple exit points can also be a stub area. However, there is no guarantee that packets exiting the area will follow an optimal path. This is due to the fact that each ABR generates a default route. There is no ability to associate traffic with a specific default routes.

All routers within the area must be configured as stub routers. This configuration is verified through the exchange of hello packets.

4.6.7.1 Not-so-stubby areas

An extension to the stub area concept is the *not-so-stubby area (NSSA)*. This alternative is documented in RFC 1587. An NSSA is similar to a stub area in that the ABR servicing the NSSA does not flood any external routes into the NSSA. The only routes flooded into the NSSA are the default route and any other routes from within the OSPF environment (for example, intra-area and inter-area).

However, unlike a stub area, an ASBR can be located within an NSSA. This ASBR can generate external routes. Therefore, the link state databases maintained within the NSSA contain the default route, routes from within the OSPF environment (for example, intra-area and inter-area routes), and the external routes generated by the ASBR within the area.

The ABR servicing the NSSA floods the external routes from within the NSSA throughout the rest of the OSPF network.

4.6.8 OSPF route summarization

Route summarization is the process of consolidating multiple contiguous routing entries into a single advertisement. This reduces the size of the link state database and the IP routing table. In an OSPF network, summarization is performed at a border router. There are two types of summarization:

- Inter-area route summarization: Inter-area summarization is performed by the ABR for an area. It is used to summarize route advertisements originating within the area. The summarized route is announcement into the backbone. The backbone receives the aggregated route and announces the summary into other areas.

- External route summarization: This type of summarization applies specifically to external routes injected into OSPF. This is performed by the ASBR distributing the routes into the OSPF network.

Figure 77 illustrates an example of OSPF route summarization.

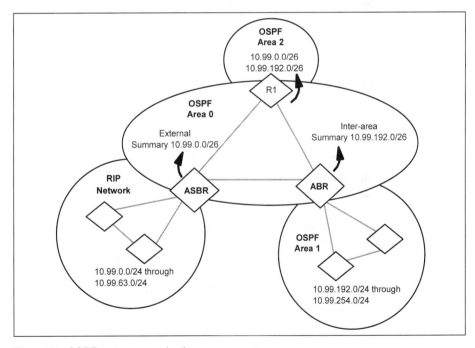

Figure 77. OSPF route summarization

In this figure, the ASBR is advertising a single summary route for the 64 subnetworks located in the RIP environment. This single summary route is flooded throughout the entire OSPF network. In addition, the ABR is generating a single summary route for the 64 subnetworks located in area 1. This summary route is flooded through area 0 and area 2. Depending of the configuration of the ASBR, the inter-area summary route may also be redistributed into the RIP network.

4.7 Enhanced Interior Gateway Routing Protocol (EIGRP)

The Enhanced Interior Gateway Routing Protocol (EIGRP) is categorized as a hybrid routing protocol. Similar to a distance vector algorithm, EIGRP uses metrics to determine network paths. However, like a link state protocol, topology updates in an EIGRP environment are event driven.

EIGRP, as the name implies, is an interior gateway protocol designed for use within an AS. In properly designed networks, EIGRP has the potential for improved scalability and faster convergence over standard distance vector algorithms. EIGRP is also better positioned to support complex, highly redundant networks.

EIGRP is a proprietary protocol developed by Cisco Systems, Inc. At the time of this writing, it is not an IETF standard protocol.

4.7.1 Features of EIGRP

EIGRP provides several benefits. Some of these benefits are also available in distance vector or link state algorithms.

- Faster convergence: EIGRP maintains a list of alternate routes that can be used if a preferred path fails. When the path fails, the new route is immediately installed in the IP routing table. No route recomputation is performed.
- Partial routing updates: When EIGRP discovers a neighboring router, each device exchanges their entire routing table. After the initial information exchange, only routing table changes are propagated. There is no periodic rebroadcasting of the entire routing table.
- Low bandwidth utilization: During normal network operations, only hello packets are transmitted through a stable network.
- CIDR and VLSM: EIGRP supports supernetting and variable length subnet masks. This allows the network administrator to efficiently allocate IP address resources.

- Route summarization: EIGRP supports the ability to summarize routing annoucements. This limits the advertisement of unnecessary subnet information.
- Multiple protocols: EIGRP can provide network layer routing for AppleTalk, IPX and IP networks.
- Unequal cost load balancing: EIGRP supports the simultaneous use of multiple unequal cost paths to a destination. Each route is installed in the IP routing table. EIGRP also intelligently load balances traffic over the multiple paths.

4.7.2 Terminology

EIGRP uses specific terminology to describe the operation of the protocol:

- Successor: For a specific destination, the successor is the neighbor router currently used for packet forwarding. This device has the least-cost path to the destination and is guaranteed not to be participating in a routing loop. To reach the target network shown in Figure 78, router B is the current successor for router A.

- Feasible Successor: A feasible successor assumes forwarding responsibility when the current successor router fails. The set of feasible successors represent the devices that can become a successor without requiring a route recomputation or introducing routing loops.

The set of feasible successors to a destination is determined by reviewing the complete list of minimum cost paths advertised by neighboring routers. From this list, neighbors that have an advertised metric less than the current routing table metric are considered feasible successors.

Figure 78 provides an example of a feasible successor relationship.

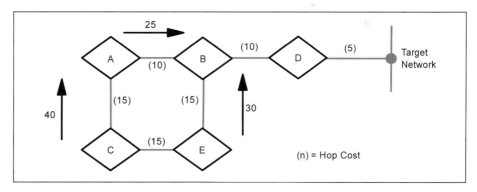

Figure 78. EIGRP feasible successors

In this diagram, the costs to reach the target network are shown. For example, the cost from router C to the target network is 40 (15 + 10 + 10 + 5). The cost from router E to the target network is 30 (15 + 10 + 5).

Router E is advertising a cost (30) that is less than the current routing table metric on router C (40). Therefore, router C recognizes router E as a a feasible successor to reach the target network. Note that the reverse is not true. The cost advertised by router C (40) is more than the current route on router E (30). Therefore, router E does not recognize router C as a feasible successor to the destination network.

- Neighbor table: EIGRP maintains a table to track the state of each adjacent neighbor. The table contains the address and interface used to reach the neighbor. It also contains the last sequence number contained in a packet from the neighbor. This allows the reliable transport mechanism of EIGRP to detect out-of-order packets.

- Topology table: EIGRP uses a topology table to install routes into the IP routing table. The topology table lists all destination networks currently advertised by neighboring routers. The table contains all the information needed to build a set of distances and vectors to each destination. This information includes:

  - Smallest bandwidth available on a segment used to reach this destination.
  - Total delay, reliability, and loading of the path.
  - Minimum MTU used on the path.
  - The feasible distance of the path. This represents the best metric along the path to the destination network. It including the metric used to reach the neighbor advertising the path.
  - The reported distance of the path. This represents the total metric along the path to a destination network as advertised by an upstream neighbor.
  - The source of the route. EIGRP marks external routes. This provides the ability to implement policy controls that customize routing patterns.

  An entry in the topology table can have one of two states:

  - Passive state: The router is not performing a route recomputation for the entry.
  - Active state: The router is performing a route recomputation for the entry. If a feasible successor exists for a route, the entry never enters this state. This avoids processor-intensive route recomputation.

- Reliable transport protocol: EIGRP can guarantee the ordered delivery of packets to a neighbor. However, not all types of packets must be reliably transmitted. For example, in a network that supports multicasting, there is no need to send individual, acknowledged hello packets to each neighbor. To provide efficient operation, reliability is provided only when needed. This improves convergence time in networks containing varying speed connections.

4.7.3 Neighbor discovery and recovery

EIGRP can dynamically learn about other routers on directly attached networks. This is similar to the Hello protocol used for neighbor discovery in an OSPF environment.

Devices in an EIGRP network exchange hello packets to verify each neighbor is operational. Like OSPF, the frequency used to exchange packets is based on the network type. Packets are exchanged at a five second interval on high bandwidth links (for example, LAN segments). Otherwise, hello packets on lower bandwidth connections are exchanged every 60 seconds.

Like OSPF, EIGRP uses a hold timer to remove inactive neighbors. This timer indicates the amount of time that a device will continue to consider a neighbor active without receiving a hello packet from the neighbor.

4.7.4 The DUAL algorithm

A typical distance vector protocol uses periodic updates to compute the best path to a destination. It uses distance, next hop, and local interface costs to determine the path. Once this information is processed, it is discarded. EIGRP does not rely on periodic updates to converge on the topology. Instead, it builds a topology table containing each of its neighbor's advertisements. Unlike a distance vector protocol, this data is not discarded.

EIGRP processes the information in the topology table to determine the best paths to each destination network. EIGRP implements an algorithm known as DUAL (Diffusing Update ALgorithm). This algorithm provides several benefits:

- The DUAL algorithm guarantees loop-free operations throughout the route computation and convergence period.
- The DUAL algorithm allows all routers to synchronize at the same time. This is unlike a RIP environment, in which the propagation of routing updates causes devices to converge at different rates.
- The DUAL algorithm allows routers not involved with a topology change to avoid route recomputation.

The DUAL algorithm is used to find the set of feasible successors for a destination. When an adverse condition occurs in the network, the alternate route is immediately added to the IP routing table. This avoids unnecessary computation to determine an alternate path. If no feasible successor is known, a route recomputation occurs. This behavior is shown in Figure 79 and Figure 80.

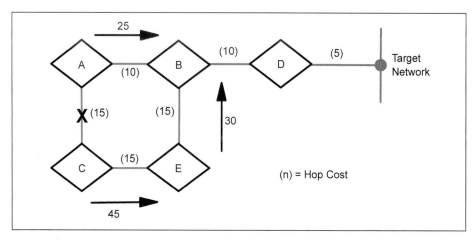

Figure 79. Using a feasible successor

In this example, router C uses router E as a feasible successor to reach the target network. If the connection between router A and router C fails, router C will immediately reroute traffic through router E. The new route is updated in the IP routing table.

4.7.4.1 Route recomputation

A route recomputation occurs when there is no known feasible successor to the destination. The process starts with a router sending a multicast query packet to determine if any neighbor is aware of a feasible successor to the destination. A neighbor replies if it has an feasible successor. If the neighbor does not have feasible successor, the neighbor may return a query indicating it also is performing a route recomputation.

Figure 80 shows an example of querying to determine a feasible successor. In this example, router E does not have a feasible successor to the target network. When the link connecting router E and router B fails, router E must determine a new path. Router E sends a multicast query to each of its neighbors. Router C has a feasible successor and responds to router E. Router E updates its IP routing table with the new path at a cost of 55.

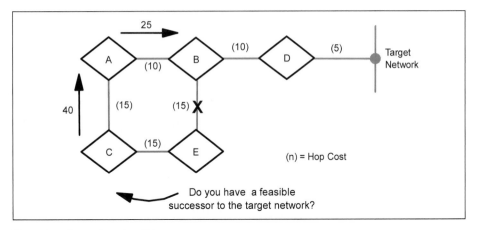

Figure 80. Query for a feasible successor

When the link to a neighbor fails, all routes that used that neighbor as the only feasible successor require a route recomputation.

4.7.4.2 EIGRP metrics

EIGRP uses a mathematical formula to determine the metric associated with a path. By default, the formula references the minimum bandwidth of a segment used to reach the destination. It also sums the delays on the path. The default formula to determine the metric is:

$$\left[\left(\frac{10^7}{minbandwith}\right) + sumofdelays\right] \times 256$$

EIGRP supports the inclusion of other measurements in the metric calculation.

4.7.5 EIGRP packet types

EIGRP uses five types of packets to establish neighbor relationships and advertise routing information:

- Hello/Acknowledgement: These packets are used for neighbor discovery. They are multicast advertised on each network segment. Unicast responses to the hello packet are returned.

  A hello packet without any data is considered an acknowledgement.

- Updates: These packets are used to convey reachability information for each destination. When a new neighbor is discovered, unicast update packets are exchanged to allow each neighbor to build their topology table. Other types of advertisements (e.g., metric changes) use multicast packets. Update packets are always transmitted reliably.

- Queries and replies: These packets are exchanged when a destination enters an active state. A multicast query packet is sent to determine if any neighbor contains a feasible successor to the destination. Unicast reply packets are sent to indicate that the neighbor does not need to go into an active state because a feasible successor has been identified. Query and reply packets are transmitted reliably.

- Request: These packets are used to obtain specific information from a neighbor. These packets are used in route server applications.

4.8 Exterior Gateway Protocol (EGP)

EGP is an exterior gateway protocol of historical merit. It was one of the first protocols developed for communication between autonomous systems. It is described in RFC 904.

EGP assumes the network contains a single backbone and a single path exists between any two autonomous systems. Due to this limitation, the current use of EGP is minimal. In practice, EGP has been replaced by BGP.

EGP is based on periodic polling using a hello/I-hear-you message exchange. These are used to monitor neighbor reachability and solicit update responses.

The gateway connecting to an AS is permitted to advertise only those destination networks reachable within the local AS. It does not advertise reachability information about its EGP neighbors outside the AS.

4.9 Border Gateway Protocol (BGP)

The Border Gateway Protocol (BGP) is an exterior gateway protocol. It was originally developed to provide a loop-free method of exchanging routing information between autonomous systems. BGP has since evolved to support aggregation and summarization of routing information.

BGP is an IETF draft standard protocol described in RFC 1771. The version described in this RFC is BGP Version 4. Following standard convention, this document uses the term BGP when referencing BGP Version 4.

4.9.1 BGP concepts and terminology

BGP uses specific terminology to describe the operation of the protocol. Figure 81 is used to illustrate this terminology.

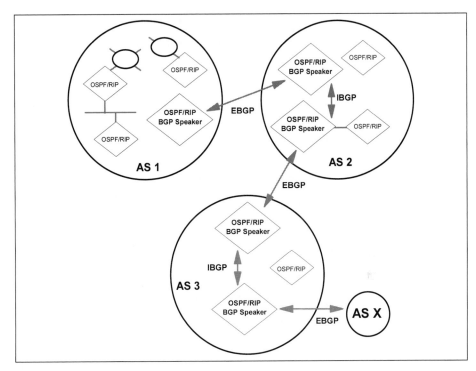

Figure 81. Components of a BGP network

- BGP speaker: A router configured to support BGP.

- BGP neighbors (peers): A pair of BGP speakers that exchange routing information. There are two types of BGP neighbors:

    - Internal (IBGP) neighbor: A pair of BGP speakers within the same AS.
    - External (EBGP) neighbor: A pair of BGP neighbors, each in a different AS. These neighbors typically share a directly connected network.

- BGP session: A TCP session connecting two BGP neighbors. The session is used to exchange routing information. The neighbors monitor the state of the session by sending keepalive messages.[1]

---

[1] This keepalive message is implemented in the application layer. It is independent of the keepalive message available in many TCP implementations.

- Traffic type: BGP defines two types of traffic:
  - Local: Traffic local to an AS either originates or terminates within the AS. Either the source or the destination IP address resides in the AS.
  - *Transit:* Any traffic that is not local traffic is transit traffic. One of the goals of BGP is to minimize the amount of transit traffic.
- AS type: BGP defines three types of autonomous systems:
  - Stub: A stub AS has a single connection to one other AS. A stub AS carries only local traffic.
  - Multihomed: A multihomed AS has connections to two or more autonomous systems. However, a multihomed AS has been configured so that it does not forward transit traffic.
  - Transit: A transit AS has connections to two or more autonomous systems and carries both local and transit traffic. The AS may impose policy restrictions on the types of transit traffic that will be forwarded.

  Depending on the configuration of the BGP devices within AS 2 in Figure 81, this autonomous system may be either a multihomed AS or a transit AS.
- AS number: A 16-bit number uniquely identifying an AS.
- AS path: A list of AS numbers describing a route through the network. A BGP neighbor communicates paths to its peers.
- Routing policy: A set of rules constraining the flow of data packets through the network. Routing policies are not defined in the BGP protocol. Rather, they are used to configure a BGP device. For example, a BGP device may be configured so that:
  - A multihomed AS can refuse to act as a transit AS. This is accomplished by advertising only those networks contained within the AS.
  - A multihomed AS can perform transit AS routing for a restricted set of adjacent autonomous systems. It does this by tailoring the routing advertisements sent to EBGP peers.
  - An AS can optimize traffic to use a specific AS path for certain categories of traffic.
- Network layer reachability information (NLRI): NLRI is used by BGP to advertise routes. It consists of a set of networks represented by the tuple <length,prefix>. For example, the tuple <14,220.24.106.0> represents the CIDR route 220.24.106.0/14.

- Routes and paths: A route associates a destination with a collection of attributes describing the path to the destination. The destination is specified in NRLI format. The path is reported as a collection of path attributes. This information is advertised in UPDATE messages. Additional information describing the UPDATE message is located in 4.9.3, "Protocol description" on page 185.

4.9.2 IBGP and EBGP communication

BGP does not replace the IGP operating within an AS. Instead, it cooperates with the IGP to establish communication between autonomous systems. BGP within an AS is used to advertise the local IGP routes. These routes are advertised to BGP peers in other autonomous systems. Figure 82 illustrates the communication that occurs between BGP peers. This example shows four autonomous systems. AS 2, AS 3 and AS 4 each have an EBGP connection to AS 1. A full mesh of IBGP sessions exists between BGP devices within AS 1.

Network 10.0.0.0/8 is located within AS 3. Using BGP, the existence of this network is advertised to the rest of the environment:

- R4 in AS 3 uses its EBGP connection to announce the network to AS 1.
- R1 in AS 1 uses its IBGP connections to announce the network to R2 and R3.
- R2 in AS 1 uses its EBGP session to announce the network into AS 2. R3 in AS 1 uses its EBGP session 5 to announce the network into AS 4.

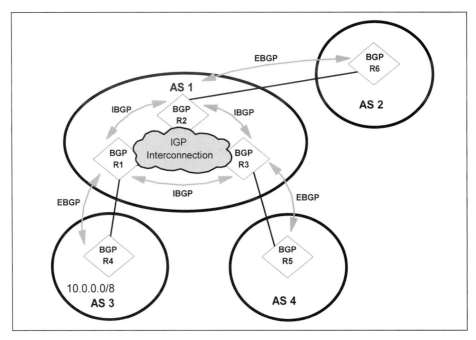

Figure 82. EBGP and IBGP communication

Several additional operational issues are shown in Figure 82:

- Role of BGP and the IGP: The diagram shows that while BGP alone carries information between autonomous systems, both BGP and the IGP are used to carry information through an AS.

- Establishing the TCP session between peers: Before establishing a BGP session, a device verifies that routing information is available to reach the peer:

  - EBGP peers: EBGP peers typically share a directly connected network. The routing information needed to exchange BGP packets between these peers is trivial.
  - IBGP peers: IBGP peers can be located anywhere within the AS. They do not need to be directly connected. BGP relies on the IGP to locate a peer. Packet forwarding between IBGP peers uses IGP-learned routes.

- Full mesh of BGP sessions within an AS: IBGP speakers assume a full mesh of BGP sessions have been established between peers in the same AS. In Figure 82, all three BGP peers in AS 1 are interconnected with BGP sessions.

  When a BGP speaker receives a route update from an IBGP peer, the receiving speaker uses EBGP to propagate the update to external peers.

Since the receiving speaker assumes a full mesh of IBGP sessions have been established, it does not propagate the update to other IBGP peers.

For example, assume there was no IBGP session between R1 and R3 in Figure 82. R1 receives the update about 10.0.0.0/8 from AS 3. R1 forwards the update to its BGP peers, namely R2. R2 receives the IBGP update and forwards it to its EBGP peers, namely R6. No update is sent to R3. If R3 needs to receive this information, R1 and R3 must be configured to be BGP peers.

4.9.3 Protocol description

BGP establishes a reliable TCP connection between peers. Sessions are established using TCP port 179. BGP assumes the transport connection will manage fragmentation, retransmission, acknowledgement, and sequencing.

When two speakers initially form a BGP session, they exchange their entire routing table. This routing information contains the complete AS path used to reach each destination. The information avoids the routing loops and counting-to-infinity behavior observed in RIP networks. Once the entire table has been exchanged, changes to the table are communicated as incremental updates.

4.9.3.1 BGP packet types

All BGP packets contain a standard header. The header specifies the BGP packet type. The valid BGP packet types include:

- OPEN[2]: This message type is used to establish a BGP session between two peer nodes.

- UPDATE: This message type is used to transfer routing information between BGP peers.

- NOTIFICATION: This message is send when an error condition is detected.

- KEEPALIVE: This message is used to determine if peers are reachable.

Figure 83 shows the flow of these message types between two autonomous systems.

---

[2] RFC 1771 uses uppercase to name BGP messages. The same convention is used in this section.

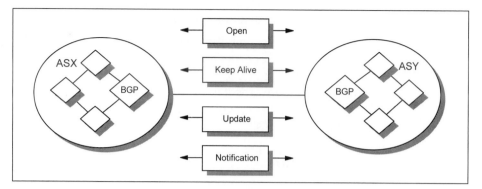

Figure 83. BGP message flows between BGP speakers

4.9.3.2 Opening and confirming a BGP connection

Once a TCP session has been established between two peer nodes, each router sends an OPEN message to the neighbor. The open message includes:

- The originating router's AS number and BGP router identifier.

- A suggested value for the hold timer. The function of this timer is discussed in the next section.

- Optional parameters. This information is used to authenticate a peer.

An OPEN message contains support for authenticating the identity of a BGP peer. However, the BGP standard does not specify a specific authorization mechanism. This allows BGP peers to select any supported authorization scheme.

An OPEN message is acknowledged by a KEEPALIVE message. Once peer routers have established a BGP connection, they can exchange additional information.

4.9.3.3 Maintaining the BGP connection

BGP does not use any transport-based keep-alive to determine if peers are reachable. Instead, BGP messages are periodically exchanged between peers. If no messages are received from the peer for the duration specified by the hold timer, the originating router assumes an error has occurred. When this happens, an error notification is sent to the peer and the connection is closed.

RFC 1771 recommends a 90 second hold timer and a 30 second keepalive timer.

4.9.3.4 Sending reachability information

Reachability information is exchanged between peers in UPDATE messages. BGP does not require a periodic refresh of the entire BGP routing table. Therefore, each BGP speaker must retain a copy of the current BGP routing table used by each peer. This information is maintained for the duration of the connection. Once neighbors have performed the initial exchange of complete routing information, only incremental updates to that information are exchanged.

An UPDATE message is used to advertise feasible routes or withdraw infeasible routes. The message may simultaneously advertise a feasible route and withdraw multiple infeasible routes from service. Figure 84 depicts the format of an UPDATE message:

- Network Layer Reachability Information (NLRI)
- Path attributes (Path attributes are discussed in 4.9.4.1, "Path attributes" on page 188)
- Withdrawn routes

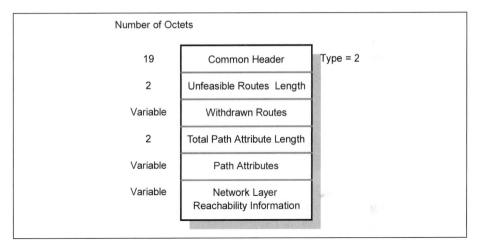

Figure 84. BGP UPDATE message

Several path attributes may be used to describe a route.

Withdrawn routes

The unfeasible routes length field indicates the total length of the withdrawn routes field.

The withdrawn routes field provides a list of IP addresses prefixes that are not feasible or are no longer in service. These addresses need to be withdrawn from the BGP routing table. The withdrawn routes are represented in the same tuple-format as the NLRI.

4.9.3.5 Notification of error conditions

A BGP device may observe error conditions impacting the connection to a peer. NOTIFICATION messages are sent to the neighbor when these conditions are detected. Once the message is sent, the BGP transport connection is closed. This means all resources for the BGP connection are deallocated. The routing table entries associated with the remote peer are marked as invalid. Finally, other peers are notified that these routes are invalid.

Notification messages include an error code and an error subcode.

The error codes provided by BGP include:

- Message header error
- OPEN message error
- UPDATE message error
- Hold timer expired
- Finite state machine error
- Cease

The error subcode further qualifies the specific error. Each error code may have multiple subcodes associated with it.

4.9.4 Path selection

BGP is a distance vector protocol. In traditional distance vector protocols, a single metric (for example, hop-count) is associated with a path. The best path is obtained by comparing the metrics of each feasible route. However, inter-AS routing complicates this process. There are no universally agreed-upon metrics that can be used to evaluate external paths. Each AS has its own set of criteria for path evaluation.

4.9.4.1 Path attributes

Path attributes are used to describe and evaluate a route. Peers exchange path attributes along with other routing information. When a device advertises a route, it may add or modify the path attributes before advertising the route to a peer. The combination of attributes are used to select the best path.

Each path attribute is placed into one of four separate categories:

- Well-known mandatory: The attribute must be recognized by all BGP implementations. It must be sent in every UPDATE message.

- Well-known discretionary: The attribute must be recognized by all BGP implementations. However, it is not required to be sent in every UPDATE message.

- Optional transitive: It is not required that every BGP implementation recognize this type of attribute. A path with an unrecognized optional transitive attribute is accepted and simply forwarded to other BGP peers.

- Optional non-transitive: It is not required that every BGP implementation recognize this type of attribute. These attributes can be ignored and not passed along to other BGP peers.

BGP defines seven attribute types to define an advertised route:

- ORIGIN: This attribute defines the origin of the path information. Valid selections are IGP (interior to the AS), EGP, or INCOMPLETE. This is a well-known mandatory attribute.

- AS_PATH: This attribute defines the set of autonomous systems which must be traversed to reach the advertised network. Each BGP device prepends its AS number onto the AS path sequence before sending the routing information to an EBGP peer. Using the sample network depicted in Figure 82 on page 184, R4 advertises network 10.0.0.0 with an AS_PATH of 3. When the update traverses AS 1, R2 prepends its own AS number to it. When the routing update reaches R6, the AS_PATH attribute for network 10.0.0.0 is <1 3>. This is a well-known mandatory attribute.

- NEXT_HOP: This attribute defines the IP address of the next hop used to reach the destination. This is a well-known mandatory attribute.

  For routing updates received over EBGP connections, the next hop is typically the IP address of the EBGP neighbor in the remote AS. BGP specifies that this next hop is passed without modification to each IBGP neighbor. As a result, each IBGP neighbor must have a route to reach the neighbor in the remote AS. Figure 85 illustrates this interaction.

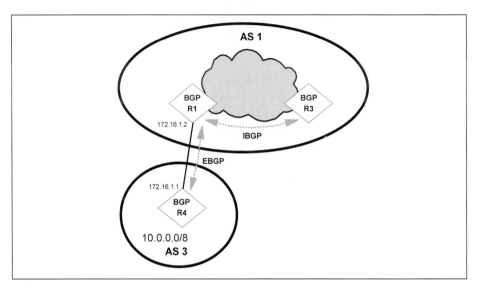

Figure 85. NEXT_HOP attribute

In this example, when a routing update for network 10.0.0.0/8 is sent from AS 3, R1 receives the update with the NEXT_HOP attribute set to 172.16.1.1. When this update is forwarded to R3, the next hop address remains 172.16.1.1. R3 must have appropriate routing information to reach this address. Otherwise, R3 will drop packets destined for AS 3 if the next hop is inaccessible.

- MULTI_EXIT_DISC (multi-exit discriminator, MED): This attribute is used to discriminate among multiple exit points to a neighboring AS. If this information is received from an EBGP peer, it is propagated to each IBGP peer. This attribute is not propagated to peers in other autonomous systems. If all other attributes are equal, the exit point with the lowest MED value is preferred. This is an optional non-transitive attribute.

- LOCAL_PREF (local preference): This attribute is used by a BGP speaker to inform other speakers within the AS of the originating speaker's degree of preference for the advertised route. Unlike MED, this attribute is used only within an AS. The value of the local preference is not distributed outside an AS. If all other attributes are equal, the route with the higher degree of preference is preferred. This is a well-known discretionary attribute.

- ATOMIC_AGGREGATE: This attribute is used when a BGP peer receives advertisements for the same destination identified in multiple, non-matching routes (that is, overlapping routes). One route describes a smaller set of destinations (a more specific prefix), other routes describe a larger set of destinations (a less specific prefix). This attribute is used by the BGP speaker to inform peers that it has selected the less specific route without selecting the more specific route. This is a well-known discretionary attribute.

A route with this attribute included may actually traverse autonomous systems not listed in the AS_PATH.

- AGGREGATOR: This attribute indicates the last AS number that formed the aggregate route, followed by the IP address of the BGP speaker that formed the aggregate route. Further information about route aggregation is located in 4.9.6, "BGP aggregation" on page 193. This is an optional transitive attribute.

4.9.4.2 Decision process

The process to select the best path uses the path attributes describing each route. The attributes are analyzed and a *degree of preference* is assigned. Since there may be multiple paths to a given destination, the route selection process determines the degree of preference for each feasible route. The path with the highest degree of preference is selected as the best path. This is the path advertised to each BGP neighbor.

Route aggregation can also be performed during this process.

Where there are multiple paths to a destination, BGP tracks each individual path. This allows faster convergence to the alternate path when the primary path fail.

4.9.5 BGP synchronization

Figure 86 shows an example of an AS providing transit service. In this example, AS 1 is used to transport traffic between AS 3 and AS 4. Within AS 1, R2 is not configured for BGP. However, R2 is used for communication between R1 and R3. Traffic between these two BGP nodes physically traverses through R2.

Using the routing update flow described earlier, the 10.0.0.0/8 network is advertised using the EBGP connection between R4 and R1. R1 passes the network advertisement to R3 using its existing IBGP connection. Since R2 is not configured for BGP, it is unaware of any networks in AS 3. A problem occurs if R3 needs to communicate with a device in AS 3. R3 passes the traffic to R2. However, since R2 does not have any routes to AS 3 networks, the traffic is dropped.

If R3 advertises the 10.0.0.0/8 network to AS 4, the problem continues. If AS 4 needs to communicate with a device in AS 3, the packets are forwarded from R5 to R3. R3 forwards the packets to R2 where they are discarded.

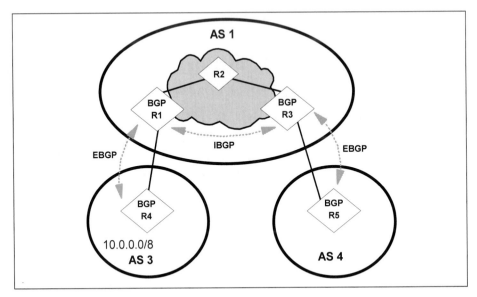

Figure 86. BGP synchronization

This situation is addressed by the synchronization rule of BGP. The rule states that a transit AS will not advertise a route before all routers within the AS have learned about the route. In this example, R3 will not advertise the existence of the networks in AS 3 until R2 has built a proper routing table. There are three methods to implement the synchronization rule:

- Enable BGP on all devices within the transit AS. In this solution, R2 would have an IBGP session with both R1 and R3. R2 learns of the 10.0.0.0/8 network at the same time it is advertised to R3. At that time, R3 announces the routes to its peer in AS 4.

- Redistribute the routes into the IGP used within the transit area. In this solution, R1 redistributes the 10.0.0.0/8 network into the IGP within AS 1. R3 learns of the network via two routing protocols: BGP and the IGP. Once R3 learns of the network via the IGP, it is certain that other routers within the AS have also learned of the routes. At that time, R3 announces the routes to its peer in AS 4.

- Encapsulate the transit traffic across the AS. In this solution, transit traffic is encapsulated within IP datagrams addressed to the exit gateway. Since this does not require the IGP to carry exterior routing information, no synchronization is required between BGP and the IGP. R3 can immediately announce the routes to its peer in AS 4.

4.9.6 BGP aggregation

The major improvement introduced in BGP Version 4 was support for CIDR and route aggregation. These features allow BGP peers to consolidate multiple contiguous routing entries into a single advertisement. It significantly enhances the scalability of BGP into large internetworking environments. These functions are illustrated in Figure 87.

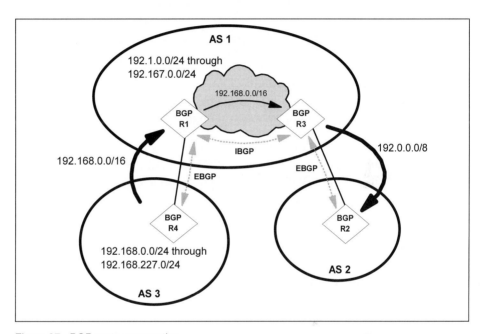

Figure 87. BGP route aggregation

This diagrams depicts three autonomous systems interconnected via BGP. In this example, networks 192.168.0.0 through 182.168.227.0 are located within AS 3. To reduce the size of routing announcements, R4 aggregates these individual networks into a single route entry prior to advertising into AS 1. The single entry 192.168.0.0/16 represents a valid CIDR supernet even though it is an illegal class C network.

BGP aggregate routes contain additional information within the AS_PATH path attribute. When aggregate entries are generated from a set of more specific routes, the AS_PATH attributes of the more specific routes are combined. For example in Figure 87, the aggregate route 192.0.0.0/8 is announced from AS 1 into AS 2. This aggregate represents the set of more specific routes deployed within AS 1 and AS 3. When this aggregate route is sent to AS 2, the AS_PATH attribute consists of <1 3>. This is done to prevent routing information loops. A loop could occur if AS 1 generated an aggregate with an AS_PATH attribute of <1>. If AS 2 had a direct connection to AS 3, the route with the less-specific AS_PATH advertised from AS 1 could generate a loop. This is because AS 2 does not know this aggregate contains networks located within AS 3.

4.9.7 BGP confederations

BGP requires that all speakers within a single AS have a fully meshed set of IBGP connections. This can be a scaling problem in networks containing a large number of IBGP peers. The use of BGP confederations addresses this problem.

A BGP confederation creates a set of autonomous systems that represent a single AS to peers external to the confederation. This removes the full mesh requirement and reduces management complexity.

Figure 88 illustrates the operation of a BGP confederation. In this sample network, AS 1 contains 8 BGP speakers. A standard BGP network would require 28 IBGP sessions to fully mesh the speakers.

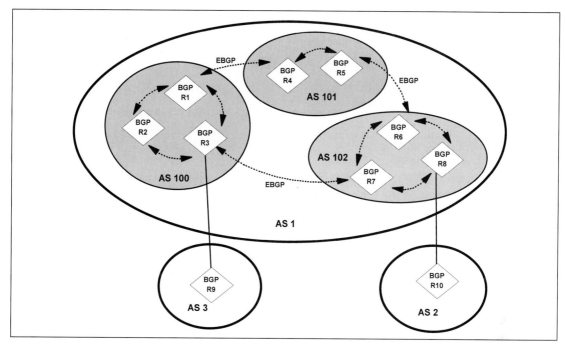

Figure 88. BGP confederations

A confederation divides the AS into a set of domains. In this example, AS 1 contains three domains. Devices within a domain have a fully meshed set of IBGP connections. Each domain also has an EBGP connection to other domains within the confederation. In the example network, R1, R2, and R3 have fully meshed IBGP sessions. R1 has an EBGP session within the confederation to R4. R3 has an EBGP session outside the confederation to R9.

Each router in the confederation is assigned a confederation ID. A member of the confederation uses this ID in all communications with devices outside the confederation. In this example, each router is assigned a confederation ID of AS 1. All communications from AS 1 to AS 2 or AS 3 appear to have originated from the confederation ID of AS 1.

Even though communication between domains within a confederation occurs with EBGP, the domains exchange routing updates as if they were connected via IBGP. Specifically, the information contained in the NEXT_HOP, MULTI_EXIT_DESC, and LOCAL_PREF attributes is preserved between domains. The confederation appears to be a single AS to other autonomous systems.

BGP confederations are described in RFC 3065. At the time of this writing, this is a proposed standard. Regardless, BGP confederations have been widely deployed throughout the Internet. Numerous vendors support this feature.

4.9.8 BGP route reflectors

Route reflectors are another solution to address the requirement for a full mesh of IBGP sessions between peers in an AS. As noted previously, when a BGP speaker receives an update from an IBGP peer, the receiving speaker propagates the update only to EBGP peers. The receiving speaker does not forward the update to other IBGP peers. Route reflectors relax this restriction. BGP speakers are permitted to advertise IBGP learned routes to certain IBGP peers.

Figure 89 depicts an environment utilizing route reflectors. R1 is configured as a route reflector for R2 and R3. R2 and R3 are route reflector clients of R1. No IBGP session is defined between R2 and R3. When R3 receives an EBGP update from AS 3, it is passed to R1 using IBGP. Since R1 is configured as a reflector, R1 forwards the IBGP update to R2.

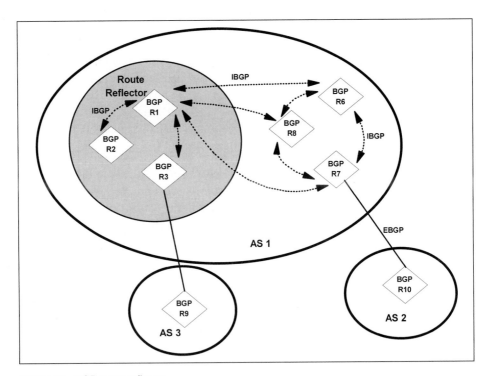

Figure 89. BGP route reflector

Figure 89 also illustrates the interaction between route reflectors and conventional BGP speakers within an AS. In this figure, R1, R2, and R3 are in the route reflector domain. R6, R7, and R8 are conventional BGP speakers containing a full mesh of IBGP peer connections. In addition, each of these speakers is peered with the route reflector. This configuration permits full IBGP communication within AS 1.

Although not shown in Figure 89, an AS can contain more than one route reflector. When this occurs, each reflector treats other reflectors as a conventional IBGP peer.

Route reflectors are described in RFC 2796. At the time of this writing, this is a proposed standard.

4.10 Routing protocol selection

The choice of a routing protocol is a major decision for the network administrator. It has a major impact to overall network performance. The selection depends on network complexity, size, and administrative policies. The protocol chosen for one type of network may not be appropriate for other types of networks. Each unique environment must be evaluated against a number of fundamental design requirements:

- Scalability to large environments: The potential growth of the network dictates the importance of this requirement. If support is needed for large, highly-redundant networks, link state or hybrid algorithms should be considered. Distance vector algorithms do not scale into these environments.

- Stability during outages: Distance vector algorithms may introduce network instability during outage periods. The counting to infinity problems (4.3.5, "Convergence and counting to infinity" on page 148) may cause routing loops or other non-optimal routing paths. Link state or hybrid algorithms reduce the potential for these problems.

- Speed of convergence: Triggered updates provide the ability to immediately initiate convergence when a failure is detected. All three types of protocols support this feature. One contributing factor to convergence is the time required to detect a failure. In OSPF and EIGRP networks, a series of hello packets must be missed before convergence begins. In RIP environments, subsequent route advertisements must be missed before convergence in initiated. These detection times increase the time required to restore communication.

- Metrics: Metrics provide the ability to groom appropriate routing paths through the network. Link state algorithms consider bandwidth when calculating routes. EIGRP improves this to include network delay in the route calculation.

- Support for VLSM: The availability of IP address ranges dictates the importance of this requirement. In environments with an constrained supply of addresses, the network administrator must develop an addressing scheme that intelligently overlays the network. VLSM is a major component of this plan. The use of private addresses ranges may also address this concern.

- Vendor interoperability: The types of devices deployed in a network indicate the importance of this requirement. If the network contains equipment from a number of vendors, standard routing protocols should be used. The IETF has dictated the operating policies for the distance vector and link state algorithms described in this document. Implementing these algorithms avoids any interoperability problems encountered with non-standard protocols.

- Ease of implementation: Distance vector protocols are the simplest routing protocol to configure and maintain. Because of this, these protocols have the largest implementation base. Limited training is required to perform problem resolution in these environments.

  In small, non-changing environments, static routes are also simple to implement. These definitions change only when sites are added or removed from the network.

The administrator must assess the importance of each of these requirements when determining the appropriate routing protocol for an environment.

4.11 Additional functions performed by the router

The main functions performed by a router relate to managing the IP routing table and forwarding data. However, the router should be able to provide information alerting other devices to potential network problems. This information is provided via the ICMP protocol described in 3.2, "Internet Control Message Protocol (ICMP)" on page 102. The information includes:

- ICMP Destination Unreachable: The destination address specified in the IP packet references an unknown IP network.
- ICMP Redirect: Redirect forwarding of traffic to a more suitable router along the path to the destination.

- ICMP Source Quench: Congestion problems (for example, too many incoming datagrams for the available buffer space) have been encountered in a device along the path to the destination.
- ICMP Time Exceeded: The Time-to-Live field of an IP datagram has reached zero. The packet is not able to be delivered to the final destination.

In addition, each IP router should support the following base ICMP operations and messages:

- Parameter problem: This message is returned to the packet's source if a problem with the IP header is found. The message indicates the type and location of the problem. The router discards the errored packet.
- Address mask request/reply: A router must implement support for receiving ICMP Address Mask Request messages and responding with ICMP Address Mask Reply messages.
- Timestamp: The router must return a Timestamp Reply to every Timestamp message that is received. It should be designed for minimum variability in delay. To synchronize the clock on the router, the UDP Time Server Protocol or the Network Time Protocol (NTP) may be used.
- Echo request/reply: A router must implement an ICMP Echo server function that receives requests sent to the router, and sends corresponding replies. The router may choose to ignore ICMP echo requests addressed to IP broadcast or IP multicast addresses.

4.12 Routing processes in UNIX-based systems

This chapter has focused on protocols available in standard IP routers. However, several of these protocols are also available in UNIX-based systems. These protocols are often implemented using one of two processes:

- routed (pronounced route-D): This is a basic routing process for interior routing. It is supplied with the majority of TCP/IP implementations. It implements the RIP protocol.

- gated (pronounced gate-D): This is a more sophisticated process allowing for both interior and exterior routing. It can implement a number of protocols including OSPF, RIP-2, and BGP-4.

Chapter 5. Transport layer protocols

This chapter provides an overview of the most important and common protocols of the TCP/IP transport layer. These include:

- User Datagram Protocol (UDP)
- Transmission Control Protocol (TCP)

By building on the functionality provided by the Internet Protocol (IP), the transport protocols deliver data to applications executing in the IP host. This is done by making use of ports as described in 5.1, "Ports and sockets" on page 201. The transport protocols can provide additional functionality such as congestion control, reliable data delivery, duplicate data suppression, and flow control as is done by TCP.

5.1 Ports and sockets

This section introduces the concepts of *port* and *socket*, which are needed to determine which local process at a given host actually communicates with which process, at which remote host, using which protocol. If this sounds confusing, consider the following:

- An application process is assigned a process identifier number (process ID), which is likely to be different each time that process is started.
- Process IDs differ between operating system platforms, hence they are not uniform.
- A server process can have multiple connections to multiple clients at a time, hence simple connection identifiers would not be unique.

The concept of ports and sockets provides a way to uniformly and uniquely identify connections and the programs and hosts that are engaged in them, irrespective of specific process IDs.

5.1.1 Ports

Each *process* that wants to communicate with another process identifies itself to the TCP/IP protocol suite by one or more ports. A port is a 16-bit number, used by the host-to-host protocol to identify to which higher level protocol or application program (process) it must deliver incoming messages. There are two types of port:

- Well-known: Well-known ports belong to standard servers, for example, Telnet uses port 23. Well-known port numbers range between 1 and 1023 (prior to 1992, the range between 256 and 1023 was used for

UNIX-specific servers). Well-known port numbers are typically odd, because early systems using the port concept required an odd/even pair of ports for duplex operations. Most servers require only a single port. Exceptions are the BOOTP server, which uses two: 67 and 68 (see 3.6, "Bootstrap protocol (BOOTP)" on page 121) and the FTP server, which uses two: 20 and 21 (see 10.1, "File Transfer Protocol (FTP)" on page 365).

The well-known ports are controlled and assigned by the Internet Assigned Number Authority (IANA) and on most systems can only be used by system processes or by programs executed by privileged users. The reason for well-known ports is to allow clients to be able to find servers without configuration information. The well-known port numbers are defined in STD 2 – Assigned Internet Numbers.

- Ephemeral: Clients do not need well-known port numbers because they initiate communication with servers and the port number they are using is contained in the UDP datagrams sent to the server. Each client process is allocated a port number for as long as it needs it by the host it is running on. Ephemeral port numbers have values greater than 1023, normally in the range 1024 to 65535. A client can use any number allocated to it, as long as the combination of <transport protocol, IP address, port number> is unique.

  Ephemeral ports are not controlled by IANA and can be used by ordinary user-developed programs on most systems.

Confusion, due to two different applications trying to use the same port numbers on one host, is avoided by writing those applications to request an available port from TCP/IP. Because this port number is dynamically assigned, it may differ from one invocation of an application to the next.

UDP, TCP and ISO TP-4 all use the same port principle. To the best possible extent, the same port numbers are used for the same services on top of UDP, TCP, and ISO TP-4.

> **Note:**
>
> Normally, a server will use either TCP or UDP, but there are exceptions. For example, domain name servers (see 8.1, "Domain Name System (DNS)" on page 279) use both UDP port 53 and TCP port 53.

5.1.2 Sockets

The socket interface is one of several *application programming interfaces* (APIs) to the communication protocols. Designed to be a generic communication programming interface, APIs were first introduced by 4.2 BSD. Although it has not been standardized, it has become a *de facto* industry standard.

4.2 BSD allowed two different communication domains: Internet and UNIX. 4.3 BSD has added the Xerox Network System (XNS) protocols, and 4.4 BSD will add an extended interface to support the ISO OSI protocols.

Let us consider the following terminologies:

- A *socket* is a special type of *file handle*, which is used by a process to request network services from the operating system.

- A *socket address* is the triple:

  <protocol, local-address, local-process>

  For example, in the TCP/IP suite:

  <tcp, 193.44.234.3, 12345>

- A *conversation* is the communication link between two processes.

- An *association* is the 5-tuple that completely specifies the two processes that comprise a connection:

  <protocol, local-address, local-process, foreign-address, foreign-process>

  In the TCP/IP suite, the following could be a valid association:

  <tcp, 193.44.234.3, 1500, 193.44.234.5, 21>

- A *half-association* is either:

  <protocol, local-address, local-process>

  or

  <protocol, foreign-address, foreign-process>

  which specify each half of a connection.

- The half-association is also called a socket or a *transport address*. That is, a socket is an endpoint for communication that can be named and addressed in a network.

Two processes communicate via *TCP sockets*. The socket model provides a process with a full-duplex byte stream connection to another process. The application need not concern itself with the management of this stream; these facilities are provided by TCP.

TCP uses the same port principle as UDP to provide multiplexing. Like UDP, TCP uses well-known and ephemeral ports. Each side of a TCP connection has a socket that can be identified by the triple <TCP, IP address, port number>. If two processes are communicating over TCP, they have a *logical connection* that is uniquely identifiable by the two sockets involved, that is, by the combination <TCP, local IP address, local port, remote IP address, remote port>. Server processes are able to manage multiple conversations through a single port. Please refer to 7.2.1, "The socket API" on page 262 for more information about socket APIs.

5.2 User Datagram Protocol (UDP)

UDP is a standard protocol with STD number 6. UDP is described by RFC 768 – User Datagram Protocol. Its status is recommended, but in practice every TCP/IP implementation that is not used exclusively for routing will include UDP.

UDP is basically an application interface to IP. It adds no reliability, flow-control, or error recovery to IP. It simply serves as a *multiplexer/demultiplexer* for sending and receiving datagrams, using ports to direct the datagrams, as shown in Figure 90. For a more detailed discussion of ports, refer to 5.1, "Ports and sockets" on page 201.

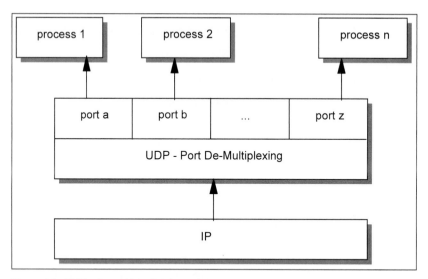

Figure 90. UDP - Demultiplexing based on ports

UDP provides a mechanism for one application to send a datagram to another. The UDP layer can be regarded as being extremely thin and consequently has low overheads, but it requires the application to take responsibility for error recovery and so on.

Applications sending datagrams to a host need to identify a target that is more specific than the IP address, since datagrams are normally directed to certain processes and not to the system as a whole. UDP provides this by using ports. The port concept is discussed in 5.1, "Ports and sockets" on page 201.

5.2.1 UDP datagram format

Each UDP datagram is sent within a single IP datagram. Although, the IP datagram may be fragmented during transmission, the receiving IP implementation will reassemble it before presenting it to the UDP layer. All IP implementations are required to accept datagrams of 576 bytes, which means that, allowing for maximum-size IP header of 60 bytes, a UDP datagram of 516 bytes is acceptable to all implementations. Many implementations will accept larger datagrams, but this is not guaranteed. The UDP datagram has a 16-byte header that is described in Figure 91.

Source Port	Destination Port
Length	Checksum
Data...	

Figure 91. UDP - Datagram format

Where:

- Source Port: Indicates the port of the sending process. It is the port to which replies should be addressed.

- Destination Port: Specifies the port of the destination process on the destination host.

- Length: The length (in bytes) of this user datagram, including the header.

- Checksum: An optional 16-bit one's complement of the one's complement sum of a pseudo-IP header, the UDP header, and the UDP data. The pseudo-IP header contains the source and destination IP addresses, the protocol, and the UDP length:

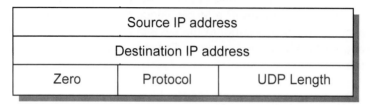

Source IP address		
Destination IP address		
Zero	Protocol	UDP Length

Figure 92. UDP - Pseudo-IP Header

The pseudo-IP header effectively extends the checksum to include the original (unfragmented) IP datagram.

5.2.2 UDP application programming interface

The application interface offered by UDP is described in RFC 768. It provides for:

- The creation of new receive ports.
- The receive operation that returns the data bytes and an indication of source port and source IP address.
- The send operation that has, as parameters, the data, source, and destination ports and addresses.

The way this interface should be implemented is left to the discretion of each vendor.

Be aware that UDP and IP do not provide guaranteed delivery, flow-control, or error recovery, so these must be provided by the application.

Standard applications using UDP include:

- Trivial File Transfer Protocol (TFTP)
- Domain Name System (DNS) name server
- Remote Procedure Call (RPC), used by the Network File System (NFS)
- Simple Network Management Protocol (SNMP)
- Lightweight Directory Access Protocol (LDAP)

5.3 Transmission Control Protocol (TCP)

TCP is a standard protocol with STD number 7. TCP is described by RFC 793 – Transmission Control Protocol. Its status is recommended, but in practice, every TCP/IP implementation that is not used exclusively for routing will include TCP.

TCP provides considerably more facilities for applications than UDP, notably error recovery, flow control, and reliability. TCP is a *connection-oriented* protocol, unlike UDP, which is *connectionless*. Most of the user application protocols, such as Telnet and FTP, use TCP.

The two processes communicate with each other over a TCP connection (InterProcess Communication - IPC), as shown in Figure 93. Please see 5.1, "Ports and sockets" on page 201 for more details about ports and sockets.

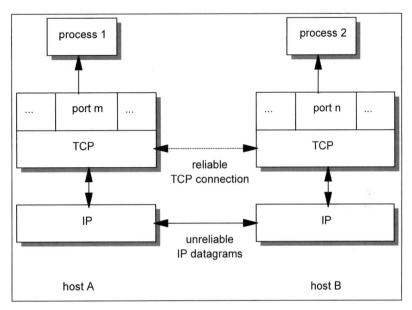

Figure 93. TCP - Connection between processes - (Processes 1 and 2 communicate over a TCP connection carried by IP datagrams.)

5.3.1 TCP concept

As noted above, the primary purpose of TCP is to provide reliable logical circuit or connection service between pairs of processes. It does *not* assume reliability from the lower-level protocols (such as IP), so TCP must guarantee this itself.

TCP can be characterized by the following facilities it provides for the applications using it:

- Stream Data Transfer: From the application's viewpoint, TCP transfers a contiguous stream of bytes through the network. The application does not have to bother with chopping the data into basic blocks or datagrams. TCP does this by grouping the bytes in TCP segments, which are passed to IP for transmission to the destination. Also, TCP itself decides how to segment the data and it can forward the data at its own convenience.

Sometimes, an application needs to be sure that all the data passed to TCP has actually been transmitted to the destination. For that reason, a push function is defined. It will push all remaining TCP segments still in storage to the destination host. The normal close connection function also pushes the data to the destination.

- Reliability: CP assigns a sequence number to each byte transmitted and expects a positive acknowledgment (ACK) from the receiving TCP. If the ACK is not received within a timeout interval, the data is retransmitted. Since the data is transmitted in blocks (TCP segments), only the sequence number of the first data byte in the segment is sent to the destination host.

  The receiving TCP uses the sequence numbers to rearrange the segments when they arrive out of order, and to eliminate duplicate segments.

- Flow Control: The receiving TCP, when sending an ACK back to the sender, also indicates to the sender the number of bytes it can receive beyond the last received TCP segment, without causing overrun and overflow in its internal buffers. This is sent in the ACK in the form of the highest sequence number it can receive without problems. This mechanism is also referred to as a window-mechanism, and we discuss it in more detail later in this chapter.

- Multiplexing: Achieved through the use of ports, just as with UDP.

- Logical Connections: The reliability and flow control mechanisms described above require that TCP initializes and maintains certain status information for each data stream. The combination of this status, including sockets, sequence numbers and window sizes, is called a logical connection. Each connection is uniquely identified by the pair of sockets used by the sending and receiving processes.

- Full Duplex: TCP provides for concurrent data streams in both directions.

5.3.1.1 The window principle

A simple transport protocol might use the following principle: send a packet and then wait for an acknowledgment from the receiver before sending the next packet. If the ACK is not received within a certain amount of time, retransmit the packet. See Figure 94 for more details.

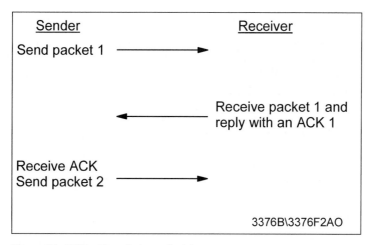

Figure 94. TCP - The window principle

While this mechanism ensures reliability, it only uses a part of the available network bandwidth.

Now, consider a protocol where the sender groups its packets to be transmitted, as in Figure 95, and uses the following rules:

- The sender can send all packets within the window without receiving an ACK, but must start a timeout timer for each of them.

- The receiver must acknowledge each packet received, indicating the sequence number of the last well-received packet.

- The sender slides the window on each ACK received.

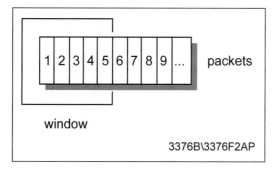

Figure 95. TCP - Message packets

In our example, the sender can transmit packets 1 to 5 without waiting for any acknowledgment:

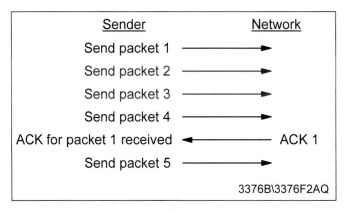

Figure 96. TCP - Window principle

At the moment the sender receives ACK 1 (acknowledgment for packet 1), it can slide its window one packet to the right:

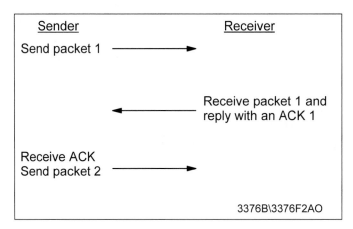

Figure 97. TCP - Message packets

At this point, the sender may also transmit packet 6.

Imagine some special cases:

- Packet 2 gets lost: The sender will not receive ACK 2, so its window will remain in position 1 (as in Figure 97). In fact, since the receiver did not receive packet 2, it will acknowledge packets 3, 4, and 5 with an ACK 1, since packet 1 was the last one received in sequence. At the sender's side, eventually a timeout will occur for packet 2 and it will be retransmitted. Note that reception of this packet by the receiver will generate ACK 5, since it has now successfully received all packets 1 to 5, and the sender's window will slide four positions upon receiving this ACK 5.

- Packet 2 did arrive, but the acknowledgment gets lost: The sender does not receive ACK 2, but will receive ACK 3. ACK 3 is an acknowledgment for *all* packets up to 3 (including packet 2) and the sender can now slide its window to packet 4.

This window mechanism ensures:

- Reliable transmission.
- Better use of the network bandwidth (better throughput).
- Flow-control, since the receiver may delay replying to a packet with an acknowledgment, knowing its free buffers are available and the window-size of the communication.

5.3.1.2 The window principle applied to TCP

The above window principle is used in TCP, but with a few differences:

- Since TCP provides a byte-stream connection, sequence numbers are assigned to each byte in the stream. TCP divides this contiguous byte stream into TCP segments to transmit them. The window principle is used at the byte level, that is, the segments sent and ACKs received will carry byte-sequence numbers and the window size is expressed as a number of bytes, rather than a number of packets.

- The window size is determined by the receiver when the connection is established and is variable during the data transfer. Each ACK message will include the window size that the receiver is ready to deal with at that particular time.

The sender's data stream can now be seen as follows:

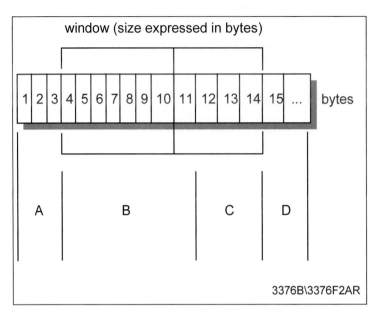

Figure 98. TCP - Window principle applied to TCP

Where:

- A: Bytes that are transmitted and have been acknowledged.
- B: Bytes that are sent but not yet acknowledged.
- C: Bytes that can be sent without waiting for any acknowledgment.
- D: Bytes that cannot be sent yet.

Remember that TCP will block bytes into segments, and a TCP segment only carries the sequence number of the first byte in the segment.

5.3.1.3 TCP segment format
The TCP segment format is shown in Figure 99.

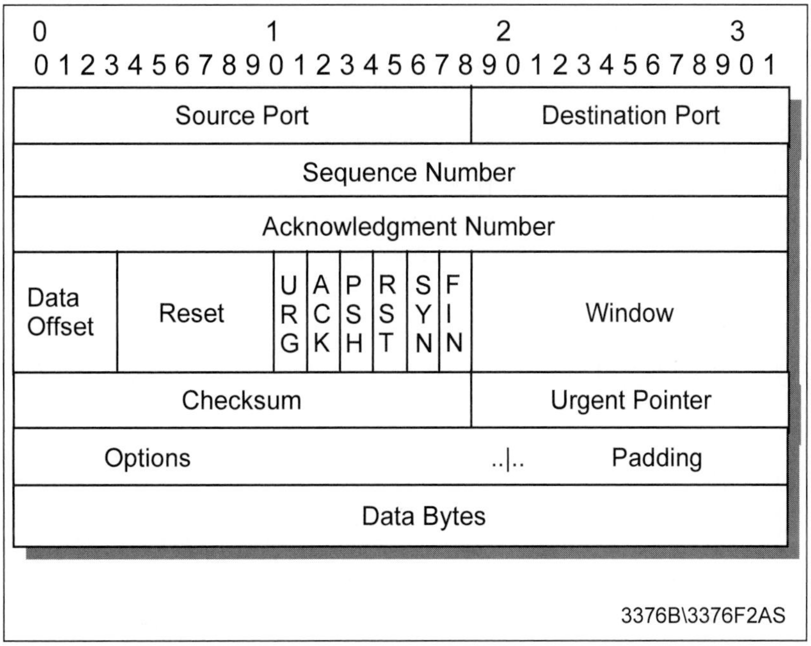

Figure 99. TCP - Segment format

Where:

- Source Port: The 16-bit source port number, used by the receiver to reply.

- Destination Port: The 16-bit destination port number.

- Sequence Number: The sequence number of the first data byte in this segment. If the SYN control bit is set, the sequence number is the initial sequence number (n) and the first data byte is n+1.

- Acknowledgment Number: If the ACK control bit is set, this field contains the value of the next sequence number that the receiver is expecting to receive.

- Data Offset: The number of 32-bit words in the TCP header. It indicates where the data begins.

- Reserved: Six bits reserved for future use; must be zero.

- URG: Indicates that the urgent pointer field is significant in this segment.

- ACK: Indicates that the acknowledgment field is significant in this segment.

- PSH: Push function.

- RST: Resets the connection.

- SYN: Synchronizes the sequence numbers.

- FIN: No more data from sender.

- Window: Used in ACK segments. It specifies the number of data bytes, beginning with the one indicated in the acknowledgment number field that the receiver (= the sender of this segment) is willing to accept.

- Checksum: The 16-bit one's complement of the one's complement sum of all 16-bit words in a pseudo-header, the TCP header, and the TCP data. While computing the checksum, the checksum field itself is considered zero.

  The pseudo-header is the same as that used by UDP for calculating the checksum. It is a pseudo-IP-header, only used for the checksum calculation, with the format shown in Figure 100.

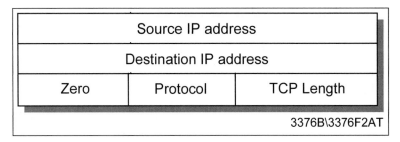

Source IP address		
Destination IP address		
Zero	Protocol	TCP Length

3376B\3376F2AT

Figure 100. TCP - Pseudo-IP header

- Urgent Pointer: Points to the first data octet following the urgent data. Only significant when the URG control bit is set.

- Options: Just as in the case of IP datagram options, options can be either:
  - A single byte containing the option number
  - A variable length option in the following format:

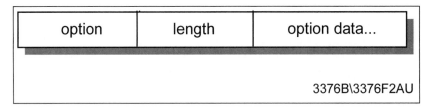

option	length	option data...

3376B\3376F2AU

Figure 101. TCP - IP datagram option - variable length option.

There are currently seven options defined:

Table 2. TCP - IP datagram options

Kind	Length	Meaning
0	-	End of option list
1	-	No-Operation
2	4	Maximum segment size
3	3	Window scale
4	2	Sack-Permitted
5	X	Sack
8	10	Timestamps

- Maximum Segment Size option: This option is only used during the establishment of the connection (SYN control bit set) and is sent from the side that is to receive data to indicate the maximum segment length it can handle. If this option is not used, any segment size is allowed. See Figure 102 for more details.

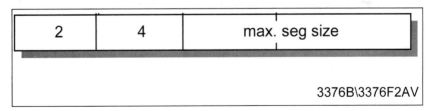

Figure 102. TCP - Maximum segment size option

- Window Scale option: This option is not mandatory. Both sides must send the Windows Scale Option in their SYN segments to enable windows scaling in their direction. The Window Scale expands the definition of the TCP window to 32 bits. It defines the 32-bit window size by using scale factor in the SYN segment over standard 16-bit window size. The receiver rebuild the 32-bit window size by using the 16-bit window size and scale factor. This option is determined while handshaking. There is no way to change it after the connection has been established. See Figure 103 for more details.

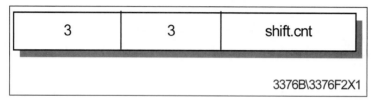

Figure 103. TCP - Window scale option

- SACK-Permitted option: This option is set when selective acknowledgment is used in that TCP connection. See Figure 104 for details.

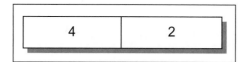

Figure 104. TCP - SACK-permitted option

- SACK option: Selective Acknowledgment (SACK) allows the receiver to inform the sender about all the segments that are received successfully. Thus, the sender will only send the segments that actually got lost. If the number of the segments that have been lost since the last SACK is too large, the SACK option will be too large. As a result, the number of blocks that can be reported by the SACK option is limited to four. To reduce this, the SACK option should be used for the most recent received data. See Figure 105 for more details.

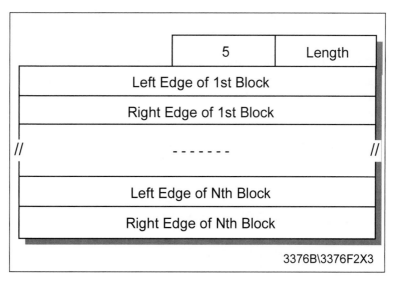

Figure 105. TCP - SACK option

- Timestamps option: The timestamps option sends a timestamp value that indicates the current value of the timestamp clock of the TCP sending the option. Timestamp Echo Value can only be used if the ACK bit is set in the TCP header. See Figure 106 for more details.

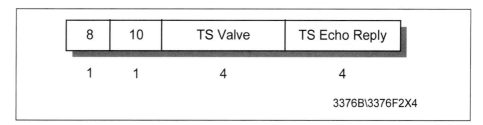

Figure 106. TCP - Timestamps option

- Padding: All zero bytes are used to fill up the TCP header to a total length that is a multiple of 32 bits.

5.3.1.4 Acknowledgments and retransmissions

TCP sends data in variable length segments. Sequence numbers are based on a byte count. Acknowledgments specify the sequence number of the next byte that the receiver expects to receive.

Consider that a segment gets lost or corrupted. In this case, the receiver will acknowledge all further well-received segments with an acknowledgment referring to the first byte of the missing packet. The sender will stop transmitting when it has sent all the bytes in the window. Eventually, a timeout will occur and the missing segment will be retransmitted.

Figure 107 illustrates and example where a window size of 1500 bytes and segments of 500 bytes are used.

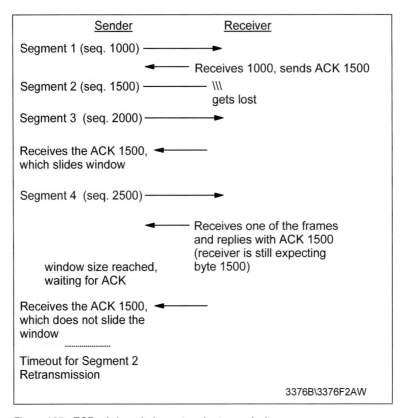

Figure 107. TCP - Acknowledgment and retransmission process

A problem now arises, since the sender does know that segment 2 is lost or corrupted, but does not know anything about segments 3 and 4. The sender should at least retransmit segment 2, but it could also retransmit segments 3 and 4 (since they are within the current window). It is possible that:

1. Segment 3 has been received, and we do not know about segment 4. It could be received, but ACK did not reach us yet, or it could be lost.
2. Segment 3 was lost, and we received the ACK 1500 upon the reception of segment 4.

Each TCP implementation is free to react to a timeout as the implementing wish. It could retransmit only segment 2, but in case 2, we will be waiting again until segment 3 times out. In this case, we lose all of the throughput advantages of the window mechanism. Or TCP might immediately resend all of the segments in the current window.

Whatever the choice, maximal throughput is lost. This is because the ACK does not contain a second acknowledgment sequence number indicating the actual frame received.

Variable timeout intervals

Each TCP should implement an algorithm to adapt the timeout values to be used for the round trip time of the segments. To do this, TCP records the time at which a segment was sent, and the time at which the ACK is received. A weighted average is calculated over several of these round trip times, to be used as a timeout value for the next segment(s) to be sent.

This is an important feature, because delays can vary in IP network, depending on multiple factors, such as the load of an intermediate low-speed network or the saturation of an intermediate IP gateway.

5.3.1.5 Establishing a TCP connection

Before any data can be transferred, a connection has to be established between the two processes. One of the processes (usually the server) issues a *passive OPEN* call, the other an *active OPEN* call. The passive OPEN call remains dormant until another process tries to connect to it by an active OPEN.

On the network, three TCP segments are exchanged:

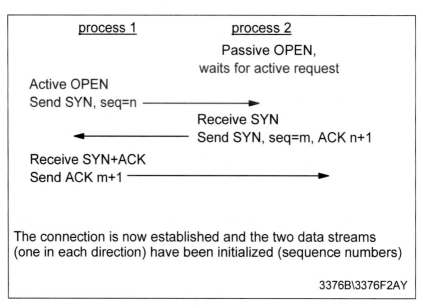

```
            process 1                    process 2
                                     Passive OPEN,
                                     waits for active request
      Active OPEN
      Send SYN, seq=n ─────────────────►
                                    Receive SYN
               ◄───────────────── Send SYN, seq=m, ACK n+1
      Receive SYN+ACK
      Send ACK m+1 ──────────────────────────────►



      The connection is now established and the two data streams
      (one in each direction) have been initialized (sequence numbers)

                                              3376B\3376F2AY
```

Figure 108. TCP - Connection establishment

This whole process is known as a *three-way handshake*. Note that the exchanged TCP segments include the initial sequence numbers from both sides, to be used on subsequent data transfers.

Closing the connection is done implicitly by sending a TCP segment with the FIN bit (no more data) set. Since the connection is full-duplex (that is, there are two independent data streams, one in each direction), the FIN segment only closes the data transfer in one direction. The other process will now send the remaining data it still has to transmit and also ends with a TCP segment where the FIN bit is set. The connection is deleted (status information on both sides) once the data stream is closed in both directions.

5.3.2 TCP application programming interface

The TCP application programming interface is not fully defined. Only some base functions it should provide are described in RFC 793 – Transmission Control Protocol. As is the case with most RFCs in the TCP/IP protocol suite, a great degree of freedom is left to the implementers, thereby allowing for optimal (operating system-dependent) implementations, resulting in better efficiency (greater throughput).

The following function calls are described in the RFC:

- Open: To establish a connection takes several parameters, such as:

- Active/passive
- Foreign socket
- Local port number
- Timeout value (optional)

This returns a local connection name, which is used to reference this particular connection in all other functions.

- Send: Causes data in a referenced user buffer to be sent over the connection. Can optionally set the URGENT flag or the PUSH flag.

- Receive: Copies incoming TCP data to a user buffer.

- Close: Closes the connection; causes a push of all remaining data and a TCP segment with FIN flag set.

- Status: An implementation-dependent call that could return information, such as:

  - Local and foreign socket
  - Send and receive window sizes
  - Connection state
  - Local connection name

- Abort: Causes all pending Send and Receive operations to be aborted, and a RESET to be sent to the foreign TCP.

Full details can be found in RFC 793 – Transmission Control Protocol.

5.3.3 TCP congestion control algorithms

One big difference between TCP and UDP is the congestion control algorithm. The TCP congestion algorithm prevents a sender from overrunning the capacity of the network (for example, slower WAN links). TCP can adapt the sender's rate to network capacity and attempt to avoid potential congestion situations. In order to understand the difference between TCP and UDP, understanding basic TCP congestion control algorithms is very helpful.

Several congestion control enhancements have been added and suggested to TCP over the years. This is still an active and ongoing research area, but modern implementations of TCP contain four intertwined algorithms as basic Internet standards:

- Slow start
- Congestion avoidance
- Fast retransmit
- Fast recovery

5.3.3.1 Slow start

Old implementations of TCP would start a connection with the sender injecting multiple segments into the network, up to the window size advertised by the receiver. While this is OK when the two hosts are on the same LAN, if there are routers and slower links between the sender and the receiver, problems can arise. Some intermediate routers cannot handle it, packets get dropped, retransmission results and performance is degraded.

The algorithm to avoid this is called slow start. It operates by observing that the rate at which new packets should be injected into the network is the rate at which the acknowledgments are returned by the other end. Slow start adds another window to the sender's TCP: the congestion window, called cwnd. When a new connection is established with a host on another network, the congestion window is initialized to one segment (for example, the segment size announced by the other end, or the default, typically 536 or 512). Each time an ACK is received, the congestion window is increased by one segment. The sender can transmit the lower value of the congestion window or the advertised window. The congestion window is flow control imposed by the sender, while the advertised window is flow control imposed by the receiver. The former is based on the sender's assessment of perceived network congestion; the latter is related to the amount of available buffer space at the receiver for this connection.

The sender starts by transmitting one segment and waiting for its ACK. When that ACK is received, the congestion window is incremented from one to two, and two segments can be sent. When each of those two segments is acknowledged, the congestion window is increased to four. This provides an exponential growth, although it is not exactly exponential, because the receiver may delay its ACKs, typically sending one ACK for every two segments that it receives.

At some point, the capacity of the IP network (for example, slower WAN links) can be reached, and an intermediate router will start discarding packets. This tells the sender that its congestion window has gotten too large. Please see Figure 109 for an overview of slow start in action.

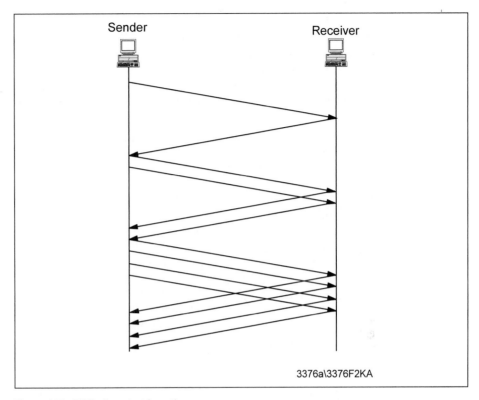

Sender

Receiver

3376a\3376F2KA

Figure 109. TCP slow start in action

5.3.3.2 Congestion avoidance

The assumption of the algorithm is that packet loss caused by damage is very small (much less than 1 percent). Therefore, the loss of a packet signals congestion somewhere in the network between the source and destination. There are two indications of packet loss:

1. A timeout occurs.

2. Duplicate ACKs are received.

Congestion avoidance and slow start are independent algorithms with different objectives. But when congestion occurs TCP must slow down its transmission rate of packets into the network, and invoke slow start to get things going again. In practice, they are implemented together.

Congestion avoidance and slow start require that two variables be maintained for each connection:

- A congestion window, cwnd

- A slow start threshold size, ssthresh

The combined algorithm operates as follows:

1. Initialization for a given connection sets cwnd to one segment and ssthresh to 65535 bytes.

2. The TCP output routine never sends more than the lower value of cwnd or the receiver's advertised window.

3. When congestion occurs (timeout or duplicate ACK), one-half of the current window size is saved in ssthresh. Additionally, if the congestion is indicated by a timeout, cwnd is set to one segment.

4. When new data is acknowledged by the other end, increase cwnd, but the way it increases depends on whether TCP is performing slow start or congestion avoidance. If cwnd is less than or equal to ssthresh, TCP is in slow start; otherwise, TCP is performing congestion avoidance.

Slow start continues until TCP is halfway to where it was when congestion occurred (since it recorded half of the window size that caused the problem in step 2), and then congestion avoidance takes over. Slow start has cwnd begin at one segment, and incremented by one segment every time an ACK is received. As mentioned earlier, this opens the window exponentially: send one segment, then two, then four, and so on.

Congestion avoidance dictates that cwnd be incremented by segsize*segsize/cwnd each time an ACK is received, where segsize is the segment size and cwnd is maintained in bytes. This is a linear growth of cwnd, compared to slow start's exponential growth. The increase in cwnd should be at most one segment each round-trip time (regardless of how many ACKs are received in that round trip time), whereas slow start increments cwnd by the number of ACKs received in a round-trip time. Many implementations incorrectly add a small fraction of the segment size (typically the segment size divided by 8) during congestion avoidance. This is wrong and should not be emulated in future releases. Please see Figure 110 for an example of TCP slow start and congestion avoidance in action.

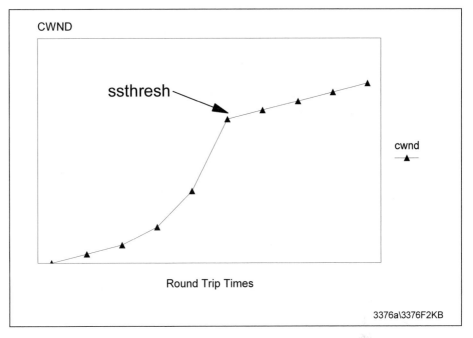

Figure 110. TCP slow start and congestion avoidance behavior in action

5.3.3.3 Fast retransmit

Fast retransmit avoids having TCP wait for a timeout to resend lost segments.

Modifications to the congestion avoidance algorithm were proposed in 1990. Before describing the change, realize that TCP may generate an immediate acknowledgment (a duplicate ACK) when an out-of-order segment is received. This duplicate ACK should not be delayed. The purpose of this duplicate ACK is to let the other end know that a segment was received out of order, and to tell it what sequence number is expected.

Since TCP does not know whether a duplicate ACK is caused by a lost segment or just a reordering of segments, it waits for a small number of duplicate ACKs to be received. It is assumed that if there is just a reordering of the segments, there will be only one or two duplicate ACKs before the reordered segment is processed, which will then generate a new ACK. If three or more duplicate ACKs are received in a row, it is a strong indication that a segment has been lost. TCP then performs a retransmission of what appears to be the missing segment, without waiting for a retransmission timer to expire. Please see Figure 111 for an overview of TCP fast retransmit in action.

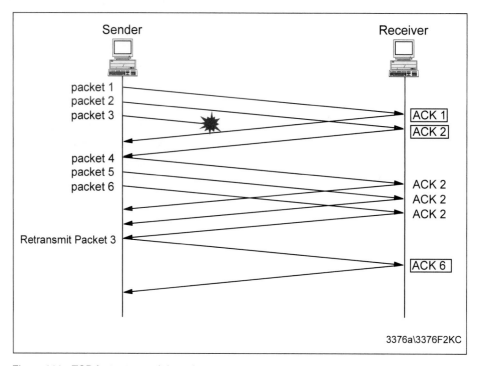

Figure 111. TCP fast retransmit in action

5.3.3.4 Fast recovery

After fast retransmit sends what appears to be the missing segment, congestion avoidance, but not slow start, is performed. This is the fast recovery algorithm. It is an improvement that allows high throughput under moderate congestion, especially for large windows.

The reason for not performing slow start in this case is that the receipt of the duplicate ACKs tells TCP more than just a packet has been lost. Since the receiver can only generate the duplicate ACK when another segment is received, that segment has left the network and is in the receiver's buffer. That is, there is still data flowing between the two ends, and TCP does not want to reduce the flow abruptly by going into slow start. The fast retransmit and fast recovery algorithms are usually implemented together as follows:

1. When the third duplicate ACK in a row is received, set ssthresh to one-half the current congestion window, cwnd, but no less than two segments. Retransmit the missing segment. Set cwnd to ssthresh plus three times the segment size. This inflates the congestion window by the number of segments that have left the network and the other end has cached (3).

2. Each time another duplicate ACK arrives, increment cwnd by the segment size. This inflates the congestion window for the additional segment that has left the network. Transmit a packet, if allowed by the new value of cwnd.

3. When the next ACK arrives that acknowledges new data, set cwnd to ssthresh (the value set in step 1). This ACK should be the acknowledgment of the retransmission from step 1, one round-trip time after the retransmission. Additionally, this ACK should acknowledge all the intermediate segments sent between the lost packet and the receipt of the first duplicate ACK. This step is congestion avoidance, since TCP is down to one-half the rate it was at when the packet was lost.

Chapter 6. IP multicast

In early IP networks, a packet could be sent to either a single device (unicast) or to all devices (broadcast). A single transmission destined for a group of devices was not possible. However, during the past few years, a new set of applications has emerged. These applications use multicast transmissions to enable efficient communication between groups of devices. Data is transmitted to a single multicast IP address and received by any device that needs to obtain the transmission.

This chapter describes the interoperation between IP multicasting, Internet Group Management Protocol (IGMP), and multicast routing protocols.

6.1 Multicast addressing

Multicast devices use Class D IP addresses to communicate. These addresses are contained in the range encompassing 224.0.0.0 through 239.255.255.255. For each multicast address, there exists a set of zero or more hosts that listen for packets transmitted to the address. This set of devices is called a *host group*. A host that sends packets to a specific group does not need to be a member of the group. The host may not even know the current members in the group. There are two types of host groups:

- Permanent: Applications that are part of this type of group have an IP address permanently assigned by the IANA. Membership in this type of host group is not permanent; a host can join or leave the group as required. A permanent group continues to exist even if it has no members. The list of IP addresses assigned to permanent host groups is included in RFC 1700. These reserved addresses include:

  - 224.0.0.0: Reserved base address
  - 224.0.0.1: All systems on this subnet
  - 224.0.0.2: All routers on this subnet
  - 224.0.0.9: All RIP2 routers

  Other address examples include those reserved for OSPF (refer to 4.6, "Open Shortest Path First (OSPF)" on page 158) They include:

  - 224.0.0.5: All OSPF routers
  - 224.0.0.6: OSPF designated routers

  An application can use DNS to obtain the IP address assigned to a permanent host group (refer to 8.1, "Domain Name System (DNS)" on page 279) using the domain mcast.net. It can determine the permanent group from an address by using a pointer query (refer to 8.1.6, "Mapping

IP addresses to domain names – pointer queries" on page 282) in the domain 224.in-addr.arpa.

- Transient: Any group that is not permanent is transient. The group is available for dynamic assignment as needed. Transient groups cease to exist when the number of members drops to zero.

6.1.1 Multicasting on a single physical network

This process is straightforward. The sending process specifies a destination IP multicast address. The device driver converts this IP address to the corresponding Ethernet address and sends the packet to the destination. The destination process informs its network device drivers that it wishes to receive datagrams destined for a given multicast address. The device driver enables reception of packets for that address.

In contrast to standard IP unicast traffic forwarding, the mapping between the IP multicast destination address and the data-link address is not done with ARP. Instead, a static mapping has been defined. In an Ethernet network, multicasting is supported if the high-order octet of the data-link address is 0x'01'. The IANA has reserved the range 0x'01005E000000' through 0x'01005E7FFFFF' for multicast addresses. This range provides 23 usable bits. The 32-bit multicast IP address is mapped to an Ethernet address by placing the low-order 23 bits of the Class D address into the low-order 23 bits of the IANA reserved address block. Figure 112 shows the mapping of a multicast IP address to the corresponding Ethernet address:

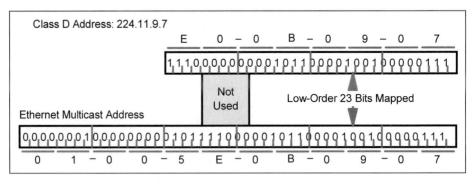

Figure 112. Mapping of Class D IP addresses to Ethernet addresses

Since the high-order five bits of the IP multicast group are ignored, 32 different multicast groups are mapped to the same Ethernet address. Because of this non-unique mapping, filtering by the device driver is required. This is done by checking the destination address in the IP header before passing the packet to the IP layer. This ensures the receiving process does not receive spurious datagrams. There are two additional reasons why filtering may be needed:

- Some LAN adapters are limited to a finite number of concurrent multicast addresses. When this limit is exceeded, they receive all multicast packets.

- The filters in some LAN adapters use a hash table value rather than the entire multicast address. If two addresses with the same hash value are used at the same time, the filter may pass excess packets.

Despite this requirement for software filtering, multicast transmissions still cause less overhead for hosts not participating in a specific session. In particular, hosts that are not participating in a host group are not listening for the multicast address. In this situation, multicast packets are filtered by lower-layer network interface hardware.

6.1.2 Multicasting between network segments

Multicast traffic is not limited to a single physical network. However, there are inherent dangers when multicasting between networks. If the environment contains multiple routers, specific precautions must be taken to ensure multicast packets do not continuously loop through the network. It is simple to create a multicast routing loop. To address this, multicast routing protocols have been developed to deliver packets while simultaneously avoiding routing loops and excess transmissions.

There are two requirements to multicast data across multiple networks:

- Determining multicast participants: A mechanism for determining if a multicast datagram needs to be forwarded on a specific network. This mechanism is defined in RFC 2236 Internet Group Management Protocol (IGMP).

- Determining multicast scope: A mechanism for determining the scope of a transmission. Unlike unicast addresses, multicast addresses can extend through the entire Internet.

  The TTL field in a multicast datagram can be used to determine the scope of a transmission. Like other datagrams, each multicast datagram has a Time To Live (TTL) field. The value contained in this field is decremented at each hop. When a host or multicast router receives a datagram, packet processing depends on both the TTL value and the destination IP address:

  - TTL = 0: A multicast datagram received with a TTL value of zero is restricted to the source host.

  - TTL = 1: A multicast datagram with a TTL value of one reaches all hosts on the subnet that are members of the group. Multicast routers decrement the value to zero. However unlike unicast datagrams, no ICMP Time Exceeded error message is returned to the source host. Datagram expiration is a standard occurrence in multicast environments.

- TTL = 2 (or more): A multicast datagram with this TTL value reaches all hosts on the subnet that are members of the group. The action performed by multicast routers depends on the specific group address:

  - 224.0.0.0 - 224.0.0.255: This range of addresses is intended for single-hop multicast applications. Multicast routers will not forward datagrams with destination addresses in this range.

    Even through multicast routers will not forward datagrams within this address range, a host must still report membership in a group within this range. The report is used to inform other hosts on the subnet that the reporting host is a member of the group.

  - Other: Datagrams with any other valid class D destination address are forwarded as normal by the multicast router. The TTL value is decremented by one at each hop.

    This allows a host to implement an *expanding ring search* to locate the nearest server listening to a specific multicast address. The host sends out a datagram with a TTL value of 1 (same subnet) and waits for a reply. If no reply is received, the host resends the datagram with a TTL value of 2. If no reply is received, the host continues to systematically increment the TTL value until the nearest server is found.

6.2 Internet Group Management Protocol (IGMP)

The Internet Group Management Protocol is used by hosts to join or leave a multicast host group. Group membership information is exchanged between a specific host and the nearest multicast router.

IGMP is best regarded as an extension to ICMP. It occupies the same position in the IP protocol stack. IGMP Version 2 is described in RFC 2236.

IGMP functions are integrated directly into IPv6 (refer to 17.3, "Internet Control Message Protocol Version 6 (ICMPv6)" on page 579). All IPv6 hosts are required to support multicasting. In IPv4, multicasting and IGMP support is optional.

6.2.1 IGMP messages

IGMP messages are encapsulated in IP datagrams. To indicate an IGMP packet, the IP header contains a protocol number of 2. The IP data field contains the 8-octet IGMP message shown in Figure 113.

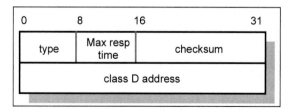

Figure 113. IGMP message format

The fields in the IGMP message contain the following information:

- Type: This field specifies the type of IGMP packet:
    - 0x'11': Specifies a membership query packet. This is sent by a multicast router. There are two sub-types of membership query messages:
        - General Query: This is used to learn which groups have members on an attached network.
        - Group-Specific Query: This is used to learn if a particular group has any members on an attached network.
    - 0x'16': Specifies a membership report packet. This is sent by a multicast host to signal participation in a specific multicast host group.
    - 0x'17': Specifies a leave group packet. This is sent by a multicast host.
- Max resp time: This field is used in membership query messages. It specifies the maximum allowed time a host can wait before sending a corresponding report. Varying this setting allows routers to tune the leave latency. This references the time between the last host leaving a group and the time the routing protocol is notified that there are no more members.
- Checksum: This field contains a 16-bit checksum.
- Class D Address: This field contains a valid multicast group address. It is used in a report packet.

Development of IGMP Version 3 has started. This version will allow receivers to subscribe to a specific set of sources within a multicast group.

6.2.2 IGMP operation

Both hosts and multicast routers participate in IGMP functions.

6.2.2.1 Host operations

To receive multicast datagrams, a host must join a host group. When a host is multi-homed, it can join groups on one or more of its attached interfaces. If a host joins the same group on multiple interfaces, the multicast messages received by the host may be different. For example, 244.0.0.1 is the group for *all* hosts on this subnet. Messages in this group received through one subnet will always be different from those on another subnet.

Multiple processes on a single host may listen for messages from the same group. When this occurs, the host joins the group once. The host internally tracks each process interested in the group.

To join a group, the host sends an IGMP membership report packet through an attached interface. The report is addressed to the desired multicast group. A host does not need to join the all hosts group (224.0.0.1). Membership in this group is automatic.

6.2.2.2 Multicast router operations

When a host attempts to join a group, multicast routers on the subnet receive the membership report packet and create an entry in their *local group database*. This database tracks the group membership of the router's directly attached networks. Each entry in the database is of the format [group, attached network]. This indicates that the attached network has at least one IP host belonging to the group. Multicast routers listen to all multicast addresses to detect these reports.

The information in the local group database is used to forward multicast datagrams. When the router receives a datagram, it is forwarded out each interface containing hosts belonging to the group.

To verify group membership, multicast routers regularly send an IGMP query message to the all hosts' multicast address. Each host that still wishes to be a member of a group sends a reply. RFC 2236 specifies this verification should occur every 125 seconds. To avoid bursts of traffic on the subnet, replies to query messages are sent using a random delay. Since routers do not track the number of hosts in each group, any host that hears another device claim membership cancels any pending membership replies. If no hosts claim membership within the specified interval, the multicast router assumes no hosts on that network are members of the group.

6.3 Multicast delivery tree

IGMP only specifies the communication occurring between receiving hosts and their local multicast router. Routing of packets between multicast routers is managed by a separate routing protocol. These protocols are described in 6.4, "Multicast forwarding algorithms" on page 236. Figure 114 shows that multicast routing protocols and IGMP operate in different sections of the *multicast delivery tree*:

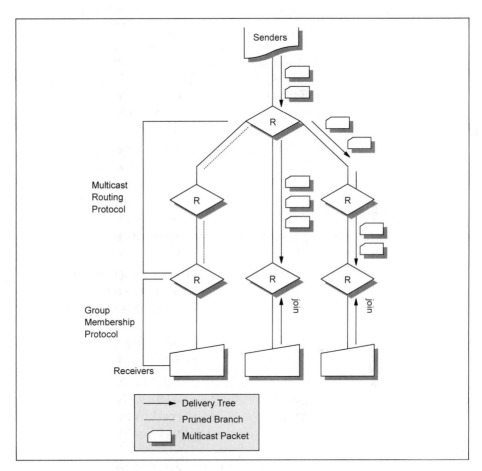

Figure 114. Multicast delivery tree

This figure shows the tree formed between a multicast sender and the set of receivers. If there are no hosts connected to a multicast router that have joined this specific group, no multicast packets for the group should be delivered to the branch connecting these hosts. The branch should be *pruned* from the delivery tree. This action reduces the size of the tree to the minimum number of branches needed to reach every group member. New sections of the tree may be dynamically added as new members join the group. This *grafts* new sections to the delivery tree.

6.4 Multicast forwarding algorithms

Multicast algorithms are used to establish paths through the network. These paths allow multicast traffic to effectively reach all group members. Each algorithm should address the following set of requirements:

- The algorithm must route data only to group members.
- The algorithm must optimize the path from source to destinations.
- The algorithm must maintain loop-free routes.
- The algorithm must provide scalable signaling functions used to create and maintain group membership.
- The algorithm must not concentrate traffic on a subset of links.

Several algorithms have been developed for use in multicast routing protocols. These algorithms have varying levels of success addressing these design requirements. Two algorithms are reviewed in the following sections.

6.4.1 Reverse path forwarding algorithm

The reverse path forwarding (RPF) algorithm uses a multicast delivery tree to forward datagrams from the source to each member in the multicast group. As shown in Figure 115, packets are replicated only at necessary branches in the delivery tree:

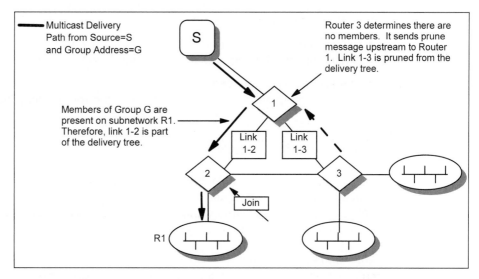

Figure 115. Reverse path forwarding (RPF)

To track the membership of individual groups, trees are calculated and updated dynamically.

The algorithm maintains a *reverse path table* used to reach each source. This table maps every known source network to the preferred interface used to reach the source. When forwarding data, if the datagram arrives through the interface used to transmit datagrams back to the source, the datagram is forwarded through every appropriate downstream interface. Otherwise, the datagram arrived through a sub-optimal path and is discarded. Using this process, duplicate packets caused by network loops are filtered.

The use of RPF provides two benefits:

- RPF guarantees the fastest delivery for multicast data. In this configuration, traffic follows the shortest path from the source to each destination.

- A different tree is computed for each source node. Packet delivery is distributed over multiple network links. This results in more efficient use of network resources.

6.4.2 Center-based tree algorithm

The center-based tree (CBT) algorithm describes another method to determine optimum paths between members of a multicast group. The algorithm describes the following steps:

- A *center point* in the network is chosen. This fixed point represents the center of the multicast group.

- Each recipient sends a join request directed towards the center point. This is accomplished using an IGMP membership report for that group.

- The request is processed by all intermediate devices located between the multicast recipient and the center point. If the router receiving the request is already a member of the tree, it marks one more interface as belonging to the group. If this is the first join request, the router forwards the request one step further towards the source.

This procedure builds a delivery tree for each multicast group. The tree is identical for all sources. Each router maintains a single tree for the entire group. This contrasts with the process used in the RPF algorithm. The RPF algorithm builds a tree for each sender in a multicast group.

Since there is no requirement for the source to be a member of the group, multicast packets from a source are forwarded toward the center point until they reach a router belonging to the tree. At this stage, the packets are forwarded using the multicast processing of the center-based tree.

The disadvantage to the center-based tree algorithm is that it may build a suboptimal path for some sources and receivers.

6.4.3 Multicast routing protocols

A number of multicast routing protocols have been developed using these algorithms:

- Distance Vector Multicast Routing Protocol (DVMRP)
- Multicast OSPF (MOSPF)
- Protocol Independent Multicast (PIM)

The remainder of this chapter details these protocols.

6.5 Distance Vector Multicast Routing Protocol (DVMRP)

DVMRP is an established multicast routing protocol. It was originally defined in RFC 1075. The standard was first implemented as the *mrouted* process available on many UNIX systems. It has since been enhanced to support RPF. DVMRP is an interior gateway protocol. It is used to build per-source per-group multicast delivery trees within an AS.

DVMRP does not route unicast datagrams. Any router that processes both multicast and unicast datagrams must be configured with two separate routing processes. Since separate processes are used, multicast and unicast traffic may not follow the same path through the network.

6.5.1 Protocol overview

DVMRP is described as a *broadcast and prune* multicast routing protocol:

- DVMRP builds per-source broadcast trees based upon routing exchanges.
- DVMRP dynamically prunes the per-source broadcast tree to create a multicast delivery tree. DVMRP uses the RPF algorithm to determine the set of downstream interfaces used to forward multicast traffic.

6.5.1.1 Neighbor discovery

DVMRP routers dynamically discover each neighbor by periodically sending neighbor probe messages on each local interface. These messages are sent to the *all-DVMRP-routers* multicast address (224.0.0.4). Each message contains a list of neighbor DVMRP routers for which neighbor probe messages have been received. This allows a DVMRP router to verify it has been seen by each neighbor.

Once a router has received a probe message that contains its address in the neighbor list, the pair of routers establish a two-way neighbor adjacency.

6.5.1.2 Routing table creation

DVMRP computes the set of reverse paths used in the RPF algorithm. To ensure all DVMRP routers have a consistent view of the path connecting to a source, a routing table is exchanged between each neighbor router. DVMRP implements its own unicast routing protocol. This routing protocol is similar to RIP.

The algorithm is based on hop counts. DVMRP requires a metric to be configured on every interface. Each router advertises the network number, mask, and metric of each interface. The router also advertises routes received from neighbor routers. Like other distance vector protocols, when a route is received, the interface metric is added to the advertised metric. This adjusted metric is used to determine the best upstream path to the source.

DVMRP has one important difference from RIP. RIP manages routing and datagram forwarding to a particular unicast destination. DVMRP manages the return path to the source of a particular multicast datagram.

6.5.1.3 Dependent downstream routers

In addition to providing a consistent view of paths to source networks, exchanging routing information provides an additional benefit. DVMRP uses this mechanism to notify upstream routers that a specific downstream router requires them to forward multicast traffic.

DVMRP accomplishes this by using the poison reverse technique (refer to 4.3.5.2, "Split horizon with poison reverse" on page 151). If a downstream router selects an upstream router as the next hop to a particular source, routing updates from the downstream router specify a metric of infinity for the source network. When the upstream router receives the advertisement, it adds the downstream router to a list of *dependent downstream routers* for this source. This technique provides the information needed to prune the multicast delivery tree.

6.5.1.4 Designated forwarder
When two or more multicast routers are connected to a multi-access network, duplicate packets may be forwarded to the network. DVMRP prevents this possibility by electing a designated forwarder for each source.

When the routers exchange their routing table, each learns the peer's metric to reach the source network. The router with the lowest metric is responsible for forwarding data to the shared network. If multiple routers have the same metric, the router with the lowest IP address becomes the designated forwarder for the network.

6.5.2 Building and maintaining multicast delivery trees
As previously mentioned, the RPF algorithm is used to forward multicast datagrams. If a datagram was received on the interface representing the best path to the source, the router forwards the datagram out a set of downstream interfaces. This set contain each downstream interface included in the multicast delivery tree.

6.5.2.1 Building the multicast delivery tree
A multicast router forwards datagrams to two types of devices: downstream dependent routers and hosts that are members of a particular multicast group. If a multicast router has no dependent downstream neighbors through a specific interface, the network is a *leaf network*. The delivery tree is built using routing information detailing these different types of destinations.

Adding leaf networks
If the downstream interface connects to a leaf network, packets are forwarded only if there are hosts that are members of the specific multicast group. The router obtains this information from the IGMP local group database. If the group address is listed in the database, and the router is the

designated forwarder for the source, the interface is included in the multicast delivery tree. If there are no group members, the interface is excluded.

Adding non-leaf networks

Initially, all non-leaf networks are included in the multicast delivery tree. This allows each downstream router to participate in traffic forwarding for each group.

6.5.2.2 Pruning the multicast delivery tree

Routers connected to leaf networks remove an interface when there are no longer any active members participating in the specific multicast group. When this occurs, multicast packets are no longer forwarded through the interface.

If a router is able to remove all of its downstream interfaces for a specific group, it notifies its upstream neighbor that it no longer needs traffic from that particular source and group pair. This notification is accomplished by sending a prune message to the upstream neighbor. If the upstream neighbor receives prune messages from each of the dependent downstream routers on an interface, the upstream router can remove this interface from the multicast delivery tree.

If the upstream router is able to prune all of its interfaces from the tree, it sends a prune message to its upstream router. This continues until all unnecessary branches have been removed from the delivery tree.

Maintaining prune information

In order to remove outdated prune information, each prune message contains a prune lifetime timer. This indicates the length of time that the prune will remain in effect. If the interface is still pruned when the timer expires, the interface is reconnected to the multicast delivery tree. If this causes unwanted multicast datagrams to be delivered to a downstream device, the prune mechanism is reinitiated.

6.5.2.3 Grafting pruned networks

Since IP multicast supports dynamic group membership, hosts may join a multicast group at any time. When this occurs, DVMRP routers use graft messages to reattach the network to the multicast delivery tree. A graft message is sent as a result of receiving a IGMP membership report for a group that has previously been pruned. Separate graft messages are sent to the appropriate upstream neighbor for each source network that has been pruned.

Receipt of a graft message is acknowledged with a graft ACK message. This allows the sender to differentiate between a lost graft packet and an inactive device. If an acknowledgment is not received within the graft timeout period, the request is retransmitted. The purpose of the graft ACK message is to acknowledge the receipt of a graft message. It does not imply any action has been taken as a result of the request. Therefore, all graft request messages are acknowledged even if they do not cause any action to be taken by the receiving router.

6.5.3 DVMRP tunnels

Some IP routers may not be configured to support native multicast routing. DVMRP provides the ability to tunnel IP multicast datagrams through networks containing non-multicast routers. The datagrams are encapsulated in unicast IP packets and forwarded through the network. This behavior is shown in Figure 116.

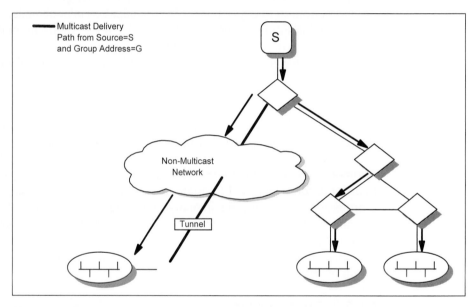

Figure 116. DVMRP tunnel

When the packet is received at the remote end of the tunnel, it is decapsulated and forwarded through the subnetwork using standard DVMRP multicast operations.

6.6 Multicast OSPF (MOSPF)

MOSPF is a multicast extension to OSPF Version 2 (refer to 4.6, "Open Shortest Path First (OSPF)" on page 158). It is defined in RFC 1584. Unlike

DVMRP, MOSPF is not a separate multicast routing protocol. It is used in networks that already utilize OSPF for unicast IP routing. The multicast extensions leverage the existing OSPF topology database to create a *source-rooted shortest path delivery tree*.

MOSPF forwards multicast datagrams using both source and destination address. This contrasts the standard OSPF algorithm, which relies solely on destination address.

6.6.1 Protocol overview

An overview of MOSPF is presented in the following sections.

6.6.1.1 Group-membership LSA

The location of every group member must be communicated to the rest of the environment. This ensures multicast datagrams are forwarded to each member. OSPF adds a new type of link state advertisement (the group-membership-LSA) to track the location of each group member. These LSAs are stored in the OSPF link state database. This database describes the topology of the AS.

6.6.1.2 Designated routers

On each network segment, one MOSPF router is selected to be the designated router (DR). This router is responsible for generating periodic IGMP host membership queries. It is also responsible for listening to the IGMP membership reports. Routers ignore any report received on a network where they are not the DR. This ensures each network segment appears in the local group database of at most one router. It also prevents datagrams from being duplicated as they are delivered to local group members.

Every router floods a group-membership-LSA for each multicast group having at least one entry in the router's local group database. This LSA is flooded throughout the OSPF area.

6.6.1.3 Shortest-path delivery trees

The path used to forward a multicast datagram is calculated by building a shortest-path delivery tree rooted at the datagram's source (refer to 4.2.3.1, "Shortest-Path First (SPF) algorithm" on page 143). This tree is built from information contained in the link state database. Any branch in the shortest-path delivery tree that does not have a corresponding group-membership-LSA is pruned. These branches do not contain any multicast members for the specific group.

Initially, shortest-path delivery trees are built when the first datagram is received. The results are cached for use by subsequent datagrams having the same source and destination. The tree is recomputed when a link state change occurs or when the cache information times out.

In an MOSPF network, all routers calculate an identical shortest-path delivery tree for a specific multicast datagram. There is a single path between the datagram source and any specific destination. This means that unlike OSPF's treatment of unicast traffic, MOSPF has no provision for equal-cost multipath.

6.6.2 MOSPF and multiple OSPF areas

OSPF allows an AS to be split into areas. While this has several traffic management benefits, it limits the topology information maintained in each router. A router is only aware of the network topology within the local area. When building shortest-path trees in these environments, the information contained in the link state database is not sufficient to describe the complete path between each source and destination. This may lead to non-optimal path selection.

Within an OSPF area, the area border router (ABR) forwards routing information and data traffic between areas. The corresponding functions in an MOSPF environment are performed by an *inter-area multicast forwarder*. This device forwards group membership information and multicast datagrams between areas. An OSPF ABR can also function as an MOSPF inter-area multicast forwarder.

Since group-membership-LSAs are only flooded within an area, a process to convey membership information between areas is required. To accomplish this, each inter-area multicast forwarder summarizes the attached areas' group membership requirements and forwards this information into the OSPF backbone. This announcement is comprised of a group-membership-LSA listing each group containing members in the non-backbone area. The advertisement performs the same function as the summary LSAs generated in a standard OSPF area.

However, unlike route summarization in a standard OSPF network, summarization for multicast group membership in MOSPF is asymmetric. Membership information for the non-backbone area is summarized into the backbone. However, this information is not readvertised into other non-backbone areas.

To forward multicast data traffic between areas, a *wild-card multicast receiver* is used. This is a router to which all multicast traffic, regardless of destination, is forwarded. In non-backbone areas, all inter-area multicast forwarders are wild-card multicast receivers. This ensures all multicast traffic originating in a non-backbone area is forwarded to a inter-area multicast forwarder. This router sends the multicast datagrams to the backbone area. Since the backbone has complete knowledge of all group membership information, the datagrams are then forwarded to the appropriate group members in other areas.

6.6.3 MOSPF and multiple autonomous systems

An analogous situation to inter-area multicast routing exists when at least one multicast device resides in another AS. In both cases, the shortest path tree describing the complete path from source to destination cannot be built.

In this environment, an ASBR in the MOSPF domain is configured as an *inter-AS multicast forwarder*. This router is also configured with an inter-AS multicast routing protocol. While the MOSPF standard does not dictate the operations of the inter-AS protocol, it does assume the protocol forwards datagrams using RPF principles. Specifically, MOSPF assumes that a multicast datagram whose source is outside the domain will enter the domain at a point that is advertising (into OSPF) the best route to the source. MOSPF uses this information to calculate the path of the datagram through the domain.

MOSPF designates an inter-AS multicast forwarder as a wild-card multicast receiver. As with inter-area communications, this ensures that the receiver remains on all pruned shortest-path delivery trees. They receive all multicast datagrams, regardless of destination. Since this device has complete knowledge of all group membership outside the AS, datagrams can be forwarded to group members in other autonomous systems.

6.6.4 MOSPF interoperability

Routers configured to support an MOSPF network can be intermixed with non-multicast OSPF routers. Both types of routers interoperate when forwarding unicast data traffic. However, forwarding IP multicast traffic is limited to the MOSPF domain. Unlike DVMRP, MOSPF does not provide the ability to tunnel multicast traffic through non-multicast routers.

6.7 Protocol Independent Multicast (PIM)

The complexity associated with MOSPF lead to the development and deployment of PIM. PIM is another multicast routing protocol. Unlike MOSPF,

PIM is independent of any underlying unicast routing protocol. It interoperates with all existing unicast routing protocols.

PIM defines two modes or operation:

- Dense mode (PIM-DM)
- Sparse mode (PIM-SM), specified in RFC 2362

Dense mode and sparse mode refer to the density of group members within an area. In a random sampling, a group is considered dense if the probability of finding at least one group member within the sample is high. This holds even if the sample size is reasonably small. A group is considered sparse if the probability of finding group members within the sample is low.

PIM provides the ability to switch between spare mode and dense mode. It also permits both modes to be used within the same group.

6.7.1 PIM dense mode

The PIM-DM protocol implements the RPF process described in 6.4.1, "Reverse path forwarding algorithm" on page 236. Specifically, when a PIM-DM device receives a packet, it validates the incoming interface with the existing unicast routing table. If the incoming interface reflects the best path back to the source, the router floods the multicast packet. The packet is sent out to every interface that has not been pruned from the multicast delivery tree.

Unlike DVMRP, PIM-DM does not attempt to compute multicast specific routes. Rather, it assumes that the routes in the unicast routing table are symmetric.

Similar to operations in a DVMRP environment, a PIM-DM device initially assumes all downstream interfaces need to receive multicast traffic. The router floods datagrams to all areas of the network. If some areas do not have receivers for the specific multicast group, PIM-DM reactively prunes these branches from the delivery tree. This reactive pruning is done because PIM-DM does not obtain downstream receiver information from the unicast routing table. Figure 117 contains an example of a PIM-DM pruning.

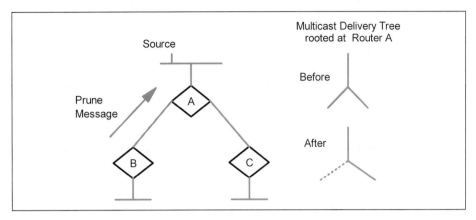

Figure 117. PIM-DM flood and prune operation

PIM-DM is relatively simple to implement. The only assumption is that a router is able to retain a list of prune requests.

6.7.1.1 PIM-DM benefits

Given the flood and prune methodology used in PIM-DM, this protocol should be used in environments where the majority of hosts within a domain need to receive the multicast data. In these environments, the majority of networks will not be pruned from the delivery tree. The overhead associated with flooding is minimal. This configuration is also appropriate when:

- Senders and receivers are in close proximity to each other.
- There are few senders and many receivers.
- The volume of multicast traffic is high.
- The stream of multicast traffic is constant.

Unlike DVMRP, PIM-DM does not support tunnels to transmit multicast traffic through non-multicast capable networks. Therefore, the network administrator must ensure each device connected to the end-to-end path is multicast-enabled.

6.7.2 PIM sparse mode

The PIM-SM protocol uses a variant of the center-based tree algorithm. In a PIM-SM network, a *rendezvous point (RP)* is analogous to the center point described in the algorithm. Specifically, an RP is the location in the network where multicast senders connect to multicast receivers. Receivers join a tree rooted at the RP. Senders register their existence with the RP. Initially, traffic from the sender flows through the RP to reach each receiver

The benefit of PIM-SM is that unlike DVMRP and PIM-DM networks, multicast data is blocked from a network segment unless a downstream device specifically asks to receive the data. This has the potential to significantly reduce the amount of traffic traversing the network. It also implies that no pruning information is maintained for locations with no receivers. This information is maintained only in devices connected to the multicast delivery tree. Because of these benefits, PIM-SM is currently the most popular multicast routing protocol used in the Internet.

6.7.2.1 Building the PIM-SM multicast delivery tree

The basic PIM-SM interaction with the RP is described below:

1. A multicast router sends periodic join messages to a group-specific RP. Each router along the path towards the RP builds and sends join requests to the RP. This builds a group-specific multicast delivery tree rooted at the RP. Like other multicast protocols, the tree is actually a reverse path tree, because join requests follow a reverse path from the receiver to the RP. This function is shown in Figure 118.

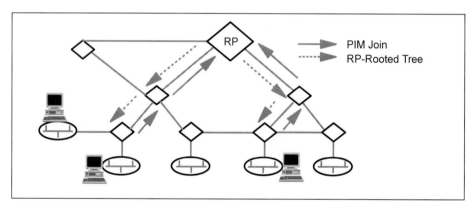

Figure 118. Creating the RP-rooted delivery tree

2. The multicast router connecting to the source initially encapsulates each multicast packet in a register message. These messages are sent to the RP. The RP decapsulates these unicast messages and forwards the data packets to the set of downstream receivers. This function is shown in Figure 119.

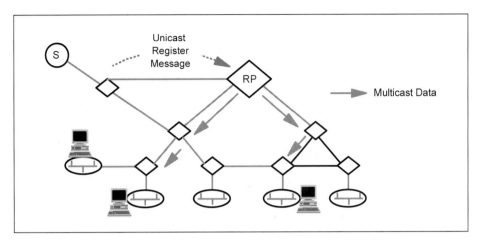

Figure 119. Registering a source

3. The RP-based delivery tree may reflect suboptimal routes to some receivers. To optimize these connections, the router may create a *source-based* multicast delivery tree. This function is shown in Figure 120.

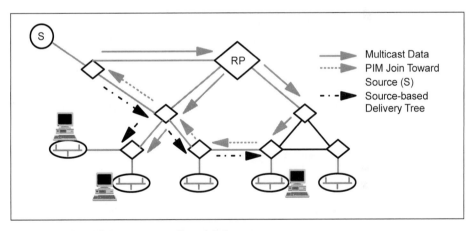

Figure 120. Establishing a source-based delivery tree

4. After the router receives multicast packets through both the source-based delivery tree and the RP-based delivery tree, PIM prune messages are sent towards the RP to prune this branch of the tree. When complete, multicast data from the source flows only through the source-based delivery tree. This function is shown in Figure 121.

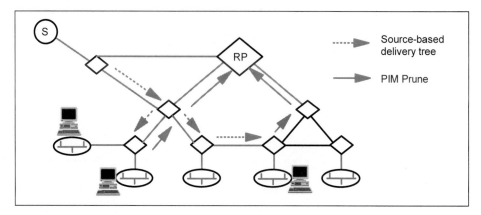

Figure 121. Eliminating the RP-based delivery tree

The switch to the source-based tree occurs after a significant number of packets have been received from the source. To implement this policy, the router monitors the quantity of packets received through the RP-based delivery tree. When this data rate exceeds a configured threshold, the device initiates the change.

6.7.2.2 RP selection

An RP is selected as part of standard PIM-SM operations. An RP is mapped to each specific multicast group. To perform this mapping, a router configured to support PIM-SM distributes a list of candidate RPs to all other routers in the environment. When a mapping needs to be performed, each router hashes the multicast group address into an IP address that represents the RP.

6.7.2.3 PIM-SM benefits

PIM-SM is optimized for environments containing a large number of multicast data streams. Each stream should flow to a relatively small number of the LAN segments. For these groups, the flooding and pruning associated with PIM-DM and DVMRP would be an inefficient use of network bandwidth. PIM-SM is also appropriate when:

- There are few receivers in a group.
- Senders and receivers are separated by WAN links.
- The stream of multicast traffic is intermittent.

Like PIM-DM, PIM-SM assumes the route obtained through the unicast routing protocol supports multicast routing. Therefore, the network administrator must ensure each device connected to the end-to-end path is multicast-enabled.

6.8 Interconnecting multicast domains

Early multicast development focused on a flat network topology. This differed from the hierarchical topology deployed in the Internet. Like the Internet, multicast developers soon realized the need to perform inter-domain routing. New classes of protocol have been proposed to address this deficiency. There are currently two approaches to interconnecting multicast domains.

6.8.1 Multicast Source Discovery Protocol (MSDP)

MSDP is a protocol to logically connect multiple PIM-SM domains. It is used to find active multicast sources in other domains. RPs in separate autonomous systems communicate through MSDP to exchange information about these multicast sources. Each domain continues to use its own RP. There is no direct dependence on other RPs for intra-domain communication.

Typically, each AS will contain one MSDP-speaking RP. Other autonomous systems create MSDP peer sessions with this RP. These sessions are used to exchange the lists of source speakers in each specific multicast group.

MSDP is not directly involved in multicast data delivery. Its purpose is to discover sources in other domains. If a device in one domain wishes to receive data from a source in another domain, the data is delivered using the standard operations within PIM-SM.

MSDP peers will usually be separated by multiple hops. All devices used to support this remote communication must be multicast capable.

MSDP relies heavily on the Multiprotocol Extensions to BGP (MBGP) for interdomain communication. An MBGP overview is presented in the 6.8.1.3, "Multiprotocol extensions for BGP-4" on page 253.

6.8.1.1 MSDP operations

To establish multicast communications between a source in one domain and receivers in other domains, MSDP uses the following steps:

- Following standard PIM-SM operations, the DR for the source sends a PIM register message to the RP. That data packet is decapsulated by the RP and forwarded down the shared tree to receivers in the same domain.

- The packet is also re-encapsulated in a *source-active (SA)* message. This message is sent to all MSDP peers. The SA message identifies the source and group. This operation occurs when the source becomes active.

When an RP for a domain receives an SA message from a MSDP peer, it determines if it has any members interested in the group described by the SA message. If there is an interested party, the RP triggers a join towards the source. Once the path has been established and the RP is forwarding data, the receiver may switch to the shortest-path tree directly to the source. This is done with standard PIM-SM conventions.

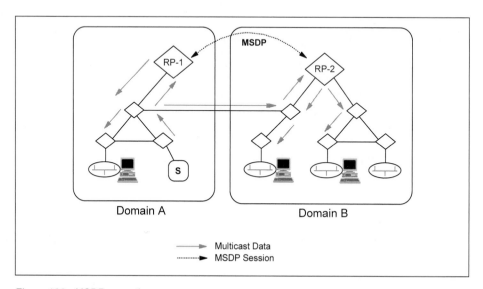

Figure 122. MSDP operations

Each MSDP peer receives and forwards SA messages. Each peer examines the MBGP routing table to determine the next-hop peer towards the originating RP. The router forwards the SA message to all MSDP peers other than the RPF peer. If the router receives the SA message from a peer that is not the next-hop peer, the message is discarded. This floods the announcements through the entire network. It is similar to the RPF processing described in 6.4.1, "Reverse path forwarding algorithm" on page 236. See Figure 122 for an overview of MSDP operations.

6.8.1.2 MSDP limitations
MSDP is not currently an IETF standard, but it is deployed in numerous network environments. Because of the periodic flood and prune messages associated with MSDP, this protocol does not scale to the address the potential needs of the Internet. It is expected that MSDP will be replaced with the Border Gateway Multicast Protocol (BGMP). This protocol is reviewed in the 6.8.2, "Border Gateway Multicast Protocol" on page 253.

6.8.1.3 Multiprotocol extensions for BGP-4

When interconnecting multicast domains, it is possible that unicast routing may select a path containing devices that do not support multicast traffic. This results in multicast join messages not reaching the intended destination.

To solve this problem, MSDP uses the MBGP protocol. This is a set of extensions allowing BGP to maintain separate routing tables for different protocols. Thus, MBGP can create routes for both unicast and multicast traffic. The multicast routes can traverse around the portions of the environment that do not support multicast. It permits links to be dedicated to multicast traffic. Alternatively, it can limit the resources used to support each type of traffic.

The information associated with the multicast routes is used by PIM to build distribution trees. The standard services for filtering and preference setting are available with MBGP. MBGP is defined in RFC 2283.

6.8.2 Border Gateway Multicast Protocol

BGMP is a multicast routing protocol that builds shared domain trees. Like PIM-SM, BGMP chooses a global root for the delivery tree. However, in BGMP, the root is a domain, not a single router. This allows connectivity to the domain to be maintained whenever any path is available to the domain.

Similar to the cooperation between an EGP and an IGP in a unicast environment, BGMP is used as the inter-domain multicast protocol. Any multicast IGP can be used internally.

BGMP operates between border routers in each domain. It does not use an RP. Join messages are used to construct trees between domains. Border routers learn from the multicast IGP whenever a host is interested in participating in an interdomain multicast group. When this occurs, the border router sends a join message to the root domain. Peer devices forward this request towards the root. This forms the shared tree used for multicast delivery.

The BGMP specification requires multicast addresses to be allocated to particular domains. The specification *suggests* the use of the Multicast Address-Set Claim (MASC) protocol to achieve this result. MASC is a separate protocol allowing domains to claim temporary responsibility for a range of addresses. The BGMP specification does not mandate the use of MASC. MASC is described in RFC 2909.

6.9 The multicast backbone

The Internet multicast backbone (MBONE) was established in March 1992. It was initially deployed to provide hands-on experience with multicast protocols. The first uses provided audio multicasting of IETF meetings. At that time, 20 sites were connected to the backbone. Two years later, simultaneous audio and video transmissions were distributed to more than 500 participants located in 15 countries. Since then, the MBONE has been used to broadcast NASA Space Shuttle missions, rock concerts and numerous technical conferences. Commercial and private use of the MBONE continues to increase.

The multicast backbone started as a virtual overlay network using much of the physical Internet infrastructure. At that time, multicast routing was not supported in standard routing devices. The first MBONE points-of-presence were UNIX systems configured with the mrouted routing process. Today, the MBONE is still operational, but multicast connectivity is natively included in many Internet routers. Efforts continue to integrate the MBONE directly into the Internet infrastructure.

6.9.1 MBONE routing

Multicast traffic does not flow to every Internet location. Until that occurs, the MBONE will consist of a set of multicast network islands. These islands are interconnected through virtual tunnels. The tunnels bridge through areas that do not support multicast traffic.

A router that needs to send multicast packets to another multicast island encapsulates the packets in unicast packets. These encapsulated packets are transmitted through the standard Internet routers. The destination address contained in the unicast packets is the endpoint of the tunnel. The router at the remote end of the tunnel removes the encapsulation header and forwards the multicast packets to the receiving devices.

An overview of an MBONE tunnel's structure is shown in Figure 123.

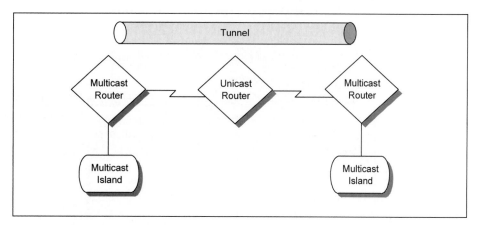

Figure 123. MBONE tunnel

MBONE tunnels have associated metric and threshold parameters. The metric parameter is used as a cost in the multicast routing algorithm. The routing algorithm uses this value to select the best path through the network. Figure 124 depicts an environment containing four multicast sites interconnected via MBONE tunnels. The tunnels have been assigned different metric values to skew traffic forwarding through the network.

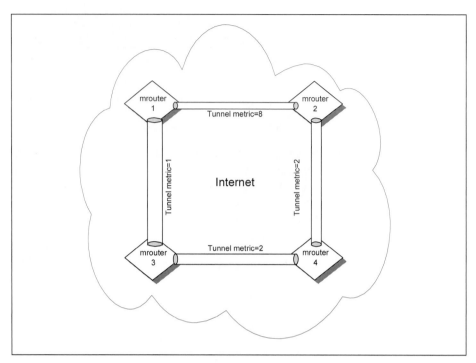

Figure 124. MBONE tunnel metric

A multicast packet sent from router 1 to router 2 should not use the tunnel directly connecting router 1 and router 2. The cost of the alternate path using router 3 and router 4 is 5 (1 + 2 + 2). This is more attractive that the direct path between router 1 and router 2; this path has a cost of 8.

The threshold parameter limits the distribution of multicast packets. It specifies a minimum TTL for a multicast packet forwarded into an established tunnel. The TTL is decremented by 1 at each multicast router.

In the future, most Internet routers will provide direct support for IP multicast. This will eliminate the need for multicast tunnels. The current MBONE implementation is only a temporary solution. It will become obsolete when multicasting is fully supported in every Internet router.

6.9.2 Multicast applications

The first multicast applications provided audio conferencing functions. These applications have increased in usability and functionality. Recently, development of multicast systems has accelerated. New and improved applications are being delivered to support:

- Multimedia conferencing: These tools have been used on the MBONE for several years. They support many-to-many audio-only or audio-video communication. When used in conjunction with whiteboard applications, these conferences enhance collaboration while requiring minimal bandwidth.

- Data distribution: These tools provide the ability to simultaneously deliver data to large numbers of receivers. For example, a central site can efficiently push updated data files to each district office.

- Gaming and Simulation: These applications have been readily available. However, the integration of multicast services allow the applications to scale to a large number of users. Multicast groups can represent different sections of the game or simulation. As users move from one section to the next, they exit and join different multicast groups.

- Real-time data multicast: These applications distribute real-time data to large numbers of users. For example, stock ticker information can be provided to sets of workstations. The use of multicast groups can tailor the information received by a specific device.

Many of these applications use UDP instead of the usual TCP transport support. With TCP, reliability and flow control mechanisms have not been optimized for real-time broadcasting of multimedia data. Frequently, the potential to lose a small percentage of packets is preferred to the transmission delays introduced with TCP.

In addition to UDP, most applications use the Real-Time Transport Protocol (refer to 13.1.1, "The Real-Time Transport Protocol (RTP)" on page 450). This protocol provides mechanisms to continuously transmit multimedia data streams through the Internet without incurring additional delays.

Chapter 7. Application structure and programming interfaces

The highest level protocols are called application protocols. They communicate with applications on other hosts and are the user-visible interface to the TCP/IP protocol suite.

7.1 Characteristics of applications

All of the higher level protocols have some characteristics in common:

- They can be user-written applications or applications standardized and shipped with the TCP/IP product. Indeed, the TCP/IP protocol suite includes application protocols such as:

  - TELNET for interactive terminal access to remote hosts.

  - FTP (file transfer protocol) for high-speed disk-to-disk file transfers.

  - SMTP (simple mail transfer protocol) as an Internet mailing system.

  These are the most widely implemented application protocols, but a lot of others exist. Each particular TCP/IP implementation will include a more or less restricted set of application protocols.

- They use either UDP or TCP as a transport mechanism. Remember that UDP (see 5.2, "User Datagram Protocol (UDP)" on page 204) is unreliable and offers no flow control, so in this case the application has to provide its own error recovery and flow control routines. It is often easier to build applications on top of TCP (see 5.3, "Transmission Control Protocol (TCP)" on page 206), a reliable, connection-oriented protocol. Most application protocols will use TCP, but there are applications built on UDP to provide better performance through reduced protocol overhead.

- Most of them use the client/server model of interaction.

7.1.1 Client/server model

TCP is a peer-to-peer, connection-oriented protocol. There are no master/slave relations. The applications, however, use a client/server model for communications (see Figure 125).

A *server* is an application that offers a service to users; a *client* is a requester of a service. An application consists of both a server and a client part, which can run on the same or on different systems.

Users usually invoke the client part of the application, which builds a request for a particular service and sends it to the server part of the application using TCP/IP as a transport vehicle.

The server is a program that receives a request, performs the required service, and sends back the results in a reply. A server can usually deal with multiple requests (multiple clients) at the same time.

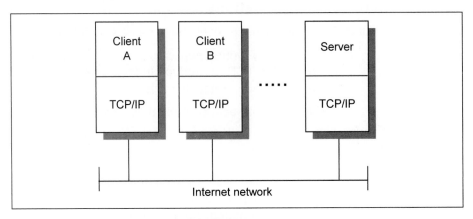

Figure 125. The client/server model of applications

Some servers wait for requests at a well-known port (see 5.1, "Ports and sockets" on page 201) so their clients know to which IP socket to direct their requests. The client uses an arbitrary port for its communication. Clients that wish to communicate with a server that does not use a well-known port must have another mechanism for learning to which port they must address their requests. This mechanism might employ a registration service such as portmap, which uses a well-known port.

7.2 Application programming interfaces (APIs)

Application programming interfaces allow developers to write applications that can make use of TCP/IP services. The following sections provide an overview of the most common APIs for TCP/IP applications.

7.2.1 The socket API

The socket interface is one of several application programming interfaces (APIs) to the communication protocols. Designed to be a generic communication programming interface, it was first introduced by the 4.2BSD UNIX-based system. Although it has not been standardized, it has become a *de facto* industry standard.

The socket interface is differentiated by the services that are provided to applications: stream sockets (connection-oriented), datagram sockets (connectionless), and raw sockets (direct access to lower layer protocols) services. Please see 5.1, "Ports and sockets" on page 201 for more detail about ports and sockets.

A variation of the BSD sockets interface is provided by the Winsock interface developed by Microsoft and other vendors to support TCP/IP applications on the Windows operating systems. Winsock 2.0, the latest version, provides a more generalized interface, allowing applications to communicate with any available transport layer protocol and underlying network services, including, but no longer limited to, TCP/IP. Please see 7.2.3, "Windows Sockets Version 2 (Winsock V2.0)" on page 271 for more information about Winsock.

7.2.1.1 Basic socket calls

The following lists some basic socket interface calls. In the next section, we see an example scenario that uses these socket interface calls.

- Initialize a socket.

  Format:

  ```
  int sockfd = socket(int family, int type, int protocol)
  ```

  Where:

    - family stands for addressing family. It can take on values such as AF_UNIX, AF_INET, AF_NS, AF_OS2, and AF_IUCV. Its purpose is to specify the method of addressing used by the socket.
    - type stands for the type of socket interface to be used. It can take on values such as SOCK_STREAM, SOCK_DGRAM, SOCK_RAW, and SOCK_SEQPACKET.
    - protocol can be UDP, TCP, IP, or ICMP.
    - sockfd is an integer (similar to a file descriptor) returned by the socket call. This will be passed as a parameter to subsequent socket calls.

- Bind (register) a socket to a port address.

  Format:

  ```
  int bind(int sockfd, struct sockaddr *localaddr, int addrlen)
  ```

  Where localaddr is the local address returned by the bind call.

  Note that after the bind call, we now have values for the first three parameters inside our 5-tuple association:

  ```
  {protocol, local-address, local-process, foreign-address, foreign-process}
  ```

- Listen for incoming connections. Indicates readiness to receive connections.

Format:

```
int listen(int sockfd, int queue-size)
```

Where queue-size indicates the number of connection requests that can be queued by the system while the local process has not yet issued the accept call.

- Accept a connection.

  Format:

  ```
  int accept(int sockfd, struct sockaddr *foreign-address, int addrlen)
  ```

  Where foreign-address is the address of the foreign (client) process returned by the accept call.

  Note that this accept call is issued by a server process rather than a client process. If there is a connection request waiting on the queue for this socket connection, accept takes the first request on the queue and creates another socket with the same properties as sockfd; otherwise, accept will block the caller process until a connection request arrives.

- Connect out to server.

  Format:

  ```
  int connect(int sockfd, struct sockaddr *foreign-address, int addrlen)
  ```

  Where foreign-address is the address of the foreign (server) process returned by the connect call.

  Note that this call is issued by a client process rather than a server process.

- Send/receive data.

  The read(), readv(sockfd, char *buffer int addrlen), recv(), readfrom(), send(sockfd, msg, len, flags), and write() calls can be used to receive and send data in an established socket association (or connection).

  Note that these calls are similar to the standard read and write file I/O system calls.

- Close a socket.

  Format:

  ```
  int close(int sockfd)
  ```

For more details, please refer to the literature listed in Appendix C, "Related publications" on page 917.

7.2.1.2 An example scenario

As an example, consider the socket system calls for a connection-oriented protocol:

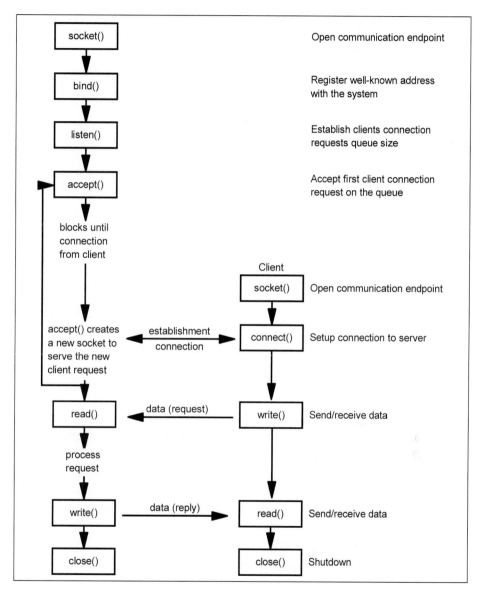

Figure 126. Socket system calls for connection-oriented protocol

The connectionless scenario is simpler, in that the listen/accept/connect stages are missed out.

Let us compare the system calls used for connection-orientated and connectionless mode:

Table 3. Socket system calls

Type	Establish	Send	Receive
Connection-orientated server	bind, listen, or accept	write or sendto	read or recvfrom
Connection-orientated client	connect	write or sendto	read or recvfrom
Connectionless server	bind	sendto	recvfrom
Connectionless client	bind	sendto	recvfrom

The socket interface is differentiated by the different services that are provided. Stream, datagram, and raw sockets each define a different service available to applications.

- Stream socket interface (SOCK_STREAM):
  Defines a reliable connection-oriented service (for example, over TCP). Data is sent without errors or duplication and is received in the same order as it is sent. Flow control is built-in to avoid data overruns. No boundaries are imposed on the exchanged data, which is considered to be a stream of bytes. An example of an application that uses stream sockets is the File Transfer Program (FTP).

- Datagram socket interface (SOCK_DGRAM):
  It defines a connectionless service (for example, over UDP). Datagrams are sent as independent packets. The service provides no guarantees; data can be lost or duplicated, and datagrams can arrive out of order. No disassembly and reassembly of packets is performed. An example of an application that uses datagram sockets is the Network File System (NFS).

- Raw socket interface (SOCK_RAW):
  It allows direct access to lower layer protocols, such as IP and ICMP. This interface is often used for testing new protocol implementations. An example of an application that uses raw sockets is the `ping` command.

7.2.2 Remote Procedure Call (RPC)

Remote Procedure Call is a standard developed by Sun Microsystems and used by many vendors of UNIX-based systems.

RPC is an application programming interface (API) available for developing distributed applications. It allows programs to call subroutines that are executed at a remote system. The caller program (called client) sends a call message to the server process, and waits for a reply message. The call message includes the procedure's parameters and the reply message contains the procedure's results. RPC also provides a standard way of encoding data in a portable fashion between different systems called External Data Representation (XDR).

7.2.2.1 RPC concept

The concept of RPC is very similar to that of an application program issuing a procedure call:

- The caller process sends a call message and waits for the reply.
- On the server side, a process is dormant awaiting the arrival of call messages. When one arrives, the server process extracts the procedure parameters, computes the results, and sends them back in a reply message.

See Figure 127 for a conceptual model of RPC.

This is only a possible model, as the Sun RPC protocol does not put restrictions on the concurrency model. In the model above, the caller's execution blocks until a reply message is received. Other models are possible; for example, the caller may continue processing while waiting for a reply, or the server may dispatch a separate task for each incoming call so that it remains free to receive other messages.

The remote procedure calls differ from local procedure calls in the following ways:

- Use of global variables as the server has no access to the caller program's address space.
- Performance may be affected by the transmission times.
- User authentication may be necessary.
- Location of server must be known.

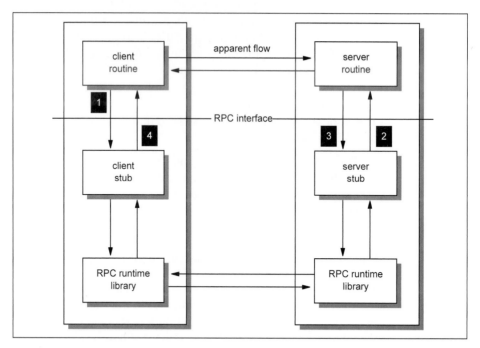

Figure 127. RPC - Remote Procedure Call model

Transport

The RPC protocol can be implemented on any transport protocol. In the case of TCP/IP, it can use either TCP or UDP as the transport vehicle. The type of the *transport* is a parameter of the RPCGEN command. In case UDP is used, remember that this does not provide reliability, so it will be up to the caller program itself to ensure this (using timeouts and retransmissions, usually implemented in RPC library routines). Note that even with TCP, the caller program still needs a timeout routine to deal with exceptional situations, such as a server crash.

The call and reply message data is formatted to the XDR standard.

RPC call message

The RPC call message consists of several fields:

- Program and procedure numbers

  Each call message contains three fields (unsigned integers) that uniquely identify the procedure to be executed:

  - Remote program number
  - Remote program version number

- Remote procedure number

The remote program number identifies a functional group of procedures, for example, a file system, which would include individual procedures such as read and write. These individual procedures are identified by a unique procedure number within the remote program. As the remote program evolves, a version number is assigned to the different releases.

Each remote program is attached to an internet port. The number of this port can be freely chosen, except for the reserved well-known-services port numbers. It is evident that the caller will have to know the port number used by this remote program.

Assigned program numbers:

00000000 - 1FFFFFFF	Defined by Sun
20000000 - 3FFFFFFF	Defined by user
40000000 - 5FFFFFFF	Transient (temporary numbers)
60000000 - FFFFFFFF	Reserved

- Authentication fields

Two fields, *credentials* and *verifier*, are provided for the authentication of the caller to the service. It is up to the server to use this information for user authentication. Also, each implementation is free to choose the varieties of supported authentication protocols. Some authentication protocols are:

- Null authentication.
- UNIX authentication. The callers of a remote procedure may identify themselves as they are identified on the UNIX system.
- DES authentication. In addition to user ID, a timestamp field is sent to the server. This timestamp is the current time, enciphered using a key known to the caller machine and server machine only (based on the *secret key* and *public key* concept of DES).

- Procedure parameters

Data (parameters) passed to the remote procedure.

RPC reply message
Several replies exist, depending on the action taken:

- SUCCESS: Procedure results are sent back to the client.
- RPC_MISMATCH: Server is running another version of RPC than the caller.
- AUTH_ERROR: Caller authentication failed.

- PROG_MISMATCH: If program is unavailable or if the version asked for does not exist or if the procedure is unavailable.

For a detailed description of the call and reply messages, see RFC 1057 – RPC: Remote Procedure Call Protocol Specification Version 2, which also contains the type definitions (typedef) for the messages in XDR language.

Portmap or portmapper

The portmap or portmapper is a server application that will map a program number and its version number to the Internet port number used by the program. Portmap is assigned the reserved (well-known service) port number 111.

Portmap only knows about RPC programs on the host it runs on. In order for portmap to know about the RPC programs, every RPC program should register itself with the local portmapper when it starts up.

The RPC client (caller) has to ask the portmap service on the remote host about the port used by the desired server program.

Normally, the calling application would contact portmap on the destination host to obtain the correct port number for a particular remote program, and then send the call message to this particular port. A variation exists when the caller also sends the procedure data along to portmap and then the remote portmap directly invokes the procedure.

See Figure 128 for more details.

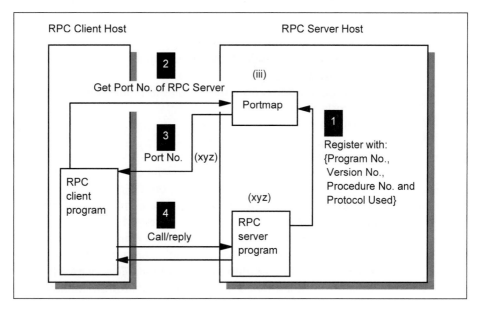

Figure 128. RPC - Portmap

RPCGEN

RPCGEN is a tool that generates C code to implement an RPC protocol. The input to RPCGEN is a file written in a language similar to C, known as the RPC language. Assuming that an input file named proto.x is used, RPCGEN produces the following output files:

- A header file called proto.h that contains common definitions of constants and macros
- Client stub source file, protoc.c
- Server stub source file, protos.c
- XDR routines source file, protox.c

7.2.3 Windows Sockets Version 2 (Winsock V2.0)

Winsock V2.0 is a network programming interface. It is basically a version of Berkeley Sockets adapted for Microsoft Windows operating systems with more functions and enhancements. The previous version of the Winsock API, Windows Sockets V1.1, is widely implemented. Therefore, Winsock V2.0 retains backwards compatibility with Winsock V1.1 but provides many more functions. One of the most significant aspects of Winsock V2.0 is that it provides a protocol-independent transport interface supporting various networking capabilities. Besides, Winsock V2.0 also supports the coexistence of multiple protocol stacks. The new functions of Winsock V2.0 can be summarized as follows:

- Support for multiple protocols
- Protocol-independent name resolution
- Quality of Service
- Protocol-independent multicast and multipoint
- Overlapped I/O and event objects
- Socket sharing
- Layered service providers

The Winsock V1.1 architecture permits only one Dynamic Link Library (DLL), WINSOCK.DLL or WSOCK32.DLL, on a system at a time, which provides the Winsock API with a way to communicate with an underlying transport protocol. This approach restricts the use of different types of Winsock implementations in conjunction with Winsock V1.1. For systems that have more than one network interface, this can become a hindrance. Winsock V2.0 provides a better solution to this problem. The Winsock V2.0 architecture allows for simultaneous support of multiple protocol stacks, interfaces, and service providers.

See Figure 129 for more details.

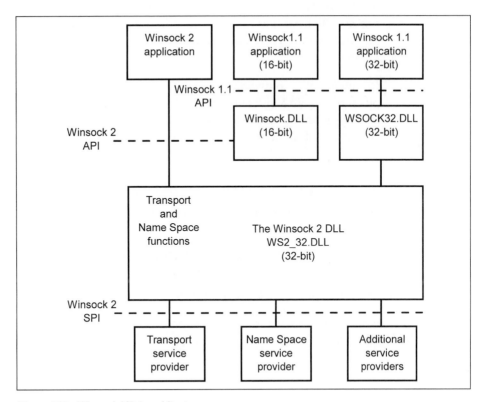

Figure 129. Winsock V2.0 architecture

7.2.4 SNMP Distributed Programming Interface (SNMP DPI)

SNMP defines a protocol that permits operations on a collection of variables. This set of variables (MIB) and a core set of variables have previously been defined. However, the design of the MIB makes provision for extension of this core set. Unfortunately, conventional SNMP agent implementations provide no means for an end user to make new variables available. The SNMP DPI addresses this issue by providing a light-weight mechanism that permits end users to dynamically add, delete, or replace management variables in the local MIB without requiring recompilation of the SNMP agent. This is achieved by writing the so-called subagent that communicates with the agent via the SNMP DPI. It is described in RFC 1592.

The SNMP DPI allows a process to register the existence of a MIB variable with the SNMP agent. When requests for the variable are received by the SNMP agent, it will pass the query on to the process acting as a subagent. This subagent then returns an appropriate answer to the SNMP agent. The SNMP agent eventually packages an SNMP response packet and sends the answer back to the remote network management station that initiated the request. None of the remote network management stations have any knowledge that the SNMP agent calls on other processes to obtain an answer.

Communication between the SNMP agent and its clients (subagents) takes place over a stream connection. This is typically a TCP connection, but other stream-oriented transport mechanisms can be used. (As an example, the VM SNMP agent allows DPI connections over IUCV.)

The SNMP Agent DPI can:

- Create and delete subtrees in the MIB
- Create a register request packet for the subagent to inform the SNMP agent
- Create response packet for the subagent to answer the SNMP agent's request
- Create a TRAP request packet.

Figure 130 shows the flow between an SNMP agent and a subagent.

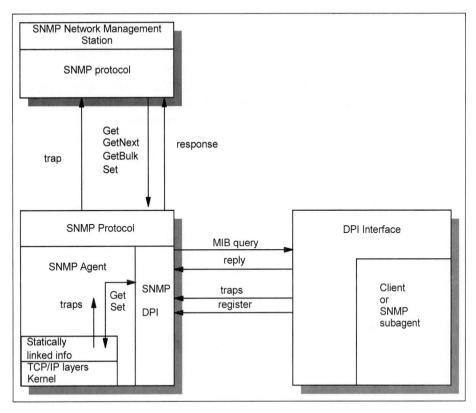

Figure 130. SNMP DPI overview

- The SNMP agent communicates with the SNMP manager via the SNMP protocol.
- The SNMP agent communicates with some statically linked-in instrumentation (potentially for the MIB II), which in turn talks to the TCP/IP layers and kernel (operating system) in an implementation dependent manner.
- An SNMP sub-agent, running as a separate process (potentially on another machine), can set up a connection with the agent. The sub-agent has an option to communicate with the SNMP agent through UDP or TCP sockets, or even through other mechanisms.
- Once the connection is established, the sub-agent issues a DPI OPEN and one or more REGISTER requests to register one or more MIB subtrees with the SNMP agent.
- The SNMP agent responds to DPI OPEN and REGISTER requests with a RESPONSE packet, indicating success or failure.

- The SNMP agent will decode SNMP packets. If such a packet contains a Get or GetNext request for an object in a subtree registered by a sub-agent, it sends a corresponding DPI packet to the sub-agent. If the request is for a GetBulk, then the agent translates it into multiple DPI GETNEXT packets and sends those to the sub-agent. However, the sub-agent can request (in the REGISTER packet) that a GETBULK be passed to the sub-agent. If the request is for a Set, then the agent uses a 2-phase commit scheme and sends the sub-agent a sequence of SET/COMMIT, SET/UNDO or SET/COMMIT/UNDO DPI packets.
- The SNMP sub-agent sends responses back via a RESPONSE packet.
- The SNMP agent then encodes the reply into an SNMP packet and sends it back to the requesting SNMP manager.
- If the sub-agent wants to report an important state change, it sends a DPI TRAP packet to the SNMP agent, which will encode it into an SNMP trap packet and send it to the manager(s).
- If the sub-agent wants to stop operations, it sends a DPI UNREGISTER and a DPI CLOSE packet to the agent. The agent sends a response to an UNREGISTER request.
- There is no RESPONSE to a CLOSE; the agent just closes the DPI connection. A CLOSE implies an UNREGISTER for all registrations that exist for the DPI connection being CLOSED.
- An agent can send DPI UNREGISTER (if a higher priority registration comes in or for other reasons) to the sub-agent. The sub-agent then responds with a DPI RESPONSE packet.
- An agent can also (for whatever reason) send a DPI CLOSE to indicate it is terminating the DPI connection.
- A sub-agent can send an ARE_YOU_THERE to verify that the connection is still open. If so, the agent sends a RESPONSE with no error, otherwise, it may send a RESPONSE with an error.

7.2.5 FTP API

The file transfer protocol (FTP) API is supplied as part of TCP/IP for OS/2. It allows applications to have a client interface for file transfer. Applications written to this interface can communicate with multiple FTP servers at the same time. It allows up to 256 simultaneous connections and enables third-party proxy transfers between pairs of FTP servers. Consecutive third-party transfers are allowed between any sequence of pairs of FTP servers. An example of such an application is FTPPM.

The FTP API tracks the servers to which an application is currently connected. When a new request for FTP service is requested, the API checks whether a connection to the server exists and establishes one if it does not exist. If the server has dropped the connection since last use, the API re-establishes it.

> **Note:**
>
> The FTP API is not reentrant. In a multithreaded program, the access to the APIs must be serialized. For example, without serialization, the program may fail if it has two threads running concurrently and each thread has its own connection to a server.

7.2.6 CICS socket interface

Customer Information Control System (CICS) is a high-performance transaction-processing system. It was developed by IBM and has product implementations in MVS/ESA, MVS, VSE, OS/400, OS/2, and AIX/6000.

CICS is the most widely used Online Transaction Processing (OLTP) system in the marketplace today. It provides a rich set of CICS *command level* APIs to the application transaction programs for data communications (using SNA) and database (using VSAM, IMS, or DB2).

Given the need for interoperability among heterogeneous network protocols, there is a requirement to enhance the CICS data communications interface to include support for TCP/IP in addition to SNA. The *IBM Sockets Interface for CICS* is a first step towards addressing this requirement.

7.2.7 IMS socket interface

The IMS socket interface is implemented in TCP/IP for OS/390 V2R5.

The IMS to TCP/IP sockets interface allows you to develop IMS message processing programs that can conduct a conversation with peer programs in other TCP/IP hosts. The applications can be either client or server applications. The IMS to TCP/IP sockets interface includes socket interfaces for IBM C/370, assembler language, COBOL, and PL/I languages to use datagram (connectionless) and stream (connection-oriented) sockets. It also provides ASCII-EBCDIC conversion routines, an ASSIST module that permits the use of conventional IMS calls for TCP/IP communications, and a Listener function to listen for and accept connection requests and start the appropriate IMS transaction to service those requests.

7.2.8 Sockets Extended

The Sockets Extended information described here is related to the implementation in MVS only.

Sockets Extended provides programmers writing in assembler language, COBOL, or PL/I with an application program interface that may be used to conduct peer-to-peer conversations with other hosts in the TCP/IP networks. You can develop applications for TSO, batch, CICS, or IMS using this API. The applications may be designed to be reentrant and multithreaded, depending upon the application requirements. Typically server applications will be multithreaded while client applications might not be.

7.2.9 REXX sockets

REXX sockets allow you to develop REXX applications that communicate over a TCP/IP network. Calls are provided to initialize sockets, exchange data via sockets, perform management activities, and close the sockets.

The REXX socket APIs are implemented in TCP/IP for MVS and OS/2.

Chapter 8. Directory and naming protocols

The TCP/IP protocol suite contains many applications, but these generally take the form of network utilities. Although these are obviously important to a company using a network, they are not, in themselves, the reason why a company invests in a network in the first place. The network exists to provide access for users, who may be both local and remote, to a company's business applications, data, and resources, which may be distributed across many servers throughout a building, city, or even the world. Those servers may be running on hardware from many different vendors and on several different operating systems. This chapter looks at methods of accessing resources and applications in a distributed network.

8.1 Domain Name System (DNS)

The Domain Name System is a standard protocol with STD number 13. Its status is recommended. It is described in RFC 1034 and RFC 1035. This section explains the implementation of the Domain Name System, and the implementation of name servers.

The early Internet configurations required users to use only numeric IP addresses. Very quickly, this evolved to the use of symbolic host names. For example, instead of typing TELNET 128.12.7.14, one could type TELNET eduvm9, and eduvm9 is then translated in some way to the IP address 128.12.7.14. This introduces the problem of maintaining the mappings between IP addresses and high-level machine names in a coordinated and centralized way.

Initially, host names to address mappings were maintained by the Network Information Center (NIC) in a single file (HOSTS.TXT), which was fetched by all hosts using FTP. This is called a *flat namespace*.

Due to the explosive growth in the number of hosts, this mechanism became too cumbersome (consider the work involved in the addition of just one host to the Internet) and was replaced by a new concept: *Domain Name System*. Hosts can continue to use a local flat namespace (the HOSTS.LOCAL file) instead of or in addition to the Domain Name System, but outside small networks, the Domain Name System is practically essential. The Domain Name System allows a program running on a host to perform the mapping of a high-level symbolic name to an IP address for any other host without the need for every host to have a complete database of host names.

8.1.1 The hierarchical namespace

Consider the internal structure of a large organization. As the chief executive cannot do everything, the organization will probably be partitioned into divisions, each of them having autonomy within certain limits. Specifically, the executive in charge of a division has authority to make direct decisions, without permission from his or her chief executive.

Domain names are formed in a similar way, and will often reflect the hierarchical delegation of authority used to assign them. For example, consider the name:

`small.itso.raleigh.ibm.com`

Here, itso.raleigh.ibm.com is the lowest level domain name, a subdomain of raleigh.ibm.com, which again is a subdomain of ibm.com, a subdomain of com. We can also represent this naming concept by a hierarchical tree (see Figure 131).

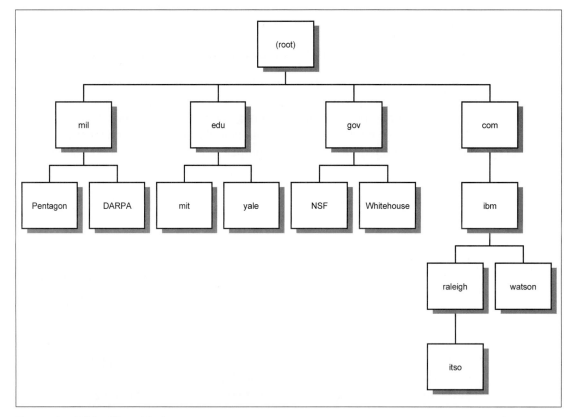

Figure 131. DNS - Hierarchical namespace

The complete structure is explained in the following sections.

8.1.2 Fully Qualified Domain Names (FQDNs)

When using the Domain Name System, it is common to work with only a part of the domain hierarchy, for example, the ral.ibm.com domain. The Domain Name System provides a simple method of minimizing the typing necessary in this circumstance. If a domain name ends in a dot (for example, wtscpok.itsc.pok.ibm.com.), it is assumed to be complete. This is termed a *fully qualified domain name (FQDN)* or an *absolute domain name*. However, if it does not end in a dot (for example, wtscpok.itsc), it is incomplete and the DNS resolver (see below) may complete this, for example, by appending a suffix such as .pok.ibm.com to the domain name. The rules for doing this are implementation-dependent and locally configurable.

8.1.3 Generic domains

The three-character top-level names are called the generic domains or the organizational domains. Table 4 shows some of the top-level domains of today's Internet domain namespace.

Table 4. DNS - Some top level Internet domains

Domain Name	Meaning
com	Commercial organizations
edu	Educational institutions
gov	Government institutions
int	International organizations
mil	U.S. military
net	Major network support centers
org	Non-profit organizations
country code	ISO 2-letter identifier for country specific domains

Since the Internet began in the United States, the organization of the hierarchical namespace initially had only U.S. organizations at the top of the hierarchy, and it is still largely true that the generic part of the namespace contains US organizations. However, only the .gov and .mil domains are restricted to the US.

At the time of writing, the U.S. Department Of Commerce - National Telecommunications and Information Administration is looking for a different organization for .us domains. As a result of this, it has been decided to change the status of the Internet Assigned Numbers Authority (IANA), which will no longer be funded and run by the U.S. Government. A new non-profit organization with an international Board of Directors will be funded by domain registries instead. On the other hand, there are some other organizations that have already begun to register new top-level domains. For current information, see the IANA Web site at:

```
http://www.iana.org
```

8.1.4 Country domains

There are also top-level domains named for the each of the ISO 3166 international 2-character country codes (from ae for the United Arab Emirates to zw for Zimbabwe). These are called the *country* domains or the *geographical* domains. Many countries have their own second-level domains underneath which parallel the generic top-level domains. For example, in the United Kingdom, the domains equivalent to the generic domains .com and .edu are .co.uk and .ac.uk (ac is an abbreviation for academic). There is a .us top-level domain, which is organized geographically by state (for example, .ny.us refers to the state of New York). See RFC 1480 for a detailed description of the .us domain.

8.1.5 Mapping domain names to IP addresses

The mapping of names to addresses consists of independent, cooperative systems called name servers. A name server is a server program that holds a master or a copy of a name-to-address mapping database, or otherwise points to a server that does, and that answers requests from the client software, called a name resolver.

Conceptually, all Internet domain servers are arranged in a tree structure that corresponds to the naming hierarchy in Figure 132 on page 285. Each leaf represents a name server that handles names for a single subdomain. Links in the conceptual tree do not indicate physical connections. Instead, they show which other name server a given server can contact.

8.1.6 Mapping IP addresses to domain names – pointer queries

The Domain Name System provides for a mapping of symbolic names to IP addresses and vice versa. While it is a simple matter in principle to search the database for an IP address with its symbolic name (because of the hierarchical structure), the reverse process cannot follow the hierarchy. Therefore, there is another namespace for the reverse mapping. It is found in the domain in-addr.arpa (arpa is used because the Internet was originally the ARPAnet).

IP addresses are normally written in dotted decimal format, and there is one layer of domain for each hierarchy. However, because domain names have the least-significant parts of the name first, but dotted decimal format has the most significant bytes first, the dotted decimal address is shown in reverse order. For example, the domain in the domain name system corresponding to the IP address 129.34.139.30 is 30.139.34.129.in-addr.arpa. Given an IP address, the Domain Name System can be used to find the matching host name. A domain name query to find the host names associated with an IP address is called a *pointer query*.

8.1.7 The distributed name space

The Domain Name System uses the concept of a *distributed name space*. Symbolic names are grouped into *zones of authority*, or more commonly *zones*. In each of these zones, one or more hosts has the task of maintaining a database of symbolic names and IP addresses and providing a server function for clients who wish to translate between symbolic names and IP addresses. These local name servers are then (through the internetwork on which they are connected) logically interconnected into a hierarchical tree of *domains*. Each zone contains a part or a *subtree* of the hierarchical tree and the names within the zone are administered independently of names in other zones. Authority over zones is vested in the name servers.

Normally, the name servers that have authority for a zone will have domain names belonging to that zone, but this is not required. Where a domain contains a subtree that falls in a different zone, the name server(s) with authority over the superior domain are said to *delegate authority* to the name server(s) with authority over the subdomain. Name servers can also delegate authority to themselves; in this case, the domain name space is still divided into zones moving down the domain name tree, but authority for two zones is held by the same server. The division of the domain name space into zones is accomplished using resource records stored in the Domain Name System.

There is an exception to this at the top level root domain, because there is no higher system to delegate authority, and we do not want all queries for fully qualified domain names to hit just one system. Hence, authority for the top level zones is shared among a set of *root name servers.*[1]

---

[1] At the time of writing there were thirteen root servers. The current list is available by anonymous FTP from ftp.rs.internic.net in the file netinfo/root-servers.txt.

Consider a query for tt.ibm.com. and let us assume that our name server does not have the answer already in its cache. The query would go to the .com root name server, which in turn would forward the query to a server with an NS record for ibm.com. At this stage, we have probably found a name server that has cached the answer we require. However, the query could be further delegated to a name server for tt.ibm.com

As a result of this scheme:

- Rather than having a central server for the database, the work that is involved in maintaining this database is off-loaded to hosts throughout the name space.
- Authority for creating and changing symbolic host names and responsibility for maintaining a database for them is delegated to the organization owning the zone (within the name space) containing those host names.
- From the user's standpoint, there is a single database that deals with these address resolutions. The user may be aware that the database is distributed, but generally need not be concerned about this.

Note:

Although domains within the namespace will frequently map in a logical fashion to networks and subnets within the IP addressing scheme, this is not a requirement of the Domain Name System. Consider a router between two subnets. It has two IP addresses, one for each network adapter, but it would not normally have two symbolic names.

8.1.8 Domain name resolution

The domain name resolution process can be summarized in the following steps:

1. A user program issues a request such as the gethostbyname() system call. (This particular call is used to ask for the IP address of a host by passing the host name.)
2. The resolver formulates a query to the name server. (Full resolvers have a local name cache to consult first; stub resolvers do not.)
3. The name server checks to see if the answer is in its local authoritative database or cache, and if so, returns it to the client. Otherwise, it will query other available name server(s), starting down from the root of the DNS tree or as high up the tree as possible.
4. The user program will finally be given a corresponding IP address (or host name, depending on the query) or an error if the query could not be

answered. Normally, the program will not be given a list of all the name servers that have been consulted to process the query.

The query/reply messages are transported by either UDP or TCP.

Domain name resolution is a client/server process. The client function (called the *resolver* or *name resolver*) is transparent to the user and is called by an application to resolve symbolic high-level names into real IP addresses or vice versa. The name server (also called a *domain name server*) is a server application providing the translation between high-level machine names and the IP addresses.

8.1.8.1 Domain name full resolver

Figure 132 shows a program called a *full resolver*, that is distinct from the user program, which forwards all queries to a name server for processing. Responses are cached by the name server for future use.

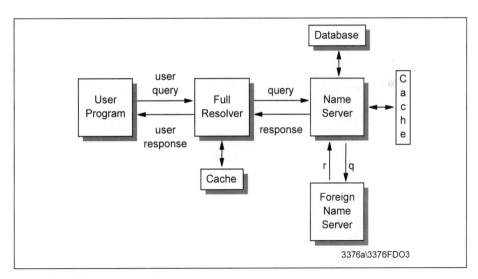

Figure 132. DNS - Using a full resolver for domain name resolution

8.1.8.2 Domain name stub resolver

Figure 133 shows a *stub resolver*, a routine linked with the user program, which forwards the queries to a name server for processing. Responses are cached by the name server, but not usually by the resolver, although this is implementation-dependent. On UNIX, the stub resolver is implemented by two library routines, gethostbyname() and gethostbyaddr(), for converting host names to IP addresses and vice versa. Other platforms have the same or equivalent routines. Stub resolvers are much more common than full resolvers.

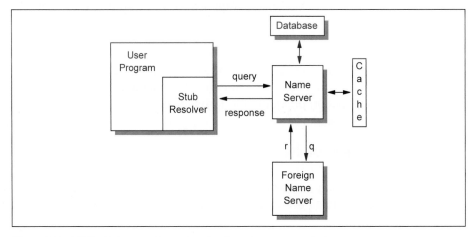

Figure 133. DNS - Using a stub resolver for domain name resolution

8.1.8.3 Domain name resolver operation

Domain name queries can be one of two types: *recursive* or *iterative* (also termed *non-recursive*). A flag bit in the domain name query specifies whether the client desires a recursive query, and a flag bit in the response specifies whether the server supports recursive queries. The difference between a recursive and an iterative query arises when the server receives a request for which it cannot supply a complete answer by itself. A recursive query requests that the server should issue a query itself to determine the requested information and return the complete answer to the client. An iterative query means that the name server should return what information it has available and also a list of additional servers for the client to contact to complete the query.

Domain name responses can be one of two types: *authoritative* and *non-authoritative*. A flag bit in the response indicates which type a response is. When a name server receives a query for a domain in a zone over which it has authority, it returns all of the requested information in a response with the authoritative answer flag set. When it receives a query for a domain over which it does not have authority, its actions depend upon the setting of the recursion desired flag in the query.

- If the recursion desired flag is set and the server supports recursive queries, it will direct its query to another name server. This will either be a name server with authority for the domain given in the query, or it will be one of the root name servers. If the second server does not return an authoritative answer (for example, if it has delegated authority to another server), the process is repeated.

When a server (or a full resolver program) receives a response, it will cache it to improve the performance of repeat queries. The cache entry is stored for a maximum length of time specified by the originator in a 32-bit *time-to-live (TTL)* field contained in the response. 172,800 seconds (two days) is a typical TTL value.

- If the recursion desired flag is not set or the server does not support recursive queries, it will return whatever information it has in its cache and also a list of additional name servers to be contacted for authoritative information.

8.1.8.4 Domain name server operation

Each name server has *authority* for zero or more zones. There are three types of name servers:

Primary   A primary name server loads a zone's information from disk, and has authority over the zone.

Secondary   A secondary name server has authority for a zone, but obtains its zone information from a primary server using a process called *zone transfer*. To remain synchronized, the secondary name servers query the primary on a regular basis (typically every three hours) and re-execute the zone transfer if the primary has been updated. A name server can operate as a primary or a secondary name server for multiple domains, or a primary for some domains and as a secondary for others. A primary or secondary name server performs all of the functions of a caching only name server.

Caching-only A name server that does not have authority for any zone is called a caching-only name server. A caching-only name server obtains all of its data from primary or secondary name servers as required. It requires at least one NS record to point to a name server from which it can initially obtain information.

When a domain is registered with the root and a separate zone of authority established, the following rules apply:

- The domain must be registered with the root administrator.
- There must be an identified administrator for the domain.

- There must be at least two name servers with authority for the zone that are accessible from outside and inside the domain to ensure no single point of failure.

It is also recommended that name servers that delegate authority also apply these rules, since the delegating name servers are responsible for the behavior of name servers under their authority.

8.1.9 Domain Name System resource records

The Domain Name System's distributed database is composed of *resource records* (RRs), which are divided into classes for different kinds of networks. We only discuss the Internet class of records. Resource records provide a mapping between domain names and *network objects*. The most common network objects are the addresses of Internet hosts, but the Domain Name System is designed to accommodate a wide range of different objects.

A zone consists of a group of resource records, beginning with a Start of Authority (SOA) record. The SOA record identifies the domain name of the zone. There will be a name server (NS) record for the primary name server for this zone. There may also be NS record(s) for the secondary name server(s) for this zone. The NS records are used to identify which of the name servers are 'authoritative' or in charge of the zone. Then come all the other resource records, which might map names to IP addresses, or aliases to names.

The general format of a resource record is:

Table 5. DNS General resource record format

Name	TTL	Class	Type	Rdata

Where:

- Name: The domain name to be defined. The Domain Name System is very general in its rules for the composition of domain names. However, it recommends a syntax for domain names which will minimize the likelihood of applications that use a DNS resolver (that is, nearly all TCP/IP applications) from misinterpreting a domain name. A domain name adhering to this recommended syntax will consist of a series of labels consisting of alphanumeric characters or hyphens, each label having a length of between 1 and 63 characters, starting with an alphabetic character. Each pair of labels is separated by a dot (period) in human readable form, but not in the form used within DNS messages. Domain names are not case-sensitive.

- ttl: The time-to-live (TTL) time in seconds that this resource record will be valid in a name server cache. This is stored in the DNS as an unsigned 32-bit value. 86400 (one day) is a typical value for records pointing to IP addresses.

- class: Identifies the protocol family. The only commonly used value is IN (the Internet system).

- type: Identifies the type of the resource in this resource record.

  The different types are described in detail in RFCs 1034, 1035 and 1706. Each type has a name and a value. Commonly used types include:

Table 6. Resource record types

Type	Value	Meaning
A	1	A host address.
CNAME	5	Canonical name. Specifies an alias name for a host.
HINFO	13	The CPU and OS used by the host. This is only a comment field.
MX	15	A mail exchange for the domain. Maps a mailbox name to a host name. See 11.1.2, "SMTP and the Domain Name System" on page 396.
NS	2	The authoritative name server for a domain.
PTR	12	A pointer to another part of the domain name space.
SOA	6	The start of a zone of authority.
WKS	11	Well-known services. Specifies some services (for example, SMTP) that are expected to be always active on this host.

- Rdata: The value depends on the type, for example:

A	A 32-bit IP address (if the class is IN)
CNAME	A domain name
MX	A 16-bit preference value (low values being preferred) followed by a domain name
NS	A host name
PTR	A domain name

Please refer to 8.2, "Dynamic Domain Name System" on page 300 for additional resource record types.

8.1.10 Domain Name System messages

All messages in the Domain Name System protocol use a single format. This format is shown in Figure 134. This frame is sent by the resolver to the name server. Only the header and the question section are used to form the query. Replies and/or forwarding of the query use the same frame, but with more sections filled in (the answer/authority/additional sections).

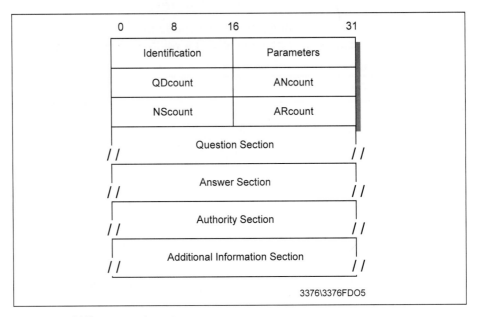

Figure 134. DNS message format

8.1.10.1 Header format

The header section is always present and has a fixed length of 12 bytes. The other sections are of variable length.

ID   A 16-bit identifier assigned by the program. This identifier is copied in the corresponding reply from the name server and can be used for differentiation of responses when multiple queries are outstanding at the same time.

Parameters A 16-bit value in the following format:

0	1	2	3	4	5	6	7	8	9	10	11	12	13	14	15
QR	Op code				AA	TC	RD	RA	Zero			Rcode			

Where:

QR Flag identifying a query (0) or a response(1)

Op code 4-bit field specifying the kind of query:

  0 Standard query (QUERY)
  1 Inverse query (IQUERY)
  2 Server status request (STATUS)

Other values are reserved for future use

AA Authoritative answer flag. If set in a response, this flag specifies that the responding name server is an authority for the domain name sent in the query.

TC Truncation flag. Set if message was longer than permitted on the physical channel.

RD Recursion desired flag. This bit signals to the name server that recursive resolution is asked for. The bit is copied to the response.

RA Recursion available flag. Indicates whether the name server supports recursive resolution.

Zero 3 bits reserved for future use. Must be zero.

Rcode 4-bit response code. Possible values are:

  0 No error.
  1 Format error. The server was unable to interpret the message.
  2 Server failure. The message was not processed because of a problem with the server.
  3 Name error. The domain name in the query does not exist. This is only valid if the AA bit is set in the response.
  4 Not implemented. The requested type of query is not implemented by name server.
  5 Refused. The server refuses to respond for policy reasons. Other values are reserved for future use.

QDcount An unsigned 16-bit integer specifying the number of entries in the question section.

ANcount An unsigned 16-bit integer specifying the number of RRs in the answer section.

NScount An unsigned 16-bit integer specifying the number of name server RRs in the authority section.

ARcount An unsigned 16-bit integer specifying the number of RRs in the additional records section.

8.1.10.2 Question section
The next section contains the queries for the name server. It contains QDcount (usually 1) entries, each in the format shown in Figure 135.

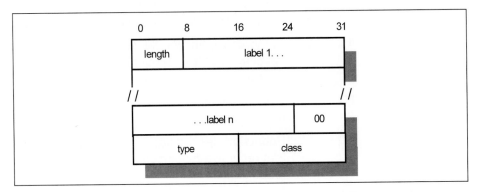

Figure 135. DNS - Question Format - all of the fields are byte-aligned. The alignment of the Type field on a 4-byte boundary is for example purposes and is not required by the format.

Where:

length A single byte giving the length of the next label.

label One element of the domain name characters (for example ibm from ral.ibm.com). The domain name referred to by the question is stored as a series of these variable length labels, each preceded by a 1-byte length.

00 X'00' indicates the end of the domain name and represents the null label of the root domain.

Type 2 bytes specifying the type of query. It can have any value from the Type field in a resource record.

Class 2 bytes specifying the class of the query. For Internet queries, this will be IN.

For example, the domain name raleigh.ibm.com would be encoded with the following fields:

```
X'07'
"raleigh"
X'03'
"ibm"
X'03'
```

```
"com"
X'00'
```

Thus, the entry in the question section for raleigh.ibm.com would require 21 bytes: 17 to store the domain name and 2 each for the Qtype and Qclass fields.

8.1.10.3 Answer, authority, and additional resource sections

These three sections contain a variable number of resource records. The number is specified in the corresponding field of the header. The resource records are in the format shown in Figure 136.

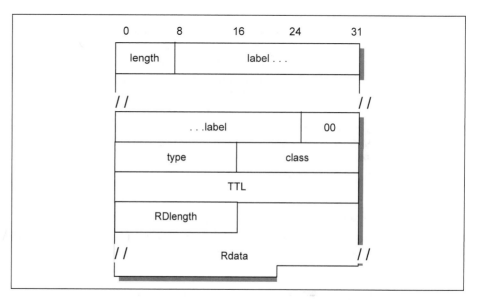

Figure 136. DNS - Answer Record Entry format - all of the fields are byte-aligned. The alignment of the Type field on a 4-byte boundary is for example purposes and is not required by the format.

Where the fields before the TTL field have the same meanings as for a question entry and:

TTL   A 32-bit time-to-live value in seconds for the record. This defines how long it can be regarded as valid.

RDlength A 16-bit length for the Rdata field.

Rdata   A variable length string whose interpretation depends on the Type field.

8.1.10.4 Message compression

In order to reduce the message size, a compression scheme is used to eliminate the repetition of domain names in the various RRs. Any duplicate domain name or list of labels is replaced with a pointer to the previous occurrence. The pointer has the form of a 2-byte field:

- The first 2 bits distinguish the pointer from a normal label, which is restricted to a 63-byte length plus the length byte ahead of it (which has a value of <64).
- The offset field specifies an offset from the start of the message. A zero offset specifies the first byte of the ID field in the header.
- If compression is used in an Rdata field of an answer, authority or additional section of the message, the preceding RDlength field contains the real length after compression is done.

Please refer to 8.2, "Dynamic Domain Name System" on page 300 for additional message formats.

8.1.11 A simple scenario

Consider a stand-alone network (no outside connections), consisting of two physical networks: one has an Internet network address 129.112, the other has a network address 194.33.7, interconnected by an IP gateway (VM2). See Figure 137 for more details.

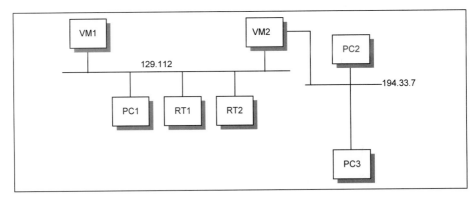

Figure 137. DNS - A simple configuration - two networks connected through an IP gateway

Let us assign the name server function to VM1. Remember that the domain hierarchical tree forms a logical tree, completely independent of the physical configuration. In this simple scenario, there is only one level in the domain tree. Let us give this configuration the domain name test.example.

The zone data for the name server will then be as shown in Figure 138.

```
;note: an SOA record has no TTL field
;
$origin test.example.                                        ;note 1
@            IN SOA VM1.test.example. ADM.VM1.test.example.
                (870611           ;serial number for data
                1800              ;secondary refreshes every 30 mn
                300               ;secondary reties every 5 mn
                604800            ;data expire after 1 week
                86400)            ;minimum TTL for data is 1 week
;
@       99999 IN NS  VM1.test.example.                       ;note 2
;
VM1     99999 IN A    129.112.1.1                            ;note 3
        99999 IN WKS 129.112.1.1 TCP (SMTP                   ;note 4
                                      FTP
                                      TELNET
                                      NAMESRV)
;
RT1     99999 IN A     129.112.1.2
              IN HINFO IBM RT/PC-AIX                         ;note 5
RT2     99999 IN A     129.112.1.3
              IN HINFO IBM RT/PC-AIX
PC1     99999 IN A     129.112.1.11
PC2     99999 IN A     194.33.7.2
PC3     99999 IN A     194.33.7.3
;
;VM2 is an IP gateway and has 2 different IP addresses
;
VM2     99999 IN A     129.112.1.4
        99999 IN A     194.33.7.1
        99999 IN WKS   129.112.1.4 TCP (SMTP FTP)
              IN HINFO IBM-3090-VM/CMS
;
4.1.112.129.in-addr.arpa.  IN  PTR  VM2                      ;note 6
;
;Some mailboxes
;
central 10   IN MX  VM2.test.example.                        ;note 7 and 8
;
;a second definition for the same mailbox, in case VM2 is down
;
central 20   IN MX  VM1.test.example.
waste   10   IN MX  VM2.test.example.
```

Figure 138. DNS - Zone data for the name server

1 The $origin statement sets the @ variable to the zone name (test.example.). Domain names that do not end with a period are suffixed with the zone name. Fully qualified domain names (those ending with a period) are unaffected by the zone name.

2 Defines the name server for this zone.

3 Defines the Internet address of the name server for this zone.

4 Specifies well-known services for this host. These are expected to always be available.

5 Gives information about the host.

6 Used for inverse mapping queries (see 8.1.6, "Mapping IP addresses to domain names – pointer queries" on page 282).

7 Will allow mail to be addressed to user@central.test.example.

8 See 11.1.2, "SMTP and the Domain Name System" on page 396 for the use of these definitions.

8.1.12 Extended scenario

Consider the case where a connection is made to a third network (129.113), which has an existing name server with authority for that zone (see Figure 139).

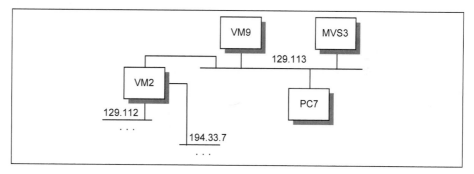

Figure 139. DNS - Extended configuration - a third network is connected to the existing configuration

Let us suppose that the domain name of the other network is tt.ibm.com and that its name server is located in VM9. All we have to do is add the address of this name server to our own name server database (in the named.ca initial cache file), and to reference the other network by its own name server. The following two lines are all that is needed to do that:

```
tt.ibm.com.          99999  IN NS  VM9.tt.ibm.com.
VM9.tt.ibm.com.      99999  IN A   129.13.1.9
```

This simply indicates that VM9 is the authority for the new network, and that all queries for that network will be directed to that name server.

8.1.13 Transport

Domain Name System messages are transmitted either as datagrams (UDP) or via stream connection (TCP).

- UDP usage: Server port 53 (decimal).

  Messages carried by UDP are restricted to 512 bytes. Longer messages are truncated and the TC bit is set in the header. Since UDP frames can be lost, a retransmission strategy is required.

- TCP usage: Server port 53 (decimal).

  In this case, the message is preceded by a 2-byte field indicating the total message frame length.

- STD 3 – Host Requirements requires that:

  - A Domain Name System resolver or server that is sending a non-zone-transfer query *must* send a UDP query first. If the answer section of the response is truncated and if the requester supports TCP, it should try the query again using TCP. UDP is preferred over TCP for queries because UDP queries have much lower overhead, and the use of UDP is essential for a heavily loaded server. Truncation of messages is rarely a problem given the current contents of the Domain Name System database, since typically 15 response records can be accommodated in the datagram, but this may change as new record types are added to the Domain Name System.

  - TCP must be used for zone transfer activities because the 512-byte limit for a UDP datagram will always be inadequate for a zone transfer.

  - Name servers must support both types of transport.

8.1.13.1 Dynamic DNS (DDNS)

The Dynamic Domain Name System (DDNS) is a protocol that defines extensions to the Domain Name System to enable DNS servers to accept requests to add, update, and delete entries in the DNS database dynamically. Because DDNS offers a functional superset to existing DNS servers, a DDNS server can serve both static and dynamic domains at the same time, a welcome feature for migration and overall DNS design.

DDNS is currently available in a non-secure and a secure flavor, defined in RFC 2136 and RFC 3007, respectively. Rather than allowing any host to update its DNS records, the secure version of DDNS uses public key security and digital signatures to authenticate update requests from DDNS hosts. IBM, for example, has fully implemented secure DDNS on its OS/2 Warp Server, AIX, OS/390, and AS/400 platforms, as well as on Windows NT.

Without client authentication, another host could impersonate an unsuspecting host by remapping the address entry for the unsuspecting host to that of its own. Once the remapping occurs, important data, such as logon passwords and mail intended for the host would, unfortunately, be sent to the impersonating host instead.

Please see 8.2, "Dynamic Domain Name System" on page 300 for more information on how DDNS works together with DHCP to perform seamless updates of reverse DNS mapping entries, and see 17.4, "DNS in IPv6" on page 595 for more information about DNS with IPv6.

8.1.14 DNS applications

Three common utilities for querying name servers are provided with many DNS implementations:

host   Obtains an IP address associated with a host name or a host name associated with an IP address.

nslookup Allows you to locate information about network nodes, examine the contents of a name server database and establish the accessibility of name servers.

dig   Allows you to exercise name servers, gather large volumes of domain name information, and execute simple domain name queries. DIG stands for Domain Internet Groper.

8.1.15 References

The following RFCs define the Domain Name System standard and the information kept in the system:

- RFC 1032 – Domain Administrator's Guide
- RFC 1033 – Domain Administrator Operations Guide
- RFC 1034 – Domain Names – Concepts and Facilities
- RFC 1035 – Domain Names – Implementation and Specification
- RFC 1101 – DNS Encoding of Networks Names and Other Types

- RFC 1183 – New DNS RR Definitions
- RFC 1480 – The US Domain
- RFC 1591 – Domain Name System Structure and Delegation
- RFC 1706 – DNS NSAP Resource Records
- RFC 3007 – Secure Domain Name System (DNS) Dynamic Update
- RFC 1995 – Incremental Zone Transfer in DNS
- RFC 1996 – A Mechanism for Prompt Notification of Zone Transfer
- RFC 2535 – Domain Name System Security Extensions
- RFC 2136 – Dynamic Updates in the Domain Name System
- RFC 3007 – Secure Domain Name System (DNS) Dynamic Updates

8.2 Dynamic Domain Name System

The Domain Name System described in 8.1, "Domain Name System (DNS)" on page 279 is a static implementation without recommendations with regard to security. In order to take advantage of DHCP, yet still to be able to locate any specific host by means of a meaningful label, such as its host name, the following extensions to DNS are required:

- A method for the host name to address mapping entry for a client in the domain name server to be updated, once the client has obtained an address from a DHCP server

- A method for the reverse address to host name mapping to take place once the client obtains its address

- Updates to the DNS to take effect immediately, without the need for intervention by an administrator

- Updates to the DNS to be authenticated to prevent unauthorized hosts from accessing the network and to stop imposters from using an existing host name and remapping the address entry for the unsuspecting host to that of its own

- A method for primary and secondary DNS servers to quickly forward and receive changes as entries are being updated dynamically by clients

In short, a secure Dynamic Domain Name System (DDNS) is necessary.

Several RFCs relate to DDNS. These are:

- RFC 2535 – Domain Name System Security Extensions

  The extensions described in this RFC provide for the storage of digital signatures and authenticated public keys in secured zones in the DNS. KEY and SIG (signature) resource record types are introduced. Three distinct services are provided:

- Distribution of keys

- Data origin authentication (by associating digital signatures with the resource records in the DNS)

- Transaction and request authentication

The RFC makes provision for any type of key and security algorithm, but by default assumes the MD5/RSA algorithm (see 21.2, "A short introduction to cryptography" on page 660).

- RFC 2136 – Dynamic Updates in the Domain Name System

This RFC introduces the UPDATE DNS message format, which is used to add or delete resource records in the DNS. The ability for updates to take effect without the DNS having to be reloaded is also described.

- RFC 1995 – Incremental Zone Transfer in DNS

This RFC introduces the IXFR DNS message type, which allows incremental transfers of DNS zone data between primary and secondary DNS servers. In other words, when an update has been made to the zone data, only the change has to be copied to other DNS servers who maintain a copy of the zone data, rather than the whole DNS database (as is the case with the AXFR DNS message type).

- RFC 1996 – Prompt Notification of Zone Transfer

This RFC introduces the NOTIFY DNS message type, which is used by a master server to inform slave servers that an update has taken place and that they should initiate a query to discover the new data.

- RFC 3007 – Secure DNS Dynamic Updates

This RFC extends recommendations from both RFC 2535 and RFC 2136 to provide a detailed description for secure dynamic DNS updates.

The above RFCs are all proposed standard protocols with elective status.

8.2.1 The UPDATE DNS message format

The DNS message format (shown in Figure 134 on page 290) was designed for the querying of a static DNS database. RFC 2136 defines a modified DNS message for updates, shown in Figure 140.

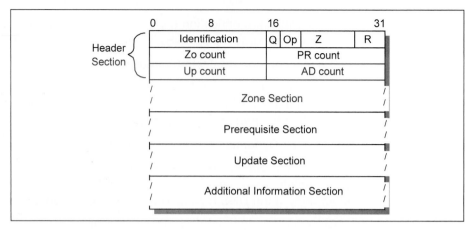

Figure 140. DDNS UPDATE message format

The header section is always present and has a fixed length of 12 bytes. The other sections are of variable length. They are:

Identification   A 16-bit identifier assigned by the program. This identifier is copied in the corresponding reply from the name server and can be used for differentiation when multiple queries/updates are outstanding at the same time.

Q   Flag identifying an update request (0) or a response (1).

Op   Opcode - The value 5 indicates an UPDATE message.

z   7-bit field set to 0 and reserved for future use.

R   Response code (undefined in update requests). Possible values are:

0   No error.

1   Format error. The server was unable to interpret the message.

2   Server failure. The message was not processed due to a problem with the server.

3	Name error. A name specified does not exist.
4	Not implemented. The type of message specified in Opcode is not supported by this server.
5	Refused. The server refuses to perform the UPDATE requested for security or policy reasons.
6	Name error. A name exists when it should not.
7	RRset error. A resource record set exists when it should not.
8	RRset error. A resource record set specified does not exist.
9	Zone Authority error. The server is not authoritative for the Zone specified.
10	Zone error. A name specified in the Prerequisite or Update sections is not in the Zone specified.
ZOcount	The number of RRs in the Zone section.
PRcount	The number of RRs in the Prerequisite section.
UPcount	The number of RRs in the Update section.
ADcount	The number of RRs in the Additional Information section.
Zone section	This section is used to indicate the zone of the records that are to be updated. As all records to be updated must belong to the same zone, the zone section has a single entry specifying the zone name, zone type (which must be SOA), and zone class.
Prerequisite section	This section contains RRs or RRsets that either must, or must not, exist, depending on the type of update.
Update section	This section contains the RRs and/or RRsets that are to be added to or deleted from the zone.

Additional information section This section can be used to pass
additional RRs that relate to the update
operation in process.

For further information on the UPDATE message format, please refer to RFC
2136.

> **Note:**
>
> The IBM implementation of DDNS uses a different UPDATE message
> format. Please see 8.2.2.6, "IBM DDNS UPDATE message format" on
> page 312.

8.2.2 The IBM implementation of DDNS

IBM's Dynamic Domain Name System (DDNS) is based on, and is a superset
of, the Internet Software Consortium's publicly available implementation of
the Berkeley Internet Name Domain (BIND) level 4.9.3 (which did not include
any security functions). See 8.2.2.4, "BIND versions" on page 310 for BIND
Version 9.1 information. The IBM implementation supports both static and
dynamic DNS domains. In dynamic domains, only authorized clients can
update their own data. RSA public-key digital signature technology is used for
client authentication.

Using IBM DHCP Server, an administrator configures (at the server) host
configuration parameters, including IP address, to automate the configuration
of IP hosts. The DDNS provides dynamic host name-to-IP address (and IP
address-to-host name) mapping for dynamic IP clients. Using DDNS, when
the client receives its new address from the DHCP server, it automatically
updates its A record on the DNS server with the new address. The IBM DHCP
server automatically updates the PTR record on behalf of the client.

8.2.2.1 DDNS mechanism

The DDNS client program, NSUPDATE, is used to update information in a
DDNS server. Dynamic updates are performed by any of the following:

Network client A host that has DHCP and DDNS client
software and can update its A and TXT
records with the current IP address
information.

DHCP server Updates PTR records with the current host
name information for the address it has just
allocated. In certain circumstances, it can also
perform updates to A records for clients that

either cannot, or do not, update the A records themselves (see 8.2.3, "Proxy A Record update (ProxyArec)" on page 313).

DDNS system administrator A system administrator can make manual changes to all resource record types in the DDNS database, or can use the NSUPDATE command from a command line to make the changes. All changes take effect immediately.

The interaction between the DDNS client, DDNS server and DHCP server is shown in Figure 141:

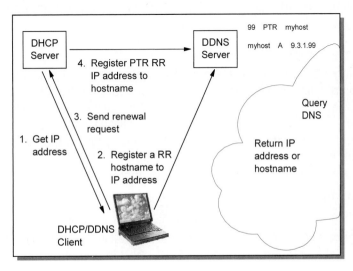

Figure 141. DDNS-to-DHCP client interaction

> **Note:**
>
> For ease of explanation, the DHCP and DDNS servers are shown as separate devices in Figure 141. In practice, it is common for these two servers to be on the same machine.

Where:

1. The DHCP makes the normal exchanges with the DHCP server to obtain configuration data (see 3.7.3, "Allocating a new network address" on page 130).

2. The DDNS client then sends an update request, including its newly obtained IP address, to the DDNS server for the resource records that are

associated with the client's host name. The client also sends its public key and signs all resource records with a digital signature. The combination of the key and the signature verifies that this client is indeed entitled to use the host name and that the information contained in the client's record is valid.

If the client's updates have been successful, the server commits the changes to its database. The client is now reachable by its host name.

3. The DHCP client sends a lease renewal request message to the DHCP server. This message includes the host name being used by the client. The DHCP server updates the PTR record (IP address-to-host name mapping) for the client on the DDNS server. An inverse query on the client's IP address to the DDNS server will now return the client's host name.

8.2.2.2 DDNS security

Having a DHCP and DDNS server in your network allows a client to automatically obtain a valid, working configuration from the network and to automatically register its presence with the DDNS server. However, this means that without authentication of the DDNS client, an unauthorized host might impersonate an unsuspecting host by copying the host name of that client. It could then update the DDNS server with its own IP address and could then intercept data (for example, logon passwords) intended for the unsuspecting host.

IBM implements RSA digital signature technology in its DDNS server and client code to authenticate the owner of the DNS records and to secure the DNS database updates. See 21.2, "A short introduction to cryptography" on page 660 for more information on RSA digital signature technology. DDNS supports two modes of securing updates for a dynamic domain, dynamic secured mode, and dynamic presecured mode. Both modes protect A records in the database from unauthorized updates.

Dynamic secured mode

When a DDNS client registers its host name for the first time, it generates an RSA key pair. A public key is sent to the DDNS server and registered for that particular host name.

The DDNS client stores the RSA key pair (with the private key encrypted) in a client key file. When the DDNS client updates the resource records on the DDNS server, the digital signature is generated by using the private key and is sent to the server with the update data. On receiving the update request, the DDNS server uses the client's public key (in the KEY resource record) to:

- Authenticate the owner of the update request to verify that the update request was signed with the corresponding private key

- Verify that the data was not changed since it was signed (to verify that no one intercepted and changed the data on the way to the name server)

In this way, only the owners of the original records, who possess the correct private key necessary to generate the correct digital signature, can update resource records that are protected by an existing KEY resource record.

In addition, a DDNS administrator can create and use a zone key for each dynamic domain. The zone key is the administrator's RSA key pair for a particular domain. This key enables the administrator to create, modify or delete any host's record in the domain, regardless of who created the records. The private key is used to generate the signature when the administrator carries out update requests and the server examines the signature to verify that update requests are from the administrator. The public key is registered in the domain data file as a KEY resource record for the domain. The private and public keys are stored in the administrator's key file on the server.

The dynamic secured mode ensures that impersonation of hosts cannot occur in a domain, but it does not prevent any DDNS client with a new host name from obtaining a working and valid configuration for the domain. The dynamic secured domain requires a minimal amount of configuration on the part of the administrator.

Dynamic presecured mode
In the presecured dynamic domain, DDNS clients must be pre-authorized by a DDNS administrator before they can create their name record. The DDNS administrator must preregister hosts and generate RSA keys for each client. This means that in presecured mode, the KEY resource record for a client must be already defined in the domain before an update from that client is accepted. The DDNS administrator must also distribute the correct, corresponding key information to each host before they create the resource records.

The presecured domain represents the most secure DNS name space available. In addition to preventing updates to A and PTR records from unknown or unauthenticated hosts, the DDNS server is able to log attempts at invalid updates and the administrator can identify MAC addresses of offending clients and can take appropriate action.

The DDNS administrator obviously has a higher workload establishing a presecured domain, but the other benefits of the dynamic domain, namely support for mobile clients and address space conservation, are still realized.

8.2.2.3 DDNS resource records

The information that composes a DNS server database is represented in the form of resource records (RRs). The RR format is shown in 8.1.9, "Domain Name System resource records" on page 288. The security mechanism introduced with DDNS introduces two new types of resource records: KEY and SIG.

1. The KEY resource record (type 25)

   This record represents a public encryption key for a name in the DDNS database. This can be a key for a zone, a host, or a user. A KEY RR is authenticated by a SIG RR. KEY RRs contain the public exponent and modulus of an encryption key.

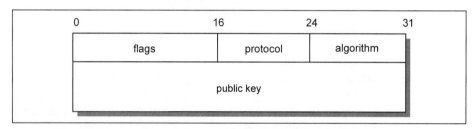

Figure 142. KEY resource record Rdata format

All resource records have the format shown in Figure 134 on page 290. Figure 142 shows the fields used within the Rdata section of a KEY resource record. The fields are:

flags   This field indicates the type of resource record for which this KEY RR is provided.

protocol   This field indicates the protocols (in addition to DDNS) that are to be secured for authentication by this KEY RR.

algorithm   This field indicates which encryption algorithm should be used with this key; in the case of IBM Dynamic IP, this field has a value of 1, which means that the RSA/MD5 algorithm is being used.

public key   The actual public key to be used for authentication. This field is structured in a public exponent length field, the public key exponent portion, and the public key modulus portion.

An example of a KEY resource record is shown below:

```
client1  IN  KEY  0x0000  0   1 AQO3P+UqipNXsuijeL3yyfJLw9PagI+NZg9oXrgYI1cSKOAo
                                 +WwPOxpEqUsjOhFsKNo4V0q6LH1LK17XcytwAI01    ;Cr=auth
```

2. The SIG resource record (type 24)

This record represents a digital signature to authenticate any resource records in a DDNS database. SIG RRs contain, within the digital signature itself, the type of resource record they are signing, the time until the signature will be valid, the time when the RR was signed, and the original time to live (TTL) value for the RR being signed.

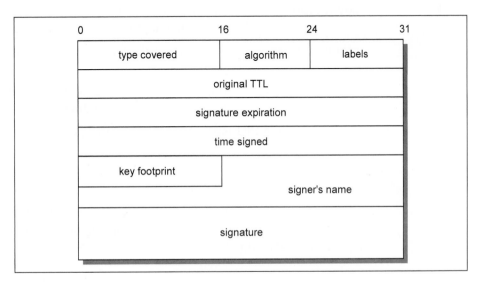

Figure 143. SIG resource record Rdata format

Figure 143 shows the fields used within the Rdata section of a SIG resource record. The fields are:

type covered   This field indicates the type of RR covered by this signature.

algorithm   This field indicates which encryption algorithm should be used with this key; in the case of IBM Dynamic IP, this field has a value of 1, which means that the RSA/MD5 algorithm is being used.

labels   This field indicates the number of labels (host and domain name strings separated by dots) in the SIG owner name.

original TTL   The original time-to-live for the signed resource record is included in order to avoid caching name servers decrement this value. This value is protected by the signature, and it is different from the TTL of the SIG record itself.

signature expiration The time until which this signature is valid. This value is represented in a number of seconds starting from 1 January 1970, GMT (ignoring leap seconds).

time signed The time when this signature was actually signed, represented in the same format as mentioned above.

key footprint This field determines, depending on the applicable encryption algorithm, how to decode the signature.

signer's name The fully qualified domain name of the signer generating this SIG RR.

signature The actual digital signature that authenticates an RR of the type indicated in the type covered field.

An example of a SIG resource record is shown below:

```
4660    IN    SIG    KEY 1 4 4660 820470267 817356268 0x8d00
                     client1.test.itsc.austin.ibm.com
                     ecK2L1zhtyVnNrI24/Viitl41reduDy7TU8dxSCoGoc9zc4IIGEy4E4uVPu
                     d4fjessH8XS+H2UVjLXhr66y6Gg==      ;Cr=auth
```

To keep data traffic and memory requirements in the DDNS server as small as possible, public encryption keys and digital signatures are converted to strings using a hash function, and they are then represented in so-called base-64 format.

> **Note:**
>
> KEY and SIG resource records always use a single line. We have indented the examples for illustration purposes only.

8.2.2.4 BIND versions

IBM offers both an enhanced version of BIND 4.9.3, and BIND 9.1under z/OS.

BIND 4.9.3 (enhanced) may still be needed for Sysplex load balancing, and also for IBM's version of DDNS.

BIND 9.1 can be made compatible with other vendor's BIND 8 and BIND 9 systems. BIND 9.1 supports DDNS function based on RFC 2136, in other words DNSSEC and TSIG security.

BIND versions are described in:

`http://www.isc.org/products/BIND`

8.2.2.5 IBM Implementation in relation to current standards

IBM implemented Dynamic DNS in 1995. This implementation was done by IBM research based on an Internet draft being discussed in the IETF at that time. In their opinion, the protocol was going to become a standard in a very short time. It is important to note that the IETF only standardizes protocol on the wire. The key management policies and the integration of DHCP and DDNS are IBM design, which is what differentiates an integrated product from a pure technology (such as an RFC-proposed standard).

The IETF did not standardize the draft from which IBM research worked. That standard evolved into the current RFC 3007 – Secure Dynamic Updates. Its resource records in the DNS are almost identical to IBM's implementation. However, the protocol on the wire is different. Also, it deals with the issue of integrating dynamic updates into secure DNS resolving (RFC 2065) and describes two modes of operation: Mode A and Mode B. In Mode A, the client-signed RRs are stored as part of the DNS data, whereas in Mode B, the server signs all the records. The IBM implementation of DDNS is actually very close to Mode A.

TSIG security is described in RFC 2845.

TSIG uses shared secrets rather than public key cryptography to secure communication between the name server and a client. It seeks to be a simpler alternative to both RFC 2065 for secure resolving and RFC 2137 for dynamic updates, in those situations where the client and the server can establish a trust relationship.

The following summary describes how IBM's implementation of Dynamic IP is different from the RFCs and also explains the reasons for that difference:

- IBM DDNS versus RFC 2137

  The logical evolution of IBM's implementation would be to move towards the RFC 2137 mechanism. This would not gain IBM any additional functionality but would ensure that IBM's DDNS clients and servers would maintain compatibility with software from other vendors complying with RFC 2137. This would become important if other vendors were developing clients or servers with this capability. At the current time, to our knowledge, no other vendor has a DDNS client or server that complies with RFC 2137, so making this change at this time would not be of any practical advantage to IBM.

- IBM DDNS versus RFC 2136\

  RFC 2136 was not designed for any authentication or expiration of resource records. It was also not designed for clients updating the DNS records. Its main design point was to allow administrators to update certain records without having to recycle the DNS. Thus, it does not have the following capabilities that are essential for the IBM integrated product:

    - No real security mechanism. It is possible to configure a list of IP addresses from where update requests to any record in the system can originate (per zone). Not only is this mechanism insecure (that is, anyone who has update capability can update anyone else's record), it is not scalable.

    - No mechanism of expiration. Thus, if a DHCP client was allocated an address and then moved away from the network, the DHCP server's IP address lease would expire after a period of time and the address would get reused, but the DNS entry would have to be manually removed.

    - No mechanism to detect out-of order update requests or prevent replay attacks. (No timestamp is associated with the update request.)

- IBM DDNS verses T-Sig

  T-Sig accomplishes the goal of providing an authentication mechanism for updates from clients. But it still does not provide an expiration mechanism. This means that if a client created its A-RR, and moved away from the network for some period of time, then the PTR record created by the DHCP server could be deleted by it but the A-RR (the host name to IP address mapping) would remain in the DNS. This has a security implication, because data intended for the old host name would be forwarded to the new holder of the IP address.

  T-Sig also has scalability issues, since the shared secret keys are theoretically unique between every client-name server pair and must be predefined in each.

  T-Sig does have a timestamp associated with its update requests, but since these timestamps are not stored with the data updated, it is questionable how out-of-order update requests or replay attacks could be effectively detected/prevented.

8.2.2.6 IBM DDNS UPDATE message format

The IBM implementation of DDNS uses the UPDATE message format shown in Figure 144.

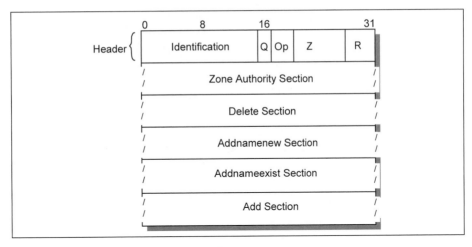

Figure 144. IBM DDNS UPDATE message format

The IBM message has a 32-bit header, which is identical to the first 32 bits of the RFC 2136 format header (see Figure 140). However, there are no "count" sections in the header. A response consists of the header only.

The body of an UPDATE message contains one or more of the following sections. Each section consists of a 1-byte type code, followed by a 1-byte count field (in units of RRs), followed by the RRs themselves:

ZONEAUTHORITY   This contains the SOA RR of the zone that is to be updated. There may only be one ZONEAUTHORITY section and it is always the first section in the body of the message.

DELETE   Used to specify RRs that are to be deleted.

ADDNAMENEW   Used to add an RR with a new name.

ADDNAMEEXIST   Used to update RRs with existing names.

ADD   Used for adding records with either new or existing names.

With the exception of the ZONEAUTHORITY section, sections in the body of the message may appear multiple times and in any order.

8.2.3 Proxy A Record update (ProxyArec)

In a DDNS environment, the client workstation requires DDNS client code to be able to update its A record on the DDNS server. The DHCP Server updates the PTR record at the DDNS server on behalf of the client.

An alternative approach is for the DHCP server to update both the PTR record *and* the A record at the DDNS server. This process is known as Proxy A Record Update (ProxyArec) and can be utilized in a situation where clients support DHCP but do not have DDNS client code. ProxyArec was discussed in the Internet draft Interaction between DHCP and DNS, but this draft has expired.

When using ProxyArec, the DDNS server cannot carry out an RSA authentication check on the client for which an update is being made; there is no interaction between the client and the DDNS server.

ProxyArec can be used in a situation where:

- Hosts are not mobile, or at least do not move from one domain to another.

- If mobile hosts have to be accommodated, then all the DHCP servers across which ProxyArec mobile hosts roam must be configured with the same RSA public/private key pair; otherwise, the digital signature verification would fail.

- The client host's DHCP program is capable of sending its fully qualified domain name (FQDN) to the DHCP server, using DHCP options 12 and 15 or 81.

- Host name hijacking is not a security concern.

The Internet draft specified the new DHCP option 81 for use with ProxyArec. Option 81 has the following format:

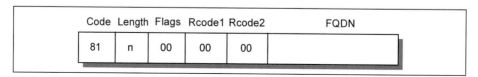

Figure 145. DHCP option 81 ProxyArec format

Where:

Flags   Has the following values:

> **0**   Client wants to retain responsibility for updating A record on DDNS server
>
> **1**   Client wants DHCP server to update A records
>
> **3**   DHCP server informs client that server assumes responsibility for A record updates (even if client wants to be responsible for update)

The default value is 1.

Rcode1 and Rcode2 Used by DHCP server to inform a DHCP client of the response code(s) from DDNS update.

FQDN Fully qualified domain name of client.

A DHCP client does not necessarily need to support option 81 in order to take advantage of ProxyArec, provided it uses options 12 and/or 15 to pass the host name to the DHCP server.

8.2.3.1 Using DDNS and ProxyArec together

In a mixed environment with both DDNS clients and clients that support DHCP only, if the DHCP server is configured for ProxyArec, the DDNS clients must be manually configured with option 81 and with Flags=0 if you wish the DDNS clients to carry out their own (secure) updates, otherwise the DHCP server will carry out all A record updates.

8.2.3.2 IBM implementation of ProxyArec

IBM has implemented an enhancement of ProxyArec that introduces a level of security. The DHCP server can be configured as being in "ProxyArec Protected" mode. In this mode, the DHCP server maintains a record of the MAC address of the client for which it created an A record initially. In a subsequent request for an update to the A record, the DHCP server checks the MAC address of the client before making the update. This gives some security against host name impersonation.

8.3 Network Information System (NIS)

The Network Information System (NIS) is not an Internet standard. It was developed by Sun Microsystems, Inc. It was originally known as the Yellow Pages.

NIS is a distributed database system which allows the sharing of system information in an AIX- or UNIX-based environment. Examples of system information that can be shared include the /etc/passwd, /etc/group, and /etc/hosts files. NIS has the following advantages:

- Provides a consistent user ID and group ID name space across a large number of systems

- Reduces the time and effort by users in managing their user IDs, group IDs, and NFS file system ownerships

- Reduces the time and effort by system administrators in managing user IDs, group IDs, and NFS file system ownerships

NIS is built on the SUN-RPC. It employs the client/server model. An NIS domain is a collection of systems consisting of:

NIS master server   Maintains *maps*, or databases, containing the system information, such as passwords and host names.

NIS slave server(s)   Can be defined to offload the processing from the master NIS server or when the NIS master server is unavailable.

NIS client(s)   The remaining systems that are served by the NIS servers.

The NIS clients do not maintain NIS maps; they query NIS servers for system information. Any changes to an NIS map is done only to the NIS master server (via RPC). The master server then propagates the changes to the NIS slave servers.

Note that the speed of a network determines the performance and availability of the NIS maps. When using NIS, the number of slave servers should be tuned in order to achieve these goals.

8.4 Lightweight Directory Access Protocol (LDAP)

The DCE architecture includes its own directory services. However, DCE, although widely implemented, is not a practical solution for every company. DCE is an "all-or-nothing" implementation. That is, in order for a company to gain the most benefit from its sophisticated security and directory services, every workstation must have a DCE client installed, every application and data server must be a DCE server, and the additional security and directory servers which make up the DCE infrastructure must also be in place. However, every company that has any kind of network has a requirement for at least some of the type of services provided by DCE.

Many network-based applications exist today that rely on their own directories (or databases) containing information describing various users, applications, files and other resources accessible from the network. For example, a company may have one directory containing information on all users and resources for their file servers and another directory containing information on all users and departments for their e-mail system. Much of the information in the two directories is common, but the two are most probably totally incompatible with each other. As the number of different networks and applications has grown, the number of specialized directories of information has also grown, resulting in islands of information that cannot be shared and are difficult to maintain. If all of this information could be maintained and accessed in a consistent and controlled manner, it would provide a focal point for integrating a distributed environment into a consistent and seamless system.

The Lightweight Directory Access Protocol (LDAP) is an open industry standard that has evolved to meet these needs. LDAP defines a standard method for accessing and updating information in a directory. LDAP is gaining wide acceptance as the directory access method of the Internet and is therefore also becoming strategic within corporate intranets. It is being supported by a growing number of software vendors and is being incorporated into a growing number of applications.

Further information on LDAP can be found in the redbook *Understanding LDAP*, SG24-4986.

8.4.1 LDAP - iightweight access to X.500

The OSI directory standard, X.500, specifies that communication between the directory client and the directory server uses the Directory Access Protocol (DAP). However, as an application layer protocol, DAP requires the entire OSI protocol stack to operate. Supporting the OSI protocol stack requires more resources than are available in many small environments. Therefore, an interface to an X.500 directory server using a less resource-intensive or lightweight protocol was desired.

LDAP was developed as a lightweight alternative to DAP. LDAP requires the lighter weight and more popular TCP/IP protocol stack rather than the OSI protocol stack. LDAP also simplifies some X.500 operations and omits some esoteric features. Two precursors to LDAP appeared as RFCs issued by the IETF, RFC 1202 – Directory Assistance Service and RFC 1249 – DIXIE Protocol Specification. These were both informational RFCs which were not proposed as standards. The directory assistance service (DAS) defined a method by which a directory client could communicate to a proxy on an OSI-capable host, which issued X.500 requests on the client's behalf. DIXIE is similar to DAS, but provides a more direct translation of the DAP. The first version of LDAP was defined in RFC 1487 – X.500 Lightweight Access, which was replaced by RFC 1777 – Lightweight Directory Access Protocol. LDAP further refines the ideas and protocols of DAS and DIXIE. It is more implementation-neutral and reduces the complexity of clients to encourage the deployment of directory-enabled applications. Much of the work on DIXIE and LDAP was carried out at the University of Michigan, which provides reference implementations of LDAP and maintains LDAP-related Web pages and mailing lists (see 8.4.10, "References" on page 335).

RFC 1777 defines the LDAP protocol itself. RFC 1777, together with the following RFCs, defines LDAP Version 2:

- RFC 1778 – The String Representation of Standard Attribute Syntaxes
- RFC 1779 – A String Representation of Distinguished Names
- RFC 1959 – An LDAP URL Format
- RFC 1960 – A String Representation of LDAP Search Filters

LDAP Version 2 has reached the status of draft standard in the IETF standardization process. Many vendors have implemented products that support LDAP Version 2. Some vendors are also implementing products that support all or parts of LDAP Version 3.

LDAP Version 3 is defined by RFC 2251 – Lightweight Directory Access Protocol (v3), which is a proposed standard. Related RFCs that are new or updated for LDAP Version 3 are:

- RFC 2252 – Lightweight Directory Access Protocol (v3): Attribute Syntax Definitions
- RFC 2253 – Lightweight Directory Access Protocol (v3): UTF-8 String Representation of Distinguished Names
- RFC 2254 – The String Representation of LDAP Search Filters
- RFC 2255 – The LDAP URL Format
- RFC 2256 – A Summary of the X.500 (96) User Schema for use with LDAPv3

LDAP defines the communication protocol between the directory client and server, but does not define a programming interface for the client. RFC 1823 – The LDAP Application Program Interface defines a C language API to access a directory using LDAP Version 2. This is an informational RFC only, but it has become a *de facto* standard. A standardized protocol and the availability of a common API on different platforms are the major reasons for the wide acceptance of LDAP. At the time of writing this book, RFC 1823 is in the process of being updated to support LDAP Version 3, but a new RFC number has not yet been assigned. This work in progress is the subject of an Internet draft The C LDAP Application Program Interface (see 8.4.10, "References" on page 335).

8.4.2 The LDAP directory server

LDAP defines a communication protocol. That is, it defines the transport and format of messages used by a client to access data in an X.500-like directory. LDAP does not define the directory service itself. An application client program initiates an LDAP message by calling an LDAP API. But an X.500 directory server does not understand LDAP messages. In fact, the LDAP client and X.500 server even use different communication protocols (TCP/IP versus OSI). The LDAP client actually communicates with a gateway process (also called a proxy or front end) that forwards requests to the X.500 directory server (see Figure 146). This gateway is known as an LDAP server. It fulfils requests from the LDAP client. It does this by becoming a client of the X.500 server. The LDAP server must communicate using both TCP/IP and OSI.

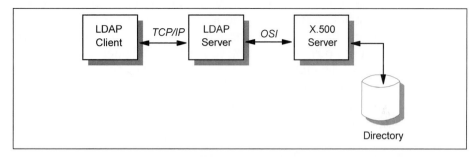

Figure 146. LDAP server acting as a gateway to an X.500 directory server

As the use of LDAP grew and its benefits became apparent, people who did not have X.500 servers or the environments to support them wanted to build directories that could be accessed by LDAP clients. This requires that the LDAP server store and access the directory itself instead of only acting as a gateway to X.500 servers (see Figure 147). This eliminates any need for the OSI protocol stack but, of course, makes the LDAP server much more complicated, since it must store and retrieve directory entries. These LDAP servers are often called stand-alone LDAP servers because they do not depend on an X.500 directory server. Since LDAP does not support all X.500 capabilities, a stand-alone LDAP server only needs to support the capabilities required by LDAP.

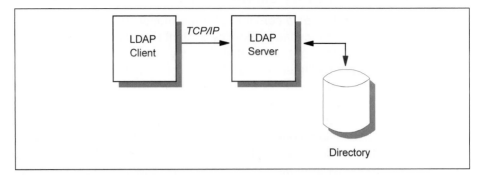

Figure 147. Stand-alone LDAP server

The concept of the LDAP server being able to provide access to local directories supporting the X.500 model, rather than acting only as a gateway to an X.500 server, is introduced in RFC 2251 – LDAP Version 3. From the client's point of view, any server that implements the LDAP protocol is an LDAP directory server, whether the server actually implements the directory or is a gateway to an X.500 server. The directory that is accessed can be called an LDAP directory, whether the directory is implemented by a stand-alone LDAP server or by an X.500 server.

8.4.3 Overview of LDAP architecture

LDAP defines the content of messages exchanged between an LDAP client and an LDAP server. The messages specify the operations requested by the client (search, modify, delete, and so on), the responses from the server, and the format of data carried in the messages. LDAP messages are carried over TCP/IP, a connection-oriented protocol, so there are also operations to establish and disconnect a session between the client and server.

The general interaction between an LDAP client and an LDAP server takes the following form:

- The client establishes a session with an LDAP server. This is known as binding to the server. The client specifies the host name or IP address and TCP/IP port number where the LDAP server is listening. The client can provide a user name and a password to properly authenticate with the server, or the client can establish an anonymous session with default access rights. The client and server can also establish a session that uses stronger security methods, such as encryption of data (see 8.4.5, "LDAP security" on page 329).

- The client then performs operations on directory data. LDAP offers both read and update capabilities. This allows directory information to be managed as well as queried. LDAP supports searching the directory for data meeting arbitrary user-specified criteria. Searching is the most common operation in LDAP. A user can specify what part of the directory to search and what information to return. A search filter that uses Boolean conditions specifies which directory data matches the search.

- When the client has finished making requests, it closes the session with the server. This is also known as unbinding.

Because LDAP was originally intended as a lightweight alternative to DAP for accessing X.500 directories, the LDAP server follows an X.500 model. The directory stores and organizes data structures known as entries. A directory entry usually describes an object, such as a person, a printer, a server, and so on. Each entry has a name called a distinguished name (DN) that uniquely identifies it. The DN consists of a sequence of parts called relative distinguished names (RDNs), much like a file name consists of a path of directory names in many operating systems, such as UNIX and OS/2. The entries can be arranged into a hierarchical tree-like structure based on their distinguished names. This tree of directory entries is called the directory information tree (DIT).

LDAP defines operations for accessing and modifying directory entries, such as:

- Searching for entries meeting user-specified criteria
- Adding an entry
- Deleting an entry
- Modifying an entry
- Modifying the distinguished name or relative distinguished name of an entry (move)
- Comparing an entry

8.4.4 LDAP models

LDAP can be better understood by considering the four models upon which it is based:

Information Describes the structure of information stored in an LDAP directory.

Naming Describes how information in an LDAP directory is organized and identified.

Functional Describes the operations that can be performed on the information stored in an LDAP directory.

Security   Describes how the information in an LDAP directory can be protected from unauthorized access.

The following sections discuss the first three LDAP models. LDAP security is covered in 8.4.5, "LDAP security" on page 329.

8.4.4.1 The information model

The basic unit of information stored in the directory is an entry, which represents an object of interest in the real world such as a person, server or organization. Each entry contains one or more attributes that describe the entry. Each attribute has a type and one or more values. For example, the directory entry for a person might have an attribute called telephoneNumber. The syntax of the telephoneNumber attribute would specify that a telephone number must be a string of numbers that can contain spaces and hyphens. The value of the attribute would be the person's telephone number, such as 919-555-1212. (A person might have multiple telephone numbers, in which case this attribute would have multiple values.)

In addition to defining what data can be stored as the value of an attribute, an attribute syntax also defines how those values behave during searches and other directory operations. The attribute telephoneNumber, for example, has a syntax that specifies:

- Lexicographic ordering.
- Case, spaces and dashes are ignored during the comparisons.
- Values must be character strings.

For example, using the correct definitions, the telephone numbers 512-838-6008, 512838-6008 and 5128386008 are considered to be the same. A few of the syntaxes that have been defined for LDAP are listed in the following table:

Table 7. Common LDAP attribute syntaxes

Syntax	Description
bin	Binary information.
ces	Case exact string, also known as a directory string. Case is significant during comparisons.
tel	Telephone number. The numbers are treated as text, but all blanks and dashs are ignored.
dn	Distinguished name.
Generalized Time	Year, month, day, and time represented as a printable string.

Syntax	Description
Postal Address	Postal address with lines separated by "$" characters.

Table 8 lists some common attributes. Some attributes have alias names that can be used wherever the full attribute name is used.

Table 8. Common LDAP attributes

Attribute, Alias	Syntax	Description	Example
commonName, cn	cis	Common name of an entry	John Smith
surname, sn	cis	A person's surname (last name)	Smith
telephoneNumber	tel	Telephone number	512-836-6008

An object class is a general description, sometimes called a template, of an object as opposed to the description of a particular object. For example, the object class person has a surname attribute, whereas the object describing John Smith has a surname attribute with the value Smith. The object classes that a directory server can store and the attributes they contain are described by *schema*. Schema define which object classes are allowed where in the directory, which attributes they must contain, which attributes are optional, and the syntax of each attribute. For example, a schema could define a person object class. The person schema might require that a person has a surname attribute that is a character string, specify that a person entry can optionally have a telephoneNumber attribute that is a string of numbers with spaces and hyphens, and so on.

Schema-checking ensures that all required attributes for an entry are present before an entry is stored. Schema also define the inheritance and subclassing of objects and where in the DIT structure (hierarchy) objects may appear. Table 9 lists a few of the common schema (object classes and their required attributes). In many cases, an entry can consist of more than one object class.

Table 9. Object classes and required attributes

Object class	Description	Required attributes
InetOrgPerson	Defines entries for a person.	commonName (cn) surname (sn) objectClass
organizationalUnit	Defines entries for organizational units.	ou objectClass
organization	Defines entries for organizations.	o objectClass

Though each server can define its own schema, for inter operability it is expected that many common schema will be standardized. There are times when new schema will be needed at a particular server or within an organization. In LDAP Version 3, a server is required to return information about itself, including the schema that it uses. A program can therefore query a server to determine the contents of the schema.

8.4.4.2 The naming model

The LDAP naming model defines how entries are identified and organized. Entries are organized in a tree-like structure called the directory information tree (DIT). Entries are arranged within the DIT based on their distinguished name (DN). A DN is a unique name that unambiguously identifies a single entry. DNs are made up of a sequence of relative distinguished names (RDNs). Each RDN in a DN corresponds to a branch in the DIT leading from the root of the DIT to the directory entry.

Each RDN is derived from the attributes of the directory entry. In the simple and common case, an RDN has the form <attribute-name>=<value>. A DN is composed of a sequence of RDNs separated by commas.

An example of a DIT is shown in Figure 148. The example is very simple, but can be used to illustrate some basic concepts. Each box represents a directory entry. The root directory entry is conceptual and does not actually exist. Attributes are listed inside each entry. The list of attributes shown is not complete. For example, the entry for the country UK (c=UK) could have an attribute called description with the value United Kingdom.

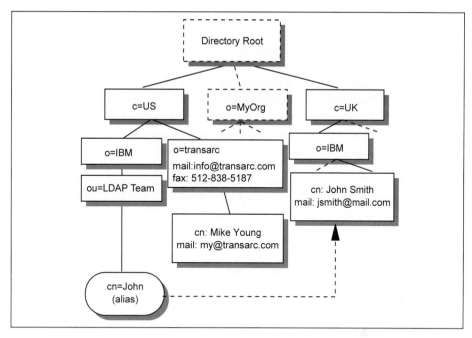

Figure 148. Example directory information tree (DIT)

It is usual to follow either a geographical or an organizational scheme to position entries in the DIT. For example, entries that represent countries would be at the top of the DIT. Below the countries would be national organizations, states, and provinces, and so on. Below this level, entries might represent people within those organizations or further subdivisions of the organization. The lowest layers of the DIT entries could represent any object, such as people, printers, application servers, and so on. The depth or breadth of the DIT is not restricted and can be designed to suit application requirements.

Entries are named according to their position in the DIT. The directory entry in the lower-right corner of Figure 148 has the DN cn=John Smith,o=IBM,c=DE.

Note:

DNs read from leaf to root as opposed to names in a file system directory which usually read from root to leaf. DCE directory entries are also named starting from the root.

The DN is made up of a sequence of RDNs. Each RDN is constructed from an attribute (or attributes) of the entry it names. For example, the DN cn=John

Smith,o=IBM,c=DE is constructed by adding the RDN cn=John Smith to the DN of the ancestor entry o=IBM,c=DE.

The DIT is described as being tree-like, implying it is not a tree. This is because of aliases. Aliases allow the tree structure to be circumvented. This can be useful if an entry belongs to more than one organization or if a commonly used DN is too complex. Another common use of aliases is when entries are moved within the DIT and you want access to continue to work as before. In Figure 148, cn=John,ou=LDAP Team,o=IBM,c=US is an alias for cn=John Smith,o=IBM,c=UK.

DNs in LDAP Version 3 are more restrictive than in LDAP V2. For example, in LDAP V2, semicolons could also be used to separate RDNs. LDAP V3 must accept the older syntax, but must not generate DNs that do not conform to the newer syntax.

As an LDAP directory can be distributed, an individual LDAP server might not store the entire DIT. A server might store the entries for a particular department and not the entries for the ancestors of the department. For example, a server might store the entries for the ITSO department at IBM. The highest node in the DIT stored by the server would be ou=ITSO,o=IBM,c=US. The server would not store entries for c=US or for o=IBM,c=US. The highest entry stored by a server is called a suffix. Each entry stored by the server ends with this suffix.

A single server can support multiple suffixes. For example, in addition to storing information about the ITSO department, the same server could store information about the sales department at Transarc. The server would then have the suffixes ou=ITSO,o=IBM,c=US and ou=sales,o=Transarc,c=US. Since a server might not store the entire DIT, servers need to be linked together in some way in order to form a distributed directory that contains the entire DIT. This is accomplished with *referrals*. A referral acts as a pointer to an entry on another LDAP server where requested information is stored. A referral is an entry of objectClass referral. It has an attribute, ref, whose value is the LDAP URL of the referred entry on another LDAP server. See 8.4.6, "LDAP URLs" on page 331, for further information.

The referral is a new feature in LDAP Version 3. Referrals allow a DIT to be partitioned and distributed across multiple servers. Portions of the DIT can also be replicated. This can improve performance and availability.

> **Note:**
>
> When an application uses LDAP to request directory information from a server, but the server only has a referral for that information, the LDAP URL for that information is passed to the client, and it is then the responsibility of that client to contact the new server to obtain the information. This is unlike the standard mechanisms of both DCE and X.500, where a directory server, if it does not contain the requested information locally, will always obtain the information from another server and pass it back to the client.

8.4.4.3 The functional model

LDAP defines operations for accessing and modifying directory entries. LDAP operations can be divided into the following three categories:

Query
Includes the search and compare operations used to retrieve information from a directory

Update
Includes the add, delete, modify, and modify RDN operations used to update stored information in a directory. These operations will normally be carried out by an administrator.

Authentication
Includes the bind, unbind, and abandon operations used to connect and disconnect to and from an LDAP server, establish access rights and protect information. For further information, please see 8.4.5, "LDAP security" on page 329.

The search operation

The most common operation is the search. This operation is very flexible and has some of the most complex options. The search operation allows a client to request that an LDAP server search through some portion of the DIT for information meeting user-specified criteria in order to read and list the result(s).

The search can be very general or very specific. The search operation allows the specification of the starting point within the DIT, how deep within the DIT to search, the attributes an entry must have to be considered a match, and the attributes to return for matched entries.

Some example searches expressed informally in English are:

- Find the postal address for `cn=John Smith,o=IBM,c=DE`.

- Find all the entries that are children of the entry `ou=ITSO,o=IBM,c=US`

- Find the e-mail address and phone number of anyone in an organization whose last name contains the characters "miller" and who also has a fax number.

To perform a search, the following parameters must be specified:

Base
A DN that defines the starting point, called the base object, of the search. The base object is a node within the DIT.

Scope
Specifies how deep within the DIT to search from the base object. There are three choices:

baseObject	Only the base object is examined.
singleLevel	Only the immediate children of the base object are examined; the base object itself is not examined.
wholeSubtree	The base object and all of its descendants are examined.

Search filter
Specifies the criteria an entry must match to be returned from a search. The search filter is a Boolean combination of attribute value assertions. An attribute value assertion tests the value of an attribute for equality, less than or equal, and so on.

Attributes to return
Specifies which attributes to retrieve from entries that match the search criteria. Since an entry may have many attributes, this allows the user to only see the attributes they are interested in. Normally, the user is interested in the value of the attributes. However, it is possible to return only the attribute types and not their values.

Alias dereferencing
Specifies if aliases are dereferenced. That is, the actual object of interest, pointed to by an alias entry, is examined. Not dereferencing aliases allows the alias entries themselves to be examined.

Limits
Searches can be very general, examining large subtrees and causing many entries to be returned. The user, (or the server), can specify time and size limits to prevent wayward searching from consuming too many resources. The size limit restricts the number of entries returned from the search. The time limit limits the total time of the search.

8.4.5 LDAP security

Security is of great importance in the networked world of computers, and this is true for LDAP as well. When sending data over insecure networks, internally or externally, sensitive information may need to be protected during transportation. There is also a need to know who is requesting the information and who is sending it. This is especially important when it comes to the update operations on a directory. The term security may be considered to cover the following four aspects:

Authentication Assurance that the opposite party (machine or person) really is who he/she/it claims to be.

Integrity Assurance that the information that arrives is really the same as what was sent.

Confidentiality Protection of information disclosure by means of data encryption to those who are not intended to receive it.

Authorization Assurance that a party is really allowed to do what it is requesting to do. This is usually checked after user authentication. In LDAP Version 3, this is currently not part of the protocol specification and is therefore implementation- (or vendor-) specific. Authorization is achieved by assigning access controls, such as read, write, or delete, for user IDs or common names to the resources being accessed. There is an Internet draft that proposes access control for LDAP (see 8.4.10, "References" on page 335).

The following sections focus on the first three aspects (since authorization is not contained in the LDAP Version 3 standard): authentication, integrity and confidentiality. There are several mechanisms that can be used for this purpose; the most important ones are discussed here. These are:

- No authentication
- Basic authentication
- Simple Authentication and Security Layer (SASL)

The security mechanism to be used in LDAP is negotiated when the connection between the client and the server is established.

8.4.5.1 No authentication

No authentication should only be used when data security is not an issue and when no special access control permissions are involved. This could be the case, for example, when your directory is an address book browsable by anybody. No authentication is assumed when you leave the password and DN field empty in the bind API call. The LDAP server then automatically assumes an anonymous user session and grants access with the appropriate access controls defined for this kind of access (not to be confused with the SASL anonymous user discussed in 8.4.5.3, "Simple Authentication and Security Layer (SASL)" on page 330).

8.4.5.2 Basic authentication

Basic authentication is also used in several other Web-related protocols, such as HTTP. When using basic authentication with LDAP, the client identifies itself to the server by means of a DN and a password, which are sent in the clear over the network (some implementations may use Base64 encoding instead). The server considers the client authenticated if the DN and password sent by the client matches the password for that DN stored in the directory. Base64 encoding is defined in the Multipurpose Internet Mail Extensions (MIME; see 11.2, "Multipurpose Internet Mail Extensions (MIME)" on page 399). Base64 is a relatively simple encryption, and it is not hard to break once the data has been captured on the network.

8.4.5.3 Simple Authentication and Security Layer (SASL)

SASL is a framework for adding additional authentication mechanisms to connection-oriented protocols. It has been added to LDAP Version 3 to overcome the authentication shortcomings of Version 2. SASL was originally devised to add stronger authentication to the IMAP protocol. SASL has since evolved into a more general system for mediating between protocols and authentication systems. It is a proposed Internet standard defined in RFC 2222 – Simple Authentication and Security Layer (SASL).

In SASL, connection protocols, such as LDAP, IMAP, and so on, are represented by profiles; each profile is considered a protocol extension that allows the protocol and SASL to work together. A complete list of SASL profiles can be obtained from the Information Sciences Institute (ISI) (see 8.4.10, "References" on page 335). Among these are IMAP4, SMTP, POP3, and LDAP. Each protocol that intends to use SASL needs to be extended with a command to identify an authentication mechanism and to carry out an authentication exchange. Optionally, a security layer can be negotiated to encrypt the data after authentication and ensure confidentiality. LDAP Version 3 includes such a command (ldap_sasl_bind()). The key parameters that influence the security method used are:

dn   This is the distinguished name of the entry which is to bind. This can be thought of as the user ID in a normal user ID and password authentication.

mechanism   This is the name of the security method that should be used. Valid security mechanisms are, currently, Kerberos Version 4, S/Key, GSSAPI, CRAM-MD5, and EXTERNAL. There is also an ANONYMOUS mechanism available, which enables authentication as an anonymous user. In LDAP, the most common mechanism used is SSL (or its successor, TLS), which is provided as an EXTERNAL mechanism.

credentials   This contains the arbitrary data that identifies the DN. The format and content of the parameter depends on the mechanism chosen. If it is, for example, the ANONYMOUS mechanism, it can be an arbitrary string or an e-mail address that identifies the user.

SASL provides a high-level framework that lets the involved parties decide on the particular security mechanism to use. The SASL security mechanism negotiation between client and server is done in the clear. Once the client and the server have agreed on a common mechanism, the connection is secure against modifying the authentication identities. However, an attacker could try to eavesdrop the mechanism negotiation and cause a party to use the least secure mechanism. In order to prevent this from happening, clients and servers should be configured to use a minimum security mechanism, provided they support such a configuration option. As stated earlier, SSL and its successor, TLS, are the mechanisms commonly used in SASL for LDAP. For details on these protocols, please refer to 21.8, "Secure Sockets Layer (SSL)" on page 747.

As no data encryption method was specified in LDAP Version 2, some vendors, for example, Netscape and IBM, added their own SSL calls to the LDAP API. A potential drawback of such an approach is that the API calls might not be compatible among different vendor implementations. The use of SASL, as specified in LDAP Version 3, should assure compatibility, although it is likely that vendor products will support only a subset of the possible range of mechanisms (maybe only SSL).

8.4.6 LDAP URLs

Since LDAP has become an important protocol on the Internet, a URL format for LDAP resources has been defined. RFC 2255 – The LDAP URL Format describes the format of the LDAP URL. LDAP URLs begin with ldap:// or ldaps://, if the LDAP server communicates using SSL. LDAP URLs can simply name an LDAP server, or can specify a complex directory search.

Some examples will help make the format of LDAP URLs clear. The following example refers to the LDAP server on the host saturn.itso.austin.ibm.com (using the default port 389):

```
ldap://saturn.itso.austin.ibm.com/
```

The following example retrieves all the attributes for the DN `o=Transarc,c=US` from the LDAP server on host saturn.itso.austin.ibm.com. Note that the port 389 is explicitly specified here as an example. Since 389 is the default port, it would not have been necessary to specify it in the URL.

```
ldap://saturn.itso.austin.ibm.com:389/o=Transarc,c=US
```

The following example retrieves all the attributes for the DN `cn=JohnSmith,ou=Austin,o=IBM,c=US`. Note that some characters are considered unsafe in URLs because they can be removed or treated as delimiters by some programs. Unsafe characters such as space, comma, brackets, and so forth should be represented by their hexadecimal value preceded by the percent sign.

```
ldap://saturn.itso.austin.ibm.com/cn=John%20Smith,ou=Austin,o=IBM,c=US
```

In this example, %20 is a space. More information about unsafe characters and URLs in general can be found in RFC 1738 – Uniform Resource Locators (URL).

8.4.7 LDAP and DCE

DCE has its own cell directory service (CDS; see 9.3.1.1, "Cell directory service" on page 350). If applications never access resources outside of their DCE cell, only CDS is required. However, if an application needs to communicate with resources in other DCE cells, the Global Directory Agent (GDA) is required. The GDA accesses a global (that is, non-CDS) directory where the names of DCE cells can be registered. This global directory (GDS) can be either a Domain Name System (DNS) directory or an X.500 directory. The GDA retrieves the address of a CDS server in the remote cell. The remote CDS can then be contacted to find DCE resources in that cell. Using the GDA enables an organization to link multiple DCE cells together using either a private directory on an intranet or a public directory on the Internet.

In view of LDAP's strong presence in the Internet, two LDAP projects have been sponsored by The Open Group to investigate LDAP integration with DCE technology.

8.4.7.1 LDAP interface for the GDA

One way LDAP is being integrated into DCE is to allow DCE cells to be registered in LDAP directories. The GDA in a cell that wants to connect to remote cells is configured to enable access to the LDAP directory (see Figure 149).

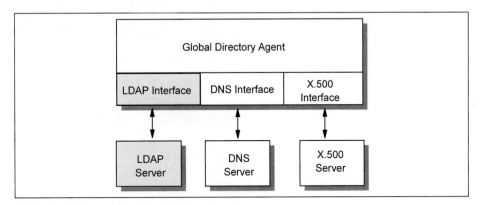

Figure 149. LDAP interface for the GDA

DCE originally only supported X.500 and DNS name syntax for cell names. LDAP and X.500 names both follow the same hierarchical naming model, but their syntax is slightly different. X.500 names are written in reverse order and use a slash (/) rather than a comma (,) to separated relative distinguished names. When the GDA is configured to use LDAP, it converts cell names in X.500 format to LDAP format to look them up in an LDAP directory.

8.4.7.2 LDAP interface for the CDS

DCE provides two programming interfaces to the Directory Service; Name Service Interface (NSI) and the X/Open Directory Service (XDS). XDS is an X.500 compatible interface used to access information in the GDS, and it can also be used to access information in the CDS. However, the use of NSI is much more common in DCE applications. The NSI API provides functionality that is specifically tailored for use with DCE client and server programs that use RPC. NSI allows servers to register their address and the type of RPC interface they support. This address/interface information is called an RPC binding and is needed by clients that want to contact the server. NSI allows clients to search the CDS for RPC binding information.

NSI was designed to be independent of the directory where the RPC bindings are stored. However, the only supported directory to date has been CDS. NSI will be extended to also support adding and retrieving RPC bindings from an LDAP directory. This will allow servers to advertise their RPC binding information in either CDS or an LDAP directory. Application programs could use either the NSI or the LDAP API when an LDAP directory is used (see Figure 150).

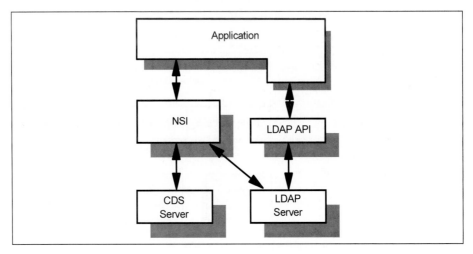

Figure 150. LDAP interface for NSI

An LDAP schema to represent RPC binding information is in the draft stage of development within the IETF.

8.4.8 The directory-enabled networks initiative (DEN)

In September 1997, Cisco Systems Inc. and Microsoft Corp. announced the so-called directory-enabled networks initiative (DEN) as a result of a collaborative work. Many companies, such as IBM, either support this initiative or even actively participate in ad hoc working groups (ADWGs). DEN represents an information model specification for an integrated directory that stores information about people, network devices, and applications. The DEN schema defines the object classes and their related attributes for those objects. As such, DEN is a key piece to building intelligent networks, where products from multiple vendors can store and retrieve topology and configuration-related data. Since DEN is a relatively new specification, products supporting it cannot be expected until about one to two years after the first draft, which was published late in 1997.

Of special interest is that the DEN specification defines LDAP Version 3 as the core protocol for accessing DEN information, which makes information available to LDAP-enabled clients and/or network devices.

DEN makes use of the Common information Model (CIM). CIM details a way of integrating different management models such as SNMP MIBs and DMTF MIFs.

More information about the DEN initiative can be found on the founder's Web sites or at:

```
http://www.dmtf.org/spec/denh.html
http://www.dmtf.org/spec/cims.html
```

8.4.9 Web-Based Enterprise Management (WBEM)

WBEM is a set of standards designed to deliver an integrated set of management tools for the enterprise. By making use of XML and CIM, it becomes possible to manage Network devices, Desktop systems, Telecom systems and Application systems, all from a Web browser. For further information, see:

```
http://www.dmtf.org/spec/wbem.html
```

8.4.10 References

Please refer to the following documents for more information about LDAP.

- RFCs

  RFC 1487 – X.500 Lightweight Directory Access Protocol

  RFC 1777 – Lightweight Directory Access Protocol

  RFC 1778 – The String Representation of Standard Attribute Syntaxes

  RFC 1779 – A String Representation of Distinguished Names

  RFC 1823 – The LDAP Application Program Interface

  RFC 1959 – An LDAP URL Format

  RFC 1960 – A String Representation of LDAP Search Filters

  RFC 2222 – Simple Authentication and Security Layer (SASL)

  RFC 2251 – Lightweight Directory Access Protocol (v3)

  RFC 2252 – Lightweight Directory Access Protocol (v3): Attribute Syntax Definitions

  RFC 2253 – Lightweight Directory Access Protocol (v3): UTF-8 String Representation of Distinguished Names

  RFC 2254 – The String Representation of LDAP Search Filters

  RFC 2255 – The LDAP URL Format

RFC 2256 – A Summary of the X.500(96) User Schema for use with LDAPv3

RFC 2820 – Access Control Requirements for LDAP

- Internet drafts

The C LDAP Application Program Interface, found at:

`http://search.ietf.org/internet-drafts/draft-ietf-ldapext-ldap-c-api-05.txt`

Access Control Model for LDAP, found at:

`http://search.ietf.org/internet-drafts/draft-ietf-ldapext-acl-model-07.txt`

- Other resources

SASL Mechanisms:

`ftp://ftp.isi.edu/in-notes/iana/assignments/sasl-mechanisms`

The University of Michigan was, and still is, an important contributor to the development of LDAP and can be considered a reliable, neutral source for extensive information:

`http://www.umich.edu/~dirsvcs/ldap`

Open source implementations of LDAP can be found at:

`http://www.OpenLDAP.org`

Chapter 9. Remote execution and distributed computing

One of the most fundamental mechanisms employed on networked computers is the ability to execute on the remote systems. That is, the user wishes to invoke an application on a remote machine. A number of application protocols exist to allow this remote execution capability, most notably the TELNET protocol. This chapter discusses some of these protocols. In addition, we discuss the concept of distributed computing.

9.1 TELNET

TELNET is a standard protocol with STD number 8. Its status is recommended. It is described in RFC 854 – TELNET Protocol Specifications and RFC 855 – TELNET Option Specifications.

The TELNET protocol provides a standardized interface, through which a program on one host (the TELNET client) can access the resources of another host (the TELNET server) as though the client were a local terminal connected to the server. See Figure 151 for more details.

For example, a user on a workstation on a LAN may connect to a host attached to the LAN as though the workstation were a terminal attached directly to the host. Of course, TELNET can be used across WANs as well as LANs.

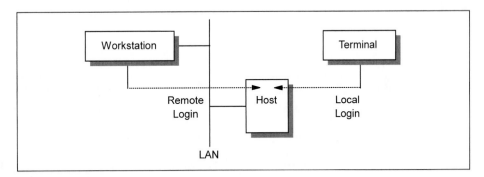

Figure 151. TELNET - Remote login using TELNET

Most TELNET implementations do not provide you with graphics capabilities.

9.1.1 TELNET operation

TELNET protocol is based on three ideas:

1. The Network Virtual Terminal (NVT) concept. An NVT is an imaginary device having a basic structure common to a wide range of real terminals. Each host maps its own terminal characteristics to those of an NVT, and assumes that every other host will do the same.

2. A symmetric view of terminals and processes.

3. Negotiation of terminal options. The principle of negotiated options is used by the TELNET protocol, because many hosts wish to provide additional services, beyond those available with the NVT. Various options may be negotiated. Server and client use a set of conventions to establish the operational characteristics of their TELNET connection via the "DO, DONT, WILL, WONT" mechanism discussed later in this chapter.

The two hosts begin by verifying their mutual understanding. Once this initial negotiation is complete, they are capable of working on the minimum level implemented by the NVT. After this minimum understanding is achieved, they can negotiate additional options to extend the capabilities of the NVT to reflect more accurately the capabilities of the real hardware in use. Because of the symmetric model used by TELNET (see Figure 152), both the host and the client may propose additional options to be used.

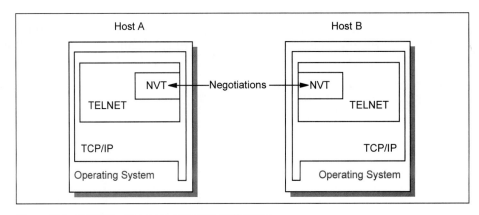

Figure 152. TELNET - The symmetric TELNET model

9.1.1.1 Network Virtual Terminal

The NVT has a printer (or display) and a keyboard. The keyboard produces outgoing data, which is sent over the TELNET connection. The printer receives the incoming data. The basic characteristics of an NVT, unless they are modified by mutually agreed options, are:

- The data representation is 7-bit ASCII transmitted in 8-bit bytes.

- The NVT is a half-duplex device operating in a line-buffered mode.

- The NVT provides a local echo function.

All of these can be negotiated by the two hosts. For example, a local echo is preferred because of the lower network load and superior performance, but there is an option for using a remote echo (see Figure 153), although no host is required to use it.

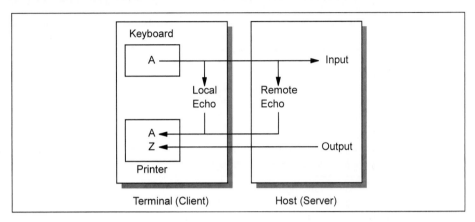

Figure 153. TELNET - Echo option

An NVT printer has an unspecified carriage width and page length. It can handle printable ASCII characters (ASCII code 32 to 126) and understands some ASCII control characters, such as:

Table 10. TELNET negotiation

Command	ASCII	Action
NULL (NUL)	0	No operation.
Line Feed (LF)	10	Moves printer to next print line, keeping the same horizontal position.
Carriage Return (CR)	13	Moves the printer to the left margin.
BELL (BEL)	7	Produces an audible or visible signal.
Backspace (BS)	8	Moves print head one character position towards the left margin.
Horizontal tab (HT)	9	Moves print head to the next horizontal tab stop.
Vertical tab (VT)	11	Moves printer to next vertical tab stop.
Form feed (FF)	12	Moves to top of next page, keeping the same horizontal position.

9.1.1.2 TELNET options

There is an extensive set of TELNET options, and the reader should consult STD 1 – Official Internet Protocol Standards for the standardization state and status for each of them. At the time of writing, the following options were defined:

Table 11. Telnet options

Num	Name	State	RFC	STD
0	Binary transmission	Standard	856	27
1	Echo	Standard	857	28
3	Suppress Go Ahead	Standard	858	29
5	Status	Standard	859	30
6	Timing mark	Standard	860	31
255	Extended options list	Standard	861	32
34	Linemode	Draft	1184	
2	Reconnection	Proposed		
4	Approximate. message size negotiation	Proposed		
7	Remote controlled trans and echo	Proposed	726	
8	Output line width	Proposed		
9	Output page size	Proposed		
10	Output carriage-return disposition	Proposed	652	
11	Output horizontal tabstops	Proposed	653	
12	Output horizontal tab disposition	Proposed	654	
13	Output formfeed disposition	Proposed	655	
14	Output vertical tabstops	Proposed	656	
15	Output vertical tab disposition	Proposed	657	
16	Output linefeed disposition	Proposed	658	
17	Extended ASCII	Proposed	698	
18	Logout	Proposed	727	
19	Byte macro	Proposed	735	
20	Data entry terminal	Proposed	1043	

Num	Name	State	RFC	STD
21	SUPDUP	Proposed	736	
22	SUPDUP output	Proposed	749	
23	Send location	Proposed	779	
24	Terminal type	Proposed	1091	
25	End of record	Proposed	885	
26	TACACS user identification	Proposed	927	
27	Output marking	Proposed	933	
28	Terminal location number	Proposed	946	
29	Telnet 3270 regime	Proposed	1041	
30	X.3 PAD	Proposed	1053	
31	Negotiate window size	Proposed	1073	
32	Terminal speed	Proposed	1079	
33	Remote flow control	Proposed	1372	
35	X Display location	Proposed	1096	
39	Telnet environment option	Proposed	1572	
40	TN3270 enhancements	Proposed	1647	
37	Telnet authentication option	Experimental	1416	
41	Telnet xauth	Experimental		
42	Telnet charset	Experimental	2066	
43	Telnet remote serial port	Experimental		
44	Telnet com port control	Experimental	2217	

All of the standard options have a status of recommended and the remainder have a status of elective. There is a historic version of the TELNET Environment Option which is not recommended; it is TELNET option 36, and was defined in RFC 1408.

Full-screen capability
Full-screen TELNET is possible provided the client and server have compatible full-screen capabilities. For example, VM and MVS provide a

TN3270-capable server. To use this facility, a TELNET client must support TN3270.

9.1.1.3 TELNET command structure

The communication between client and server is handled with internal commands, which are not accessible by users. All internal TELNET commands consist of 2 or 3-byte sequences, depending on the command type.

The Interpret As Command (IAC) character is followed by a command code. If this command deals with option negotiation, the command will have a third byte to show the code for the referenced option. See Figure 154 for more details.

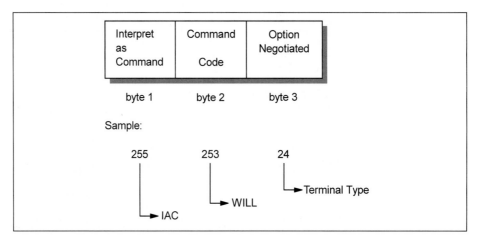

Figure 154. TELNET - Internal TELNET command proposes negotiation about terminal type

Some of the possible command codes are:

Table 12. Command codes

Command	Code	Comments
SE	240	End of sub-negotiation parameters.
NOP	241	No operation.
Data Mark	242	The data stream portion of a synch. This should always be accompanied by a TCP urgent notification.
Break	243	NVT character BRK.
Go Ahead	249	The GA signal.

Command	Code	Comments
SB	250	Start of sub-negotiation of option indicated by the immediately following code.
WILL	251	Shows desire to use, or confirmation of using, the option indicated by the code immediately following.
WONT	252	Shows refusal to use or continue to use the option.
DO	253	Requests that other party uses, or confirms that you are expecting the other party to use, the option indicated by the code immediately following.
DONT	254	Demands that the other party stop using, or confirms that you are no longer expecting the other party to use, the option indicated by the code immediately following.
IAC	255	Interpret As command. Indicates that what follows is a TELNET command, not data.

9.1.1.4 Option negotiation

Using internal commands, TELNET is able to negotiate options in each host. The starting base of negotiation is the NVT capability: each host to be connected must agree to this minimum. Every option can be negotiated by the use of the four command codes WILL, WONT, DO, and DONT. In addition, some options have sub-options: if both parties agree to the option, they use the SB and SE commands to manage the sub-negotiation. A simplified example of how option negotiation works is shown below:

Table 13. Option negotiation

Send	Reply	Meaning
DO transmit binary	WILL transmit binary	
DO window size	WILL window size	Can we negotiate window size?
SB Window size 0 80 0 24 SE		Specify window size.
DO terminal type	WILL terminal type	Can we negotiate terminal type?
SB terminal type SE		Send me your terminal characteristics.
	SB terminal type IBM=3278-2 SE	My terminal is a 3278-2.
DO echo	WONT echo	

The terminal types are defined in STD 2 – Assigned Numbers.

9.1.1.5 TELNET basic commands

The primary goal of the TELNET protocol is the provision of a standard interface for hosts over a network. To allow the connection to start, the TELNET protocol defines a standard representation for some functions:

IP	Interrupt Process
AO	Abort Output
AYT	Are You There
EC	Erase Character
EL	Erase Line
SYNCH	Synchronize

9.1.2 Terminal emulation (Telnet 3270)

Telnet may be used to make a TCP/IP connection to an SNA host. However, telnet 3270 is used to provide 3270 telnet emulation (TN3270). The following differences between traditional telnet and 3270 terminal emulation make it necessary for additional telnet options specifically for TN3270 to be defined:

- 3270 terminal emulation uses block mode rather than line mode.

- 3270 terminal emulation uses the EBCDIC character set rather than the ASCII character set.

- 3270 terminal emulation uses special key functions, such as ATTN and SYSREQ.

The TN3270 connection over telnet is accomplished by the negotiation of the following three different telnet options:

1. Terminal type

2. Binary transmission

3. End of record

A TN3270 server must support these characteristics during initial client/server session negotiations. Binary transmission and end of record options can be sent in any order during the TN3270 negotiation. Please note that TN3270 does not use any additional options during the TN3270 negotiation; it uses normal telnet options. After a TN3270 connection is established, additional options can be used. These options are TELNET-REGIME, SUPPRESS-GO-AHEAD, ECHO, and TIMING-MARK.

Terminal type option is a string that specifies the terminal type for the host, such as IBM 3278-3. The -3 following 3278 indicates the use of an alternate screen size other than the standard size of 24x80. The binary transmission telnet option states that the connection will be other than the initial NVT mode. If the client or server want to switch to NVT mode, they should send a command that disables binary option. A 3270 data stream consists of a command and related data. Since the length of the data associated with the command may vary, every command and its related data must be separated with the IAC EOR sequence. For this purpose, the EOR telnet option is used during the negotiation.

Other important issues for a TN3270 connection are the correct handling of the ATTN and SYSREQ functions. The 3270 ATTN key is used in SNA environments to interrupt the current process. The 3270 SYSREQ key is used in SNA environments to terminate the session without closing the connection. However, SYSREQ and ATTN commands cannot be sent directly to the TN3270 server over a telnet connection. Most of the TN3270 server implementations convert the BREAK command to an ATTN request to the host via the SNA network. On the client side, a key or combination of keys are mapped to BREAK for this purpose. For the SYSREQ key, either a telnet Interrupt Process command can be sent or a SYSREQ command can be sent imbedded into a TN3270 data stream. Similarly, on the client side, a key or combination of keys are mapped for SYSREQ.

There are some functions that cannot be handled by traditional TN3270. Some of these issues are;

1. TN3270 does not support 328x types of printers.
2. TN3270 cannot handle SNA BIND information.
3. There is no support for the SNA positive/negative response process.
4. The 3270 ATTN and SYSREQ keys are not supported by all implementations.
5. TN3270 cannot map telnet sessions into SNA device names.

9.1.3 TN3270 enhancements (TN3270E)

The 3270 structured field allows non-3270 data to be carried in 3270 data. Therefore, it is possible to send graphics, IPDS printer data streams and others. The structured field consists of a structured field command and one or more blocks following the command. However, not every TN3270 client can support all types of data. In order for clients to be able to support any of these functions, the supported range of data types should be determined when the telnet connection is established. This process requires additions to TN3270. To overcome the shortcomings of traditional TN3270, TN3270 extended attributes are defined. Please refer to RFC 2355 for detailed information about TN3270 enhancements (TN3270E).

In order to use the extended attributes of TN3270E, both the client and server should support TN3270E. If neither side supports TN3270E, traditional TN3270 can be used. Once both sides have agreed to use TN3270E, they begin to negotiate the subset of TN3270E options. These options are device-type and a set of supported 3270 functions, which are:

- Printer data stream type
- Device status information
- The passing of BIND information from server to client
- Positive/negative response exchanges

9.1.3.1 Device-type negotiation

Device-type names are NVT ASCII strings and all uppercase. When the TN3270E server issues the DEVICE-TYPE SEND command to the client, the server replies with a device type, a device name, or a resource name followed by the DEVICE-TYPE REQUEST command. The device-types are:

Table 14. TN3270E Device-types - Terminals

Terminal	Terminal-E	Screen size
IBM-3278-2	IBM-3278-2-E	24 row x 80 col display
IBM-3278-3	IBM-3278-3-E	32 row x 80 col display
IBM-3278-4	IBM-3278-4-E	43 row x 80 col display
IBM-3278-5	IBM-3278-5-E	27 row x 132 col display
IBM-DYNAMIC	n/a	n/a

Table 15. TN3270E device-types - Printers

Printer
IBM-3287-1

Since the 3278 and 3287 are commonly used devices, device-types are restricted to 3278 and 3287 terminal and printer types to simplify the negotiation. This does not mean that other types of devices cannot be used. Simply, the device-type negotiation determines the generic characteristic of the 3270 device that will be used. More advanced functions of 3270 data stream supported by the client are determined by the combination of read partition query and query reply.

The -E suffix indicates the use of extended attributes, such as partition, graphics, extended colors, and alternate character sets. If the client and the server have agreed to use extended attributes and negotiated on a device with the -E suffix, such as an IBM-DYNAMIC device or printer, both sides must be able to handle the 3270 structured field. The structured field also allows 3270 telnet clients to issue specific 3270 data stream to host applications that the client is capable of using.

From the point of TN3270E client, it is not always possible or easy to know device names available on the network. The TN3270E server should assign the proper device to the client. This is accomplished by using a device pool that is defined on the TN3270E server. Basically, these device pools contain SNA network devices, such as terminals and printers. In other words, The TN3270E implementation maps TN3270 sessions to specific SNA logical unit (LU) names, thus effectively turning them into SNA devices. The device pool not only defines SNA network devices but also provides some other important functions for a TN3270E session. Some of these are:

- It is possible to assign one or more printers to a specific terminal device.
- It is possible to assign a group of devices to a specific organization.
- A pool can be defined that has access to only certain types of applications on the host.

The TN3270E client can issue CONNECT or ASSOCIATE commands to connect or associate the sessions to certain types of resources. However, this resource must not conflict with the definition on the server and the device-type determined during the negotiation.

9.1.4 References

Please refer to the following RFCs for more information on telnet:

- RFC 854 – TELNET Protocol Specifications
- RFC 855 – TELNET Option Specifications.
- RFC 2355 – TN3270 Enhancements

9.2 Remote Execution Command protocol (REXEC and RSH)

Remote EXEcution Command Daemon (REXECD) is a server that allows execution of jobs submitted from a remote host over the TCP/IP network. The client uses the REXEC or Remote Shell Protocol (RSH) command to transfer the job across to the server. Any standard output or error output is sent back to the client for display or further processing.

9.2.1 Principle of operation

REXECD is a server (or daemon). It handles commands issued by foreign hosts, and transfers orders to slave virtual machines for job execution. The daemon performs automatic login and user authentication when an user ID and password are entered.

The REXEC command is used to define user ID, password, host address, and the process to be started on the remote host. On the other hand, RSH does not require you to send a user name and password; it uses a host access file instead. Both server and client are linked over the TCP/IP network. REXEC uses TCP port 512 and RSH uses TCP port 514. See Figure 155 for more details.

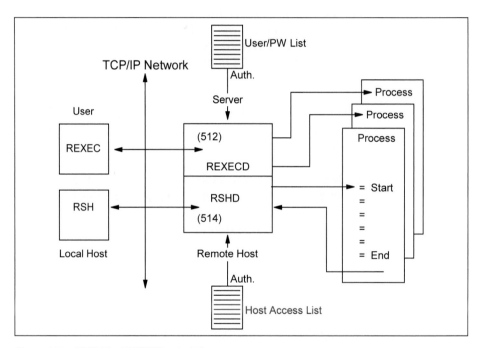

Figure 155. REXEC - REXECD principle

9.3 Introduction to the Distributed Computing Environment (DCE)

Distributed Computing Environment (DCE) is an architecture, a set of open standard services and associated APIs used to support the development and administration of distributed applications in a multiplatform, multivendor environment.

DCE is the result of work from the Open Systems Foundation (now called the Open Group), a collaboration of many hardware vendors, software vendors, customers, and consulting firms. The OSF began in 1988 with the purpose of supporting the research, development, and delivery of vendor-neutral technology and industry standards. One such standard developed was DCE. DCE Version 1.0 was released in January 1992.

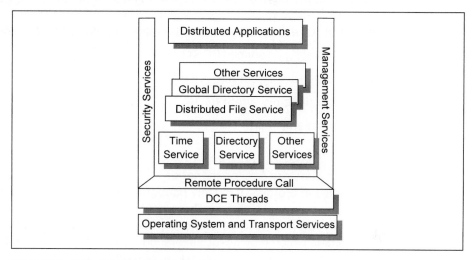

Figure 156. DCE architectural components

As shown in Figure 156, DCE includes the following major services:

- Directory service
- Security service
- Distributed time service
- Distributed file service
- Threads
- Remote Procedure Call

All the services above have Application Program Interfaces (APIs) that allow the programmer to use these functions. These services are described in more detail in the following pages.

The DCE architecture does not specifically require that TCP/IP should be used for transport services, but few other protocols today meet the open and multivendor requirements of the DCE design goals. In practice, the vast majority, if not all, implementations of DCE are based on TCP/IP networks.

9.3.1 DCE directory service

When working in a large, complex network environment, it is important to keep track of the locations, names, and services (and many other details) of the participants and resources in that network. It is also important to be able to access this information easily. To enable this, information should be stored in a logical, central location and should have standard interfaces for accessing the information. The DCE cell directory service does exactly this.

The DCE Directory Service has the following major components:

- Cell directory service (CDS)
- Global directory service (GDS)
- Global directory agent (GDA)
- Application Program Interface (API)

9.3.1.1 Cell directory service

The cell directory service manages a database of information about the resources in a group of closely cooperating hosts, which is called a cell. A DCE cell is very scalable and may contain many thousands of entities. Typically, even fairly large corporate companies will be organized within a single cell, which may cover several countries. The Directory Service database contains a hierarchical set of names, which represent a logical view of the machines, applications, users, and resources within the cell. These names are usually directory entries within a directory unit. Often, this hierarchical set of names is also called the namespace. Every cell requires at least one DCE server configured with the cell directory service (a directory server).

The CDS has two very important characteristics: it can be distributed, and it can be replicated. Distributed means that the entire database does not have to reside on one physical machine in the cell. The database can logically be partitioned into multiple sections (called replicas), and each replica can reside on a separate machine. The first instance of that replica is the master replica, which has read/write access. The ability of the cell directory to be split into several master replicas allows the option of distributing the management responsibility for resources in different parts of the cell. This might be particularly important if the cell covers, say, several countries.

Each master replica can be replicated. That is, a copy of this replica can be made on a different machine (which is also a directory server). This is called a read-only replica. Read-only replicas provide both resilience and performance enhancement by allowing a host machine to perform lookups to the nearest available replica.

Replicas are stored in a clearinghouse. A clearinghouse is a collection of directory replicas at a particular server. All directory replicas must be part of a clearinghouse (although not necessarily the same one).

The Cell Directory Service makes use of the DCE security service. When the CDS initializes, it must authenticate itself to the DCE security service. This prevents a fraudulent CDS from participating in the existing cell.

Figure 157 shows the directory structure of the CDS namespace. As you can see, the namespace is organized in a hierarchical manner.

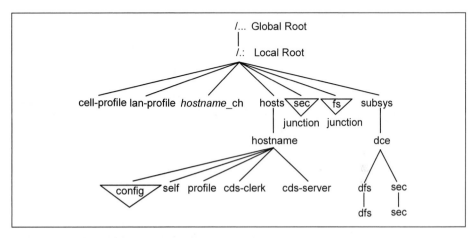

Figure 157. DCE - CDS namespace directory structure

Not all DCE names are stored directly in the DCE directory service. Resource entries managed by some services, such as the security service (sec) and the distributed file system (fs), connect into the namespace by means of specialized CDS entries called junctions. A junction entry contains binding information that enables a client to connect to a directory server outside of the directory service.

The security namespace is managed by the registry service of the DCE security component, and the DFS namespace is managed by the fileset location database (FLDB) service of DFS.

9.3.1.2 Global directory service and agent
The cell directory service is responsible for knowing where resources are within the cell. However, in a multi-cell network, each cell is part of a larger hierarchical namespace, called the global directory namespace. The global directory service (GDS) allows us to resolve the location of resources in

foreign cells. This is the case when a company wants to connect their cells together, or to the Internet.

In order to find a resource in another cell, a communication path needs to exist between the two cells. This communication path can currently be one of two types:

- CCITT X.500
- Internet Domain Name Services (DNS)

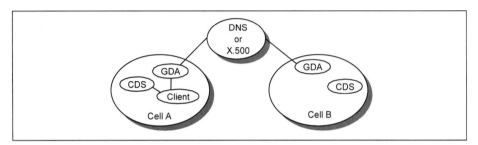

Figure 158. DCE - Global directory agent

In order for intercell communications to be accomplished, another component, the global directory agent, is required. The global directory agent (GDA) is the intermediary between the local cell and the Global Directory Service. In Figure 158, if the CDS does not know the location of a resource, it tells the client to ask the GDA for assistance. The GDA knows to which global namespace it is connected and queries the GDS (either DNS or X.500) for the name of the foreign cell directory server with which to communicate. Once in direct communication with the foreign cell directory server, the network name of the resource requested can be found. The global directory agent is the component that provides communications support for either DNS or X.500 environments.

9.3.2 DCE security service

Security is always a concern in a networked environment. In a large, distributed environment, it is even more crucial to ensure that all participants are valid users who access only the data with which they are permitted to work. The two primary concerns are authentication and authorization. Authentication is the process of proving or confirming the identity of a user or service. Authorization is the process of checking a user's level of authority when an access attempt is made. For example, if a user tries to make a change when read-only access has been granted, then the update attempt will fail.

The DCE security service ensures secure communications and controlled access to resources in this distributed environment. It is based on the Massachusetts Institute of Technology's Project Athena, which produced Kerberos. Kerberos is an authentication service that validates a user or service. The current DCE security service (DCE 1.2.2) is based on Kerberos Version 5.

Since the DCE security service must be able to validate users and services, it must also have a database to hold this information. This is indeed the case. The DCE security service maintains a database of principals, accounts, groups, organizations, policies, properties, and attributes. This database is called the registry. Figure 159 shows a pictorial representation of the registry tree. The registry is actually part of the cell directory namespace, although it is stored on a separate server.

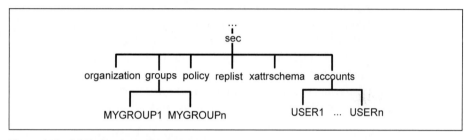

Figure 159. DCE - Registry directory structure

The DCE security service consists of several components:

Authentication service   Handles the process of verifying that principals are correctly identified. This also contains a *ticket granting service*, which allows the engagement of secure communications.

Privilege service   Supplies a user's privilege attributes to enable them to be forwarded to DCE servers.

Registry service   Maintains the registry database, which contains accounts, groups, principals, organizations, and policies.

Access control list facility   Provides a mechanism to match a principal's access request against the access controls for the resource.

Login facility	Provides the environment for a user to log in and initialize the security environment and credentials.

These services allow for user authentication, secure communication, authorized access to resources, and proper enforcement of security.

The DCE security service communicates with the cell directory service to advertise its existence to the other systems that are part of the cell. The DCE security service also uses the distributed time service to obtain timestamps for use in many of its processes.

9.3.2.1 Authentication service

The role of the authentication service is to allow principals to positively identify themselves and participate in a DCE network. Both users and servers authenticate themselves in a DCE environment, unlike security in most other client/server systems, where only users are authenticated. There are two distinct steps to authentication. At initial logon time, the Kerberos third-party protocol is used within DCE to verify the identity of a client requesting to participate in a DSS network. This process results in the client obtaining credentials, which form the basis for setting up secure sessions with DCE servers when the user tries to access resources.

In DCE Version 1.1, the idea of preauthentication was introduced, which is not present in the Kerberos authentication protocols. Preauthentication protects the security server from a rogue client trying to guess valid user IDs in order to hack into the system. In DCE 1.1 there are three protocols for preauthentication:

No preauthentication	This is provided to support DCE clients earlier than Version 1.1.
Timestamps	This is used by DCE Version 1.1 clients that are unable to use the third-party protocol. An encrypted timestamp is sent to the security server. The timestamp is decrypted and if the time is within five minutes, the user is considered preauthenticated. This option should be specified for cell administrators and non-interactive principals.
Third-party	This is the default used by DCE Version 1.1 (and later) clients. It is similar to the timestamps protocol, but additional information about the client is also encrypted in various keys.

The login and authentication process using the third-party preauthentication protocol is shown in Figure 160.

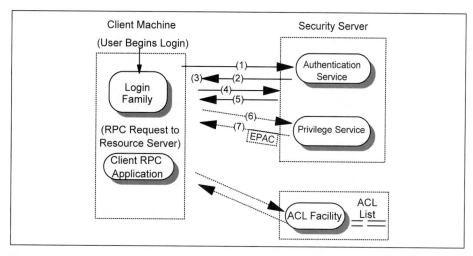

Figure 160. DCE - Authentication and login using third-party protocol

This process is described in detail below:

1. The user issues a request to log into the cell. However, the user must first be authenticated. The client creates two random conversation keys, one of them based on the machine session key. The login facility on the client then uses these keys and the supplied password to encrypt a request for an authentication ticket (ticket granting ticket, or TGT) from the security server.

2. The authentication service (AS) on a security server receives the request. The AS looks up the machine session key from the registry to decrypt the request. (Note that by knowing the machine session key, the security server proves to be valid for the cell. A false server would not know the machine session key.) If the decryption is successful and the timestamp is within five minutes, the AS encrypts a TGT using one of the client conversation keys provided. When successful, this encrypted TGT is returned to the client.

3. The client receives the TGT envelope and decrypts it using one of the client conversation keys it provided. Also included is a conversation key for the AS. Note that the TGT itself is encrypted with a conversation key of the AS. This valid TGT is proof that the user is now authenticated.

4. Now the user needs his authorization credentials, known as extended privilege attribute certificate (EPAC), from the privilege service (PS). Therefore, it must construct a privilege ticket granting ticket (PTGT)

request to retrieve this from the PS. To communicate with the PS, the client sends a request to the AS to contact the PS. This request is encrypted with the conversation key of the AS.

5. The AS receives this request. Using the secret key of the PS, the AS generates a conversation key for the client to use when contacting the PS. This is returned to the client and encrypted again with the AS conversation key. The client receives the envelope and decrypts it (using the conversation key) and discovers the conversation key for the PS. The client can now send a privilege service ticket to the PS.

6. The PS receives the request and decrypts it with its secret key successfully. This proves that the service ticket is legitimate, which also implies that the AS involved is also legitimate. From this, the PS knows that the client and the AS are valid. The PS constructs the EPAC, which lists the user's standard and extended registry attributes, including group membership. The PS creates more conversation keys and sends the EPAC and other information in an encrypted PTGT envelope to the client.

7. The client decrypts the PTGT envelope using the PS conversation key. Also, the client has the conversation key information and an encrypted PTGT (which the client cannot decrypt, since it is encrypted using the AS secret key).

8. Now, the client wants to contact an application server. To do so, it sends the PTGT to the AS and requests a service ticket for the application server. The AS receives the PTGT and decrypts it to obtain the EPAC information. It encrypts the EPAC information with the secret key of the application server and also provides a conversation key for the application server. This information is encrypted with the conversation key of the AS (which the client knows) and is returned to the client.

9. The client decrypts the envelope and discovers the application server's secret conversation key. Using this key, it can now contact the application server. By correctly decrypting the request from the client, the application server is able to determine that the client has been authenticated and by responding to the client, the client knows that it was, indeed, the real application server that it has contacted. The two will then establish a *mutually authenticated* session.

In addition to the extensive use of secret keys during logon, third-party authentication makes use of timestamps to ensure that the conversation is protected against intruders and eavesdropping. Timestamps make impersonation techniques, such as record and playback, ineffective. Also, the actual user password entered at logon time does not flow to the server as such. Instead, it is used as an encryption key for the initial logon messages which are then decrypted by the security server using its own copy of the password stored in the registry database.

If the security server is not able to authenticate the client for some reason, such as the entering an invalid password, an error is returned and the logon is terminated. However, if the exchange completes with the client being successfully authenticated, the security server returns credentials which are then used by the client to establish sessions with other DCE servers, such as resource and directory servers. These credentials contain information in the form of a privilege ticket granting ticket (PTGT) and extended privilege attribute certificate (EPAC):

EPAC   This is a validated list supplied by the security server containing the client's name, groups the client belongs to, and the extended registry attributes for the authenticated client (if any were defined and associated with their account). A client must present its EPAC (acquired during third-party authentication) to any server the client wishes to connect to in order to access its resources.

PTGT   A PTGT is a privilege ticket granting ticket. It contains the EPAC, which has all the relevant information about a user (UUID, group membership, ERAs, and so on). The PTGT is what is actually passed from a DCE client to a DCE server when it needs to access resources.

Public key support

The latest version of DCE (DCE Version 1.2.2) introduces the option of using public key technology (such as that from RSA or smart cards) to support login. Using this technology, the long-term key (or password) for a user (or other DCE object) does not need to be stored at the security server, providing enhanced security in the event of compromise of the security server. Administrators can specify that some principals may use the pre-DCE 1.2 mechanisms while others have access to the public key mechanism. DCE 1.2.2 retains full interoperability with previous DCE releases. At login, public key users receive credentials that allow them to use the current (Kerberos-based) DCE authentication mechanism. A new pre-authentication protocol is used. The login client does not have to determine whether a given user is public key-capable prior to requesting credentials.

9.3.3 DCE threads

Traditional applications (written in languages such as C, COBOL, and so on) have many lines of programming code which usually execute in a sequential manner. At any time, there is one point in the program that is executing. This can be defined as single threading. A thread is a single unit of execution flow within a process. Better application performance can often be obtained when a program is structured so that several areas can be executed concurrently. This is called multithreading. The capability of executing multiple threads is also dependent on the operating system.

In a distributed computing environment based on the client/server model, threads provide the ability to perform many procedures at the same time. Work can continue in another thread while the thread waiting for a specific response is blocked (for example, waiting for response from the network). A server may issue concurrent procedure call processing. While one server thread is waiting for an I/O operation to finish, another server thread can continue working on a different request.

To function well, thread support needs to be integrated into the operating system. If threads are implemented at the application software level instead of within the operating system, performance of multithreaded applications may seem slow.

The DCE thread APIs are either user-level (in operating systems that do not support threads, such as Windows 3.x) or kernel threads (such as AIX and OS/2). They are based on the POSIX 1003.4a Draft 4 standard. Since OS/2 also has threads, the programmer can use DCE threads or OS/2 threads.

DCE threads can be *mapped* onto OS/2 threads through special programming constructs. However, in order to write portable applications that can run on different platforms, only DCE threads should be used. In many cases, there is little performance difference resulting from this mapping.

9.3.4 DCE remote procedure call

The DCE remote procedure call (RPC) architecture is the foundation of communication between the client and server within the DCE environment.

> **Note:**
>
> The DCE RPC is conceptually similar to the ONC RPC (see 7.2.2, "Remote Procedure Call (RPC)" on page 266), but the protocol used on the wire is not compatible.

RPCs provide the ability for an application program's code to be distributed across multiple systems, which can be anywhere in the network.

An application written using DCE RPCs has a client portion, which usually issues RPC requests, and a server portion, which receives RPC requests, processes them, and returns the results to the client. RPCs have three main components:

- The interface definition language (IDL) and its associated compiler. From the specification file, it generates the header file, the client stub and the server stub. This allows an application to issue a remote procedure call in the same manner that it would issue a local procedure call.

- The network data representation, which defines the format for passing data, such as input and output parameters. This ensures that the bit-ordering and platform-specific data representation can be converted properly once it arrives at the target system. This process of preparing data for an RPC call is called marshalling.

- The run-time library, which shields the application from the details of network communications between client and server nodes.

The application programmer may choose to use multiple threads when making RPC calls. This is because an RPC is synchronous; that is, when an RPC call is made, the thread that issued the call is blocked from further processing until a response is received.

Remote procedure calls can be used to build applications that make use of other DCE facilities, such as the cell directory service (CDS) and the security service. The CDS may be used to find servers or to advertise a server's address for client access. The security service might be used to make authenticated RPCs that enable various levels of data integrity and encryption using the commercial data masking facility (CDMF), data encryption standard (DES), and other functions such as authorization.

9.3.5 Distributed time service

Keeping the clocks on different hosts synchronized is a difficult task as the hardware clocks do not typically run at the same rates. This presents problems for distributed applications that depend on the ordering of events that happen during their execution. For example, let us say that a programmer is compiling some code on a workstation and some files are also located on a server. If the workstation and the server do not have their time synchronized, it is possible that the compiler may not process a file, because the date is older than an existing one on the server. In reality, the file is newer, but the clock on the workstation is slow. As a result, the compiled code will not reflect the latest source code changes. This problem becomes more acute in a large cell where servers are distributed across multiple time zones.

The DCE distributed time service (DTS) provides standard software mechanisms to synchronize clocks on the different hosts in a distributed environment. It also provides a way of keeping a host's time close to the absolute time. DTS is optional. It is not a required core service for the DCE cell. However, if DTS is not implemented, the administrator must use some other means of keeping clocks synchronized for all the systems in the cell.

The distributed time service has several components. They are:

- Local time server
- Global time server
- Courier and backup courier time server

9.3.5.1 Local time server

The local time server is responsible for answering time queries from time clerks on the LAN. Local time servers also query each other to maintain synchronization on the LAN. If a time clerk cannot contact the required number of local time servers (as specified by the minservers attribute), it must contact global time servers through a CDS lookup.

It is recommended that there are at least three local time servers per LAN. This ensures that the time on the LAN is synchronized. The task of synchronization across multiple LANs in the cell is performed by global and courier time servers.

9.3.5.2 Global time server

A global time server (GTS) advertises itself in the cell directory service namespace so that all systems can find it easily. A GTS participates in the local LAN in the same way that local time servers do, but it has an additional responsibility. It also gives its time to a courier time server, which is located in a different LAN.

9.3.5.3 Courier roles

Local and global time servers can also have a courier role; they can be couriers, backup couriers, or non-couriers. The courier behaves similarly to other local time servers, participating in the time synchronization process. However, the courier does not look at its own clock. It requests the time from a global time server located in another LAN or in another part of the cell. Because the time is imported from another part of the network, this enables many remote LAN segments in all parts of the cell to have a very closely synchronized time value.

The backup courier role provides support in the event that the primary courier for that LAN is not available. The backup couriers will negotiate to elect a new courier and thus maintain the proper time synchronization with the global time servers. Note that even if a courier time server is not defined, local time servers and clerks will try to contact a global time server if they cannot contact the minimum number of servers from the local segment.

The default for time servers is the non-courier role. As long as enough local time servers can be contacted, they will not contact a global time server.

In a large or distributed network, local time servers, global time servers, and courier time servers automatically and accurately make the process of time synchronization function.

9.3.6 Distributed file service (DFS)

The distributed file service is not really a core component of DCE, but it is an application that is integrated with, and uses, the other DCE services. DFS provides global file sharing. Access to files located anywhere in interconnected DCE cells is transparent to the user. To the user, it appears as if the files were located on a local drive. DFS servers and clients may be heterogeneous computers running different operating systems.

The origin of DFS is Transarc Corporation's implementation of the Andrew File System (AFS) from Carnegie-Mellon University (see 10.4, "The Andrew File System (AFS)" on page 383). DFS conforms to POSIX 1003.1 for file system semantics and POSIX 1003.6 for access control security. DFS is built onto, and integrated with, all of the other DCE services, and was developed to address identified distributed file system needs, such as:

- Location transparency
- Uniform naming
- Good performance
- Security
- High availability
- File consistency control
- NFS interoperability

DFS follows the client/server model, and it extends the concept of DCE cells by providing DFS administrative domains, which are an administratively independent collection of DFS server and client systems within a DCE cell.

There may be many DFS file servers in a cell. Each DFS file server runs the file exporter service that makes files available to DFS clients. The file exporter is also known as the protocol exporter. DFS clients run the cache manager, which is an intermediary between applications that request files from DFS servers. The cache manager translates file requests into RPCs to the file exporter on the file server system, and stores (caches) file data on disk or in memory to minimize server accesses. It also ensures that the client always has an up-to-date copy of a file.

The DFS file server can serve two different types of file systems:

- Local file system (LFS), also known as the episode file system
- Some other file system, such as the UNIX File System (UFS)

Full DFS functionality is only available with LFS and includes:

- High performance
- Log-based, fast restarting filesets for quick recovery from failure
- High availability with replication, automatic updates and automatic bypassing of failed file server
- Strong security with integration to the DCE security service providing ACL authorization control

9.3.6.1 File naming

DFS uses the cell directory service (CDS) name /.:/fs as a junction to its self-administered namespace (see Figure 157 on page 351). DFS objects of a cell (files and directories) build a file system tree rooted in /.:/fs of every cell. Directories and files can be accessed by users anywhere on the network, using the same file or directory names, no matter where they are physically located, since all DCE resources are part of a global namespace.

As an example of DFS file naming, to access a particular file from within a cell, a user might use the following name:

```
/.:/fs/usr/woodd/games/tictactoe.exe
```

From outside the cell, using GDS (X.500) format, the following name would be used:

```
/.../C=US/O=IBM/OU=ITSC/fs/usr/woodd/games/tictactoe.exe
```

or in DNS format:

```
/.../itsc.ibm.com/usr/woodd/games/tictactoe.exe
```

9.3.6.2 DFS performance

Performance is one of the main goals of DFS, and it achieves it by including features such as:

Cache manager   Files requested from the server are stored in cache at the client so that the client does not need to send requests for data across the network every time the user needs a file. This reduces load on the server file systems and minimizes network traffic, thereby improving performance.

Multithreaded servers DFS servers make use of DCE threads support to efficiently handle multiple file requests from clients.

RPC pipes The RPC pipe facility is extensively used to transport large amounts of data efficiently.

Replication Replication support allows efficient load-balancing by spreading out the requests for files across multiple servers.

9.3.6.3 File consistency

Using copies of files cached in memory at the client side could potentially cause problems when the file is being used by multiple clients in different locations. DFS uses a token mechanism to synchronize concurrent file accesses by multiple users and ensure that each user is always working with the latest version of a file. The whole process is transparent to the user.

9.3.6.4 Availability

LFS file sets can be replicated on multiple servers for better availability. Every fileset has a single read/write version and multiple read-only replicas. The read/write version is the only one that can be modified. Every change in the read/write fileset is reflected in the replicated filesets. If there is a crash of a server system housing a replicated fileset, the work is not interrupted, and the client is automatically switched to another replica.

9.3.6.5 DFS security

DCE security provides DFS with authentication of user identities, verification of user privileges, and authorization control. Using the DCE security's ACL mechanism, DFS provides more flexible and powerful access control than that typically provided by an operating system (for example, UNIX read, write, and execute permissions).

9.3.6.6 DFS/NFS interoperability

DFS files can be exported to NFS so that NFS clients can access them as unauthenticated users. This requires an NFS/DFS authenticating gateway facility, which may not be available in every implementation.

9.3.7 References

For additional information on DCE, please refer to one of the following IBM redbooks:

Understanding OSF DCE 1.1 for AIX and OS/2, SG24-4616

DCE Cell Design Considerations, SG24-4746

Administering DCE and DFS 2.1 for AIX (and OS/2 Clients), SG24-4714

Security on the Web Using DCE Technology, SG24-4949

For information on the most current release of DCE (Version 1.2.2), view the Open Group Web site at:

`http://www.opengroup.org/dce`

Chapter 10. File related protocols

The TCP/IP protocol suite provides a number of protocols for the manipulation of files. In general, there are two different mechanisms for accessing remote files. The most simple mechanism is by transferring the particular file to the local machine. In this case, multiple copies of the same file are likely to exist. File Transfer Protocol (FTP) and Trivial File Transfer Protocol (TFTP) both employ this mechanism of file sharing.

An alternate approach to accessing files is via the use of the file system. In this case, the operating machine on the local host provides the necessary functionality to access the file on the remote machine. The user and application on the local machine are not aware that the file actually resides on the remote machine; they just read and write the file through the file system as if it were on the local machine. In this case, only one copy of the file exists, and the file system is responsible for coordinating updates. The Network File System (NFS) and the Andrew File System (AFS) provide this type of functionality.

10.1 File Transfer Protocol (FTP)

FTP is a standard protocol with STD Number 9. Its status is recommended. It is described in RFC 959 – File Transfer Protocol (FTP) and updated in RFC 2228 – FTP Security Extensions.

Copying files from one machine to another is one of the most frequently used operations. The data transfer between client and server can be in either direction. The client can send a file to the server machine. It can also request a file from this server.

To access remote files, the user must identify himself or herself to the server. At this point, the server is responsible for authenticating the client before it allows the file transfer.

From an FTP user's point of view, the link is connection-oriented. In other words, it is necessary to have both hosts up and running TCP/IP to establish a file transfer.

10.1.1 Overview of FTP

FTP uses TCP as a transport protocol to provide reliable end-to-end connections. The FTP server listens to connections on port 20 and 21. Two connections are used: the first is for login and follows the TELNET protocol.

The second is for managing the data transfer. As it is necessary to log into the remote host, the user must have a user name and a password to access files and directories. The user who initiates the connection assumes the client function, while the server function is provided by the remote host.

On both sides of the link, the FTP application is built with a protocol interpreter (PI), a data transfer process (DTP), and a user interface (see Figure 161).

The user interface communicates with the protocol interpreter, which is in charge of the control connection. This protocol interpreter has to communicate any necessary control commands to the remote system.

On the opposite side of the link, the protocol interpreter, besides its function of responding to the TELNET protocol, has to initiate the data connection. During the file transfer, the data management is performed by DTPs. After a user's request is completed, the server's PI has to close the data connection.

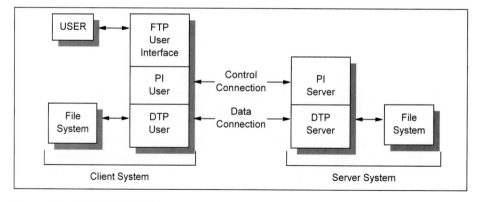

Figure 161. FTP - FTP principle

10.1.2 FTP operations

When using FTP, the user will perform some or all of the following operations:

- Connect to a remote host
- Select a directory
- List files available for transfer
- Define the transfer mode
- Copy files to or from the remote host
- Disconnect from the remote host

10.1.2.1 Connecting to a remote host

To execute a file transfer, the user begins by logging into the remote host. This is the primary method of handling the security. The user must have a user ID and password for the remote host, unless using anonymous FTP, which is described in 10.1.6, "Anonymous FTP" on page 371.

There are four commands that are used:

Open   Selects the remote host and initiates the login session.

User   Identifies the remote user ID.

Pass   Authenticates the user.

Site   Sends information to the foreign host that is used to provide services specific to that host.

10.1.2.2 Selecting a directory

When the control link is established, the user can use the cd (change directory) subcommand to select a remote directory to work with. Obviously, the user can only access directories for which the remote user ID has the appropriate authorization. The user can select a local directory with the lcd (local change directory) command. The syntax of these commands depends upon the operating system in use.

10.1.2.3 Listing files available for transfer

This task is performed using the dir or ls subcommands.

10.1.2.4 Specifying the transfer mode

Transferring data between dissimilar systems often requires transformations of the data as part of the transfer process. The user has to decide on two aspects of the data handling:

- The way the bits will be moved from one place to another

- The different representations of data upon the system's architecture

This is controlled using two subcommands:

Mode   Specifies whether the file is to be treated as having a record structure in a byte stream format.

        Block   Logical record boundaries of the file are preserved.

        Stream   The file is treated as a byte stream. This is the default, and provides more efficient transfer but may not produce the desired results when working with a record-based file system.

Type   Specifies the character sets used for the data.

  ASCII   Indicates that both hosts are ASCII-based, or that if one is ASCII-based and the other is EBCDIC-based, that ASCII-EBCDIC translation should be performed.

  EBCDIC   Indicates that both hosts use an EBCDIC data representation.

  Image   Indicates that data is to be treated as contiguous bits packed in 8-bit bytes.

Because these subcommands do not cover all possible differences between systems, the SITE subcommand is available to issue implementation-dependent commands.

10.1.2.5 Transferring files
The following commands can be used to copy files between FTP clients and servers:

Get   Copies a file from the remote host to the local host.

Mget   Copies multiple files from the remote to the local host.

Put   Copies a file from the local host to the remote host.

Mput   Copies multiple files from the local host to the remote host.

10.1.2.6 Using passive mode
Passive mode reverses the direction of establishment of the data transfer connection. The FTP server on the remote host selects a port and informs the FTP client program which port to use when the client connects to the server on the remote host. Since passive mode allows the FTP server to create a ephemeral port for the connection, we no longer need to put a dangerous service listener on a fixed port. Also, having both the control connection and the data connection initiated from the same side (client side) makes it easier to configure filtering rules for firewalls. Therefore, this mode is also referred to as firewall-friendly mode. Please see 21.3.4.2, "An example: FTP proxy server" on page 685 for more detail about FTP proxy server and passive mode.

10.1.2.7 Using proxy transfer
Proxy transfer allows the clients that have a slow connection to use a third-party transfer between two remote servers. A client that is connected to a server opens an FTP connection to another server using that server by issuing the `proxy open` command. For example, client A wants to download a file from server B but the connection is slow. In this case, client A can first

connect to server C and then issue the `proxy open server_B` command to log into server B. Client A sends `proxy get filename` to transfer the file from server B to server C.

10.1.2.8 Terminating the transfer session

The following commands are used to end an FTP session:

Quit   Disconnects from the remote host and terminates FTP. Some implementations use the BYE subcommand.

Close   Disconnects from the remote host but leaves the FTP client running. An `open` command can be issued to work with a new host.

10.1.3 Reply codes

In order to manage these operations, the client and server conduct a dialog using the TELNET convention. The client issues commands, and the server responds with *reply codes*. The responses also include comments for the benefit of the user, but the client program uses only the codes.

Reply codes are three digits long, with the first digit being the most significant:

Table 16. FTP reply codes - The second and third digits provide more details about the response

Reply code	Description
1xx	Positive preliminary reply.
2xx	Positive completion reply.
3xx	Positive intermediate reply.
4xx	Transient negative completion reply.
5xx	Permanent negative completion reply.

10.1.3.1 Example

For each user command, shown like `this`, the FTP server responds with a message beginning with a 3-digit reply code, shown like this:

```
FTP foreignhost
220 service ready
USERNAME cms01
331 user name okay
PASSWORD xyxyx
230 user logged in
TYPE Image
200 command okay
```

10.1.4 FTP scenario

A LAN user has to transfer a file from a workstation to a system running VM. The file has to be transferred from the workstation's disk drive to the minidisk 191 owned by CMS user cms01. There is no Resource Access Control Facility (RACF) installed. The symbolic name corresponding to an Internet address is host01.itsc.raleigh.ibm.com. See Figure 162 for more details.

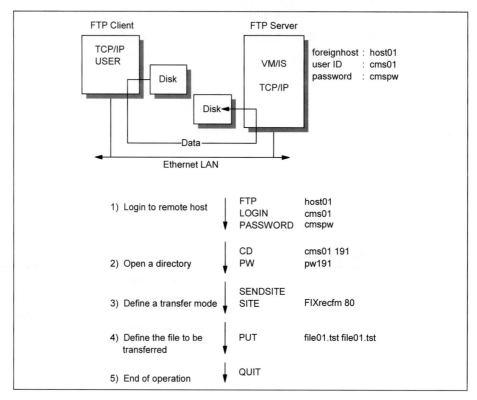

Figure 162. FTP - FTP scenario

10.1.5 A sample FTP session

Figure 163 illustrates an FTP session as seen from an FTP client program.

```
[C:\SAMPLES] ftp host01.itsc.raleigh.ibm.com
Connected to host01.itsc.raleigh.ibm.com.
220 host01 FTP server (Version 4.1 Sat Nov 23 12:52:09 CST 1991) ready.
Name (rs60002): cms01
331 Password required for cms01.
Password: xxxxxx
230 User cms01 logged in.
ftp> put file01.tst file01.tst
200 PORT command successful.
150 Opening data connection for file01.tst (1252 bytes).
226 Transfer complete.
local: file01.tst remote: file01.tst
1285 bytes received in 0.062 seconds (20 Kbytes/s)
ftp> close
221 Goodbye.
ftp> quit
```

Figure 163. FTP - A sample FTP session

10.1.6 Anonymous FTP

Many TCP/IP sites implement what is known as *anonymous FTP*, which means that these sites allow public access to some file directories. The remote user only needs to use the login name *anonymous* and password *guest* or some other common password conventions, for example, the user's Internet e-mail ID. The password convention used on a system is explained to the user during the login process.

10.1.7 Remote job entry using FTP

The FTP server on MVS allows sending job control language (JCL) to the internal reader. With this feature, a kind of remote job entry (RJE) for TCP/IP can be implemented. It uses the site filetype=jes subcommand to indicate that the file sent is not really a file, but a job. The FTP server on MVS then transfers the job to the job entry system (JES) for spooling and execution. The individual spool files can be received with the get subcommand of FTP.

10.2 Trivial File Transfer Protocol (TFTP)

The TFTP protocol is a standard protocol with STD number 33. Its status is elective and it is described in RFC 1350 – The TFTP Protocol (Revision 2). Updates to TFTP can be found in the following RFCs: 1785, 2347, 2348, and 2349.

TFTP file transfer is a disk-to-disk data transfer, as opposed to, for example, the VM SENDFILE command, a function that is considered in the TCP/IP world as a mailing function, where you send out the data to someone's mailbox (reader in the case of VM).

TFTP is an extremely simple protocol to transfer files. This is deliberate, so that it can be easily implemented. Some diskless devices use TFTP to download their firmware at boot time.

TFTP is implemented on top of UDP (User Datagram Protocol). The TFTP client initially sends read/write request via port 69, then the server and the client determines the port that they will use for the rest of the connection. TFTP lacks most of the features of FTP (see 10.1, "File Transfer Protocol (FTP)" on page 365). The only thing it can do is read/write a file from/to a server.

> **Note:**
>
> TFTP has no provisions for user authentication; in that respect, it is an insecure protocol.

10.2.1 TFTP usage

The command TFTP <hostname> takes you to the interactive prompt, where you can enter subcommands, such as the following:

Connect <host>	Specify destination host ID
Mode <ascii/binary>	Specify the type of transfer mode
Get <remote filename> [<local filename>]	Retrieve a file
Put <remote filename> [<local filename>]	Store a file
Verbose	Toggle verbose mode, which displays additional information during file transfer, on or off
Quit	Exit TFTP

For a full list of these commands, see the user's guide of your particular TFTP implementation.

10.2.2 Protocol description

Any transfer begins with a request to read or write a file. If the server grants the request, the connection is opened and the file is sent in blocks of 512 bytes (fixed length). Blocks of the file are numbered consecutively, starting at 1. Each data packet must be acknowledged by an acknowledgment packet before the next one can be sent. Termination of the transfer is assumed on a data packet of less than 512 bytes.

Almost all errors will cause termination of the connection (lack of reliability). If a packet gets lost in the network, a timeout will occur, after which a retransmission of the last packet (data or acknowledgment) will take place.

There was a serious bug, known as the Sorcerer's Apprentice Syndrome, in RFC 783. It may cause excessive retransmission by both sides in some network delay scenarios. It was documented in RFC 1123 and was corrected in RFC 1350. OACK packet was added to the TFTP packets as an extension. This is described in RFC 2347. For details, please refer to the RFCs.

10.2.2.1 TFTP packets

There are six types of packets:

Table 17. TFTP packet types

Opcode	Operation
1	Read Request (RRQ)
2	Write Request (WRQ)
3	Data (DATA)
4	Acknowledgment (ACK)
5	Error (ERROR)
6	Option Acknowledgment (OACK)

The TFTP header contains the *opcode* associated with the packet. See Figure 164 for more details.

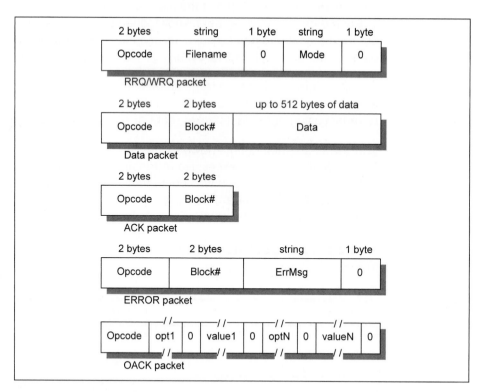

Figure 164. TFTP - TFTP packets

10.2.2.2 Data modes

Three modes of transfer are currently defined in RFC 1350:

NetASCII US-ASCII, as defined in the USA Standard Code for Information Interchange with modifications specified in RFC 854 – Telnet Protocol Specification and extended to use the high order bit. (That is, it is an 8-bit character set, unlike US-ASCII, which is 7-bit.)

Octet   Raw 8-bit bytes, also called binary.

Mail   This mode was originally defined in RFC 783 and was declared obsolete by RFC 1350. It allowed for sending mail to a user rather than transferring to a file.

The mode used is indicated in the Request for Read/Write packet (RRQ/WRQ).

10.2.3 TFTP multicast option

This option allows multiple clients to get files simultaneously from the server using the multicast packets. For example, when two similar machines are remotely booted, they can retrieve the same config file simultaneously by adding the multicast option to the TFTP option set. TFTP multicast option is described in RFC 2090.

Here is the TFTP read request packet, which is modified to include the multicast option:

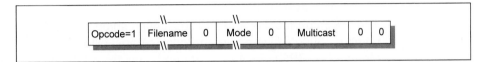

Figure 165. TFTP - Read request packet with multicast option

If the server accepts the multicast, it sends an option acknowledgment (OACK) packet to the server including the multicast option. This packet consists of the multicast address and a flag that specifies whether the client should send acknowledgments (ACK).

10.2.4 Security issues

Since TFTP does not have any authentication mechanism, the server should protect the host files. Generally, TFTP servers do not allow write access and only allow read access to public directories. Some server implementations also have a host access list.

10.3 Network File System (NFS)

The SUN Microsystems Network File System (NFS) protocol enables machines to share file systems across a network. The NFS protocol is designed to be machine-, operating system-, and transport protocol-independent. This is achieved through implementation on top of Remote Procedure Call (see 7.2.2, "Remote Procedure Call (RPC)" on page 266). RPC establishes machine independence by using the External Data Representation convention.

SUN-NFS is a proposed standard protocol. Its status is elective. The current NFS specifications can be found in RFC 1813 – NFS: NFS Version 3 Protocol Specification and RFC 3010 – NFS version 4 Protocol.

10.3.1 NFS concept

NFS allows authorized users to access files located on remote systems as if they were local. Two protocols serve this purpose:

1. The mount protocol specifies the remote host and file system to be accessed and where to locate them in the local file hierarchy.
2. The NFS protocol does the actual file I/O to the remote file system.

Both the mount and NFS protocols are RPC applications (caller/server concept) and are transported by both TCP and UDP.

10.3.1.1 Mount protocol

The mount protocol is an RPC application shipped with NFS. It is program number 100005. The mount protocol is transported by both TCP and UDP. Mount is an RPC server program and provides a total of six procedures:

NULL Does nothing. Useful for server response testing.

MNT Mount function. Returns a file handle pointing to the directory.

DUMP Returns the list of all mounted file systems.

UMNT Removes a mount list entry.

UMNTALL Removes all mount list entries for this client.

EXPORT Returns information about the available file systems.

The MOUNT call returns a file handle to the directory. The file handle is a variable-length array of 64 bytes maximum, which will be used subsequently by the client to access files. File handles are a fundamental part of NFS because each directory and file will be referenced through a handle. Some implementations will encrypt the handles for security reasons. (For example, NFS on VM can optionally use the VM encryption programs to provide this function.)

The user interface to this RPC application is provided through the MOUNT command. The user issues a MOUNT command to locate the remote file system in his or her own file hierarchy.

For example, consider a VM NFS server. The concept of subdirectories (hierarchical file system) does not exist here; there are only minidisks (to be considered as one directory each). Now consider an AIX client. (AIX does have a subdirectory file system.) The client can access the user 191 VM minidisk as its local subdirectory /u/vm/first by issuing the MOUNT command:

```
MOUNT -o options
      host:user.191,ro,pass=password,record=type,names=action
      /u/vm/first
```

Where:

options   System options, such as message size.

host   The TCP/IP name of the remote host.

user   VM user ID.

191   Minidisk address.

pass=   Link password that will allow the NFS machine to access the minidisk.

record=   Specifies what translation processing is to be done on the CMS records:

    binary No processing performed.

    text   Code conversion between EBCDIC (server) and ASCII (client).

    nl   EBCDIC-to-ASCII translation, and new line characters are interpreted as CMS record boundaries.

names=   Specifies the handling of a file name:

    fold   File names supplied by the client are translated to uppercase.

    mixed File names are used as supplied by the client.

If no name translation option is specified, case folding is performed and, in addition, client names that are not valid in CMS will be converted into valid CMS names.

The result is that the VM minidisk is now seen by the client machine as a local subdirectory:

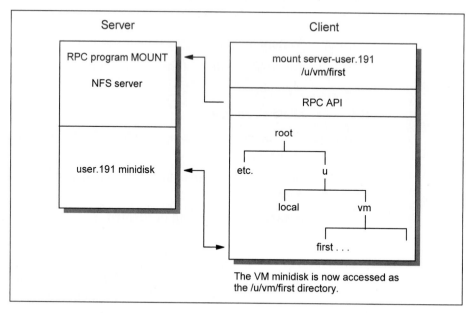

Figure 166. NFS - The client mounts the VM minidisk user.191 as its local directory

Obviously, the previous command:

```
MOUNT -o options host:user.191,ro,pass=password,record=type,names=action
/u/vm/first
```

has three parts:

1. -o options is the client part. It has to be understood by the NFS client only. This means it depends on the client host and is documented in the client's documentation.
2. host:user.191,ro,....,names=action is the server part. The syntax depends on the server's file system. (Obviously, user.191 does not mean anything to an MVS NFS server.) Refer to the documentation of the NFS server to know what parameters it will accept.
3. /u/vm/first is a client part and is called the *mount point*, that is, where the remote file system will be hooked on the local file system.

The UMOUNT command removes the remote file system from the local file hierarchy. Continuing the example above, the following command will remove the /u/vm/first directory:

```
UMOUNT /u/vm/first
```

10.3.1.2 NFS protocol

NFS is the RPC application program providing file I/O functions to a remote host, once it has been requested through a MOUNT command. It has program number 100003 and sometimes uses IP port 2049. As this is not an officially assigned port and several versions of NFS (and mount) already exist, port numbers may change. It is advised to go to Portmap (port number 111) (see "Portmap or portmapper" on page 270) to obtain the port numbers for both the Mount and NFS protocols. The NFS protocol is transported by both TCP and UDP.

The NFS program supports 22 procedures, providing for all basic I/O operations, such as:

ACCESS	Resolves the access rights, according to the set of permissions of the file for that user.
LOOKUP	Searches for a file in the current directory and if found, returns a file handle pointing to it plus information on the file's attributes.
READ/WRITE	Basic read/write primitives to access the file.
RENAME	Renames a file.
REMOVE	Deletes a file.
MKDIR, RMDIR	Creation/deletion of subdirectories.
GET, SET-ATTR	Gets or sets file attributes.

Other functions are also provided.

These correspond to most of the file I/O primitives used in the local operating system to access local files. In fact, once the remote directory is mounted, the local operating system just has to re-route the file I/O primitives to the remote host. This makes all file I/Os look alike, regardless of whether the file is located locally or remotely. The user can operate his or her normal commands and programs on both kinds of files; in other words, this NFS protocol is completely transparent to the user (see Figure 167).

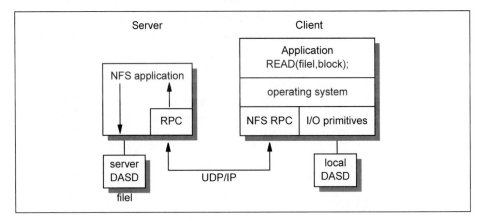

Figure 167. NFS - File I/O intercepted at the operating system level, transparent to the user

10.3.1.3 File integrity

Since NFS is a stateless protocol, there is a need to protect the file integrity of the NFS-mounted files. Many implementations have the Lock Manager protocol for this purpose. Sometimes, multiple processes might open the same file simultaneously. If the file is opened for merely read access, every process will get the most current data. If there is more than one processes writing to the file at one time, the changes made by writers should be coordinated and at the same time the most accurate changes should be given to the readers. If some part of the file is cached on each client's local system, it becomes a more complicated job to synchronize the writers and readers accordingly. Though they might not occur so frequently, these incidents should be taken into consideration.

Lock manager protocol

This protocol allows client and server processes to exclude the other processes when they are writing to the file. When a process locks the file for exclusive access, no other process can access the file. When a process locks the file for shared access, the other processes can share the file but cannot initiate an exclusive access lock. If any other process request conflicts with the locking state, either the process waits until the lock is removed or it may return an error message.

10.3.1.4 NFS file system

NFS assumes a hierarchical file system (directories). Files are unstructured streams of uninterpreted bytes; that is, files are seen as a contiguous byte stream, without any record-level structure.

This is the kind of file system used by AIX and PC/DOS, so these environments will easily integrate an NFS client extension in their own local file system. File systems used in VM and MVS lend themselves less readily to this kind of extension.

With NFS, all file operations are *synchronous*. This means that the file-operation call only returns when the server has completed all work for this operation. In case of a write request, the server will physically write the data to disk and if necessary, update any directory structure, before returning a response to the client. This ensures file integrity.

NFS also specifies that servers should be *stateless*. That is, a server does not need to maintain any extra information about any of its clients in order to function correctly. In case of a server failure, clients only have to retry a request until the server responds, without having to reiterate a mount operation.

10.3.1.5 Cache File System

The Cache File System (CacheFS) provides the ability to cache one file system on another. CacheFS accomplishes caching by mounting remote directories on the local system. Whenever the client needs a mounted file, it first refers to local cache. If the requested file exists, it is accessed locally. Otherwise, the file is retrieved from the server using NFS. In case of reading the file sequentially, the future data is retrieved for future access to the cache. This procedure increases the file access speed. It depends on the implementation to store the cache on Random Access Memory (RAM) or disk. If the amount of the data is not too large, it is better to use RAM for much faster access to the cache.

CacheFS periodically checks the cached data for the data accuracy, sweeps out the inaccurate data from the cache, and retrieves the current data from the server to the cache. CacheFS is proper for the cases in which the files are not changed frequently. In other circumstances, CacheFS reduces server and network loads and improves performance for clients on slow links.

10.3.2 NFS Version 4

There are some enhancements to NFS in Version 4:

- Elimination of need for mount protocol with NFS, by means of a root file handle, a public file handle, and pseudo file systems, which fill in the gaps in the exported directory names.
- New security at the RPC layer, based on GSS-API.
- Support for RPCSEC_GSS, described in RFC 2203.

- Support for Kerberos 5, LIPKEY, and SPKM-3 security.

- New volatile style file handle, to help server implementations cope with file system reorganizations.

- Compound commands for performance (lookup and read in one operation).

- Delegation of status and locks by server to a given client, for caching/performance reasons.

- Internationalization in the form of 16/32 bit character support for file names, by means of the UTF-8 encoding.

10.3.3 WebNFS

WebNFS is an enhanced version of the standard NFS. WebNFS allows the clients to access files over wide area networks (WANs). Since as a transport protocol UDP is fast for local area networks (LANs), many implementations use UDP for the standard NFS. However, a TCP connection is much more reliable for wide area networks. Most of the new NFS implementations support TCP and UDP. WebNFS clients first attempt to use a TCP connection. If it fails or refused, it then uses a UDP connection. WebNFS can easily recover from dropped lines and recover the lost data.

10.3.3.1 Pathname evaluation

The standard NFS version 3 is designed for LANs. The amount of time for each LOOKUP request is not significant. As a result of this, the NFS protocol permits only one single pathname request at a time. When we consider a WAN or the Internet, to request the pathname and evaluate the pathname might cause significant delays. This process is very expensive, especially for files that are several directories away. WebNFS can handle retrieving the entire pathname and evaluate it.

10.3.3.2 NFS URL

This scheme allows the NFS clients to go over the Internet, just like other Internet applications. The URL scheme is based on the common Internet scheme syntax. The NFS URL is described in RFC 2224. The general form of the NFS URL scheme is the following:

```
nfs://<host>:<port><url-path>
```

The port is optional. If it is not specified, the default value is 2049. The WebNFS server evaluates the path using a multi-component lookup relative to the public file handle.

10.3.4 References

The following RFCs provide detailed information on NFS:

- RFC 1813 – NFS Version 3 Protocol Specification
- RFC 2054 – WebNFS Client Specification
- RFC 2055 – WebNFS Server Specification
- RFC 2203 – RPCSEC_GSS Protocol Specification.
- RFC 2224 – NFS URL Scheme
- RFC 3010 – NFS version 4 Protocol

10.4 The Andrew File System (AFS)

The Andrew File System (AFS) is a distributed file system used in non-DCE environments. DCE DFS was based upon AFS, and the two file systems are similar in architecture.

AFS offers high availability, by storing information on more than one server. It is also designed to work over WANs or the Internet, unlike NFS Version 3.

The latest version (AFS 3) has the following attributes:

Single logical shared namespace Every AFS user shares the same uniform name space. File names are independent of both the user's and the file's physical locations. Groups of client and server machines are known as cells.

Client caching Data is cached on client machines to reduce subsequent data requests directed at file servers, which reduces network and server loads. Servers keep track of client caches through callbacks, guaranteeing cache consistency without constant queries to the server to see if the file has changed.

RPCs AFS uses its remote procedure call (RPC) reads and writes for efficient data transfer across the network.

Security Kerberos-based authentication requires that users prove their identities before accessing network services. Once authenticated, AFS access control lists

	(ACLs) give individual users or groups of users varying levels of authority to perform operations on the files in a directory.
Replication	Replication techniques are used for file system reliability. Multiple copies of applications and data may be replicated on multiple file servers within a cell. When accessing this information, a client will choose among the available servers. Replication also reduces the load on any particular server by placing frequently accessed information on multiple servers.
Management utilities	Backup, reconfiguration, and routine maintenance are all done without any system down time and files remain available to users during these operations. This is done by creating online clones of volumes (subsets of related files).

AFS commands are RPC-based. Administrative commands can be issued by any authenticated administrator from any client workstation. System databases track file locations, authentication information, and access control lists. These databases are replicated on multiple servers, and are dynamically updated as information changes.

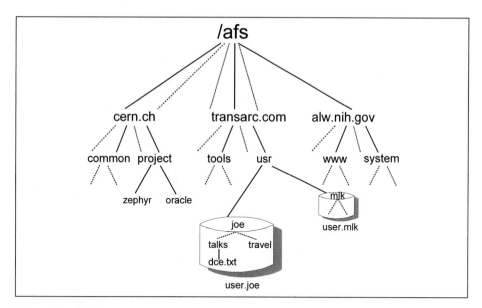

Figure 168. AFS 3 name space

Figure 168 shows an example of an AFS namespace. user.joe is a *volume*, which is a group of files managed as a single unit. Any user, situated anywhere in the network, can access Joe's dce.txt file by using the file name:

```
/afs/transarc.com/usr/joe/talks/dce.txt
```

Further information on AFS can be found at the Transarc Web site at:

```
http://www.transarc.com/
```

Chapter 11. Mail applications

Electronic mail (e-mail) is probably the most widely used TCP/IP application. For most people, it has become an integral part of everyday life. This chapter provides an overview of the TCP/IP application protocols dealing with electronic mail.

11.1 Simple Mail Transfer Protocol (SMTP)

The basic Internet mail protocols provide mail (note) and message exchange between TCP/IP hosts; facilities have been added for the transmission of data that cannot be represented as 7-bit ASCII text. There are three standard protocols that apply to mail of this kind. Each is recommended. The term Simple Mail Transfer Protocol (SMTP) is frequently used to refer to the combined set of protocols, since they are so closely inter-related, but strictly speaking, SMTP is just one of the three. Normally, it is evident from the context which of the three protocols is being referred to. Whenever some doubt might exist, we refer to the STD or RFC numbers to avoid ambiguity. The three standards are:

- A standard for exchange of mail between two computers (STD 10/RFC 821), which specifies the protocol used to send mail between TCP/IP hosts. This standard is SMTP itself.

- A standard (STD 11) on the format of the mail messages, contained in two RFCs. RFC 822 describes the syntax of mail header fields and defines a set of header fields and their interpretation. RFC 1049 describes how a set of document types other than plain text ASCII can be used in the mail body (the documents themselves are 7-bit ASCII containing imbedded formatting information: PostScript, Scribe, SGML, TEX, TROFF, and DVI are all listed in the standard).

  The official protocol name for this standard is MAIL.

- A standard for the routing of mail using the Domain Name System, described in RFC 974. The official protocol name for this standard is DNS-MX.

STD 10/RFC 821 dictates that data sent via SMTP is 7-bit ASCII data, with the high-order bit cleared to zero. This is adequate in most instances for the transmission of English text messages, but is inadequate for non-English text or non-textual data. There are two approaches to overcoming these limitations:

- Multipurpose Internet Mail Extensions (MIME), defined in RFCs 2045 to 2049, which specifies a mechanism for encoding text and binary data as 7-bit ASCII within the mail envelope defined by RFC 822. MIME is described in 11.2, "Multipurpose Internet Mail Extensions (MIME)" on page 399.

- SMTP service extensions, which define a mechanism to extend the capabilities of SMTP beyond the limitations imposed by RFC 821. There are three current RFCs that describe SMTP service extensions:

  - A standard for a receiver SMTP to inform a sender SMTP which service extensions it supports (RFC 1869).

    RFC 1869 modifies RFC 821 to allow a client SMTP agent to request that the server respond with a list of the service extensions that it supports at the start of an SMTP session. If the server SMTP does not support RFC 1869, it will respond with an error and the client can either terminate the session or attempt to start a session according to the rules of RFC 821. If the server does support RFC 1869, it can also respond with a list of the service extensions that it supports. A registry of services is maintained by IANA. The initial list defined in RFC 1869 contains those commands listed in RFC 1123 – Requirements for Internet Hosts – Application and Support as optional for SMTP servers.

    Other service extensions are defined via RFCs in the usual manner. The next two RFCs define specific extensions:

  - A protocol for 8-bit text transmission (RFC 1652) that allows an SMTP server to indicate that it can accept data consisting of 8-bit bytes. A server that reports that this extension is available to a client must leave the high order bit of bytes received in an SMTP message unchanged if requested to do so by the client.

    The MIME and SMTP Service Extension approaches are complementary rather than competing standards. In particular, RFC 1652 is titled SMTP Service Extension for 8-bit-MIMEtransport, since the MIME standard allows messages to be declared as consisting of 8-bit data rather than 7-bit data. Such messages cannot be transmitted by SMTP agents that strictly conform to RFC 821, but can be transmitted when both the client and the server conform to RFCs 1869 and 1652. Whenever a client SMTP attempts to send 8-bit data to a server that does not support this extension, the client SMTP must either encode the message contents into a 7-bit representation compliant with the MIME standard or return a permanent error to the user.

This service extension does not permit the sending of arbitrary binary data, because RFC 821 defines the maximum length of a line that an SMTP server is required to accept as 1000 characters. Non-text data could easily have sequences of more than 1000 characters without a <CRLF> sequence.

> **Note:**
>
> The service extension specifically limits the use of non-ASCII characters (those with values above decimal 127) to message bodies. They are *not* permitted in RFC 822 message headers.

- A protocol for message size declaration (RFC 1870) that allows a server to inform a client of the maximum size message it can accept. Without this extension, a client can only be informed that a message has exceeded the maximum size acceptable to the server (either a fixed upper limit or a temporary limit imposed by a lack of available storage space at the server) after transmitting the entire message. When this happens, the server discards the failing message. If both client and server support the message size declaration extension, the client may declare an estimated size of the message to be transferred and the server will return an error if the message is too large.

Each of these SMTP Service Extensions is a draft standard protocol and each has a status of elective.

11.1.1 How SMTP works

SMTP (that is, STD 11/RFC 821) is based on *end-to-end delivery*; an SMTP client will contact the destination host's SMTP server directly to deliver the mail. It will keep the mail item being transmitted until it has been successfully copied to the recipient's SMTP. This is different from the store-and-forward principle that is common in many mailing systems, where the mail item may pass through a number of intermediate hosts in the same network on its way to the destination and where successful transmission from the sender only indicates that the mail item has reached the first intermediate hop.

In various implementations, there is a possibility to exchange mail between the TCP/IP SMTP mailing system and the locally used mailing systems. These applications are called *mail gateways* or *mail bridges*. Sending mail through a mail gateway can alter the end-to-end delivery specification, since SMTP will only guarantee delivery to the mail-gateway host, not to the real destination host, which is located beyond the TCP/IP network. When a mail gateway is used, the SMTP end-to-end transmission is host-to-gateway,

gateway-to-host, or gateway-to-gateway; the behavior beyond the gateway is not defined by SMTP. CSNET provides an interesting example of mail gateway service. Started as a low-cost facility to interconnect scientific and corporate research centers, CSNET operates a mail gateway service that allows subscribers to send and receive mail across the Internet using only a dial-up modem. The mail gateway polls the subscribers at regular times, delivers mail that was addressed to them, and picks up the outgoing mail. Although this is not a direct end-to-end delivery, it has proven to be a very useful system.

Each message has:

- A header, or envelope, the structure of which is strictly defined by RFC 822.

  The mail header is terminated by a null line (that is, a line with nothing preceding the <CRLF> sequence). However, some implementations (for example, VM, which does not support zero-length records in files) may interpret this differently and accept a blank line as a terminator.

- Contents

  Everything after the null (or blank) line is the message body, which is a sequence of lines containing ASCII characters (that is, characters with a value less than 128 decimal).

RFC 821 defines a client/server protocol. As usual, the client SMTP is the one that initiates the session (that is, the sending SMTP) and the server is the one that responds (the receiving SMTP) to the session request. However, since the client SMTP frequently acts as a server for a user mailing program, it is often simpler to refer to the client as the sender SMTP and to the server as the receiver SMTP.

11.1.1.1 Mail header format
The user normally does not have to worry about the message header, since it is taken care of by SMTP itself. A short reference is included below for completeness.

RFC 822 contains a complete lexical analysis of the mail header. The syntax is written in a form known as the augmented Backus-Naur Form (BNF). RFC 822 contains a description of augmented BNF, and many RFCs that are related to RFC 822 use this format. RFC 822 describes how to parse a mail header to a *canonical representation*, unfolding continuation lines, deleting insignificant spaces, removing comments, and so on. The syntax is powerful, but relatively difficult to parse. A basic description is given here, which should be adequate for the reader to interpret the meaning of simple mail headers that he or she encounters. However, this description is too great a simplification to understand the details workings of RFC 822 mailers; for a full description, refer to RFC 822.

Briefly, the header is a list of lines, of the form:

```
field-name: field-value
```

Fields begin in column 1. Lines beginning with white space characters (SPACE or TAB) are continuation lines that are unfolded to create a single line for each field in the canonical representation. Strings enclosed in ASCII quotation marks indicate single tokens within which special characters such as the colon are not significant. Many important field values (such as those for the To and From fields) are *mailboxes*. The most common forms for these are:

```
octopus@garden.under.the.sea
The Octopus <octopus@garden.under.the.sea>
"The Octopus" <octopus@garden.under.the.sea>
```

The string The Octopus is intended for human recipients and is the name of the mailbox owner. The string octopus@garden.under.the.sea is the machine-readable address of the mailbox. (The angle brackets are used to delimit the address but are not part of it.) One can see that this form of addressing is closely related to the Domain Name System concept. In fact, the client SMTP uses the Domain Name System to determine the IP address of the destination mailbox.

Some frequently used fields are:

Table 18. SMTP - Mail header frequently used fields

Keyword	Value
to	Primary recipients of the message.
cc	Secondary (carbon-copy) recipients of the message.
from	Identity of sender.
reply-to	The mailbox to which responses are to be sent. This field is added by the originator.
return-path	Address and route back to the originator. This field is added by the final transport system that delivers the mail.
Subject	Summary of the message. This is usually provided by the user.

11.1.1.2 Mail exchange

The SMTP design is based on the model of communication shown in Figure 169. As a result of a user mail request, the sender SMTP establishes a two-way connection with a receiver SMTP. The receiver SMTP can be either the ultimate destination or an intermediate (mail gateway). The sender SMTP will generate commands that are replied to by the receiver SMTP.

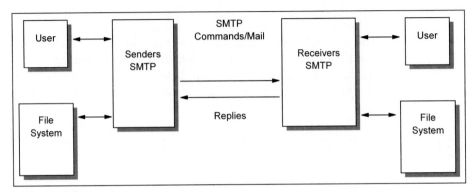

Figure 169. SMTP - Model for SMTP

SMTP mail transaction flow

Although mail commands and replies are rigidly defined, the exchange can easily be followed in Figure 170 on page 394. All exchanged commands/replies/data are text lines, delimited by a <CRLF>. All replies have a numeric code at the beginning of the line. The steps of this flow are:

1. The sender SMTP establishes a TCP connection with the destination SMTP and then waits for the server to send a 220 Service ready message or a 421 Service not available message when the destination is temporarily unable to proceed.

2. HELO (HELO is an abbreviation for hello) is sent, to which the receiver will identify himself or herself by sending back its domain name. The sender-SMTP can use this to verify if it contacted the right destination SMTP.

   If the sender SMTP supports SMTP Service Extensions as defined in RFC 1869, it may substitute an EHLO command in place of the HELO command. A receiver SMTP that does not support service extensions will respond with a 500 Syntax error, command unrecognized message. The sender SMTP should then retry with HELO, or if it cannot transmit the message without one or more service extensions, it should send a QUIT message.

If a receiver-SMTP supports service extensions, it responds with a multi-line 250 OK message, which includes a list of service extensions that it supports.

3. The sender now initiates the start of a mail transaction by sending a MAIL command to the receiver. This command contains the reverse-path which can be used to report errors. Note that a path can be more than just the user mailbox@host domain name pair. In addition, it can contain a list of routing hosts. Examples of this are when we pass a mail bridge, or when we provide explicit routing information in the destination address. If accepted, the receiver replies with a 250 OK.

4. The second step of the actual mail exchange consists of providing the server SMTP with the destinations for the message. There can be more than one recipient. This is done by sending one or more RCPTTO:<forward-path> commands. Each of them will receive a reply 250 OK if the destination is known to the server, or a 550 No such user here if it is not.

5. When all RCPT commands are sent, the sender issues a DATA command to notify the receiver that the message contents are following. The server replies with 354 Start mail input, end with <CRLF>.<CRLF>. Note the ending sequence that the sender should use to terminate the message data.

6. The client now sends the data line by line, ending with the 5-character sequence <CRLF>.<CRLF> line upon which the receiver acknowledges with a 250 OK or an appropriate error message if anything went wrong.

7. We now have several possible actions:

   - The sender has no more messages to send. He or she will end the connection with a QUIT command, which will be answered with a 221 Service closing transmission channel reply.
   - The sender has no more messages to send, but is ready to receive messages (if any) from the other side. He or she will issue the TURN command. The two SMTPs now switch their role of sender/receiver and the sender (previously the receiver) can now send messages by starting with step 3 above.
   - The sender has another message to send, and simply goes back to step 3 to send a new MAIL command.

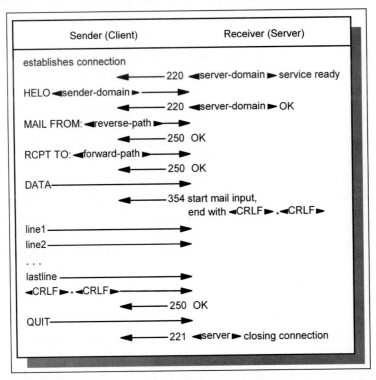

Figure 170. SMTP - Normal SMTP data flow - one mail message to one destination mailbox

The SMTP destination address (mailbox address)

Its general form is local-part@domain-name and can take several forms:

user@host	For a direct destination on the same TCP/IP network.
user%remote-host@gateway-host	For a user on a non-SMTP destination remote-host, via the mail gateway gateway-host.
@host-a,@host-b:user@host-c	For a relayed message. This contains explicit routing information. The message will first be delivered to host-a, who will resend (relay) the message to host-b. Host-b will then forward the message to the real destination host-c. Note that the message is stored on each of the intermediate hosts, so we do not

have an end-to-end delivery in this case.

In the above description, only the most important commands were mentioned. All of them are commands that must be recognized in each SMTP implementation. Other commands exist, but most of those are only optional; that is, the RFC standard does not require them to be implemented everywhere. However, they implement very interesting functions such as relaying, forwarding, mailing lists, and so on.

For a full list of command verbs, see RFC 821 Simple Mail Transfer Protocol and RFC 1123 Requirements for Internet Hosts – Application and Support. For details of SMTP service extensions, see RFC 1869 SMTP Service Extensions, RFC 1652 SMTP Service Extension for 8-bit-MIMEtransport and RFC 1870 SMTP Service Extension for Message Size Declaration.

Example
In the following scenario, user abc at host vm1.stockholm.ibm.com sends a note to users xyz, opq and rst at host delta.aus.edu. The lines preceded by R: are lines sent by the receiver; the S: lines are sent by the sender.

```
R: 220 delta.aus.edu Simple Mail Transfer Service Ready
S: HELO stockholm.ibm.com
R: 250 delta.aus.edu
S: MAIL FROM:<abc@stockholm.ibm.com>
R: 250 OK
S: RCPT TO:<xyz@delta.aus.edu>
R: 250 OK
S: RCPT TO:<opq@delta.aus.edu>
R: 550 No such user here
S: RCPT TO:<rst@delta.aus.edu>
R: 250 OK
S: DATA
R: 354 Start mail input, end with <CRLF>.<CRLF>
S: Date: 23 Jan 89  18:05:23
S: From: Alex B. Carver <abc@stockholm.ibm.com>
S: Subject: Important meeting
S: To:  <xyz@delta.aus.edu>
S: To:  <opq@delta.aus.edu>
S: cc:  <rst@delta.aus.edu>
S:
S: Blah blah blah
S: etc.....
S: .
R: 250 OK
S: QUIT
R: 221 delta.aus.edu Service closing transmission channel
```

Figure 171. SMTP - An example scenario

Note that the message header is part of the data being transmitted.

11.1.2 SMTP and the Domain Name System

If the network is using the domain concept, an SMTP cannot simply deliver mail sent to TEST.IBM.COM by opening a TCP connection to TEST.IBM.COM. It must first query the name server to find out to which host (again a domain name) it should deliver the message.

For message delivery, the name server stores resource records (RRs) known as MX RRs. They map a domain name to two values:

- A preference value. As multiple MX resource records may exist for the same domain name, a preference (priority) is assigned to them. The lowest preference value corresponds to the most preferred record. This is useful whenever the most preferred host is unreachable; the sending SMTP then tries to contact the next (less preferred) host.

- A host name.

It is also possible that the name server responds with an empty list of MX RRs. This means that the domain name is in the name server's authority, but has no MX assigned to it. In this case, the sending SMTP may try to establish the connection with the host name itself.

An important recommendation is given in RFC 974. It recommends that after obtaining the MX records, the sending SMTP should query for well-known services (WKS) records for this host, and should check that the referenced host has SMTP as a WKS-entry.

> **Note**
>
> This is only an option of the protocol but is already widely implemented.

Here is an example of MX resource records:

```
fsc5.stn.mlv.fr.        IN    MX 0  fsc5.stn.mlv.fr.
                        IN    MX 2  psfred.stn.mlv.fr.
                        IN    MX 4  mvs.stn.mlv.fr.
                        IN    WKS   152.9.250.150 TCP (SMTP)
```

In the above example, mail for fsc5.stn.mlv.fr should, by preference, be delivered to the host itself, but in case the host is unreachable, the mail might also be delivered to psfred.stn.mlv.fr or to mvs.stn.mlv.fr (if psfred.stn.mlv.fr is also unreachable).

11.1.2.1 Addressing mailboxes on server systems

When a user employs a server system for all mail functions, the mailbox address seen by other SMTP users refers exclusively to the mail server system. For example, if two OS/2 systems are named:

```
hayes.itso.ral.ibm.com
```

and

```
itso180.itso.ral.ibm.com
```

with the first one being used as an UltiMail client and the second as an UltiMail server, the mailbox address might be:

```
hayes@itso180.itso.ral.ibm.com
```

This mailbox address would appear in the From: header field of all outgoing mail and in the SMTP commands to remote servers issued by the UltiMail server system.

When the user uses a POP server, however, the mailbox address on outbound mail items contains the workstation's host name (for example, steve@hayes.itso.ral.ibm.com). In this case, the sender should include a Reply-To: field in the mail header to indicate that replies should *not* be sent to the originating mailbox. For example, the mail header might look like this:

```
Date: Fri, 10 Feb 95 15:38:23
From: steve@hayes.itso.ral.ibm.com
To: "Steve Hayes" <tsgsh@gford1.warwick.uk.ibm.com>
Reply-To: hayes@itso180.itso.ral.ibm.com
Subject: Test Reply-To: header field
```

The receiving mail agent is expected to send replies to the Reply-To: address and not the From: address.

Using the Domain Name System to direct mail

An alternative approach to using the Reply-To: header field is to use the Domain Name System to direct mail to the correct mailbox. The administrator for the domain name server (with authority for the domain containing the user's workstation and the name server) can add MX resource records to the Domain Name System to direct mail appropriately, as described in 11.1.2, "SMTP and the Domain Name System" on page 396. For example, the following MX records indicate to the client SMTPs that if the SMTP server on hayes.itso.ral.ibm.com is not available, there is a mail server on itso.180.ral.ibm.com (9.24.104.180) that should be used instead:

```
itso180.itso.ral.ibm.com.   IN    WKS  9.24.104.180 TCP (SMTP)
hayes.itso.ral.ibm.com.     IN    MX 0 hayes.itso.ral.ibm.com.
                            IN    MX 1 itso180.itso.ral.ibm.com.
```

11.1.3 References

A detailed description of the SMTP, MAIL and DNS-MX standards can be found in the following RFCs:

- RFC 821 – Simple Mail Transfer Protocol
- RFC 822 – Standard for the format of ARPA Internet text messages
- RFC 974 – Mail Routing and the Domain System
- RFC 1049 – A Content Type Header Field for Internet messages
- RFC 1652 – SMTP Service Extension for 8-bit-MIMEtransport

11.2 Multipurpose Internet Mail Extensions (MIME)

MIME is a draft-standard protocol. Its status is elective.

Electronic mail (as described in 11.1, "Simple Mail Transfer Protocol (SMTP)" on page 387) is probably the most widely used TCP/IP application. However, SMTP (that is, an STD 10/RFC 821-compliant mailing system) is limited to 7-bit ASCII text with a maximum line length of 1000 characters, which results in a number of limitations:

- SMTP cannot transmit executable files or other binary objects. There are a number of ad hoc methods of encapsulating binary items in SMTP mail items, for example:

  - Encoding the file as pure hexadecimal

  - The UNIX uuencode and uudecode utilities that are used to encode binary data in the UUCP mailing system, to overcome the same limitations of 7-bit transport

  - The Andrew Toolkit representation

  None of these can be described as a *de facto* standard. Uuencode is perhaps the most pervasive, due to the pioneering role of UNIX systems in the Internet.

- SMTP cannot transmit text data that includes national language characters, since these are represented by code points with a value of 128 (decimal) or higher in all character sets based on ASCII.

- SMTP servers may reject mail messages over a certain size. Any given server may have permanent and/or transient limits on the maximum amount of mail data it can accept from a client at any given time.

- SMTP gateways that translate from ASCII to EBCDIC and vice versa do not use a consistent set of code page mappings, resulting in translation problems.

- Some SMTP implementations or other mail transport agents (MTAs) in the Internet do not adhere completely to the SMTP standards defined in RFC 821. Common problems include:

  - Removal of trailing white space characters (TABs and SPACEs).

  - Padding of all lines in a message to the same length.

  - Wrapping of lines longer than 76 characters.

  - Changing of new line sequences between different conventions. (For example, <CR> characters may be converted to <CRLF> sequences.)

- Conversion of TAB characters to multiple SPACEs.

MIME is a standard that includes mechanisms to solve these problems in a manner that is highly compatible with existing RFC 822 standards. Because mail messages are frequently forwarded through mail gateways, it is not possible for an SMTP client to distinguish between a server that manages the destination mailbox and one that acts as a gateway to another network. Since mail that passes through a gateway may be tunnelled through further gateways, some or all of which may be using a different set of messaging protocols, it is not possible in general for a sending SMTP to determine the lowest common denominator capability common to all stages of the route to the destination mailbox. For this reason, MIME assumes the worst: 7-bit ASCII transport, which may not strictly conform to or be compatible with RFC 821. It does not define any extensions to RFC 821, but limits itself to extensions within the framework of RFC 822. Thus, a MIME message is one which can be routed through any number of networks that are loosely compliant with RFC 821 or are capable of transmitting RFC 821 messages.

MIME is a draft-standard protocol with a status of elective. It is described in five parts:

- Protocols for including objects other than US ASCII text mail messages within the bodies of messages conforming to RFC 822. These are described in RFC 2045.

- General structure of the MIME media typing system, which defines an initial set of media types. This is described in RFC 2046.

- A protocol for encoding non-US ASCII text in the header fields of mail messages conforming to RFC 822. This is described in RFC 2047.

- Various IANA registration procedures for MIME-related facilities. This is described in RFC 2048.

- MIME conformance criteria. This is described in RFC 2049.

Although RFC 2045 provides a mechanism suitable for describing non-textual data from X.400 messages in a form that is compatible with RFC 822, it does not say how X.400 message parts are to be mapped to MIME message parts. The conversion between X.400 and MIME is defined in RFCs 1494, 2156, and 1496, which update the protocols for the conversion between RFC 822 and X.400.

The MIME standard was designed with the following general order of priorities:

1. Compatibility with existing standards, such as RFC 822.

There are two areas where compatibility with previous standards is not complete:

a. RFC 1049 (which is part of STD 11) described a Content-Type: field used to indicate the type of (ASCII text) data in a message body. PostScript or SGML would allow a user mail agent to process it accordingly. MIME retains this field, but changes the values that are defined for it. Since the correct response for a mail agent on encountering an unknown value in this field is basically to ignore it, this does not raise any major compatibility concerns.

b. RFC 934 discussed encapsulation of messages in the context of message forwarding and defined encapsulation boundaries: lines indicating the beginning and end of an encapsulated message. MIME retains broad compatibility with RFC 934, but does not include the quoting mechanism used by RFC 934 for lines in encapsulated messages that could otherwise be misinterpreted as boundaries.[1]

The most important compatibility issue is that the standard form of a MIME message is readable with an RFC 821-compliant mail reader. This is, of course, the case. In particular the default encoding for MIME message bodies is no encoding at all, just like RFC 822.

2. Robustness across existing practice. As noted above, there are many widely deployed MTAs in the Internet that do not comply with STD 10/RFC 821. The encoding mechanisms specified in RFC 2045 are designed to always circumvent the most common of these (folding of lines as short as 76 characters and corruption of trailing white space characters) by only transmitting short lines with no trailing white space characters, and allowing encoding of any data in a mail safe fashion.

---

[1] The reason for this departure is that MIME allows for deeply nested encapsulation, but encodes text in such a way as to reversibly spill text lines at or before column 76 to avoid the lines being spilled irreversibly by non-conforming SMTP agents. The RFC 934 quoting mechanism can result in lines being lengthened with each level of encapsulation, possibly past column 76.

> **Note:**
>
> MIME does *not* require mail items to be encoded; the decision is left to the user and/or the mail program. For binary data transmitted across (7-bit) SMTP, encoding is invariably required, but for data consisting mostly of text, this may not be the case.
>
> The preferred encoding mechanism for mostly text data is that, at a minimum, it is mail-safe with any compliant SMTP agent on an ASCII system and at maximum is mail-safe with all known gateways and MTAs. The reason why MIME does not require maximum encoding is that the encoding hampers readability when the mail is transmitted to non-MIME compliant systems.

3. Ease of extension. RFC 2045 categorizes elements of mail bodies into seven *content-types*, which have *subtypes*. The content-type/subtype pairs in turn have parameters that further describe the object concerned. The RFC defines a mechanism for registering new values for these and other MIME fields with the Internet Assigned Numbers Authority (IANA). This process is itself updated by RFC 2048.

   For the current list of all MIME values, consult STD 2 – Assigned Internet Numbers. The remainder of this chapter describes only the values and types given in RFC 2045.

One consequence of this approach is that, to quote RFC 2045, "some of the mechanisms [used in MIME] may seem somewhat strange or even baroque at first. In particular, compatibility was always favored over elegance."

Because RFC 822 defines the syntax of message headers (and deliberately allows for additions to the set of headers it describes) but not the composition of message bodies, the MIME standard is largely compatible with RFC 822, particularly the RFC 2045 part that defines the structure of message bodies and a set of header fields that are used to describe that structure.

MIME can be seen as a high-level protocol; since it works entirely within the boundaries of STD 10 and STD 11, it does not involve the transport layer (or lower layers) of the protocol stack at all.

11.2.1 How MIME works

A MIME-compliant message must contain a header field with the following verbatim text:

```
MIME-Version: 1.0
```

As is the case with RFC 822 headers, the case of MIME header field names are never significant, but the case of field values may be, depending on the field name and the context. For the MIME fields described below, the values are case-insensitive unless stated otherwise.

The general syntax for MIME header fields is the same as that for RFC 822, so the following field is valid, because parenthetical phrases are treated as comments and ignored:

```
MIME-Version: 1.0 (this is a comment)
```

The following five header fields are defined for MIME:

MIME-Version As noted above, this must have the value 1.0.

Content-Type This describes how the object within the body is to be interpreted. The default value is text/plain; charset=us-ascii, which indicates unformatted 7-bit ASCII text data (which is a message body by the RFC 822 definition).

Content-Transfer-Encoding This describes how the object within the body was encoded so that it could be included in the message in a mail-safe form.

Content-Description A plain text description of the object within the body, which is useful when the object is not readable (for example, audio data).

Content-ID A world-unique value specifying the content of this part of this message.

The first two of these fields are described in more detail in the following sections.

11.2.2 The Content-Type field

The body of the message is described with a Content-Type field of the form:

```
Content-Type: type/subtype ;parameter=value ;parameter=value
```

The allowable parameters are dependent on the type and subtype. Some type/subtype pairs have no parameters, some have optional ones, some have mandatory ones, and some have both. The subtype parameter *cannot* be omitted, but the whole field can, in which case the default value is text/plain.

There are seven standard content-types:

1. Text

   A single subtype is defined:

   a. plain: Unformatted text. The character set of the text may be specified with the charset parameter. The following values are permitted:

   b. us-ascii: The text consists of ASCII characters in the range 0 to 127 (decimal). This is the default (for compatibility with RFC 822).

   c. iso-8859-x: Where x is in the range 1 to 9 for the different parts of the ISO-8859 standard. The text consists of ISO characters in the range 0 to 255 (decimal). All of the ISO-8859 character sets are ASCII-based with national language characters and so on in the range 128 to 255. Note that if the text contains no characters with values above 127, the character set should be specified as us-ascii, because it can be adequately represented in that character set.

   Further subtypes may be added to describe other readable text formats (such as word processor formats), which contain formatting information for an application to enhance the appearance of the text, provided that the correct software is not required to determine the meaning of the text.

2. Multipart

   The message body contains multiple objects of independent data types. In each case, the body is divided into parts by lines called encapsulation boundaries. The contents of the boundary are defined with a parameter in the content-type field, for example:

   ```
   Content-Type: multipart/mixed; boundary="1995021309105517"
   ```

   The boundary should not appear in any of the parts of the message. It is case-sensitive and consists of 1-70 characters from a set of 75 that are known to be very robust through mail gateways, and it may not end in a space. (The example uses a 16-digit decimal timestamp.) Each encapsulation boundary consists of the boundary value prefixed by a <CRLF> sequence and two hyphens (for compatibility with RFC 934). The final boundary that marks the end of the last part also has a suffix of two hyphens. Within each part there is a MIME header, which, like ordinary mail headers, is terminated by the sequence <CRLF><CRLF> but may be blank. The header fields define the content of the encapsulated message.

   Four subtypes are defined:

   a. Mixed: The different parts are independent but are transmitted together. They should be presented to the recipient in the order that they appear in the mail message.

b. Parallel: This differs from the mixed subtype only in that no order is ascribed to the parts and the receiving mail program can, for example, display all of them in parallel.

c. Alternative: The different parts are alternative versions of the same information. They are ordered in increasing faithfulness to the original, and the recipient's mail system should display the best version to the user.

d. Digest: This is a variant on multipart/mixed where the default type/subtype is message/rfc822 (see below) instead of text/plain. It is used for the common case where multiple RFC 822 or MIME messages are transmitted together.

An example of a complex multipart message is shown in Figure 172.

```
MIME-Version: 1.0
From: Steve Hayes <steve@hayessj.bedfont.uk.ibm.com>
To:    Matthias Enders <enders@itso180.itso.ral.ibm.com>
Subject: Multipart message
Content-type: multipart/mixed; boundary="1995021309105517"

This section is called the preamble. It is after the header but before the first
boundary. Mail readers which understand multipart messages must ignore this.
--1995021309105517

The first part. There is no header, so this is text/plain with
charset=us-ascii by default. The immediately preceding <CRLF> is part of the
<CRLF><CRLF> sequence that ends the null header. The one at the end is part of the
next boundary, so this part consists of five lines of text with four <CRLF>s.
--1995021309105517
Content-type: text/plain; charset=us-ascii
Comments: this header explicitly states the defaults

One line of text this time, but it ends in a line break.

--1995021309105517
Content-Type: multipart/alternative; boundary=_
Comments:     An encapsulated multipart message!

Again, this preamble is ignored. The multipart body contains a still image and a
video image encoded in Base64. See 11.2.3.5, "Base64 encoding" on page 413. One
feature is that the character "_" which is allowed in multipart boundaries never
occurs in Base64 encoding so we can use a very simple boundary!
--_
Content-type: text/plain

This message contains images which cannot be displayed at your terminal.
This is a shame because they're very nice.

--_
Content-type: image/jpeg
Content-transfer-encoding: base64
Comments: This photograph is to be shown if the user's system cannot display MPEG
videos. Only part of the data is shown in this book
because the reader is unlikely to be wearing MIME-compliant spectacles.

Qk1OAAAAAAAAE4EAABAAAAAQAEAAPAAAAABAAgAAAAAAAAAAAAAAAAAAAAABAAAAAQAAAAA
AAAAAAAAAAAAAAAAAAAAAAAB4VjQSAAAAAAAgAAAkgAAAJKAAKoAAACqAIAAqpIAAMHBwQDJyckA
/9uqAKpJAAD/SQAAAG0AAFVtAACqbQAA/20AAAAkAABVkgAAqiQAAP+SAAAAtgAAVbYAAKq2AAD/
<base64 data continues for another 1365 lines>
--_
Content-type: video/mpeg
Content-transfer-encoding: base64

AAABswoAeBn//+CEAAABsgAAAOgAAAG4AAAAAAAAQAAT/////wAAAGy//8AAAEBQ/ZlIwwBGWCX
+pqMiJQDjAKywS/1NRrtXcTCLgzVQymqqHAf0sL1sMgMq4SWLCwOTYRdgyAyrhNYsLhhF3DLjAGg
BdwDXBv3yMV8/4tzrp3zsAWIGAJg1IBKTeFFI2IsgutIdfuSaAGCTsBVnWdz8afdMMAMgKgMEkPE
<base64 data continues for another 1839 lines>
--_--
That was the end of the nested multipart message.   This is the epilogue.
Like the preamble it is ignored.
--1995021309105517--
And that was the end of the main multipart message. That's all folks!
```

Figure 172. MIME - A complex multipart example

Where:

message The body is an encapsulated message, or part of one. Three subtypes are defined:

    rfc822   The body itself is an encapsulated message with the syntax of an RFC 822 message. It is required that at least one of From:, Subject,: or Date: be present.

Note:

RFC 822 refers to the syntax of the encapsulated message envelopes and does not, for example, preclude MIME messages.

---

    partial   This type is used to allow fragmentation of large mail items in a similar way to IP fragmentation. Because SMTP agents may impose upper limits on maximum mail sizes, it may be necessary to send large items as fragments. The intent of the message/partial mail items is that the fragmentation is transparent to the recipient. The receiving user agent should re-assemble the fragments to create a new message with identical semantics to the original. There are three parameters for the Content-Type: field:

        id=   A unique identifier common to all parts of the message.

        number=   The sequence number of this part, with the first part being numbered 1.

        total=   The total number of parts. This is optional on all but the last part. The last part is identified by the fact that it has the same value for the number and total parameters.

The original message is always a message according to RFC 822 rules. The first part is syntactically equivalent to a message/rfc822 message (that is, the body itself contains message headers), and the subsequent parts are syntactically equivalent to text/plain messages. When re-building the message, the RFC 822 header fields are taken from the top-level message, not from the enclosed message, with the exception of those fields that cannot be copied from the inner message to the outer when fragmentation is performed (for example, the Content-Type: field).

> **Note:**
>
> It is explicitly permitted to fragment a message/partial message further. This allows mail gateways to freely fragment messages in order to ensure that all parts are small enough to be transmitted. If this were not the case, the mail agent performing the fragmentation would have to know the smallest maximum size limit that the mail items would encounter en route to the destination.

external-body This type contains a pointer to an object that exists elsewhere. It has the syntax of the message/rfc822 type. The top-level message header defines how the external object is to be accessed, using the access-type: parameter of the Content-Type: field and a set of additional parameters that are specific to the access type. The intent is for the mail reader to be able to synchronously access the external object using the specified access type. The following access types are defined:

ftp File Transfer Protocol. The recipient will be expected to supply the necessary user ID and password. For security reasons, these are never transmitted with the message.

tftp Trivial File Transfer Protocol.

anon-ftp Anonymous FTP.

local-file The data is contained in a file accessible directly via the recipient's local file system.

mail-server The data is accessible via a mail server. Unlike the others, this access is necessarily asynchronous.

When the external object has been received, the desired message is obtained by appending the object to the message header encapsulated within the body of the message/external-body message. This encapsulated message header defines how the resulting message is to be interpreted. (It is required to have a Content-ID: and will normally have a Content-Type: field.) The encapsulated message body is not used (the real message body is elsewhere, after all) and it is therefore termed the phantom body. There is one exception to this: if the access-type is mail-server, the phantom body contains the mail server commands necessary to extract the real message body. This is because mail server syntaxes vary widely so it is much simpler to use the otherwise redundant phantom body than to codify a syntax for encoding arbitrary mail server commands as parameters on the Content-Type: field.

3. Image

The body contains image data requiring a graphical display or some other device such as a printer to display it. Two subtypes are defined initially:

a. jpeg: The image is in JPEG format, JFIF encoding.

b. gif: GIF format.

4. Video

The body contains moving image data (possibly with synchronized audio) requiring an intelligent terminal or multimedia workstation to display it. A single subtype is defined initially:

a. mpeg: MPEG format.

5. Audio

The body contains image data requiring a speaker and sound card (or similar hardware) to display it. A single subtype is defined initially:

a. basic: A lowest common denominator format in the absence of any de facto standards for audio encoding. Specifically, it is single-channel 8-bit ISDN mu-law encoding at a sample rate of 8kHz.

6. Application

This type is intended for types that do not fit into other categories, and particularly for data to be processed by an application program before being presented to the user, such as spreadsheet data. It is also intended for application programs that are intended to be processed as part of the mail reading process (for example, see the PostScript type below). This type of usage poses serious security risks unless an implementation ensures executable mail messages are run in a safe or *padded cell* environment.

Two subtypes are defined initially:

a. PostScript: Adobe Systems PostScript (Level 1 or Level 2).

PostScript security issues: Although PostScript is often thought of as a format for printer data, it is a programming language and the use of a PostScript interpreter to process application/PostScript types poses serious security problems. Any mail reader that automatically interprets PostScript programs is equivalent, in principle, to one that automatically runs executable programs it receives. RFC 2046 outlines the issues involved.

b. octet-stream: This subtype indicates general binary data consisting of 8-bit bytes. It is also the subtype that a mail reader should assume on encountering an unknown type or subtype. Any parameters are permitted, and RFC mentions two: a type= parameter to inform the recipient of the general type of the data, and padding= to indicate a bit stream encoded in a byte stream. (The padding value is the number of trailing zero bits added to pad the stream to a byte boundary.)

Implementations are recommended to offer the user the option of using the data as input to a user program or storing it in a file. An optional "Content-Disposition:" field, described in RFC 2183, allows the specification of the preferred name of such a file.

Security issues: The RFCs strongly recommend against an implementation automatically executing an application/octet-stream part or using it as input to a program specified in the mail header. To do so would expose the receiving system to serious security risks and could impact the integrity of any networks that the system is connected to.

Obviously, there are many types of data that do not fit into any of the subtypes above. Cooperating mail programs may, in keeping with the rules of RFC 822, use types and/or subtypes beginning with X- as private values. No other values are permitted unless they have first been registered with the Internet Assigned Numbers Authority (IANA). See RFC 2048 for more details. The intention is that few, if any, additional types will be needed, but that many subtypes will be added to the set.

11.2.3 The Content-Transfer-Encoding field

As already noted, SMTP agents and mail gateways can severely constrain the contents of mail messages that can be transmitted safely. The MIME types described above list a rich set of different types of objects that can be included in mail messages and the majority of these do not fall within these constraints. Therefore, it is necessary to encode data of these types in a fashion that can be transmitted, and to decode them on receipt. RFC 2045 defines two forms of encoding that are mail safe. The reason for two forms rather than one is that it is not possible, given the small set of characters known to be mail safe, to devise a form that can both encode text data with minimal impact to the readability of the text and yet can encode binary data that consists of characters distributed randomly across all 256 byte values compactly enough to be practical.

These two encodings are used only for bodies and not for headers. Header encoding is described in 11.2.4, "Using non-ASCII characters in message headers" on page 416. The Content-Transfer-Encoding: field defines the encoding used. Although cumbersome, this field name emphasizes that the encoding is a feature of the transport process and not an intrinsic property of the object being mailed. Although there are only two encodings defined, this field can take on *five* values. (As usual, the values are case-insensitive.) Three of the values actually specify that no encoding has been done; where they differ is that they imply different reasons for why this is the case. This is a subtle but important point. MIME is not restricted to SMTP as a transport agent, despite the prevalence of (broadly) SMTP-compliant mail systems on the Internet. It therefore allows a mail agent to transmit data that is not mail-safe by the standards of SMTP (that is, STD 10/RFC 821). If such a mail item reaches a gateway to a more restrictive system, the encoding mechanism specified allows the gateway to decide on an item-by-item basis whether the body must be encoded to be transmitted safely.

The five encodings are:

- 7-bit (the default if the Content-Transfer-Encoding: header is omitted)
- 8-bit
- Binary
- Quoted-Printable
- Base64

These are described in the sections that follow.

11.2.3.1 7-bit encoding

7-bit encoding means that no encoding has been done and the body consists of lines of ASCII text with a length of no more than 1000 characters. It is therefore known to be mail-safe with any mail system that *strictly* conforms with STD 10/RFC 821. This is the default, since these are the restrictions which apply to pre-MIME STD 11/RFC 822 messages.

11.2.3.2 8-bit encoding

8-bit encoding implies that lines are short enough for SMTP transport, but that there may be non-ASCII characters (that is, octets with the high-order bit set). Where SMTP agents support the SMTP service extension for 8-bit-MIMEtransport, described in RFC 1652, 8-bit encoding is possible. Otherwise, SMTP implementations should set the high-order bit to zero, so 8-bit encoding is not valid.

11.2.3.3 Binary encoding

Binary encoding indicates that non-ASCII characters may be present and that the lines may be too long for SMTP transport. (That is, there may be sequences of 999 or more characters without a CRLF sequence.) There are currently no standards for the transport of unencoded binary data by mail based on the TCP/IP protocol stack, so the only case where it is valid to use binary encoding in a MIME message sent on the Internet or other TCP/IP based network is in the header of an external-body part (see the message/external-body type above). Binary encoding would be valid if MIME were used in conjunction with other mail transport mechanisms, or with a hypothetical SMTP service extension that did support long lines.

11.2.3.4 Quoted-printable encoding

This is the first of the two real encodings and it is intended to leave text files largely readable in their encoded form.

- It represents non-mail safe characters by the hexadecimal representation of their ASCII characters.

- It introduces reversible (soft) line breaks to keep all lines in the message to a length of 76 characters or less.

Quoted-printable encoding uses the equal sign as a quote character to indicate both of these cases. It has five rules which are summarized as follows:

1. Any character except one that is part of a new line sequence (that is, a X' 0D0A' sequence on a text file) can be represented by =XX, where XX are

two uppercase hexadecimal digits. If none of the other rules apply, the character must be represented as XX.

2. Any character in the range X'21' to X'7E', except for X'3D' ("="), can be represented as the ASCII character.

3. ASCII TAB (X'09') and SPACE (X'20') can be represented as the ASCII character, except when it is the last character on the line.

4. A line break must be represented by a <CRLF> sequence (X'0D0A'). When encoding binary data, X'0D0A' is not a line break and should be coded, according to rule 1, as =0D=0A.

5. Encoded lines cannot be longer than 76 characters (excluding the <CRLF>). If a line is longer than this, a soft line break must be inserted at or before column 75. A soft line break is the sequence =<CRLF> (X'3D0D0A').

This scheme is a compromise between readability, efficiency, and robustness. Since rules 1 and 2 use the phrase "may be encoded," implementations have a fair degree of latitude on how many characters are quoted. If as few characters are quoted as possible within the scope of the rules, then the encoding will work with well-behaved ASCII SMTP agents. Adding the following set of ASCII characters to the list of those to be quoted is adequate for well-behaved EBCDIC gateways:

```
! " # $ @ [ \ ] ^ ` { | } ~
```

For total robustness, it is better to quote *every* character except for the 73-character set known to be invariant across all gateways, that is the letters and digits (A-Z, a-z and 0-9) and the following 11 characters:

```
' ( ) + , - . / : = ?
```

> **Note:**
>
> This invariant list does not even include the SPACE character. For practical purposes, when encoding text files, only a SPACE should be quoted. Otherwise, at the end of a line readability is severely impacted.

11.2.3.5 Base64 encoding

This encoding is intended for data that does not consist mainly of text characters. Quoted-Printable replaces each non-text character with a 3-byte sequence which is grossly inefficient for binary data. Base64 encoding works by treating the input stream as a bit stream, regrouping the bits into shorter bytes, padding these short bytes to 8 bits, and then translating these bytes to characters that are known to be mail-safe. As noted in the previous section, there are only 73 safe characters, so the maximum byte length usable is 6 bits, which can be represented by 64 unique characters (hence the name Base64). Since the input and output are both byte streams, the encoding has to be done in groups of 24 bits (that is 3 input bytes and 4 output bytes). The process can be seen as follows:

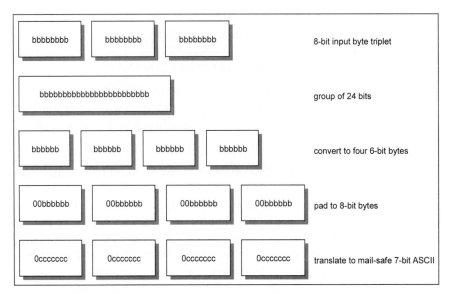

Figure 173. MIME - Base64 Encoding - How 3 input bytes are converted to 4 output bytes in the Base64 encoding scheme.

The translate table used is called the *Base64 Alphabet*:

Table 19. MIME - The Base64 Alphabet

Base64 value	ASCII char	Base64 value	ASCII char	Base64 value	ASCII char	Base64 value	ASCII char
0	A	16	Q	32	g	48	w
1	B	17	R	33	h	49	x
2	C	18	S	34	i	50	Y
3	D	19	T	35	j	51	Z
4	E	20	U	36	k	52	0
5	F	21	V	37	l	53	1
6	G	22	W	38	m	54	2
7	H	23	X	39	n	55	3

Base64 value	ASCII char	Base64 value	ASCII char	Base64 value	ASCII char	Base64 value	ASCII char
8	I	24	Y	40	o	56	4
9	J	25	Z	41	p	57	5
10	K	26	a	42	q	58	6
11	L	27	b	43	r	59	7
12	M	28	c	44	s	60	8
13	N	29	d	45	t	61	9
14	O	30	e	46	u	62	+
15	P	31	f	47	v	63	/

One additional character (the = character) is needed for padding. Because the input is a byte stream that is encoded in 24-bit groups, it will be short by zero, 8, or 16 bits, as will the output. If the output is of the correct length, no padding is needed. If the output is 8 bits short, this corresponds to an output quartet of two complete bytes, a short byte, and a missing byte. The short byte is padded with two low-order zero bits. The missing byte is replaced with an = character. If the output is 16 bits short, this corresponds to an output quartet of one complete byte, a short byte, and two missing bytes. The short byte is padded with 6 low-order zero bits. The two missing bytes are replaced with an = character. If zero characters (that is, As) were used, the receiving agent would not be able to tell, when decoding the input stream, if the trailing X'00' characters in the last or last two positions of the output stream were data or padding. With pad characters, the number of "="s (0, 1 or 2) gives the length of the input stream modulo 3 (0, 2 or 1 respectively).

11.2.3.6 Conversion between encodings

The Base64 encoding can be freely translated to and from the binary encoding without ambiguity, since both treat the data as an octet-stream. This is also true for the conversion from Quoted-Printable to either of the other two (in the case of the Quoted-Printable to Binary conversion, the process can be viewed as involving an intermediate binary encoding) by converting the quoted character sequences to their 8-bit form, deleting the soft line breaks and replacing hard line breaks with <CRLF> sequences. This is not strictly true of the reverse process, since Quoted-Printable is actually a record-based system. There is a semantic difference between a hard line break and an imbedded =0D=0A sequence. (For example, when decoding Quoted-Printable on a EBCDIC record-based system such as VM, hard line breaks map to record boundaries, but =0D=0A sequences map to X'0D25' sequences.)

11.2.3.7 Multiple encodings

MIME does *not* allow nested encodings. Any Content-Type that recursively includes other Content-Type fields (notably the multipart and message types) cannot use a Content-Transfer-Encoding other than 7-bit, 8-bit, or binary. All encodings must be done at the innermost level. The purpose of this restriction is to simplify the operation of user mail agents. If nested encodings are not permitted, the structure of the entire message is always visible to the mail agent without the need to decode the outer layer(s) of the message.

This simplification for user mail agents has a price: complexity for gateways. Because a user agent can specify an encoding of 8-bit or binary, a gateway to a network where these encodings are not safe must encode the message before passing it to the second network. The obvious solution, to simply encode the message body and to change the Content-Transfer-Encoding: field, is not allowed for the multipart or message types, since it would violate the restriction described above. The gateway must therefore correctly parse the message into its components and re-encode the innermost parts as necessary.

There is one further restriction: messages of type message/partial must *always* have 7-bit encoding. (8-bit and binary are also disallowed.) The reason for this is that if a gateway needs to re-encode a message, it requires the entire message to do so, but the parts of the message may not all be available together. (Parts may be transmitted serially because the gateway is incapable of storing the entire message at once or they may even be routed independently via different gateways.) Therefore, message/partial body parts must be mail safe across lowest common denominator networks; that is, they must be 7-bit encoded.

11.2.4 Using non-ASCII characters in message headers

All of the mechanisms above refer exclusively to bodies and not to headers. The contents of message headers must still be coded in US-ASCII. For header fields that include human-readable text, this is not adequate for languages other than English. A mechanism to include national language characters is defined by the second part of MIME (RFC 2047). This mechanism differs from the Quoted-Printable encoding, which would be used in a message body for the following reasons:

- The format of message headers is strictly codified by RFC 822, so the encoding used by MIME for header fields must work within a narrower set of constraints than that used for bodies.

- Message relaying programs frequently change message headers, for example, re-ordering header fields, deleting some fields but not others, re-ordering mailboxes within lists, or spilling fields at different positions than the original message.

- Some message handling programs do not correctly handle some of the more arcane features of RFC 822 (such as the use of the \ character to quote special characters, such as < and >).

The approach used by MIME is to reserve improbable sequences of legal ASCII characters that are not syntactically important in RFC 822 for use with this protocol. Words in header fields that need national characters are replaced by *encoded words*, which have the form:

```
=?charset?encoding?word?=
```

Where:

charset The value allowed for the charset parameter used with text/plain MIME type, that is: "us-ascii" or "iso-8859-1" through" iso-8859-9".

encoding B or Q. B is identical to the Base64 encoding used in message bodies. Q is similar to the Quoted-Printable encoding but uses _ to represent X' 20' (ASCII SPACE).[2] Q encoding requires the encoding of _ characters and does not allow line breaks. Any printable ASCII character other than _, = and SPACE may be left unquoted within an encoded word unless it would be syntactically meaningful when the header field is parsed according to RFC 822.

charset and encoding are both case-insensitive.

word A string of ASCII text characters other than SPACE, which conforms to the rules of the encoding given.

An encoded word must have no imbedded white space characters (SPACE or TAB), can be up to 75 characters long, and cannot be on a line that is greater than 76 characters long (excluding the <CRLF>). These rules ensure that gateways will not fold encoded words in the middle of the word. Encoded words can generally be used in the human-readable parts of header fields. For example, if a mailbox is specified in the following form:

```
The Octopus <octopus@garden.under.the.sea>
```

---

[2] The underscore character is not strictly mail-safe, but it is used because the use of any other character to indicate a SPACE would seriously hamper readability.

an encoded word could be used in the The Octopus section but not in the address part between the < and the >. RFC 2047 specifies precisely where encoded words can be used with reference to the syntax of RFC 822.

11.2.5 References

A detailed description of MIME can be found in the following RFCs:

- RFC 2045 – MIME (Multipurpose Internet Mail Extensions) Part One: Format of Internet Message Bodies
- RFC 2046 – MIME (Multipurpose Internet Mail Extensions) Part Two: Media Types
- RFC 2047 – MIME (Multipurpose Internet Mail Extensions) Part Three: Message Header Extensions for Non-ASCII Text
- RFC 2048 – MIME (Multipurpose Internet Mail Extensions) Part Four: Registration Procedures
- RFC 2049 – MIME (Multipurpose Internet Mail Extensions) Part Five: Conformance Criteria and Examples
- RFC 2156 – MIXER (MIME Internet X.400 Enhanced Relay): Mapping between X.400 and RFC 822/MIME
- RFC 2159 – A MIME Body Part for FAX
- RFC 2183 – Communicating Presentation Information in Internet Messages
- RFC 2231 – MIME Parameter Value and Encoded Word Extensions

11.3 Post Office Protocol (POP)

The Post Office Protocol, Version 3 is a standard protocol with STD number 53. Its status is elective. It is described in RFC 1939. The older Post Office Protocol Version 2 is an historic protocol with a status of not recommended.

The Post Office Protocol is an electronic mail protocol with both client (sender/receiver) and server (storage) functions. POP3 supports basic functions (download and delete) for electronic mail retrieval. More advanced functions are supported by IMAP4 (see 11.4, "Internet Message Access Protocol Version 4 (IMAP4)" on page 420).

POP3 clients establish a TCP connection to the server using port 110. When the connection is established, the POP3 server sends a greeting message to the client. The session then enters the *authentication state*. The client must send its identification to the server while the session is in this state. If the server verifies the ID successfully, the session enters the *transaction state*. In this state, the client can access the mailbox. When the client sends the QUIT command, the session enters the *Update state* and the connection is then closed.

11.3.1 POP3 commands and responses

POP3 commands consist of a keyword and possibly one or more arguments following the keyword. Keywords are three or four characters long and separated by one space character from arguments. Each argument must be up to 40 characters long.

The server sends a response to the command that was issued by the client. This response must be up to 512 characters and begin with a status indicator which shows whether the reply is positive or negative. These indicators are (+OK) or (-ERR). The server must send these indicators in upper case.

Here are the three states for a POP3 session:

- Authorization state

  In this state, the client sends identification to the server. This is implemented in two ways (More information on authentication is described in RFC 1734):

  - Using USER and PASS commands
  - Using APOP command

- Transaction state

  In this state, the client can issue commands for listing, retrieving, and deleting. Please note that the deleting action is not taken in this state. The client must send the QUIT command and then the server goes to the update state.

- Update state

  In this state, the server updates the mailbox according to the commands received from the client in the transaction state and the TCP connection ends. If the connection is broken for any reason before the `quit` command is received from the client, the server does not enter the update state. Thus, the server will not update anything.

11.3.1.1 Important POP3 commands

Here are some important POP3 commands and their descriptions:

USER name   User name for authentication.

PASS password   Password for authentication.

STAT	To get the number of messages and total size of the messages.
LIST [msg]	If a message number is specified, the size of this mail is listed (if it exists). If not, all messages will be listed with the message sizes.
RETR msg	This command sends the whole message to the client.
DELE msg	This command deletes the specified message.
NOOP	The server does not do anything, just sends a positive response.
RSET	This command cancels previous delete requests if they exist.
QUIT	If entered in the authorization state, it merely ends the TCP connection. If entered in the transaction state, it first updates the mailbox (deletes any messages requested previously) and then ends the TCP connection.

11.3.2 References

A detailed description of the Post Office Protocol can be found in the following RFCs:

- RFC 937 – Post Office Protocol – Version 2
- RFC 1939 – Post Office Protocol – Version 3

11.4 Internet Message Access Protocol Version 4 (IMAP4)

The Internet Message Access Protocol, Version 4 is a proposed standard protocol. Its status is elective. It is described in RFC 2060.

IMAP4 is an electronic messaging protocol with both client and server functions. Similar to POP, IMAP4 servers store messages for multiple users to be retrieved upon client requests, but IMAP4 clients have more capabilities in doing so than POP clients. IMAP4 allows clients to have multiple remote mailboxes to retrieve messages from and to choose any of those at any time. IMAP4 clients can specify criteria for downloading messages, such as not transferring large messages over slow links. Also, IMAP4 always keeps messages on the server and replicates copies to the clients. Transactions performed by disconnected clients are effected on server mailboxes by periodic re-synchronization of client and server. Let us discuss the underlying electronic mail models of IMAP4 first, in order to understand the IMAP4 functions clearly. These are described in detail in RFC 1733 - Distributed Electronic Mail Models In IMAP4.

11.4.1 IMAP4 underlying electronic mail models

IMAP4 supports all three major electronic mail models. These models are offline, online, and disconnected use models.

In the offline model, a client periodically connects to the server and downloads the mail messages. Mail messages are deleted on the server. Therefore, mail is processed locally on the client. An example of a mail protocol that uses this model is POP3. Please see 11.3, "Post Office Protocol (POP)" on page 418 for further information.

In the online model, clients make changes on the server. This is often done by means of a remote file system protocol, such as NFS. In other words, mail is held on the server, but processed by software on the client. Please see 10.3, "Network File System (NFS)" on page 375 for further information.

The disconnected use model is composite of offline and online models. In this model, a client downloads the data and makes changes on it locally, then at a later time uploads it to server. An example of a mail program that can use this model is Lotus Notes mail.

These three models have some advantages and disadvantages. Since IMAP4 supports all these models, the client is able to switch to another model, for example, if the connection is too slow and there is a large message in the mailbox. An IMAP4 client can retrieve a small part of the message, change that part and then reconnect to the server and upload that part again.

IMAP4 is aware of MIME multipart messages. It is possible, with the FETCH command, to just download part of the nth MIME encapsulated message.

11.4.2 IMAP4 commands and responses

Similar to the POP3 (see 11.3, "Post Office Protocol (POP)" on page 418), IMAP4 clients establish a TCP connection to the server using port 143. When the connection is established, the server sends a greeting message. After that, the client and the server exchange data interactively. Whenever the client sends a command, the server sends a completion result response to this command. The server can also send data for any other reason. All commands and responses are in the form of lines ending with CRLF.

All client commands begin with a different identifier which is called a *tag*. The server may not respond to the commands in the order in which they were received. Let us say a command that has the tag ABC005 is sent and then another command, which has tag ABC006, is sent. If it takes less time to process the second command, the server responds to the ABC006 command first with a line beginning with the relevant tag (In this case, ABC006). A unique tag must be used for every command sent.

In two cases, the client command is not sent completely on one line. When this happens, no other commands can be sent until either a continuation or a BAD response is received. These cases are:

1. When sending a literal string from client to the server, the client sends the {', length, '} sequence, and then waits for the server to respond with a line beginning with +. After which, the rest of the string is sent.

2. During the authentication stage, the client also has to wait for the + continuation line.

The server sends a command completion response to the command that was issued by the client. This response begins with the same tag of the relevant command and a status indicator following by the tag, which shows that the operation result is either positive or negative. These indicators are OK, NO, or BAD.

All data responses and status responses begin with (*), which are called untagged responses. These are sent by the server at any time (even if a command has not completed). As an example, if a new mail message arrives during the session, the server sends the relevant flag to notify the client.

11.4.3 Message numbers

There are two methods used to identify the messages: the unique identifier and the message sequence number. Some of the attributes are shown in the following sections. Please refer to RFC 2060 for details.

11.4.3.1 Unique identifier (UID) message attribute

Every message has a 32-bit identifier, which, when it is combined with a unique identifier validity value, forms a 64-bit value. When a new message is added to the mailbox, a higher UID, than those added previously, is assigned to that message. Unique identifiers do not have to be contiguous. Unique identifiers also persist in to other sessions. In this way, if the clients disconnect, the client can use the same values from the previous session in the next session.

Each mailbox has a unique identifier validity value. If it is not possible to use the same value for the next session, then a new value must be greater than the value that was used in the previous session. For example, if a mailbox is deleted in one session and a new one created with the same name in the next session, the client may not realize that this is a new mailbox, since the mailbox name is the same. In this case, the unique identifier validity value should be changed. The unique identifier validity value is sent with the mailbox selection to the client as UIDVALIDITY.

11.4.3.2 Message sequence number message attribute

The message sequence number shows the relative position of the message in the mailbox. It must be in ascending order. The message sequence number is subject to change during the session or in the next session. If a new message is added, the number of total messages (including the new message) is assigned to that message. The total number of the messages and the message sequence number of the newest message must always be kept the same, in order to correctly assign the message sequence number to each new mail message. If a message is removed permanently, then the message sequence numbers must be recalculated in that session.

11.4.3.3 Flags message attribute

Flags are used to show the current status of the message. There are two types of flags: permanent and session-only. All system flags begin with a \. Please refer to RFC 2060 for details.

\Seen	Message has been read.
\Answered	Message has been answered.
\Flagged	Message is marked for special attention.
\Deleted	Message is deleted for later permanent removal.
\Draft	Message has been completed.
\Recent	Message has arrived recently and this is the first session after its arrival. This flag cannot be changed by the client.

11.4.4 IMAP4 states

Similar to POP3 (see 11.3, "Post Office Protocol (POP)" on page 418), the IMAP4 session works in different states. Some commands are valid for certain states and some of the commands are valid for all states. If the client sends a command that is not appropriate for that state, the server responds with an error message. This error message may vary. The server might send either BAD or NO depending on the implementation. Here are the four states for IMAP4:

Non-authenticated state In this state, the client sends identification to the server.

Authenticated state In this state, the client must select a mailbox to proceed.

Selected state In this state, a mailbox has been successfully selected.

Logout state In this state, the connection is ended either by the request of the client or any other reason.

A flow diagram of an IMAP4 session is shown in Figure 174.

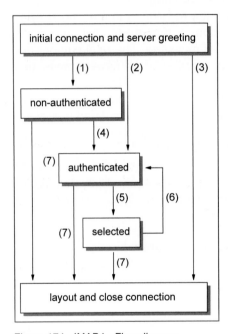

Figure 174. IMAP4 - Flow diagram

Where:

(1)	Connection without pre-authentication (OK greeting)

(2)	Pre-authenticated connection (PREAUTH greeting)

(3)	Rejected connection (BYE greeting)

(4)	Successful LOGIN or AUTHENTICATE command

(5)	Successful SELECT or EXAMINE command

(6)	CLOSE command, or failed SELECT or EXAMINE command

(7)   LOGOUT command, server shutdown, or connection closed

11.4.5 Client commands

Most of the IMAP4 commands must be used in the corresponding state. Some of them can be used in more than one state. The following list shows the commands and the states in which they are used:

- In any state

  The following commands are valid for this state:

  - CAPABILITY: This command sends a request a list of functions that the server supports.

  - NOOP: This command does nothing. It can be used to reset the inactivity autologout timer on the server.

  - LOGOUT: This command sends a request to end the connection.

- In a non-authenticated state

  All commands in any state and the following commands are valid for this state:

  - AUTHENTICATE: This command requests a special authentication mechanism with an argument from the server. If the server does not support that mechanism, the server sends an error message.

  - LOGIN: This command sends the user name and password in plain text.

- In an authenticated state

  All commands in any state and the following commands are valid for this state:

  - SELECT: This command selects a mailbox.

  - EXAMINE: This command also selects a mailbox, but access to the mailbox with this command is read-only.

  - CREATE: This command creates a mailbox with a given name. It is not allowed to create INBOX or any other existing mailbox.

  - DELETE: This command permanently removes the mailbox with the given name.

  - RENAME: This command changes the name of the mailbox.

  - SUBSCRIBE: This command adds the specified mailbox to the subscription list (which can be obtained by the LSUB command).

- UNSUBSCRIBE: This command removes the specified mailbox name from the subscription list.
- LIST: This command requests a subset of names from the complete set of all names available from the server.
- LSUB: This command requests a subset of names from the subscription list.
- STATUS: This command requests the status of the given mailbox name. The server checks the flags and send the status according to the status of the flags.
- APPEND: This command appends a message text to the given mailbox as a new message.

- In selected state

  All commands in any state, all commands in authenticated state, and the following commands are valid for this state:

  - CHECK: This command requests resolution of the state of the selected mailbox in the memory and the disk.
  - CLOSE: This command permanently removes all messages from the currently selected mailbox that were previously marked as deleted and returns to authenticated state from selected state.
  - EXPUNGE: This command permanently removes all messages from the currently selected mailbox that were previously marked as deleted.
  - SEARCH: This command searches the mailbox for the messages that match given searching criteria.
  - FETCH: This command retrieves data associated with a message in the selected mailbox.
  - STORE: This command updates the message with the data which was retrieved by a FETCH command.
  - COPY: This command copies the specified message to the end of the specified destination mailbox.
  - UID: This command returns unique identifier instead of message sequence numbers. This command is used with other commands.

11.4.6 References

A detailed description of the IMAP protocol can be found in:

- RFC 1733 – Distributed Electronic Mail Models in IMAP4
- RFC 2060 – Internet Message Access Protocol – Version 4rev1

Chapter 12. The World Wide Web

This chapter introduces some of the protocols and applications that have made the task of using the Internet both easier and very popular over the past couple of years. In fact, World Wide Web traffic, which mostly uses the Hypertext Transfer Protocol (HTTP), greatly surpasses any other application protocol (such as Telnet and FTP) as using the most bandwidth across the Internet. Modern computer operating systems provide Web browser applications by default, some even provide Web servers, thus making it ever easier for end users and businesses to explore and exploit the vast capabilities of worldwide networked computing.

The World Wide Web is a global hypertext system that was initially developed in 1989 by Tim Berners Lee at the European Laboratory for Particle Physics, CERN in Switzerland to facilitate an easy way of sharing and editing research documents among a geographically dispersed group of scientists.

In 1993, the Web started to grow rapidly, which was mainly due to the National Center for Supercomputing Applications (NCSA) developing a Web browser program called Mosaic, an X Windows-based application. This application provided the first graphical user interface to the Web and made browsing more convenient. Today, there are Web browsers and servers available for nearly all platforms. The rapid growth in popularity of the Web is due to the flexible way people can navigate through worldwide resources in the Internet and retrieve them.

The number of Web servers is also increasing rapidly and the traffic over port 80, which is the well-known port for HTTP Web servers, on the NSF backbone has had a phenomenal rate of growth too. The NSFNET, however, was converted back to a private research network in 1995; therefore comprehensive statistics of backbone traffic are not as easily available today.

12.1 Web browsers

Generally, a browser is referred to as an application that provides access to a Web server. Depending on the implementation, browser capabilities and hence structures may vary. A Web browser, at a minimum, consists of an Hypertext Markup Language (HTML) interpreter and HTTP client which is used to retrieve HTML Web pages. Besides this basic requirement, many browsers also support FTP, NNTP, e-mail (POP and SMTP clients), among other features, with an easy-to-manage graphical interface. Figure 175 on page 428 illustrates a basic Web browser structure.

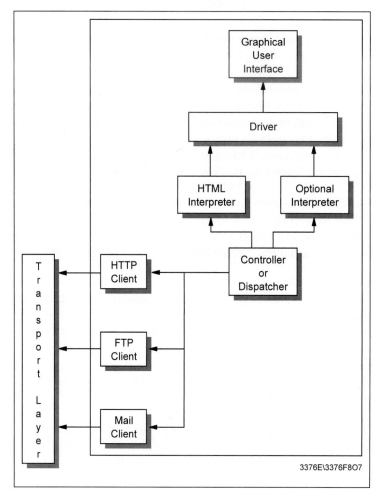

Figure 175. Structure of a Web browser

As with many other Internet facilities, the Web uses a client/server processing model. The Web browser is the client component. Examples of Web browsers include Mosaic, Netscape Navigator, and Microsoft Internet Explorer. Web browsers are responsible for formatting and displaying information, interacting with the user, and invoking external functions, such as Telnet, or external viewers for data types that Web browsers do not directly support. Web browsers have become the "universal client" for the GUI workstation environment, in much the same way that the ability to emulate popular terminals such as the DEC VT100 or IBM 3270 allows connectivity and access to character-based applications on a wide variety of computers. Web browsers are widely available for all popular GUI workstation platforms and are inexpensive.

12.2 Web servers

Web servers are responsible for servicing requests for information from Web browsers. The information can be a file retrieved from the server's local disk, or it can be generated by a program called by the server to perform a specific application function.

There are a number of public-domain Web servers available for a variety of platforms including most UNIX variants, as well as personal computer environments such as Windows NT. Some well-known public domain servers are CERN, NCSA httpd, and Apache servers.

The IBM HTTP Server (current version V1.3.19) is based on the Apache HTTP Server, which is the most popular server on the Web. This HTTP Server runs on AIX, Solaris, Windows NT, Window 2000, HP-UX, and Linux. Other versions include the IBM HTTP Server for AS/400 and the IBM HTTP Server for OS/390 which completes the IBM offering on a wide range of platforms. IBM has enhanced the Apache-powered HTTP Server. For example, IBM has added SSL for secure transactions and offers full support, when part of the WebSphere bundle. IBM HTTP Server features include:

- Easy installation.
- Support for SSL and TLS secure connections.
- Fast Response Cache Accelerator.
- IBM support as part of the WebSphere bundle.
- Hardware crypto support.
- Administration Server that helps to administer and configure IHS servers.
- Help information that uses the easy-to-navigate design that is common to all WebSphere products.

For more information, please reference:

`http://www.software.ibm.com/webservers`

12.3 Hypertext Transfer Protocol (HTTP)

HTTP 1.1 is a draft standard protocol. It is described in RFC 2616. The older HTTP 1.0 is an informational protocol and described in RFC 1945.

The hypertext transfer protocol is a protocol designed to allow the transfer of Hypertext Markup Language (HTML) documents. HTML is a tag language used to create hypertext documents. Hypertext documents include links to other documents that contain additional information about the highlighted term or subject. Such documents may contain other elements apart from text, such as graphic images, audio and video clips, Java applets, and even virtual reality worlds (which are described in VRML, a scripting language for that kind of elements). See 12.4.1.1, "Hypertext Markup Language (HTML)" on page 441 for more information on HTML.

12.3.1 Overview of HTTP

HTTP is based on request-response activity. A client, running an application called a browser, establishes a connection with a server and sends a request to the server in the form of a request method. The server responds with a status line, including the message's protocol version and a success or error code, followed by a message containing server information, entity information and possible body content.

An HTTP transaction is divided into four steps:

1. The browser opens a connection.
2. The browser sends a request to the server.
3. The server sends a response to the browser.
4. The connection is closed.

On the Internet, HTTP communication generally takes place over TCP connections. The default port is TCP 80, but other ports can be used. This does not preclude HTTP from being implemented on top of any other protocol on the Internet, or on other networks. HTTP only presumes a reliable transport; any protocol that provides such guarantees can be used.

Except for experimental applications, current practice requires that the connection be established by the client prior to each request and closed by the server after sending the response. Both clients and servers should be aware that either party may close the connection prematurely, due to user action, automated timeout, or program failure, and should handle such closing in a predictable and desirable fashion. In any case, the closing of the connection by either or both parties always terminates the current request, regardless of its status.

In simple terms, HTTP is a stateless protocol because it does not keep track of the connections. To load a page including two graphics, for example, a graphic-enabled browser will open three TCP connections: One for the page and two for the graphics. Most browsers, however, are able to handle several of these connections simultaneously.

This behavior can be rather resource-intensive if one page consists of a lot of elements, as quite a number of Web pages do. HTTP 1.1, as defined in RFC 2616, alleviates this problem to the extent that one TCP connection will be established per type of element on a page, and all elements of that kind will be transferred over the same connection respectively. These deviates from HTTP 1.0 by making the connections persistent.

However, if a request depends on the information exchanged during a previous connection, then this information has to be kept outside the protocol. One way of tracking such persistent information is the use of cookies. A cookie is a set of information that is exchanged between a client Web browser and a Web server during an HTTP transaction. The maximum size of a cookie is 4 KB. All these pieces of information, or cookies, are then stored in one single file and placed in the directory of the Web browser. If cookies are disabled, that file is automatically deleted. A cookie can be retrieved and checked by the server at any subsequent connection. Because cookies are regarded as a potential privacy exposure, a Web browser should allow the user to decide whether or not he or she will accept cookies from a particular server. While cookies merely serve the purpose of keeping some kind of state for HTTP connections, secure client and server authentication is provided by the Secure Sockets Layer (SSL) which is described in 21.8, "Secure Sockets Layer (SSL)" on page 747.

12.3.2 HTTP operation

In most cases, the HTTP communication is initiated by the user agent requesting a resource on the origin server. In the simplest case, the connection is established via a single connection between the user agent and the origin server as shown in Figure 176.

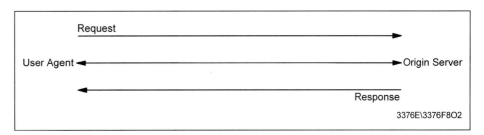

Figure 176. HTTP - Single client/server connection

In some cases, there is no direct connection between the user agent and the origin server. There is one (or more) intermediary between the user agent and origin server, such as a proxy, gateway, or tunnel. Requests and responses are evaluated by the intermediaries and forwarded to the destination or another intermediary in the request-response chain as shown in Figure 177.

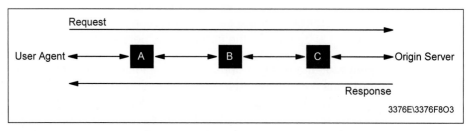

Figure 177. HTTP - Client/server connection with intermediaries in between

As described in 21.3.4, "Application level gateway (proxy)" on page 682, a proxy can handle the content of the data and therefore modify the data accordingly. When a request comes to a proxy, it rewrites all or part of the message and forwards the message to the next destination. A gateway receives the message and sends the message to the underlying protocols with an appropriate format. A tunnel does not deal with the content of the message, therefore it simply forwards the message as it is.

Proxies, and gateways in general, can handle the caching of HTTP messages. This can dramatically reduce the response time and IP traffic on the network. Since tunnels cannot understand the message content, they cannot store cached data of HTTP messages. In the previous figure (Figure 177), if one of the intermediaries (A, B, and C) employs an internal cache for HTTP messages, the user agent can get a response from the intermediary if it is previously cached from the origin server in the response chain. Figure 178 illustrates that A has a cached copy of an earlier response from the origin server in the response chain. Hence, if the server response for the request is not already cached in the user agent's internal cache, it can directly be obtained from A.

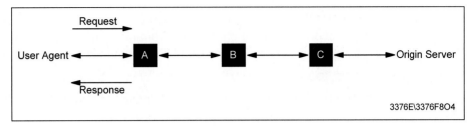

Figure 178. HTTP - Cached server response

Caching is not applicable to all server responses. Caching behavior can be modified by special requests to determine which server responses can or cannot be cached. For this purpose, server responses can be marked as non-cachable, public, or private (cannot be cached in a public cache). Cache behavior and cachable responses are discussed in 12.3.2.11, "HTTP caching" on page 439.

12.3.2.1 Protocol parameters

Some of the HTTP protocol parameters are given below. Please refer to RFC 2616 for the full list and details.

- HTTP version

  HTTP uses a <major>.<minor> numbering scheme to indicate the versions of the protocol. The furthermost connection will be performed according to the protocol versioning policy. The <major> number is incremented when there are significant changes in protocol, such as changing a message format. The <minor> number is incremented when the changes do not affect the message format.

  The version of HTTP messages is sent by an HTTP-Version field in the first line of the message. The HTTP-Version field is in the following format (refer to RFC 2822 for augmented Backus-Naur Form.):

  ```
  HTTP-Version  =   "HTTP" "/" 1*DIGIT "." 1*DIGIT
  ```

- Uniform Resource Identifiers (URI)

  Uniform Resource Identifiers are generally referred to as WWW addresses and combination of Uniform Resource Locators (URL) and Uniform Resource Names (URN). In fact, URIs are strings that indicate the location and name of the source on the server. Please see RFC 2616 and RFC 2396 for more detail about the URI and URL syntax.

- HTTP URL

  The HTTP URL scheme allows you to locate network resources via HTTP protocol. It is based on the URI Generic Syntax and described in RFC 2396. The general syntax of a URL scheme is shown below:

  ```
  HTTP_URL = "http" "//" host [ ":" port ] [ abs_path ]
  ```

  The port number is optional. If it is not specified, the default value is 80.

12.3.2.2 HTTP message

HTTP messages consist of the following fields:

- Message types

  A HTTP message can be either a client request or a server response. The following string indicates the HTTP message type:

  ```
  HTTP-message   =   Request | Response
  ```

- Message headers

  HTTP message header field can be one of the following:

  - General header

  - Request header

  - Response header

  - Entity header

- Message body

  Message body can be referred to as entity body if there is no transfer coding has been applied. Message body simply carries the entity body of the relevant request or response.

- Message length

  Message length indicates the length of the message body if it is included. The message length is determined according to the criteria that is described in RFC 2616 in detail.

- General header fields

  General header fields can apply both request and response messages. Currently defined general header field options are as follows:

  - Cache-Control

  - Connection

  - Date

  - Pragma

- Transfer-Encoding

- Upgrade

- Via

12.3.2.3 Request

A request message from a client to a server includes the method to be applied to the resource, the identifier of the source, and the protocol version in use. A request message field is as follows:

```
Request  =  Request-Line
              *( general-header | request-header | entity-header )
               CRLF
               [ message-body ]
```

Please refer to RFC 2616 for detailed information.

12.3.2.4 Response

An HTTP server returns a response after evaluating the client request. A response message field is as follows:

```
Request  =  Request-Line
              *( general-header | request-header | entity-header )
               CRLF
               [ message-body ]
```

Please refer to RFC 2616 for detailed information.

12.3.2.5 Entity

Either the client or server might send Entity in the request message or the response message, unless otherwise indicated. Entity consists of the following:

- Entity header fields
- Entity body

12.3.2.6 Persistent connections

A significant difference between HTTP 1.1 and earlier versions of HTTP is that HTTP 1.1 uses persistent connection as the default. In earlier version implementations, a separate TCP connection is established for each URL and clients have to make multiple requests for images and associated data on the same URL. This approach was causing congestion and performance problems on the network. Persistent HTTP connections have a number of advantages, most notably the reduction in TCP connections and subsequently, of waiting times.

12.3.2.7 Method definitions

Currently defined methods are as follows:

- Safe and idempotent methods

  Methods considered not to cause side effects are referred to as *safe*. Idempotent methods are GET, HEAD, PUT and DELETE.

- OPTIONS

  This method allows the client to determine the options or requirements associated with a source or capabilities of a server, without any resource retrieval.

- GET

  This method allows the client to retrieve the data which was determined by the request URI.

- HEAD

  This method allows the client to retrieve metainformation about the entity which does not require you to transfer the entity body.

- POST

  The post function is determined by the server.

- PUT

  This method is similar to the post method with one important difference which is the URI in post request identifies the resource that will handle enclosed entity.

- DELETE

  This methods requests that the server delete the source determined by the request URI.

- TRACE

  Trace method allows the client to see how the message was retrieved at the other side for testing and diagnostic purposes.

12.3.2.8 Status code definitions

The status code definitions are as follows:

- Informational (1xx)

  Informational status codes indicate a provisional response. Currently defined codes are as follows:

  - 100 Continue
  - 101 Switching Protocols

- Successful (2xx)

  This class of codes indicates that a particular request was successfully received, understood and accepted. Currently defined codes are as follows:

  - 200 OK
  - 201 Created
  - 202 Accepted
  - 203 Non-Authoritative Information
  - 204 No Content
  - 205 Reset Content
  - 206 Partial Content

- Redirection (3xx)

  This class of codes indicates that an action is required from the user agent in order to complete the request. Currently defined codes are as follows:

  - 300 Multiple Choices
  - 301 Moved Permanently
  - 302 Moved Temporarily
  - 303 See Other
  - 304 Not Modified
  - 305 Use Proxy

- Client error (4xx)

  This class of codes indicates client errors. Currently defined codes are as follows:

  - 400 Bad Request
  - 401 Unauthorized
  - 402 Payment Required
  - 403 Forbidden
  - 404 Not Found
  - 405 Method Not Allowed
  - 406 Not Acceptable
  - 407 Proxy Authentication Required
  - 408 Request Timeout
  - 409 Conflict
  - 410 Gone
  - 411 Length Required
  - 412 Precondition Failed
  - 413 Request Entity Too Large
  - 414 Request-URI Too Long
  - 415 Unsupported Media Type

- Server error (5xx)

  This class of codes indicate client errors. Currently defined codes are as follows:

  - 500 Internal Server Error
  - 501 Not Implemented
  - 502 Bad Gateway
  - 503 Service Unavailable
  - 504 Gateway Timeout
  - 505 HTTP Version Not Supported

12.3.2.9 Access authentication

HTTP provides an authentication mechanism to allow servers to define access permissions on resources and clients to use these resources. The authentication method can be one of the following:

- Basic authentication scheme

  Basic authentication is based on user IDs and passwords. In this authentication scheme, the server will permit the connection only if the user ID and password are validated. In basic authentication, user IDs and passwords are not encrypted. They are encoded in base64 format (see 11.2.3.5, "Base64 encoding" on page 413). Therefore, the use of SSL or TLS is highly recommended.

- Digest authentication scheme

  Digest authentication scheme is an extension to HTTP and described in RFC 2617. In this authentication scheme, the user ID and a digest containing a hash value of the password are sent to the server. The server computes a similar digest and grants access to the protected resources if the two digests are equal. Notice that if the digest authentication is enabled, what is sent over the network is not simply an encrypted form of the password, which could be decrypted if one had the correct key, but is a one-hash value of the password, which cannot be decrypted. So digest authentication provides a higher level of security than the base-64 encoded password. Unfortunately, digest authentication is not yet supported by all browsers.

12.3.2.10 Content negotiation

In order to find the best handling for different types of data, the correct representation for a particular entity body should be negotiated.

There are three types of negotiation:

- Server-driven negotiation

  The representation for a response is determined according to the algorithms located at the server.

- Agent-driven negotiation

  If the representation for a response is determined according to the algorithms located.

- Transparent negotiation

  This is a combination of both server-driven and agent-driven negotiation. It is accomplished by a cache that includes a list of all available representations.

12.3.2.11 HTTP caching

One of the most important features of HTTP is caching capability. Since HTTP is a distributed information-based protocol, caching can improve the performance significantly. There are a number of functions that come with the HTTP 1.1 protocol to use caching efficiently and properly.

In most cases, client requests and server responses can be stored in a cache within a reasonable amount of time, to handle the corresponding future requests. If the response is in the cache and is accurate, there is no need to request another response from the server. This approach not only reduces the network bandwidth requirement, but also increases the speed. There is a mechanism that the server estimates a minimum time in which the response message will be valid. That means, an expiration time is determined by the server for that particular response message. Therefore, within this time, the message can be used without referring to the server.

Consider that this time is exceeded and there is a need for that response message. The data inside the message might have been changed (or not) after the expiration date. To be able to ensure whether the data is changed or not, a validation mechanism is defined as follows:

Expiration mechanism   In order to decide whether the data is fresh or not, an expiration time should be determined. In most cases, the origin server explicitly defines the expiration time for a particular response message within that message. If this is the case, the cached data can be used to send from cache for subsequent requests within the expiration time.

If the origin server did not define any expiration time, there are some methods to estimate/calculate a reasonable expiration time (such as the Last-Modified time). Since this is not originated from the server, they should be used cautiously.

Validation mechanism

When the expiration time is exceeded, there is a possibility that the data is stale. In order to ensure the validation of the response message, the cache has to check with the origin server (or possibly an intermediate cache with a fresh response) whether the response message is still usable. HTTP 1.1 provides conditional methods for this purpose.

When an origin server sends a full response, it attaches some sort of validator to the message. This will then be used as a *cache validator* by the user agent or the proxy cache. The client (user agent or the proxy cache) generates a conditional request with a cache validator attached to it. The server then evaluates the message and responds with a special code (usually, 304 (Not Modified)) and no entity body. Otherwise, the server sends the full response (including the entity body). This approach avoids an extra round-trip if the validator does not match and also avoids sending the full response if the validator matches.

Please refer to RFC 2616 for more details about HTTP caching.

12.4 Content

A Web server can serve static or dynamic (generated by a program upon invocation) content. This section discusses some commonly used technologies used to provide content and to facilitate interaction between a Web server and an application server that is not typically directly accessible to a client (for example, a Web browser).

12.4.1 Static content

Static content, or static pages, usually consist of data associated with a URL that does not change very often and does not depend on any client input. That is not to say that static content does not change at all, as a Web page may be updated frequently. This content is usually in the form of some markup language, such as HTML or XML.

12.4.1.1 Hypertext Markup Language (HTML)

HTML is one of the major attractions of the Web. It has an architected set of tags that should be understood by all Web browsers and Web servers, although as new features are added to HTML, they may not be supported by older Web browsers. These tags are device independent. The same document can be sent from a personal computer, an AIX or UNIX machine, or a mainframe, and the Web browser on any client machine can understand the HTML tags and build the data stream to display it on the target device. HTML tags describe basic elements of a Web document, such as headers, paragraphs, text styles, and lists. There are also more sophisticated tags to create tables and to include interactive elements, such as forms, scripts or Java applets.

Once document writers and programmers have mastered HTML, those skills are applicable to any operating system on any machine, provided that it has a Web browser.

Since HTML supports hypertext, it allows document writers to include links to other HTML documents. Those documents might be on the same machine as the original or they might be on a machine on another network on the other side of the world; such is the power of HTML links.

12.4.1.2 Extensible Markup Language (XML)

Extensible Markup Language (XML) describes a class of data objects called XML documents which are stored on computers, and partially describes the behavior of programs that process these objects. XML is an application profile, or restricted form, of SGML. The goal of XML is to enable generic SGML to be served, received, and processed on the Web in the way that is now possible with HTML. XML has been designed for ease of implementation and for interoperability with both SGML and HTML.

12.4.2 Client-side dynamic content

The extension of functionality into the client has led to the development of technologies to leverage dynamic content on the client's side.

12.4.2.1 Programs and applets

When a Java program is started from inside an HTML (Web) page, it is called a Java applet, as opposed to a Java program, which is executed from the command line or otherwise on the local system. Applets are downloaded via the Web browser from a server and, by definition, are somewhat limited in the way they can use resources of the local system.

Originally, Java applets were not supposed to touch anything local (outside of its Java Virtual Machine (JVM)), and could only communicate back to the server it was downloaded from. With Java 1.1, applets can be signed with security keys and certificates and can therefore be authenticated. Thus, an applet can be authorized to access local resources, such as file systems, and it may communicate with other systems.

12.4.2.2 JavaScript

JavaScript is an HTML extension and programming language, developed by Netscape, which is a simple object-based language compatible with Java. JavaScript programs are embedded as a source directly in an HTML document. They can control the behavior of forms, buttons and text elements. It is used to create dynamic behavior in elements of the Web page. In addition, it can be used to create forms whose fields have built-in error checking routines.

12.4.3 Server-side dynamic content

The complement of client-side dynamic content generation is, of course, server-side content generation. By executing the necessary functions of the server's side, this technology can leverage a server's processing power and its ability to coordinate requests with objects.

12.4.3.1 Common Gateway Interface (CGI)

The Common Gateway Interface (CGI) is a means of allowing a Web server to execute a program that is provided by the Web server administrator, rather than retrieving a file. CGI programs allow a Web server to generate a dynamic response, usually based on the client's input. A number of popular Web servers support the CGI, and a variety of programming languages can be used to develop programs that interface with CGI. However, CGI programs are not easily portable across platforms, unless using PERL.

12.4.3.2 Server-specific APIs

Some Web servers offer specific APIs that allow developers to create programs that can be invoked for special purposes upon certain events. Those APIs are usually quite powerful, but offer no portability across Web server platforms. The most popular server-specific APIs are Netscape Server API (NSAPI) and Microsoft Internet Information Server API (ISAPI).

12.4.3.3 Servlets

In order to spare resources on clients and networks, Java applets can be executed on the server rather than downloaded and started at the client. Such programs are then referred to as servlets. Though that method requires a significantly more powerful server, it is highly suitable for environments with medialess systems, such as network computers (see Appendix A, "Platform implementations" on page 889). This method is usually very portable across platforms and incurs little processing overhead.

12.4.3.4 Server-side includes (SSI)

This is a technology that a Java-enabled Web server (meaning, a Web server with a servlet engine) can use to convert a section of an HTML file into an alternative dynamic portion each time the document is sent to the client's browser. This dynamic portion invokes an appropriate servlet and passes to it the parameters it needs. The replacement is performed at the server and it is completely transparent to the client. Pages that use this technology have the extension .shtml instead of .html (or .htm).

12.4.3.5 Java Server Pages (JSP)

This is an easy-to-use solution for generating HTML (or other markup languages such as XML) pages with dynamic content. A JSP file contains combinations of HTML tags, NCSA tags (special tags that were the first method of implementing server-side includes), <SERVLET> tags, and JSP syntax. JSP files have the extension .jsp. One of the many advantages of JSP is that it enables programmers to effectively separate the HTML coding from the business logic in Web pages. JSP can be used to access reusable components, such as servlets, JavaBeans (reusable Java objects), and Java-based Web applications. JSP also supports embedding inline Java code within Web pages. JSPs are typically compiled into servlets for execution.

12.4.4 Objects

One main thrust in developing content on the Web is the use of objects. In general, objects allow for decreased application development cost and effort by promoting the re-usability of code. In addition, they allow for cooperation and coordination between different processes (and machines) by enabling operations that change the state of particular objects. That is, the term object is sometimes used to describe an implementation of reusable data structures and functions, but can also be used to described the instantiation of those data structures and functions.

12.4.4.1 JavaBeans

According to its inventors at JavaSoft, a JavaBean is a reusable software component that can be manipulated visually by using a builder tool. The JavaSoft definition allows for a broad range of components that can be thought of as beans.

JavaBeans can be visual components, such as buttons or entry fields, or even an entire spreadsheet application. JavaBeans can also be non-visual components, encapsulating business tasks or entities, such as processing employee paychecks, a bank account, or even an entire credit rating component. Non-visual beans still have a visual representation, such as an icon and/or name, to allow visual manipulation. While this visual representation may not appear to the user of an application, non-visual beans are depicted on-screen so developers can work with them.

JavaBeans can only be manipulated and reused if they are built in a standardized way. To build beans, JavaSoft provides the JavaBeans API, an architecture that defines a software component model for Java. The JavaBeans architecture delivers four key benefits:

- Support for a range of component granularity, as beans may come in different shapes and sizes.

- Portability, as the API is platform neutral. A bean, especially non-visual components developed under Windows, for example, should behave the same whether it is run under Windows, AIX, Solaris, or even z/OS, OS/400.

- Uniform, high-quality API; ideally, every platform that supports Java will support the entire JavaBeans API.

- Simplicity; the API is simple, universal and compact, easy to learn and begin to use.

The JavaBeans API defines the distinguishing characteristics of a bean, specifically, how they look and feel.

12.4.4.2 CORBA

Common Object Request Broker Architecture (CORBA) is a standard for distributed applications in which computers remotely invoke methods on objects residing on other computers. CORBA allows interconnection of objects and application regardless of language, location, or computer architecture.

An application is enabled to use distributed objects by using the Object Request Broker (ORB). The ORB transparently forwards remote object requests (for example, a method invocation) to the appropriate server objects, dispatches the requests and returns the results (for example, a method return value).

The Internet Inter-ORB Protocol (IIOP) is a communications protocol based on the CORBA specifications provided by the Object Management Group (OMG). Further information about the Object Management Group can be found at the OMG home page at the following URL:

```
http://www.omg.org/
```

12.4.4.3 Enterprise JavaBeans
An Enterprise JavaBean (EJB) is a Java component that can be combined with other EJBs and other Java components to create a distributed, multi-tiered application. Figure 179 shows the EJB environment. An EJB client, such as a Servlet or Java application, interacts with the EJB server via Remote Method Invocation (RMI) to access the objects (EJBs), which it coordinates. The actual object data is contained in some data source.

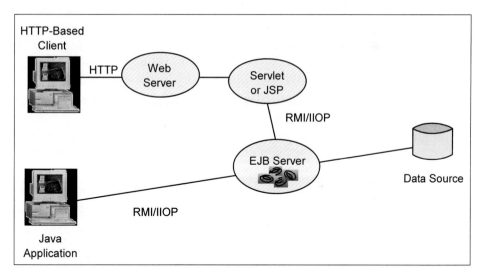

Figure 179. The Enterprise JavaBean environment

Remote Method Invocation (RMI)
RMI is a standard protocol for communication between Java objects residing on different computers. RMI provides a way for client and server applications to invoke methods across a distributed network of clients and servers running the JVM. You can invoke methods on the remote RMI object like you would on a local Java object. RMI is cross-platform, but not cross-language (Java only).

Sun Microsystems, with IBM and others, has recently developed a more portable version of RMI, which uses the Object Management Group's (OMG) Internet Inter-ORB protocol. IIOP is necessary for J2EE deployments to be interoperable with CORBA systems.

Types of EJBs

There are two types of Enterprise JavaBeans (EJB):

- Entity EJBs: They encapsulate permanent data, which is stored in a data source such as a database or a file system, and associated methods to manipulate that data. In most cases, an entity bean must be accessed in some transactional manner. Instances of an entity bean are unique and they can be accessed by multiple users.

  For example, the information about a bank account can be encapsulated in an entity bean. An account entity bean might contain an account ID, an account type (checking or savings), a balance variable, and methods to manipulate these variables.

- Session EJBs: They encapsulate ephemeral (nonpermanent) data associated with a particular EJB client. Unlike the data in an entity bean, the data in a session bean is not stored in a permanent data source and no harm is caused if this data is lost. However, a session bean can update data in an underlying database, usually by accessing an entity bean. A session bean can also participate in a transaction.

  When created, instances of a session bean are identical, though some session beans can store semipermanent data that makes them unique at certain points in their life cycle. A session bean is always associated with a single client; attempts to make concurrent calls result in an exception being thrown.

  For example, the task associated with transferring funds between two bank accounts can be encapsulated in a session bean. Such a transfer session bean can find two instances of an account entity bean (by using the account IDs), and then subtract a specified amount from one account and add the same amount to the other account.

12.4.5 Developing content with IBM Web Application Servers

To develop and optimize powerful Web application servers and solutions, IBM offers, among others, the following products on a variety of server platforms:

WebSphere Application Server An application server environment based on Java servlets and open standards, such as XML, CORBA and JDBC. WebSphere application server allows the

	development and object component distribution from simple Web publishing to enterprise transaction processing. WebSphere application server leverages the power of existing Web servers, such as IBM HTTP Server, Apache, Netscape Enterprise Server and Microsoft Internet Information Server.
WebSphere Edge Server	Provides enhanced caching, filtering, server monitoring, proxy, scalability and high availability functions to Web servers. Its functionality includes the ability to cache Java Server Page (JSP) technology and servlet results. In addition, it provides both reverse proxy caching, which improves Web server response time and forward proxy caching, to reduce network bandwidth requirements.
Lotus Domino	Domino is a messaging and collaboration, Web application and workflow server platform. It offers a rich set of server (Notes, HTTP, NNTP, SMTP, POP, IMAP, LDAP), client and security (SSL, hierarchical certificate-based authentication, multi-level access control list authorization) functions and a consistent user and development interface for corporate applications.

More information on the IBM e-business Web servers can be found at the following URL:

`http://www.software.ibm.com/webservers`

12.5 References

Please see the following RFCs for more information on Internet protocols and applications:

- RFC 1945 – Hypertext Transfer Protocol – HTTP/1.0
- RFC 2109 – HTTP State Management Mechanism
- RFC 2396 – Uniform Resource Identifiers (URI): Generic Syntax

- RFC 2616 – Hypertext Transfer Protocol – HTTP/1.1
- RFC 2617 – HTTP Authentication: Basic and Digest Access Authentication
- RFC 2822 – Standard for the Format of ARPA Internet Text Messages

Chapter 13. Multimedia protocols

The increased processing power available in desktop computers has resulted in the development of a wide range of multimedia applications. These applications leverage the existing network infrastructure to deliver video-based and audio-based applications to end users. The network is no longer used solely to support traditional data transmission.

These applications provide enhanced abilities for two-way videoconferencing, audio broadcasting, whiteboard collaboration, interactive training and IP telephony. With these applications, video and audio streams are transferred through the network between peers or between clients and servers.

This chapter provides a description of two peer protocols used to facilitate these applications. The Real-Time Transport Protocol (RTP) and the Real-Time Control Protocol (RTCP) are used to synchronize and control traffic flows in multimedia applications. The chapter concludes with an analysis of the current state of IP telephony standards. Applications using these standards rely heavily on RTP and RTCP to deliver service.

13.1 Real-Time Protocols: RTP and RTCP

The real-time transport protocol standards were developed by the Audio-Video Transport Working Group within the Internet Engineering Task Force (IETF). The basic standards are documented in RFC 1889 and RFC 1890.

To use real-time services in an application, two protocols must be implemented:

- The Real-Time Transport Protocol (RTP) provides the transport of real-time data packets.
- The RTP Control Protocol (RTCP) monitors the quality of service provided to existing RTP sessions.

Final versions of these standards were published in January 1996. They detail the functions expected to be common across all types of real-time applications. To accommodate new real-time applications, the architecture was intentionally left incomplete. Unlike conventional protocols, RTP is tailored through modifications and additions to headers as needed. This allows the protocol to easily adapt to new audio and video standards.

13.1.1 The Real-Time Transport Protocol (RTP)

RTP implements the transport features needed to provide synchronization of multimedia data streams.

Consider an application utilizing both video and audio components. RTP may be used to mark the packets associated with the individual video and audio streams. This allows the streams to be synchronized at the receiving host. Figure 180 shows the operation of RTP in a multimedia transmission. Audio and video data are encapsulated in RTP packets prior to transmission from the sender to the receiver.

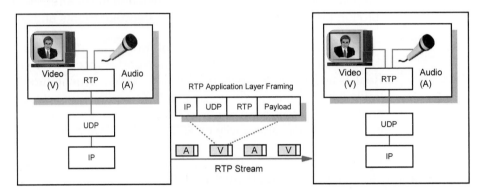

Figure 180. RTP operation in a multimedia environment

If the multimedia application does not utilize RTP services, the receiver may not be able to associate the corresponding audio and video packets. This can be attributed to the varying levels of network performance provided during a multimedia session. Congestion or other transient conditions within the environment can cause packets to be lost or reordered during transit. This can delay delivery of packets by varying amounts of time. This behavior causes quality problems with typical multimedia applications.

The standards specify that RTP can be used with any appropriate network or transport protocol. In practice, multimedia applications typically use RTP in conjunction with UDP. This allows the application to utilize the multiplexing and checksum services provided by UDP. RTP is often implemented to support multicast applications.

The RTP protocol alone does not include any mechanism to provide guaranteed delivery or other quality of service functions. The standard does not prevent out-of-sequence packet delivery, nor does it assume that the underlying network is reliable and delivers packets in-sequence. RTP also does not prevent the occurrence of network congestion. Designers of each application must determine if these levels of service are acceptable.

13.1.1.1 RTP header format

The header of an RTP packet has the following format, illustrated in Figure 181.

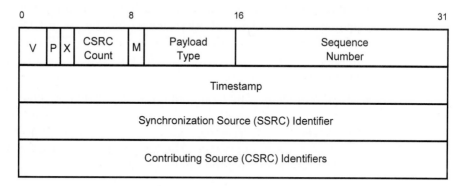

Figure 181. RTP header fields

The first 12 octets are required in every RTP packet. The list of CSRC identifiers is present only when inserted by a mixer (see 13.1.4, "RTP translators and mixers" on page 459). The individual fields have the following interpretation:

- V: Indicates the RTP version.

- P: Contains the padding bit. If this field is set, the packet contains a set of padding octets that are not part of the payload. This function is used by certain encryption algorithms.

- X: Contains the extension bit. If this field is set, a header extension follows the fixed header.

- CSRC Count: This field contains the number of contributing source identifiers that follow the fixed header.

- M: This field allows significant events to be marked in the packet stream (that is, frame boundaries).

- Payload type: Specifies the format of the payload in the RTP packet. An RTP sender emits a single RTP payload type at any given time. Refer to page 452 for further information regarding the contents of the payload type field.

- Sequence number: The sequence number is used by the receiver to restore packet sequence and detect packet loss. Refer to page 453 for further information regarding the contents of the sequence number field.

- Timestamp: The timestamp contains a value representing the time when the payload data was sampled. Refer to page 454 for further information regarding the timestamp field.

- SSRC identifier: The Synchronization Source is a randomly chosen identifier for an RTP host. All packets from the same source contain the same SSRC identifier. Each device in the same RTP session must have a unique SSRC identifier. This enables the receiver to group packets for playback.

- CSRC identifiers: The Contributing Source field contains a list of the sources for the payload in the current packet. This field is used when a mixer (see 13.1.4, "RTP translators and mixers" on page 459) combines different streams of packets. The information contained in this field allows the receiver to identify the original senders.

13.1.1.2 Protocol services

RTP provides end-to-end transport services for applications transmitting real-time data. These services include:

- Payload type identification

- Sequence numbering

- Timestamping

Payload type identification:

An RTP packet can contain portions of either audio or video data streams. To differentiate between these streams, the sending application includes a payload type identifier within the RTP header. The identifier indicates the specific encoding scheme used to create the payload. The receiving application uses this identifier to determine the appropriate decoding algorithm. Table 20 shows the payload types that are supported.

Table 20. RTP payload types

Audio		Video	
Payload type	Encoding name	Payload type	Encoding name
0	PCMU	24	unassigned
1	1016	25	CelB
2	G726-32	26	JPEG
3	GSM	27	unassigned

Audio		Video	
4	G723	28	nv
5	DVI4 (8 KHz)	29	unassigned
6	DVI4 (16 KHz)	30	unassigned
7	LPC	31	H261
8	PCMA	32	MPV
9	G722	33	MP2T
10	L16 Stereo	34	H263
11	L16 Mono	35-71	unassigned
12	QCELP	72-76	reserved
13	reserved	77-95	unassigned
14	MPA	96-127	dynamic
15	G728	dynamic	BT656
16	DVI4	dynamic	H263-1998
17	DVI4	dynamic	MP1S
18	G729	dynamic	MP2P
19	reserved	dynamic	BMPEG
20-23	unassigned		
dynamic	GSM-EFR		
dynamic	L8		
dynamic	RED		
dynamic	VDVI		

This list is maintained by the Internet Assigned Numbers Authority (IANA). It may be enhanced as new audio and video formats are developed. Although RTP was primarily designed to support multimedia data, it is not limited to audio and video traffic. Any application producing continuous data streams can use RTP services.

Several encoding schemes can specify a dynamic payload type. Systems deploying these encoding schemes dynamically agree on the payload type identifier.

Sequence numbering
Sequence numbers are used by the receiving RTP host to restore the original packet order. The receiver is able to detect packet loss using the information in this field.

The sequence number increments by one for each RTP data packet sent. The initial value of the sequence number is randomly determined. This makes hacking attacks on encryption more difficult. A random number is used even if the source device does not encrypt the RTP packet. The packets may flow through a translator that does provide encryption services.

Timestamping

Time stamps are used in RTP to synchronize packets from different sources. The timestamp represents the sampling (creation) time of the first octet in the RTP data packet. It is derived from a clock that increments monotonically and linearly. The resolution of the timer depends on the desired synchronization accuracy required by the application.

It is possible that several consecutive RTP packets may have the same time stamp. For example, this can occur when a single video frame is transmitted in multiple RTP packets. Since the payloads of these packets were logically generated at the same instant, the timestamps remain constant. The initial value of the timestamp is random. Figure 182 shows an example of time stamp generation in a video application.

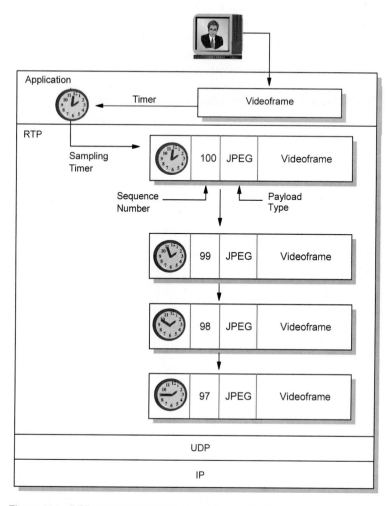

Figure 182. RTP packet generation in a video application

13.1.2 The Real-Time Control Protocol

To manage real-time delivery, many applications require feedback about the
current performance of the network. This function is provided by the
Real-Time Control Protocol (RTCP). The protocol is based on periodic
transmissions of control packets to all participants in a session.

The primary function of RTCP is to provide feedback about the quality of RTP
data distribution. This is comparable to the flow and congestion control
functions provided by other transport protocols. Feedback provided by each
receiver is used to diagnose distribution faults. By sending feedback to all

participants in a session, the device observing problems can determine if the problem is local or remote. This also enables a managing entity (i.e., a network service provider) who is not a participant in the session to receive the feedback information. The network provider can then act as a third party monitor to diagnose network problems.

RTCP uses a UDP connection for communication. This is separate from any UDP connection used by the RTP protocol. Figure 183 shows the cooperation of the RTP and the RTCP protocols.

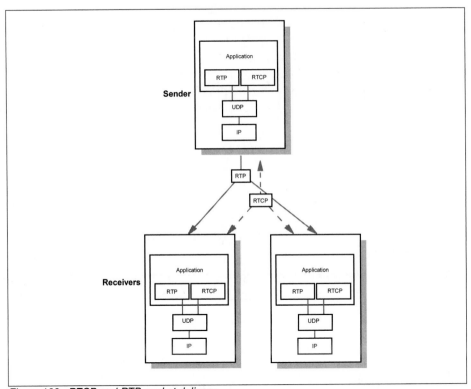

Figure 183. RTCP and RTP packet delivery

The RTCP architecture defines five types of control information used to report current performance:

- Sender report: An RTCP sender report is sent by the source of an RTP data stream. It provides the transmission and reception statistics observed by the sender. This report is sent as a multicast packet processed by all RTP session participants. The packet format for this report is detailed in section 13.1.3, "RTCP packet format" on page 457.

- Receiver report: An RTCP receiver report provides reception statistics for participants that are not active senders. A sender report is issued if a device has sent any data packets during the interval since issuing the last report, otherwise a receiver report is issued.

- Source description report: A source description packet is used by an RTP sender to provide local capability information. The currently defined source descriptions include:
    - CNAME: A unique name for the source.
    - NAME: The real name of the source.
    - EMAIL: The e-mail address of the application user.
    - PHONE: The phone number of the application user.
    - LOC: The geographic location of the application user.
    - TOOL: The specific application or tool name.
    - NOTE: Additional notes about the source.
    - PRIV: Private extensions.

- BYE: The RTCP bye message is used by a source when it leaves a conference. This is used when a mixer shuts down. The bye message is used to indicate all sources contributing to the session.

- APP: The APP packet is intended for experimental use as new applications and features are developed. After testing and if wider use is justified, it is recommended that each APP packet be registered with the Internet Assigned Numbers Authority.

13.1.3 RTCP packet format

Figure 184 shows the format of a RTCP sender report. The report is grouped in three sections. The first section contains the header. This section specifies the packet type, length, and sender identification.

The second section contains sender information. The third section contains receiver report blocks. The packet may contain several receiver report blocks. This allows the sender to report feedback from RTP packets received from other senders.

The format of the sender report is shown for clarity. The formats for the other four report types are similar.

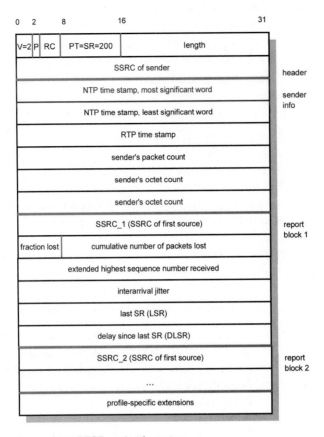

Figure 184. RTCP packet format

The fields in the packet are used to:

- V: This field indicates the version.

- P: This field indicates if additional padding is located at the end of the packet.

- RC: This field contains the number of report blocks in this packet.

- PT: This field contains the report type.

- Length: This field contains the packet length.

- SSRC of sender: This field contains the SSRC identifies of the host sending this packet.

- NTP timestamp: This field contains the absolute time reported by NTP. This protocols counts the number seconds since January 1, 1900.

- RTP timestamp: This field contains the timestamp from the RTP packets according to the sender.

- Sender's packet count: This field contains the total number of RTP data packets transmitted by the sender since the start of the transmission.

- Sender's octet count: This field contains the total number of payload bytes transmitted by the sender since the start of the transmission.

- SSRC_n: This field contains the SSRC identifier of another RTP sender from which this sender has received packets. The number of report blocks with different sender SSRCs depends on the number of other sources that were heard by this sender since the last report.

- Fraction lost: This field contains the fraction of RTP data packets that were lost since the previous sender report or receiver report was sent from the source SSRC_n.

- Cumulative number of packets lost: This field indicates the total number of lost RTP packets from source SSRC_n.

- Extended highest sequence number received: This field contains the highest sequence number that was received in an RTP packet from the source SSRC_n.

- Interarrival jitter: This field contains the estimated variance of the interarrival times from the appropriate source. If the packets arrive regularly, the jitter value is zero. If the packets arrive irregularly, the jitter value is high.

- Last SR timestamp (LSR): This field contains the middle 32 bits from the 64-bit NTP timestamp received in the last RTCP sender report packet from the source SSRC_n.

- Delay since last SR (DLSR): This field contains the delay between receiving the last SR packet from the source SSRC_n and the sending of the current exception report block in units of 1/65536 seconds.

13.1.4 RTP translators and mixers

The RTP protocol supports the use of translators and mixers to modify the RTP packet stream. These devices are used when some participants in a multimedia session need to receive data in different formats.

13.1.4.1 RTP translating

RTP translators are used to change the type of data in an RTP packet. Figure 185 depicts an environment where RTP translators are used. In this example, three videoconferencing workstations are exchanging MPEG traffic over a high-speed local area network. Each workstation is generating MPEG data at a rate of 1.5 Mbps. Another workstation connected via a lower-speed serial connection wishes to participate on the videoconference. The bandwidth of this connection is not sufficient to support the video streams.

One solution for this problem is changing all workstations to a video format, producing less traffic (e.g., H.261 with 256 Kbps). However, reducing the data bit rate also reduces the overall quality of the video.

An alternate solution uses RTP translation devices. In this solution, packets containing MPEG data from the LAN-attached workstations are converted to a format generating a lower-speed bit rate prior to forwarding to the serially-attached workstation. In this example, each individual MPEG video stream is converted to an H.261 video stream. This reduces each 1.5 Mbps stream to a 256 Kbps stream. The individual H.261 streams can then be transmitted through the serial connection. The three LAN-attached workstations continue to use the higher-quality MPEG format for communication with each other.

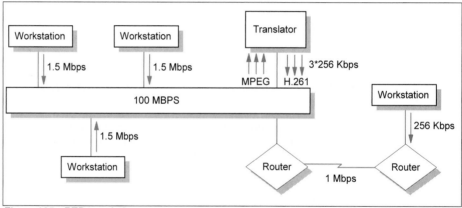

Figure 185. RTP translation

The translated RTP packets are forwarded with their synchronization source identifier intact. This allows receivers of the translated RTP packets to identify the original source. The receiver is unable to detect the presence of a translator unless it is aware of the payload type used by the original source.

One common use of RTP translators provides interoperability with application-level firewalls. In this configuration, participants in a conference are not directly reachable via IP multicast. They are located behind a firewall that does not pass IP multicast packets. Translators may be used to support these participants. Two translators are installed, one on either side of the firewall. One translator is configured to funnel all multicast packets through a

secure tunnel to the partner translator located inside the firewall. This
translator forwards information as multicast packets to the group restricted
within the site's internal network.

13.1.4.2 RTP mixing

RTP mixers are used to combine multiple data streams into a single RTP
stream. These devices are used to support audio transmissions applications
where there are only one or two simultaneous speakers. RTP mixing is not
usable in video application environments.

Figure 186 depicts an environment where RTP mixing is used. In this
example, three participants in an audio conference are connected to a 1
Mbps LAN. Each participant produces a PCM audio stream at a rate of 64
Kbps. A fourth workstation connected via a lower-speed serial connection
wishes to participate in the audio conference. The bandwidth of this
connection is not sufficient to support the combined 192 Kbps produced by
the existing three participants. An RTP mixer merges the three sender
streams into a single 64 Kbps stream. This allows the new station to join the
conference.

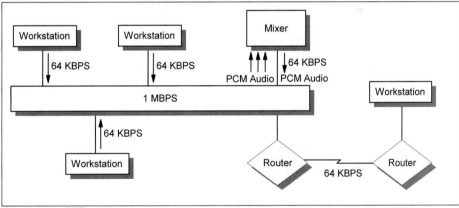

Figure 186. RTP mixing

In the example shown in Figure 186, the payload type of the incoming and
outgoing packets remain the same. However, it is possible to combine RTP
mixing and RTP translating in the same environment. This would be required
if the workstation shown in Figure 186 is connected via a lower-speed
modem. In this configuration, the payload format of the outgoing stream must
be changed to a lower bandwidth specification (e.g., GSM audio producing
8-16 Kbps).

When multiple input streams are processed by the RTP mixer, it is possible that the timing of the different source streams is not synchronized. When this occurs, the mixer generates new timing for the single output stream. The SSRC field of the output stream contains the mixer's SSRC identifier. To allow the receiver to identify the original sources of the audio data, the mixer includes the SSRC identifiers of each original source. This information is included in the CSRC identifier list contained in the RTP packet header.

13.1.5 Real-time applications

Many existing real-time applications provide support for videoconferencing, IP telephony or media streaming. As reviewed in Section 6.9.2, "Multicast applications" on page 256, most MBONE tools use RTP to provide real-time data delivery. The following list reviews several additional real-time multimedia applications:

- QuickTime: QuickTime is an application from Apple Computer, Inc. that provides digital video and media streaming. It provides live streaming features that eliminate the need to download files to the local environment. It can provide fast, high quality broadcasting performance. It supports the RTP and RTSP standards for streaming content over the Internet.

- RealAudio and RealVideo: RealNetworks, Inc. develop applications for the delivery of digital media. They provide high-quality audio and video streaming. These applications support RTP and RTSP.

- NetMeeting: NetMeeting is an application developed by Microsoft Corp. that provides IP telephony, white boarding, text chats, and application and file sharing. The applications support RTP and RTSP.

- CU-seeMe: CU-seeMe is a set of applications provided by CUseeMe Networks, Inc. These provide Internet video chat software supporting video, audio, text and whiteboard communications. It uses RTP for real-time transmissions.

- IP/TV: This is a client/server video application provided by Cisco Systems, Inc. The software supports several high quality video and audio standards (e.g., MPEG, H.261). Live video, scheduled video, and video on demand are all provided with IP/TV.

- Real-Time Streaming Protocol (RTSP): RTSP establishes and controls several time-synchronized streams of continuous audio and video. Sources of data can include both live data feeds and stored clips. During an RTSP session, an RTSP client may open and close many reliable transport connections to the server to issue RTSP requests. Alternatively, it may use a connectionless transport protocol, such as UDP. The streams controlled by RTSP may use RTP, but the operation of RTSP does not depend on this protocol. RTSP is not typically responsible for the delivery of the data streams, although interleaving of the media stream with the control stream is possible.

13.2 IP telephony

IP telephony products (also referred to as Voice over IP) provide the ability to transport voice traffic over an IP network. This can be done in any IP network type including the Internet, corporate intranets, or local area networks. In these environments, a voice signal is digitized and enclosed in an IP packet. The packet is then transmitted across the IP network.

Standard protocols providing the signaling structures required to merge voice traffic into data networks are currently being developed. These protocols provide the ability to locate users, negotiate capabilities, and establish calls.

There are several drivers causing the convergence of voice and data networks:

- Corporations have deployed large-scale data networks and expect cost savings and reduced expenses with a merged multimedia network.

- New applications are integrating voice and data. These applications provide improvements to existing business processes. Examples of these applications include computer-supported collaborative work efforts, web-enabled call centers, and integrated voice and e-mail.

13.2.1 Introduction

For IP telephony to succeed, several key issues need to be addressed. Some issues stem from the fact that IP networks were originally designed for transporting data. Other issues are concerned with the potential growth and scalability of the environment. At a minimum, an IP telephony network must provide:

- Quality: Communications quality must be at least equal to the level currently provided by the Plain Old Telephone System (POTS) network. End-to-end delay has a major impact to the perceived quality. This delay includes the time for a calling device to collect and encode a set of voice samples. It also includes the time required to transmit these encoded samples through the network. Excessive delay can cause several problems in IP telephony environments:

    - Voice echo is caused by signal reflection of the speakers voice. It can also be present in conventional POTS networks. However, voice echo becomes a major problem in Voice over IP (VoIP or IP telephony) networks because the delay in these networks usually exceeds the delay in POTS networks. Echo becomes a significant quality problem when the total delay exceeds 50 milliseconds. To minimize the impact caused by this problem, echo cancellation equipment must be used.

- Talker overlap can also occur when the delay is excessive. Traffic prioritization features must be used to control network delays so that this problem is minimized.

- Voice clarity is also impacted by the overall performance of the IP network. Lost or late-arriving voice packets can adversely impact perceived clarity. Digitization and compression schemes used to convert voice signals to IP packets may also impact voice clarity.

• Usability: The functionality and ease of operation of the VoIP network must be at least equal to the level currently provided by the POTS network. IP telephony networks will not be generally accepted if the services require complex dialing plans, have a large percentage of call drops, or require significant time to complete a call.

• Scalability: VoIP systems have the potential to provide high-quality services at a much lower cost than the existing Public Switched Telephone Network (PSTN). This creates the possibility of high growth rates in these services. IP telephony systems must be extensible to support these potential growth rates.

• Interoperability and Integration: IP telephony environments must operate with similar products from different vendors. They must also work with the existing PSTN. These different networks must appear as a single environment to users of these services.

13.2.2 The IP telephony protocol stack

An IP telephony environment is comprised of a number of individual protocols. These protocols interoperate in a hierarchical fashion to provide the required services. The protocol interaction can be represented as a stack, similar to the method used to represent many other communications systems.

One way to depict the stack is to divide the protocols into two functional sections, which are illustrated in Figure 187.

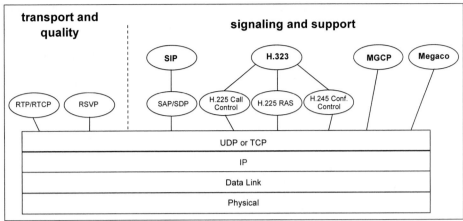

Figure 187. The IP telephony protocol stack

The two sections of the protocol stack provide the following functions:

- Transport and quality protocols: These protocols are used to transport the the actual voice traffic.

- Signaling and support protocols: The majority of IP telephony activities have been devoted to developing signaling protocols. These protocols locate users, negotiate capabilities, and manage voice calls. There are currently four major signaling protocols:

  - International Telecommunications Union Telecommunications Standardization Sector (ITU-T) Recommendation H.323
  - Session Initiation Protocol (SIP)
  - Media Gateway Control Protocol (MGCP)
  - ITU-T Recommendation H.248/Media Gateway Controller (Megaco)

These protocols are incompatible and often provide redundant functions. When they are used in the same environment, communication between these protocols requires a converter or gateway.

The remainder of this chapter describes each current signaling protocol.

13.2.3 ITU-T recommendation H.323

H.323 is an ITU-T standard originally developed for multimedia videoconferencing over packet-switched networks. The standard was later extended to include IP telephony requirements. At the time of this writing, it is the most widely deployed call processing protocol.

The initial version of H.323 was developed very rapidly. Work started in the ITU-T in May 1995 and was completed by June of 1996. Since that time, three additional versions have been published.

There are four components in a standard H.323 network:

- Terminals
- Gateways
- Gatekeepers
- Multipoint control units

13.2.3.1 Terminals

Terminals are the LAN client endpoints in an IP telephony network. An H.323 terminal can communicate with other H.323 terminals, an H.323 gateway, or an H.323 MCU.

All terminals must support voice communication. Support for video and data is optional. H.323 specifies the operations required for different types of terminals to work together. All H.323 terminals must support the set of protocols described in Section 13.2.3.6, "H.323 protocol stack" on page 468.

H.323 terminals support multipoint conversations and provide the ability to initiate ad-hoc conferences. They also have multicast features which allow multiple people to participate in a call without centralized mixing or switching.

13.2.3.2 Gateways

Gateways enable standard telephones to use VoIP services. They provide communication between H.323 terminals and terminals connected to either an IP-based network or another H.323 gateway. The gateway functions as a translator, providing the interface between the PSTN and the IP network.

The gateway is responsible for mapping the call signaling and control protocols between dissimilar networks. It is also responsible for media mapping (i.e., multiplexing, rate matching, audio transcoding) between the networks.

13.2.3.3 Gatekeepers

Gatekeepers are the most important component in an H.323 environment. A network of H.323 terminals and gateways under the control of a particular gatekeeper forms an integrated sub-network within the larger IP network environment. The gatekeeper's functions include:

- Directory server: Using information obtained during terminal registration, this function translates an H.323 alias address to an IP (transport) address. This allows the user to have meaningful, unchanging names to reference other users in the system. These names are arbitrary and may appear similar to those used in e-mail or voice mail applications.

- Supervisory: The gatekeeper may be used to grant permission to make a call. This can be used to apply bandwidth limits reducing the likelihood of congestion within the network.

- Call signaling: The gatekeeper may perform call routing functions to provide supplementary services. It can also provide Multipoint Controller functionality supporting calls with a large number of participants.

- Call management: The gatekeeper may be used to perform call accounting and call management.

13.2.3.4 Multipoint control units (MCUs)

A multipoint control unit (MCU) is an endpoint in the network. It provides the ability for three or more terminals or gateways to participate in a multipoint conference. An MCU provides conference management, media switching and multipoint conferencing.

There are three types of multipoint conferences:

- Centralized: All terminals have point-to-point communication streams with the MCU. The MCU is responsible for management of the conference. It receives, processes, and sends the voice packets to other terminals.

- Decentralized: Terminals communicate directly with each other. An MCU is not directly involved.

- Mixed multipoint: This represents a mixture of centralized and decentralized conferences. The MCU ensures operations of the conference are transparent to the each terminal.

13.2.3.5 H.323 sample configuration

Figure 188 shows an H.323 network configuration. The IP based network is connected to the PSTN through H.323-to-PSTN gateways.

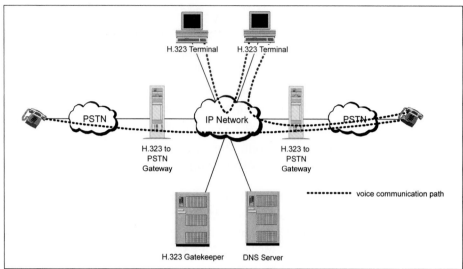

Figure 188. H.323 network elements

The diagram shows three types of connections:

- Native H.323 terminals can communicate through the IP network infrastructure.

- H.323 terminals attached to the IP network can communicate with standard phones in the PSTN. In this configuration, the H.323 gateway provides interoperability between IP-connected H.323 terminals and other audio devices connected to a non-IP based network.

- Two standard PSTN telephones can communication through the IP network infrastructure. In this configuration, the IP network is used purely for transport services.

13.2.3.6 H.323 protocol stack

The H.323 specification is an umbrella recommendation. Various components of H.323 are defined by other ITU-T standards. Figure 189 shows the suite of H.323 definitions.

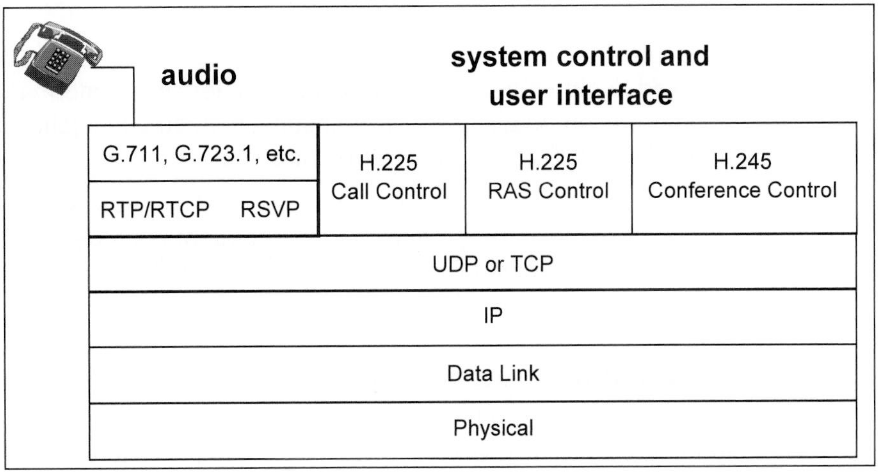

Figure 189. The H.323 protocol stack

The sub-protocols encompassing the H.323 standards include:

- H.225 call control: This protocol provides call signaling and control functions. In networks without a gatekeeper, call signaling messages are passed directly between the calling and called endpoints. In networks that contain a gatekeeper, these messages are initially exchanged between the calling endpoint and the gatekeeper. H.225 call control messages use TCP transport services.

- H.225 registration, admission and signaling (RAS) control: The RAS channel is used for communication between the endpoints and the gatekeeper. The protocol defines standard procedures for gatekeeper discovery, endpoint registration, endpoint location, and admissions control. H.225 RAS messages use UDP transport services.

- H.245 conference control: This specifies the protocol used after a call establishment phase has completed. H.245 is used to negotiate the media channels used by RTP and RTCP. The protocol defines standard procedures for exchanging capabilities, determining master and slave assignments and controlling conferences.

- G.711, G.723.1: Section 13.2.8, "Voice encoding and compression" on page 476 contains further information regarding these encoding and compression specifications.

- Real-time Transport Protocol (RTP): This protocol allows the receiver to detect packet loss. It also provides timing information that allows the receiver to compensate for variable packet arrival times (i.e., jitter).

Further information detailing RTP functions is located in Section 13.1.1, "The Real-Time Transport Protocol (RTP)" on page 450.

- Real-time Control Protocol (RTCP): This protocol accompanies RTP. It is used to obtain network status and QoS feedback information. Further information detailing RTCP functions is located in section 13.1.2, "The Real-Time Control Protocol" on page 455.

- Resource Reservation Protocol (RSVP): A host uses RSVP to request a specific QoS from the network. The request is processed by each node along the session path. The devices reserve the appropriate resources to support the application data stream.

13.2.4 Session Initiation Protocol (SIP)

SIP is an application layer signaling protocol used to initiate, modify and terminate calls. This allows clients, VoIP gateways and other communication systems to communicate. Functionally, the services and features provided by SIP are similar to H.323 Version 2.

SIP was originally developed in late 1996 as a way of inviting users to join an MBONE session. Development of additional features continued and an RFC describing the protocol was issued in 1998. The basic standard is documented in RFC 2543. Once the RFC was published, developers started to accept the protocol as a telephony standard.

There are two components in a standard SIP network:

- User agent
- Network server

13.2.4.1 User agent

A user agent resides in every SIP end station. It contains two components:

- A User Agent Client (UAC) is responsible for issuing SIP requests.
- A User Agent Server (UAS) is responsible for receiving and responding to requests.

A user agent is equivalent to an H.323 terminal.

13.2.4.2 Network servers

SIP network servers are used to support advanced calling functions. There are three types of network servers:

- Redirect Servers are used during call initiation to determine the address of the called device. This information is returned to the calling device.

- Proxy Servers provide application layer routing of SIP requests and responses. When the server receives a request, it forwards the request to a next hop server having more information about the location of the called device.

- Registrar Servers are used to record the SIP address and the associated IP address of a device.

SIP Network servers usually implement a combination of the different server types. The network servers are the functional equivalent to an H.323 gatekeeper.

13.2.4.3 SIP architecture

SIP architects used the Internet model during the development of the standard. As such, the architecture of SIP is similar to the architecture of HTTP. Both systems use a *request-response* model for communication. The calling device sends a request to the called device. The called device chooses to accept or reject the request and returns the response to the initiator.

SIP leverages other features of HTTP. The message formats in SIP are based on HTTP. SIP reuses most of the header fields, encoding rules and error codes of HTTP. This provides a readable, text-based format for displaying information.

A SIP address is referred to as a SIP Uniform Resource Locator (SIP-URL). It has the format sip:username@hostname.domain. This address is used to identify an individual device or group of devices. It allows a user to initiate a call by selecting a link in a standard browser.

13.2.4.4 SIP protocol stack

In a SIP environment, voice calls are carried using RTP, as is done with H.323. The main difference between SIP and H.323 is how call signaling and control is achieved. The SIP protocol stack is shown in Figure 190.

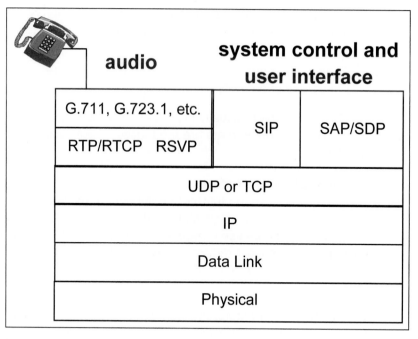

Figure 190. The SIP protocol stack

SIP relies on additional standards to provide signaling and control functions. These include:

- Session Description Protocol (SDP): SDP is a protocol providing session announcement and session invitation in a multimedia environment. This allows the recipients of the session announcement to participate in the session. Details of this protocol are documented in RFC 2327.

- Session Announcement Protocol (SAP): SAP is another protocol for advertising multicast conferences and sessions. It is intended to announce the existence of long-lived wide-area multicast sessions.

13.2.5 Media Gateway Control Protocol (MGCP)

MGCP is an alternate call signaling protocol. It was originally developed to address perceived deficiencies of H.323. It provides the ability to separate a telephone gateway into a set of components. These components form a master-slave relationship. The master component is called a call agent. The slave components are called gateways.

The MGCP model assumes the core contains the intelligence to implement enhanced services. Endpoint phones have minimal technical features. This is unlike the SIP architecture where the intelligence resides in the network endpoints. The MGCP model can be viewed as a benefit for carriers, since it enables the delivery of enhanced services through low cost endpoints.

Development of the architectures that form MGCP started in mid-1998. The IETF published the MGCP RFC in late-1999. Basic MGCP functionality is described in RFC 2705. The standard provides an application programming interface (API) and a corresponding protocol (MGCP).

There are two components in a standard MGCP network:

- Call agents
- Gateway

13.2.5.1 Call agents

A call agent directs the operations of a gateway. The intelligence required to perform call operations resides in the call agent. These devices are also responsible for signaling and call processing functions.

An MGCP network does not need to integrate with an H.323 network. However, since the MGCP call agent implements signaling functions, it can appear as an H.323 gatekeeper.

13.2.5.2 Gateway

A gateway is responsible for converting between the audio signals used in the PSTN and the data packets used in IP networks. Examples of gateways include:

- Trunking gateways provide an interface between a traditional PSTN telephone network and a VoIP network. These gateways typically manage a large number of circuits.

- Residential gateways provide an interface between a traditional telephony end user (analog RJ-11) and a VoIP network. These include interfaces to cable modems and xDSL devices.

Since MGCP is a master/slave protocol, a gateway is expected to execute the commands provided by a call agent.

13.2.6 Media Gateway Controller (Megaco)

Similar to the use of MGCP in an IP telephony network, Megaco addresses the relationship between a gateway and a call agent. However, unlike MGCP, Megaco supports a broader range of networks including ATM. This makes the protocol applicable to a much wider range of media gateways.

After the MGCP standard was approved, additional proposals and enhancements were submitted to the IETF. The Megaco protocol combines these different standards into a single architecture. It is the result of joint development by the ITU and the IETF.

Megaco has been architected to support gateways ranging in size from a single port to thousands of ports. There are two components in a standard Megaco network:

- Terminations
- Contexts

13.2.6.1 Terminations

Terminations represent streams entering or leaving the gateway. Some terminations, typically representing ports on the gateway, are automatically created when the device activates. Other terminations are created when required. These represent transient flows through the network, such as RTP traffic flows and VoIP streams.

13.2.6.2 Contexts

Terminations are placed into contexts. This occurs when two or more termination streams are connected together. A simple call may have two terminations per context (one termination representing the end device and the other termination representing the connection to the network). A conference call may have numerous terminations per context, each termination representing one leg of the conference.

Megaco uses a series of commands to manipulate terminations and contexts. For example, the ADD command adds a termination to a context. The MOVE command moves a termination from one context to another. These commands are sent from the call agent to the gateway.

13.2.7 Signaling protocol functional comparison

There were several drivers leading to the development of multiple signaling standards:

- The protocols were developed by different standards organizations. For example, H.323 was developed by the ITU. Traditionally, this organization developed standards for circuit switched environments. The SIP standard was developed by the Internet Engineering Task Force (IETF). Traditionally, this organization developed data network standards.

- The protocols were developed at different times. H.323 dates to early 1995. SIP development was not standardized until 1999.

Each signaling protocols has advantages and disadvantages.

13.2.7.1 Deployment

H.323 was the earliest major VoIP signaling protocol. It has long been promoted as the standard for interoperability. Since it was the first major protocol option, the standard has a much larger market presence. It was originally adopted by traditional telephony providers and vendors because they were familiar with the concept and architecture. However, as providers seek to develop enhanced services, the industry appears to be migrating from H.323 to SIP.

Since the Megaco standard provides a superset of the functions provided by the MGCP standard, support for MGCP appears to be losing momentum.

13.2.7.2 Protocol complexity and scalability

H.323 is a relatively complex protocol. Many services require interaction between the numerous sub-protocols encompassing the standard. This is a disadvantage for IP telephony applications because it increases complexity. The complexity adversely impacts the time required to develop new features based on this standard.

SIP leverages existing maturity of HTTP. HTTP has been proven to support large-scale network environments. These scalability enhancements, developed throughout the evolution of HTTP have been included in SIP. This allows SIP to potentially scale to very large environments.

13.2.7.3 Interoperability

Interoperability includes consistency between different vendor implementations of the standard and also between different versions of the same standard:

- Between vendor implementations: Service definitions in H.323 are very detailed and few interoperability issues occur. SIP is highly flexible and extensible, however, minimal safeguards have been established to prevent one vendor from extending the protocol differently than another vendor.

- Between versions: H.323 has taken steps to ensure compatibility among different versions. Conversely, newer versions of SIP may discard older features that received minimal support. This reduces protocol complexity, but causes incompatibility between versions. Some features implemented in older SIP versions may not be supported in the newer versions.

13.2.7.4 Ease of implementation

H.323 signaling is encoded using ASN.1 notation. This encoding requires complex parsing and complicates implementation and debugging efforts. Conversely, SIP messages are text-based. This type of encoding provides easier implementation and debugging.

13.2.7.5 Quality of service support

Quality of service features in H.323 and SIP are comparable. Both protocols have similar call set-up times. In addition, both H.323 and SIP have no direct support for resource reservation. Each relies on the RSVP standard to reserve network resources.

13.2.7.6 Acceptance

SIP, MGCP, and Megaco have the backing of the IETF. This is one of the most recognized standards bodies.

13.2.8 Voice encoding and compression

Transmitting uncompressed voice packets across the network can consume a large amount of bandwidth. To alleviate this problem, specific devices are used to encode and compress voice packets before transmission. Partner devices are used to decompress and decode the same packets when they arrive at their destination.

The use of these devices adds delay to the overall time required to deliver the voice packets:

- The hardware performing the compression causes a delay as it buffers the data to evaluate specific voice segments.

- The hardware performing the compression causes additional delay as it conducts the actual computation to compress the speech.

To reduce the impact of this delay, a balance must be determined between voice quality and bandwidth consumption. This balance is unique to the mix of specific voice and data applications and will vary from one environment to the next.

There are a number of existing standards used to provide voice compression including:

- G.711: This standard encodes non-compressed speech streams running at 64 Kbps. This is well within the bandwidth limits of a LAN, but not optimal for transmission outside the local network. This standard provides toll-quality speech. All H.323 terminals must support the G.711 voice standard for speech compression

- G.723.1: This standard provides a relatively high degree of compression with an output bit rate of either 5.3 or 6.4 Kbps. Among compression standards, G.723.1 provides toll-quality performance at a very low bit rate. It has been chosen as the default encoder for IP telephony by the International Multimedia Teleconferencing Consortium (IMTC) VoIP Forum.

  Implementations of this standard can be CPU intensive. This may adversely impact the ability to provide a scalable solution using G.723.1.

- G.729A: This standard also provides a relatively high degree of compression with an output bit rate of 8 Kbps. It provides near toll-quality performance. This standard was selected as the alternate default encoder for the IMTC VoIP Forum.

Chapter 14. Wireless Application Protocol (WAP)

Wireless Application Protocol (WAP) is the *de facto* worldwide standard for providing Internet communications and advanced services on digital mobile devices, such as handheld phones, pagers, and other wireless devices. This protocol is an open, global specification that allows users of the referenced digital devices to securely access and interact with Internet, intranet, and extranet applications and services.

According to researchers, there will be more than 530 million wireless subscribers by the end of 2001. Some estimates report that the number of wireless subscribers will be more than one billion by the year 2004. Most of the phones sold in the near future will have multimedia capabilities that include:

- Retrieving e-mail
- Accessing data from company databases
- Executing stock trading
- Bill paying
- Making travel reservations
- Running other exciting applications

Based on these forecasts, wireless service providers, manufacturers of handheld devices, and software development companies see a huge new market of information-hungry users.

The WAP Forum was founded in June 1997, by Ericsson, Motorola, Nokia, and Phone.com. It has drafted a global wireless specification for all wireless networks. The forum is contributing to various industry groups, like wireless service providers, handset manufacturers, infrastructure providers, and software developers. The forum has also provided the specifications to standards bodies like ARIB, CDG, ECMA, ETSI, TIA, and W3C. Today, more than 400 members, including IBM, belong to the WAP Forum.

14.1 The WAP environment

Wireless data networks present many communications challenges, compared to wired networks. For example, the wireless communication environment is constrained because wireless links have:

- Less bandwidth
- More latency
- Less connection stability
- Less predictable availability

As a result, protocols that provide wireless applicability must be tolerant of these types of problems. In addition, machines using these wireless links are limited in terms of processing power and other functionality. For example, wireless devices lack the traditional desktop GUI like the Web browser. Other fundamental limitations for handheld, wireless devices include:

- Life of battery
- Less powerful CPUs
- Less memory
- Restricted power consumption
- Smaller displays
- Different input devices (for example, phone keypad and voice input)
- Lack of a mouse

Today's user application requirements will primarily be information inquiries rather than transaction processing. For example, users may only view what emails are received instead of reading the contents of the e-mail on the small screen, or looking at stock quotes rather than doing stock trading. However, it is assumed that other tasks, like executing banking transactions, will be required in the not-so-distant future. This would require reliable data transmission, message privacy, integrity, and authentication. As a result, these functions must be included as part of the specifications of WAP.

14.2 Key elements of the WAP specifications

WAP defines an open standard architecture and set of protocols to implement wireless Internet access. The key elements of the WAP specification include:

- Definition of the WAP programming model (see Figure 191 on page 481)
- The Wireless Markup Language (WML) (see 14.3, "Wireless Markup Language (WML) and WMLScript" on page 486)
- A specification for a microbrowser
- A lightweight protocol stack (see 14.5, "Overview of the WAP protocol stack" on page 495)
- A framework for wireless telephony

14.2.1 Overview of the WAP programming model

The WAP architecture illustrated in Figure 191 describes:

- The WAP client (the handheld device or WAP terminal)
- The WAP gateway
- The Web server

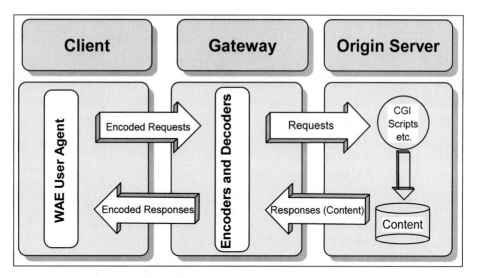

Figure 191. WAP programming model

This programming model is similar to the Web programming model. Programmers will see it as an advantage because they will meet a well-known interface based on client/server technology.

In order to solve the constraints of handheld devices (WAP terminals), there is a gateway protocol between the client and Web server. The gateway translates the traditional Web content into compact encoded formats. This reduces the size and number of packets traveling over the wireless network. Therefore, two connections are established via this gateway or proxy, with different protocols between client and proxy (WSP/WTP) and between proxy and Web server (TCP/IP HTTP).

14.2.1.1 WAP client

The client, also known as wireless application environment (WAE) user agent is a component of the WAP terminal. It consists of a microbrowser and the WAP protocol stack (see Figure 197 on page 496) in order to handle the execution of all requests and responses going through the WAP layered structure. For example this includes:

- Session establishment
- Data transport connection-less or connection-oriented
- Setting up a secure environment including:
    - Applying encryption and authentication
    - Encoding of outgoing requests
- Decoding of incoming responses to minimize bandwidth

The microbrowser is the interface to the user and to the WAP-content coming from the Internet or intranet. Two primary standards are supported by the microbrowser:

- Encoded Wireless Markup Language (WML)
- Compiled Wireless Markup Language Script (WMLScript)

See 14.3, "Wireless Markup Language (WML) and WMLScript" on page 486 for more details.

14.2.1.2 WAP gateway

The gateway works as a WAP proxy. It receives requests from the client, transforms an HTTP message, and sends it (based on the Uniform Resource Locator (URL)) to the addressed Web server. When the Web server returns the response, the gateway transforms it again into a bit-coded output. It then sends it to the mobile network, which directs it to the WAP client. This method allows the data content and applications to be hosted in standard Web servers using traditional Web technology.

The WAP gateway is also able to work as a WAP application server (see Figure 193 on page 486). This solution does not need a Web server. It can be used to support end-to-end security configurations. This could be for applications which require higher access control or a guarantee of service, like those used for Wireless Telephony Application (WTA) (see 14.5.2, "Wireless Telephony Application (WTA)" on page 498).

The WAP gateway decreases the response time to the WAP terminal by aggregating data from different Web servers and caching frequently used information. It also divides large HTTP responses into smaller transmission units before sending the responses to the client.

The WAP gateway can also interface with subscriber databases and use information to dynamically customize WML pages for a certain group of users.

The WAP gateway provides transition between the Internet and different non-voice mobile services. These might be services such as Short Message Services (SMS), Circuit Switched Data (CSD), or General Packet Radio Services (GPRS).

14.2.1.3 Origin server

The client's microbrowser requests Wireless Markup Language (WML) pages. These WML pages are stored on the origin server, which might be a Web server, connected via the Internet or intranet. WML pages may also be stored in an application server installed in the gateway itself. A WML page consists of a WML deck. One WML deck is divided into one or more WML cards. A WML card can be regarded as a unit of interaction. Services let the user navigate back and forth between cards from one or several WML pages. WML, especially designed for WAP terminals, provides a smaller set of markup tags than HTML. It is based on HTTP 1.1. WML decks may also contain WMLScripts, another way of coding Web pages.

14.2.2 WAP network configurations

The WAP network may be designed using two configurations:

- The first configuration describes the client's access via a WAP gateway to a Web server. This configuration will be used when traditional Web services with HTTP connections are used.

- The second configuration allows the client to access a WAP application server directly without traversing an IP network. In this case the WAP gateway is not used. This solution will mainly be used for wireless telephony applications. These are applications, such as phone books, broadcast information about weather or traffic conditions, and stock quotes.

In order to save hardware costs, all functions of the WAP application server may also be implemented in the WAP gateway.

14.2.2.1 Usage of a WAP gateway

This type of configuration, illustrated in Figure 192, consists of two connections:

- The first connection is between the client and a WAP gateway.

- The second connection is between the WAP gateway and the Web server.

While the first connection uses the Wireless Session Protocol (WSP) and the Wireless Transaction Protocol (WTP), the second connection uses the traditional Hypertext Transfer Protocol (HTTP), which runs above TCP. The proxy gateway maintains the two connections as one logical connection between the client and the Web server.

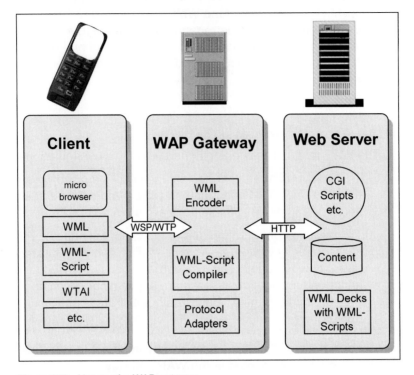

Figure 192. Usage of a WAP gateway

Client-server flow

The client-server flow is as follows:

1. A client asking for a particular service from an origin server submits a request to this server using the WML user agent (refer to Figure 198 on page 497).

2. The WML user agent uses the URL addressing scheme operation to find the origin server. URLs are used to address applications on a Web server, for example, a Common Gateway Interface (CGI).[1]

3. The client's request is transmitted to the gateway using WSP/WTP.

4. The gateway does the bit-encoding, transforms the request into an HTTP message, and sends it to the Web server (addressed by the URL).

5. The origin server replies to the request by returning a single deck (refer to 14.3.1, "WML" on page 486), if it is stored in textual format in the origin server.

6. The deck is transmitted to the gateway.

[1] Essentially, the Common Gateway Interface (CGI) script is an executable entity that produces content as output.

7. On its way through the gateway, the textual format of each deck has to be converted into a format that is better suited for over-the-air transmission to WAP terminals. This conversion is done by the gateway using the WML encoder to convert the textual format into a binary format.

8. The gateway sends the encoded content to the client via the WAP protocol stack layers (refer to Figure 197 on page 496) over the wireless network.

9. At the client's WAP terminal, the data is received and can be displayed and interpreted, for example, by a microbrowser.

There are also some additional optimization procedures based on negotiation between the gateway and the client. The client may submit one or more additional requests via the WML user agent. These requests may also address WMLScripts, which can be received from the origin server at the WMLScript user agent.

The procedure in the gateway differs from the WML procedure. When the gateway receives a WMLScript, then:

- A WMLScript compiler takes the script as input
- Compiles it into a byte code
- Sends it to the WAP terminal, using the WAP protocol stack layer via the wireless network

14.2.2.2 Usage of a WAP application server

The usage of the WAP gateway is not mandatory. Encoding and compiling textual content need not be done in a gateway. It is conceivable that some origin servers have implemented WML encoders and WMLScript compilers. This could also be done in WAP application servers, as shown in Figure 193.

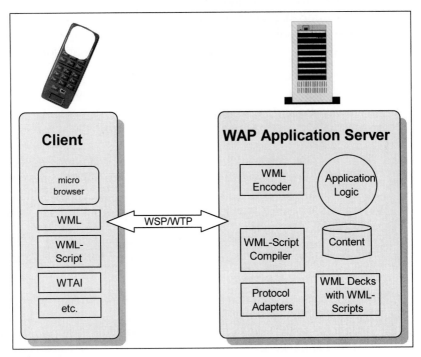

Figure 193. Usage of a WAP application server

14.3 Wireless Markup Language (WML) and WMLScript

Clients interact with origin servers through the WAP application entity (WAE) layer. WAE consist of user agents and services (see Figure 198 on page 497). The WML user agent offers two different services for communication between the client and the server:

- WML
- WMLScript

14.3.1 WML

WML is a tag-based document language. It is optimized for specifying presentation and user interaction on devices such as telephones and other wireless mobile terminals especially designed for narrow-band transmission. WML has implemented a deck and card structure. This allows the application to specify documents (commonly referred to as decks) made up of multiple cards. The user interacts with these WML cards in that it:

- Navigates forwards and backwards
- Reviews its contents

- May enter request information
- May meet choices
- Moves on to another card

There may be instructions which invoke services on origin servers within the cards. WML decks are stored as files on an origin server. They are fetched from the servers when required. The decks can also be dynamically generated by a content generator running on an origin server. Each card in a deck contains a specification for a particular user interaction.

WML provides a variety of features. For example:

- Support for text and images

  It includes output presentation with emphasis elements (for example, bold, italic, big, and so on), with line breaks models (for example, line wrapping and line wrapping suppression), and tab columns that support simple tabbing alignment.

- Support for user input

  Several elements to solicit user input are supported. The elements can be combined into one or more cards. WML includes text entry control for text and password input. Text entry fields may be masked, preventing the user from entering incorrect character types. WML provides options, such as selection control, that allows the user to present a list of options which can set data, navigate among cards, or invoke scripts. Also, task initiation controls may be set up.

- Navigation and history stack

  WML allows several navigation mechanisms using URLs. Navigation includes HTML-style hyperlinks, intercard navigation elements, and history navigation elements.

- International support

  WML uses the Universal Character set of ISO/IEC-1046. Currently, this character set is identical to Unicode 2.0.

- Narrow-band optimization

  There are various technologies to optimize communication on a narrow-band terminal. For example, multiple user interactions (cards) are executed in one data transfer (a deck).

- State and context management

  WML exposes a flat context control, which means that each WML text input can introduce variables. The state of the variables can be used to modify the contents of a parameterized card without having to communicate with the server.

14.3.1.1 WML example

This example, illustrated in Figure 194, shows WML consisting of one deck, beginning with <WML> and ending with </WML>. The deck contains two cards. Cards begin with <CARD> and end with </CARD>.

The first card controls the welcome panel. The second card provides the input function including variables. It also gives the user the choice to select between two processing options.

The sample in Figure 194 navigates the user through the welcome panel. Two variables, *N* and *S,* are offered for the subsequent input. For the variable *S,* the user may enter 0 or 1.

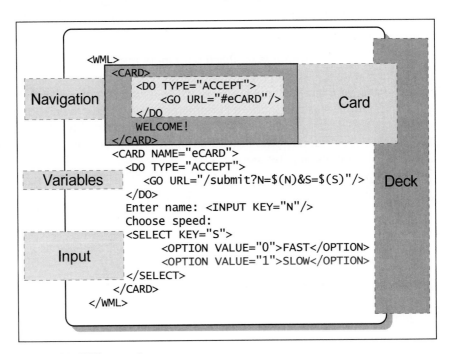

Figure 194. WML example

14.3.2 WMLScript

WMLScript is a lightweight procedural language. It enhances the standard browsing and presentation facilities of WML. For example:

- It adds intelligence to the client.

- It allows to create programming loops.
- It executes conditionals.

WMLScript is derived from JavaScript WWW scripting language. Thus, procedural logic can be brought to WML decks. WMLScript provides the application programmer with a variety of interesting capabilities:

- The ability to check the validity of user input before it is sent to the content server
- The ability to access device facilities and peripherals
- The ability to interact with the user without introducing round-trips to the origin server (for example, display an error message).

14.4 Push architecture

The design of the client/server model allows only the clients to make requests of a service from the server. The server responds by transmitting the information to the client. This type of information exchange is called *pull technology,* because the client pulls the information from the server.

The WWW method is a typical example of the pull technology. The client enters an URL to retrieve information from the Web server. The Web server sends the information to the client for displaying the Web page on the Web browser.

Following traditional Web technology, wireless service providers could not send messages to the client without a request being made. In order to make this service possible, the push architecture was designed.

In contrast, the WAP architecture defines, in addition, a *push technology,* as shown in Figure 195. This technology is also based on the client-server model, but there is no explicit request from the client to the server. The push transactions are initiated by the server only. It is used to transmit information to a WAP terminal without a previous user action.

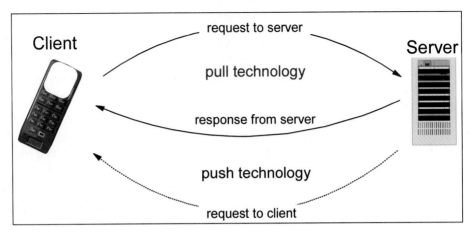

Figure 195. Comparison of pull vs. push technology

14.4.1 Push framework

Within TCP/IP, information requests to a server can be initiated from the client only. However, information service providers also need a way to contact clients without an outstanding client request. For example, a mail service provider wants to notify a WAP client that e-mails are in the client's mailbox, and also wants to provide all the senders' names, or to deliver the newest stock quotes, headlines news, and weather and traffic conditions that the WAP client has subscribed to.

This kind of transaction, where the server is the initiator of the connection with a WAP client, is a new feature. It is designed under the name *push initiator,* as illustrated in Figure 196.

Since the WAP client is located in the WAP domain and the server is in the Internet, both do not share the push initiator protocol. Therefore, again, gateway support is needed to provide this functionality. A gateway that performs pushing is called a *push proxy gateway* (PPG).

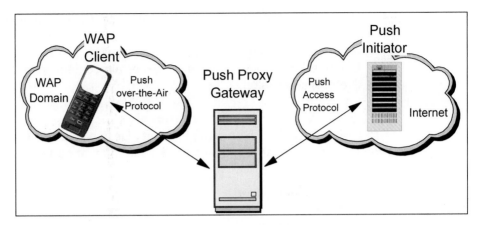

Figure 196. Push framework

If the push initiator wants to send out information to WAP clients, it contacts the push proxy gateway (PPG). It uses traditional Internet protocols together with the push access protocol (PAP). The PPG forwards the pushed content to the WAP domain, where it is transmitted over the air using the push over-the-air protocol (OTA).

The PPG may have the capability to tell the push initiator about the state of the delivery of the message to the client. But this may take some time, since the WAP client may not be online. If the client is online, it may accept or reject the pushed content.

The PAP uses XML messages, which may be tunneled through HTTP through the Internet.

14.4.2 Push proxy gateway (PPG)

The PPG is the access point for content pushes from the Internet to the mobile network. It does everything that is necessary for this kind of operation, such as:

- Authentication
- Security
- Client control

As owner of the gateway, it decides who may get access to the WAP domain and who is allowed to push messages.

14.4.2.1 Overview of PPG services

The services of the push proxy gateway include:

- Push initiator identification authentication, access control
- Parsing of and error detection in content control information
- Client discovery services
- Address resolution
- Binary encoding and compilation of certain content types to improve OTA
- Protocol conversion

14.4.2.2 Access from the Internet side

PPG accepts contents from the Internet side, which is divided into several parts using multipart/related content type. The first part contains the information for the PPG, for example:

- Recipient information
- Time-outs
- Callback requests

The PPG will acknowledge the parsing of this control information. If the push initiator requests, it may also call back a pushing server when the final status of the push submission to the WAP client has been reached, and will report about the status (delivered, cancelled, or expired).

14.4.2.3 PPG's pushed content delivery

PPG tries to find the correct WAP client and, if successful, delivers the content using the push over-the-air protocol. The trial to deliver is limited by the timeout specified for the client. This timeout may be set by the push initiator or the policies of the mobile operator.

PPG may have implemented addressing aliasing schemes to enable special multi- and broadcast functions. This requires the translation of special addresses into broadcast operation. The push initiator may also query client capabilities and preferences to create a better formatted content for a particular WAP terminal.

14.4.3 Push access control protocol (PAP)

The push initiator uses PAP to push content via a PPG to the WAP domain. PAP is carried over an HTTP 1.1 tunnel. PAP carries an XML-style entity.

14.4.3.1 PAP operations

PAP supports the following operations:

- Push submission (initiator to PPG)

The push message contains a control entity, which provide delivery instructions for the PPG, a content entity, which is the textual content for the WAP terminal, and, optionally, a capability entity.

Depending on the message type (WML or WMLScript), PPP will convert this message into more bandwidth-optimized form before forwarding over-the-air through (OTA). Also, encrypting may be done sending the message to the client.

- Result notification (PPG to initiator)

  If the push initiator has requested confirmation of successful delivery, a notification message is returned to the push initiator. This gives the push initiator the awareness that the WAP client has also acknowledged successful delivery to the PPG.

- Push cancellation (initiator to PPG)

  This XML-entity is sent from the push initiator to the PPG, requesting that a previously submitted content should be cancelled. The PPG responds, if the cancellation was successful or not.

- Status query (initiator to PPG)

  The push initiator requests the status of delivery during the 2-way process to the WAP client:

  - First way: push initiator -> PPG

  - Second way: PPG -> client

- Client capabilities query (initiator to PPG)

  The push initiator requests, from the PPG, information about the capabilities of a particular WAP terminal. The PPG responds with a multipart/related message in two parts:

  - The first part is about the execution of the message itself.

  - In the second part, the capabilities of the WAP terminal defined by the user agent profiles group is reported.

14.4.4 Service indication

The service indication (SI) content type enables the sending of notifications to end users in an asynchronous manner (for example, new emails, and so on). An SI contains a short message and a uniform resource indicator (URI), indicating a service.

The message is presented to the end user upon reception. The end user may now select to either start the service immediately or postpone it for a later execution. If the SI is postponed, the client stores it in order to enable the user for later SI handling.

14.4.5 Push over-the-air protocol (OTA)

OTA is responsible for transmitting the content from the PPG to the client's user agent over the wireless network.

OTA may use a WSP session to deliver the content. However, a WSP session works in a connection-oriented mode and has to be established by a client prior to delivery of the pushed content. In this case, where there is no active WSP session, a session initiation application in the client has to establish the session. This new function in the client works like a server, who listens to session requests from OTA-servers and responds by setting up a WSP session for the push purpose.

The client may verify the identity information of the OTA-server against a list of such servers before attempting any push session.

14.4.6 Client-side infrastructure

A connection-oriented push requires an active WSP session. As explained in 14.4.5, "Push over-the-air protocol (OTA)" on page 494, the client needs a special *session initiation application* (SIA) in order to set up the push session with the PPG. After receiving a session request from PPG, SIA establishes a session with the PPG and reports which client applications accept content over the newly opened session. SIA may also ignore the session request from the PPG in case there is no suitable application available or installed.

When the client receives pushed content, a dispatcher looks at the push message header to determine its destination application. This dispatcher is responsible for rejecting content, in case the destination application is not installed. It is also responsible for confirming operations to the PPG.

14.4.7 Security

In a trusted environment, several questions may arise. For example:

- How can the push initiator be authenticated?
- What role does PPG play in a security and trusted model?
- What are the access control policies for a push initiator and pushed content?
- How can a client authenticate something if it has no certificates?

14.4.7.1 Authenticating a push initiator

Some of the following solutions may be used to implement a security environment between a push initiator and the PPG:

- Use of session level certificates (TSL and SSL)

  If the push content traverses the Internet between push initiator and PPG, TSL or SSL can be used.

- Use of object-level certificates

  Certificates could be used to sign and/or encrypt the pushed content on an end-to-end basis. This would strengthen the level of confidence in the content authenticity at the client's end.

- HTTP authentication

  The basic authentication through user ID and password is available. In addition, HTTP authentication, for example, based on digests, may be implemented.

- Combination of technologies

  Another approach could be combining technologies by using TLS/SSL session with a PPG, while HTTP authentication could be used to authenticate the push initiator. Signed and/or encrypted content could then be sent over this authenticated session

14.4.7.2 Client authentication

If a client and a PPG are able to create a trusted environment, the PPG can authenticate a push initiator on behalf of that client, that is, trust can be transitive. A trust situation can be established between client and PPG by maintaining a list of trusted PPGs in a client system. Push initiators own a certificate or public key for end-to-end authentication of the origin server.

14.5 Overview of the WAP protocol stack

The WAP protocol stack consists of a number of protocols that provide functionality throughout the traditional networking layered stack model. This is outlined in Figure 197.

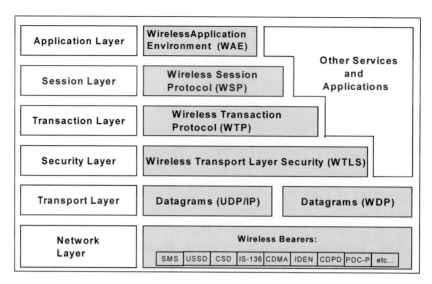

Figure 197. WAP protocol stack

14.5.1 Wireless application environment (WAE)

This layer contains similar WWW functions and mobile phone technologies. It includes a microbrowser environment that contains functionality such as WML, WML-Script, and Wireless Telephony Application (WTA).

WTA enables the user to interact with mobile-phone features and other user agents not specified by WAE, such as calender or phone book functions. For further information, see 14.5.2, "Wireless Telephony Application (WTA)" on page 498

WAE includes different user agents to execute different services (see Figure 198 on page 497). The user agent is the interface to the user and to the current selected service on the wireless device. WML, WMLScript, and WTA are examples of these services. The user agent uses a Uniform Resource Locator (URL) to address servers for a specific service content. The user agent sends a request with a URL for a service to the WAP gateway/proxy. The WAP gateway/proxy resolves the URL by an IP host address.

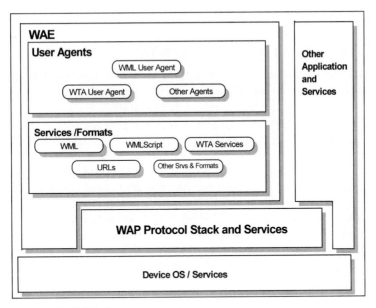

Figure 198. WAP client components

WAE defines a set of content formats for interoperable data exchange. The way of data exchange is dependent on the data and the targeted WAE user agents. The two main formats are the encoded WML and the WMLScript byte code formats. These formats are mainly designed for WAP terminals to minimize computational power and for lower bandwidth usage. There are, in addition, formats for data types such as:

- Images

  It supports multiple choices of pixel depth, color space tables, small encoding, very low CPU and RAM encoding and presentation demands, and availability of common tools, and so on.

- Multipart messages

  It supports multipart-encoding scheme optimized for exchanging multiple typed content over WSP (see 14.5.3, "Wireless Session Protocol (WSP)" on page 498).

- User agent-specific formats

  This is a function which supports two additional formats for exchanging data among user agents: electronic business card (vCard 2.1), and electronic calendaring and scheduling exchange format (vCalender 1.0) specified by IMC.

WAE also defines WTA-specific formats to support wireless telephone applications.

14.5.2 Wireless Telephony Application (WTA)

WTA provides tools for building telephony applications. It is primarily designed for network operators, carriers, and equipment vendors. Network security and reliability is a major consideration. Extensions are added to the standard WML/WMLScript browser to support an additional WTA Application Programming Interface (WTAI).

WTAI includes the following functions: call control, network text messaging, phone book interface, indicator control, and event processing.

Since WTA is beyond the TCP/IP scope, we will not discuss it further. Please see the official documentation of the WAP forum at:

www.wapforum.org

14.5.3 Wireless Session Protocol (WSP)

WSP establishes a reliable session between the client (see Figure 197 on page 496) and the server, which is the WAP gateway/proxy and releases that session in an orderly manner. WSP session establishment agrees on common level of protocol functionality using the capability of negotiation. WSP exchanges content between client and server using compact encoding, and also controls communication interrupt. Communication interrupt happens with change of a bearer, such as SMS (see Figure 197 on page 496).

WSP defines two protocols:

1. Connection-mode session services over a transaction service

   This mode will be used for long-lived connections. A session state is maintained. There is reliability for data sent over a connection-mode session.

2. Non-confirmed, connection-less services over a datagram transport service.

   This service is suitable when applications do not need reliable delivery of data and do not care about confirmation. It can be used without actually having established a session.

WSP provides semantics and mechanisms based on Hypertext Transport Protocol (HTTP) 1.1, and enhancements for wireless networks and its WAP terminals.

14.5.3.1 Basic functionality

The core of the WSP design is a binary form of HTTP 1.1.

Content headers are used to define content type, character set encoding, languages, and so on. Compact binary encoding is defined for the well-known headers to reduce protocol overhead. A compact data format is supported that provides content headers for each component within the composite data object. This is a semantically equivalent binary form of the MIME-multipart/multimixed format used by HTTP 1.1.

As part of the session establishment process, request and response headers that remain constant over the life of the session can be exchanged between the service users in the client and the server. WSP will pass through client and server session headers, as well as request and response headers, without additions or removals.

The life cycle of a WSP session is not tied to the underlying transport protocol. A session re-establishment protocol has been defined that allows sessions to be suspended and resumed without the overhead of initial establishment. This allows a session to be suspended while idle to release network resources or save battery power. The session may be resumed over a different bearer network.

14.5.3.2 Layer-to-layer communication

Communications between layers and between entities within the session layer are accomplished through service primitives. They represent the logical exchange of information and control between the session layer and adjacent layers.

Service primitives consist of commands and their respective response associated with the service provided and parameters. For example:

```
X-service.type (parameter)
```

Where X designates the layer providing the service; for WSP, it is S.

For the service.type, see the following table:

Table 21.   Service primitives

Type	Abbreviation	Description
Request	req	Used when a higher level requests a service from a lower level.

Type	Abbreviation	Description
Indication	ind	Used to notify the next higher layer of activities to the peer (such as an invocation request) or to the provider of the service (such as a protocol generated event).
Response	res	A layer uses the response to acknowledge receipt of indication from the next lower layer.
Confirm	cnf	The layer providing the requested service uses confirm to report successfully completion of the activity.

When using service primitives, additional parameters may be possible. They describe certain types of parameters. For example:

- Addresses

  They describe client and server addresses to establish the session.

- Headers and body

  They describe the HTTP entity-body. The headers distinguish between requests and responses sent from client to the server or reverse. The body contains the content of the message.

- Capabilities

  These are service facilities, for example:

  - Largest transaction data unit

  - Set of code page names

  - Maximum of outstanding requests

  The capabilities may be negotiated between the client and the server.

- Push identifier

  It indicates that the received message is a push transaction of the session that is pending on the service interface.

- Reason

  The service provider uses the reason type to report the cause of a particular state of a primitive (for example, protocol error, disconnect mode, session suspended, and session resumed).

Service primitive sample
The behavior of service primitives is illustrated in Figure 199, using a time sequence chart.

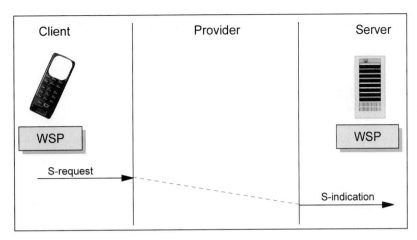

Figure 199. Non-confirmed service

Figure 199 depicts a simple non-confirmed service. The client invokes a S-request primitive, which results in an S-indication primitive in the server (WSP peer layer). The dashed line represents the propagation through the provider over a period of time.

14.5.3.3 Session services and operations

WSP is designed to function above transaction services, and also directly on datagram services without using the WTP layer. This means WSP may communicate with WDP (see 14.5.6, "Wireless Datagram Protocol (WDP)" on page 519) or with WTP (see 14.5.4, "Wireless Transaction Protocol (WTP)" on page 511), depending on the architecture of the application. Figure 200 on page 502 shows two sessions from a WAP client to a WAP proxy (further connections to Web server are not depicted).

One WAE application (see dashed line) uses services from the session layer (WSP), the transport layer (WDP), and the network layer in the WAP client, when it sends a message over the wireless network to the WAP proxy. In the WAP proxy, the equivalent peer layers are also used to reach the receiving WAE.

The other WAE application (see solid line) uses additionally services from the transaction layer (WTP). This is because an additional class of services is required for particular transactions (see "WSP connection-mode using wireless transaction protocol (WTP)" on page 507).

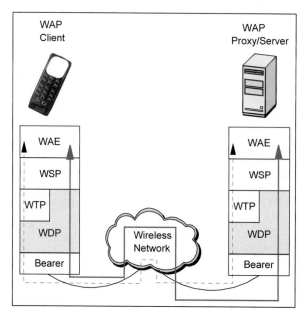

Figure 200. Client/server connection flow

WSP connection-mode - overview

Connection-mode session services provide two standard facilities:

- Session management facility

  Session management facility allows a client to connect with a server based on agreement of facilities and options to use. During session establishment, the client may also exchange attribute information for the duration of the session. While session establishment can only be done by the client, sessions can be terminated by both. The peer is invoked if one side tries to terminate the session. The user agent is also notified.

- Exception reporting facility

  Exception reporting facility allows the service provider to notify the user about events during the session.

There are some other facilities that are controlled through negotiation capabilities during session establishment. These are:

- Method invocation facility

  Method invocation facility permits the client to ask the server to execute an operation and return the result to the client. These operations may be compared with HTTP methods like GET, PUT, and so on (see RFC 2616), or user-defined operations, which fit into the same request/reply or transaction pattern. The service users are notified about completion of the operation whether it was successful or failed.

- Push facility

Push facility allows the server to send unsolicited information to the client. The sent information is non-confirmed. Delivery may be not reliable.

- Confirmed push facility

Confirmed push facility is the same function as described in the previous paragraph. However, this unsolicited information forces an acknowledgment from the client to the server.

- Session resume facility

Session resume facility allows both peers to suspend the session. The current session state is preserved. Further communication via this session is not possible until the client resumes the session. This function can also be used to switch the session to an alternate bearer.

WSP connection-mode - negotiation capability

Information that is related to the operation of a session service provider is handled through capabilities. Capability negotiation is used between peers to agree on an acceptable level of service.

The peer who starts the negotiation process is the initiator and the other peer is the responder. The initiator only proposes a set of capabilities. The responder agrees or rejects the proposal.

Negotiations are about capabilities, such as:

- A list of alternate addresses for the same requested service
- An agreement on size of the largest size of transaction data
- Header code pages
- Maximum outstanding method requests
- Maximum outstanding push requests

WSP connection-mode - operations

Figure 201 on page 505 shows a sample of a successful session establishment process through the client with subsequent invocation of an action in a server. Several service primitives are used on the client and the server side.

- Service primitives

  S-Connect   It is used to initiate the session establishment and to notify the successful execution. Several parameters are provided, such as *client address* (session originator), *server address* (session target), *client and server headers* (application-level parameters to indicate, that request and response headers of both partners are used throughout the session), and *requested and negotiated capabilities* for the duration of the session (for example, list of alias-addresses, client send data unit size, server send data unit size, maximum outstanding method requests, and maximum outstanding push requests).

S-MethodInvoke   It is used to request an operation to be executed by a server. This service primitive can be used only together with *S-MethodResult,* which returns the result from the server to the client after the execution. The following parameters are valid: *Client and server transaction id* (to distinguish between several pending transactions over the same session), *method* (tells which operation has to be used (either an HTTP method like GET or PUT, or one of the extension methods established during capability negotiation)), *Request Uniform Resource Identifier* (*URI*) to determine to which entity the operation applies, *request headers* (equivalent to HTTP headers), and *request body* (contains the data associated with the request).

S-MethodResult   This service primitive returns the response to an operation request. It can be invoked only after a preceding S-MethodInvoke has occurred. The following parameters may be used for this service primitive: *Client and server transaction ID* (distinguishes between pending transactions), *status* (Tells, through the equivalent of the HTTP status code (RFC 2613), the state of the requested operation invoked by S-MethodInvoke through the client), *response headers* (as described under S-MethodeInvoke, the response body, the data associated with the response or, if the status indicates an error, contains further detailed error information), and *acknowledgment headers* (may be used to return some information back to the server).

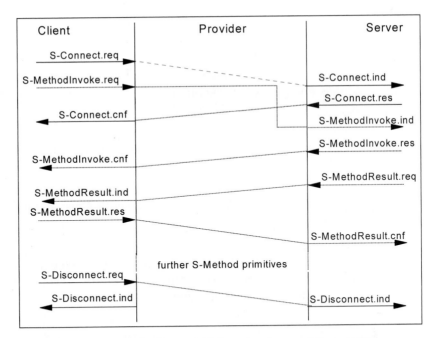

Figure 201. Normal session flow: establishment, actions and disconnection

- Usage of primitives:

  Primitives are used to send an information (commands or data) to the session partner via the provider's network.

  - In order to send an information, the primitive request type ***.req* is used.

  - When the communication partner receives the sent information, it notifies the services in the same peer layer that a command is received and notifies the upper layer that there is data for the upper layer. This notification is done through a primitive of the type indication with a ***.ind extension.

  - If, in the session establishment process, the option *confirmation of requests* is negotiated, a primitive of the type response with the extension ***.res is returned to the sender of the previous request.

  - The receiver of the response informs its upper layer and its services in the same layer about the reception through a primitive of the type with a ***.cnf extension.

  The meaning of the extensions are:

  - ***.req = request

- ***.ind = indication
- ***.res = response
- ***.cnf = confirm

- Description of the flow for a normal session establishment, session actions and session termination.

  The client's session layer starts with a S-Connect.req request. The server's session layer notifies its upper layer (application layer) through an S-Connect.ind indication that a connection request is received.

  The server uses the S-Connect.res response primitive to acknowledge reception of the indication primitive. The client's session layer uses the confirm primitive to report that the activity (S-Connect.req) has been completed successfully.

  During the session initiation process, the client's session layer may start immediately with sending S-MethodInvoke.req requests asking for an execution on the server's machine. This request indicates that the upper layer has to execute an operation on the server's side.

  The server sends a S-MethodInvoke.res response to the client confirming that the previous S-MethodInvoke.req request was completed successfully. The client is informed through S-Method.cnf.

  After execution of the operation by the server, it sends the result to the client through S-MethodResult.req. The client indicates the upper layer (the application layer) through S-Method.Result.ind the receipt of the returned data.

  Since the session partner have negotiated confirmation of all requests (***.req), the client confirms the S-MethodResult.req request with an S-MethodResult.res. response.

  Further requests and responses may use this session.

  The active session may by terminated in this example by issuing a S-Disconnect.req request to the server through the client. The server sends a S-Diconnect.ind to the session services in the session layer, which finishes the session. Session services on the client side will be informed to take down the session through S-Diconnect.ind.

Since the session layer does not provide any sequencing between multiple overlapping method invocations, the indications may be delivered in a different order than the sent request. The same is valid also for responses and confirmations, as well as for the corresponding S-MethodResult primitives. The application has to handle the sequencing.

There are some other session service primitives which are not used in the samples of the WSP connection-mode. These are:

S-Suspend   Suspends a session.

S-Resume   Resumes a session which was suspended.

S-Exception   Reports events.

S-MethodAbort   Aborts an operation request that is not yet complete.

S-Push   Sends unsolicited information from the server

S-ConfirmedPush   Sends unsolicited information from the server; however, the client has to confirm this information.

S-PushAbort   Rejects a push operation for a confirmed push.

WSP connection-less

The connection-less session service provides non-confirmed facilities. They can be used to exchange content entities between layers. Like the connection-mode service, the connection-less service is asymmetric, which means no sequencing of messages.

This service is used mainly for the push facility.

The following service primitives are defined:

- S-Unit-MethodInvoke
- S-Unit-MethodResult
- S-Unit-Push

WSP connection-mode using wireless transaction protocol (WTP)

The following section describes the operation of when WSP sessions are run over wireless transaction protocol (WTP) services (see 14.5.4, "Wireless Transaction Protocol (WTP)" on page 511).

The advantage of using WTP transaction within WSP sessions is comparable to TCP. WTP provides reliable transmissions, selectively defined re-transmission of lost packets, segmentation, and re-assembly of large messages and controlled data flow between sender and receiver.

Another advantage is the usage of WTP transaction classes. Three transaction classes allow you to define datagram transmission. These are:

Class 0   Unconfirmed invoke message with no result message, mainly used for unreliable push within a session using the same socket association.

Class 1 Confirmed invoke message with no result message, which is mainly used by WSP to realize a reliable push service

Class 2 Confirmed invoke message with one confirmed result message is the basic request/response transaction service used by WSP for method invocations.

The following table shows when these three transaction classes are used:

Table 22. WTP facilities and transaction classes

WSP facility	WTP transaction classes
Session Management	Class 0 and Class 2
Method Invocation	Class 2
Session Resume	Class 0 and Class 2
Push	Class 0
Confirmed Push	Class 1

In order to show the cooperation between session services and transaction services, some diagrams are added. These are samples of different transaction services used by session services:

- Normal session establishment using transaction class 2

- Normal session termination using transaction class 0

- Normal session suspend and resume using transaction class 0

- Normal method invocation using transaction class 2

Normal session establishment

Figure 202 shows the normal session establishment process.

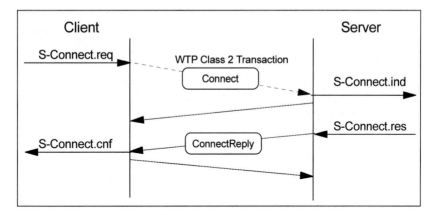

Figure 202. WSP WTP normal session establishment

Normal session termination

Figure 203 shows the normal session termination process.

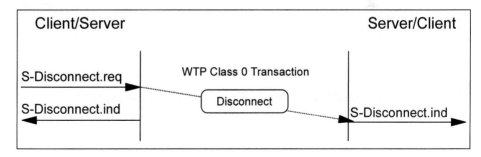

Figure 203. WSP WTP normal session termination

Normal session suspend and resume
Figure 204 shows the normal session suspend and resume process.

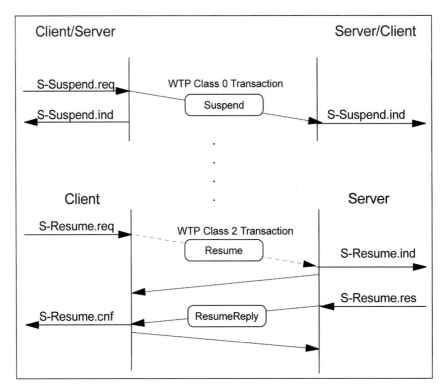

Figure 204. WSP WPT normal session suspend and resume

Normal method invocation

Figure 205 shows the normal method invocation process.

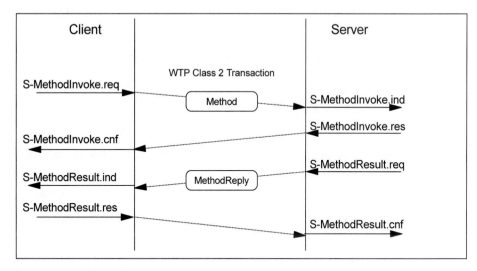

Figure 205. WSP WTP normal method invocation

14.5.3.4 Event processing

Sessions are distinguished by an unique session identifier, which is valid during the duration of the session. Each session is associated with a peer quadruplet address. This quadruplet consists of:

- Client address
- Client port
- Server address
- Server port

Incoming transaction are assigned to a particular session based on the peer address quadruplet. This kind of session addressing scheme allows one session to be bound to a peer address quadruplet at a time.

14.5.4 Wireless Transaction Protocol (WTP)

WTP provides a mechanism especially designed for WAP terminals with limited resources over networks, and with low to medium bandwidth. This technology allows more subscribers on the same network, due to reduced bandwidth utilization.

WTP provides unreliable and reliable data transfer based on request/reply paradigm. Unlike TCP, there is no connection setup and tear down. Compared to TCP, where a SYN and ACK flow is started before the first data are transmitted, WTP carries data already in the first packet of the protocol exchange.

WTP works message oriented, not stream oriented, like TCP.

14.5.4.1 WTP classes of operation

There are three classes of operation:

- Class 0: Unconfirmed invoke message with no result message

  This is a Datagram that can be sent within the context of an existing WSP session.

- Class 1: Confirmed invoke message with no result message

  This is used for data push, where no response from the destination is expected.

- Class 2: Confirmed invoke message with one confirmed result message

  One single request produces a single reply

14.5.4.2 Layer-to-layer communication

Service primitives are used to control the transaction traffic between the layers of the client and server. These service primitives have a similar syntax, as described for WSP.

```
X - generic name. type (parameters)
```

where X designates the layer providing the service. For the transaction layer, it is TR. The primitive types and their abbreviations are the same as described under WSP (see Table 21 on page 499).

There are three primitives for the service to the upper layer:

TR-Invoke	Initiates a new transaction.
TR-Result	Sends back a result of a previously initiated transaction.
TR-Abort	Aborts an existing transaction.

14.5.4.3 Example of a WSP-WTP sequence flow

Figure 206 on page 513 depicts the flow of a primitive sequence and shows the relationship between WSP and WTP request and responses. The flow is based on a class 2 transaction, a reliable, confirmed message exchange.

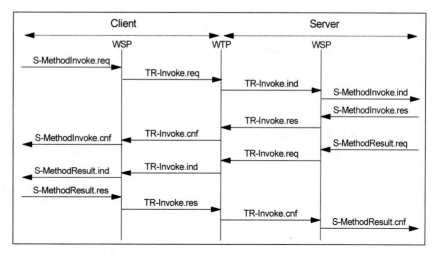

Figure 206. WSP-WTP primitive sequence for request-response

The first sequence is initiated through a client application (for example, an inquiry for a service), which starts with a S-MethodInvoke.req operation to the server application within a session.

The second sequence is a response from the server to confirm to WSP in the client stack that the invoke message (the inquiry) has been received by the server.

The third sequence returns the result request (reply to the inquiry) from the server to the client.

The fourth sequence confirms the receipt to the server that the reply was received correctly.

In order to control the message flow of the transaction layer peers WTP, uses two types of messages:

- Data messages that carry user data
- Control messages:
  - They are used for acknowledgments, error reporting, and so on.
  - Other control messages, which do not carry user data.

14.5.4.4 Summary of the WTP support
WTP supports:

- Retransmission of lost packets

- Selective retransmission

- Segmentation and re-assembly

- Port number addressing (UDP port numbers are used)

- Data flow control

14.5.5 Wireless Transport Layer Security (WTLS)

14.5.5.1 Overview

Many applications on the Web today require a secure connection between a client and the application server. WTLS is the security protocol to ensure secure transactions on WAP terminal. WTLS is based upon the industry-standard Transport Layer Security (TLS) protocol, formerly known as Secure Socket Layer (SSL).

WTLS has been optimized for use over narrow-band communication channels. It ensures data integrity, privacy, authentication, and denial-of-service protection. For Web applications, that employ standard Internet security techniques with TLS, the WAP gateway automatically and transparently manages wireless security with minimal overhead. It provides end-to-end security and application-level security. This includes security facilities for en-/decrypting, strong authentication, integrity, and key management. WTLS complies with regulations on the use of cryptographic algorithms and key lengths in different countries.

WTLS employs special adapted mechanisms for the wireless environment. For example, long existing secure sessions, optimized handshake procedures for the wireless network, and simple data reliability for operation over datagram bearers.

Figure 207 on page 515 shows the location of WTLS in the WAP architecture model and the internal WTLS architecture with its different WTLS protocols.

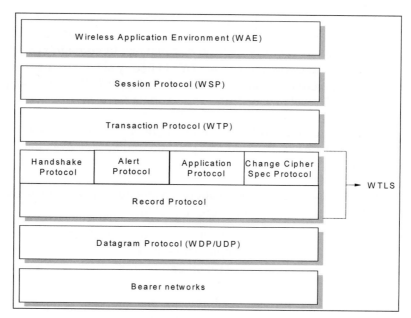

Figure 207. WTLS within the WAP architecture and WTLS components

14.5.5.2 WTLS layer goals

The primary goal is to provide security between client and server in terms of:

Privacy   Data sent is not presented in clear text to make it difficult for another network user to look at the data. This is done through encrypting the data stream.

Data integrity   If a network user where able to change the sent data, it should be detected by the client or server that sent the data. This is done through message digests.

Authentication   A network partner can be sure that he or she is connected with the true desired partner and not with someone else who pretends to be it. This is done through digital certificates.

Denial of service Rejecting and detecting data that is not successfully verified. This is done through a WTLS function.

14.5.5.3 Overview of the WTLS protocols

WTLS operates on connection-oriented and/or datagram transport protocols. Security functions are executed as an option above the transport layer.

WTLS connection management

WTLS connection management provides a secure communication between client and server. Several steps are needed within the connection establishment process through negotiations to agree to security parameters between the client and server. This is nearly similar to a secure connection establishment process via secure socket layer (SSL) (please see 21.8, "Secure Sockets Layer (SSL)" on page 747).

Security parameters for the secure connection establishment process may include, for example, cryptographic algorithms, key exchange procedures, and authentication.

Service primitives provide support to initiate this secure connection. The following service primitives are available:

SEC-Create	Initiates a secure connection with the following optional parameters: - Client certificates - Key exchange suites - Cipher suites - Compression methods - Key refreshing rules - Session ID
SEC-Exchange	Performs public-key authentication or key exchange with a client.
SEC-Commit	Initiated when the handshake is completed and either peer requests to switch to the agreed connection state.
SEC-Terminate	Terminates the connection.
SEC-Exception	Informs the other partner about warning level alerts.
SEC-Create-Request	The server requests the client to initiate a new handshake.

Protocol overview

Figure 208 shows the location of WTLS within the WAP layer model and the WTLS protocols.

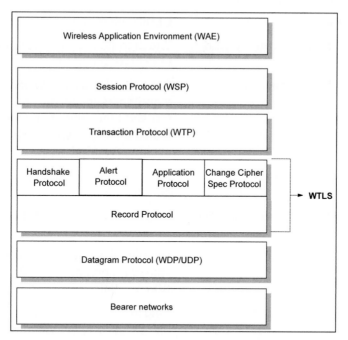

Figure 208. WTLS within the WAP architecture model and WTLS protocols

- Record protocol

  The record protocol is the interface to the upper layer (transaction or session layer) and to the lower layer (transport layer).

  The record protocol receives messages from the upper layer to be transmitted. It optionally compresses the data, applies a message authentication code (MAC), and encrypts and transmits the message.

  Received data is decrypted, verified, decompressed, and delivered to a higher layer of the client.

  Four protocols are defined that cooperate very closely with the record protocol in a client implementation environment:

  - Handshake protocol

    This protocol consists of three sub-protocols that allow peers to agree to security parameters for the record layer. The handshake protocol is responsible for the negotiation process between the client and server. These parameters are negotiated during the handshake:

    Session identifier   Identifies an active and resumeable secure session.

Protocol version	WTLS protocol version number.
Peer certificate	Certificate of the peer.
Compression method	The algorithm used to compress data prior to encryption.
Cipher spec	Specifies the bulk data encryption algorithm (such as null, RC5, DES, and so on) and MAC algorithm (such as SHA-1). It also defines cryptographic attributes, such as the MAC size.
Master secret	20 bytes secret shared between client and server.
Sequence number mode	Sequence numbering scheme used in this secure connection.
Key refresh	Defines how often some connection state values (encryption key, MAC secret, and IV) calculations are performed.
Is resumeable	Flag indicating whether the secure session can be used to initiate new secure connection.

- Change cipher spec protocol

  The change cipher spec is sent by the client or server to notify the other partner that subsequent records will be sent under the newly negotiated cipher spec and keys. This message is sent during the handshake after the security parameters have been agreed upon, but before the verifying finished message is sent.

- Alert protocol

  Alert messages contain information about the severity of the message and a description of the alert. Messages of a fatal level may terminate the secure connection.

- User data protocol

  Consist of the payload which the WAP client intends to send.

Further information about cryptographic computations may be obtained from 21.2, "A short introduction to cryptography" on page 660.

14.5.6 Wireless Datagram Protocol (WDP)

WDP provides a consistent service to the upper layers (security, transaction, and session) of the WAP architecture. This allows for applications to operate transparently over different available bearer services. It communicates transparently over the different bearer services supported by multiple network types. WDP is a connection-less, unreliable datagram service. It supports port number addressing. The port number points to the higher layer level of WDP. This may be WTP, WTLS, WSP, or an application.

In order to support the different bearer services with its specific capabilities and characteristics, an adaptation is required to keep WDP as a common layer for the various bearer services. Thus, WDP, with its kind of adaptation layer, cooperates with its underlying bearer layer. Figure 209 shows the general WDP structure.

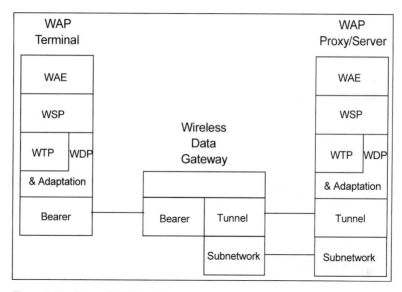

Figure 209. General WDP architecture

WDP messages are sent by the WAP terminal to the wireless data gateway using the bearer services. The wireless data gateway has the choice to pass WDP packets on to the WAP proxy/server via a tunneling protocol, which is the interface between the gateway that provides bearer service and the WAP proxy server. For example, if the bearer service were an GSM SMS, the gateway would be a GSM SMSC and would support a specific tunneling protocol to interface the SMSC to other servers. It is also possible to use a subnetwork as a common technology in order to connect two communication devices. This connection could be, for example, via a wide-area network based on TCP/IP or frame relay, or a LAN operating TCP/IP over Ethernet. The WAP proxy/server may offer application content or may operate as gateway between the wireless WTP protocols and the wired Internet.

When used over an IP network layer, UDP is used instead of WDP.

14.5.6.1 Bearer layer
The bearer layer is a bearer service, such as:

- IS-136 (GUTS, R-Data, DSD, and Packet Data)
- GSM (SMS, USSD, GPRS, and CSD)
- CDPD
- IDEN
- Flex and ReFLEX
- PHS
- PDC
- CDMA

14.5.6.2 WDP service primitives
Service primitives are used to control the transaction traffic between the layers of the client and server. These service primitives have a similar syntax to that described for WSP.

```
X - generic name. type (parameters)
```

where X designates the layer providing the service. For the WDP layer, it is T. The primitive types and their abbreviations are the same as described for WSP (see Table 21 on page 499).

There are two primitives for the service layer:

T-DUnitdata   Transmits data as datagram.
T-DError   WDP may also receive a T-DError primitive if the requested transmission cannot be executed by the WDP protocol layer.

14.5.6.3 Mapping WDP for IP
User datagram protocol (UDP), as a connection-less datagram service, is used as the WDP protocol for any wireless bearer network where IP is used as a routing protocol. UDP provides port based addressing (destination and source port). IP provides the segmentation and re-assembly.

The following bearer services are known to have adopted UDP as a WDP definition:

GSM Circuit-Switched Data, GSM GPRS, ANSI-136 R-Data, ANSI-136 Circuit-Switched Data, GPRS-136, CDPD, CDMA Circuit-Switched Data, CDMA Packet Data, PDC Circuit-Switched Data, PDC Packet Data, iDEN Circuit-Switched Data, iDEN Packet Data, PHS Circuit-Switched Data, DECT connection oriented services, and DECT packet switched services.

14.5.6.4 Mapping of WDP for other bearer services

There are a variety of services which map WDP, such as GSM SMS, ANSI-136 GHOST and USSD, and so on.

14.6 Protocol summary

Figure 210 shows the protocol structure of a WAP environment connected to a TCP/IP network. The purpose of this figure is to point out the different protocols used in the different environments, and what protocol conversion the WAP proxy/gateway has to do. In addition to this protocol conversion, the gateway has, after converting HTML code into WML code, to encode the content to a binary form in order to minimize bandwidth.

Protocol conversion is required only if HTML code is used for requests and responses on a connection to a Web server. If WML content or WMLScripts are retrieved from the Web server, then there is no protocol conversion necessary.

The WAP client initiates a session with the WAP proxy/gateway, using a reliable transaction, for retrieval of information from the Web server. The client selects, from the microbrowser's menu, the desired service by clicking on this line. This starts the transaction using an associated Uniform Resource Locator (URL), which identifies the Web target (IP address and port number for the Web server).

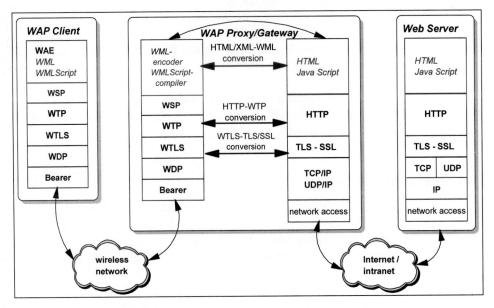

Figure 210. Protocol structure for a WAP and an Internet/intranet environment

If security is a concern for this session, a secure WTLS connection between the WAP client and the WAP proxy/gateway will be set up. Encryption, authentication and certificates are negotiated during the handshake process for the secure session. Please note that there is no secure end-to-end connection between the WAP client and the Web server, because each environment (the WAP and the TCP/IP environment) has different security protocols. If there is a security requirement for the connection between the WAP proxy/gateway and the Web server, a second secure connection path has to be established using TLS or SSL.

The WAP proxy/gateway will resolve the URL into a real IP address via internal cache or using domain name services, and will create the HTTP-, TCP-, and IP-header structure.

When the creation process for all headers is finished, the WAP proxy/gateway will set up an HTTP/TCP connection with the Web server and sends out a traditional IP datagram to the Internet/intranet. The path through the Internet or intranet is router controlled.

The Web server receives the HTTP request. It retrieves the desired Web page, WML deck, or WMLScript, and then responds to the HTTP request with its content to the WAP proxy/gateway, which is the other end of the HTTP/TCP connection.

The WAP proxy/gateway encodes the content (if it is WLM based), compiles the content (if it is WMLScript), or does protocol conversion into WML (if it is HTML code). It then associates the encoded response to the appropriate session and transaction, prepares the WSP/WTP/WDP header structure, and sends the data out to WAP client.

Chapter 15. Network management

With the growth in size and complexity of the TCP/IP-based internetworks the need for network management became very important.

The Internet Architecture Board (IAB) issued an RFC 1052 detailing its recommendation, which adopted two different approaches:

- Simple Network Management Protocol (SNMP).
- ISO Common Management Information Services/Common Management Information Protocol (CMIS/CMIP).

The IAB said that, in the short term, SNMP should be used. SNMP became so popular that it has become the industry-wide standard for reporting management data for an IP based network.

15.1 Simple Network Management Protocol and MIB overview

The SNMP network management framework consists of:

- A large number of managed nodes, each with an SNMP entity (agent). An SNMP agent is a server at a managed host that responds to SNMP requests from managers. An agent must be present at each IP host in order to enable management of that host by a SNMP manager. The SNMP agent manages/supports the Management Information Base (MIB) on the IP host on which it resides.

- At least one SNMP entity with management applications (manager). An SNMP manager is an application that runs on a management station that typically requests management data from an SNMP agent using the SNMP protocol.

- The management information database (MIB) for each entity. MIBs are the representation of the data objects that are managed by the agents. MIBs are represented using ASN.1 notation.

- A protocol to carry management information between the entities. The protocol that is used between an agent and the manager is SNMP. The protocol used between an agent and a sub-agent can be DPI/SMUX/AgentX or any proprietary protocol.

The IAB recommends that all IP and TCP implementations be network manageable using SNMP, that is, all hosts, gateways, and other IP aware devices should implement at least MIB-II.

Note that the historic protocols Simple Gateway Monitoring Protocol (SGMP, RFC 1028) and MIB-I (RFC 1156) are not recommended for use.

SNMP is an Internet standard protocol. Its status is recommended. Its current specification can be found in RFC 1157 Simple Network Management Protocol (SNMP).

MIB-II is an Internet standard protocol. Its status is recommended. Its current specification can be found in RFC 1213 Management Information Base for Network Management of TCP/IP-based internetworks: MIB-II.

More information can be found in:

1. SMI (RFC 1155) - Describes how managed objects contained in the MIB are defined. (It is discussed in 15.2, "Structure and identification of management information (SMI)" on page 526.)

2. MIB-II (RFC 1213) - Describes the managed objects contained in the MIB. (It is discussed in 15.3, "Management Information Base (MIB)" on page 528.)

3. SNMP (RFC 1157) - Defines the protocol used to manage these objects. (It is discussed in 15.4, "Simple Network Management Protocol (SNMP)" on page 532.)

15.2 Structure and identification of management information (SMI)

The SMI defines the rules for how managed objects are described and how management protocols can access these objects. The description of managed objects is made using a subset of the ASN.1 (Abstract Syntax Notation 1, ISO standard 8824), a data description language. The object type definition consists of five fields:

- Object: A textual name, termed the *object descriptor*, for the object type along with its corresponding *object identifier* defined below.

- Syntax: The abstract syntax for the object type. It can be a choice of SimpleSyntax (Integer, Octet String, Object Identifier, Null) or an ApplicationSyntax (NetworkAddress, Counter, Gauge, TimeTicks, Opaque) or other application-wide types (see RFC 1155 for more details).

- Definition: A textual description of the semantics of the object type.

- Access: One of read-only, read-write, write-only or not-accessible.

- Status: One of mandatory, optional, or obsolete.

As an example, we can have:

```
OBJECT
        sysDescr { system 1 }
Syntax   OCTET STRING
Definition This value should include the full name and version
           identification of the system's hardware type, software
           operating system, and networking software. It is
           mandatory that this contain only printable ASCII
           characters.
Access   read-only.
Status   mandatory.
```

This example shows the definition of an object contained in the Management Information Base (MIB). Its name is sysDescr and it belongs to the system group (see 15.3, "Management Information Base (MIB)" on page 528).

A managed object not only has to be described but identified, too. This is done using the ASN.1 Object Identifier in the same way as a telephone number, reserving group of numbers to different locations. In the case of TCP/IP-based network management the number allocated was 1.3.6.1.2 and SMI uses it as the base for defining new objects.

The number 1.3.6.1.2 is obtained by joining groups of numbers with the following meaning:

- The first group defines the node administrator:
  - (1) for ISO
  - (2) for CCITT
  - (3) for the joint ISO-CCITT
- The second group for the ISO node administrator defines (3) for use by other organizations.
- The third group defines (6) for the use of the U.S. Department of Defense (DoD).
- In the fourth group the DoD has not indicated how it will manage its group so the Internet community assumed (1) for its own.
- The fifth group was approved by IAB to be:
  - (1) for the use of OSI directory in the Internet
  - (2) for objects identification for management purposes
  - (3) for objects identification for experimental purposes
  - (4) for objects identification for private use.

In the example the "{ system 1 }" beside the object name means that the object identifier is 1.3.6.1.2.1.1.1. It is the first object in the first group (system) in the Management Information Base (MIB).

15.3 Management Information Base (MIB)

The MIB defines the objects that may be managed for each layer in the TCP/IP protocol. There are two versions: MIB-I and MIB-II. MIB-I was defined in RFC 1156, and is now classified as an *historic* protocol with a status of *not recommended*.

MIB-II is described in RFC 1213. The group definitions are:

Table 23. Management Information Base II (MIB-II) group definitions

Group	Objects for	#
System	Basic system information	7
Interfaces	Network attachments	23
AT	Address translation	3
IP	Internet protocol	42
ICMP	Internet control message protocol	26
TCP	Transmission control protocol	19
UDP	User datagram protocol	7
EGP	Exterior gateway protocol	18
SNMP	SNMP applications entities	39
Legend: # = Number of objects in the group		

There is also space in the definition for a Transmission group, for describing the underlying media.

Each managed node supports only those groups that are appropriate. For example, if there is no gateway, the EGP group need not be supported. If a group is appropriate, all objects in that group must be supported.

The list of managed objects defined has been derived from those elements considered essential. This approach of taking only the essential objects is not restrictive, since the SMI provides extensibility mechanisms such as definition of a new version of the MIB and definition of private or non-standard objects.

Below are some examples of objects in each group. The complete list is defined in RFC 1213. Please also refer to RFC 2011, RFC 2012 and RFC 2013 for updated information of IP, TCP and UDP.

- System Group

  - sysDescr - Full description of the system (version, HW, OS)
  - sysObjectID - Vendor's object identification
  - sysUpTime - Time since last re-initialization
  - sysContact - Name of contact person
  - sysServices - Services offered by device

- Interfaces Group

  - ifIndex - Interface number
  - ifDescr - Interface description
  - ifType - Interface type
  - ifMtu - Size of the largest IP datagram
  - ifAdminisStatus - Status of the interface
  - ifLastChange - Time the interface entered in the current status
  - ifINErrors - Number of inbound packets that contained errors
  - ifOutDiscards - Number of outbound packets discarded

- Address Translation Group

  - atTable - deprecated (MIB-I).
  - atEntry - deprecated (MIB-I).
  - atIfIndex - IfIndex interface number.
  - atPhysAddress - The media-dependent physical address
  - atNetAddress - The network address corresponding to the
    media-dependent physical address

- IP Group

  - ipForwarding - Indication of whether this entity is an IP gateway
  - ipInHdrErrors - Number of input datagrams discarded due to errors in
    their IP headers
  - ipInAddrErrors - Number of input datagrams discarded due to errors in
    their IP address
  - ipInUnknownProtos - Number of input datagrams discarded due to
    unknown or unsupported protocol
  - ipReasmOKs - Number of IP datagrams successfully re-assembled
  - ipRouteDest - Destination IP address

- ICMP Group

  - icmpInMsgs - Number of ICMP messages received
  - icmpInDestUnreachs - Number of ICMP destination-unreachable
    messages received
  - icmpInTimeExcds - Number of ICMP time-exceeded messages
    received

- icmpInSrcQuenchs - Number of ICMP source-quench messages received
- icmpOutErrors - Number of ICMP messages not sent due to problems within ICMP

- TCP Group

  - tcpRtoAlgorithm - Algorithm to determine the timeout for retransmitting unacknowledged octets
  - tcpMaxConn - Limit on the number of TCP connections the entity can support
  - tcpActiveOpens - Number of times TCP connections have made a direct transition to the SYN-SENT state from the CLOSED state
  - tcpInSegs - Number of segments received, including those received in error
  - tcpConnRemAddress - The remote IP address for this TCP connection
  - tcpInErrs - Number of segments discarded due to format error
  - tcpOutRsts - Number of resets generated

- UDP Group

  - udpInDatagrams - Number of UDP datagrams delivered to UDP users
  - udpNoPorts - Number of received UDP datagrams for which there was no application at the destination port
  - udpInErrors - Number of received UDP datagrams that could not be delivered for reasons other than the lack of an application at the destination port
  - udpOutDatagrams - Number of UDP datagrams sent from this entity

- EGP Group

  - egpInMsgs - Number of EGP messages received without error
  - egpInErrors - Number of EGP messages with errors
  - egpOutMsgs - Number of locally generated EGP messages
  - egpNeighAddr - The IP address of this entry's EGP neighbor
  - egpNeighState - The EGP state of the local system with respect to this entry's EGP neighbor

This is not the complete MIB definition but it is presented as an example of the objects defined in each group. These modules currently support IPv4.

To illustrate this, the Interfaces Group contains two top-level objects: the number of interface attachments on the node (ifNumber) and a table containing information on those interfaces (ifTable). Each entry (ifEntry) in that table contains the objects for a particular interface. Among those, the interface type (ifType) is identified in the MIB tree using the ASN.1 notation by 1.3.6.1.2.1.2.2.1.3. and for a token-ring adapter the value of the corresponding variable would be 9, which means iso88025-tokenRing (see Figure 211).

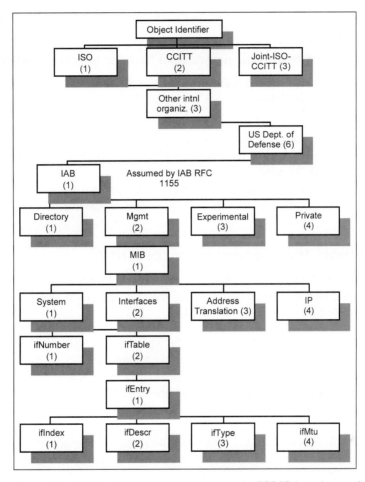

Figure 211. MIB-II - Object identifier allocation for TCP/IP-based network

15.3.1 IBM-specific MIB part

IBM has added the following objects in the MIB-II database:

```
* IBM SNMP agent DPI UDP port
DPI_port                1.3.6.1.4.1.2.2.1.1.    number        2

* IBM "ping" round-trip-time table
RTTaddr                 1.3.6.1.4.1.2.2.1.3.1.  internet     60
minRTT                  1.3.6.1.4.1.2.2.1.3.2.  number       60
maxRTT                  1.3.6.1.4.1.2.2.1.3.3.  number       60
```

```
averRTT              1.3.6.1.4.1.2.2.1.3.4.   number        60
RTTtries             1.3.6.1.4.1.2.2.1.3.5.   number        60
RTTresponses         1.3.6.1.4.1.2.2.1.3.6.   number        60
```

Where:

- DPI_port returns the port number between the agent and the subagent.

- *RTT* allows an SNMP manager to ping remote hosts. RTT stands for Round Trip Time table.

  - RTTaddr: host address
  - minRTT: minimum round trip time
  - maxRTT: maximum round trip time
  - aveRTT: average round trip time
  - RTTtries: number of pings yet to be performed
  - RTTresponses: number of responses received

15.4 Simple Network Management Protocol (SNMP)

The SNMP added the improvement of many years of experience in SGMP and allowed it to work with the objects defined in the MIB with the representation defined in the SIM.

RFC 1157 defines the Network Management Station (NMS) as the one that executes network management applications (NMA) that monitor and control network elements (NE) such as hosts, gateways and terminal servers. These network elements use a management agent (MA) to perform the network management functions requested by the network management stations. The Simple Network Management Protocol (SNMP) is used to communicate management information between the network management stations and the agents in the network elements (see Figure 212 for more details).

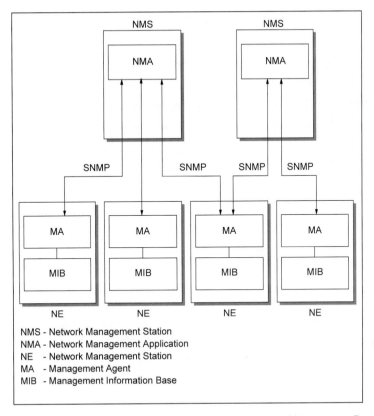

Figure 212. SNMP - Components of the Simple Network Management Protocol

All the management agent functions are only alterations (set) or inspections (get) of variables limiting the number of essential management functions to two and avoiding more complex protocols. In the other direction, from NE to NMS, a limited number of unsolicited messages (traps) are used to indicate asynchronous events. In the same way, trying to preserve the simplicity, the interchange of information requires only an unreliable datagram service and every message is entirely and independently represented by a single transport datagram. This means also that the mechanisms of the SNMP are generally suitable for use with a wide variety of transport services. RFC 1157 specifies the exchange of messages via the UDP protocol, but a wide variety of transport protocols can be used.

The entities residing at management stations and network elements that communicate with one another using the SNMP are termed SNMP application entities. The peer processes that implement it are the protocol entities. An SNMP agent with some arbitrary set of SNMP application entities is called an

SNMP community, where each one is named by a string of octets that need to be unique only to the agent participating in the community.

A message in the SNMP protocol consists of a version identifier, an SNMP community name and a protocol data unit (PDU). It is mandatory that all implementations of SNMP support the five PDUs:

GetRequest   Retrieve the values of a specific object from the MIB.

GetNextRequest Walk through portions of the MIB.

SetRequest   Alter the values of a specific object from the MIB.

GetResponse   Response from a GetRequest, a GetNextRequest and a SetRequest.

Trap   Capability of the network elements to generate events to network management stations such as agent initialization, agent restart and link failure. There are seven trap types defined in RFC 1157: coldStart, warmStart, linkDown, linkUp, authenticationFailure, egpNeighborLoss and enterpriseSpecific.

The formats of these messages are a illustrated in Figure 213.

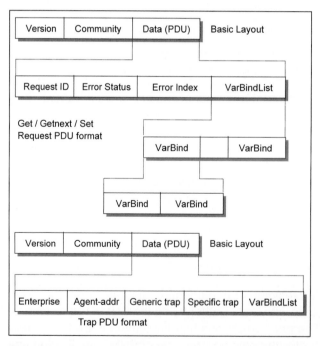

Figure 213. SNMP message format - Request, set and trap PDU format

There are three versions of SNMP available, usually referred as SNMPv1, SNMPv2, and SNMPv3, respectively. The security functions provided by the SNMP protocols are categorized into the following two models:

- Community-based security model, whose data is protected by nothing more than a password, namely the community name. This level of security is provided by the SNMPv1 and SNMPv2c Community-Based Security Model.

- User-based security model (USM), which provides different levels of security, based on the user accessing the managed information. To support this security level, the SNMPv3 framework defines several security functions, such as USM for authentication and privacy and view-based access control model (VACM), which provides the ability to limit access to different MIB objects on a per-user basis, and the use of authentication and data encryption for privacy.

15.5 Simple Network Management Protocol Version 2 (SNMPv2)

The framework of Version 2 of the Simple Network Management Protocol (SNMPv2) was published in April 1993 and consists of 12 RFCs including the first, RFC 1441, which is an introduction. In August 1993, all 12 RFCs became a proposed standard with the status elective.

This framework consists of the following disciplines:

- Structure of Management Information (SMI)

  Definition of the OSI ASN.1 subset for creating MIB modules. See RFC 2578 for a description.

- Textual conventions

  Definition of the initial set of textual conventions available to all MIB modules. See RFC 2579 for a description.

- Protocol operations

  Definition of protocol operations with respect to the sending and receiving of PDUs. See RFC 1905 for a description.

- Transport mappings

  Definition of mapping SNMPv2 onto an initial set of transport domains because it can be used over a variety of protocol suites. The mapping onto UDP is the preferred mapping. The RFC also defines OSI, DDP, IPX etc. See RFC 1906 for a description.

- Protocol instrumentation

Definition of the MIB for SNMPv2. See RFC 1907 for a description.

- Administrative framework

Definition of the administrative infrastructure for SNMPv2, the user-based security model for SNMPv2 and the community-based SNMPv2. See RFCs 1909, 1910 and 1901 for descriptions.

- Conformance statements

Definition of the notation compliance or capability of agents. See RFC 2580 for a description.

The following sections describe the major differences and improvements from SNMPv1 to SNMPv2.

15.5.1 SNMPv2 entity

An SNMPv2 entity is an actual process that performs network management operations by generating and/or responding to SNMPv2 protocol messages by using the SNMPv2 protocol operations. All possible operations of an entity can be restricted to a subset of all possible operations that belong to a particular administratively defined party (please refer to 15.5.2, "SNMPv2 party" on page 536). An SNMPv2 entity could be member of multiple SNMPv2 parties. The following local databases are maintained by an SNMPv2 entity:

- One database for all parties known by the SNMPv2 entity which could be:
  - Operation realized locally
  - Operation realized by proxy interactions with remote parties or devices
  - Operation realized by other SNMPv2 entities
- Another database that represents all managed object resources that are known to that SNMPv2 entity.
- And at least a database that represents an access control policy that defines the access privileges accorded to known SNMPv2 parties.

An SNMPv2 entity can act as an SNMPv2 agent or manager.

15.5.2 SNMPv2 party

An SNMPv2 party is a conceptual, virtual execution environment whose operation is restricted, for security or other purposes, to an administratively defined subset of all possible operations of a particular SNMPv2 entity (please refer to 15.5.1, "SNMPv2 entity" on page 536). Architecturally, each SNMPv2 party comprises:

- A single, unique party identity.

- A logical network location at which the party executes, characterized by a transport protocol domain and transport addressing information.

- A single authentication protocol and associated parameters by which all protocol messages originated by the party are authenticated as to origin and integrity.

- A single privacy protocol and associated parameters by which all protocol messages received by the party are protected from disclosure.

15.5.3 GetBulkRequest

The GetBulkRequest is defined in RFC 1905 and is thus part of the protocol operations. A GetBulkRequest is generated and transmitted as a request of an SNMPv2 application. The purpose of the GetBulkRequest is to request the transfer of a potentially large amount of data, including, but not limited to, the efficient and rapid retrieval of large tables. The GetBulkRequest is more efficient than the GetNextRequest in case of retrieval of large MIB object tables. The syntax of the GetBulkRequest is:

```
GetBulkRequest [ non-repeaters = N, max-repetitions = M ]
                ( RequestedObjectName1,
                  RequestedObjectName2,
                  RequestedObjectName3 )
```

Where:

RequestedObjectName1, 2, 3 MIB object identifier such as sysUpTime etc. The objects are in a lexicographically ordered list. Each object identifier has a binding to at least one variable. For example, the object identifier ipNetToMediaPhysAddress has a variable binding for each IP address in the ARP table and the content is the associated MAC address.

N Specifies the non-repeaters value, which means that you request only the contents of the variable next to the object specified in your request of the first N objects named between the parentheses. This is the same function as provided by the GetNextRequest.

M Specifies the max-repetitions value, which means that you request from the remaining (number of requested objects -

N) objects the contents of the M variables next to your object specified in the request. Similar to an iterated GetNextRequest but transmitted in only one request.

With the GetBulkRequest you can efficiently get the contents of the next variable or the next M variables in only one request.

Assume the following ARP table in a host that runs an SNMPv2 agent:

```
Interface-Number   Network-Address   Physical-Address    Type

        1              10.0.0.51      00:00:10:01:23:45   static
        1              9.2.3.4        00:00:10:54:32:10   dynamic
        2              10.0.0.15      00:00:10:98:76:54   dynamic
```

An SNMPv2 manager sends the following request to retrieve the sysUpTime and the complete ARP table:

```
GetBulkRequest [ non-repeaters = 1, max-repetitions = 2 ]
               ( sysUpTime,
                 ipNetToMediaPhysAddress,
                 ipNetToMediaType )
```

The SNMPv2 entity acting in an agent role responds with a response PDU:

```
Response (( sysUpTime.0 =  "123456" ),
          ( ipNetToMediaPhysAddress.1.9.2.3.4 =
                                "000010543210" ),
          ( ipNetToMediaType.1.9.2.3.4 =  "dynamic" ),
          ( ipNetToMediaPhysAddress.1.10.0.0.51 =
                                "000010012345" ),
          ( ipNetToMediaType.1.10.0.0.51 =  "static" ))
```

The SNMPv2 entity acting in a manager role continues with:

```
GetBulkRequest [ non-repeaters = 1, max-repetitions = 2 ]
               ( sysUpTime,
                 ipNetToMediaPhysAddress.1.10.0.0.51,
                 ipNetToMediaType.1.10.0.0.51 )
```

The SNMPv2 entity acting in an agent role responds with:

```
Response (( sysUpTime.0 =  "123466" ),
          ( ipNetToMediaPhysAddress.2.10.0.0.15 =
                                  "000010987654" ),
          ( ipNetToMediaType.2.10.0.0.15 =
```

```
                                          "dynamic" ),
          ( ipNetToMediaNetAddress.1.9.2.3.4 =
                                          "9.2.3.4" ),
          ( ipRoutingDiscards.0 =  "2" ))
```

This response signals the end of the table to the SNMPv2 entity acting in a manager role. With the GetNextRequest you would have needed four requests to retrieve the same information. If you had set the max-repetition value of the GetBulkRequest to three, in this example, you would have needed only one request.

15.5.4 InformRequest

An InformRequest is generated and transmitted as a request from an application in an SNMPv2 manager entity that wishes to notify another application, acting also in an SNMPv2 manager entity, of information in the MIB view[1] of a party local to the sending application. The packet is used as an indicative assertion to the manager of another party about information accessible to the originating party (manager-to-manager communication across party boundaries). The first two variables in the variable binding list of an InformRequest are sysUpTime.0 and snmpEventID.i[2] respectively. Other variables may follow.

15.6 MIB for SNMPv2

This MIB defines managed objects that describe the behavior of the SNMPv2 entity.

> **Note:**
>
> This is not a replacement of the MIB-II.

Following are some object definitions to get an idea of the contents:

```
sysName OBJECT-TYPE
     SYNTAX      DisplayString (SIZE (0..255))
     MAX-ACCESS  read-write
     STATUS      current
     DESCRIPTION
             "An administratively-assigned name for this managed node.
             By convention, this is the node's fully-qualified domain
             name. If the name is unknown, the value is the zero-length
             string."
```

[1] A MIB view is a subset of the set of all instances of all object types defined according to SMI.
[2] snmpEventID.i is an SNMPv2 manager-to-manager MIB object that shows the authoritative identification of an event.

```
     ::= { system 5 }
warmStart NOTIFICATION-TYPE
     STATUS   current
     DESCRIPTION
             "A warmStart trap signifies that the SNMPv2
             entity, acting in an agent role, is reinitializing
             itself such that its configuration is unaltered."
     ::= { snmpTraps 2 }
```

15.7 The new administrative model

It is the purpose of the administrative model for SNMPv2 to define how the administrative framework is applied to realize effective network management in a variety of configurations and environments.

The model entails the use of distinct identities for peers that exchange SNMPv2 messages. Thus, it represents a departure from the community-based administrative model of the original SNMPv1. By unambiguously identifying the source and intended recipient of each SNMPv2 message, this new strategy improves upon the historical community scheme both by supporting a more convenient access control model and allowing for effective use of asymmetric (public key) security protocols in the future. Please refer to Figure 214 for the new message format.

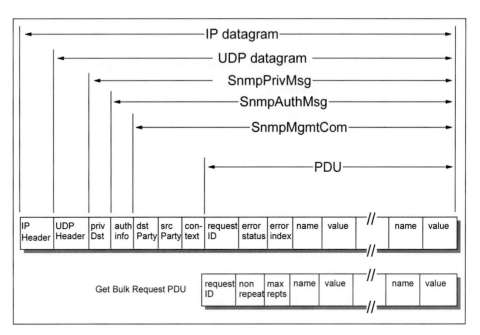

Figure 214. SNMP Version 2 message format

- PDU

    Includes one of the following protocol data units:

    - GetNextRequest

    - GetRequest

    - Inform

    - Report

    - Response

    - SNMPv2-Trap

    - SetRequest

    The GetBulkRequest has a different PDU format, as shown above (refer to 15.5.3, "GetBulkRequest" on page 537).

    > **Note:**
    >
    > The SNMP trap now has the same format as all the other requests.

- SnmpMgmtCom (SNMP Management Communication)

  Adds the source party ID (srcParty), the destination party ID (dstParty) and the context to the PDU. The context specifies the SNMPv2 context containing the management information referenced by the communication.

- SnmpAuthMsg

  This field is used as authentication information from the authentication protocol used by that party. The SnmpAuthMsg is serialized according to ASN.1 BER[3] and can then be encrypted.

- SnmpPrivMsg SNMP Private Message

  An SNMPv2 private message is an SNMPv2 authenticated management communication that is (possibly) protected from disclosure. A private destination (privDst) is added to address the destination party.

The message is then encapsulated in a normal UDP/IP datagram and sent to the destination across the network.

For further information please refer to the above mentioned RFCs.

15.8 Simple Network Management Protocol Version 3 (SNMPv3)

SNMPv3 is described in RFC 2570, RFC 2571, RFC 2572, RFC 2573 and RFC 2574. SNMPv3 is an extension to the existing SNMP architecture.

SNMPv3 supports the following:

- A new SNMP message format
- Authentication for messages
- Security for messages
- Access control
- Continued support for SNMPv2

The User-based Security Model (USM), described in RFC 2574, specifies using MD5 and hashing algorithms. This provides data integrity, security and privacy. There is support for the authentication protocols HMAC-MD5-96, HMAC-SHA-96, and optional support for the encryption protocol CBC-DES.

The View-based Access Control Model (VACM) in RFC 2575, shows how to define views which are subsets of the full MIB tree. Access control is then available for these views.

---

[3] ASN.1 BER specifies the Basic Encoding Rules for OSI Abstract Syntax Notation One, according to ISO 8825.

Since SNMP has a modular structure, changes to individual modules do not impact the other modules directly. This allows you to easily define SNMPv3 over the existing model. For example, to add a new SNMP message format, it is sufficient to upgrade the message processing model. Furthermore, since it is needed to support SNMPv1 and SNMPv2 messages as well, it can be achieved by adding the new SNMPv3 message module into the message processing subsystem. The Figure 215 illustrates this structure.

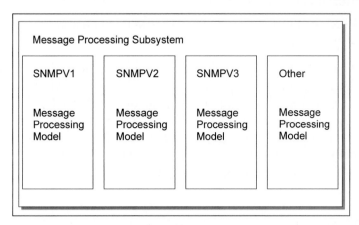

Figure 215. SNMP - Message processing subsystem

15.8.1 Single authentication and privacy protocol

The authentication protocol provides a mechanism by which SNMPv3 management communications, transmitted by a party, can be reliably identified as having originated from that party.

The privacy protocol provides a mechanism by which SNMPv3 management communications transmitted to a party are protected from disclosure.

Principal threats against which the SNMPv3 security protocol provides protection are:

- Modification of information
- Masquerade
- Message stream modification
- Disclosure

The following security services provide protection against the above threats:

- Data integrity

Provided by the MD5 message digest algorithm. A 128-bit digest is calculated over the designated portion of a SNMPv3 message and included as part of the message sent to the recipient.

- Data origin authentication

Provided by prefixing each message with a secret value shared by the originator of that message and its intended recipient before digesting.

- Message delay or replay

Provided by including a timestamp value in each message.

- Data confidentiality

Provided by the symmetric privacy protocol which encrypts an appropriate portion of the message according to a secret key known only to the originator and recipient of the message. This protocol is used in conjunction with the symmetric encryption algorithm, in the cipher block chaining mode, which is part of the Data Encryption Standard (DES). The designated portion of an SNMPv3 message is encrypted and included as part of the message sent to the recipient.

15.9 References

The following RFCs define the Simple Network Management Protocol and the information kept in a system:

- RFC 1052 – IAB Recommendations for the Development of Internet Network Management Standards
- RFC 1085 – ISO Presentation Services on Top of TCP/IP-Based Internets
- RFC 1155 – Structure and Identification of Management Information for TCP/IP-Based Internets
- RFC 1157 – A Simple Network Management Protocol (SNMP)
- RFC 1213 – Management Information Base for Network Management of TCP/IP-Based Internets: MIB-II
- RFC 1215 – Convention for Defining Traps for Use with the SNMP
- RFC 1228 – SNMP-DPI: Simple Network Management Protocol Distributed Programming Interface
- RFC 1239 – Reassignment of Experimental MIBs to Standard MIBs
- RFC 1351 – SNMP Administrative Model
- RFC 1352 – SNMP Security Protocols
- RFC 1441 – Introduction to Version 2 of the Internet-Standard Network Management Framework
- RFC 1592 – Simple Network Management Protocol Distributed Protocol Interface Version 2.0
- RFC 1748 – IEEE 802.5 Token-Ring MIB

- RFC 1901 – Introduction to Community-Based SNMPv2
- RFC 1904 – Conformance Statements for Version 2 of the Simple Network Management Protocol (SNMPv2)
- RFC 1905 – Protocol Operations for Version 2 of the Simple Network Management Protocol (SNMPv2)
- RFC 1906 – Transport Mappings for Version 2 of the Simple Network Management Protocol (SNMPv2)
- RFC 1907 – Management Information Base for Version 2 of the Simple Network Management Protocol (SNMPv2)
- RFC 1909 – An Administrative Infrastructure for SNMPv2
- RFC 1910 – User-Based Security Model for SNMPv2
- RFC 2011 – SNMPv2 Management Information Base for the Internet Protocol Using SMIv2
- RFC 2012 – SNMPv2 Management Information Base for the Transmission Control Protocol Using SMIv2
- RFC 2013 – SNMPv2 Management Information Base for the User Datagram Protocol Using SMIv2
- RFC 2570 – Introduction to Version 3 of the Internet-standard Network Management Framework.
- RFC 2571 – An Architecture for Describing SNMP Management Frameworks.
- RFC 2572 – Message Processing and Dispatching for the Simple Network Management Protocol (SNMP).
- RFC 2573 – SNMP Applications
- RFC 2574 – User-based Security Model (USM) for SNMPv3.
- RFC 2575 – View-based Access Control Model (VACM) for the Simple Network Management Protocol (SNMP)
- RFC 2578 – Structure of Management Information for Version 2 of the Simple Network Management Protocol (SNMPv2)
- RFC 2579 – Textual Conventions for Version 2 of the Simple Network Management Protocol (SNMPv2).
- RFC 2580 – Conformance Statements for SMIv2
- RFC 2742 – Definitions of Managed Objects for Extensible SNMP Agents

Chapter 16. Utilities

In this chapter, we briefly cover some miscellaneous application protocols and utilities.

16.1 Remote printing (LPR and LPD)

The line printer requester (LPR) allows access to printers on other computers running the line printer daemon (LPD) as though they were on your computer. The clients provided (LPR, LPQ, LPRM or LPRMON or LPRPORTD) allow the user to send files or redirect printer output to a remote host running a remote print server (LPD). Some of these clients can also be used to query the status of a job, as well as to delete a job. For more information about remote printing, see RFC 1179.

16.2 X Window system

The X Window system (hereafter referred to as X) is one of the most widely used *graphical user interface (GUI)*, or bitmapped-window display systems. It is supported by all major workstation vendors, and is used by a large and growing number of users worldwide. The X Window system offers more than just a raw environment. It also offers a platform for uniquely incorporated commercial packages. In addition to writing application software, some industry groups have created proprietary software packages and standards for interfaces that leverage the display capabilities of the X Window system. These packages are then integrated into applications to improve the look and feel of them.

The two most significant commercial packages in this area are the Open Software Foundation's *MOTIF* and UNIX International's *Open Look*. X was the brainchild of Robert Scheifler, Jim Gettys, and others at MIT, as part of *Project Athena*, a research project devoted to the examination of very large networks of personal computers and workstations. (For an overview of the Project Athena, please refer to *Project Athena: Supporting Distributed Computing at MIT.*) As part of this study, a unifying window system environment extending over all systems was deemed necessary. X was envisioned as this window system, one that could be used among the varied heterogeneous computers and networks.

As Project Athena progressed, X evolved into a portable network-based window system. Much of the early work on X was derived from an existent Stanford window system called W. In fact, the name X was simply a play on the previous name W. The MIT X Consortium, founded in 1988, is dedicated to the advancement of the X Window System and to the promotion of cooperation within the computer industry in standardizing the X Window System interfaces.

Current X releases contain two numbers: the *version number* indicating major protocol or standards revisions, and a *release number* indicating minor changes. At the time of writing, the latest version is X11 Release 6.4, also known as X11R6.4. The latest release of OSF/MOTIF is V2.1.10 (based on X11R5). Major revisions of X are incompatible, but there is backward compatibility with minor releases within major revision categories.

The aim of X was to allow the user to control all sessions from one screen, with applications either running in a window, or in separate virtual terminals but with an icon on the primary screen reminding him or her of the existence of that application (the same function as OS/2 Presentation Manager).

The X Window System provides the capability of managing both local and remote windows. Remote windows are established through TCP/IP, and local windows through the use of BSD *sockets*. Some of the important features of X11R6.4 is that it provides access to remote applications over the Internet. Since the internet connections are relatively slow, there is a need to compress the data and send accordingly. For this purpose the Low Bandwidth X (LBX) extension is added in the latest release. Another issue that comes with the Internet is security. The latest X window release has security function to overcome this problem.

16.2.1 Functional concept

Basically there are two parts communicating with each other:

1. The application, which gets input from the user, executes code, and sends output back to the user. Instead of reading and writing directly to a display, the application uses the Xlib programming interface to send and receive data to/from the user's terminal. The application part is also called the X client.

2. The user's terminal, running a display-managing software which receives/sends data from/to the application and is called the X server.

See Figure 216 for more details.

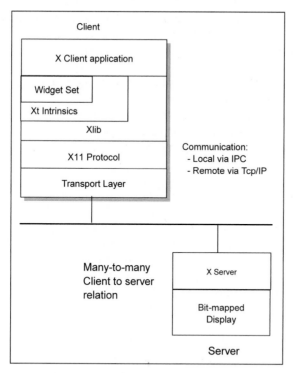

Figure 216. Concept of X Window system - Clients and servers communicating together.

Terminology:

X Server This is a dedicated program that provides display services on a graphic terminal, on behalf of a user, at the request of the user's X client program. It controls the screen and handles the keyboard and the mouse (or other input devices) for one or more X clients. Equally, it is responsible for output to the display, the mapping of colors, the loading of fonts and the keyboard mapping. Typically X server programs run on high-performance graphic PCs and workstations, as well as X terminals, which are designed to run only the X server program.

An X Font Service protocol is available to allow the X servers to delegate the task of managing fonts to a font server. The X11R6.4 X server supports LBX, security, printing and AddGroup extensions.

X Client	This is the actual *application* and is designed to employ a graphical user interface to display its output. Typically, many X clients compete for the service of one X server per display per user. Conflict for services are resolved by the X Window Manager, a separate entity altogether. *Xterm* and *Xclock* are two examples of X clients.
	Since the X11R6 release, X client uses the MIT-KERBEROS-5 authorization scheme. Once the connection is established, Xdm initiates the authentication over Xlib to authorize the client to the server.
X Window Manager	This is an X client program usually located on the workstation where the X server runs. While windows can be created without a window manager in place, a window manager permits windows to be resized, moved, and otherwise modified on demand.
X Protocol	This runs within the network connection, and allows requests and responses between client and server. It uses a reliable byte stream connection (that is TCP) and describes the format of messages exchanged between client and server over this connection.
Xlib	The rudimentary application programming interface is contained in the Xlib. It is a collection of C primitive subroutines embedded in all X clients, which gives the lowest level access to the X protocol. The procedures in Xlib translate client requests to X protocol requests, parse incoming messages (events, replies, and errors) from the X server, and provide several additional utilities, such as storage management and operating system-independent operations. It is possible to write application programs entirely with Xlib. In fact, most existing X clients are or were developed in this fashion. Other significant functions of Xlib are device-independent color, international languages, local customs and character string encodings support.
X Toolkits	The complexity of the low-level Xlib interface and of the underlying X protocol is handled by an increasing variety of available X *toolkits*. The X toolkits are

software libraries that provide high-level facilities for implementing common user-interface *objects* such as buttons, menus, and scroll bars, as well as layout tools for organizing these objects on the display. The basis for a family of toolkits is provided with the standard X releases from MIT. The library, called the X Intrinsics or Xt, forms the building blocks for sets of user interface objects called *widgets*.

Widgets

For toolkits based on the X Intrinsics, a common interface mechanism called a *widget* is used. A widget is essentially an X window plus some additional data and a set of procedures for operating on that data. Widgets are a client-side notion only. Neither the X server nor the X protocol understand widgets. A sample widget set, *Xaw*, more commonly referred to as the *Athena Widget Set*, is distributed by MIT with the X11 source.

16.2.1.1 Functionality

The following paragraphs outline the functional operation of the X Window System.

- X client and X server can be on different hosts. Then they use the TCP/IP protocol to communicate over the network. They can also be on the same machine, using IPC (inter-process communication) to communicate (through sockets).

- There is only one X server per terminal. Multiple X client applications can communicate with this one X server. The duty of the X server is to display the application windows and to send the user input to the appropriate X client application.

- It is up to the X client to maintain the windows that it created. It is notified by *events* from the X server whenever something is changed on the display by other clients. However, they don't have to care about which part of their windows are visible when they are drawing or redrawing their windows.

- The X server keeps track of the visibility of the windows, by maintaining *stacks*. A stack contains all "first generation" children of a parent window. A child window can also be a parent window by having one or more child windows itself, which are again held in a *substack*. The *primary stack* is the stack that holds all the windows located directly below the root. See Figure 217 for an illustration. Subwindows can only be fully visible when their parent is on the top of its respective stack and mapped to the display.

- X server itself has no management functions; it only performs window clipping according to its stacks. Every client is responsible for its own windows. There is a *window manager* which manipulates the top-level windows of all the clients. The window manager is not part of the X server but is itself a client. As soon as the window manager changes something on the screen (for instance, resizing a window), it makes the X server send out an exposure event to all the other clients.

- The client applications send *request messages* to the X server, which replies with a *reply message* or an *error message*. The X server can also send *event messages* to the applications. Event messages indicate changes to the windows (and their visibility), and user input (mouse and keyboard).

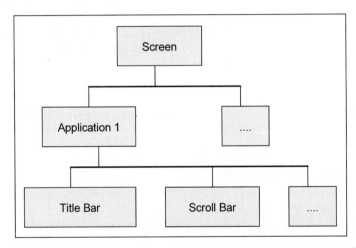

Figure 217. X Window system window structure - each window is a child of another window

Applying this client/server concept gives the following advantages:

- Applications don't have to know the hardware characteristics of the terminal.

- Applications don't have to be on the same computer as the terminal.

- Programs written to Xlib are portable.

- New terminal types can be added by providing an appropriate X server.

- The programmers do not have to deal with the communications. They just write graphic applications to Xlib, regardless of whether the users will be remote or local.

16.2.2 Protocol

An X Window System protocol can be implemented on top of any reliable byte stream transport mechanism. It uses a simple block protocol on top of the stream layer. Four kinds of messages are used:

- Request format: Requests flow from the client application to the X server.

major	length	minor	data

Figure 218. X Window request format

Where:

- Major and minor are opcodes, each 1-byte long.

- Length is 2-bytes long.

- Data can be zero or more bytes, depending on the request.

- Reply format: 32-byte block.

- Error format: 32-byte block.

- Event format: 32-byte block.

Reply, error and event messages are sent by the X server to the X client applications.

Displays are always numbered from zero. For TCP connections, display number N is associated with port 5800+N (hex 5800) and port 5900+N. The X server treats connections on the 58xx ports as connections with hosts that use the low-order byte first format, and the 59xx ports as high-order byte first.

There are more than a hundred different possible requests, each corresponding to an Xlib application call. As this document is not a programmer's guide, we will not deal with the Xlib functions. RFC 1013 – X Window System Protocol, Version 11 contains the 1987 alpha update of the X11 protocol. For documentation on the current release X11R6, please contact either MIT or a commercial computer books publisher.

16.3 Network News Transfer Protocol (NNTP)

One application that is particularly popular on the Internet is Network News, also known as Usenet News. Based on the Network News Transfer Protocol (NNTP), users on the Internet can view and contribute to news groups covering topics such as science, education, computers, business, politics, recreation, sports, and many more. News groups are stored on news servers. NNTP is used for both server-to-server and client-to-server communication.

- Clients use a news agent application, such as the IBM NewsReader/2, to retrieve articles from one or more news groups, and to post articles to one or more news groups. For more information about NNTP, see RFC 977 – Network News Transfer Protocol

16.4 Finger protocol

Finger is a draft-standard protocol. Its status is elective. The current finger specification can be found in RFC 1288 – The Finger User Information Protocol.

The `finger` command displays information about users of a remote host. `finger` is a UNIX command. Its format is:

```
finger user@host
```
or
```
finger @host
```

The information provided by the `finger` command about a user depends on the implementation of the finger server. If a user is not specified, the information will typically be a list of all users currently logged on to this host.

Connections are established through TCP port 79 (decimal). The client sends an ASCII command string, ending with <CRLF>. The server responds with one or more ASCII strings, until the server closes the connection.

16.5 Netstat

The `netstat` command is used to query TCP/IP about the network status of the local host. The exact syntax of this command is very implementation-dependent. See the *User's Guide* or the *Command Reference Manual* of your implementation for full details. It is a useful tool for debugging purposes.

In general, `netstat` will provide information on:

- Active TCP connections at this local host
- State of all TCP/IP servers on this local host and the sockets used by them
- Devices and links used by TCP/IP

• The IP routing tables (gateway tables) in use at this local host

The `netstat` command is implemented in all IBM software TCP/IP products.

Part 3. Advanced concepts and new technologies

Chapter 17. IP Version 6

The Internet is growing extremely rapidly. The latest Internet Domain Survey[1], conducted in January 2000, counted over 109.5 million hosts. The IPv4 addressing scheme, with a 32-bit address field, provides for over 4 billion possible addresses, so it might seem more than adequate to the task of addressing all of the hosts on the Internet, since there appears to be room to accommodate 40 times as many Internet hosts. Unfortunately, this is not the case for a number of reasons, including the following:

- An IP address is divided into a network portion and a local portion which are administered separately. Although the address space within a network may be very sparsely filled, allocating a portion of the address space (range of IP addresses) to a particular administrative domain makes all addresses within that range unavailable for allocation elsewhere.

- The address space for networks is structured into Class A, B, and C networks of differing sizes, and the space within each needs to be considered separately.

- The IP addressing model requires that unique network numbers be assigned to all IP networks, whether or not they are actually connected to the Internet.

- It is anticipated that growth of TCP/IP usage into new areas outside the traditional connected PC will shortly result in a rapid explosion of demand for IP addresses. For example, widespread use of TCP/IP for interconnecting hand-held devices, electronic point-of-sale terminals or for Web-enabled television receivers (all devices that are now available) will enormously increase the number of IP hosts.

These factors mean that the address space is much more constrained than our simple analysis would indicate. This problem is called *IP Address Exhaustion*. Methods of relieving this problem are already being employed, but eventually, the present IP address space will be exhausted. The Internet Engineering Task Force (IETF) set up a working group on *Address Lifetime Expectations (ALE)* with the express purpose of providing estimates of when exhaustion of the IP will become an intractable problem. Their final estimates (reported in the ALE working group minutes for December 1994) were that the IP address space would be exhausted at some point between 2005 and 2011. Since then, their position may have changed somewhat, in that the use of CIDR (Classless Inter Domain Routing - see 3.1.7, "Classless Inter-Domain Routing (CIDR)" on page 86) and the increased use of DHCP

---

[1] Source: Internet Software Consortium (http://www.isoc.org/)

may have relieved pressure on the address space, but on the other hand, current growth rates are probably exceeding that expectation.

Apart from address exhaustion, other restrictions in IPv4 also call for the definition of a new IP protocol:

1. Even with the use of CIDR, routing tables, primarily in the IP backbone routers, are growing too large to be manageable.

2. Traffic priority, or class of service, is vaguely defined, scarcely used, and not at all enforced in IPv4, but highly desirable for modern real-time applications.

In view of these issues, the IETF established an IPng (IP next generation) working group and published RFC 1752 –The Recommendation for the IP Next Generation Protocol. Eventually, the specification for Internet Protocol, Version 6 (IPv6) was produced in RFC 1883. It has since been obsoleted by RFC 2460.

17.1 IPv6 overview

IPv6 offers the following significant features:

- A dramatically larger address space, which is said to be sufficient for at least the next 30 years

- Globally unique and hierarchical addressing, based on prefixes rather than address classes, to keep routing tables small and backbone routing efficient

- A mechanism for the autoconfiguration of network interfaces

- Support for encapsulation of itself and other protocols

- Class of service that distinguishes types of data

- Improved multicast routing support (in preference to broadcasting)

- Built-in authentication and encryption

- Transition methods to migrate from IPv4

- Compatibility methods to coexist and communicate with IPv4

17.2 The IPv6 header format

The format of the IPv6 packet header has been simplified from its counterpart in IPv4. The length of the IPv6 header is increased to 40 bytes (from 20 bytes) and contains two 16-byte addresses (source and destination), preceded by 8 bytes of control information, as shown in Figure 219. The IPv4 header (see Figure 27 on page 91) has two 4-byte addresses preceded by 12 bytes of control information and possibly followed by option data. The reduction of the control information and the elimination of options in the header for most IP packets are intended to optimize the processing time per packet in a router. The infrequently used fields that have been removed from the header are moved to optional extension headers when they are required.

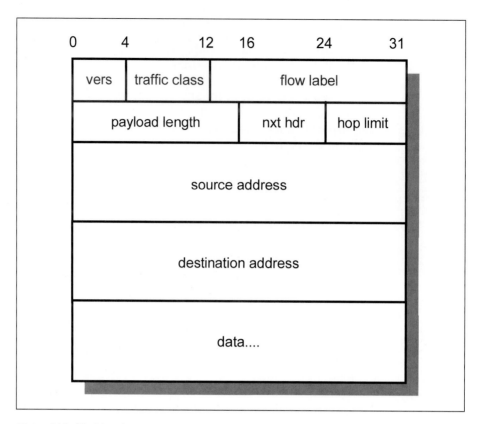

0	4	12	16	24	31

vers | traffic class | flow label

payload length | nxt hdr | hop limit

source address

destination address

data....

Figure 219. IPv6 header

Where:

Vers
4-bit Internet Protocol version number: 6.

Traffic class
8-bit traffic class value. See 17.2.4, "Traffic class" on page 578.

Flow label
20-bit field. See 17.2.5, "Flow labels" on page 579 below.

Payload length
The length of the packet in bytes (excluding this header) encoded as a 16-bit unsigned integer. If length is greater than 64 KB, this field is 0 and an option header (Jumbo Payload) gives the true length.

Next header
Indicates the type of header immediately following the basic IP header. It may indicate an IP option header or an upper layer protocol. The protocol numbers used are the same as those used in IPv4 (see the list in 3.1,

"Internet Protocol (IP)" on page 65). The next header field is also used to indicate the presence of extension headers, which provide the mechanism for appending optional information to the IPv6 packet. The following values will appear in IPv6 packets, in addition to those mentioned for IPv4.

41 IPv6 Header
45 Interdomain Routing Protocol
46 Resource Reservation Protocol
58 IPv6 ICMP Packet

The following values are all extension headers:

0 Hop-by-Hop Options Header
43 IPv6 Routing Header
44 IPv6 Fragment Header
50 Encapsulating Security Payload
51 IPv6 Authentication Header
59 No Next Header
60 Destination Options Header

The different types of extension header are discussed in 17.2.2, "Extension headers" on page 565.

Hop limit   This is the IPv4 TTL field but it is now measured in hops and not seconds. It was changed for two reasons:

- IP normally forwards datagrams faster than one hop per second and the TTL field is always decremented on each hop, so, in practice, it is measured in hops and not seconds.

- Many IP implementations do not expire outstanding datagrams on the basis of elapsed time.

The packet is discarded once the hop limit is decremented to zero.

Source address   A 128-bit address. IPv6 addresses are discussed in 17.2.3, "IPv6 addressing" on page 572.

Destination address A 128-bit address. IPv6 addresses are discussed in 17.2.3, "IPv6 addressing" on page 572.

A comparison between the IPv4 and IPv6 header formats will show that a number of IPv4 header fields have no direct equivalents in the IPv6 header.

- Type of Service

  Type of service issues in IPv6 will be handled using the *flow* concept, described in 17.2.5, "Flow labels" on page 579.

- Identification, Fragmentation Flags, and Fragment Offset

  Fragmented packets have an extension header rather than fragmentation information in the IPv6 header. This reduces the size of the basic IPv6 header. Since higher level protocols, particularly TCP, tend to avoid fragmentation of datagrams (this reduces the IPv6 header overhead for the normal case). As noted below, IPv6 does not fragment packets en route to their destinations, only at the source.

- Header Checksum

  Because transport protocols implement checksums, and because IPv6 includes an optional authentication header that can also be used to ensure integrity, IPv6 does *not* provide checksum monitoring of IP packets.

  Both TCP and UDP include a pseudo IP header in the checksums they use, so in these cases, the IP header in IPv4 is being checked twice.

  TCP and UDP, and any other protocols using the same checksum mechanisms running over IPv6, will continue to use a pseudo IP header although, obviously, the format of the pseudo IPv6 header will be different from the pseudo IPv4 header. ICMP, IGMP, and any other protocols that do not use a pseudo IP header over IPv4 will use a pseudo IPv6 header in their checksums.

- Options

  All optional values associated with IPv6 packets are contained in extension headers, ensuring that the basic IP header is always the same size.

17.2.1 Packet sizes

All IPv6 nodes are expected to dynamically determine the maximum transmission unit (MTU) supported by all links along a path (as described in RFC 1191 – Path MTU Discovery) and source nodes will only send packets that do not exceed the Path MTU. IPv6 routers will therefore not have to fragment packets in the middle of multihop routes and allow much more efficient use of paths that traverse diverse physical transmission media. IPv6 requires that every link supports an MTU of 1280 bytes or greater.

17.2.2 Extension headers

Every IPv6 packet starts with the basic header. In most cases, this will be the only header necessary to deliver the packet. Sometimes, however, it is necessary for additional information to be conveyed along with the packet to the destination or to intermediate systems on route (information that would previously have been carried in the Options field in an IPv4 datagram). Extension headers are used for this purpose.

Extension headers are placed immediately after the IPv6 basic packet header and are counted as part of the payload length. Each extension header (with the exception of 59) has its own 8-bit *Next Header field* as the first byte of the header that identifies the type of the following header. This structure allows IPv6 to chain multiple extension headers together. Figure 220 shows an example packet with multiple extension headers.

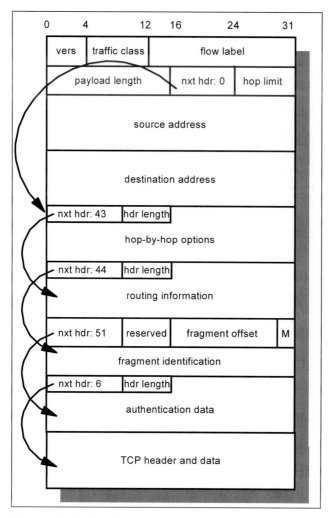

Figure 220. IPv6 packet containing multiple extension headers

The length of each header varies, depending on type, but is always a multiple of 8 bytes. There are a limited number of IPv6 extension headers, any one of which may be present only once in the IPv6 packet (with the exception of the Destination Options Header - 60, which may appear more than once). IPv6 nodes that originate packets are required to place extension headers in a specific order (numeric order, with the exception of 60), although IPv6 nodes that receive packets are not required to verify that this is the case. The order is important for efficient processing at intermediate routers. Routers will generally only be interested in the hop-by-hop options and the routing header. Once the router has read this far, it does not need to read further in the packet and can immediately forward. When the Next Header field contains a value other than one for an extension header, this indicates the end of the IPv6 headers and the start of the higher level protocol data.

IPv6 allows for encapsulation of IPv6 within IPv6 ("tunneling"). This is done with a Next Header value of 41 (IPv6). The encapsulated IPv6 packet may have its own extension headers. Because the size of a packet is calculated by the originating node to match the path MTU, IPv6 routers should not add extension headers to a packet, but instead should encapsulate the received packet within an IPv6 packet of their own making (which may be fragmented, if necessary).

With the exception of the Hop-by-Hop header (which must immediately follow the IP header if present) and, sometimes, the Destination Options header (see 17.2.2.6, "Destination options header" on page 572), extension headers are not processed by any router on the packet's path except the final one.

17.2.2.1 Hop-by-hop header

A Hop-by-hop header contains options that must be examined by every node the packet traverses, as well as the destination node. It must immediately follow the IPv6 header (if present) and is identified by the special value 0 in the Next Header field of the IPv6 basic header. (This value is not actually a protocol number but a special case to identify this unique type of extension header).

Hop-by-hop headers contain variable length options of the following format (commonly known as the *Type-Length-Value (TLV)* format):

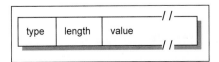

Figure 221. IPv6 Type-ILngth-Value (TLV) option format

Where:

Type   The type of the option. The option types all have a common format:

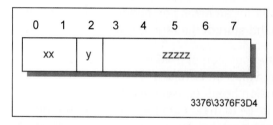

Figure 222. IPv6 Type-Length-Value (TLV) option type format

Where:

xx   A 2-bit number, indicating how an IPv6 node that does not recognize the option should treat it:

      0   Skip the option and continue.

      1   Discard the packet quietly.

      2   Discard the packet and inform the sender with an ICMP Unrecognized Type message.

      3   Discard the packet and inform the sender with an ICMP Unrecognized Type message unless the destination address is a multicast address.

y   If set, this bit indicates that the value of the option may change en route. If this bit is set, the entire Option Data field is excluded from any integrity calculations performed on the packet.

zzzzz   The remaining bits define the option:

      0   Pad1
      1   PadN
      194   Jumbo Payload Length

Length   The length of the option value field in bytes.

Value   The value of the option. This is dependent on the type.

Hop-by-hop header option types

You may have noticed that each extension header is an integer multiple of 8 bytes long, in order to retain 8-byte alignment for subsequent headers. This is done, not purely for "neatness," but because processing is much more efficient if multibyte values are positioned on natural boundaries in memory (and today's processors have natural word sizes of 32 or 64 bits).

In the same way, individual options are also aligned so that multibyte values are positioned on their natural boundaries. In many cases, this will result in the option headers being longer than otherwise necessary, but still allow nodes to process packets more quickly. To allow this alignment, two padding options are used in Hop-by-Hop headers.

Pad1   A X'00' byte used for padding a single byte. Longer padding sequences should be done with the PadN option.

PadN   An option in the TLV format (described above). The length byte gives the number of bytes of padding after the minimum two that are required.

The third option type in a Hop-by-Hop header is the *Jumbo Payload Length*. This option is used to indicate a packet with a payload size in excess of 65,535 bytes (which is the maximum size that can be specified by the 16-bit Payload Length field in the IPv6 basic header). When this option is used, the Payload Length in the basic header must be set to zero. This option carries the total packet size, less the 40 byte basic header. See Figure 225 for details.

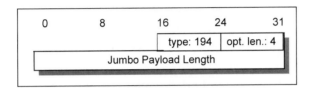

Figure 223. Jumbo payload length option

17.2.2.2 Routing header

The path that a packet takes through the network is normally determined by the network itself. Sometimes, however, the source may wish to have more control over the route taken by the packet. It may wish, for example, for certain data to take a slower but more secure route than would normally be taken. The routing header (see Figure 224) allows a path through the network to be predefined. The routing header is identified by the value 43 in the preceding Next Header field. It has its next header field as the first byte and a single byte routing type as the second byte. The only type defined initially is type 0 - Strict/Loose Source Routing, which operates in a similar way to source routing in IPv4 (see 3.1.8.3, "IP datagram routing options" on page 97).

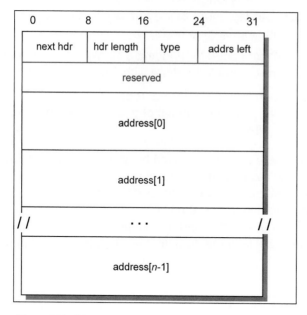

Figure 224. IPv6 routing header

Where:

Next hdr   The type of header after this one.

Hdr length   Length of this routing header, not including the first 8 bytes.

Type   Type of routing header. Currently, this can only have the value 0, meaning Strict/Loose Source Routing.

Segments left   Number of route segments remaining, that is, number of explicitly listed intermediate nodes still to be visited before reaching the final destination.

Address 1..n   A series of 16-byte IPv6 addresses that comprise the source route.

The first hop on the required path of the packet is indicated by the destination address in the basic header of the packet. When the packet arrives at this address, the router swaps the next address from the router extension header with the destination address in the basic header. The router also decrements the segments left field by one, then forwards the packet.

17.2.2.3 Fragment header

As discussed in 17.2.1, "Packet sizes" on page 564, the source node determines the MTU for a path before sending a packet. If the packet to be sent is larger than the MTU, the packet is divided into pieces, each of which is a multiple of 8 bytes and carries a fragment header. The fragment header is identified by the value 44 in the preceding Next Header field and has the following format:

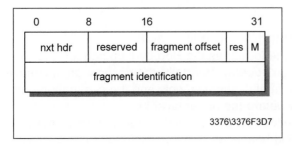

Figure 225. IPv6 fragment header

Where:

Nxt hdr   The type of next header after this one.

Reserved   8-bit reserved field; initialized to zero for transmission and ignored on reception.

Fragment offset   A 13-bit unsigned integer giving the offset, in 8-byte units, of the following data relative to the start of the original data before it was fragmented.

Res   2-bit reserved field; initialized to zero for transmission and ignored on reception.

M   More flag. If set, it indicates that this is not the last fragment.

Fragment identification   This is an unambiguous identifier used to identify fragments of the same datagram. This is very similar to the IPv4 Identifier field, but it is twice as wide.

17.2.2.4 Authentication header

The authentication header is used to ensure that a received packet has not been altered in transit and that it really came from the claimed sender. The authentication header is identified by the value 51 in the preceding Next Header field. The format of the authentication header and further details on authentication can be found in 21.5.2, "Authentication Header (AH)" on page 702.

17.2.2.5 Encapsulating Security Payload

The Encapsulated Security Payload (ESP) is a special extension header, in that it can appear anywhere in a packet between the basic header and the upper layer protocol. All data following the ESP header is encrypted. For further details, please see 21.5.3, "Encapsulating Security Payload (ESP)" on page 708.

17.2.2.6 Destination options header

This has the same format as the Hop-by-Hop header, but it is only examined by the destination node(s). Normally, the destination options are only intended for the final destination only and the destination options header will be immediately before the upper layer header. However, destination options can also be intended for intermediate nodes, in which case they must precede a routing header. A single packet may therefore include two destination options headers. Currently, only the Pad1 and PadN types of options are specified for this header (see 17.2.2.1, "Hop-by-hop header" on page 567). The value for the preceding Next Header field is 60.

17.2.3 IPv6 addressing

The IPv6 address model is specified in RFC 2373 – IP Version 6 Addressing Architecture. IPv6 uses a 128-bit address instead of the 32-bit address of IPv4. That theoretically allows for as many as 340,282,366,920,938,463,463,374,607,431,768,211,456 addresses. Even when used with the same efficiency as today's IPv4 address space, that would still allow for 50,000 addresses per square meter of land on Earth.

IPv6 addresses are represented in the form of eight hexadecimal numbers divided by colons, for example:

```
FE80:0000:0000:0000:0001:0800:23e7
:f5db
```

To shorten the notation of addresses, leading zeroes in any of the groups can be omitted, for example:

```
FE80:0:0:0:1:800:23e7:f5db
```

Finally, a group of all zeroes, or consecutive groups of all zeroes, can be substituted by a double colon, for example:

```
FE80::1:800:23e7:f5db
```

> **Note:**
>
> The double colon shortcut can be used only once in the notation of an IPv6 address. If there are more groups of all zeroes that are not consecutive, only one may be substituted by the double colon; the others would have to be noted as 0.

The IPv6 address space is organized using format prefixes, similar to telephone country and area codes, that logically divide it in the form of a tree, so that a route from one network to another can easily be found. The following prefixes have been assigned so far:

Table 24. :IPv6 - Format prefix allocation

Allocation	Prefix (bin)	Start of address range (hex)	Mask length (bits)	Fraction of address space
Reserved	0000 0000	0:: /8	8	1/256
Reserved for NSAP	0000 001	200:: /7	7	1/128
Reserved for IPX	0000 010	400:: /7	7	1/128
Aggregatable Global Unicast Addresses	001	2000:: /3	3	1/8
Link-local Unicast	1111 1110 10	FE80:: /10	10	1/1024
Site-local Unicast	1111 1110 11	FEC0:: /10	10	1/1024
Multicast	1111 1111	FF00:: /8	8	1/256
Total Allocation				15%

IPv6 defines the following types of addresses:

- Unicast Address

    A unicast address is an identifier assigned to a single interface. Packets sent to that address will only be delivered to that interface. Special purpose unicast addresses are defined as follows:

- Loopback address (::1): This address is assigned to a virtual interface over which a host can send packets only to itself. It is equivalent to the IPv4 loopback address 127.0.0.1.

- Unspecified address (::):This address is used as a source address by hosts while performing autoconfiguration. It is equivalent to the IPv4 unspecified address 0.0.0.0.

- IPv4-compatible address (::<IPv4_address>): Addresses of this kind are used when IPv6 traffic needs to be tunneled across existing IPv4 networks. The endpoint of such tunnels can be either hosts (automatic tunneling) or routers (configured tunneling). IPv4-compatible addresses are formed by placing 96 bits of zero in front of a valid 32-bit IPv4 address. For example, the address 1.2.3.4 (hex 01.02.03.04) becomes ::0102:0304.

- IPv4-mapped address (::FFFF:<IPv4_address>): Addresses of this kind are used when an IPv6 host needs to communicate with an IPv4 host. This requires a dual stack host or router for header translations. For example, if an IPv6 node wishes to send data to host with an IPv4 address of 1.2.3.4, it uses a destination address of ::FFFF:0102:0304.

- Link-local address: Addresses of this kind can be used only on the physical network that a host's interface is attached to.

- Site-local address: Addresses of this kind cannot be routed into the Internet. They are the equivalent of IPv4 networks for private use (10.0.0.0, 176.16.0.0-176.31.0.0, 192.168.0.0-192.168.255.0).

- Global Unicast Address Format

  The Global Unicast address format, as specified in RFC 2374 – An IPv6 Aggregatable Global Unicast Address *Format* is expected to become the predominant format used for IPv6 nodes connected to the Internet. The aggregatable address can be split into three sections that relate to the three-level hierarchy of the Internet, namely:

  - Public Topology: Providers and exchanges that provide public Internet transit services.

  - Site Topology: Local to an organization that does not provide public transit service to nodes outside of the site.

  - Interface Identifiers: Identify interfaces on links.

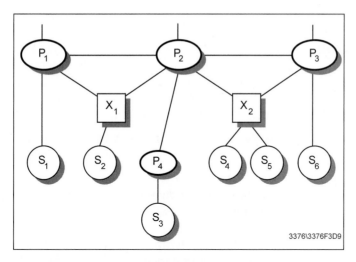

Figure 226. Global unicast address format - three-level hierarchy

The Global Unicast Address Format is designed for the infrastructure shown in Figure 226. P1, P2, and P3 are backbone providers. P4 is a smaller provider that obtains services from P2. Exchanges (X1 and X2), which are analogous to exchanges in a telephone network, will allocate addresses. Subscribers (S1-S6) have the choice of connecting directly to a provider or to an exchange (in which case they must also subscribe to a provider for backbone service). Organizations connecting via an exchange have the flexibility to be able to change their backbone provider without having to change their IP addresses.

The format of the aggregatable global unicast address is shown in Figure 227.

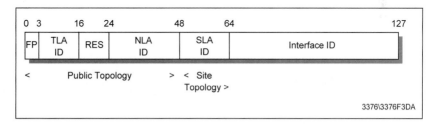

Figure 227. Global unicast address format

Where:

FP   Format Prefix (001).

TLA ID   Top-Level Aggregation Identifier. These are the top level in the routing hierarchy. Internet top-level routers will need a routing table entry for every active TLA ID. This will be a maximum of 8,192 entries, which compares with around 50,000 entries in today's IPv4 top-level routers.

RES   Reserved for future use. This will allow growth in the number of either TLA IDs or NLA IDs in the future (if this becomes necessary).

NLA ID   Next-Level Aggregation Identifier. Used by organizations assigned a TLA ID (who may be providers) to create their own addressing hierarchy and to identify sites. The 24-bit NLA ID space allows each organization to provide service to as many sites as the current total number of networks supported by IPv4.

SLA ID   Site-Level Aggregation Identifier. This field is used by an individual organization to create its own local addressing hierarchy. The 16-bit field allows for up to 65,535 individual subnets.

- Multicast Address

  A multicast address is an identifier assigned to a set of interfaces on multiple hosts. Packets sent to that address will be delivered to all interfaces corresponding to that address. (See 6.2, "Internet Group Management Protocol (IGMP)" on page 232 for more information on IP multicasting.) There are no broadcast addresses in IPv6, their function being superseded by multicast addresses. Figure 228 shows the format of an IPv6 multicast address:

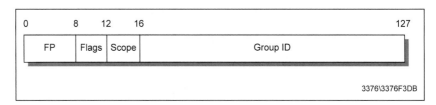

Figure 228. IPv6 multicast address format

Where:

FP   Format Prefix - 1111 1111.

Flags   Set of four flag bits. Only the low order bit currently has any meaning, as follows:

          0000 Permanent address assigned by a numbering authority.

          0001 Transient address. Addresses of this kind can be established by applications as required. When the application ends, the address will be released by the application and can be reused.

Scope   4-bit value indicating the scope of the multicast. Possible values are:

          0 Reserved
          1 Confined to interfaces on the local node (node-local)
          2 Confined to nodes on the local link (link-local)
          5 Confined to the local site
          8 Confined to the organization
          E Global scope
          F Reserved

Group ID Identifies the multicast group.

          For example, if the NTP servers group is assigned a permanent multicast address, with a group ID of &hex.101, then:

- FF02::101 means all NTP servers on the same link as the sender.

- FF05::101 means all NTP servers on the same site as the sender.

Certain special purpose multicast addresses are pre-defined as follows:

FF01::1   All interfaces node-local. Defines all interfaces on the host itself.

FF02::1   All nodes link-local. Defines all systems on the local network.

FF01::2   All routers node-local. Defines all routers local to the host itself.

FF02::2   All routers link-local. Defines all routers on the same link as the host.

FF05::2   All routers site-local. Defines all routers on the same site as the host.

FF02::B   Mobile agents link-local.

FF02::1:2 All DHCP agents link-local.

FF05::1:3 All DHCP servers site-local.

A more complete listing of reserved multicast addresses may be found in RFC 2375 – IPv6 Multicast Address Assignments.

This RFC also defines a special multicast address known as the *solicited node address*, which has the format FF02::1:FFxx:xxxx, where xx xxxx is taken from the last 24-bits of a nodes unicast address. For example, the node with the IPv6 address of 4025::01:800:100F:7B5B belongs to the multicast group FF02::1:FF 0F:7B5B. The solicited node address is used by ICMP for neighbor discovery and to detect duplicate addresses. Please see 17.3, "Internet Control Message Protocol Version 6 (ICMPv6)" on page 579 for further details.

- Anycast address

An anycast address is a special type of unicast address that is assigned to interfaces on multiple hosts. Packets sent to such an address will be delivered to the nearest interface with that address. Routers determine the nearest interface based upon their definition of distance, for example, hops in case of RIP or link state in case of OSPF.

Anycast addresses use the same format as unicast addresses and are indistinguishable from them. However, a node that has been assigned an anycast address must be configured to be aware of this fact.

RFC 2373 currently specifies the following restrictions on anycast addresses:

  - An anycast address must not be used as the source address of a packet.

  - Any anycast address may only be assigned to a router

A special anycast address, the *subnet-router address*, is predefined. This address consists of the subnet prefix for a particular subnet followed by trailing zeroes. This address may be used when a node needs to contact a router on a particular subnet and it does not matter which router is reached (for example, when a mobile node needs to communicate with one of the mobile agents on its "home" subnet).

17.2.4 Traffic class

The 8-bit traffic class field allows applications to specify a certain priority for the traffic they generate, thus introducing the concept of *Class of Service*. This enables the prioritization of packets, as in Differentiated Services. For a comparison of how priority traffic may be handled in an IPv4 network, please see 22.1, "Why QoS?" on page 781.

17.2.5 Flow labels

IPv6 introduces the concept of a *flow*, which is a series of related packets from a source to a destination that requires a particular type of handling by the intervening routers, for example, real-time service. The nature of that handling can either be conveyed by options attached to the datagrams (that is, by using the IPv6 Hop-by-Hop options header) or by a separate protocol (such as resource reservation protocol; see 22.2.2, "The Resource Reservation Protocol (RSVP)" on page 790). The handling requirement for a particular flow label is known as the *state information*; this is cached at the router. When packets with a known flow label arrive at the router, the router can efficiently decide how to route and forward the packets without having to examine the rest of the header for each packet.

There may be multiple active flows between a source and a destination, as well as traffic that is not associated with any flow. Each flow is distinctly labelled by the 24-bit flow label field in the IPv6 packet. See RFC 2460 and RFC 1809 for further details on the use of the flow label.

17.3 Internet Control Message Protocol Version 6 (ICMPv6)

The IP protocol concerns itself with moving data from one node to another. However, in order for IP to perform this task successfully, there are many other functions that need to be carried out: error reporting, route discovery, and diagnostics, to name a few. All these tasks are carried out by the Internet Control Message Protocol (see 3.2, "Internet Control Message Protocol (ICMP)" on page 102). In addition, ICMPv6 carries out the tasks of conveying multicast group membership information, a function that was previously performed by the IGMP protocol in IPv4 (see 6.2, "Internet Group Management Protocol (IGMP)" on page 232) and address resolution, previously performed by ARP (see 3.4, "Address Resolution Protocol (ARP)" on page 114).

ICMPv6 messages and their use are specified in RFC 2463 – Internet Control Message Protocol (ICMPv6) for the Internet Protocol Version 6 (IPv6) Specification and RFC 2461 – Neighbor Discovery for IP Version 6 (IPv6). Both RFCs are draft standards with a status of elective.

Every ICMPv6 message is preceded by an IPv6 header (and possibly some IP extension headers). The ICMPv6 header is identified by a Next Header value of 58 in the immediately preceding header.

ICMPv6 messages all have a similar format, shown in Figure 229.

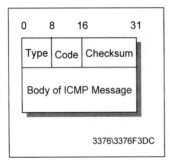

```
0   8    16        31

Type  Code  Checksum

Body of ICMP Message

                 3376\3376F3DC
```

Figure 229. ICMPv6 general message format

Where:

Type   There are two classes of ICMPv6 messages. Error messages have a Type from 0 to 127. Informational messages have a Type from 128 to 255.

1	Destination Unreachable
2	Packet Too Big
3	Time (Hop Count) Exceeded
4	Parameter Problem
128	Echo Request
129	Echo Reply
130	Group Membership Query
131	Group Membership Report
132	Group Membership Reduction
133	Router Solicitation
134	Router Advertisement
135	Neighbor Solicitation
136	Neighbor Advertisement
137	Redirect Message

Code   Varies according to message type.

Checksum   Used to detect data corruption in the ICMPv6 message and parts of the IPv6 header.

Body of message Varies according to message type.

For full details of ICMPv6 messages for all types, please refer to RFC 2463 and RFC 2461.

17.3.1 Neighbor discovery

Neighbor discovery is an ICMPv6 function that enables a node to identify other hosts and routers on its links. The node needs to know of at least one router, so that it knows where to forward packets if a target node is not on its local link. Neighbor discovery also allows a router to redirect a node to use a more appropriate router if the node has initially made an incorrect choice.

17.3.1.1 Address resolution

Figure 230 shows a simple Ethernet LAN segment with four IPv6 workstations.

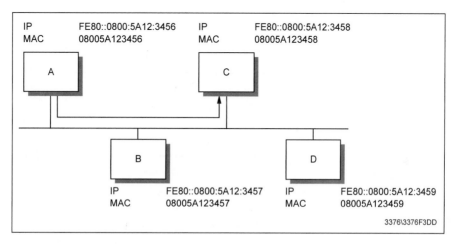

Figure 230. IPv6 address resolution

Workstation A needs to send data to workstation B. It knows the IPv6 address of workstation B, but it does not know how to send a packet, because it does not know its MAC address. To find this information, it sends a *neighbor solicitation* message, of the format shown in Figure 231.

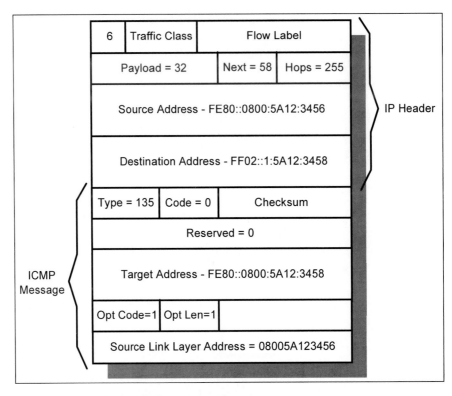

Figure 231. Neighbor solicitation message format

Notice the following important fields in the IP header of this packet:

Next   58 (for the following ICMP message header).

Hops   Any solicitation packet that does *not* have hops set to 255 is discarded; this ensures that the solicitation has not crossed a router.

Destination address This address is the *solicited node address* for the target workstation (a special type of multicast; see page 578). Every workstation *must* respond to its own solicited node address but other workstations will simply ignore it. This is an improvement over ARP in IPv4, which uses broadcast frames that have to be processed by every node on the link.

In the ICMP message itself, notice:

Type 135 (Neighbor Solicitation).

Target address This is the known IP address of the target workstation.

Source link layer address This is useful to the target workstation and saves it from having to initiate a neighbor discovery process of its own when it sends a packet back to the source workstation.

The response to the neighbor solicitation message is a *neighbor advertisement*, which has the following format:

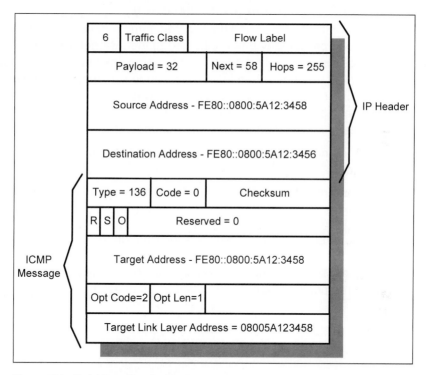

Figure 232. Neighbor advertisement message

The neighbor advertisement is addressed directly back to Workstation A. The ICMP message option contains the target IP address together with the target's link layer (MAC) address. Note also the following flags in the advertisement message:

R Router Flag. This bit is set on if the sender of the advertisement is a router.

S Solicited Flag. This bit is set on if the advertisement is in response to a solicitation.

O Override Flag. When this bit is set on, the receiving node must update an existing cached link layer entry in its neighbor cache.

Once Workstation A receives this packet, it commits the information to memory in its neighbor cache, then forwards the data packet that it originally wanted to send to Workstation C.

Neighbor advertisement messages may also be sent by a node to force updates to neighbor caches if it becomes aware that its link layer address has changed.

17.3.1.2 Router and prefix discovery

Figure 230 on page 581 shows a very simple network example. In a larger network, particularly one connected to the Internet, the neighbor discovery process is used to find nodes on the same link in exactly the same way. However, it is more than likely that a node will need to communicate, not just with other nodes on the same link, but with nodes on other network segments that may be anywhere in the world. In this case, there are two important pieces of information that a node needs to know:

1. The address of a router that the node can use to reach the rest of the world

2. The prefix (or prefixes) that define the range of IP addresses on the same link as the node that can be reached without going through a router.

Routers use ICMP to convey this information to hosts, by means of *router advertisements*. The format of the router advertisement message is shown in Figure 233. The message will generally have one or more attached options; all three possible options are shown in this example.

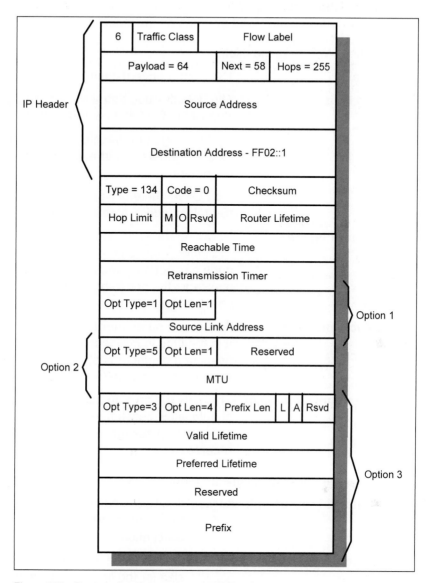

Figure 233. Router advertisement message format

Notice the following important fields in the IP header of this packet:

Next   58 (for the following ICMP message header).

Hops   Any advertisement packet that does *not* have hops set to 255 is discarded. This ensures that the packet has not crossed a router.

Destination address This address is the special multicast address defining all systems on the local link.

In the ICMP message itself:

Type   134 (router advertisement).

Hop limit   The default value that a node should place in the Hop Count field of its outgoing IP packets.

M   1-bit Managed Address Configuration Flag (see 17.3.2, "Stateless address autoconfiguration" on page 590).

O   1-bit Other Stateful Configuration Flag (see 17.3.2, "Stateless address autoconfiguration" on page 590).

Router lifetime   How long the node should consider this router to be available. If this time period is exceeded and the node has not received another router advertisement message, the node should consider this router to be unavailable.

Reachable time   This sets a parameter for all nodes on the local link. It is the time in milliseconds that the node should assume a neighbor is still reachable after having received a response to a neighbor solicitation.

Retransmission timer This sets the time, in milliseconds, that nodes should allow between retransmitting neighbor solicitation messages if no initial response is received.

The three possible options in a router advertisement message are:

Option 1 (source link address) Allows a receiving node to respond directly to the router without having to do a neighbor solicitation.

Option 5 (MTU)   Specifies the maximum transmission unit size for the link. For some media, such as Ethernet, this value is fixed, so this option is not necessary.

Option 3 (Prefix)   Defines the address prefix for the link. Nodes use this information to determine when they do, and do not, need to use a router. Prefix options used for this purpose have the L (link) bit set on. Prefix options are also used as part of address configuration, in which case the A bit is set on. Please see 17.3.2, "Stateless address autoconfiguration" on page 590 for further details.

A router constantly sends unsolicited advertisements at a frequency defined in the router configuration. A node may, however, wish to obtain information about the nearest router without having to wait for the next scheduled advertisement (for example, a new workstation that has just attached to the network). In this case, the node can send a *router solicitation message*. The format of the router solicitation message is shown in Figure 234.

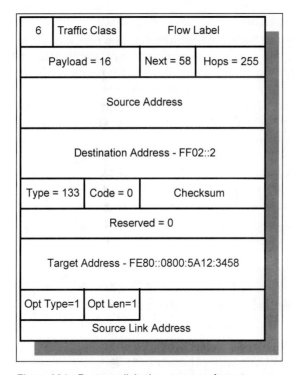

Figure 234. Router solicitation message format

Notice the following important fields in the IP header of this packet: break.

Next   58 (for the following ICMP message header).

Hops   Any advertisement packet that does *not* have hops set to 255 is discarded. This ensures that the packet has not crossed a router.

Destination address This address is the special multicast address defining all routers on the local link.

In the ICMP message itself:

Type 133 (Router Solicitation)

Option 1 (source link address) Allows the receiving router to respond directly to the node without having to do a neighbor solicitation.

Each router that receives the solicitation message responds with a router advertisement sent *directly* to the node that sent the solicitation (not to the all systems link-local multicast address).

17.3.1.3 Redirection

The router advertisement mechanism ensures that a node will always be aware of one or more routers through which it is able to connect to devices outside of its local links. However, in a situation where a node is aware of more than one router, it is likely that the default router selected when sending data will not always be the most suitable router to select for every packet. In this case, ICMPv6 allows for *redirection* to a more efficient path for a particular destination.

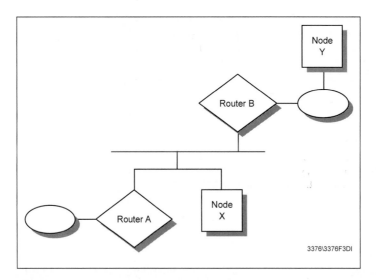

Figure 235. Redirection

Consider the simple example shown in Figure 235. Node X is aware of routers A and B, having received router advertisement messages from both.

Node X wishes to send data to Node Y. By comparing Node Y's IP address against the local link prefix, Node X knows that Node Y is not on the local link, and that it must therefore use a router. Node X selects router A from its list of default routers and forwards the packet. Obviously, this is not the most efficient path to Node Y. As soon as router A has forwarded the packet to Node Y (via router B), router A sends a *redirect* message to Node X. The format of the redirect message (complete with IP header) is shown in Figure 236.

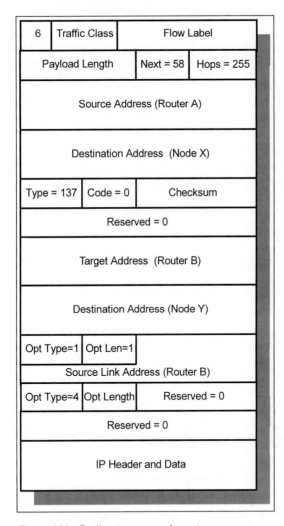

Figure 236. Redirect message format

The fields to note in the message are: break.

Type	137 (Redirect).
Target address	This is address of the router that should be used when trying to reach Node Y.
Destination address	Node Y's IP address.
Option 2 (target link layer address)	Gives link address of router B so that Node X can reach it without a neighbor solicitation.
Option 4 (redirected header)	Includes the original packet sent by node X, full IP header and as much of the data that will fit, so that the total size of the redirect message does not exceed 576 bytes.

17.3.1.4 Neighbor unreachability detection

An additional responsibility of the neighbor discovery function of ICMPv6 is *neighbor unreachability detection* (NUD).

A node actively tracks the reachability state of the neighbors to which it is sending packets. It may do this in two ways: either by monitoring the upper layer protocols to see if a connection is making forward progress (for example, TCP acknowledgments are being received), or it may issue specific neighbor solicitations to check that the path to a target host is still available. When a path to a neighbor appears to be failing, then appropriate action is taken to try and recover the link. This may include restarting the address resolution process or deletion of a neighbor cache entry, so that a new router may be tried in order to find a working path to the target.

NUD is used for all paths between nodes, including host-to-host, host-to-router, and router-to-host. NUD may also be used for router-to-router communication, if the routing protocol being used does not already include a similar mechanism. For further information on neighbor unreachability detection, please refer to RFC 2461.

17.3.2 Stateless address autoconfiguration

Although the 128-bit address field of IPv6 solves a number of problems inherent in IPv4, the size of the address itself represents a potential problem to the TCP/IP administrator. Because of this, IPv6 has been designed with the capability to automatically assign an address to an interface at initialization time, with the intention that a network can become operational with minimal to no action on the part of the TCP/IP administrator. IPv6 nodes will generally always use autoconfiguration to obtain their IPv6 address. This may be achieved using DHCP (see 17.5, "DHCP in IPv6" on page 598), which is known as *stateful* autoconfiguration, or by *stateless* autoconfiguration, which is a new feature of IPv6 and relies on ICMPv6.

The stateless autoconfiguration process is defined in RFC 2462 – IPv6 Stateless Address Autoconfiguration. It consists of the following steps:

1. During system startup, the node begins the autoconfiguration by obtaining an interface token from the interface hardware, for example, a 48-bit MAC address on token-ring or Ethernet networks.

2. The node creates a tentative link-local unicast address. This is done by combining the well-known link-local prefix (FE80::/10) with the interface token.

3. The node attempts to verify that this tentative address is unique by issuing a neighbor solicitation message with the tentative address as the target. If the address is already in use, the node will receive a neighbor advertisement in response, in which case the autoconfiguration process stops. (Manual configuration of the node is then required.)

4. If no response is received, the node assigns the link-level address to its interface. The host then sends one or more router solicitations to the all-routers multicast group. If there are any routers present, they will respond with a router advertisement. If no router advertisement is received, the node should attempt to use DHCP to obtain an address and configuration information. If no DHCP server responds, the node continues using the link-level address and can communicate with other nodes on the same link only.

5. If a router advertisement *is* received in response to the router solicitation, then this message contains several pieces of information that tells the node how to proceed with the autoconfiguration process (see Figure 233). break.

M flag   Managed address configuration

If this bit is set, the node should use DHCP to obtain its IP address.

O flag   Other stateful configuration.

If this bit is set then the node uses DHCP to obtain other configuration parameters.

Prefix option   If the router advertisement has a prefix option with the A bit (autonomous address configuration flag) set on, then the prefix is used for stateless address autoconfiguration.

6. If stateless address configuration is to be used, the prefix is taken from the router advertisement and added to the interface token to form the global unicast IP address, which is assigned to the network interface.

7. The working node will continue to receive periodic router advertisements. If the information in the advertisement changes, the node must take appropriate action.

Note that it is possible to use both stateless and stateful configuration simultaneously. It is quite likely that stateless configuration will be used to obtain the IP address, but DHCP will then be used to obtain further configuration information. However, plug-and-play configuration is possible in both small and large networks without the requirement for DHCP servers.

The stateless address configuration process, together with the fact that more than one address can be allocated to the same interface, also allows for the graceful renumbering of all the nodes on a site (for example, if a switch to a new network provider necessitates new addressing) without disruption to the network. For further details, please refer to RFC 2462.

17.3.3 Multicast Listener Discovery (MLD)

The process used by a router to discover the members of a particular multicast group is known as *Multicast Listener Discovery* (MLD). MLD is a subset of ICMPv6 and provides the equivalent function of IGMP for IPv4 (see 6.2, "Internet Group Management Protocol (IGMP)" on page 232). This information is then provided by the router to whichever multicast routing protocol is being used, so that multicast packets are correctly delivered to all links where there are nodes listening for the appropriate multicast address.

MLD is specified in RFC 2710 - Multicast Listener Discovery (MLD) for IPv6. MLD uses ICMPv6 messages of the format shown in Figure 237.

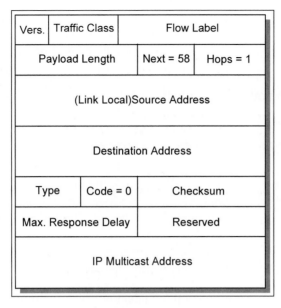

Vers.	Traffic Class	Flow Label	
Payload Length		Next = 58	Hops = 1
(Link Local)Source Address			
Destination Address			
Type	Code = 0	Checksum	
Max. Response Delay		Reserved	
IP Multicast Address			

Figure 237. MLD message format

Note the following fields in the IPv6 header of the message:

Next   58 (for the following ICMPv6 message header).

Hops   Always set to 1.

Source address   A link-local source address is used.

In the MLD message itself, notice:

Type   There are three types of MLD message:

                130   Multicast Listener Query

                      There are two types of queries:

                        • General queryUsed to find which multicast addresses are being listened for on a link.

                        • Multicast-address-specific queryUsed to find if any nodes are listening for a specific multicast address on a link.

                131   Multicast listener report

                      Used by a node to report that it is listening to a multicast address.

132	Multicast listener done
	Used by a node to report that it is ceasing to listen to a multicast address.
Code	Set to 0 by sender and ignored by receivers.
Max response delay	This sets the maximum allowed delay before a responding report must be sent. This parameter is only valid in query messages. Increasing this parameter can prevent sudden bursts of high traffic if there a lot of responders on a network.
Multicast address	In a query message, this field is set to zero for a general query, or set to the specific IPv6 multicast address for a multicast-address-specific query.
	In a response or done message, this field contains the multicast address being listened for.

A router users MLD to learn which multicast addresses are being listened for on each of its attached links. The router only needs to know that nodes listening for a particular address are present on a link; it does not need to know the unicast address of those listening nodes, or how many listening nodes are present.

A router periodically sends a General Query on each of its links to the all nodes link-local address (FF02::1). When a node listening for any multicast addresses receives this query, it sets a delay timer (which may be anything between 0 and maximum response delay) for each multicast address for which it is listening. As each timer expires, the node sends a *multicast listener report* message containing the appropriate multicast address. If a node receives another node's report for a multicast address while it has a timer still running for that address, then it stops its timer and does not send a report for that address. This prevents duplicate reports being sent and, together with the timer mechanism, prevents excess, or bursty traffic being generated.

The router manages a list of, and sets a timer for, each multicast address it is aware of on each of its links. If one of these timers expires without a report being received for that address, the router assumes that no nodes are still listening for that address, and the address is removed from the list. Whenever a report *is* received, the router resets the timer for that particular address.

When a node has finished listening to a multicast address, if it was the last node on a link to send a report to the router (that is, its timer delay was not interrupted by the receipt of another node's report), then it sends a *multicast listener done* message to the router. If the node *was* interrupted by another node before its timer expired, then it assumes that other nodes are still listening to the multicast address on the link and therefore does not send a done message.

When a router receives a done message, it sends a multicast-address-specific message on the link. If no report is received in response to this message, the router assumes that there are no nodes still listening to this multicast address and removes the address from its list.

17.4 DNS in IPv6

With the introduction of 128-bit addresses, IPv6 makes it even more difficult for the network user to be able to identify another network user by means of the IP address of his or her network device. The use of the Domain Name Service therefore becomes even more of a necessity (please see 8.1, "Domain Name System (DNS)" on page 279).

A number of extensions to DNS are specified to support the storage and retrieval of IPv6 addresses. These are defined in RFC 1886 – DNS Extensions to Support IP Version 6, which is a proposed standard with elective status. However, there is also work in progress on usability enhancements to this RFC, described in an Internet draft of the same name.

The following extensions are specified:

- A new resource record type, AAAA, which maps the domain name to the IPv6 address
- A new domain, which is used to support address-to-domain name lookups
- A change to the definition of existing queries, so that they will perform correct processing on both A and AAAA record types

17.4.1 Format of IPv6 resource records

RFC 1886 defines the format of the AAAA record as similar to an A resource record, but with the 128-bit IPv6 address encoded in the data section, and a Type value of 28 (decimal).

A special domain, IP6.INT, is defined for inverse (address-to-host name) lookups (similar to the *in-addr.arpa* domain used in IPv4). As in IPv4, the address must be entered in reverse order, but hexadecimal digits are used rather than decimal notation.

For example, the inverse domain name entry for the IPv6 address:

```
2222:0:1:2:3:4:5678:9abc
```

is:

```
c.b.a.9.8.7.6.5.4.0.0.0.3.0.0.0.2.0.0.0.1.0.0.0.0.0.0.0.2.2.2.2.IP6.INT.
```

So, if the above address relates to the node ND1.test.com, we might expect to see the following entries in the name server zone data:

```
$origin test.com.

ND1     99999 IN AAAA 2222:0:1:2:3:4:5678:9abc

cba98765400030002000100000002222.IP6.INT. IN  PTR ND1 [2]
```

17.4.1.1 Proposed changes to resource records

The IPv6 addressing system has been designed to allow for multiple addresses on a single interface and to facilitate address renumbering (for example, when company changes one of its service providers). Using the AAAA resource record format specified in RFC 1886 would require a major administrative effort in the event of a renumbering change. The current version of the Internet draft DNS Extensions to Support IP Version 6 proposes changes to the format of the AAAA resource record to simplify network renumbering.

The proposed format of the data section of the AAAA record is shown in Figure 238.

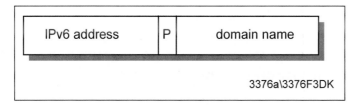

Figure 238. AAAA resource record - proposed data format

---

[2] All characters making up the reversed IPv6 address in this PTR entry should be separated by a period(.). These have been omitted in this example for clarity.

Where:

IPv6 address   128-bit address (contains only the lower bits of the address)

P   Prefix Length (0-128)

Domain name   The domain name of the prefix

To see how this format works, consider the example shown in Figure 239.

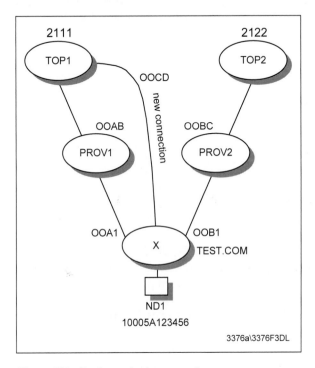

Figure 239. Prefix numbering example

Site X is multihomed to two providers, PROV1 and PROV2. PROV1 gets its transit services from top-level provider TOP1. PROV2 gets its service from TOP2. TOP1 has the top-level aggregate (TLA ID + format prefix) of 2111 (see Figure 227 on page 575). TOP2 has the TLA of 2222.

TOP1 has assigned the next-level aggregate (NLA) of 00AB to PROV1. PROV2 has been assigned the NLA of 00BC by TOP2.

PROV1 has assigned the subscriber identifier 00A1 to site X. PROV2 has assigned the subscriber identifier 00B1 to site X.

Node ND1, at site X, which has the interface token of 10005A123456, is therefore configured with the following two IP addresses:

```
2111:00AB:00A1::1000:5A12:3456
2222:00BC:00B1::1000:5A12:3456
```

Site X is represented by the domain name test.com. Each provider has their own domain, top1.com, top2.com, prov1.com and prov2.com. In each of these domains an IP6 subdomain is created that is used to hold prefixes. The node ND1 can now be represented by the following entries in the DNS:

```
ND1.TEST.COM AAAA ::1000:5A12:3456 80
IP6.TEST.COM

IP6.TEST.COM AAAA 0:0:00A1:: 32 IP6.PROV1.COM
IP6.TEST.COM AAAA 0:0:00B1:: 32 IP6.PROV2.COM

IP6.PROV1.COM AAAA 0:00AB:: 16 IP6.TOP1.COM

IP6.PROV2.COM AAAA 0:00BC:: 16 IP6.TOP2.COM

IP6.TOP1.COM AAAA 2111::

IP6.TOP2.COM AAAA 2222::
```

This format simplifies the job of the DNS administrator considerably and makes renumbering changes much easier to implement. Say, for example, site X decides to stop using links from providers PROV1 and PROV2 and invests in a connection direct from the top-level service provider TOP1 (who allocates the next-level aggregate 00CD to site X). The only change necessary in the DNS would be for the two IP6.TEST.COM entries to be replaced with a single entry, as follows:

```
IP6.TEST.COM AAAA 0:00CD:: 16 IP6.TOP1.COM
```

> **Note:**
>
> Note that the proposed AAAA resource record format is currently a work in progress only. An alternative draft of A6 resource records is also currently under consideration. It is unclear which of these technologies will become the standard at this time.

17.5 DHCP in IPv6

Although IPv6 introduces stateless address autoconfiguration, DHCP retains its importance as the stateful alternative for those sites that wish to have more control over their addressing scheme. Used together with stateless autoconfiguration, DHCP provides a means of passing additional configuration options to nodes once they have obtained their addresses. (See 3.7, "Dynamic Host Configuration Protocol (DHCP)" on page 126 for a detailed description of DHCP.)

There is currently no RFC covering DHCP in IPv6, although there is work in progress described in two Internet drafts, *Dynamic Host Configuration Protocol for IPv6 (DHCPv6)* and *Extensions for the Dynamic Host Configuration Protocol for IPv6.*

17.5.1 Differences between DHCPv6 and DHCPv4

DHCPv6 has some significant differences to DHCPv4, as it takes advantage of some of the inherent enhancements of the IPv6 protocol. Some of the principal differences are as follows:

- As soon as a client boots, it already has a link-local IP address, which it can use to communicate with a DHCP server or a relay agent.
- The client uses multicast addresses to contact the server, rather than broadcasts.
- IPv6 allows the use of multiple IP addresses per interface and DHCPv6 can provide more than one address when requested.
- Some DHCP options are now unnecessary. Default routers, for example, are now obtained by a client using IPv6 neighbor discovery.
- DHCP messages (including address allocations) appear in IPv6 message extensions, rather than in the IP header as in IPv4.
- There is no requirement for BOOTP compatibility.
- There is a new reconfigure message, which is used by the server to send configuration changes to clients (for example, the reduction in an address lifetime). Clients must continue to listen for reconfigure messages once they have received their initial configuration.

17.5.2 DHCPv6 messages

The following DHCPv6 messages are currently defined:

DHCP Solicit   This is an IP multicast message. The DHCP client forwards the message to FF02::1:2, the well-known multicast address for all DHCP agents (relays and servers). If received by a relay, the relay forwards the message to FF05::1:3, the well-known multicast address for all DHCP servers.

DHCP Advertise	This is a unicast message sent in response to a DHCP Solicit. A DHCP server will respond directly to the soliciting client, if on the same link, or via the relay agent, if the DHCP Solicit was forwarded by a relay. The advertise message may contain one or more extensions (DHCP options).
DHCP Request	Once the client has located the DHCP server, the DHCP request (unicast message) is sent to request an address and/or configuration parameters. The request must be forwarded by a relay if the server is not on the same link as the client. The request may contain extensions (options specified by the client) that may be a subset of all the options available on the server.
DHCP Reply	An IP unicast message sent in response to a DHCP request (may be sent directly to the client or via a relay). Extensions contain the address and/or parameters committed to the client.
DHCP Release	An IP unicast sent by the client to the server, informing the server of resources that are being released.
DHCP Reconfigure	An IP unicast or multicast message, sent by the server to one or more clients, to inform them that there is new configuration information available. The client must respond to this message with a DHCP request to request these new changes from the server.

For further details of DHCPv6, please refer to the latest Internet drafts. Note that exact numbering of the drafts is subject to change. You can find the drafts at:

`http://www.ietf.org/internet-drafts/draft-ietf-dhc-dhcpv6-19.txt`

17.6 Mobility support in IPv6

At time of writing, there is no RFC covering mobility support in IPv6, although there is work in progress on the subject, described in a current Internet draft called Mobility Support in IPv6.

Certain enhancements in the IPv6 protocol lend themselves particularly to the mobile environment. For example, unlike Mobile IPv4, there is no requirement for routers to act as "foreign agents" on behalf of the mobile node (see Chapter 19, "Mobile IP" on page 629), as neighbor discovery and address autoconfiguration allow the node to operate away from home without any special support from a local router. Also, most packets sent to a mobile node while it is away from its home location can be tunneled by using IPv6 routing (extension) headers, rather than a complete encapsulation, as used in Mobile IPv4, which reduces the overhead of delivering packets to mobile nodes.

For further information on mobility support in IPv6, please refer to the latest Internet draft at:

```
http://www.ietf.org/internet-drafts/draft-ietf-mobileip-ipv6-14.txt
```

17.7 Internet transition - Migrating from IPv4 to IPv6

If the Internet is to realize the benefits of IPv6, then a period of transition will be necessary when new IPv6 hosts and routers deployed alongside existing IPv4 systems. RFC 2893– Transition Mechanisms for IPv6 Hosts and Routers and RFC2185 – Routing Aspects of IPv6 Transition define a number of mechanisms to be employed to ensure both compatibility between old and new systems and a gradual transition that does not impact the functionality of the Internet. These techniques are sometimes collectively termed *Simple Internet Transition (SIT)*. The transition employs the following techniques:

- Dual-stack IP implementations for hosts and routers that must interoperate between IPv4 and IPv6.

- Imbedding of IPv4 addresses in IPv6 addresses. IPv6 hosts will be assigned addresses that are interoperable with IPv4, and IPv4 host addresses will be mapped to IPv6.

- IPv6-over-IPv4 tunneling mechanisms for carrying IPv6 packets across IPv4 router networks.

- IPv4/IPv6 header translation.This technique is intended for use when implementation of IPv6 is well advanced and only a few IPv4-only systems remain.

The techniques are also adaptable to other protocols, notably Novell IPX, which has similar internetwork layer semantics and an addressing scheme that can be easily mapped to a part of the IPv6 address space.

17.7.1 Dual IP stack implementation - the IPv6/IPv4 node

The simplest way to ensure that a new IPv6 node maintains compatibility with existing IPv4 systems is to provide a dual IP stack implementation. An IPv6/IPv4 node can send and receive either IPv6 packets or IPv4 datagrams, depending on the type of system with which it is communicating. The node will have both a 128-bit IPv6 address and a 32-bit IPv4 address, which do not necessarily need to be related. Figure 240 shows a dual stack IPv6/IPv4 system communicating with both IPv6 and IPv4 systems on the same link.

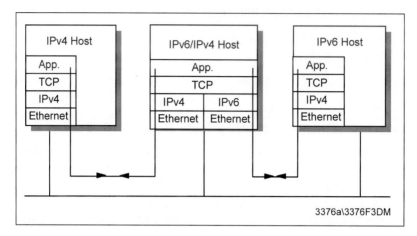

Figure 240. IPv6/IPv4 dual stack system

The IPv6/IPv4 node may use stateless or stateful autoconfiguration to obtain its IPv6 address. It may also use any method to obtain its IPv4 address, such as DHCP, BOOTP, or manual configuration. However, if the node is to perform automatic tunneling, then the IPv6 address must be an IPv4-compatible address, with the low order 32-bits of the address serving as the IPv4 address. (See 17.2.3, "IPv6 addressing" on page 572)

Conceptually, the dual stack model envisages a doubling-up of the protocols in the internetwork layer only. However, related changes are obviously needed in all transport-layer protocols in order to operate when using either stack. Application changes are also needed if the application is to exploit IPv6 capabilities, such as the increased address space of IPv6.

When an IPv6/IPv4 node wishes to communicate with another system, it needs to know the capabilities of that system and which type of packet it should send. The DNS plays a key role here. As described in 17.4, "DNS in IPv6" on page 595, a new resource record type, AAAA, is defined for mapping host names to IPv6 addresses. The results of a name server lookup determine how a node will attempt to communicate with that system. The records found in the DNS for a node depend on which protocols it is running:

- IPv4-only nodes only have A records containing IPv4 addresses in the DNS.

- IPv6/IPv4 nodes that can interoperate with IPv4-only nodes have AAAA records containing IPv4-compatible IPv6 addresses and A records containing the equivalent IPv4 addresses.

- IPv6-only nodes that cannot interoperate with IPv4-only nodes have only AAAA records containing IPv6 addresses.

Because IPv6/IPv4 nodes make decisions about which protocols to use based on the information returned by the DNS, the incorporation of AAAA records in the DNS is a prerequisite to interoperability between IPv6 and IPv4 systems. Note that name servers do not necessarily need to use an IPv6-capable protocol stack, but they must support the additional record type.

17.7.2 Tunneling

When IPv6 or IPv6/IPv4 systems are separated from other similar systems that they wish to communicate with by older IPv4 networks, then IPv6 packets must be tunneled through the IPv4 network.

IPv6 packets are tunnelled over IPv4 very simply; the IPv6 packet is encapsulated in an IPv4 datagram, or in other words, a complete IPv4 header is added to the IPv6 packet. The presence of the IPv6 packet within the IPv4 datagram is indicated by a protocol value of 41 in the IPv4 header.

There are two kinds of tunneling of IPv6 packets over IPv4 networks: *automatic* and *configured*.

17.7.2.1 Automatic tunneling

Automatic tunneling relies on IPv4-compatible addresses. The decision to when to tunnel is made by an IPv6/IPv4 host that has a packet to send across an IPv4-routed network area, and it follows the following rules:

- If the destination is an IPv4 or an IPv4-mapped address, send the packet using IPv4 because the recipient is not IPv6-capable. Otherwise, if the destination is on the same subnet, send it using IPv6, because the recipient is IPv6-capable.

- If the destination is not on the same subnet but there is at least one default router on the subnet that is IPv6-capable, or there is a route configured to an IPv6 router for that destination, then send it to that router using IPv6. Otherwise, if the address is an IPv4-compatible address, send the packet using automatic IPv6-over-IPv4 tunneling. Otherwise, the destination is a node with an IPv6-only address that is connected via an IPv4-routed area, which is not also IPv6-routed. Therefore, the destination is unreachable.

> **Note**
>
> The IP address must be IPv4-compatible for tunneling to be used. Automatic tunneling cannot be used to reach IPv6-only addresses, because they cannot be addressed using IPv4. Packets from IPv6/IPv4 nodes to IPv4-mapped addresses are not tunnelled to because they refer to IPv4-only nodes.

The rules listed above emphasize the use of an IPv6 router in preference to a tunnel for three reasons:

- There is less overhead, because there is no encapsulating IPv4 header.
- IPv6-only features are available.
- The IPv6 routing topology will be used when it is deployed in preference to the pre-existing IPv4 topology.

A node does not need to know whether it is attached to an IPv6-routed or an IPv4-routed area; it will always use an IPv6 router if one is configured on its subnet and will use tunneling if one is not (in which case it can infer that it is attached to an IPv4-routed area).

Automatic tunneling may be either host-to-host, or it may be router-to-host. A source host will send an IPv6 packet to an IPv6 router if possible, but that router may not be able to do the same, and will have to perform automatic tunneling to the destination host itself. Because of the preference for the use of IPv6 routers rather than tunneling, the tunnel will always be as "short" as possible. However, the tunnel will always extend all of the way to the destination host, because IPv6 uses the same hop-by-hop routing paradigm, a host cannot determine if the packet will eventually emerge into an IPv6-complete area before it reaches the destination host. In order to use a tunnel that does not extend all of the way to the recipient, configured tunneling must be used.

The mechanism used for automatic tunneling is very simple:

- The encapsulating IPv4 datagram uses the low-order 32 bits of the IPv6 source and destination addresses to create the equivalent IPv4 addresses and sets the protocol number to 41 (IPv6).
- The receiving node's network interface layer identifies the incoming packets (or packets if the IPv4 datagram was fragmented) as belonging to IPv4 and passes them upwards to the IPv4 part of the dual IPv6/IPv4 internetwork layer.

- The IPv4 layer then receives the datagram in the normal way, re-assembling fragments if necessary, notes the protocol number of 41, then removes the IPv4 header and passes the original IPv6 packet "sideways" to the IPv6 part of the internetwork layer.

- The IPv6 code then processes the original packet as normal. Since the destination IPv6 address in the packet is the IPv6 address of the node (an IPv4-compatible address matching the IPv4 address used in the encapsulating IPv4 datagram), the packet is at its final destination. IPv6 then processes any extension headers as normal and then passes the packet's remaining payload to the next protocol listed in the last IPv6 header.

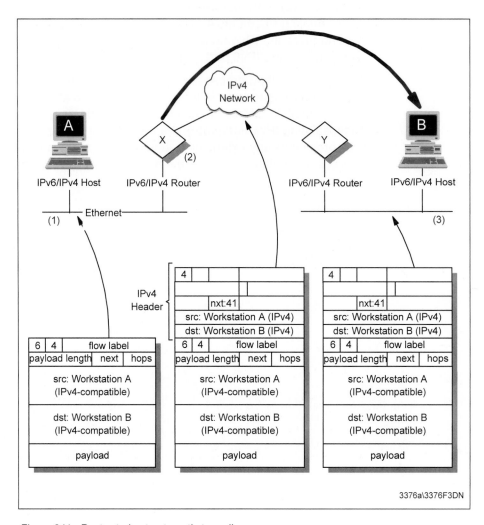

Figure 241. Router-to-host automatic tunneling

Figure 241 shows two IPv6/IPv4 nodes separated by an IPv4 network. Both workstations have IPv4-compatible IPv6 addresses. Workstation A sends a packet to workstation B, as follows:

1. Workstation A has received router solicitation messages from an IPv6-capable router (X) on its local link. It forwards the packet to this router.

2. Router X adds an IPv4 header to the packet, using IPv4 source and destination addresses derived from the IPv4-compatible addresses. The

packet is then forwarded across the IPv4 network, all the way to workstation B. This is *router-to-host* automatic tunneling.

3. The IPv4 datagram is received by the IPv4 stack of workstation B. As the Protocol field shows that the next header is 41 (IPv6), the IPv4 header is stripped from the datagram and the remaining IPv6 packet is then handled by the IPv6 stack.

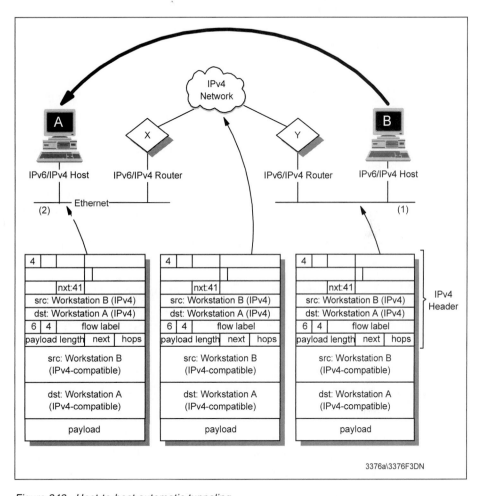

Figure 242. Host-to-host automatic tunneling

In Figure 242, workstation B responds as follows:

1. Workstation B has no IPv6-capable router on its local link. It therefore adds an IPv4 header to its own IPv6 frame and forwards the resulting IPv4

datagram directly to the IPv4 address of workstation A via the IPv4 network. This is *host-to-host* automatic tunneling.

2. The IPv4 datagram is received by the IPv4 stack of workstation A. As the Protocol field shows that the next header is 41 (IPv6), the IPv4 header is stripped from the datagram and the remaining IPv6 packet is then handled by the IPv6 stack.

17.7.2.2 Configured tunneling

Configured tunneling is used for host-router or router-router tunneling of IPv6-over-IPv4. The sending host or the forwarding router is configured so that the route, as well as having a next hop, also has a *tunnel end* address (which is always an IPv4-compatible address). The process of encapsulation is the same as for automatic tunneling, except that the IPv4 destination address is not derived from the low-order 32 bits of the IPv6 destination address, but from the low-order 32 bits of the tunnel end. The IPv6 destination and source addresses do *not* need to be IPv4-compatible addresses in this case.

When the router at the end of the tunnel receives the IPv4 datagram, it processes it in exactly the same way as a node at the end of an automatic tunnel. When the original IPv6 packet is passed to the IPv6 layer in the router, it recognizes that it is not the destination, and the router forwards the packet on to the final destination as it would for any other IPv6 packet.

It is, of course, possible that after emerging from the tunnel, the IPv6 packet is tunnelled again by another router.

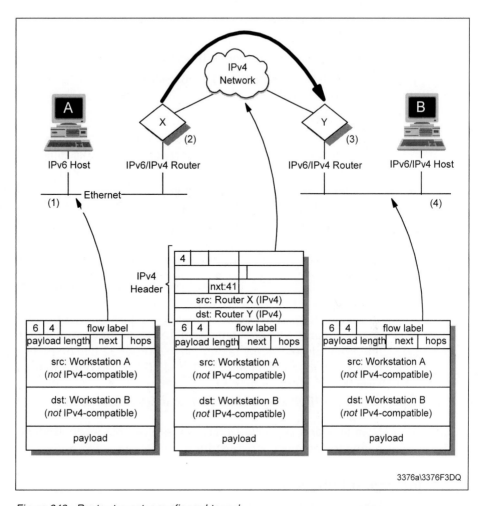

Figure 243. Router-to-router configured tunnel

Figure 243 shows two IPv6-only nodes separated by an IPv4 network. A router-to-router tunnel is configured between the two IPv6/IPv4 routers X and Y.

1. Workstation A constructs an IPv6 packet to send to workstation B. It forwards the packet to the IPv6 router advertising on its local link (X).

2. Router X receives the packet, but has no direct IPv6 connection to the destination subnet. However, a tunnel has been configured for this subnet. The router therefore adds an IPv4 header to the packet, with a destination address of the tunnel-end (router Y) and forwards the datagram over the IPv4 network.

3. The IPv4 stack of router Y receives the frame. Seeing the Protocol field value of 41, it removes the IPv4 header, and passes the remaining IPv6 packet to its IPv6 stack. The IPv6 stack reads the destination IPv6 address, and forwards the packet.

4. Workstation B receives the IP6 packet.

17.7.3 Header translation

Installing IPv6/IPv4 nodes allows for backward compatibility with existing IPv4 systems. However, when migration of networks to IPv6 reaches an advanced stage, it is likely that new systems being installed will be IPv6 only. Therefore, there will be a requirement for IPv6-only systems to communicate with the remaining IPv4-only systems. Header translation is required for IPv6-only nodes to interoperate with IPv4-only nodes. Header translation is performed by IPv6/IPv4 routers on the boundaries between IPv6 routed areas and IPv4 routed areas.

The translating router strips the header completely from IPv6 packets and replaces it with an equivalent IPv4 header (or the reverse). In addition to correctly mapping between the fields in the two headers, the router must convert source and destination addresses from IPv4-mapped addresses to real IPv4 addresses (by taking the low-order 32 bits of the IP address). In the reverse direction, the router adds the ::FFFF /96 prefix to the IPv4 address to form the IPv4-mapped address. If either the source or the destination IPv6 address is IPv6 only, the header cannot be translated.

Note that for a site with even just one IPv4 host, every IPv6 node with which it needs to communicate must have an IPv4-mapped address.

17.7.4 Interoperability summary

Whether two nodes can interoperate depends upon their capabilities and their addresses.

An IPv4 node can communicate with:

- Any IPv4 node on the local link
- Any IPv4 node via an IPv4 router
- Any IPv6 node with IPv4-mapped address via a header translator

An IPv6 node (IPv6-only address) can communicate with:

- Any IPv6 node on the local link

- Any IPv6 node via an IPv6 router on the local link (may require tunneling through IPv4 network from the router)

An IPv6 node (IPv4-mapped address) can communicate with:
- Any IPv6 node on the local link
- Any IPv6 node via an IPv6 router on the local link (may require tunneling through IPv4 network from the router)
- Any IPv4 node via a header translator

An IPv6/IPv4 node (IPv4-compatible address) can communicate with:
- Any IPv4 node on the local link
- Any IPv4 node via an IPv4 router on the local link
- Any IPv6 node on the local link
- Any IPv6 node via an IPv6 router on the local link (may require tunneling through IPv4 network from the router)
- Any IPv6/IPv4 node (IPv4-compatible address) via host-to-host tunnel

17.8 The drive towards IPv6

The driving forces for the introduction of IPv6 networks are likely to be requirements for new facilities that require IPv6, or exhaustion of the IPv4 address space. Which of these is seen as more important will vary between organizations. For example, commercial organizations with large, long-established internal IPv4 networks are unlikely to upgrade thousands of working IPv4 hosts and routers, unless they have a problem with the address space within their own networks. They will, however, be likely to invest in IPv6 deployment if new business-critical applications require facilities that are only available on IPv6 or if they require connectivity to other organizations that are using IPv6-only addresses.

Businesses that are implementing IP networks for the first time, however, may be interested in some of the capabilities of IPv6, such as the address autoconfiguration. However, anyone thinking of implementing IPv6 today needs to be aware that the protocol is still, as of today, very much under development. It may be said that IPv4 is also still under development, as new RFCs and Internet drafts are constantly being produced, but for IPv6, certain key protocols, such as DHCP, are still at Internet draft stage only at time of writing. The Internet backbone today consists of IPv4 routers and, until such time as the IPv6 protocols have been widely used and tested, the owners of these production routers are unlikely to put them at risk by upgrading them to IPv6.

One off-shoot of the IETF IPng (next generation) project was the development of the 6Bone, which is an Internet-wide IPv6 virtual network, layered on top of the physical IPv4 Internet. The 6Bone consists of many islands supporting IPv6 packets, linked by tunnels across the existing IPv4 backbone. The 6Bone is widely used for testing of IPv6 protocols and products. It is expected that, as confidence grows in IPv6 and more products with IPv6 capability become available, the 6Bone will eventually be replaced by a production backbone of ISP and user network IPv6 capable routers.

17.9 References

The following RFCs contain detailed information on IPv6:

- RFC 1752 –The Recommendation for the IP Next Generation Protocol
- RFC 1883 – Internet Protocol, Version 6 (IPv6)
- RFC 2460 – Internet Protocol, Version 6 (IPv6)
- RFC 1191 – Path MTU Discovery
- RFC 2373 – IP Version 6 Addressing Architecture
- RFC 2374 – An IPv6 Aggregatable Global Unicast Address Format
- RFC 2375 – IPv6 Multicast Address Assignments
- RFC 2463 – Internet Control Message Protocol (ICMPv6) for the Internet Protocol Version 6 (IPv6) Specification
- RFC 2461 – Neighbor Discovery for IP Version 6 (IPv6)
- RFC 2462 – IPv6 Stateless Address Autoconfiguration
- RFC 1886 – DNS Extensions to Support IP Version 6
- RFC 2893 – Transition Mechanisms for IPv6 Hosts and Routers
- RFC 2185 – Routing Aspects of IPv6 Transition

Chapter 18. Multiprotocol Label Switching (MPLS)

The Multiprotocol Label Switching (MPLS) standard represents the current effort in the continued evolution of multilayer switching. The primary goal of MPLS is the integration of label swapping paradigms with traditional network layer routing. This integration bring efficiencies in data forwarding as well as positioning the network for advanced QoS functions.

Initial MPLS efforts focused on IPv4; however, the core technology is extensible to other network layer protocols. MPLS is also not limited to a specific link layer technology; it can function on any media over which network layer packets can pass.

Basic MPLS specifications are documented in RFC 3031. At the time of this writing, the RFC is in proposed standard status. As development of the technology continues, enhancements will be documented in subsequent RFCs.

18.1 MPLS overview

In an MPLS environment, conventional layer-3 or network layer routing (that is, IP routing) is used to determine a path through the network. Once the path is determined, data packets are then switched through each node as they traverse the network.

18.1.1 Conventional routing model

In a traditional connectionless network, every router runs a layer-3 routing algorithm. As a packet traverses through the network, each router along the path makes an independent forwarding decision for that packet. Using information contained in the packet header, as well as information obtained from the routing algorithm, the router chooses a next hop destination for the packet. In an IP network, this process involves matching the destination address stored in the IP header of each packet with the most specific route obtained from the IP routing table. This comparison process determines the next hop destination for the packet. This analysis and classification of the layer-3 header can be processor-intensive. In a traditional connectionless environment, this activity occurs at every node along the end-to-end path.

18.1.2 MPLS forwarding model

In an MPLS environment, optimum paths through the network are identified in advance. Then, as data packets enter the MPLS network, ingress devices use information in the layer-3 header to assign the packets to one of the predetermined paths. This assignment is used to append a *label* referencing the end-to-end path into the packet. The label accompanies the data packet as it traverses the network. Subsequent routers along the path use the information in the label to determine the next hop device. Because these devices only manipulate information in the label, processor-intensive analysis and classification of the layer-3 header occurs only at the ingress point.

18.1.3 Additional benefits

In additional to reducing the processing requirements on devices in the core of the network, MPLS has a number of additional advantages over conventional layer-3 routing, which are detailed in the followign sections.

18.1.3.1 Traffic engineering

Traffic engineering is the process of selecting network paths so that the resulting traffic patterns achieve a balanced utilization of resources.

Routing based on conventional interior gateway protocol (IGP) algorithms may select network paths that result in unbalanced resource utilization. In these environments, some network resources are overutilized, while others are underutilized. A limited degree of engineering can be provided by manipulating the IGP metrics associated with network links. However, this effort is difficult to manage in environments with a large number of redundant paths.

To achieve the benefits of traffic engineering, MPLS can be used in-conjunction with IGP algorithms. MPLS provides the ability to specify the specific route data packets should use to traverse the network. This explicit routing of data packets ensures a particular stream of data uses a specific path. By monitoring and managing these data streams, efficient utilization of network resources can be achieved. Explicit routing has been available through the source routing options of traditional IP routing. However, because this is a processor-intensive activity, its usage has been limited. MPLS makes the efficient use of explicit routing possible.

MPLS also provides the ability to analyze fields outside the IP packet header when determining the explicit route for a data packet. For example, the network administrator can develop traffic flow policies based on how or where a packet entered the network. In a traditional network, this information is only available at the ingress point. The additional analysis provides the administrator with a higher level of control, resulting in a more predictable level of service.

18.1.3.2 Quality of Service routing

QoS routing is the ability to choose a route for a particular data stream so that the path provides a desired level of service. These levels of service can specify acceptable levels of bandwidth, delay, or packet loss in the network. This provides the intelligence to deliver different levels of service based on overall network policies.

Providing a network path delivering a desired QoS often requires the use of explicit routing. For example, it is straightforward to allocate a path for a particular stream requiring a specific bandwidth allocation. However, it is possible that the combined bandwidth of multiple streams may exceed existing capacity. In this scenario, individual streams, even those between the same ingress and egress nodes, may need to be individually routed. This requires a finer level of granularity than that provided by standard traffic engineering.

There are two approaches to providing QoS routing in an MPLS environment:

- The MPLS label contains class of service (CoS) information. As traffic flows through the network, this information can be used to intelligently prioritize traffic at each network hop.

- The MPLS network can provision multiple paths between ingress and egress devices. Each path is engineered to provide a different level of service. Traffic is then intelligently assigned to an appropriate path as it enters the network.

These approaches simply classify packets into a class of service category. Local network administration policies actually determine the service provided to each category.

18.1.3.3 Multiprotocol support

The Multiprotocol Label Switching standard provides support for existing network layer protocols, including IPv4, IPv6, IPX, and AppleTalk. The standard also provides link layer support for Ethernet, token-ring, FDDI, ATM, frame relay, and point-to-point links. Activities continue to extend this standard to other protocols and network types.

18.2 Components of an MPLS network

This section details key concepts and terminology used in an MPLS environment.

18.2.1 Terminology

The following sections define the terms that are used with MPLS.

18.2.1.1 Forwarding equivalency class (FEC)

An FEC is a group of layer-3 packets that are forwarded in the same manner. All packets in this group follow the same network path and have the same prioritization. Packets within an FEC may have different layer-3 header information. However, to simply make a forwarding decision, these packets are indistinguishable.

Common examples of FEC groups are:

- A set of packets that have the same most specific route in the IP routing table.
- A set of packets that have the same most specific route in the IP routing table and the same IP type of service setting.

In an MPLS network, an FEC is identified by a label.

18.2.1.2 Label and labeled packet

As stated above, a label identifies a unique FEC. MPLS devices forward all identically labeled packets in the same way.

A label is locally significant between a pair of MPLS devices. It represents an agreement between the two devices describing the mapping between a label and an FEC. The fact that labels are locally significant enhances the scalability of MPLS into large environments, because the same label need not be used at every hop.

The MPLS label can be located at different positions in the data frame, depending on the layer-2 technology used for transport. If the layer-2 technology supports a label field, the MPLS label is encapsulated in the native label field. In an ATM network, the VPI/VCI fields can be used to store an MPLS label. Similarly, the DLCI field can be used to store an MPLS label in frame relay networks.

If the layer-2 technology does not natively support a label, the MPLS label resides in an encapsulation header appended specifically for this purpose. The header is located between the layer-2 header and the IP header. This use of a dedicated header permits MPLS service over any layer-2 technology (see Figure 244).

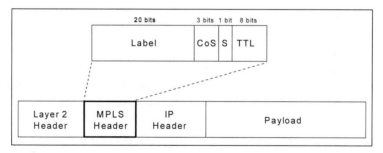

Figure 244. The 32-bit MPLS header

The contents of the MPLS header include:

- A label field that contains the actual value of the MPLS label.
- A CoS field that can be used to affect the queueing and discard algorithms applied to the packet as it traverses the network.
- A S (stack) field that supports a hierarchical label stack.
- A TTL (time-to-live) field that supports conventional IP TTL functionality.

A labeled packet is a packet into which a label has been encoded. To support enhanced MPLS functions, the packet may actually contain more than one label. This is known as a label stack. The stack establishes an ordered relationship between individual labels. The stack is implemented using the last-in, first-out model. This feature is further discussed in 18.2.4, "Label stack and label hierarchies" on page 620.

18.2.1.3 Label stack router (LSR)
A label stack router is an MPLS node that is also capable of forwarding native layer-3 packets. There are two important types of LSRs in an MPLS network:

- An *ingress node* connects the MPLS network with a node that does not execute MPLS functionality. The ingress node handles traffic as it enters the MPLS network.

- An *egress node* connects the MPLS network with a node that does not execute MPLS functionality. The egress node handles traffic as it leaves the MPLS network.

18.2.1.4 Next hop label forwarding entry (NHLFE)
An NHLFE is used by an MPLS node to forward packets. There is at least one NHLFE for each FEC flowing through the node. Each node is responsible for maintaining an NHLFE information base containing the following information:

- The packet's next hop address.

- The operation performed on the label stack:
  - Replace the label at the top of the stack with a specified new label. This is known as *popping* the old label and *pushing* a new label.
  - Pop the label at the top of the stack.
  - Replace the label at the top of the stack with a specified new label, and then push one or more specified new labels onto the label stack. When this action is complete, the stack will contain at least two MPLS labels.
- The data link encapsulation used to transmit the packet (optional).
- The label stack encoding used to transmit the packet (optional).
- Any other information needed in order to properly process the packet.

18.2.1.5 Incoming label map (ILM)
The ILM is used by an MPLS node to forward labeled packets. The label in an incoming packet is used as a reference to the ILM. The ILM information allows the node to select a set of NHLFEs containing forwarding instructions.

The ILM may map a label to a group of NHLFEs. This provides the ability to load balance over multiple equal-cost paths.

18.2.1.6 FEC-to-NHLFE map (FTN)
The FTN is used by an MPLS node to process packets that arrive unlabeled, but need to be labeled before forwarding. An unlabeled data packet is assigned a specific FEC at the ingress MPLS node. This FEC is used as a reference to the FTN. The FTN map allows the node to select a set of NHLFEs containing forwarding instructions. This activity is performed at the ingress node of the MPLS network.

The FTN may map a label to a group of NHLFEs. This provides the ability to load balance over multiple equal cost paths.

18.2.2 Label swapping
Label swapping is the process used by an MPLS node to forward a data packet to the next hop device. This process is used regardless of whether the packet arrives labeled or unlabeled. The process is similar to the method used in ATM and frame relay networks to forward traffic through a virtual circuit.

18.2.2.1 Forwarding a labeled packet
An MPLS node examines the label at the top of the stack of an incoming packet. It uses the ILM to map the label to an NHLFE. The NHLFE indicates

where to forward the packet and the operation to perform on the label stack. Using this information, the node encodes a new label stack and forwards the resulting packet.

18.2.2.2 Forwarding an unlabeled packet

An MPLS node examines the network layer header and any other pertinent information required to determine an FEC. The node uses the FTN to map the FEC to an NHLFE. Processing is now identical to a labeled packet. The NHLFE indicates where to forward the packet and the operation to perform on the label stack. Using this information, the node encodes a new label stack and forwards the resulting packet.

The following diagram depicts label swapping in an MPLS environment:

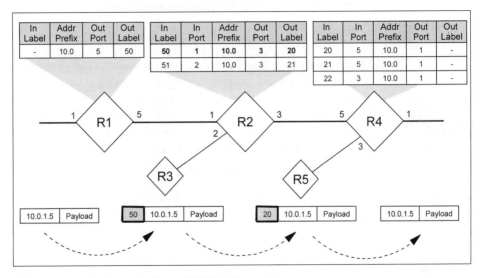

Figure 245. Label swapping in an MPLS environment

> **Note**
>
> In a label swapping environment, the next hop router is always determined from MPLS information. This may cause the packet to traverse a different path than the one obtained using conventional routing algorithms

18.2.2.3 Penultimate hop popping

This is the ability to pop an MPLS label at the penultimate node rather than at the egress node. From an architectural perspective, this type of processing is permitted. The purpose of a label is to forward a packet through the network to the egress node. Once the penultimate node has decided to send the packet to the egress node, the label no longer has any function. It does not need to be included in the packet.

The penultimate node pops the stack and forwards the packet based on the next hop address obtained from the NHLFE. When the egress node receives the packet, one of two activities will occur:

- The packet contains a label. This will occur when the penultimate node processed a packet with at least two labels. In this scenario, the label now at the top of the stack is the label the egress node needs to process to make a forwarding decision.

- The packet does not contain a label. In this scenario, the LSP egress receives a standard network layer packet. The node uses the local IP routing table to make a forwarding decision.

18.2.3 Label switched path (LSP)

An LSP represents a set of MPLS nodes traversed by packets belonging to a specific FEC. The set is an ordered, unidirectional list. Traffic flows from the node at the head-end of the list toward the node at the tail-end of the list. The LSP for the traffic flow shown in Figure 245 is <R1, R2, R4>.

In an MPLS network, LSPs can be established in one of two ways:

- Independent LSP control: Each LSR makes an independent decision to bind a label to an FEC. It then distributes the label to its peer nodes. This is similar to conventional IP routing; each node makes an independent decision as to how to forward a packet.

- Ordered LSP control: An LSR binds a label to a particular FEC only if it is the egress LSR for that FEC, or if it has already received a label binding for that FEC from its next hop for that FEC. In an environment implementing traffic engineering policies, ordered LSP control is used to ensure that traffic in a particular FEC follows a specific path.

18.3, "Label distribution protocols" on page 624 details the procedures used to exchange label information in an MPLS environment.

18.2.4 Label stack and label hierarchies

A labeled packet can contain more than one label. The labels are maintained in a last-in, first-out stack. The stack implements an ordered hierarchy among the set of labels.

This hierarchy is used when an MPLS node delivers a packet to a partner MPLS node, but the nodes are not consecutive routers on the hop-by-hop path for the packet. In this situation, a tunnel is created between the two MPLS nodes. The tunnel is implemented as an LSP and label switching is used to forward traffic through the tunnel.

The set of traffic sent through the tunnel constitutes an FEC. Each LSR in the tunnel must assign a label to that FEC.

To send a packet through the tunnel, the tunnel ingress node pushes a label understood by the tunnel egress node onto the label stack. The tunnel ingress node then pushes a label understood by the next hop node and forwards the data packet through the tunnel.

For example, a network may contain an LSP <R1, R2, R3, R4>. In this example, R2 and R3 are not directly connected, but are peers endpoints of an LSP tunnel. The actual sequence of LSRs traversed through the network is <R1, R2, R21, R22, R3, R4>. The following figure shows this configuration:

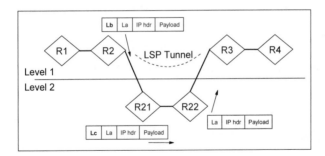

Figure 246. LSP tunnels

A packet traversing this network travels along a level-1 LSP <R1, R2, R3, R4> and then, when traveling from R2 to R3, uses a level-2 LSP <R2, R21, R22, R3>. From the perspective of the level-1 LSP, R2's peer devices are R1 and R3. From the level-2 perspective, R2's peer device is R21.

Using this diagram, the following actions occurs when a packet is sent through the LSP tunnel:

- R2 receives a labeled packet from R1. The packet containing a single label. The depth of the label stack is one.

- R2 pops this label and pushes a label understood by R3. This label is called La.

- R2 must also include a label understood by R21. R2 pushes the label on top of the existing level-1 label. This label is called Lb. The label stack contains two entries.

- R2 forwards the packet to R21.

- R21 pops the level-2 label (Lb) appended by R2 and pushes a level-2 label understood by R22. This label is called Lc. R21 does not process the level-1 label. The label stack contains two entries.

- R21 forwards the packet to R22.

- R22 reviews the level-2 label appended by R21 and realizes it is the penultimate hop in the R2-R3 tunnel. R22 pops the level-2 label (Lc) and forwards the packet to R3. The label stack contains one entry.

18.2.5 MPLS stacks in a BGP environment

The network shown in Figure 247 shows three autonomous systems. The environment contains two classes of IP routing:

- Each autonomous system runs an IGP to maintain connectivity within the AS. For example, R2, R21, R22, and R3 may use OSPF to maintain routes within AS 2.

- Each autonomous systems runs BGP to maintain connectivity between autonomous systems. For example, border routers R1, R2, R3, and R4 use BGP to exchange inter-AS routing information.

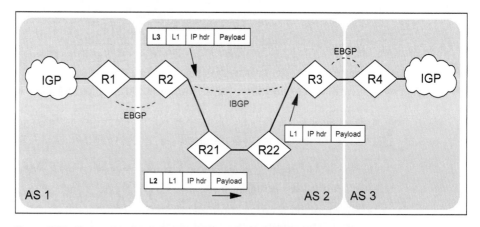

Figure 247. Connecting autonomous systems in an MPLS environment

In this sample network, it is desirable to avoid distributing BGP-learned routes to devices which are not BGP border routers (for example, R21, R22). This minimizes the CPU processing required to maintain the IP routing table on these devices. It also eliminates the need to run a BGP routing algorithm on these devices.

The use of an MPLS LSP stack can be used to implement this environment. In this configuration, BGP routes are distributed only to BGP peers, and not to interior routers that lie along the hop-by-hop path between peers. LSP tunnels are configured so that:

- Each peer distributes a label for each address prefix that it distributes via BGP. These labels are distributed to peers within the same AS.
- The IGP maintains a host route for each BGP border router. Each interior router distributes a label for the host route to each IGP neighbor.

Consider a situation where R2 receives an unlabeled packet destined for a network connected via AS 3. The packet may have originated from a LAN segment locally connected to R2 or another LAN segment within AS 2. The packet would have been previously labeled if it had originated in AS1.

- R2 searches the local IP forwarding table to determine the most specific route for the required destination address. The route will have be learned via BGP. The BGP next hop will be R3.
- R3 has previously bound a label for the longest match and distributed this label to R2. This label is called L1.
- Since all devices within AS 2 participate in the IGP, a route to R3 appears in the routing table of all devices within AS 2:
  - R22 has previously bound a label for R3 and distributed this label to R21. This label is called L2.
  - R21 has previously bound a label for R3 and distributed this label to R2. This label is called L3.
- R2 prepares the data packet destined for AS 3 by creating a label stack. The initial entry on the stack is created by pushing the L1 label. The top entry on the stack is created by pushing the L3 label. The labeled packet is then sent to the next hop, R21.
- R21 receives the labeled packet and reviews the top entry in the stack. Using the information in the NHLFE, R21 replaces the L3 label in the stack with the L2 label. The labeled packet is then sent to the next hop, R22.
- R22 receives the labeled packet and reviews the top entry. Since R22 is the penultimate hop on the R2-R3 tunnel, R22 pops the L2 label on the stack and forwards the data packet to R3. The label stack now contains a single entry as it is forwarded to R3.

- R3 receives the labeled data packet and reviews the L1 label on the stack. Using information in the NHLFE, R3 replaces the old label with a label bound by R4 and forwards the packet.

Note

Whenever an MPLS node pushes a label on to an already labeled packet, the new label must correspond to an FEC whose LSP egress is the node that assigned the new label.

18.3 Label distribution protocols

A label distribution protocol is a set of procedures that allows one MPLS node to distribute labels to other peer nodes. This specification is used by an LSR to notify another LSR of an assigned label and its associated meaning. This exchange establishes a common agreement between peers.

Each MPLS node participates in a local IGP to determine the network topology and populate the routing table. Label distribution protocols use this information to establish labels. After a distribution protocol has run in each node, the entire MPLS network should have a complete set of paths and associated labels.

Label distribution protocols also encompasses any negotiations between peers needed to learn MPLS capabilities of each peer.

18.3.1 Types of label distribution protocols

The MPLS architecture does not specify a required distribution protocol nor does it assume there is only a single protocol. Because of this, there are a number of different standards under development. These standards can be placed into one of two categories:

18.3.1.1 Extensions to existing protocols

Proposals have been made to existing protocols so that label distribution information is included within existing data flows. Two examples of this are:

- BGP extensions: In many cases, FECs are used to identify address prefixes distributed by BGP peers. It may be advantageous to have these same devices distribute MPLS labels. Further, the use of BGP route reflectors to distribute labels can provide significant scalability enhancements.

- RSVP extensions: This proposal enhances the RSVP standard to include support for establishing and distributing LSP information. This enables the allocation of resources along the end-to-end path.

18.3.1.2 Development of new protocols

New protocols are also being developed with the sole purpose of distributing labels. These stand-alone protocols do not rely on the presence of specific routing protocols at every hop along the path. This is useful in situations in which an LSP must traverse nodes that do not support one of the existing protocols that has been extended to include label distribution functions.

18.3.2 Label distribution methods

There are two methods to initiate communication between MPLS nodes to exchange of label information:

- Downstream-on-demand: An LSR can request a label binding for a particular FEC. The request is made to the next hop MPLS node for that FEC.

- Unsolicited downstream: An LSR can distribute bindings to LSRs that have not explicitly requested the information.

Both of these distribution techniques can be used in the same network at the same time. For a given set of peers, the upstream LSR and the downstream LSR must agree on the technique to be used.

18.4 Stream merge

Stream merge is the aggregation of a large number of data flows into a single downstream flow. The device performing the merge consolidates the individual streams so that they are treated as a single stream by subsequent MPLS nodes. The merged stream is represented by a single label. Once the merged packets are transmitted, any information that the packets arrived with different incoming labels is lost.

Stream merge is a major component of MPLS scalability.

18.4.1 Merging in a frame-based environment

Stream merge in a frame based environment is straightforward. The device performing the merge maps multiple upstream labels into a single downstream label. There is no change to any existing MPLS label swapping procedures.

18.4.2 Merging in an ATM environment

Stream merge in an ATM environment is more complex. In ATM, data packets are encapsulated in an AAL5 PDU and sent as ATM cells. These cells have a specific VPI/VCI value. All cells within the VPI/VCI are transmitted in sequence. It is mandatory that all ATM switches along the data path maintain cell order. The device reassembling the PDU expects the cells to be contiguous and received in the correct sequence.

Problems occur if straightforward MPLS stream merging occurs in an ATM environment. In this scenario, cells from multiple incoming VCs are interleaved into a single outgoing VC. Problems occur with reconstructing the original PDUs, because the ATM cell header does not contain information to restore original order.

There are two methods to avoid cell interleaving during stream merge in an ATM environment:

- VC merge allows multiple incoming VCs to be merged into a single outgoing VC. The MPLS node performing the merge keeps the cells from one AAL5 frame separated from the cells of another AAL5 frame. To accomplish this, the ATM switch delays sending cells from one frame while cells from another frame are transmitted. When the end of frame indicator is reached, the next frame can be transmitted in entirety. This type of buffering and store-and-forward capability is not typically available in existing ATM switches.

- VP merge allows multiple VPs to be merged into a single outgoing VP. Separate VCIs within the merged VP are used to distinguish frames from multiple sources.

  VP merge has the advantage in that it is compatible with a higher percentage of deployed ATM gear, making it deployable in existing networks. VP merge also has the advantage that it does not introduce delays at the merge points, and does not introduce any new buffering requirements.

  The main disadvantage to VP merge is that is requires coordination of VCI assignments within each VP.

The MPLS architecture specifies support for both VP merge and VC merge. ATM switches participating in MPLS must be able to determine if neighboring switches perform VP merge, VC merge, or no merge.

18.5 Multiprotocol Lambda Switching

Increased data network complexities are driving architectures that provide cost-effective and scalable solutions. These solutions must also provide performance optimization features. Some of these requirements are addressed by the MPLS standard. These same business requirements are applicable to the underlying optical transport network (OTN). As a result, standards bodies are starting to develop specifications for incorporating MPLS functions into optical cross-connect (OXC) devices. This effort is called called MPλS.

There are several benefits to extending MPLS functions into optical networks:

- The activity can leverage techniques developed for MPLS to provide a methodology for real-time provisioning of optical channels. This promotes faster development of these technologies.

- The activity can provide a uniform approach to network management for both data and optical environments. This simplifies overall management efforts.

- The effort can provide a single architecture allowing an LSP to traverse a mix of router and OXC devices. This positions the network to provide real bandwidth on demand facilities.

- The effort positions IP routers for the eventual incorporation of high-capacity Dense Wave Division Multiplexing (DWDM) capabilities.

The extension of MPLS functions into optical network is based on a number of similarities between the two types of networks:

- In MPLS, an LSP describes the point-to-point path traversed by a set of labeled packets. In MPλS, an optical channel trail is used to describe the point-to-point optical connection between two access points.

- In an MPLS network, an LSR establishes a relationship between an <input port, input label> tuple and <output port, output label> tuple. Similarly, in an optical transport network, an OXC establishes a relationship between an <input port, input optical channel> tuple and <output port, output optical channel> tuple. Once established, these relationships cannot be altered by the contents of any data packet.

- In an MPLS network, an LSR discovers, distributes, and maintains state information associated with the network. An OXC is responsible for these same functions in an OTN.

- In an MPLS network, an LSR is responsible for creating and maintaining LSPs associated with existing traffic engineering policies. An OXC is responsible for the same functions in an OTN.

- In an MPLS network, an LSP is unidirectional. In an OTN, an optical channel trail is also unidirectional.

In a MPλS environment, it will be possible to represent the fiber within the OTN as a set of links, each link representing a set of channels. An IP routing protocol (with extensions) will distribute information about the optical network topology, available bandwidth, and other pertinent state information. The information will be used to compute explicit routes for optical channel trails. MPLS distribution protocols will then create these trails.

As development of this technology continues, important distinctions between an MPLS network and an OTN must be addressed:

- In an MPLS network, forwarding information is carried as part of the label contained in each data packet. In an OTN, switching information is implied from the wavelength or optical channel.

- In an OTN, there is no concept of label merging. An OXC cannot merge several wavelengths into one wavelength.

- An OXC cannot perform label push or pop operations. In an optical domain, the analog of a label is a wavelength. There is no concept of pushing or popping wavelengths in current optical technologies.

Chapter 19. Mobile IP

The increasingly mobile nature of the workforce presents problems with regard to configuration and operation of mobile network devices. It is possible to allocate multiple sets of configuration parameters to a device, but this obviously means increased workload for the administrator and the user. Perhaps more importantly, however, is that this type of configuration is wasteful with respect to the number of IP addresses allocated.

In DHCP and DDNS environments, DHCP provides a device with a valid IP address for the point at which it is attached to the network. DDNS provides a method of locating that device by its host name, no matter where that device happens to be attached to a network and what IP address it has been allocated. An alternative approach to the problem of dealing with mobile devices is provided in RFC 2002 – IP Mobility Support. IP Mobility Support, commonly referred to as Mobile IP, is a proposed standard, with a status of elective.

19.1 Mobile IP overview

Mobile IP allows a device to maintain the same IP address (its *home address*) wherever it attaches to the network. (Obviously, a device with an IP address plugged into the wrong subnet will normally be unreachable.) However, the mobile device also has a *care-of* address, which connects to the subnet where it is currently located. The care-of address is managed by a *home agent*, which is a device on the home subnet of the mobile device. Any packet addressed to the IP address of the mobile device is intercepted by the home agent and then forwarded on to the care-of address through a tunnel. Once it arrives at the end of the tunnel, the datagram is delivered to the mobile device. The mobile node generally uses its home address as the source address of all datagrams that it sends.

Mobile IP can help resolve address shortage problems and reduce administrative workload, because each device that needs to attach to the network at multiple locations only requires a single IP address.

The following terminology is used in a mobile IP network configuration:

Home address The static IP address allocated to a mobile node. It does not change, no matter where the node attaches to the network.

Home network A subnet with a network prefix matching the home address of the mobile node. Datagrams intended for the home address of the mobile node will always be routed to this network.

Tunnel   The path followed by an encapsulated datagram.

Visited network   A network to which the mobile node is connected (other than the node's home network).

Home agent   A router on the home network of the mobile node that maintains current location information for the node and tunnels datagrams for delivery to the node when it is away from home.

Foreign aAgent   A router on a visited network that registers the presence of a mobile node and detunnels and forwards datagrams to the node that have been tunneled by the mobile node's home agent.

19.2 Mobile IP operation

Mobility agents (home agents and foreign agents) advertise their presence on the network by means of *agent advertisement* messages, which are ICMP router advertisement messages with extensions (see 19.3, "Mobility agent advertisement extensions" on page 632). A mobile node may also explicitly request one of these messages with an agent solicitation message. When a mobile node connects to the network and receives one of these messages, it is able to determine whether it is on its home network or a foreign network. If the mobile node detects that it is on its home network, it will operate normally, without the use of mobility services. In addition, if it has just returned to the home network, having previously been working elsewhere, it will deregister itself with the home agent. This is done through the exchange of a registration request and registration reply.

If, however, the mobile node detects, from an agent advertisement, that it has moved to a foreign network, then it obtains a care-of address for the foreign network. This address may be obtained from the foreign agent (a foreign agent care-of address, which is the address of the foreign agent itself), or it may be obtained by some other mechanism, such as DHCP (in which case, it is known as a co-located care-of address). The use of co-located care-of addresses has the advantage that the mobile node does not need a foreign agent to be present at every network that it visits, but it does require that a pool of IP addresses be made available for visiting mobile nodes by the DHCP server.

Note that communication between a mobile node and a foreign agent takes place at the link layer level. It cannot use the normal IP routing mechanism, because the mobile node's IP address does not belong to the subnet in which it is currently located.

Once the mobile node has received its care-of address, it needs to register itself with its home agent. This may be done through the foreign agent, which forwards the request to the home agent, or directly with the home agent (see 19.4, "Mobile IP registration process" on page 634).

Once the home agent has registered the care-of address for the mobile node in its new position, any datagram intended for the home address of the mobile node is intercepted by the home agent and tunneled to the care-of address. The tunnel endpoint may be at a foreign agent (if the mobile node has a foreign agent care-of address), or at the mobile node itself (if it has a co-located care-of address). Here the original datagram is removed from the tunnel and delivered to the mobile node.

The mobile node will generally respond to the received datagram using standard IP routing mechanisms.

Mobile IP operation is shown in Figure 248.

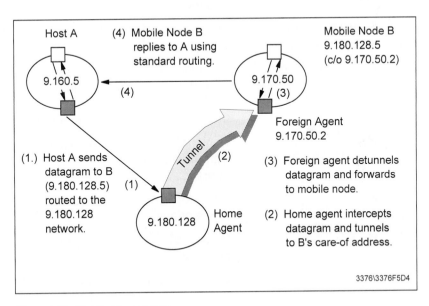

Figure 248. Mobile IP operation

19.3 Mobility agent advertisement extensions

The mobility agent advertisement consists of an ICMP router Advertisement with one or more of the following extensions:

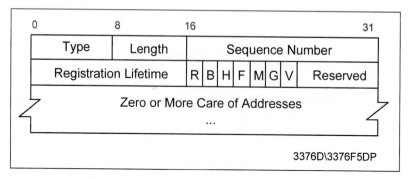

Figure 249. Mobility agent advertisement extension

Where:

Type   16

Length   (6+[4*N]), where N is the number of care-of addresses advertised.

Sequence number   The number of advertisements sent by this agent since it was initialized.

Registration lifetime   The longest lifetime, in seconds, that this agent will accept a Registration Request. A value of 0xffff indicates infinity. This field bears no relationship with the lifetime field in the router advertisement itself.

R   Registration required; mobile node must register with this agent rather than use a co-located care-of address.

B   Busy; foreign agent cannot accept additional registrations.

H   Home Agent; this agent offers service as a home agent on this link.

F   Foreign Agent; this agent offers service as a foreign agent on this link.

M   Minimal encapsulation; this agent receives tunneled datagrams that use minimal encapsulation.

G	GRE encapsulation; this agent receives tunneled datagrams that use GRE encapsulation.
V	Van Jacobson header compression; this agent supports use of Van Jacobson header compression over the link with any registered mobile node.
Reserved	This area is ignored.
Care-of Address(es)	The care-of address(es) advertised by this agent. At least one must be included if the F bit is set.

Note that a foreign agent may be too busy to service additional mobile nodes at certain times. However, it must continue to send agent advertisements (with the B bit set) so that mobile nodes that are already registered will know that the agent has not failed or that they are still in range of the foreign agent.

The prefix lengths extension may follow the mobility agent advertisement extension. It is used to indicate the number of bits that should be applied to each router address (in the ICMP router advertisement portion of the message), when network prefixes are being used for move detection (see 19.7, "Move detection" on page 638). See Figure 250 for more details

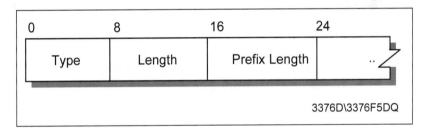

Figure 250. Prefix-lengths extension

Where:

Type	19
Length	The number of router address entries in the router advertisement portion of the agent advertisement.
Prefix length(s)	The number of leading bits that make up the network prefix for each of the router addresses in the router advertisement portion of the agent advertisement. Each prefix length is a separate byte, in the order that the router addresses are listed.

19.4 Mobile IP registration process

RFC 2002 defines two different procedures for mobile IP registration: the mobile node may register via a foreign agent, which relays the registration to the mobile node's home agent, or it may register directly with its home agent. The following rules are used to determine which of these registration processes is used:

- If the mobile node has obtained its care-of address from a foreign agent, it must register via that foreign agent.

- If the mobile node is using a co-located care-of address, but has received an agent advertisement from a foreign agent on this subnet (which has the R bit (registration required) set in that advertisement), then it should register via the agent. This mechanism allows for accounting to take place on foreign subnets, even if DHCP and co-located care-of address is the preferred method of address allocation.

- If the mobile node is using a co-located care-of address but has not received such an advertisement, it must register directly with its home agent.

- If the mobile node returns to its home network, it must deregister directly with its home agent.

The registration process involves the exchange of registration request and registration reply messages, which are UDP datagrams. The registration request is sent to port 434. The request consists of a UDP header, followed by the fields shown in Figure 251.

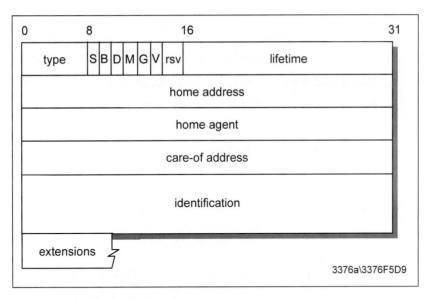

Figure 251. Mobile IP - Registration request

Where:

Type   1

S   Simultaneous bindings; if this bit is set, the home agent should keep any previous bindings for this node as well as adding the new binding. The home agent will then forward any datagrams for the node to multiple care-of addresses. This capability is particularly intended for wireless mobile nodes.

B   Broadcast datagrams; if this bit is set, the home agent should tunnel any broadcast datagrams on the home network to the mobile node.

D   Decapsulation by mobile node; the mobile node is using a co-located care-of address and will, itself, decapsulate the datagrams sent to it.

M   Minimal encapsulation should be used for datagrams tunneled to the mobile node.

G   GRE encapsulation should be used for datagrams tunneled to the mobile node.

V   Van Jacobson compression should be used over the link between agent and mobile node.

rsv	Reserved bits; sent as zero.
Lifetime	The number of seconds remaining before the registration will be considered expired. A value of zero indicates a request for deregistration. 0xffff indicates infinity.
Home address	The home IP address of the mobile node.
Home agent	The IP address of the mobile node's home agent.
Care-of address	The IP address for the end of the tunnel.
Identification	A 64-bit identification number constructed by the mobile node and used for matching registration requests with replies.
Extensions	A number of extensions are defined, all relating to authentication of the registration process. Please see RFC 2002 for full details.

The mobility agent responds to a registration request with a registration reply and with a destination port copied from the source port of the registration request. The registration reply is of the format shown in Figure 252.

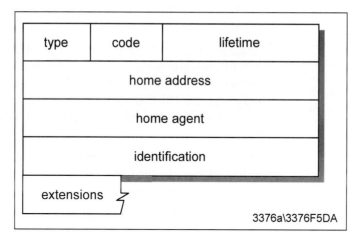

Figure 252. Mobile IP - Registration reply

Where:

Type	3
Code	Indicates the result of the registration request:
	0 Registration accepted.

1	Registration accepted, but simultaneous bindings unsupported.
64-88	Registration denied by foreign agent.
128-136	Registration denied by home agent.

Lifetime   The number of seconds remaining before the registration is considered expired. (Code field must be 0 or 1.)

Home address   Home IP address of the mobile node.

Home agent   IP address of the mobile node's home agent.

Identification   A 64-bit identification number used for matching registration requests with replies.

Extensions   A number of extensions are defined, all relating to authentication of the registration process.

For full details of these messages, please refer to RFC 2002.

19.5 Tunneling

The home agent examines the destination IP address of all datagrams arriving on the home network. If the address matches with any of the mobile nodes currently registered as being away from home, then the home agent tunnels (using IP in IP encapsulation) the datagram to the care-of address for that mobile node. It is likely that the home agent will also be a router on the home network. In this case, it is likely that it will receive datagrams addressed for a mobile node that is *not* currently registered as being away from home. In this case, the home agent assumes that the mobile node is at home, and forwards the datagram to the home network.

When a foreign agent receives a datagram sent to its advertised care-of address, it compares the inner destination address with its list of registered visitors. If it finds a match, the foreign agent forwards the decapsulated datagram to the appropriate mobile node. If there is no match, the datagram is discarded. (The foreign agent must not forward such a datagram to the original IP header, otherwise a routing loop will occur.)

If the mobile node is using a co-located care-of address, then the end of the tunnel lies at the mobile node itself. The mobile node is responsible for decapsulating the datagrams received from the home agent.

19.6 Broadcast datagrams

If the home agent receives a broadcast datagram, it should not forward it to mobile nodes unless the mobile node specifically requested forwarding of broadcasts in its registration request. In this case, it will forward the datagram in one of the following manners:

- If the mobile node has a co-located care-of address, the home agent simply encapsulates the datagram and tunnels it directly to the care-of address.

- If the mobile node has a foreign agent care-of address, the home agent first encapsulates the broadcast in a unicast datagram addressed to the home address of the node. It then encapsulates and tunnels this datagram to the care-of address. In this way, the foreign agent, when it decapsulates the datagram, knows to which of its registered mobile nodes it should forward the broadcast.

19.7 Move detection

Mobile IP is designed not just for mobile users who regularly move from one site to another and attach their laptops to different subnets each time, but also for truly dynamic mobile users (for example, users of a wireless connection from an aircraft). Two mechanisms are defined that allow the mobile node to detect when it has moved from one subnet to another. When the mobile node detects that it has moved, it must re-register with a care-of address on the new foreign network. The two methods of move detection are as follows:

1. Foreign agents are consistently advertising their presence on the network by means of agent advertisements. When the mobile node receives an agent advertisement from its foreign agent, it starts a timer based on the lifetime field in the advertisement. If the mobile node has not received another advertisement from the same foreign agent by the time the lifetime has expired, then the mobile node assumes that it has lost contact with that agent. If, in the meantime, it has received an advertisement from *another* foreign agent, it may immediately attempt registration with the new agent. If it has not received any further agent advertisements, it should use Agent solicitation to try and locate a new foreign agent with which to register.

2. The mobile node checks whether any newly received agent advertisement is on the same subnet as its current care-of address. If the network prefix is different, the mobile node assumes that it has moved. On expiration of

its current care-of address, the mobile node registers with the foreign agent that sent the new agent advertisement.

19.7.1 Returning home

When the mobile node receives an agent advertisement from its own home agent, it knows that it has returned to its home network. Before deregistering with the home agent, the mobile node must configure its routing table for operation on the home subnet.

19.8 ARP considerations

Mobile IP requires two extensions to ARP to cope with the movement of mobile nodes. These are:

Proxy ARP An ARP reply sent by one node on behalf of another that is either unable or unwilling to answer an ARP request on its own behalf.

Gratuitous ARP An ARP packet sent as a local broadcast packet by one node that causes all receiving nodes to update an entry in their ARP cache.

When a mobile node is registered as being on a foreign network, its home agent will use proxy ARP in response to any ARP request seeking the mobile node's MAC address. The home agent responds to the request giving its own MAC address.

When a mobile node moves from its home network and registers itself with a foreign network, the home agent does a gratuitous ARP broadcast to update the ARP caches of all local nodes on the network. The MAC address used is again the MAC address of the home agent.

When a mobile node returns to its home network, having been previously registered at a foreign network, gratuitous ARP is again used to update ARP caches of all local nodes, this time with the real MAC address of the mobile node.

19.9 Mobile IP security considerations

The mobile computing environment has many potential vulnerabilities with regard to security, particularly if wireless links are in use, which are particularly exposed to eavesdropping. The tunnel between a home agent and the care-of address of a mobile node could also be susceptible to interception, unless a strong authentication mechanism is implemented as part of the registration process. RFC 2002 specifies implementation of keyed MD5 for the authentication protocol and advocates the use of additional mechanisms (such as encryption) for environments where total privacy is required.

Chapter 20. Integrating other protocols with TCP/IP

With the increase in popularity of the TCP/IP protocol suite, many networks now implement multiple networking protocols (aside from TCP/IP). Examples include System Network Architecture (SNA), Advanced Peer-to-Peer Networking (APPN), and NetBIOS. To reduce the expense of maintaining parallel networks, a number of techniques can be employed to integrate these networking protocols with TCP/IP. Usually, one network infrastructure is chosen to provide connectivity while other protocol data is carried over this infrastructure. Because of IP's ubiquitous deployment and platform popularity, IP has become the network protocol of choice in today's networks.

While multiprotocol transport networking (MPTN) attempts to create a mapping between network protocols, most popular integration methods make use of data encapsulation, which provides the ability to transmit data of one type of network protocol over another by enveloping data units of one protocol within the data units of another. In this sense, the encapsulated protocol data is seen as data payload to the underlying network infrastructure.

20.1 Enterprise Extender

The Enterprise Extender network connection is a simple set of extensions to the existing open high performance routing (HPR) technology. It performs an efficient integration of the HPR frames using UDP/IP packets. To the HPR network, the IP backbone is a logical link. To the IP network, the SNA traffic is UDP datagrams that are routed without any hardware or software changes to the IP backbone. Unlike gateways, there is no protocol transformation, and unlike common tunneling mechanisms, the integration is performed at the routing layers without the overhead of additional transport functions. The advanced technology enables efficient use of the intranet infrastructure for support of IP-based client accessing SNA-based data (for example, TN2370 emulators or Web browsers using services such as IBM Host On-Demand), as well as SNA clients using any of the SNA LU types.

Enterprise Extender seamlessly routes packets through the network protocol "edges," eliminating the need to perform costly protocol translation and the store-and-forward associated with transport-layer functions. Unlike Data Link Switching (DLSw), for example, there are no TCP retransmit buffers and timers and no congestion control logic in the router, because it uses connectionless UDP and the congestion control is provided end system to end system. Because of these savings, the "edge" routers have less work to do and can perform the job they do best which is forwarding packets instead of incurring protocol translation overhead and maintaining many TCP connections. This technology, then, allows the data center routers to handle larger networks and larger volumes of network traffic, thus providing more capacity for the money.

20.1.1 Performance and recovery

The Enterprise Extender also provides many of the traffic control features that SNA users have come to expect. Using Class of Service (COS), SNA applications specify the nature of the services they require from the network (for example, interactive or batch). Included in this specification is the required traffic priority. Most routers support some form of prioritized queuing. In IBM routers, this function is called the Bandwidth Reservation System (BRS). Enterprise Extender exploits this existing function by mapping the SNA priority to the UDP port numbers that routers can easily use to determine the appropriate priority. Defaults for these port numbers have been registered with the Internet Assigned Numbers Authority (IANA).

Network failures, even in a network of combined technologies, can be handled successfully. Unlike other technologies, such as Data Link Switching, Enterprise Extender can switch around failures that occur at the edges of the SNA and IP protocols. Since HPR can switch between routes as required and Enterprise Extender provides the flexibility for those routes to include an IP backbone, Enterprise Extender makes it possible for SNA networks to use the IP attachment as alternate and backup routes for the SNA network.

20.2 Data Link Switching

Data Link Switching (DLSw) was issued by IBM in March 1993 and is documented in RFC 1795. Its state is informational.

20.2.1 Introduction

Data Link Switching is a forwarding mechanism for the IBM SNA and IBM NetBIOS protocols. It does not provide full routing, but instead provides switching at the data link layer and encapsulation in TCP/IP for transport over the Internet. Routers of other vendors can participate if they comply to the above RFC or without DLSw capability as intermediate routers, because the DLSw connection exists only between the two end routers.

20.2.2 Functional description

DLSw was developed to provide support for SNA and NetBIOS in multiprotocol routers. Since SNA and NetBIOS are basically connection-oriented protocols, the data link control procedure that they use on the LAN is IEEE 802.2 Logical Link Control (LLC) Type 2. DLSw also accommodates SNA protocols over WAN links via the SDLC protocol.

IEEE 802.2 LLC Type 2 was designed with the assumption that the network transit delay would be small and predictable (for example, a local LAN). Therefore, LLC uses a fixed timer for detecting lost frames. When bridging is used over wide area lines (especially at lower speeds), the network delay is larger and can vary greatly based upon congestion. When the delay exceeds the timeout value, LLC attempts to retransmit. If the frame is not actually lost, only delayed, it is possible for the LLC Type 2 procedures to become confused, and as a result, the link is eventually taken down.

Given the use of LLC Type 2 services, DLSw addresses the following bridging problems:

- DLC timeouts
- DLC acknowledgments over the WAN
- Flow and congestion control
- Broadcast control of search packets
- Source-route bridging hop count limits

NetBIOS also makes extensive use of datagram services that use LLC Type 1. In this case, DLSw addresses the last two problems in the above list. The principal difference between DLSw and bridging is that DLS terminates the data link control, whereas bridging does not. Figure 253 illustrates this difference based upon two end systems operating with LLC Type 2 services.

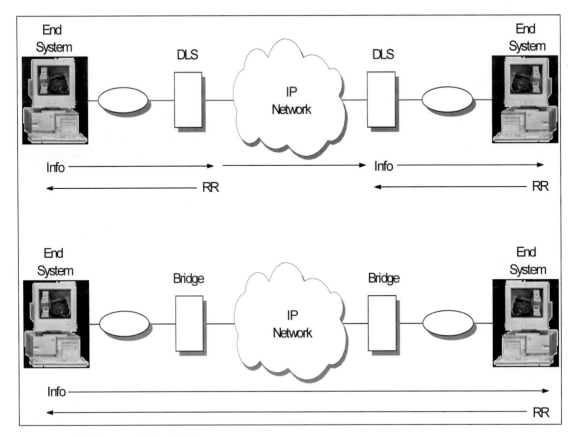

Figure 253. DLSw compared to bridging

In traditional bridging, the data link control is end-to-end. DLSw terminates the LLC Type 2 connection at the switch. This means that the LLC Type 2 connections do not cross the wide area network. The DLS multiplexes LLC connections onto a TCP connection to another DLS. Therefore, the LLC connections at each end are totally independent of each other. It is the responsibility of the data link switch to deliver frames that it has received from an LLC connection to the other end. TCP is used between the data link switches to guarantee delivery of frames.

As a result of this design, LLC timeouts are limited to the local LAN. (For example, they do not traverse the wide area.) Also, the LLC Type 2 acknowledgments (RRs) do not traverse the WAN, thereby reducing traffic across the wide area links. For SDLC links, polling and poll response occurs locally, not over the WAN. Broadcast of search frames is controlled by the data link switches once the location of a target system is discovered. Finally, the switches can now apply back pressure to the end systems to provide flow and congestion control.

DLSw uses LAN addressing to set up connections between SNA systems. SDLC-attached devices are defined with MAC addresses to enable them to communicate with LAN-attached devices. For NetBIOS systems, DLSw uses the NetBIOS name to forward datagrams and to set up connections for NetBIOS sessions. For circuit establishment, SNA systems send TEST (or in some cases, XID) frames to the null (x'00') SAP. NetBIOS systems have an address resolution procedure, based upon the name query and name recognized frames, that is used to establish an end-to-end circuit.

Since DLSw can be implemented in multiprotocol routers, there may be situations where both bridging and switching are enabled. SNA frames can be identified by their link SAP. Typical SAP values for SNA are x'04', x'08', and x'0C'. NetBIOS always uses a link SAP value of x'F0'.

For further details, please refer to RFC 1795.

20.3 Multiprotocol Transport Network (MPTN)

Multiprotocol transport networking (MPTN), developed by IBM, is an open architecture for:

- Mixed-protocol networking: running applications associated with one network protocol over different network protocols

- Network concatenation: connection matching applications across networks of different protocols through gateways

20.3.1 Requirements for mixed-protocol networking

With the growth of networking in general and local area networks in particular, many large customer networks have become confederations of individual networks running different networking protocols. This heterogeneity has arisen for a number of reasons. Some of these include:

- Shift of customer interest away from selecting a particular networking architecture in favor of finding solutions to business problems, regardless of the specific network protocol required

- Inter-enterprise information exchange requirement, for example, direct manufacturing, order placement, or billing systems

- Company mergers requiring interconnection

20.3.2 MPTN architecture

Networking protocols generally provide three types of functions:

- Transport
- Naming and addressing
- Higher level functions

Transport functions are those that provide the basic facility for two partners to communicate, either through connections or in a connectionless manner through datagrams. Naming and addressing conventions define how entities are known and how they are to be found. The higher level functions include allocation of the connections to users and control of their use. Not all networking protocols support higher level functions. SNA and OSI do; TCP/IP and NetBIOS do not.

MPTN separates transport functions from higher level functions and from the address formats seen by the users of the protocol. Its goal is to allow any higher level protocol using the corresponding address structure to run over any transport function. The division of functions between transport and higher level was chosen because the transport level is the highest level at which there are common functions that can be reasonably mapped across protocols. At other levels, the number of services is either too large or too small to provide a practical division.

20.3.3 MPTN methodology

MPTN architecture solves the above requirements by defining a new canonical interface to a set of transport services that concatenate connections across multiple networking protocols. When an application is written for a particular transport service, it may be written so that it makes assumptions about the particular transport service. Thus, it may appear to be transport-specific in the services that it uses. For example, applications written to the NetBEUI interface may request a message be broadcast. In environments where a particular service is not natively supported over the underlying transport network, MPTN provides compensation. In essence, MPTN frees up applications so that they are able to operate over different transport networks.

Another way of thinking about this is that (in the OSI model) functions, from the session layer up, are users of transport services or transport users. These services are in turn provided by functions from the transport layer down. MPTN defines a boundary interface, called the transport-layer protocol boundary (TLPB), which clearly delineates this distinction between transport user and transport provider. This is shown graphically in Figure 254.

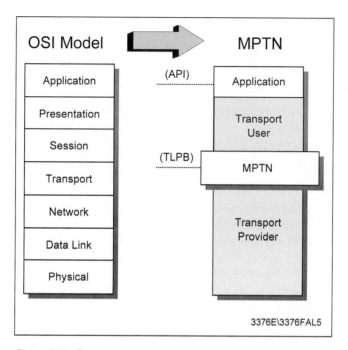

Figure 254. Transport-layer protocol boundary

20.3.4 MPTN major components

MPTN functions appear in four types of nodes:

- MPTN access node

  An MPTN access node contains the transport-layer protocol boundary (TLPB), which provides a semantic interface so that higher level protocols or application interfaces written for a particular transport protocol can be transported over another protocol with no apparent change. Such a node can run application programs independent of the underlying transport network and can run application programs on different underlying transport networks.

  The applications in the MPTN access node are generally written to an existing application programming interface (API). The API uses the functions of the native communications protocol. When transport-level MPTN functions are accessed, the API will be converted to access these functions instead of the native communication protocol, while keeping the same interface to the application program. For example, the NetBEUI application interface is written to use the NetBIOS communications protocol. To use another protocol stack below the transport layer, the NetBEUI API must be made to invoke the MPTN functions. After this is done, all programs using NetBEUI on this MPTN access node can communicate via, for example, SNA, TCP/IP, OSI, and other protocols, with another NetBEUI application within the MPTN network. All this is possible without the original application program requiring any changes.

- MPTN address mapping server node

An address mapping server node is an MPTN node with a special function that provides a general address mapping service to the address mapping client component of other MPTN nodes, access, or gateway, connected to the same transport provider network.

- MPTN multicast server node

A multicast server node is an MPTN node with a special function, the multicast server, which manages multicast and broadcast distribution of datagrams in networks that do not provide the service as a natural consequence of their design. For example, a NetBIOS transport network is designed to support multicast distribution of datagrams while an SNA network is not. The multicast server operates in cooperation with the address mapping server to provide a multicast service where this capability does not exist within the services offered by the transport network.

- MPTN gateway node

An MPTN gateway connects two transport networks to provide an end-to-end service over both of them for one or more transport user protocols. There are two types of gateways: nonnative-to-nonnative, with respect to the supported transport user protocol, and native-to-nonnative, with respect to the supported transport user protocol.

In the case of nonnative-to-native, one of the transport providers connected to the gateway node is native to the transport user. This type of gateway allows access to an end node that has no MPTN function. When one side is native, the MPTN protocol (of the nonnative side) terminates in the gateway (refer to Figure 255).

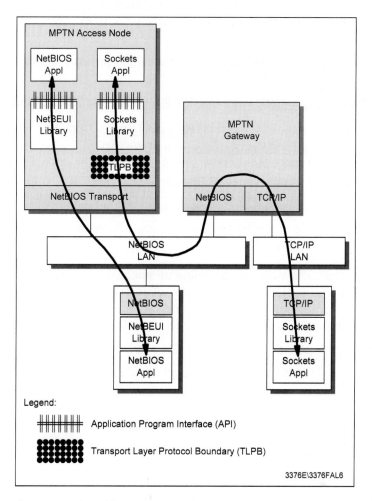

Figure 255. An MPTN network - nonnative-to-native gateway

20.4 NetBIOS over TCP/IP

For some time, the NetBIOS service has been a dominant mechanism for networking of personal computers in a LAN environment. NetBIOS is a vendor-independent software interface (API), not a protocol. There is no official NetBIOS specification, although in practice, the NetBIOS version described in the IBM publication *LAN Technical Reference: 802.2 and NetBIOS APIs*, SC30-3587 is used as reference.

The NetBIOS service has some specific characteristics that limit its use in certain wide area network environments:

- NetBIOS workstations address each other using NetBIOS names. NetBIOS relies on the broadcast technique to register and find NetBIOS names on the network.
- NetBIOS uses a flat name space, which bears no relationship to the domain name system.
- NetBIOS generally uses the 802.2 interface, so it is not routeable.

One solution to overcome these limitations is found in RFC 1001 – Protocol Standard for a NetBIOS Service on a TCP/UDP Transport: Concepts and Methods and RFC 1002 – Protocol Standard for a NetBIOS Service on a TCP/UDP Transport: Detailed Specifications.

As the titles suggest, these RFCs define a method of implementing NetBIOS services on top of the Transmission Control Protocol (TCP) and User Datagram Protocol (UDP).

RFCs 1001 and 1002 do not define an encapsulation technique; they define the mapping of NetBIOS services to UDP/IP and TCP/IP. For example, once a NetBIOS session has been established, sockets-send commands will be used over a TCP connection to send NetBIOS session data.

From the point of view of a network application, written to the NetBIOS interface, there is no change to the NetBIOS service. An application is unaware of the change in the underlying protocol.

The NetBIOS service running over TCP and UDP is logically represented in Figure 256.

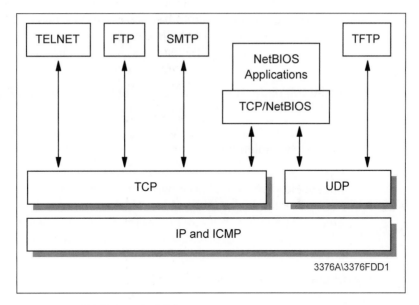

Figure 256. TCP/IP and NetBIOS

RFC 1001 introduces a number of new concepts to facilitate NetBIOS operation in a TCP/IP environment:

• NetBIOS scope

  The NetBIOS scope is a group of computers across which a NetBIOS name is known. In a standard NetBIOS configuration, using broadcast techniques, all the computers in this group would be able to contact each other. The NetBIOS over TCP/IP implementation must provide an alternative method for this group to communicate with each other, particularly as they may be spread across subnets. An internetwork may support multiple, non-intersecting NetBIOS scopes. Each NetBIOS scope has a *scope identifier*, which is a character string in a format compatible with the domain name system.

• NetBIOS end node

  Computers using NetBIOS over TCP/IP are known as NetBIOS end nodes. RFC 1001 defines the following three types of end node:

  - Broadcast (B) node: Uses local broadcast UDP datagrams to establish connections and distribute datagrams. Because broadcast datagrams cannot typically cross routers, B nodes (as defined in RFC 1001) can only establish communications within a single network segment.

- Point-to-Point (P) node: Relies on a NetBIOS name server (NBNS) to establish connections with other nodes and on a NetBIOS datagram distributor (NBDD) for datagram distribution. P nodes neither generate, or listen for broadcast UDP packets, and use directed unicast packets only.

- Mixed (M) node: A mixed node is a combination of both B and P nodes. It uses both unicast (to a NBNS) and broadcast packets

A fourth node type, the hybrid (H) node, although not defined in the RFCs, is also widely implemented:

- Hybrid (H) Node: The hybrid node is also a combination of B and P nodes. However, the H node will always attempt to contact a NetBIOS name server initially, using unicast packets, and will only resort to broadcast packets in the event that this is unsuccessful. The H node has an advantage over the M node in that it limits the generation of unwanted broadcast packets.

• NetBIOS Name Server (NBNS)

The NBNS registers the NetBIOS name/IP address of each P, M, or H node when it is initialized. Whenever a node wishes to contact another node by means of its NetBIOS name, it uses the NBNS to obtain the corresponding IP address for that node. NetBIOS names are combined with their scope identifiers and stored in an encoded form (which is a valid domain system name) in the NBNS.

• NetBIOS Datagram Distributor (NBDD)

• The NBDD extends the NetBIOS datagram distribution service to the internet environment. When an end node wishes to broadcast a datagram, the node sends a unicast datagram, which contains the scope of the broadcast to the NBDD. The NBDD sends a NetBIOS datagram to each end node within the specified NetBIOS scope, using the services of the NBNS to obtain the relevant IP addresses. (In practice, it is likely that the NBNS and NBDD will be implemented on the same device.)

20.4.1 NetBIOS Name Server (NBNS) implementations

NetBIOS name servers dynamically register NetBIOS-to-IP mappings for P, H, and M node workstations as they are initialized and respond to requests for those mappings. The NBNS is the simplest NetBIOS over IP solution to manage, as it removes the requirement for manual configuration of files, either on the client workstations, or on the DNS.

20.4.1.1 Microsoft Windows Internet Name Service (WINS)

Windows Internet Name Service (WINS) is Microsoft's implementation of an NBNS. WINS only supports Microsoft's proprietary clients with its implementation of native NetBIOS and NetBIOS over TCP/IP.

Each Microsoft client needs to be configured with the IP address of a primary WINS server, and, optionally, with the IP address of a secondary WINS server. Whenever a client starts, it will attempt to register its NetBIOS name and IP address with the primary WINS server. The registration occurs when services or applications are started (for example, Workstation or Messenger), and is sent directly to the primary WINS server. If the name is not already registered to another client, the server responds with a message detailing the NetBIOS name that has been registered, and the name time-to-live (TTL). If the client attempts three times to register its name with the primary server and fails, the client will attempt to register its name with the secondary server. If the secondary server also fails to respond, the client will revert to broadcasting in order to register its name.

The name registrations are made on a temporary basis, and the client is responsible for maintaining the lease of the registered name. At one-eighth of the TTL, the client will attempt to refresh its name registration with the primary WINS server. If the client does not receive a response from the server, it will continue to attempt to refresh the registration every two minutes until half the TTL has expired. At this point it will repeat the procedure, but this time using the secondary WINS server.

With WINS enabled, the client acts as an H node client for name registration. For resolution, it is H node with a few modifications. The sequence used by a WINS client for name resolution is:

1. Check to see if it is the local machine name.
2. Check the local cache. (Any resolved name is placed in a cache for 10 minutes.)
3. Try to use the primary WINS server. (Use the secondary server if the primary does not answer after three attempts).
4. Try a name query broadcast.
5. Check the LMHOSTS file (If the computer is configured to use LMHOSTS).
6. Try the HOSTS file.
7. Try the DNS.

For further information on NetBIOS over TCP/IP, please refer to RFC 1001 and RFC 1002.

Chapter 21. TCP/IP security

This chapter discusses security issues regarding TCP/IP networks and provides an overview of solutions to prevent security exposures or problems before they can occur. The field of network security in general and of TCP/IP security in particular is too wide to be dealt with in an all encompassing way in this book, so the focus of this chapter is on the most common security exposures and measures to counteract them. Because many, if not all, security solutions are based on cryptographic algorithms, we also provide a brief overview of this topic for the better understanding of concepts presented throughout this chapter.

21.1 Security exposures and solutions

This section gives an overview of some of the most common attacks on computer security, and it presents viable solutions to those exposures and lists actual implementations thereof.

21.1.1 Common attacks against security

For thousands of years, people have been guarding the gates to where they store their treasures and assets. Failure to do so usually resulted in being robbed, victimized by society, or even killed. Though things are usually not as dramatic anymore, they can still become very bad. Modern day IT managers have realized that it is equally important to protect their communications networks against intruders and saboteurs from both inside and outside. One does not have to be overly paranoid to find some good reasons as to why this is the case:

- Tapping the wire: To get access to cleartext data and passwords
- Impersonation: To get unauthorized access to data or to create unauthorized e-mails, orders, etc.
- Denial-of-service: To render network resources non-functional
- Replay of messages: To get access to information and change it in transit
- Guessing of passwords: To get access to information and services that would normally be denied (dictionary attack)
- Guessing of keys: To get access to encrypted data and passwords (brute-force attack)
- Viruses: To destroy data

Though these attacks are not exclusively specific to TCP/IP networks, they should be considered potential threats to anyone who is going to base their network on TCP/IP, which is the most prevalent protocol used. TCP/IP is an open protocol, and as such, hackers find easy prey by trying the above.

21.1.2 Solutions to network security problems

Network owners should try to protect themselves with the same zealousness that intruders use to search for a way to get into the network. To that end, we have provided some solutions to effectively defend a network from an attack, specifically against the attacks mentioned above. It has to be noted that any of these solutions only solve a single (or a very limited number) of security problems. Therefore, a combination of several such solutions should be considered in order to guarantee a certain level of safety and security. These solutions include:

- Encryption: To protect data and passwords

- Authentication by digital signatures and certificates: To verify who is sending data over the network

- Authorization: To prevent improper access

- Integrity checking and message authentication codes: To protect against improper alteration of messages

- Non-repudiation: To make sure that an action cannot be denied by the person who performed it

- One-time passwords and two-way random number handshakes: To mutually authenticate parties of a conversation

- Frequent key refresh, strong keys and prevention of deriving future keys: To protect against breaking of keys (cryptanalysis)

- Address concealment: To protect against denial-of-service attacks

Table 25 matches common problems and security exposures to the solutions listed above:

Table 25. Security exposures and protections

Problem/exposure	Remedy
How to prevent wire tappers from reading messages?	Encrypt messages, typically using a shared secret key (secret keys offer a tremendous performance advantage over public/private keys).
How to distribute the keys in a secure way?	Use a different encryption technique, typically public/private key.

Problem/exposure	Remedy
How to prevent keys from becoming stale, and how to protect against guessing of future keys by cracking current keys?	Refresh keys frequently and do not derive new keys from old ones (use perfect forward secrecy).
How to prevent retransmission of messages by an impostor (replay attack)?	Use sequence numbers (timestamps are usually unreliable for security purposes).
How to ensure a message has not been altered in transit?	Use message digests (hash or one-way functions).
How to ensure the message digest has not also been compromised?	Use digital signatures by encrypting the message digest with a secret or private key (origin authentication, non-repudiation).
How to ensure the message and signature originated from the desired partner?	Use two-way handshakes involving encrypted random numbers (mutual authentication).
How to ensure handshakes are exchanged with the right partners (man-in-the-middle attack)?	Use digital certificates (binding of public keys to permanent identities).
How to prevent improper use of services by otherwise properly authenticated users?	Use a multi-layer access control model.
How to protect against viruses?	Restrict access to outside resources; run anti-virus software on every server and workstation that has contact to outside data, and update that software frequently.
How to protect against unwanted or malicious messages (denial of service attacks)?	Restrict access to internal network using filters, firewalls, proxies, packet authentication, conceal internal address and name structure, etc.

In general, keep your network tight towards the outside, but also keep a watchful eye at the inside because most attacks are mounted from inside a corporate network.

21.1.3 Implementations of security solutions

The following protocols and systems are commonly used to provide various degrees of security services in a computer network. They are discussed at length throughout the rest of this chapter.

- IP filtering

- Network Address Translation (NAT)
- IP Security Architecture (IPsec)
- SOCKS
- Secure Shell (SSH)
- Secure Sockets Layer (SSL)
- Application proxies
- Firewalls
- Kerberos and other authentication systems (AAA servers)
- Secure Electronic Transactions (SET)

Figure 257 illustrates where these security solutions fit within the TCP/IP layers.

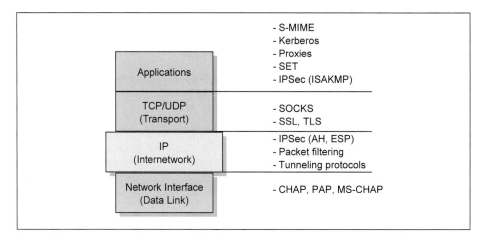

Figure 257. Security solutions in the TCP/IP layers

Table 26 summarizes the characteristics of some of the security solutions mentioned before and compares them to each other. This should help anyone who needs to devise a security strategy to determine what combination of solutions would achieve a desired level of protection.

Table 26. Security solution implementations - a comparison

	Access Control	Encryption	Authenti-cation	Integrity Checking	Perfect Forward Security	Address Conceal-ment	Session Monitoring
IP filtering	y	n	n	n	n	n	n

	Access Control	Encryption	Authenti-cation	Integrity Checking	Perfect Forward Security	Address Conceal-ment	Session Monitoring
NAT	y	n	n	n	n	y	y (connection)
IPsec	y	y (packet)	y(packet)	y (packet)	y	y	n
SOCKS	y	n	y (client/ user)	n	n	y	y (connection)
SSL	y	y (data)	y (system/ user)	y		n	y
Application Proxy	y	normally no	y (user)	y	normally no	y	y (connection and data)
AAA servers	y (user)	n	y (user)	n	n	n	n

An overall security solution can, in most cases, only be provided by a combination of the listed options. Your particular security requirements need to be specified in a security policy and should be, for example, enforced by using a firewall.

21.1.4 Network security policy

An organization's overall security policy must be determined according to security and business needs analysis. Since a firewall relates to network security only, a firewall has little value unless the overall security policy is properly defined.

Network security policy defines those services that will be explicitly allowed or denied, how these services will be used, and the exceptions to these rules. Every rule in the network security policy should be implemented on a firewall and/or remote access server (RAS). Generally, a firewall uses one of the following methods.

Everything not specifically permitted is denied
This approach blocks all traffic between two networks except for those services and applications that are permitted. Therefore, each desired service and application should be implemented one by one. No service or application that might be a potential hole on the firewall should be permitted. This is the most secure method, denying services and applications unless explicitly allowed by the administrator. On the other hand, from the point of users, it might be more restrictive and less convenient.

Everything not specifically denied is permitted

This approach allows all traffic between two networks except for those services and applications that are denied. Therefore, each untrusted or potentially harmful service or application should be denied one by one. Although this is a flexible and convenient method for the users, it could potentially cause some serious security problems.

Remote access servers should provide authentication of users and should ideally also provide for limiting certain users to certain systems and/or networks within the corporate intranet (authorization). Remote access servers must also determine if a user is considered roaming (can connect from multiple remote locations) or stationary (can connect only from a single remote location), and if the server should use call-back for particular users once they are properly authenticated.

Generally, anonymous access should at best, be granted to servers in a demilitarized zone (DMZ, see 21.3.6.4, "Screened subnet firewall (demilitarized zone)" on page 693). All services within a corporate intranet should require at least password authentication and appropriate access control. Direct access from the outside should always be authenticated and accounted.

21.2 A short introduction to cryptography

The purpose of this chapter is to introduce the terminology and give a brief overview of the major cryptographic concepts that relate to TCP/IP security implementations. The information presented here only scratches the surface. Some issues are left open or not mentioned at all.

21.2.1 Terminology

Let's start with defining some very basic concepts.

Cryptography

Put simply, cryptography is the science of keeping your data and communications secure. To achieve this goal, techniques such as *encryption, decryption* and *authentication* are used. With the recent advances in this field, the frontiers of cryptography have become blurred. Every procedure consisting of transforming data based on methods that are difficult to reverse can be considered cryptography. The key factor to strong cryptography is the difficulty of reverse engineering. You might be amazed to know that simple methods, such as password-scrambled word processor documents or compressed archives, can be broken in a matter of minutes by a hacker using an ordinary PC. *Strong* cryptography means that the computational effort needed to retrieve your cleartext messages without knowing the proper keys makes the retrieval infeasible. In this context, infeasible means something like this: If all the computers in the world were assigned to the problem, they would have to work tens of thousands of years until the solution was found. The process of retrieval is called *cryptanalysis*. An attempted cryptanalysis is an *attack*.

Encryption and decryption - cryptographic algorithms

Encryption is the transformation of a cleartext message into an unreadable form in order to hide its meaning. The opposite transformation, which retrieves the original cleartext, is the decryption. The mathematical function used for encryption and decryption is the *cryptographic algorithm* or *cipher*.

The security of a cipher might be based entirely on keeping its functionality a secret, in which case it is a *restricted* cipher. There are many drawbacks to restricted ciphers. It is very difficult to keep an algorithm a secret when it is used by many people. If it is incorporated in a commercial product, then it is only a matter of time and money before it is reverse engineered. For these reasons, the currently used algorithms are *keyed*, that is, the encryption and decryption makes use of a parameter, known as the *key*. The key can be chosen from a set of possible values, called the *keyspace*. The keyspace usually is huge, the bigger the better. The security of these algorithms rely entirely on the key, not on their internal secrets. In fact, the algorithms themselves are usually public and are extensively analyzed for possible weaknesses.

> **Note:**
>
> Do not trust new, unknown, or unpublished algorithms. The principle of keyed ciphers is shown in Figure 258.

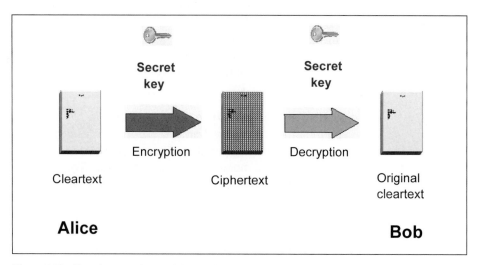

Figure 258. Keyed encryption and decryption

> **Note:**
>
> It is common in cryptographic literature to denote the first participant in a protocol as Alice and the second one as Bob. They are the "crypto couple."

Authentication, integrity, and non-repudiation

Encryption provides confidentiality to messages. When communicating over an untrusted medium, such as the Internet, you may also need, in addition to confidentiality:

- Authentication - A method for verifying that the sender of a message is really who he or she claims to be. Any intruder masquerading as someone else is detected by authentication.

- Integrity checking - A method for verifying that a message has not been altered along the communication path. Any tampered message sent by an intruder is detected by an integrity check. As a side effect, communication errors are also detected.

- Non-repudiation - The possibility to prove that the sender has really sent the message. When algorithms providing non-repudiation are used, the sender is not able to later deny the fact that he or she sent the message in question.

21.2.2 Symmetric or secret-key algorithms

Symmetric algorithms are keyed algorithms where the decryption key is the same as the encryption key. These are conventional cryptographic algorithms where the sender and the receiver must agree on the key *before* any secured communication can take place between them. Figure 258 illustrates a symmetric algorithm. There are two types of symmetric algorithms: *block algorithms*, which operate on the cleartext in blocks of bits, and *stream algorithms*, which operate on a single bit (or byte) of cleartext at a time.

Block ciphers are used in several *modes*. Electronic Codebook Mode (ECB) is the simplest; each block of cleartext is encrypted independently. Given a block length of 64 bits, there are 2^{64} possible input cleartext blocks, each of them corresponding to exactly one out of 2^{64} possible ciphertext blocks. An intruder might construct a codebook with known cleartext-ciphertext pairs and mount an attack. Because of this vulnerability, the Cipher Block Chaining (CBC) mode is often used, where the result of the encryption of the previous block is used in the encryption of the current block, thus each ciphertext block is dependent not just on the corresponding plaintext block, but on all previous plaintext blocks.

The algorithms often make use of initialization vectors (IVs). These are variables independent of the keys and are good for setting up the initial state of the algorithms.

A well-known block algorithm is the Data Encryption Standard (DES), which is a worldwide standard cipher developed by IBM. DES operates on 64-bit blocks and has a key length of 56 bits, often expressed as a 64-bit number, with every eighth bit serving as parity bit. From this key, 16 subkeys are derived, which are used in the 16 rounds of the algorithm.

DES produces ciphertexts the same length as the cleartext and the decryption algorithm is exactly the same as the encryption, the only difference being the subkey schedule. These properties make it very suitable for hardware implementations.

Although DES is aging (its origins date back to the early '70s), the algorithm itself is still considered secure. The most practical attack against it is *brute-force* decryption, with all possible keys, looking for a meaningful result. The problem with DES is the key length. Given enough time and computers, a brute-force attack against the 56-bit key might be feasible; that's why a new mode of DES, called triple-DES, or 3DES, has recently gained popularity. With triple-DES, the original DES algorithm is applied in three rounds, with two or three different keys. This encryption is thought to be unbreakable for a long time, even with the foreseeable technological advances taken into account.

An exportable version of DES is IBM's Commercial Data Masking Facility, or CDMF, which uses a 40-bit key.

Another, more recent block algorithm is the International Data Encryption Algorithm (IDEA). This cipher uses 64-bit blocks and 128-bit keys. It was developed in the early '90s and aimed to replace DES. It is cryptographically strong and faster than DES. Despite this, there is no widespread commercial acceptance, mainly because it is relatively new and not fully analyzed. The most significant use of IDEA is in the freeware secure e-mail package Pretty Good Privacy (PGP).

An example of a stream algorithm is A5, which is used to encrypt digital cellular telephony traffic in the GSM standard, widely used in Europe.

The advantage of the symmetric algorithms is their efficiency. They can be easily implemented in hardware. A major disadvantage is the difficulty of key management. A secure way of exchanging the keys must exist, which is often very hard to implement.

21.2.3 Asymmetric or public-key algorithms

These algorithms address the major drawback of symmetric ciphers, the requirement of the secure key-exchange channel. The idea is that two different keys should be used: a public key which, as the name implies, is known to everyone, and a private key, which is to be kept in tight security by the owner. The private key cannot be determined from the public key. A cleartext encrypted with the public key can only be decrypted with the corresponding private key. A cleartext encrypted with the private key can only be decrypted with the corresponding public key. Thus, if someone sends a message encrypted with the recipient's public key, it can be read by the intended recipient only. The process is shown in Figure 259, where Alice sends an encrypted message to Bob.

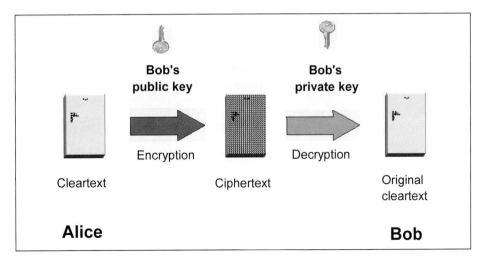

Figure 259. Encryption using the recipient's public key

As the public key is available to anyone, privacy is assured without the need for a secure key-exchange channel. Parties who wish to communicate retrieve each other's public key.

21.2.3.1 Authentication and non-repudiation

An interesting property of the public-key algorithms is that they can provide authentication. The private key is used for encryption. Since anyone has access to the corresponding public key and can decrypt the message, this provides no privacy. However, it authenticates the message. If one can successfully decrypt it with the claimed sender's public key, then the message has been encrypted with the corresponding private key, which is known by the real sender only. Thus, the sender's identity is verified. Encryption with the private key is used in *digital signatures*. The principle is shown in Figure 260. Alice encrypts her message with her private key ("signs" it), in order to enable Bob to verify the authenticity of the message.

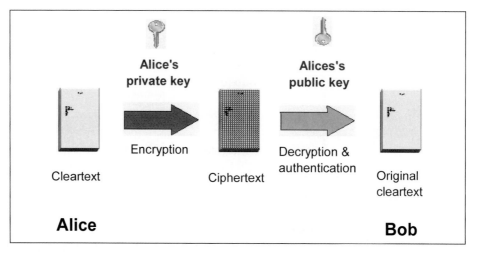

Figure 260. Authentication by encrypting with a private key

Going a step further, encrypting with the private key gives non-repudiation too. The mere existence of such an encrypted message testifies that the originator has really sent it, because only he or she could have used the private key to generate the message. Additionally, if a timestamp is included, then the exact date and time can also be proven. There are protocols involving trusted third parties that prevent the sender from using phony timestamps.

21.2.3.2 Examples of public-key algorithms

Algorithms based on public keys can be used for a variety of purposes. Two common applications are:

1. Encryption (see "RSA public key algorithm" on page 667)
2. Generation of shared keys for use with symmetric key algorithms (see "Diffie-Hellman key exchange" on page 668)

The most popular public-key algorithm is the *de facto* standard RSA, named after its three inventors: Ron Rivest, Adi Shamir and Leonard Adleman. The security of RSA relies on the difficult problem of factoring large numbers. The public and private keys are functions of two very large (200 digits or even more) prime numbers. Given the public key and the ciphertext, an attack would be successful if it could factor the product of the two primes. RSA has resisted many years of extensive attacks. As computing power grows, keeping RSA secure is a matter of increasing the key length (unlike DES, where the key length is fixed).

Another public-key algorithm, actually the very first ever invented, is *Diffie-Hellman*. This is a key-exchange algorithm; that is, it is used for securely establishing a shared secret over an insecure channel. The communicating parties exchange public information from which they derive a key. An eavesdropper cannot reconstruct the key from the information that went through the insecure channel. More precisely, the reconstruction is computationally infeasible. The security of Diffie-Hellman relies on the difficulty of calculating discrete logarithms in finite fields. After the shared secret has been established, it can then be used to derive keys for use with symmetric key algorithms such as DES.

Diffie-Hellman makes the secure derivation of a shared secret key possible, but it does not authenticate the parties. For authentication, another public-key algorithm must be used, such as RSA.

Unfortunately, public-key algorithms, while providing for easier key management, privacy, authentication, and non-repudiation, also have some disadvantages. The most important one is that they are slow and difficult to implement in hardware. For example, RSA is 100 to 10,000 times slower than DES, depending on implementation. Because of this, public-key algorithms generally are not used for bulk encryption. Their most important use is key exchange and authentication. Another notable disadvantage is that they are susceptible to certain cryptanalytic attacks to which symmetric algorithms are resistant.

Therefore, a good cryptographic system (*cryptosystem*) makes use of both worlds. It uses public-key algorithms in the session establishment phase for authentication and key exchange, then a symmetric one for encrypting the consequent messages.

For the interested reader, we give more detailed information of the two most important asymmetric algorithms, which involves modular arithmetic. An arithmetic operation modulo m means that the result of that operation is divided by m and the remainder is taken. For example: 3 * 6 mod 4 = 2, since 3 * 6 = 18 and dividing 18 by 4 gives us 2 as the remainder.

RSA public key algorithm
RSA is used in the ISAKMP/Oakley framework as one of the possible authentication methods. The principle of the RSA algorithm is as follows:

1. Take two large primes, p and q.

2. Find their product n = pq; n is called the modulus.

3. Choose a number, e, less than n and relatively prime to (p-1)(q-1) which means that e and (p-1)(q-1) have no common factor other than 1.

4. Find its inverse, d mod (p-1)(q-1) which means that ed = 1 mod (p-1)(q-1).

e and d are called the public and private exponents, respectively. The public key is the pair (n,e); the private key is d. The factors p and q must be kept secret or destroyed.

A simplified example of RSA encryption would be the following:

1. Suppose Alice wants to send a private message, m, to Bob. Alice creates the ciphertext c by exponentiating:

   $c = m^e \bmod n$

   where e and n are Bob's public key.

2. Alice sends c to Bob.

3. To decrypt, Bob exponentiates:

   $m = c^d \bmod n$

   and recovers the original message; the relationship between e and d ensures that Bob correctly recovers m. Since only Bob knows d, only Bob can decrypt the ciphertext.

A simplified example of RSA authentication would be the following:

1. Suppose Alice wants to send a signed message, m, to Bob. Alice creates a digital signature s by exponentiating:

   $s = m^d \bmod n$

   where d and n belong to Alice's private key.

2. She sends s and m to Bob.

3. To verify the signature, Bob exponentiates and checks if the result, compares to m:

   $m = s^e \bmod n$

   where e and n belong to Alice's public key.

Diffie-Hellman key exchange

The Diffie-Hellman key exchange is a crucial component of the ISAKMP/Oakley framework. In the earliest phase of a key negotiation session, there is no secure channel in place. The parties derive shared secret keys using the Diffie-Hellman algorithm. These keys will be used in the next steps of the key negotiation protocol.

The outline of the algorithm is the following:

1. The parties (Alice and Bob) share two public values, a modulus m and an integer g; m should be a large prime number.

2. Alice generates a large random number a and computes:

    $$X = g^a \bmod m$$

3. Bob generates a large random number b and computes:

    $$Y = g^b \bmod m$$

4. Alice sends X to Bob.

5. Bob computes:

    $$K1 = X^b \bmod m$$

6. Bob sends Y to Alice.

7. Alice computes:

    $$K2 = Y^a \bmod m$$

Both K1 and K2 are equal to g^{ab} mod m. This is the shared secret key. No one is able to generate this value without knowing a or b. The security of the exchange is based on the fact that is extremely difficult to inverse the exponentiation performed by the parties. (In other words, to calculate discrete logarithms in finite fields of size m.) Similar to RSA, advances in adversary computing power can be countered by choosing larger initial values, in this case a larger modulus m.

Please see 21.5.5, "The Internet Key Exchange protocol (IKE)" on page 721 for more details on how ISAKMP/Oakley uses Diffie-Hellman exchanges.

21.2.4 Hash functions

Hash functions (also called message digests) are fundamental to cryptography. A hash function is a function that takes variable-length input data and produces fixed length output data (the hash value), which can be regarded as the "fingerprint" of the input. That is, if the hashes of two messages match, it is highly probable that the messages are the same.

Cryptographically useful hash functions must be *one-way*, which means that they should be easy to compute, but infeasible to reverse. An everyday example of a one-way function is mashing a potato; it is easy to do, but once mashed, reconstructing the original potato is rather difficult.

A good hash function should also be *collision-resistant*. It should be hard to find two different inputs that hash to the same value. As any hash function maps an input set to a smaller output set, theoretically it is possible to find collisions. The point is to provide a unique digital "fingerprint" of the message, that identifies it with high confidence, much like a real fingerprint identifying a person.

A hash function that takes a key as a second input parameter and its output depends on both the message and the key is called a *message authentication code (MAC)*, as shown in Figure 261.

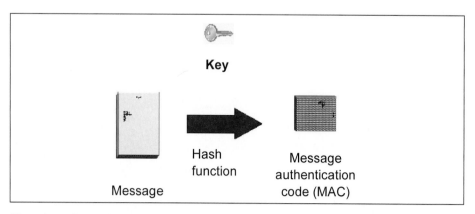

Figure 261. Generating a message authentication code (MAC)

Put simply, if you encrypt a hash, it becomes a MAC. If you add a secret key to a message, then hash the concatenation, the result is a MAC. Both symmetric and asymmetric algorithms can be used to generate MACs.

Hash functions are primarily used to assure integrity and authentication :

- The sender calculates the hash of the message and appends it to the message.
- The recipient calculates the hash of the received message and then compares the result with the transmitted hash.
- If the hashes match, the message was not tampered with.
- If the encryption key (symmetric or asymmetric) is only known by a trusted sender, a successful MAC decryption indicates that the claimed and actual senders are identical.

See Figure 262 for an illustration of the procedure. The Message* and MAC* notations reflect the fact that the message might have been altered while crossing the untrusted channel.

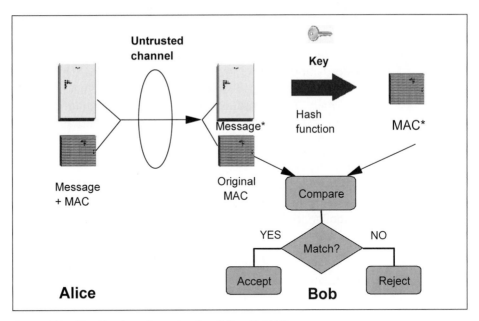

Figure 262. Checking integrity and authenticity with MAC

One could argue that the same result can be obtained with any kind of encryption, because if an intruder modifies an encrypted message, the decryption will result in nonsense, thus tampering can be detected. The answer is that many times only integrity and/or authentication is needed, maybe with encryption on some of the fields of the message. Also encryption is very processor-intensive. Examples include the personal banking machine networks, where only the PINs are encrypted, however MACs are widely used. Encrypting all the messages in their entirety would not yield noticeable benefits and performance would dramatically decrease.

The encryption of a hash with the private key is called a *digital signature*. It can be thought of as a special MAC. Using digital signatures instead of encrypting the whole message with the private key leads to considerable performance gains and a remarkable new property. The authentication part can be decoupled from the document itself. This property is used, for example, in the Secure Electronic Transactions (SET) protocol.

The encryption of a secret key with a public key is called a *digital envelope*. This is a common technique used to distribute secret keys for symmetric algorithms.

21.2.4.1 Examples of hash functions

The most widely used hash functions are MD5 and Secure Hash Algorithm 1 (SHA-1). MD5 was designed by Ron Rivest (co-inventor of RSA). SHA-1 is largely inspired from MD5 and was designed by the National Institute of Standards and Technology (NIST) and the National Security Agency (NSA) for use with the Digital Signature Standard (DSS). MD5 produces a 128-bit hash, while SHA-1 produces a 160-bit hash. Both functions encode the message length in their output. SHA-1 is regarded as more secure, because of the larger hashes it produces.

Neither MD5 nor SHA-1 takes a key as an input parameter, hence in their original implementation, they cannot be used for MAC calculation. However, for this purpose, it is easy to concatenate a key with the input data and apply the function to the result.

Note:

In practice, for example in IPsec, more sophisticated schemes are often used.

Keyed MD5 and keyed SHA-1

Using MD5 and SHA-1 in keyed mode is simple. The shared secret key and the data to be protected are both input to the hash algorithm. In the following IPsec example, the datagram is combined with the key, and the output hash value is placed in the Authentication Data field of the AH header, as it is shown in Figure 263.

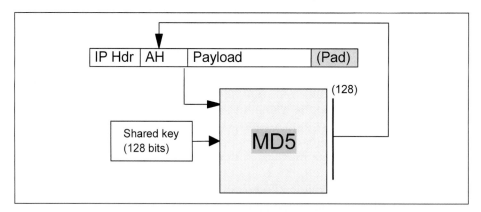

Figure 263. Keyed MD5 processing

Keyed SHA-1 operates in the same way, the only difference being the larger 160-bit hash value.

HMAC-MD5-96 and HMAC-SHA-1-96

A stronger method is the Hashed Message Authentication Code (HMAC), proposed by IBM. HMAC itself is not a hash function, rather a cryptographically strong way to use a specific hash function for MAC calculation.

To show how HMAC works, consider MD5 as an example. The base function is applied twice in succession. In the first round, the input to MD5 is the shared secret key and the datagram. The 128-bit output hash value and the key is input again to the hash function in the second round. The left-most 96 bits of the resulting hash value are used as the MAC for the datagram. See Figure 264 for an illustration.

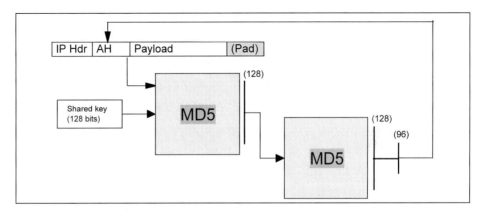

Figure 264. HMAC-MD5-96processing

HMAC-SHA-1-96 operates in the same way, except that the intermediary results are 160 bits long.

Digital Signature Standard (DSS)

As mentioned previously, a hash value encrypted with the private key is called a *digital signature* and is illustrated in Figure 265.

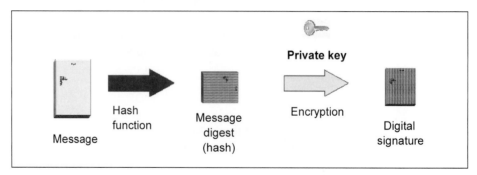

Private key

Message   Hash function   Message digest (hash)   Encryption   Digital signature

Figure 265. Generating a digital signature

One authentication method that can be used with ISAKMP/Oakley is DSS which was selected by NIST and NSA to be the digital authentication standard of the U.S. government. The standard describes the Digital Signature Algorithm (DSA) used to sign and verify signatures of message digests produced with SHA-1.

A brief description of DSA is given below:

1. Choose a large prime number, p, usually between 512 and 1024 bits long.

2. Find a prime factor q of (p-1), 160 bits long.

3. Compute:

    $$g = h^{(p-1)/q} \bmod p$$

    where h is a number less than (p-1) and the following is true:

    $$h^{(p-1)/q} > 1$$

4. Choose another number x, less than q, as the sender's private key.

5. Compute:

    $$y = g^x \bmod p$$

    and use that as the sender's public key. The pair (x,y) is sometimes referred to as the long-term key pair.

6. The sender signs the message as follows:

    a. Generate a random number, k, less than q.
    b. Compute:

        $$r = (g^k \bmod p) \bmod q$$
        $$s = (k^{-1}(SHA1(m) + xr)) \bmod q$$

    The pair (k,r) is sometimes referred to as the per-session key pair, and the signature is represented by the pair (r,s).

7. The sender sends (m,r,s).

8. The receiver verifies the signature as follows:

Compute:

```
w=s⁻¹ mod q
u1=(SHA1(m)*w) mod q
u2=(rw) mod q
v=((g^u1 y^u2) mod p) mod q
```

9. If v=r, then the signature is verified.

21.2.5 Digital certificates and certification authorities

As mentioned in 21.2.3.1, "Authentication and non-repudiation" on page 665, with public-key cryptography, the parties retrieve each other's public key. However, there are security exposures here. An intruder could replace some real public keys with his or her own public key, and then mount a so-called *man-in-the-middle attack*.

For example, the intruder places himself between Alice and Bob. He can trick Bob by sending him one of his own public keys as if it were Alice's. The same applies to Alice. She thinks she uses Bob's public key, but the sour reality is that she actually uses the intruder's. So the clever intruder can decrypt the confidential traffic between the two and remain undetected. For example, a message sent by Alice and encrypted with "Bob's" public key lands at the intruder, who decrypts it, learns its content, then re-encrypts it with Bob's real public key. Bob has no way to realize that Alice is using a phony public key.

An intruder could also use impersonation, claiming to be somebody else, for example an online shopping mall, fooling innocent shoppers.

The solution to these serious threats is the *digital certificate*. A digital certificate is a file that binds an identity to the associated public key. This binding is validated by a trusted third party, the *certification authority (CA)*. A digital certificate is signed with the private key of the certification authority, so it can be authenticated. It is only issued after a verification of the applicant. Apart from the public key and identification, a digital certificate usually contains other information too, such as:

- Date of issue

- Expiration date

- Miscellaneous information from issuing CA (for example, serial number)

> **Note:**
>
> There is an international standard in place for digital certificates: The ISO X.509 protocols.

The parties retrieve each other's digital certificate and authenticate it using the public key of the issuing certification authority. They have confidence that the public keys are real, because a trusted third party vouches for them. This helps protect against both man-in-the-middle and impersonation attacks.

It is easy to imagine that one CA cannot cover all needs. What happens when Bob's certificate is issued by a CA unknown to Alice? Can she trust that unknown authority? Well, this is entirely her decision, but to make life easier, CAs can form a hierarchy, often referred to as the *trust chain*. Each member in the chain has a certificate signed by it superior authority. The higher the CA is in the chain, the tighter security procedures are in place. The root CA is trusted by everyone and its private key is top secret.

Alice can traverse the chain upwards until she finds a CA that she trusts. The traversal consists of verifying the subordinate CA's public key and identity using the certificate issued to it by the superior CA.

When a trusted CA is found in the chain, Alice is assured that Bob's issuing CA is trustworthy. This is all about delegation of trust. We trust your identity card if somebody who we trust signs it. And if the signer is unknown to us, we can go upward and see who signs for the signer, etc.

An implementation of this concept can be found in the SET protocol, where the major credit card brands operate their own CA hierarchies that converge to a common root. Lotus Notes authentication, as another example, is also based on certificates, and it can be implemented using hierarchical trust chains. PGP also uses a similar approach, but its trust chain is based on persons and it is a distributed Web rather than a strict hierarchical tree.

21.2.6 Random-number generators

An important component of a cryptosystem is the random-number generator. Many times random session keys and random initialization variables (often referred to as initialization vectors) are generated. For example, DES requires an explicit initialization vector and Diffie-Hellman relies on picking random numbers which serve as input for the key derivation.

The quality, that is the randomness of these generators, is more important than you might think. The ordinary random function provided with most programming language libraries is good enough for games, but not for cryptography. Those random-number generators are rather predictable; if you rely on them, be prepared for happy cryptanalysts finding interesting correlations in your encrypted output.

The fundamental problem faced by the random-number generators is that the computers are ultimately deterministic machines, so real random sequences cannot be produced. As John von Neumann ironically said: "Anyone who considers arithmetical methods of producing random digits is, of course, in a state of sin." That's why the term *pseudorandom generator* is more appropriate.

Cryptographically strong pseudorandom generators must be unpredictable. It must be computationally infeasible to determine the next random bit, even with total knowledge of the generator.

A common practical solution for pseudorandom generators is to use hash functions. This approach provides sufficient randomness and it can be efficiently implemented. Military-grade generators use specialized devices that exploit the inherent randomness in physical phenomena. An interesting solution can be found in the PGP software. The initial seed of the pseudorandom generator is derived from measuring the time elapsed between the keystrokes of the user.

21.2.7 Export/import restrictions on cryptography

U.S. export regulations changed in 1996, which put cryptography under the control of the Commerce Department. It had formerly been treated as a munition. This is a significant step in liberalizing the export of cryptographic products.

According to the new export regulations, a license may be granted to export a 56-bit key encryption algorithm if a company has an approved key recovery plan. The key recovery plan must be implemented in 2 years and the license is granted on a 6 month basis. Financial institutions could be exempted from the key recovery plan restrictions.

In 1997 IBM was granted the license to export DES as long as it was used in similar ways as other products that have been approved. In 1998, the export of strong encryption products (such as triple-DES) was allowed for banking applications.

In September 1998, the White House announced further liberalization of U.S. export restrictions on cryptographic material and key recovery requirements, which can be summarized as follows:

- The key recovery requirement for export of 56-bit DES and equivalent products is eliminated. This includes products that use 1024-bit asymmetric key exchanges together with 56-bit symmetric key algorithms.

- Export of unlimited strength encryption (for example, 3DES) under license exceptions (with or without key recovery) is now broadened to include others besides the financial industry for 45 countries. This includes subsidiaries of U.S firms, insurance, health and medical (excluding biochemical and pharmaceutical manufacturers), and online merchants for the purpose of securing online transactions (excluding distributors of items considered munitions).

  For the latter, recoverable products will be granted exceptions world wide (excluding terrorist countries) without requiring a review of foreign key recovery agents.

- Export of recoverable products will be granted to most commercial firms, for a broad range of countries, in the major commercial markets (excluding items on the U.S. munitions list).

- Export licenses to end users may be granted on a case-by-case basis.

More information can be obtained from the U.S. Department of Commerce:

```
http://www.bxa.doc.gov/Encryption/
```

According to the law in France, any product capable of enciphering/deciphering user data should be granted a license from the French government before being marketed. Customers need to be authorized to use such products on a case-by-case basis. In reality, two major and useful exceptions exist:

1. Routinely, licenses are granted that allow banks to use DES products on a global basis (no case-by-case authorization required).
2. Routinely, global licenses are granted that allow anybody to use weak encryption (RC2/RC4 with 40-bit keys).

21.3 Firewalls

Firewalls have significant functions in an organization's security policy. Therefore, it is important to understand these functions and apply them to the network properly. This chapter explains the firewall concept, network security, firewall components and firewall examples.

21.3.1 Firewall concept

A firewall is a system (or group of systems) that enforces a security policy between a secure internal network and an untrusted network such as the Internet. Firewalls tend to be seen as a protection between the Internet and a private network. But generally speaking, a firewall should be considered as a means to divide the world into two or more networks: one or more secure networks and one or more non-secure networks.

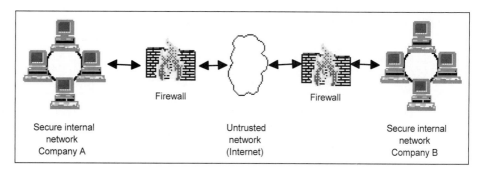

Figure 266. A firewall Illustration

A firewall can be a PC, a router, a midrange, a mainframe, a UNIX workstation, or a combination of these that determines which information or services can be accessed from the outside and who is permitted to use the information and services from outside. Generally, a firewall is installed at the point where the secure internal network and untrusted external network meet which is also known as a *choke point*.

In order to understand how a firewall works, consider the network to be a building to which access must be controlled. The building has a lobby as the only entry point. In this lobby, receptionists welcome visitors, security guards watch visitors, video cameras record visitor actions and badge readers authenticate visitors who enter the building.

Although these procedures may work well to control access to the building, if an unauthorized person succeeds in entering, there is no way to protect the building against this intruder's actions. However, if the intruder's movements are monitored, it may be possible to detect any suspicious activity.

Similarly, a firewall is designed to protect the information resources of the organization by controlling the access between the internal secure network and the untrusted external network (please see Figure 267). However, it is important to note that even if the firewall is designed to permit the trusted data to pass through, deny the vulnerable services, and prevent the internal network from outside attacks, a newly created attack may penetrate the firewall at any time. The network administrator must examine all logs and alarms generated by the firewall on a regular basis. Otherwise, it is generally not possible to protect the internal network from outside attacks.

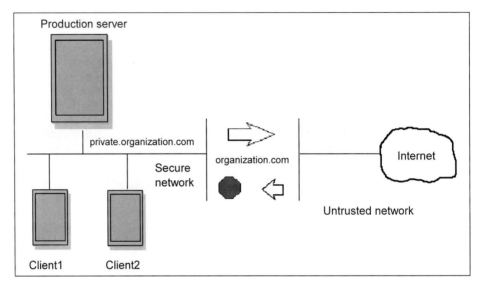

Figure 267. A firewall controls traffic between the secure network and the Internet

21.3.2 Components of a firewall system

As mentioned previously, a firewall can be a PC, a midrange, a mainframe, a UNIX workstation, a router, or combination of these. Depending on the requirements, a firewall can consist of one or more of the following functional components:

1. Packet-filtering router

2. Application level gateway (proxy)

3. Circuit level gateway

Each of these components has different functions and shortcomings. Generally, in order to build an effective firewall, these components are used together.

21.3.3 Packet-filtering router

Most of the time, packet-filtering is accomplished by using a router that can forward packets according to filtering rules. When a packet arrives at the packet-filtering router, the router extracts certain information from the packet header and makes decisions according to the filter rules as to whether the packet will pass through or be discarded (see Figure 268). The following information can be extracted from the packet header:

- Source IP address
- Destination IP address
- TCP/UDP source port
- TCP/UDP destination port
- ICMP message type
- Encapsulated protocol information (TCP, UDP, ICMP or IP tunnel)

The packet-filtering rules are based on the network security policy (see 21.1.4, "Network security policy" on page 659). Therefore, packet-filtering is done by using these rules as input. When determining the filtering rules, outside attacks must be taken into consideration, as well as service level restrictions and source/destination level restrictions.

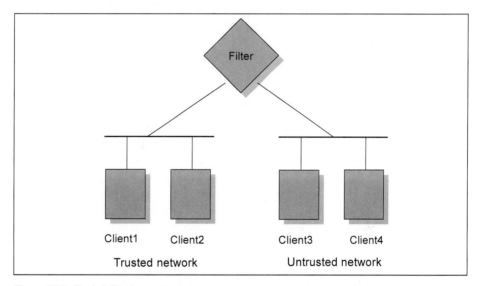

Figure 268. Packet filtering router

Service level filtering

Since most services use well-known TCP/UDP port numbers, it is possible to allow or deny services by using related port information in the filter. For example, an FTP server listens for connections on TCP port 21, and for a non-passive mode client, makes outbound data connections from port 20. Therefore, to permit FTP connections to pass through to a secure network, the router could be configured to permit packets which contain 20 and 21 as the TCP port in its header. On the other hand, there are some applications, such as NFS, which use RPC and use different ports for each connection. Allowing these kind of services might cause security problems.

Source/destination level filtering

The packet-filtering rules allow a router to permit or deny a packet according to the destination or the source information in the packet header. In most cases, if a service is available, only that particular server is permitted to outside users. Other packets that have another destination or no destination information in their headers are discarded.

Advanced filtering

As mentioned previously (see 21.1.1, "Common attacks against security" on page 655), there are different types of attacks that threaten the privacy and network security. Some of them can be discarded by using advanced filtering rules such as checking IP options, fragment offset and so on.

Packet-filtering limitations

Packet-filtering rules are sometimes very complex. When there are exceptions to existing rules, it becomes much more complex. Although, there are a few testing utilities available, it is still possible to leave some holes in the network security. Packet filters do not provide an absolute protection for a network. For some cases, it might be necessary to restrict some set of information (for example, a command) from passing through to the internal secure network. It is not possible to control the data with packet filters because they are not capable of understanding the contents of a particular service. For this purpose, an application level control is required.

21.3.4 Application level gateway (proxy)

An application level gateway is often referred to as a *proxy*. An application level gateway provides higher level control on the traffic between two networks in that the contents of a particular service can be monitored and filtered according to the network security policy. Therefore, for any desired application, the corresponding proxy code must be installed on the gateway in order to manage that specific service passing through the gateway (see Figure 269).

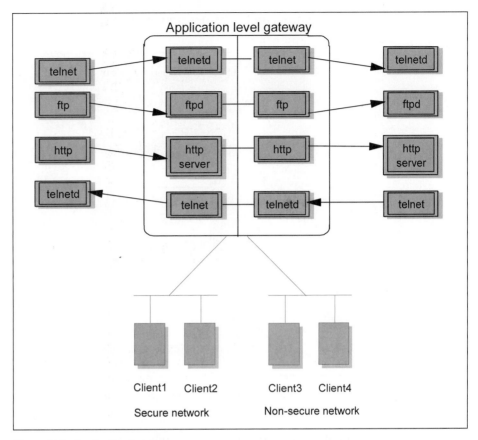

Figure 269. Application level gateway

A proxy acts as a server to the client and as a client to the destination server. A virtual connection is established between the client and the destination server. Though the proxy seems to be *transparent* from the point of view of the client and the server, the proxy is capable of monitoring and filtering any specific type of data, such as commands, before sending it to the destination. For example, an FTP server is permitted to be accessed from outside. In order to protect the server from any possible attacks the FTP proxy in the firewall can be configured to deny PUT and MPUT commands.

A proxy server is an application-specific relay server that runs on the host that connects a secure and a non-secure network. The purpose of a proxy server is to control exchange of data between the two networks at an application level instead of an IP level. By using a proxy server, it is possible to disable IP routing between the secure and the non-secure network for the application protocol the proxy server is able to handle, but still be able to

exchange data between the networks by relaying it in the proxy server.
Figure 270 shows an FTP proxy server.

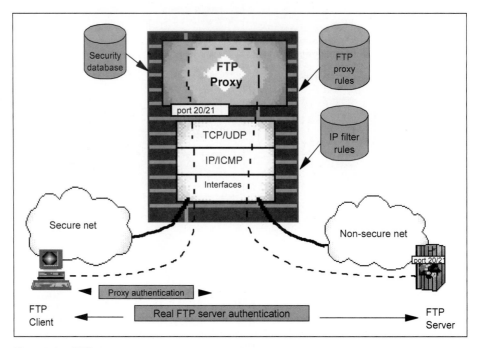

Figure 270. FTP proxy server

Please note that in order for any client to be able to access the proxy server, the client software must be specifically modified. In other words, the client and server software should support the proxy connection. In the previous example, the FTP client must authenticate itself to the proxy first. If it is successfully authenticated, the FTP session starts based on the proxy restrictions. Most proxy server implementations use more sophisticated authentication methods such as security ID cards. This mechanism generates a unique key which is not reusable for another connection. Two security ID cards are supported by IBM Firewall: the SecureNet card from Axent and the SecureID card from Security Dynamics.

Compared with IP filtering, application level gateways provide much more comprehensive logging based on the application data of the connections. For example, an HTTP proxy can log the URLs visited by users. Another feature of application level gateways is that they can use strong user authentication. For example, when using FTP and TELNET services from the unsecure network, users can be forced to authenticate themselves to the proxy. Figure 271 shows a proxy server TCP segment flow example.

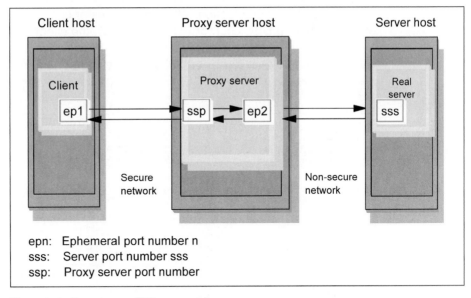

Figure 271. Proxy server TCP segment flow

21.3.4.1 Application level gateway limitations
A disadvantage of application level gateways is that, in order to achieve a connection via a proxy server, the client software should be changed to support that proxy service. This can sometimes be achieved by some modifications in user behavior rather than software modification. For example, to connect to a TELNET server over a proxy, the user usually has to be authenticated by the proxy server then by the destination TELNET server. This requires two user steps to make a connection rather than one. However, a modified TELNET client can make the proxy server transparent to the user by specifying the destination host rather than proxy server in the TELNET command.

21.3.4.2 An example: FTP proxy server
Most of the time, in order to use the FTP proxy server, users must have a valid user ID and password. On UNIX systems, users also should be defined as users of the UNIX system.

FTP can be used in one of two modes:

1. Normal mode

2. Passive mode

In normal mode, the FTP client first connects to the FTP server port 21 to establish a control connection. When data transfer is required (for example, as the result of a DIR, GET, or PUT command), the client sends a PORT command to the server instructing the server to establish a data connection from the server's data port (port 20) to a specified ephemeral port number on the client host.

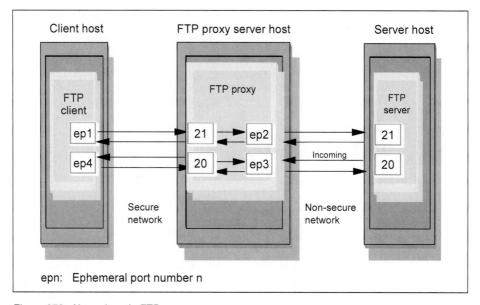

Figure 272. Normal mode FTP proxy

In an FTP proxy server situation, normal mode means that we have to allow inbound TCP connections from the non-secure network to the FTP proxy host. Notice in Figure 272 how a connection is established from the FTP server port 20 in the non-secure network to the FTP proxy server's ephemeral port number. To allow this to happen, IP filtering rules are used that allow inbound connection requests from port 20 to an ephemeral port number on the FTP proxy host. This is normally not an IP filter rule. It is sometimes better to add a custom filter rule configuration, because it would allow a cracker to run a program on port 20 and scan all the port numbers above 1023, which, in its simplest form, might result in a denial of service situation. Some firewalls handle this correctly by building a table of outgoing FTP requests and matching up the corresponding incoming data transfer request.

A much more firewall-friendly mode is the passive mode of operation, as shown in Figure 271. This mode has been dubbed a firewall-friendly FTP and is described in RFC 1579 Firewall-Friendly FTP.

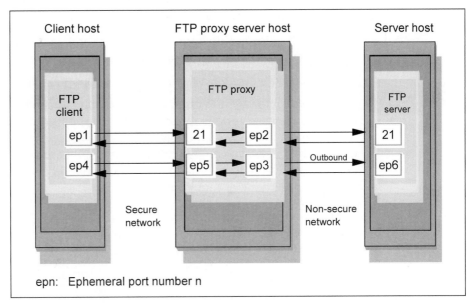

Figure 273. Passive mode FTP proxy (firewall-friendly FTP)

In passive mode, the FTP client again establishes a control connection to the server's port 21. When data transfer has to start, the client sends a PASV command to the server. The server responds with a port number for the client to contact, in order to establish the data connection, and the client then initiates the data connection.

In this setup, to establish connections to both port 21 and any ephemeral port number in the non-secure network, an ephemeral port number is used on the FTP proxy host. Here, we do not need a rule that allows inbound connections to ephemeral port numbers, because we are now connecting outwards.

21.3.5 Circuit level gateway

A circuit level gateway relays TCP connections and does not provide any extra packet processing or filtering. Some circuit level gateways can handle UDP packets. A circuit level gateway can be said to be a special type of application level gateway. This is because the application level gateway can be configured to pass all information once the user is authenticated, just as the circuit level gateway (see Figure 274). However, in practice, there are significant differences between them, such as:

- Circuit level gateways can handle several TCP/IP applications as well as UDP applications without any extra modifications on the client side for each application. Thus, this makes circuit level gateways a good choice to satisfy user requirements.

- Circuit level gateways do not provide packet processing or filtering. Thus, a circuit level gateway is generally referred to as a *transparent* gateway.

- Application level gateways have a lack of support for UDP.

- Circuit level gateways are often used for outbound connections, whereas application level gateways (proxy) are used for both inbound and outbound connections. Generally, in cases of using both types combined, circuit level gateways can be used for outbound connections and application level gateways can be used for inbound connections to satisfy both security and user requirements.

Circuit level gateways can sometimes handle incoming UDP packets or TCP connections. However a client on the secure side, must inform the gateway to expect such packets. SOCKS v5 has this capability.

A well known example of a circuit level gateway is SOCKS (refer to 21.6, "SOCKS" on page 739 for more information). Because the data flows over SOCKS are not monitored or filtered, a security problem may arise. To minimize security problems, trusted services and resources should be used on the outside network (untrusted network).

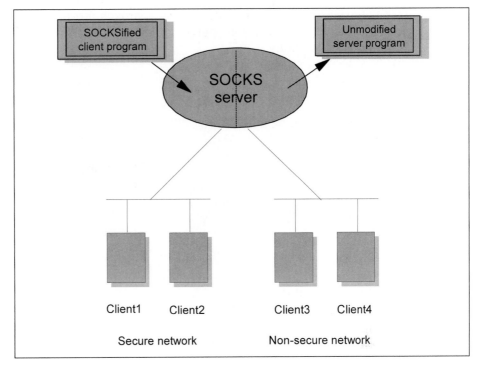

Figure 274. Circuit level gateway

21.3.6 Types of firewall

A firewall consists of one or more software elements that run on one or more hosts. The hosts may be general purpose computer systems or specialized such as routers. There are four important examples of firewalls. These are:

1. Packet-Filtering Firewall
2. Dual-Homed Gateway Firewall
3. Screened Host Firewall
4. Screened Subnet Firewall

21.3.6.1 Packet-filtering firewall

The packet-filtering firewall is commonly used because it is inexpensive (please see Figure 275). The firewall is just a router sitting between the external network and the internal secure network Packet-filtering rules are defined to permit or deny traffic, see "Packet-filtering router" on page 680.

Generally, a packet-filtering firewall is configured to deny any service if it is not explicitly permitted. Although this approach prevents some potential attacks, the firewall is still open to attacks which result from improper filter rule configurations.

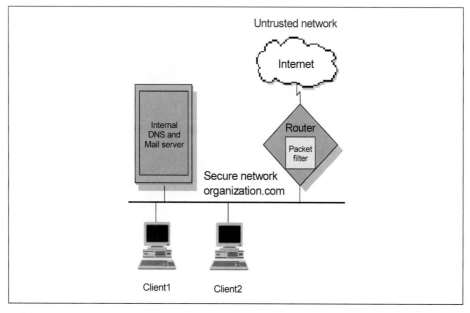

Figure 275. Packet-filtering firewall

The filter will allow some of the hosts on the internal network to be directly accessed from the external network. Such hosts should have their own authorization mechanism and need to be updated regularly in case of any attacks.

21.3.6.2 Dual-homed gateway firewall

A dual-homed host has at least two network interfaces and therefore at least two IP addresses. IP forwarding is disabled in the firewall, hence all IP traffic between the two interfaces is broken at the firewall (please see Figure 276). Thus, there is no way for a packet to pass the firewall except via the related proxy or SOCKS service. Unlike the packet filtering firewalls, dual-homed gateway firewalls make sure that any attack that comes from an unknown service will be blocked. A dual-homed gateway implements the method in which everything not specifically permitted is denied.

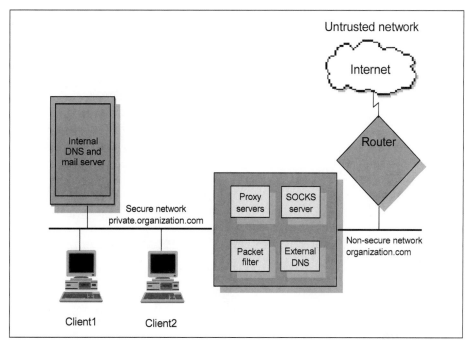

Figure 276. Dual-homed firewall

If an information server (such as a Web or FTP server) needs to be located to give access to both inside and outside users, it can either be installed inside the protected network or it can be installed between the firewall and the router, which is relatively insecure. If it is installed beyond the firewall, the firewall must have the related proxy services to give access to the information server from inside the secure network. If the information server is installed between the firewall and the router, the router should be capable of packet filtering and configured accordingly. This type of firewall is called a screened host firewall and discussed in 21.3.6.3, "Screened host firewall" on page 691.

21.3.6.3 Screened host firewall

This type of firewall consists of a packet filtering router and an application level gateway. The host containing the application level gateway is known as a bastion host. The router is configured to forward all untrusted traffic to the bastion host and in some cases also to the information server (please see Figure 277). Since the internal network is on the same subnet as the bastion host, the security policy may allow internal users to access outside networks directly or force them to use proxy services to access the outside network. This can be achieved by configuring the router filter rules so that the router only accepts outbound traffic originating from the bastion host.

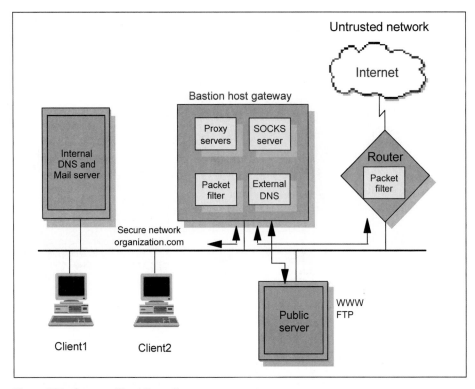

Figure 277. Screened host firewall

This configuration allows an information server to be placed between the router and the bastion host. Again, the security policy determines whether the information server will be accessed directly by either outside users or internal users or if it will be accessed via bastion host. If strong security is needed, traffic from both the internal network to the information server and from outside to the information server can go through the bastion host.

In this configuration, the bastion host can be a standard host or, if a more secure firewall system is needed, it can be a dual-homed host. In this case, all internal traffic to the information server and to the outside through the router is automatically forced to pass the proxy server on the dual-homed host. The bastion host is then the only system that can be accessed from the outside. No one should be permitted to log on to the bastion host, otherwise an intruder may log on the system and change the configuration to bypass the firewall.

21.3.6.4 Screened subnet firewall (demilitarized zone)

This type of firewall consists of two packet filtering routers and a bastion host. Screened subnet firewalls provide the highest level security among the different firewall types (please see Figure 278). This is achieved by creating a demilitarized zone (DMZ) between the external and internal network, so that the outer router only permits access from the outside to the bastion host (possibly to the information server) and the inner router only permits access from the internal network to the bastion host. The routers force all inbound and outbound traffic through the Bastion host. This provides strong security because an intruder has to penetrate three separate systems to reach the internal network.

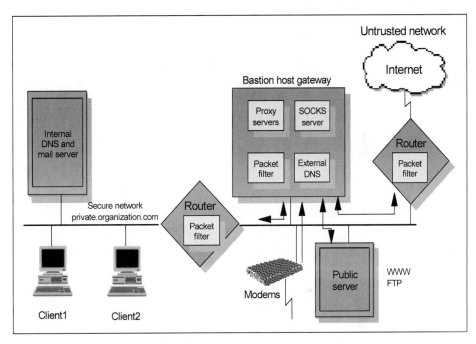

Figure 278. Screened subnet firewall

One of the significant benefits of the DMZ is that since the routers force the systems on both external and internal networks to use the bastion host, there is no need for the bastion host to be a dual-homed host. This provides much faster throughput than achieved by a dual-homed host. Of course, this is complicated and some security problems could be caused by improper router configurations.

21.4 Network Address Translation (NAT)

This section explains Network Address Translation (NAT). NAT is also known as IP masquerading. It provides a mapping between internal IP addresses and officially assigned external addresses.

Originally, NAT was suggested as a short-term solution to the problem of IP address depletion. Also, many organizations have, in the past, used locally assigned IP addresses, not expecting to require Internet connectivity.

NAT is defined in RFC 3022.

21.4.1 NAT concept

The idea of NAT is based on the fact that only a small number of the hosts in a private network are communicating outside of that network. If each host is assigned an IP address from the official IP address pool only when they need to communicate, then only a small number of official addresses are required.

NAT might be a solution for networks that have private address ranges or unofficial addresses and want to communicate with hosts on the Internet. In fact, most of the time, this can also be achieved by implementing a firewall. Hence, clients that communicate with the Internet by using a proxy or SOCKS server do not expose their addresses to the Internet, so their addresses do not have to be translated anyway. However, for any reason, when proxy and SOCKS are not available, or do not meet specific requirements, NAT might be used to manage the traffic between the internal and external network without advertising the internal host addresses.

Consider an internal network that is based on the private IP address space, and the users want to use an application protocol for which there is no application gateway; the only option is to establish IP-level connectivity between hosts in the internal network and hosts on the Internet. Since the routers in the Internet would not know how to route IP packets back to a private IP address, there is no point in sending IP packets with private IP addresses as source IP addresses through a router into the Internet.

As shown in Figure 279, NAT takes the IP address of an outgoing packet and dynamically translates it to an officially assigned global address. For incoming packets it translates the assigned address to an internal address.

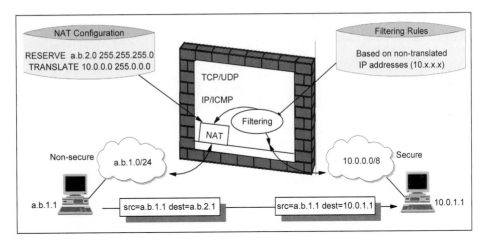

Figure 279. Network Address Translation (NAT)

From the point of two hosts that exchange IP packets with each other, one in the secure network and one in the non-secure network, NAT looks like a standard IP router that forwards IP packets between two network interfaces (please see Figure 280).

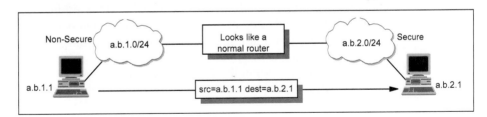

Figure 280. NAT seen from the non-secure network

21.4.2 Translation mechanism

For each outgoing IP packet, the source address is checked by the NAT configuration rules. If a rule matches the source address, the address is translated to a global address from the address pool. The predefined address pool contains the addresses that NAT can use for translation. For each incoming packet, the destination address is checked if it is used by NAT. When this is true, the address is translated to the original internal address. Figure 281 shows the NAT configuration.

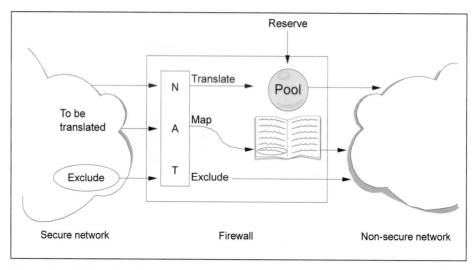

Figure 281. NAT configuration

If NAT translates an address for an IP packet, the checksum is also adjusted. For FTP packets, the task is even more difficult, because the packets can contain addresses in the data of the packet. For example, the FTP PORT command contains an IP address in ASCII. These addresses should also be translated correctly and checksum updates and even TCP sequence and acknowledgement updates should be made accordingly.

NAT looks like a normal IP router to the systems which use it. In order to make the routing tables work, the IP network design should choose addresses as if connecting two or more IP networks or subnets through a router. The NAT IP addresses need to come from separate networks or subnets, and the addresses need to be unambiguous with respect to other networks or subnets in the non-secure network. If the non-secure network is the Internet, the NAT addresses need to come from a public network or subnet, in other words, the NAT addresses need to be assigned by IANA.

The assigned addresses should be reserved in a pool, in order to use them when needed. If connections are established from the secure network, NAT can just pick the next free public address in the NAT pool and assign that to the requesting secure host. NAT keeps track of which internal IP addresses are mapped to which external IP addresses at any given point in time, so it will be able to map a response it receives from the external network into the corresponding secure IP address.

When NAT assigns IP addresses on a demand basis, it needs to know when to return the external IP address to the pool of available IP addresses. There is no connection setup or tear-down at the IP level, so there is nothing in the IP protocol itself that NAT can use to determine when an association between a secure IP address and a NAT non-secure IP address is no longer needed. Since TCP is a connection-oriented protocol, it is possible to obtain the connection status information from TCP header (whether connection is ended or not), whereas UDP does not include such information. Therefore, a timeout value should be configured that instructs NAT how long to keep an association in an idle state before returning the external IP address to the free NAT pool. Generally, the default value for this parameter is 15 minutes.

Network administrators also need to instruct NAT whether all the secure hosts are allowed to use NAT or not. This can be done by using corresponding configuration commands. If hosts in the non-secure network need to initiate connections to hosts in the secure network, NAT should be configured in advance as to which non-secure NAT address matches which secure IP address. Thus, a static mapping should be defined to allow connections from non-secure networks to a specific host in the internal network. The external name server may, for example, have an entry for a mail gateway that runs on a computer in the secure network. The external name server resolves the public host name of the internal mail gateway to the statically mapped IP address (the external address), and the remote mail server sends a connection request to this IP address. When that request comes to NAT on the non-secure interface, NAT looks into its mapping rules to see if it has a static mapping between the specified non-secure public IP address and a secure IP address. If so, it translates the IP address and forwards the IP packet into the secure network to the internal mail gateway.

Please note that the non-secure NAT addresses as statically mapped to secure IP addresses should not overlap with the addresses specified as belonging to the pool of non-secure addresses NAT can use on a demand basis.

21.4.3 NAT limitations

NAT works fine for IP addresses in the IP header. Some application protocols exchange IP address information in the application data part of an IP packet, and NAT will generally not be able to handle translation of IP addresses in the application protocol. Currently, most of the implementations handle the FTP protocol. It should be noted that implementation of NAT for specific applications that have IP information in the application data is more sophisticated than the standard NAT implementations.

Another important limitation of NAT is that NAT changes some of the address information in an IP packet. When end-to-end IPsec authentication is used, a packet whose address has been changed will always fail its integrity check under the AH protocol, since any change to any bit in the datagram will invalidate the integrity check value that was generated by the source. Since IPsec protocols offer some solutions to the addressing issues that were previously handled by NAT, there is no need for NAT when all hosts that compose a given virtual private network use globally unique (public) IP addresses. Address hiding can be achieved by IPsec's tunnel mode. If a company uses private addresses within its intranet, IPsec's tunnel mode can keep them from ever appearing in cleartext from in the public Internet, which eliminates the need for NAT. (Please see 21.5, "The IP security architecture (IPsec)" on page 698 and 21.11, "Virtual private networks (VPN) overview" on page 755 for details about IPsec and VPN.)

21.5 The IP security architecture (IPsec)

This section examines, in detail, the IPsec framework and its three main components, Authentication Header (AH), Encapsulating Security Payload (ESP), and Internet Key Exchange (IKE). The header formats, the specific cryptographic features and the different modes of application are discussed.

IPsec adds integrity checking, authentication, encryption and replay protection to IP packets. It is used for end-to-end security and also for creating secure tunnels between gateways.

IPsec was designed for interoperability. When correctly implemented, it does not affect networks and hosts that do not support it. IPsec is independent of the current cryptographic algorithms; it can accommodate new ones as they become available. It works both with IPv4 and IPv6. In fact, IPsec is a mandatory component of IPv6.

IPsec uses state-of-the-art cryptographic algorithms. The specific implementation of an algorithm for use by an IPsec protocol is often called a *transform*. For example, the DES algorithm used by ESP is called the ESP DES-CBC transform. The transforms, like the protocols, are published in the RFCs.

21.5.1 Concepts

Two major IPsec concepts should be clarified: Security Associations and tunneling. These concepts are described in the following sections.

21.5.1.1 Security Associations

The concept of a Security Association (SA) is fundamental to IPsec. An SA is a unidirectional (simplex) logical connection between two IPsec systems, uniquely identified by the following triple:

```
<Security Parameter Index, IP destination address, security protocol>
```

The definition of the members is as follows:

Security parameter index (SPI) This is a 32-bit value used to identify different SAs with the same destination address and security protocol. The SPI is carried in the header of the security protocol (AH or ESP). The SPI has only local significance, as defined by the creator of the SA. SPI values in the range 1 to 255 are reserved by the Internet Assigned Numbers Authority (IANA). The SPI value of 0 must be used for local implementation-specific purposes only. RFC 2406 states that a value of 0 must not be transmitted. Generally, the SPI is selected by the destination system during SA establishment.

IP destination address This address can be a unicast, broadcast, or multicast IP address. However, currently SA management mechanisms are defined only for unicast addresses.

Security protocol This can be either AH or ESP.

An SA can be in either of two modes, transport or tunnel, depending on the mode of the protocol in that SA. You can find the explanation of these protocol modes later in this chapter.

SAs are simplex, hence, for bidirectional communication between two IPsec systems, there must be two SAs defined, one in each direction.

A single SA gives security services to the traffic carried by it either by using AH or ESP, but not both. In other words, for a connection that should be protected by both AH and ESP, two SAs must be defined for each direction. In this case, the set of SAs that define the connection is referred to as an *SA bundle*. The SAs in the bundle do not have to terminate at the same endpoint. For example, a mobile host could use an AH SA between itself and a firewall and a nested ESP SA that extends to a host behind the firewall.

An IPsec implementation maintains two databases related to SAs:

Security Policy Database (SPD) The Security Policy Database specifies what security services are to be offered to the IP traffic, depending on factors such as source, destination, whether it is inbound, outbound, etc. It contains an ordered list of policy entries, separate for inbound and outbound traffic. These entries might specify that some traffic must bypass the IPsec processing, some must be discarded, and the rest must be processed by the IPsec module. Entries in this database are similar to firewall rules or packet filters.

Security Association Database (SAD) The Security Association Database contains parameter information about each SA, such as AH or ESP algorithms and keys, sequence numbers, protocol mode and SA lifetime. For outbound processing, an SPD entry points to an entry in the SAD. That is, the SPD determines which SA is to be used for a given packet. For inbound processing, the SAD is consulted to determine how the packet must be processed.

Note:

The user interface of an IPsec implementation usually hides or presents these databases in a more friendly way.

21.5.1.2 Tunneling

Tunneling or encapsulation is a common technique in packet-switched networks. It consists of wrapping a packet in a new one. That is, a new header is attached to the original packet. The entire original packet becomes the payload of the new one, as is shown in Figure 282.

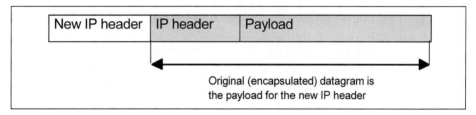

New IP header	IP header	Payload

Original (encapsulated) datagram is
the payload for the new IP header

Figure 282. IP tunneling

In general, tunneling is used to carry traffic of one protocol over a network that does not support that protocol directly. For example, NetBIOS or IPX can be encapsulated in IP to carry it over a TCP/IP WAN link. In the case of IPsec, IP is tunneled through IP for a slightly different purpose: To provide total protection, including the header of the encapsulated packet. If the encapsulated packet is encrypted, an intruder cannot figure out, for example, the destination address of that packet. (Without tunneling, he or she could.) The internal structure of a private network can be concealed in this way.

Tunneling requires intermediate processing of the original packet while en-route. The destination specified in the outer header, usually an IPsec firewall or router, receives the tunneled packet, extracts the original packet, and sends it to the ultimate destination. The processing overhead is compensated by the extra security.

A notable advantage of IP tunneling is the possibility to exchange packets with private IP addresses between two intranets over the public Internet, which requires globally unique addresses. Since the encapsulated header is not processed by the Internet routers, only the endpoints of the tunnel (the gateways) need to have globally assigned addresses; the hosts in the intranets behind them can be assigned private addresses (for example, 10.x.x.x). As globally unique IP addresses are becoming a scarce resource, this interconnection method gains importance.

> **Note:**
>
> IPsec tunneling is modeled after RFC 2003 *IP Encapsulation within IP.* It was originally designed for Mobile IP, an architecture that allows a mobile host to keep its home IP address even if attached to remote or foreign subnets. See 19.1, "Mobile IP overview" on page 629.

21.5.2 Authentication Header (AH)

AH is used to provide integrity and authentication to IP datagrams. Replay protection is also possible. Although its usage is optional, the replay protection service must be implemented by any IPsec-compliant system. The services are connectionless, that is they work on a per-packet basis. AH is used in two modes, transport mode and tunnel mode.

AH authenticates as much of the IP datagram as possible. In transport mode some fields in the IP header change en-route and their value cannot be predicted by the receiver. These fields are called *mutable* and are not protected by AH. The mutable IPv4 fields are:

- Type of service (TOS)
- Flags
- Fragment offset
- Time to live (TTL)
- Header checksum

When protection of these fields is required, tunneling should be used. The payload of the IP packet is considered immutable and is always protected by AH.

AH is identified by protocol number 51, assigned by the IANA. The protocol header (IPv4, IPv6, or extension) immediately preceding the AH header contains this value in its protocol (IPv4) or Next header (IPv6, extension) field.

AH processing is applied only to non-fragmented IP packets. However, an IP packet with AH applied can be fragmented by intermediate routers. In this case, the destination first reassembles the packet and then applies AH processing to it. If an IP packet that appears to be a fragment (offset field is non-zero, or the More Fragments bit is set) is input to AH processing, it is discarded. This prevents the so-called *overlapping fragment attack*, which misuses the fragment reassembly algorithm in order to create forged packets and force them through a firewall.

Packets that fail authentication are discarded and never delivered to upper layers. This mode of operation greatly reduces the chances of successful denial of service attacks, which aim to block the communication of a host or gateway by flooding it with bogus packets.

21.5.2.1 AH format
The AH format is described in RFC 2402.

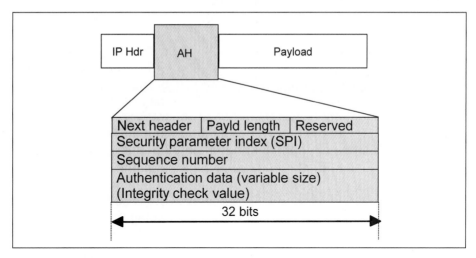

Figure 283. AH format

Figure 283 shows the position of the Authentication Header fields in the IP packet. The fields are as follows:

Next header

The next header *t* is an 8-bit field that identifies the type of what follows. The value of this field is chosen from the set of IP protocol numbers defined in the most recent Assigned Numbers RFC from the Internet Assigned Numbers Authority (IANA). In other words, the IP header protocol field is set to 51, and the value which would have gone in the protocol field goes in the AH next header field.

Payload length

This field is 8 bits long and contains the length of the AH header expressed in 32-bit words, minus 2. It does not relate to the actual payload length of the IP packet as a whole. If default options are used, the value is 4 (three 32-bit fixed words plus three 32-bit words of authentication data minus two).

Reserved

This field is reserved for future use. Its length is 16 bits and it is set to zero.

Security parameter index (SPI)

This field is 32 bits in length. See "Security parameter index (SPI) This is a 32-bit value used to identify different SAs with the same destination address and security protocol. The SPI is carried in the header of the security protocol (AH or ESP). The SPI has only local significance, as defined by the creator of the SA. SPI values in the range 1 to 255 are reserved by the Internet Assigned Numbers Authority (IANA). The SPI value of 0 must be used for local implementation-specific purposes only. RFC 2406 states that a value of 0 must not be transmitted. Generally, the SPI is selected by the destination system during SA establishment." on page 699 for a definition.

Sequence number

This 32-bit field is a monotonically increasing counter, which is used for replay protection. Replay protection is optional; however, this field is mandatory. The sender always includes this field and it is at the discretion of the receiver to process it or not. At the establishment of an SA, the sequence number is initialized to zero. The first packet transmitted using the SA has a sequence number of 1. Sequence numbers are not allowed to repeat. Thus the maximum number of IP packets that can be transmitted on any given SA is $2^{32}-1$. After the highest sequence number is used, a new SA and consequently a new key is established. Anti-replay is enabled at the sender by default. If upon SA establishment the receiver chooses not to use it, the sender need not be concerned with the value in this field anymore.

Authentication data　　　This is a variable-length field containing the Integrity Check Value (ICV), and is padded to 32 bits for IPv4 or 64 bits for IPv6. The ICV for each packet is calculated with the algorithm selected at SA initialization. As its name implies, it is used by the receiver to verify the integrity of the incoming packet.

In theory, any MAC algorithm can be used to calculate the ICV. The specification requires that HMAC-MD5-96 and HMAC-SHA-1-96 must be supported. The old RFC 1826 requires Keyed MD5. In practice, Keyed SHA-1 is also used. Implementations usually support two to four algorithms.

When doing the ICV calculation, the mutable fields are considered to be filled with zero.

21.5.2.2 Ways of using AH

AH can be used in two ways: Transport mode and tunnel mode.

AH in transport mode　　In this mode, the authentication header is inserted immediately after the IP header, as it is shown in Figure 284. If the datagram already has IPsec header(s), then the AH is inserted before them.

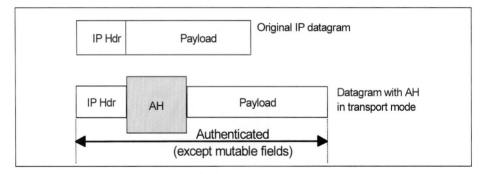

Figure 284. Authentication Header in transport mode

Transport mode is used by hosts, not by gateways. Gateways are not required to support transport mode.

The advantage of transport mode is less processing overhead. The disadvantage is that mutable fields are not authenticated.

AH in tunnel mode   With this mode, the tunneling concept is applied, a new IP datagram is constructed and the original IP datagram is made the payload of it. AH in transport mode is applied to the resulting datagram. See Figure 285 for an illustration.

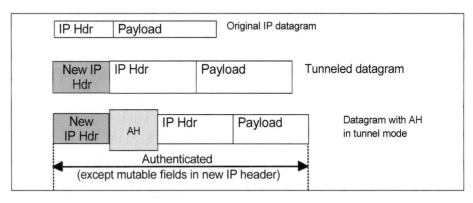

Figure 285. Authentication Header in tunnel mode

Tunnel mode is used whenever either end of a security association is a gateway. Thus, between two firewalls, tunnel mode is always used.

Gateways often also support transport mode. This mode is allowed when the gateway acts as a host, that is, in cases when traffic is destined to the gateway itself. For example, SNMP commands could be sent to the gateway using transport mode.

In tunnel mode the outer headers' IP addresses do not need to be the same as the inner headers' addresses. For example, two security gateways can operate an AH tunnel which is used to authenticate all traffic between the networks they connect together. This is a very typical mode of operation.

The advantages of tunnel mode include total protection of the encapsulated IP datagram and the possibility of using private addresses. However, there is extra processing overhead associated with this mode.

> **Note:**
>
> The original AH specification in RFC 1825 only mentions tunnel mode in passing, not as a requirement. Because of this, there are IPsec implementations based on that RFC that do not support AH in tunnel mode.

21.5.2.3 IPv6 considerations

AH is an integral part of IPv6 (see 17.2.2, "Extension headers" on page 565). In an IPv6 environment, AH is considered an end-to-end payload and it appears after hop-by-hop, routing, and fragmentation extension headers. The destination options extension header(s) could appear either before or after the authentication header. Figure 286 illustrates the positioning of AH in transport mode for a typical IPv6 packet. The position of the extension headers marked with * is variable, if present at all.

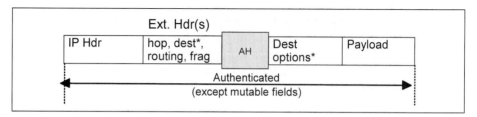

Figure 286. AH in transport mode for IPv6

For a detailed description of AH in IPv6 please refer to RFC 2402.

21.5.3 Encapsulating Security Payload (ESP)

ESP is used to provide integrity check, authentication, and encryption to IP datagrams. Optional replay protection is also possible. These services are connectionless, in that they operate on a per-packet basis. The set of desired services are selectable upon SA establishment. However, some restrictions apply:

- Integrity check and authentication are used together.
- Replay protection is selectable only in conjunction with integrity check and authentication.
- Replay protection can be selected only by the receiver.

Encryption can be selected independently of other services. It is highly recommended that, if encryption is enabled, integrity check and authentication be turned on. If only encryption is used, intruders could forge packets in order to mount cryptanalytic attacks.

Although both authentication (with integrity check) and encryption are optional, at least one of them is always selected, otherwise you would not be using ESP.

ESP is identified by protocol number 50, as assigned by the IANA. The protocol header (IPv4, IPv6, or extension) immediately preceding the AH header will contain this value in its protocol (IPv4) or the next header field (IPv6, extension).

ESP processing is applied only to non-fragmented IP packets. However, an IP packet with ESP applied can be fragmented by intermediate routers. In this case, the destination first reassembles the packet and then applies ESP processing to it. If an IP packet that appears to be a fragment is input to ESP processing (offset field is non-zero, or the More Fragments bit is set), it is discarded. This prevents the overlapping fragment attack mentioned in 21.5.2, "Authentication Header (AH)" on page 702.

If both encryption and authentication with integrity check are selected, then the receiver first authenticates the packet and, only if this step was successful, proceeds with decryption. This mode of operation saves computing resources and reduces the vulnerability to denial of service attacks.

21.5.3.1 ESP packet format

The current ESP packet format is described in RFC 2406. It contains important modifications compared to the previous ESP specification, RFC 1827. The information in this section is based on RFC 2406.

The format of the ESP packet is more complicated than that of the AH packet. There is not only an ESP header, but also an ESP trailer and ESP authentication data (see Figure 287). The payload is located (encapsulated) between the header and the trailer, hence the name of the protocol.

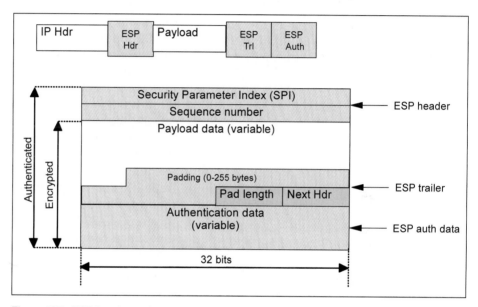

Figure 287. ESP header and trailer

The following fields are part of an ESP packet:

Security Parameter Index (SPI) This field is 32 bits in length. See "Security parameter index (SPI) This field is 32 bits in length. See "Security parameter index (SPI) This is a 32-bit value used to identify different SAs with the same destination address and security protocol. The SPI is carried in the header of the security protocol (AH or ESP). The SPI has only local significance, as defined by the creator of the SA. SPI values in the range 1 to 255 are reserved by the Internet Assigned Numbers Authority (IANA). The

Sequence number

SPI value of 0 must be used for local implementation-specific purposes only. RFC 2406 states that a value of 0 must not be transmitted. Generally, the SPI is selected by the destination system during SA establishment." on page 699 for a definition." on page 703 for the definition.

This 32-bit field is a monotonically increasing counter. See "Sequence number This 32-bit field is a monotonically increasing counter, which is used for replay protection. Replay protection is optional; however, this field is mandatory. The sender always includes this field and it is at the discretion of the receiver to process it or not. At the establishment of an SA, the sequence number is initialized to zero. The first packet transmitted using the SA has a sequence number of 1. Sequence numbers are not allowed to repeat. Thus the maximum number of IP packets that can be transmitted on any given SA is 232-1. After the highest sequence number is used, a new SA and consequently a new key is established. Anti-replay is enabled at the sender by default. If upon SA establishment the receiver chooses not to use it, the sender need not be concerned with the value in this field anymore." on page 704 for the definition.

Notes

1. Typically, the anti-replay mechanism is not used with manual key management.

2. The original ESP specification in RFC 1827 did not discuss the concept of sequence numbers. Older IPsec implementations that are based on that RFC can therefore not provide replay protection.

Payload data

The payload data field is mandatory. It consists of a variable number of bytes of data described by the next header field. This field is encrypted with the cryptographic algorithm selected during SA establishment. If the algorithm requires initialization vectors, these are also included here.

The ESP specification requires support for the DES algorithm in CBC mode (DES-CBC transform). Often, other encryption algorithms are also supported, such as triple-DES and CDMF, in the case of IBM products.

Padding

Most encryption algorithms require that the input data must be an integral number of blocks. Also, the resulting ciphertext (including the padding, pad length and next header fields) must terminate on a 4-byte boundary, so the next header field is right-aligned. For this reason, padding is included. It can also be used to hide the length, of the original messages. However, this could adversely impact the effective bandwidth. Padding is an optional field (but needed for some algorithms).

> **Note:**
>
> The encryption covers the payload data, padding, pad length and next header fields.

Pad length

This 8-bit field contains the number of the preceding padding bytes. It is always present, and the value of 0 indicates no padding.

Next header

The next header is an 8-bit mandatory field that shows the data type carried in the payload, for example an upper-level protocol identifier such as TCP. The

| Authentication data | values are chosen from the set of IP protocol numbers defined by the IANA. |

Authentication data   This field is variable in length and contains the ICV calculated for the ESP packet from the SPI to the next header field inclusive. The authentication data field is optional. It is included only when integrity check and authentication have been selected at SA initialization time.

The ESP specifications require two authentication algorithms to be supported: HMAC with MD5 and HMAC with SHA-1. Often the simpler keyed versions are also supported by IPsec implementations.

Notes

1. The IP header is not covered by the ICV.

2. The original ESP specification in RFC 1827 discusses the concept of authentication within ESP in conjunction with the encryption transform. That is, there is no Authentication Data field and it is left to the encryption transforms to eventually provide authentication.

21.5.3.2 Ways of using ESP

Like AH, ESP can be used in two ways: Transport mode and tunnel mode.

ESP in transport mode

In this mode, the ESP header is inserted right after the IP header, as it is shown in Figure 288. If the datagram already has IPsec header(s), then the ESP header is inserted before any of those. The ESP trailer and the optional authentication data are appended to the payload.

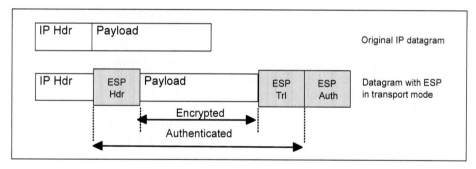

Figure 288. ESP in transport mode

ESP in transport mode provides neither authentication nor encryption for the IP header. This is a disadvantage, since false packets might be delivered for ESP processing. The advantage of transport mode is the lower processing overhead.

As in the case of AH, ESP in transport mode is used by hosts, not gateways. Gateways are not required to support transport mode.

ESP in tunnel mode

As expected, this mode applies the tunneling principle. A new IP packet is constructed with a new IP header. ESP is then applied, as in transport mode, this is illustrated in Figure 289. Since the original datagram becomes the payload data for the new ESP packet, it is completely protected, if both encryption and authentication are selected. However, the new IP header is still not protected.

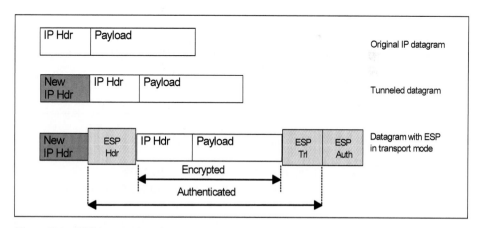

Figure 289. ESP in tunnel mode

The tunnel mode is used whenever either end of a security association is a gateway. Thus, between two firewalls the tunnel mode is always used.

Gateways often also support transport mode. This mode is allowed when the gateway acts as a host, that is in cases when traffic is destined to the gateway itself. For example, SNMP commands could be sent to the gateway using transport mode.

In tunnel mode the outer header's IP addresses does not need to be the same as the inner headers' addresses. For example two security gateways may operate an ESP tunnel which is used to secure all traffic between the networks they connect together. Hosts are not required to support tunnel mode.

The advantages of tunnel mode are total protection of the encapsulated IP datagram and the possibility of using private addresses. However, there is an extra processing overhead associated with this mode.

21.5.3.3 IPv6 considerations

As with AH, ESP is an integral part of IPv6 (see 17.2.2, "Extension headers" on page 565). In an IPv6 environment, ESP is considered an end-to-end payload and it appears after hop-by-hop, routing, and fragmentation extension headers. The destination options extension header(s) could appear either before or after the AH header. Figure 290 illustrates the positioning of the AH header in transport mode for a typical IPv6 packet. The position of the extension headers marked with * is variable, if present at all.

For more details, please refer to RFC 2406.

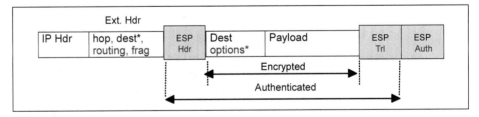

Figure 290. ESP in transport mode for IPv6

21.5.3.4 Two authentication protocols

Knowing about the security services of ESP, one might ask if there is really a requirement for AH. Why does ESP authentication not cover the IP header as well? There is no official answer to these questions, but here are some points that justify the existence of two different IPsec authentication protocols:

- ESP requires strong cryptographic algorithms to be implemented, whether it will actually be used or not. There are restrictive regulations on strong cryptography in some countries. It might be troublesome to deploy ESP-based solutions in such areas. However, authentication is not regulated and AH can be used freely around the world.

- Often, only authentication is needed. AH is more performant compared to ESP with authentication only, because of the simpler format and lower processing overhead. It makes sense to use AH in these cases.

- Having two different protocols means finer-grade control over an IPsec network and more flexible security options. By nesting AH and ESP, for example, one can implement IPsec tunnels that combine the strengths of both protocols.

21.5.4 Combining IPsec protocols

The AH and ESP protocols can be applied alone or in combination. Given the two modes of each protocol, there is quite a number of possible combinations. To make things more complicated, the AH and ESP SAs do not need to have identical endpoints. Luckily, out of the many possibilities, only a few make sense in real-world scenarios.

> **Note:**
>
> RFC 2406 describes mandatory combinations that must be supported by each IPsec implementation. Other combinations may also be supported, but this might impact interoperability.

We mentioned in 21.5.1.1, "Security Associations" on page 699, that the combinations of IPsec protocols are realized with SA bundles.

There are two approaches for an SA bundle creation:

- Transport adjacency: Both security protocols are applied in transport mode to the same IP datagram. This method is practical for only one level of combination.

- Iterated (nested) tunneling: The security protocols are applied in tunnel mode, in sequence. After each application, a new IP datagram is created and the next protocol is applied to it. This method has no limit in the nesting levels. However, more than three levels are impractical.

These approaches can be combined. For example, an IP packet with transport adjacency IPsec headers can be sent through nested tunnels.

When designing a VPN, one should limit the number of IPsec processing stages. In our view, three stages is the limit beyond which further processing has no benefits. Two stages are sufficient for almost all cases.

Note that, in order to be able to create an SA bundle in which the SAs have different endpoints, at least one level of tunneling must be applied. Transport adjacency does not allow for multiple source/destination addresses, because only one IP header is present.

The practical principle of the combined usage is that, upon the receipt of a packet with both protocol headers, the IPsec processing sequence should be authentication followed by decryption. It is common sense not to bother with decryption of packets of uncertain origin.

Following the above principle, the sender first applies ESP and then AH to the outbound traffic. In fact, this sequence is an explicit requirement for transport mode IPsec processing. When using both ESP and AH, a new question arises: Should ESP authentication be turned on? AH authenticates the packet anyway. The answer is simple.

Turning on ESP authentication makes sense only when the ESP SA extends beyond the AH SA. For example, ESP could be used end-to-end, while AH only goes as far as the remote gateway. In this case, not only does it make sense to use ESP authentication, but it is highly recommended to do so to avoid spoofing attacks within the intranet.

As far as the modes are concerned, transport mode is usually used between the endpoints of a connection and tunnel mode is usually used between two machines when at least one of them is a gateway.

Let's take a look at the different ways of using the IPsec protocols, from the simplest to the more complicated nested setups.

21.5.4.1 Case 1: End-to-end security

As shown in Figure 291, two hosts are connected through the Internet (or an intranet) without any IPsec gateway between them. They can use ESP, AH or both. Either transport or tunnel mode can be applied.

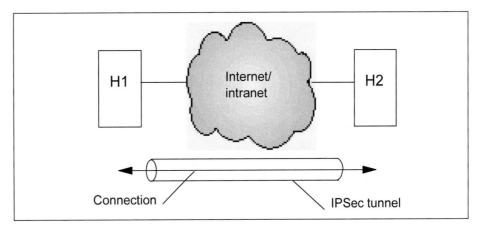

Figure 291. End-to-end security

The combinations required to be supported by any IPsec implementation are the following:

- Transport Mode
    - AH alone
    - ESP alone
    - AH applied after ESP (transport adjacency)
- Tunnel Mode
    - AH alone
    - ESP alone

21.5.4.2 Case 2: Basic VPN support

Virtual private networks (VPNs) are described in 21.11, "Virtual private networks (VPN) overview" on page 755.

Figure 292 illustrates the simplest IPsec VPN. The gateways G1 and G2 run the IPsec protocol stack. The hosts in the intranets are not required to support IPsec.

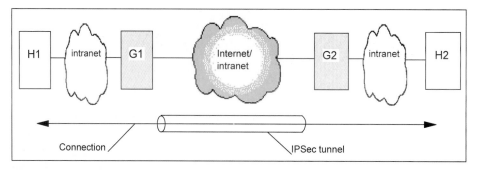

Figure 292. Basic VPN support

In this case, the gateways are required to support only tunnel mode, either with AH or ESP.

Combined tunnels between gateways

Although gateways are required to support either an AH tunnel or ESP tunnel, it is often desirable to have tunnels between gateways that combine the features of both IPsec protocols.

The IBM IPsec implementations support this type of combined AH-ESP tunnels. The order of the headers is user selectable by setting the tunnel policy.

A combined tunnel between gateways does not mean that iterated tunneling takes place. Since the SA bundle comprising the tunnel have identical endpoints, it is inefficient to do iterated tunneling. Instead, one IPsec protocol is applied in tunnel mode and the other in transport mode, which can be conceptually thought of as a combined AH-ESP tunnel. An equivalent approach is to IP tunnel the original datagram and then apply transport adjacency IPsec processing to it. The result is that we have an outer IP header followed by the IPsec headers in the order set by the tunnel policy, then the original IP packet, as is shown in the figure below. This is the packet format in a combined AH-ESP tunnel between two IBM firewalls.

> **Note:**
>
> ESP authentication data was not present in early implementations of the IBM firewall.

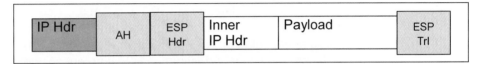

Figure 293. Combined AH-ESP tunnel

21.5.4.3 Case 3: End-to-end security with VPN support

This case is a combination of cases 1 and 2 and does not raise new IPsec requirements for the machines involved (see Figure 294). The big difference from case 2 is that now the hosts are also required to support IPsec.

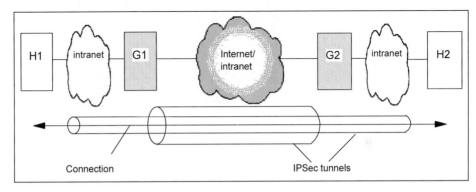

Figure 294. End-to-end security with VPN support

In a typical setup, the gateways use AH in tunnel mode, while the hosts use ESP in transport mode. An enhanced security version could use a combined AH-ESP tunnel between the gateways. In this way, the ultimate destination addresses would be encrypted, the whole packet traveling the Internet would be authenticated and the carried data double encrypted. This is the only case when three stages of IPsec processing might be useful, however, at a cost; the performance impact is considerable.

AH tunneling of ESP transport

Let us look in more detail at the common combination of using AH tunneling to protect ESP traffic in transport mode.

Figure 295 shows in detail how this combination is realized. Consider that host H1 in Figure 294 sends an IP packet to host H2. Here is what happens:

1. Host H1 constructs the IP packet and applies ESP transport to it. H1 then sends the datagram to gateway G1, the destination address being H2.

2. Gateway G1 realizes that this packet should be routed to G2. Upon consulting its IPsec databases (SPD and SAD) G1 concludes that AH in tunnel mode must be applied before sending the packet out. It does the required encapsulation. Now the IP packet has the address of G2 as its destination, the ultimate destination H2 being encapsulated.

3. Gateway G2 receives the AH-tunneled packet. It is destined to itself, so it authenticates the datagram and strips off the outer header. G2 sees that the payload is yet another IP packet (that one sent by H1) with destination H2, so it forwards to H2. G2 does not care that this packet has an ESP header.

4. Finally H2 receives the packet. As this is the destination, ESP-transport processing is applied and the original payload retrieved.

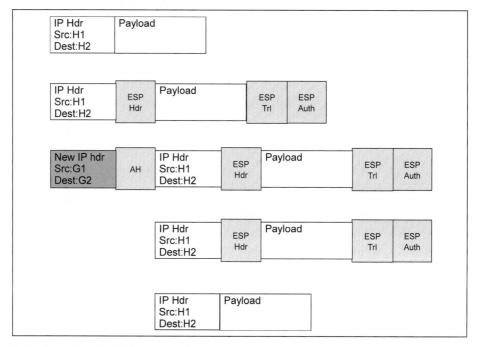

Figure 295. Nesting of IPsec protocols

21.5.4.4 Case 4: Remote access
This case, shown in Figure 296, applies to remote hosts that use the Internet to reach a server in the organization protected by a firewall. The remote host typically uses a PPP dial-in connection to an ISP.

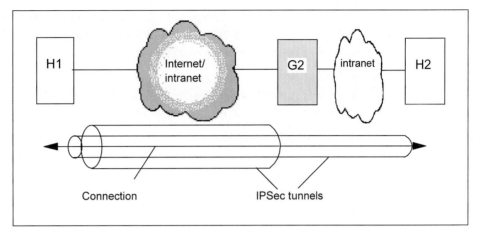

Figure 296. Remote access

Between the remote host H1 and the firewall G2, only tunnel mode is required. The choices are the same as in case 2. Between the hosts themselves, either tunnel mode or transport mode can be used, with the same choices as in case 1.

A typical setup is to use AH in tunnel mode between H1 and G2 and ESP in transport mode between H1 and H2. Older IPsec implementations that do not support AH in tunnel mode cannot implement this.

It is also common to create a combined AH-ESP tunnel between the remote host H1 and the gateway G2. In this case H1 can access the whole intranet using just one SA bundle, whereas if it were using the setup shown in Figure 296, it only could access one host with one SA bundle.

21.5.5 The Internet Key Exchange protocol (IKE)

The Internet Key Exchange (IKE) framework, previously referred to as ISAKMP/Oakley, supports automated negotiation of Security Associations, and automated generation and refresh of cryptographic keys. The ability to perform these functions with little or no manual configuration of machines is a critical element to any enterprise-scale IPsec deployment.

Before describing the details of the key exchange and update messages, some explanations are necessary:

- Internet security association and key management protocol (ISAKMP)

    A framework that defines the management of security associations (negotiate, modify, delete) and keys, and it also defines the payloads for exchanging key generation and authentication data. ISAKMP itself does not define any key exchange protocols, and the framework it provides can be applied to security mechanisms on the network, transport or application layer, and also to itself.

- Oakley

  A key exchange protocol that can be used with the ISAKMP framework to exchange and update keying material for security associations.

- Domain of interpretation (DOI)

  Definition of a set of protocols to be used with the ISAKMP framework for a particular environment; also a set of common definitions shared with those protocols regarding syntax of SA attributes and payload contents, namespace of cryptographic transforms, etc. In relation to IPsec, the DOI instantiates ISAKMP for use with IP.

- Internet key exchange (IKE)

  A protocol that uses parts of ISAKMP and parts of the Oakley and SKEME key exchange protocols to provide management of keys and security associations for the IPsec AH and ESP protocols and for ISAKMP itself.

21.5.5.1 Protocol overview

ISAKMP requires that all information exchanges must be both encrypted and authenticated, so that no one can eavesdrop on the keying material. The keying material will be exchanged only among authenticated parties. This is required because the ISAKMP procedures deal with initializing the keys, so they must be capable of running over links where no security can be assumed to exist.

In addition, the ISAKMP methods have been designed with the explicit goals of providing protection against several well-known exposures:

- Denial of service: The messages are constructed with unique *cookies* that can be used to quickly identify and reject invalid messages without the need to execute processor-intensive cryptographic operations.

- Man-in-the-Middle: Protection is provided against the common attacks such as deletion of messages, modification of messages, reflecting messages back to the sender, replaying of old messages, and redirection of messages to unintended recipients.

- Perfect Forward Secrecy (PFS): Compromise of past keys provides no useful clues for breaking any other key, whether it occurred before or after the compromised key. That is, each refreshed key will be derived without any dependence on predecessor keys.

The following authentication methods are defined for IKE:

1. Pre-shared key

2. Digital signatures (DSS and RSA)

3. Public key encryption (RSA and revised RSA)

The robustness of any cryptography-based solution depends much more strongly on keeping the keys secret than it does on the actual details of the chosen cryptographic algorithms. Hence, the IETF IPsec Working Group has prescribed a set of extremely robust Oakley exchange protocols. It uses a 2-phase approach:

Phase 1
This set of negotiations establishes a master secret from which all cryptographic keys will be derived for protecting the users' data traffic. In the most general case, public key cryptography is used to establish an ISAKMP security association between systems and to establish the keys that will be used to protect the ISAKMP messages that will flow in the subsequent phase 2 negotiations. Phase 1 is concerned only with establishing the protection suite for the ISAKMP messages themselves, but it does not establish any security associations or keys for protecting user data.

In phase 1, the cryptographic operations are the most processor-intensive, but need only be done infrequently, and a single phase 1 exchange can be used to support multiple subsequent phase 2 exchanges. As a rule of thumb, phase 1 negotiations are executed once a day or maybe once a week, while phase 2 negotiations are executed once every few minutes.

Phase 2
Phase 2 exchanges are less complex, since they are used only after the security protection suite negotiated in phase 1 has been activated. A set of communicating systems negotiate the security associations and keys that will protect user data exchanges. Phase 2 ISAKMP messages are protected by the ISAKMP security association generated in phase 1. Phase 2 negotiations generally occur more frequently than phase 1. For example, a typical application of a phase 2 negotiation is to refresh the cryptographic keys once every two to three minutes.

Permanent identifiers
The IKE protocol also offers a solution even when the remote host's IP address is not known in advance. ISAKMP allows a remote host to identify itself by a *permanent* identifier, such as a name or an e-mail address. The ISAKMP phase 1 exchanges will then authenticate the remote host's permanent identity using public key cryptography:

- Certificates create a binding between the permanent identifier and a public key. Therefore, ISAKMP's certificate-based phase 1 message exchanges can authenticate the remote host's permanent identify.

- Since the ISAKMP messages themselves are carried within IP datagrams, the ISAKMP partner (for example, a firewall or destination host) can associate the remote host's dynamic IP address with its authenticated permanent identity.

21.5.5.2 Initializing security associations with IKE

This section outlines how ISAKMP/Oakley protocols initially establish security associations and exchange keys between two systems that wish to communicate securely.

In the remainder of this section, the parties involved are named Host-A and Host-B. Host-A will be the initiator of the ISAKMP phase 1 exchanges, and Host-B will be the responder. If needed for clarity, subscripts A or B will be used to identify the source of various fields in the message exchanges.

21.5.5.3 IKE phase 1 - Setting up ISAKMP security associations

The security associations that protect the ISAKMP messages themselves are set up during the phase 1 exchanges. Since we are starting "cold" (no previous keys or SAs have been negotiated between Host-A and Host-B), the phase 1 exchanges will use the ISAKMP Identity Protect exchange (also known as Oakley Main Mode). Six messages are needed to complete the exchange:

- Messages 1 and 2 negotiate the characteristics of the security associations. Messages 1 and 2 flow in the clear for the initial phase 1 exchange, and they are unauthenticated.
- Messages 3 and 4 exchange nonces (random values) and also execute a Diffie-Hellman exchange to establish a master key (SKEYID). Messages 3 and 4 flow in the clear for the initial phase 1 exchange, and they are unauthenticated.
- Messages 5 and 6 exchange the required information for mutually authenticating the parties' identities. The payloads of messages 5 and 6 are protected by the encryption algorithm and keying material established with messages 1 through 4.

The detailed description of the phase 1 messages and exchanged information follows.

IKE phase 1, message 1

Since Host-A is the initiating party, it will construct a cleartext ISAKMP message (message 1) and send it to Host-B. The ISAKMP message itself is carried as the payload of a UDP packet, which in turn is carried as the payload of a normal IP datagram (see Figure 297).

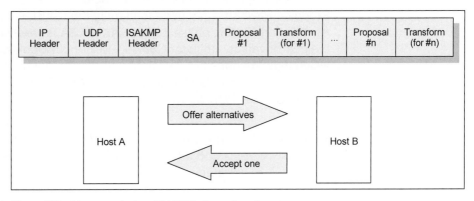

Figure 297. Message 1 of an ISAKMP phase 1 exchange

The source and destination addresses to be placed in the IP header are those of Host-A (initiator) and Host-B (responder), respectively. The UDP header will identify that the destination port is 500, which has been assigned for use by the ISAKMP protocol. The payload of the UDP packet carries the ISAKMP message itself.

In message 1, Host-A, the initiator, proposes a set of one or more protection suites for consideration by Host-B, the responder. Hence, the ISAKMP message contains at least the following fields in its payload:

ISAKMP header   The ISAKMP header in message 1 will indicate an exchange type of Main Mode, and will contain a Message ID of 0. Host-A will set the Responder Cookie field to 0, and will fill in a random value of its choice for the Initiator Cookie, denoted as Cookie-A.

Security Association   The Security Association field identifies the Domain of Interpretation (DOI). Since the hosts plan to run IPsec protocols between themselves, the DOI is simply IP.

Proposal Payload   Host-A's Proposal Payload will specify the protocol PROTO_ISAKMP and will set the SPI value to 0.

Transform Payload   The Transform Payload will specify KEY_OAKLEY. For the KEY_OAKLEY transform, Host-A must also specify the relevant attributes: namely, the authentication method to be used, the pseudo-random function to be used, and the encryption algorithm to be used.

IKE phase 1, message 2

In message 1, Host-A proposed one or more candidate protection suites to be used to protect the ISAKMP exchanges. Host-B uses message 2 to indicate which one, if any, it will support. If Host-A proposed just a single option, Host-B merely needs to acknowledge that the proposal is acceptable.

The source and destination addresses to be placed in the IP header are those of Host-B (responder) and Host-A (initiator), respectively. The UDP header will identify that the destination port is 500, which has been assigned for use by the ISAKMP protocol. The payload of the UDP packet carries the ISAKMP message itself.

The message contents will be as follows:

ISAKMP Header   The ISAKMP Header in message 2 will indicate an exchange type of Main Mode, and will contain a Message ID of 0. Host-B will set the Responder Cookie field to a random value, which we will call Cookie-B, and will copy into the Initiator Cookie field the value that was received in the Cookie-A field of message 1. The value pair <Cookie-A, Cookie-B>

will serve as the SPI for the ISAKMP Security Association.

Security Association The Security Association field identifies the Domain of Interpretation (DOI). Since the hosts plan to run IPsec protocols between themselves, the DOI is simply IP.

Proposal Payload Host-B's Proposal Payload will specify the protocol PROTO_ISAKMP and will set the SPI value to 0.

Transform Payload The Transform Payload will specify KEY_OAKLEY. For the KEY_OAKLEY transform, the attributes that were accepted from the proposal offered by Host-A are copied into the appropriate fields.

At this point, the properties of the ISAKMP Security Association have been agreed to by Host-A and Host-B. The identity of the ISAKMP SA has been set equal to the pair <Cookie-A, Cookie-B>. However, the identities of the parties claiming to be Host-A and Host-B have not yet been authoritatively verified.

IKE phase 1, message 3
The third message of the phase 1 ISAKMP exchange begins the exchange of the information from which the cryptographic keys will eventually be derived (see Figure 298).

> **Important:**
>
> None of the messages themselves carry the actual cryptographic keys. Instead, they carry inputs that will be used by Host-A and Host-B to derive the keys locally.

The ISAKMP payload will be used to exchange two types of information:

Diffie-Hellman public value The Diffie-Hellman public value g^x from the initiator. The exponent x in the public value is the private value that must be kept secret.

Nonce The nonce N_i from the initiator. (Nonce is a fancy name for a value that is considered to be random according to some very strict mathematical guidelines.)

ID If the RSA public key is used for authentication, the nonces are encrypted with the public key of the other party. Likewise for the IDs of either party, which are then also exchanged at this stage.

If authentication with revised RSA public key is used, the KE and ID payloads are encrypted with a secret key that is derived from the nonces and the encryption algorithm agreed to in messages 1 and 2, thus avoiding one CPU-intensive public key operation.

Certificates may optionally be exchanged in either case of public key authentication, as well as a hash value thereof.

These values are carried in the Key Exchange, and the Nonce and the ID fields, respectively.

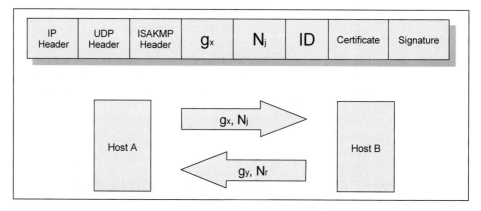

Figure 298. Message 3 of an ISAKMP phase 1 exchange

IKE phase 1, message 4
After receiving a Diffie-Hellman public value and a nonce from Host-A, Host-B will respond by sending to Host-A its own Diffie-Hellman public value (g^y from the responder) and its nonce (N_r from the responder).

Generating the Keys (phase 1)
At this point, each host knows the values of the two nonces (N_i and N_r). Each host also knows its own private Diffie-Hellman value (x and y) and also knows its partner's public value (g^x or g^y). Hence each side can construct the composite value g^{xy}. And finally, each side knows the values of the initiator cookie and the responder cookie.

Given all these bits of information, each side can then independently compute identical values for the following quantities:

- SKEYID: This collection of bits is sometimes referred to as keying material, since it provides the raw input from which actual cryptographic keys will be derived later in the process. It is obtained by applying the agreed-to keyed pseudorandom function (prf) to the known inputs:

  - For digital signature authentication:

    $$\texttt{SKEYID = prf}(N_i, N_r, g^{xy})$$

  - For authentication with public keys:

    $$\texttt{SKEYID = prf(hash}(N_i, N_r), \texttt{CookieA, CookieB})$$

  - For authentication with a pre-shared key:

    $$\texttt{SKEYID = prf(pre-shared key}, N_i, N_r)$$

- Having computed the value SKEYID, each side then proceeds to generate two cryptographic keys and some additional keying material:

  - SKEYID_d is keying material that will be subsequently used in phase 2 to derive the keys that will be used in non-ISAKMP SAs for protecting user traffic:

    $$\texttt{SKEYID\_d = prf(SKEYID}, g^{xy}, \texttt{CookieA, CookieB, 0})$$

  - SKEYID_a is the key used for authenticating ISAKMP messages:

    $$\texttt{SKEYID\_a = prf(SKEYID, SKEYID\_d}, g^{xy}, \texttt{CookieA, CookieB, 1})$$

  - SKEYID_e is the key used for encrypting ISAKMP exchanges:

    $$\texttt{SKEYID\_e = prf(SKEYID, SKEYID\_a}, g^{xy}, \texttt{CookieA, CookieB, 2})$$

At this point in the protocol, both Host-A and Host-B have derived identical authentication and encryption keys that they will use to protect the ISAKMP exchanges. And they have also derived identical keying material from which they will derive keys to protect user data during phase 2 of the ISAKMP negotiations. However, at this point, the two parties' identities still have not been authenticated to one another.

IKE phase 1, message 5

At this point in the phase 1 flows, the two hosts will exchange identity information with each other to authenticate themselves. As shown in Figure 299, the ISAKMP message will carry an identity payload, a signature payload, and an optional certificate payload. Host-A uses message 5 to send information to Host-B that will allow Host-B to authenticate Host-A.

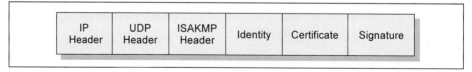

Figure 299. Message 5 of an ISAKMP phase 1 exchange

When an actual certificate is present in the Certificate Payload field, the receiver can use the information directly, after verifying that it has been signed with a valid signature of a trusted certificate authority. If there is no certificate in the message, then it is the responsibility of the receiver to obtain a certificate using some implementation method. For example, it may send a query to a trusted certificate authority using a protocol such as LDAP, or it may query a secure DNS server, or it may maintain a secure local cache that maps previously used certificates to their respective ID values, or it may send an ISAKMP Certificate Request message to its peer, who must then immediately send its certificate to the requester.

> **Note:**
>
> The method for obtaining a certificate is a local option, and is not defined as part of IKE. In particular, it is a local responsibility of the receiver to check that the certificate in question is still valid and has not been revoked.

There are several points to bear in mind:

- At this stage of the process, all ISAKMP payloads, whether in phase 1 or phase 2, are encrypted, using the encryption algorithm (negotiated in messages 1 and 2) and the keys (derived from the information in messages 3 and 4). The ISAKMP header itself, however, is still transmitted in the clear.

- In phase 1, IPsec's ESP protocol is not used; that is, there is no ESP header. The recipient uses the Encryption Bit in the Flags field of the ISAKMP header to determine if encryption has been applied to the message. The pair of values <CookieA, CookieB>, which serve as an SPI for phase 1 exchanges, provide a pointer to the correct algorithm and key to be used to decrypt the message.

- The digital signature, if used, is not applied to the ISAKMP message itself. Instead, it is applied to a hash of information that is available to both Host-A and Host-B.
- The identity carried in the identity payload does not necessarily bear any relationship to the source IP address; however, the identity carried in the identity payload must be the identity to which the certificate, if used, applies.

Host-A (the initiator) will generate the following hash function, and then place the result in the Signature Payload field:

```
HASH_I = prf(SKEYID, g^x, g^y, CookieA, CookieB, SA_p, ID_A)
```

If digital signatures were used for authentication, this hash will also be signed by Host-A.

ID_A is Host-A's identity information that was transmitted in the identity payload of this message, and SA_p is the entire body of the SA payload that was sent by Host-A in message 1, including all proposals and all transforms proposed by Host-A. The cookies, public Diffie-Hellman values, and SKEYID were explicitly carried in messages 1 through 4, or were derived from their contents.

IKE phase 1, message 6
After receiving message 5 from Host-A, Host-B will verify the identity of Host-A by validating the hash.

If digital signatures were used for authentication, the signature of this hash will be verified by Host-B.

If this is successful, then Host-B will send message 6 to Host-A to allow Host-A to verify the identity of Host-B.

The structure of message 6 is the same as that of message 5, with the obvious changes that the identity payload and the certificate payload now pertain to Host-B.

```
HASH_R = prf(SKEYID, g^y, g^x, CookieB, CookieA, SA_p, ID_B)
```

Notice that the order in which Diffie-Hellman public values and the cookies appear has been changed, and the final term now is the Identity Payload that Host-B has included in message 6.

If digital signatures were used for authentication, this hash will also be signed by Host-B, which is different from the one previously signed by Host-A.

When Host-A receives message 6 and verifies the hash or digital signature, the phase 1 exchanges are then complete. At this point, each participant has authenticated itself to its peer. Both have agreed on the characteristics of the ISAKMP Security Associations, and both have derived the same set of keys (or keying material).

Miscellaneous phase 1 facts
There are several miscellaneous facts worth noting:

- Regardless of the specific authentication mechanism that is used, there will be six messages exchanged for Oakley Main Mode. However, the content of the individual messages will differ, depending on the authentication method.

- Although Oakley exchanges make use of both encryption and authentication, they do not use either IPsec's ESP or AH protocol. ISAKMP exchanges are protected with application-layer security mechanisms, not with network layer security mechanisms.

- ISAKMP messages are sent using UDP. There is no guaranteed delivery for them.

- The only way to identify that an ISAKMP message is part of a phase 1 flow rather than a phase 2 flow is to check the Message ID field in the ISAKMP Header. For phase 1 flows, it must be 0, and (although not explicitly stated in the ISAKMP documents) for phase 2 flows, it must be non-zero.

21.5.5.4 IKE phase 2 - Setting up protocol security associations
After having completed the phase 1 negotiation process to set up the ISAKMP Security Associations, Host-A's next step is to initiate the Oakley phase 2 message exchanges (also known as Oakley Quick Mode) to define the security associations and keys that will be used to protect IP datagrams exchanged between the pair of users. (In the Internet drafts, these are referred to somewhat obtusely as "non-ISAKMP SAs.")

Because the purpose of the phase 1 negotiations was to agree on how to protect ISAKMP messages, all ISAKMP phase 2 payloads, but not the ISAKMP header itself, must be encrypted using the algorithm agreed to by the phase 1 negotiations.

When Oakley Quick Mode is used in phase 2, authentication is achieved via the use of several cryptographically based hash functions. The input to the hash functions comes partly from phase 1 information (SKEYID) and partly from information exchanged in phase 2. Phase 2 authentication is based on certificates, but the phase 2 process itself does not use certificates directly. Instead, it uses the SKEYID_a material from phase 1, which itself was authenticated via certificates.

Oakley Quick Mode comes in two forms:

- Without a Key Exchange attribute, Quick Mode can be used to refresh the cryptographic keys, but does not provide the property of Perfect Forward Secrecy (PFS).
- With a Key Exchange attribute, Quick Mode can be used to refresh the cryptographic keys in a way that provides PFS. This is accomplished by including an exchange of public Diffie-Hellman values within messages 1 and 2.

> **Note:**
>
> PFS apparently is a property that is very much desired by cryptography experts, but strangely enough, the specs treat PFS as optional. They mandate that a system must be capable of handling the Key Exchange field when it is present in a Quick Mode message, but do not require a system to include the field within the message.

The detailed description of the phase 2 messages and exchanged information follows below:

IKE phase 2, message 1
Message 1 of a Quick Mode Exchange allows Host-A to authenticate itself, to select a nonce, to propose security association(s) to Host-B, to execute an exchange of public Diffie-Hellman values, and to indicate if it is acting on its own behalf or as a proxy negotiator for another entity. An overview of the format of message 1 is shown in Figure 300.

> **Note:**
>
> Inclusion of a key exchange field is optional. However, when Perfect Forward Secrecy is desired, it must be present.

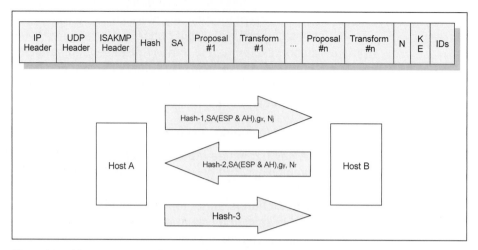

Figure 300. Message 1 of an ISAKMP phase 2 Quick Mode Exchange

Since we have assumed that Host-A and Host-B are each acting on their own behalf, the user identity fields illustrated in Figure 300 will not be present. The message will consist of:

ISAKMP Header The ISAKMP Header will indicate an exchange type of Quick Mode, will include a non-zero Message-ID chosen by Host-A, will include the initiator and responder cookie values chosen in phase 1 (that is, Cookie-A and Cookie-B), and will turn on the encryption flag to indicate that the payloads of the ISAKMP message are encrypted according to the algorithm and key negotiated during phase 1.

Hash A Hash Payload must immediately follow the ISAKMP header. HASH_1 uses the keyed pseudo-random function that was negotiated during the phase 1 exchanges, and is derived from the following information:

- SKEYID_a was derived from the phase 1 exchanges.
- M-ID is the message ID of this message.
- SA is the Security Association payload carried in this message, including all proposals that were offered.

- Nonce is a new value different from the one used in phase 1.
- KE is the public Diffie-Hellman value carried in this message. This quantity is chosen by Host-A, and is denoted as g_{qm}^x. Note that this is not the same quantity as g^x that was used in the phase 1 exchanges.
- IDs, which can identify either the endpoints of the phase 1 exchange or endpoints on whose behalf the protocol SA should be negotiated (proxy IDs when IKE is used in client mode). These can subsequently be different from the IDs used in phase 1.

Note:

The use of KE and ID is optional, depending if PFS is desired.

```
HASH_1 = prf(SKEYID_a, M-ID, SA, N_qmi, KE, ID_qmi, ID_qmr)
```

Security Association	Indicate IP as the Domain of Interpretation.
Proposal, Transform Pairs	There can be one or more of these pairs in this message. The first proposal payload will be numbered 1, will identify an IPsec protocol to be used, and will include an SPI value that is randomly chosen by Host-A for use with that protocol. The proposal payload will be followed by a single transform payload that indicates the cryptographic algorithm to be used with that protocol. The second proposal payload will be numbered 2, etc.
Nonce payload	This contains the nonce N^{qmi} that was chosen randomly by Host-A.
KE	This is the key exchange payload that will carry the public Diffie-Hellman value chosen by Host-A, g_{qm}^x. There is also a field called Group, that indicates the prime number and generator used in the Diffie-Hellman exchange.

ID payload   Specifies the endpoints for this SA.

IKE phase 2, message 2
After Host-B receives message 1 from Host-A and successfully authenticates
it using HASH_1, it constructs a reply, message 2, to be sent back to Host-A.
The Message ID of the reply will be the same one that Host-A used in
message 1.

Host-B will choose new values for the following:

Hash   The hash payload now carries the value HASH_2,
                                which is defined as:

$$\text{HASH\_2} = \text{prf}(\text{SKEYID\_a}, N_{qmi}, M\text{-}ID, SA, N_{qmr}, KE, ID_{qmi}, ID_{qmr})$$

Security Association The Security Association payload only describes the
                        single chosen proposal and its associated transforms,
                        not all of the protection suites offered by Host-A.
                        Host-B also chooses an SPI value for the selected
                        protocol. Host-B's SPI does not depend in any way on
                        the SPI that Host-A assigned to that protocol when it
                        offered the proposal. That is, it is not necessary that
                        SPI_A be the same as SPI_B; it is only necessary that
                        they each be non-zero and that they each be
                        randomly chosen.

Nonce   Nonce payload now carries N_r, a random value
                                chosen by Host-B.

KE   Key exchange payload now carries Host-B's public
                                Diffie-Hellman value, $g_{qm}{}^y$.

                                At this point, Host-A and Host-B have exchanged
                                nonces and public Diffie-Hellman values. Each one
                                can use this in conjunction with other information to
                                derive a pair of keys, one for each direction of
                                transmission.

Generating the keys (phase 2)
Using the nonces, public Diffie-Hellman values, SPIs, protocol code points
exchanged in messages 1 and 2 of phase 2, and the SKEYID value from
phase 1, each host now has enough information to derive two sets of keying
material.

- When PFS is used:

  - For data generated by Host-A and received by Host-B, the keying
    material is:

$$\mathrm{KEYMAT_{AB}} = \mathrm{prf}(\mathrm{SKEYID\_d},\ g_{qm}{}^{xy},\ \mathrm{protocol},\ \mathrm{SPI_B},\ N_{qmi},\ N_{qmr})$$

- For data generated by Host-B and received by Host-A, the keying material is:

$$\mathrm{KEYMAT_{BA}} = \mathrm{prf}(\mathrm{SKEYID\_d},\ g_{qm}{}^{xy},\ \mathrm{protocol},\ \mathrm{SPI_A},\ N_{qmi},\ N_{qmr})$$

• When PFS is not used:

- For data generated by Host-A and received by Host-B, the keying material is:

$$\mathrm{KEYMAT_{AB}} = \mathrm{prf}(\mathrm{SKEYID\_d},\ \mathrm{protocol},\ \mathrm{SPI_B},\ N_{qmi},\ N_{qmr})$$

- For data generated by Host-B and received by Host-A, the keying material is:

$$\mathrm{KEYMAT_{BA}} = \mathrm{prf}(\mathrm{SKEYID\_d},\ \mathrm{protocol},\ \mathrm{SPI_A},\ N_{qmi},\ N_{qmr})$$

Note:

Depending on the particular case, Host-A may need to derive multiple keys for the following purposes:

• Generating the integrity check value for transmitted datagrams
• Validating the integrity check value of received datagrams
• Encrypting transmitted datagrams
• Decrypting received datagrams

Likewise, Host-B needs to derive the mirror image of the same keys. For example, the key that Host-B uses to encrypt its outbound messages is the same key that Host-A uses to decrypt its inbound messages, etc.

IKE phase 2, message 3

At this point, Host-A and Host-B have exchanged all the information necessary for them to derive the necessary keying material. The third message in the Quick Mode exchange is used by Host-A to prove its alive state, which it does by producing a hash function that covers the message ID and both nonces that were exchanged in messages 1 and 2. Message 3 consists only of the ISAKMP header and a hash payload that carries:

$$\mathrm{HASH\_3} = \mathrm{prf}(\mathrm{SKEYID\_a},\ 0,\ \mathrm{M\text{-}ID},\ N_{qmi},\ N_{qmr})$$

When Host-B receives this message and verifies the hash, then both systems can begin to use the negotiated security protocols to protect their user data streams.

21.5.5.5 Negotiating multiple Security Associations
It is also possible to negotiate multiple security associations, each with its own set of keying material, within a single 3-message Quick Mode exchange.

The message formats are very similar to the previously illustrated ones, so only the differences will be highlighted below:

- Message 1 will carry multiple security association payloads, each offering a range of protection suites.

- HASH_1 will cover the entire set of all offered Security Associations carried in message 1. That is, each Security Association and all of its offered proposals are included.

- In message 2, for each offered SA, Host-B will select a single protection suite. That is, if n SAs are open for negotiation, then Host-B will choose n protection suites, one from each proposal.

- As was the case for HASH_1, HASH_2 will now cover the entire set of all offered security associations carried in message 1. That is, each security association and all of its offered proposals are included.

- After messages 1 and 2 have been exchanged, then Host-A and Host-B will be able to generate the keying material for each of the accepted protection suites, using the same formulas as in on page 736, applied individually for each accepted SA. Even though the nonces and the public Diffie-Hellman values are the same for all selected suites, the keying material derived for each selected protection suite will be different because each proposal will have a different SPI.

- Because multiple security associations have been negotiated, it is a matter of local choice as to which one is used to protect a given datagram. A receiving system must be capable of processing a datagram that is protected by any SA that has been negotiated. That is, it would be legal for a given source host to send two consecutive datagrams to a destination system, where each datagram was protected by a different SA.

21.5.5.6 Using IKE with remote access
The critical element in the remote access scenario is the use of Oakley to identify the remote host by name, rather than by its dynamically assigned IP address. Once the remote host's identity has been authenticated and the mapping to its dynamically assigned IP address has been ascertained, the remainder of the processes are the same as we have described for the other

scenarios. For example, if the corporate intranet is considered to be trusted, then the remote host needs to establish a single SA between itself and the firewall. But if the corporate intranet is considered to be untrusted, then it may be necessary for the remote host to set up two SAs: one between itself and the firewall, and a second between itself and the destination host.

Recall that a single ISAKMP phase 1 negotiation can protect several subsequent phase 2 negotiations. Phase 1 ISAKMP negotiations use computationally intensive public key cryptographic operations, while phase 2 negotiations use the less computationally intensive symmetric key cryptographic operations. Hence, the heavy computational load only occurs in phase 1, which will only be executed when the dial-up connection is first initiated.

The principal points that pertain to the remote access case are:

- The remote host's dynamically assigned address is the one that is placed in the IP header of all ISAKMP messages.

- The remote host's permanent identifier (such as an e-mail address) is the quantity that is placed in the ID field of the ISAKMP phase 1 messages.

- The remote host's certificate used in the ISAKMP exchange must be associated with the remote host's permanent identifier.

- In traffic-bearing datagrams, the remote host's dynamically assigned IP address will be used. This is necessary since the destination IP address that appears in the datagram's IP header is used in conjunction with the SPI and protocol type to identify the relevant IPsec security association for processing the inbound datagram.

21.6 SOCKS

SOCKS is a standard for circuit-level gateways. It does not require the overhead of a more conventional proxy server where a user has to consciously connect to the firewall first before requesting the second connection to the destination (please see Figure 301).

The user starts a client application with the destination server IP address. Instead of directly starting a session with the destination server, the client initiates a session to the SOCKS server on the firewall. The SOCKS server then validates that the source address and user ID are permitted to establish onward connection into the nonsecure network, and then creates the second session.

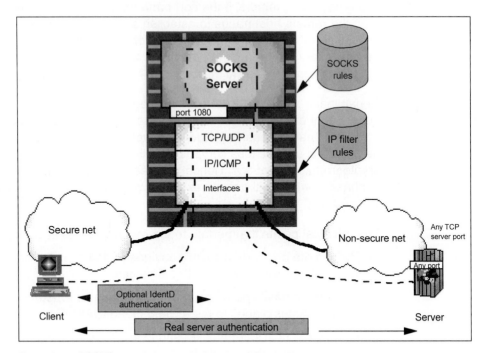

Figure 301. SOCKS server

SOCKS needs to have new versions of the client code (called SOCKSified clients) and a separate set of configuration profiles on the firewall. However, the server machine does not need modification; indeed it is unaware that the session is being relayed by the SOCKS server. Both the client and the SOCKS server need to have SOCKS code. The SOCKS server acts as an application-level router between the client and the real application server. SOCKSv4 is for outbound TCP sessions only. It is simpler for the private network user, but does not have secure password delivery so it is not intended for sessions between public network users and private network applications. SOCKSv5 provides for several authentication methods and can therefore be used for inbound connections as well, though these should be used with caution. SOCKSv5 also supports UDP-based applications and protocols.

The majority of Web browsers are SOCKSified and you can get SOCKSified TCP/IP stacks for most platforms. For additional information, refer to RFC 1928, RFC 1929, RFC 1961 and the following URL:

```
http://www.socks.nec.com
```

21.6.1 SOCKS Version 5 (SOCKSv5)

SOCKS version 5 is a proposed standard protocol with a status of elective. It is described in RFC 1928.

Application-level gateways provide secure connections for some applications such as TELNET, FTP and SMTP. However, it is not easy to write proxy code for each new application. Generally, the proxy service becomes available after some time, even if the service can be used directly and application level gateways do not allow UDP connections. SOCKSv5 satisfies all these shortcomings and requirements with a strong authentication mechanism and the hiding of addresses from a non-secure network. Although, supporting UDP might seem to be vulnerable, it can be configured to pass UDP for particular users and particular applications only.

The SOCKSv5 concept is based on SOCKSv4 with some extensions such as UDP support, new and various sophisticated authentication methods and extended addressing schemes to cover domain-name and IPv6. SOCKSv5 supports a range of authentication methods, including:

1. User name/password authentication

2. One-time password generators

3. Kerberos

4. Remote Authentication Dial-In User Services (RADIUS)

5. Password Authentication Protocol (PAP)

6. IPsec Authentication method

SOCKSv5 also supports the following encryption standards:

1. DES

2. Triple DES

3. IPsec

The following tunneling protocols are supported:

1. PPTP

2. L2F

3. L2TP

The following key management systems are supported:

1. SKIP

2. ISAKMP/Oakley

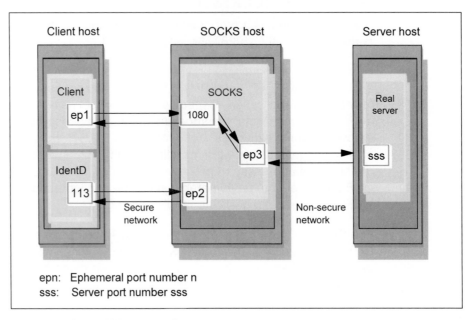

Figure 302. Socks TCP segment flow

The SOCKSv5 server listens for connections on a given port, usually 1080. According to the connection type (TCP or UDP), the steps discussed in the following sections are taken to establish a connection.

21.6.1.1 SOCKSv5 TCP connection

To establish a connection using TCP, the client first sends a TCP packet which contains session request information via port 1080 to the server (please see Figure 302). If the access permissions allow this operation and the connection request succeeds, the client enters an authentication negotiation. In this state, the authentication type is determined, after which the client sends a relay request. The SOCKSv5 server evaluates the request and either establishes the connection or rejects it. The client sends the following message, which contains a version identifier and method options:

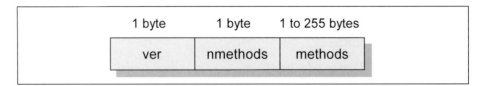

Figure 303. SOCKSv5 - Version identifier and method selection message format

Where:

VER　　　　　　　*Indicates the version of SOCKS. For SOCKSv5, the value is hexadecimal X'05'.*

NMETHODS　　　Indicates the number of the methods appeared in the methods field.

METHODS　　　Indicates the supported authentication and encapsulation methods.

The server responds by the following message:

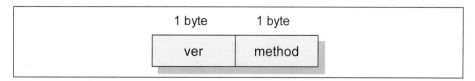

Figure 304. SOCKSv5 - Selected method message format

The hexadecimal values for current standard METHODS are as follows:

X'00'　　　　　　NO AUTHENTICATION REQUIRED

X'01'　　　　　　GSSAPI

X'02'　　　　　　USERNAME/PASSWORD

X'03' to X'7F'　　IANA ASSIGNED

X'80' to X'FE'　　RESERVED FOR PRIVATE METHODS

X'FF'　　　　　　NO ACCEPTABLE METHODS

All implementations should support USERNAME/PASSWORD and GSSAPI authentication methods.

SOCKSv5 Connect

Once authentication is completed successfully, the client sends the request details. If an encapsulation method is negotiated during the method negotiation, the selected encapsulation method must be applied for the following messages. The detail request message format issued by the client is as follows:

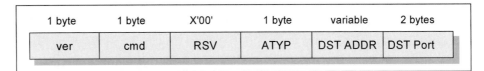

1 byte	1 byte	X'00'	1 byte	variable	2 bytes
ver	cmd	RSV	ATYP	DST ADDR	DST Port

Figure 305. SOCKSv5 - Detail request message format

Where:

VER   Socks protocol version. For SOCKSv5, the value is hexadecimal X'05'.

CMD   SOCKS command in octets.

         X'01'   CONNECT

         X'02'   BIND

         X'03'   UDP ASSOCIATE

RSV   Reserved for future use.

ATYP   Address types in octets.

         X'01'   IPv4 address

         X'03'   Domain-name

         X'04'   IPv6 address

DST.ADDR   Desired destination address.

DST.PORT   Desired destination port in network octet order.

An IPv4 address is stored as 4 bytes. An IPv6 address is stored in 16 bytes.

A domain name is stored as a length byte, then a fully qualified domain name. There is no trailing null at the end of the domain name.

The server evaluates the request detail message and replies with one or more messages. Here is the reply message format issued by the server:

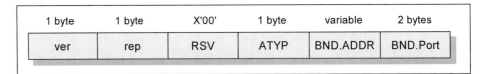

1 byte	1 byte	X'00'	1 byte	variable	2 bytes
ver	rep	RSV	ATYP	BND.ADDR	BND.Port

Figure 306. SOCKSv5 - Server reply message format

Where:

VER	Socks protocol version. For SOCKSv5, the value is hexadecimal X'05'.

REP	Reply field:	
	X'00'	Succeeded
	X'01'	General SOCKS server failure
	X'02'	Connection not allowed by ruleset
	X'03'	Network unreachable
	X'04'	Host unreachable
	X'05'	Connection refused
	X'06'	TTL expired
	X'07'	Command not supported
	X'08'	Address type not supported
	X'09' to X'FF'	Unassigned

RSV	Reserved for future use.	

ATYP	Address types in octets.	
	X'01'	IPv4 address
	X'03'	Domain name
	X'04'	IPv6 address

BND.ADDR	Server bound address.
BND.PORT	Server bound port in network octet order.

SOCKSv5 BIND

If you wish to accept an incoming connection from the Internet, then you use the same request and reply format as described above for SOCKSv5 Connect, setting the CMD field to BIND. However, you will receive two reply packets.

The 1st reply contains the IP address and port number that the SOCKS server has put a listener on.

When the remote system calls into the SOCKS server, you get a 2nd reply with the BND.ADDR and BIND.Port fields containing details of the remote server.

21.6.1.2 SOCKSv5 UDP Connection

To be able use a UDP connection over a SOCKS server, the client first issues the UDP ASSOCIATE command to the SOCKSv5 server. The SOCKSv5 server then assigns a UDP port to which the client sends all UDP datagrams. Each UDP datagram has a UDP request header. The UDP request header format is as follows:

2 bytes	1 byte	1 byte	variable	2 bytes	variable
RSV	frag	ATYP	DST.ADDR	DST.Port	data

Figure 307. SOCKSv5 - UDP datagram request header format

Where:

RSV   Reserved for future use. All bytes are zero.

FRAG   Current fragment number.

ATYP   Address types in octets.

    X'01'   IPv4 address

    X'03'   Domain-name

    X'04'   IPv6 address

DST.ADDR   Desired destination address.

DST.PORT   Desired destination port in network octet order.

DATA   User data.

The UDP relay server gets the IP address of the client which sends UDP datagrams to the port specified by DST.PORT. It will then discard any datagram that comes from another source.

21.7 Secure Shell (I)

SSH can be used to secure connections between systems. It allows application traffic such as that generated by TELNET, FTP POP3, or even X Windows to be both encrypted and compressed. Compression is useful over slow modem links. Implementations can allow the user a choice of encryption methods.

Client software often offers both SSH1 and SSH2 support. The user is authenticated by password or public/private key.

SSH1 offers Blowfish, DES, 3DES and RC4 encryption ciphers.

SSH2 offers 3DES, RC4 and Twofish encryption ciphers.

21.7.1 SSH overview

SSH establishes a single TCP/IP connection from the client to the server. The traffic sent down this connection is encrypted, and optionally compressed using LempleZiv compression. Public/private keys can be used to verify both the user, and the identity of the remote system.

21.7.1.1 SSH and X Windows

X Window sessions may be passed through the SSH connection. The SSH server generates a new DISPLAY variable (and xauth key) for the remote X Window's clients. SSH forwards the X Windows traffic to the user's local X Server. The user has to supply his own X Server application; make sure it is listening on localhost.

21.7.1.2 SSH port forwarding

SSH offers the ability to map TCP/IP ports across systems. For example, you can configure SSH to copy data between a port on the client's localhost and the servers POP3 port. By running a POP3 client and pointing it at localhost, you establish a secure encrypted session over which to read e-mail.

21.8 Secure Sockets Layer (SSL)

SSL is a security protocol that was developed by Netscape Communications Corporation, along with RSA Data Security, Inc. The primary goal of the SSL protocol is to provide a private channel between communicating applications, which ensures privacy of data, authentication of the partners, and integrity.

21.8.1 SSL overview

SSL provides an alternative to the standard TCP/IP socket API that has security implemented within it. Hence, in theory it is possible to run any TCP/IP application in a secure way without changing the application. In practice, SSL is only widely implemented for HTTP connections, but Netscape Communications Corp. has stated an intention to employ it for other application types, such as NNTP and Telnet and there are several such implementations freely available on the Internet. IBM, for example, is using SSL to enhance security for TN3270 sessions in its Host On-Demand and eNetwork Communications Server products.

SSL is composed of two layers:

- At the lower layer, a protocol for transferring data using a variety of predefined cipher and authentication combinations, called the *SSL Record Protocol*. Figure 308 illustrates this and contrasts it with a standard HTTP socket connection. Note that this diagram shows SSL as providing a simple socket interface, on which other applications can be layered. In reality, current implementations have the socket interface embedded within the application and do not expose an API that other applications can use.

- On the upper layer, a protocol for initial authentication and transfer of encryption keys, called the *SSL Handshake Protocol*.

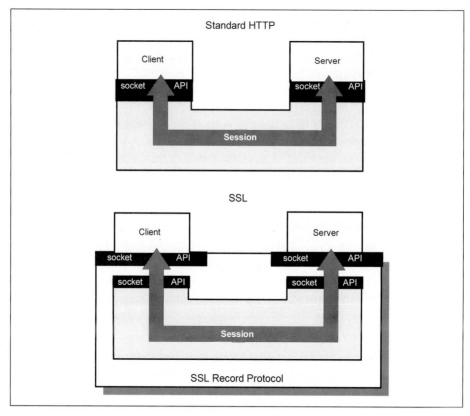

Figure 308. SSL - Comparison of standard and SSL sessions

An SSL session is initiated as follows:

- On the client (browser) the user requests a document with a special URL that commences https: instead of http:, either by typing it into the URL input field, or by clicking on a link.

- The client code recognizes the SSL request and establishes a connection through TCP port 443 to the SSL code on the server.
- The client then initiates the SSL handshake phase, using the SSL Record Protocol as a carrier. At this point, there is no encryption or integrity checking built in to the connection.

The SSL protocol addresses the following security issues:

Privacy   After the symmetric key is established in the initial handshake, the messages are encrypted using this key.

Integrity   Messages contain a message authentication code (MAC) ensuring the message integrity.

Authentication   During the handshake, the client authenticates the server using an asymmetric or public key. It can also be based on certificates.

SSL requires each message to be encrypted and decrypted and therefore has a high performance and resource overhead.

21.8.1.1 Differences between SSL V2.0 and SSL V3.0

There is backward compatibility between SSL V2.0 and SSL V3.0. An SSL V3.0 server implementation should be able accept the connection request from an SSL V2.0 client. The main differences between SSL V2.0 and SSL V3.0 are as follows:

- SSL V2.0 does not support client authentication.
- SSL V3.0 supports more ciphering types in the CipherSpec.

21.8.2 SSL protocol

The SSL protocol is located at the top of the transport layer. SSL is also a layered protocol itself. It simply takes the data from the application layer, reformats it and transmits it to the transport layer. SSL handles a message as follows:

- Sender

  Performs the following tasks:

    - Takes the message from upper layer
    - Fragments the data to manageable blocks
    - Optionally compresses the data
    - Applies a Message Authentication Code (MAC)
    - Encrypts the data
    - Transmits the result to the lower layer

- Receiver

  Performs the following tasks:

  - Takes the data from lower layer
  - Decrypts
  - Verifies the data with the negotiated MAC key
  - Decompresses the data if compression was used
  - Reassembles the message
  - Transmits the message to the upper layer

An SSL session works in different states. These states are *session* and *connection* states. The SSL handshake protocol (see 21.8.2.2, "SSL handshake protocol" on page 751) coordinates the states of the client and the server. In addition, there are read and write states defined to coordinate the encryption according to the change cipher spec messages.

When either party sends a change cipher spec message, it changes the pending write state to current write state. Again, when either party receives a change cipher spec message, it changes the pending read state to the current read state.

The session state includes the following components:

Session identifier   An arbitrary byte sequence chosen by the server to identify an active or resumable session state.

Peer certificate   Certificate of the peer. This field is optional; it can be empty.

Compression method   The compression algorithm.

Cipher spec   Specifies data encryption algorithm (such as null, DES) and a MAC algorithm.

Master secret   48-byte shared secret between the client and the server.

Is resumable   A flag indicating whether the session can be used for new connections.

The connection state includes the following components:

Server and client random An arbitrary byte sequence chosen by the client and server for each connection.

Server write MAC secret The secret used for MAC operations by the server.

Client write MAC secret The secret used for MAC operations by the client.

Server write key The cipher key for the server to encrypt the data and the client to decrypt the data.

Client write key The cipher key for the client to encrypt the data and the server to decrypt the data.

Initialization vectors Initialization vectors store the encryption information.

Sequence numbers A sequence number indicates the number of the message transmitted since the last change cipher spec message. Both the client and the server maintain sequence numbers.

21.8.2.1 Change cipher spec protocol

The change cipher spec protocol is responsible for sending change cipher spec messages. At any time, the client can request to change current cryptographic parameters such as handshake key exchange. Following the change cipher spec notification, the client sends a handshake key exchange and if available, certificate verify messages, and the server sends a change cipher spec message after processing the key exchange message. After that, the newly agreed keys will be used until the next change cipher spec request. The change cipher spec message is sent after the hello messages during the negotiation.

21.8.2.2 SSL handshake protocol

The SSL handshake protocol allows the client and server to determine the required parameters for an SSL connection such as protocol version, cryptographic algorithms, optional client or server authentication, and public-key encryption methods to generate shared secrets. During this process all handshake messages are forwarded to the SSL record layer to be encapsulated into special SSL messages. Figure 309 illustrates an SSL handshake process.

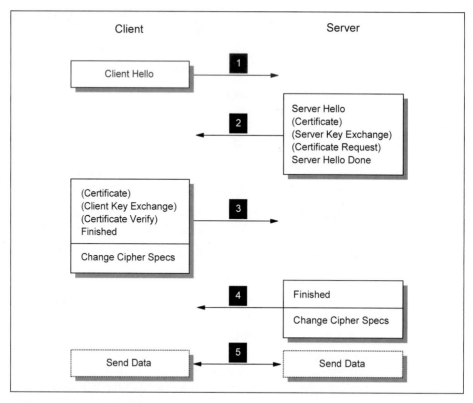

Figure 309. SSL - Handshake process

The SSL handshake process detailed in Figure 309 is explained in more detail in the following:

- Step 1: The client sends a connection request with a client hello message. This message includes:
  - Desired version number.
  - Time information (the current time and date in standard UNIX 32-bit format).
  - Optionally session-ID. If it is not specified the server will try to resume previous sessions or return an error message
  - Cipher suites. (List of the cryptographic options supported by the client. These are authentication modes, key exchange methods, encryptions and MAC algorithms.)
  - Compression methods supported by the client.
  - A random value.

- Step Two: The server evaluates the parameters sent by the client hello message and returns a server hello message that includes the following parameters which were selected by the server to be used for the SSL session:
  - Version number
  - Time information (the current time and date in standard UNIX 32-bit format)
  - Session ID
  - Cipher suite
  - Compression method
  - A random value

  Following the server hello message the server sends the following messages:
  - Server certificate if the server is required to be authenticated
  - A server key exchange message if there is no certificate available or the certificate is for signing only
  - A certificate request if the client is required to be authenticated

  Finally, the server sends a server hello done message and begins to wait for the client response.

- Step Three: The client sends the following messages:
  - If the server has sent a certificate request, the client must send a certificate or a no certificate message.
  - If the server has sent a server key exchange message, the client sends a client key exchange message based on the public key algorithm determined with the hello messages.
  - If the client has sent a certificate, the client verifies the server certificate and sends a certificate verify message indicating the result.

  The client then sends a finished message indicating the negotiation part is completed. The client also sends a change cipher spec message to generate shared secrets. It should be noted that this is not controlled by the handshake protocol, the change cipher spec protocol manages this part of the operation.

- Step Four: The server sends a finished message indicating the negotiation part is completed. The server then sends the change cipher spec message.

- Step Five: Finally, the session partners separately generate an encryption key, in which they derive the keys to use in the encrypted session that follows from the master key. The Handshake protocol changes the state to the connection state. All data taken from the application layer is transmitted as special messages to the other party.

There is significant additional overhead in starting up an SSL session compared with a normal HTTP connection. The protocol avoids some of this overhead by allowing the client and server to retain session key information and to resume that session without negotiating and authenticating a second time.

Following the handshake, both session partners have generated a master key. From that key they generate other session keys, which are used in the symmetric-key encryption of the session data and in the creation of message digests. The first message encrypted in this way is the finished message from the server. If the client can interpret the finished message, it means:

- Privacy has been achieved, because the message is encrypted using a symmetric-key bulk cipher (such as DES or RC4).
- The message integrity is assured, because it contains a Message Authentication Code (MAC), which is a message digest of the message itself plus material derived from the master key.
- The server has been authenticated, because it was able to derive the master key from the pre-master key. As this was sent using the server's public key, it could only have been decrypted by the server (using its private key). Note that this relies on the integrity of the server's public key certificate.

21.8.2.3 SSL record protocol
Once the master key has been determined, the client and server can use it to encrypt application data. The SSL record protocol specifies a format for these messages. In general they include a message digest to ensure that they have not been altered and the whole message is encrypted using a symmetric cipher. Usually, this uses the RC2 or RC4 algorithm, although DES, triple-DES and IDEA are also supported by the specification.

The U.S. National Security Agency (NSA), a department of the United States federal government, imposed restrictions on the size of the encryption key that can be used in software exported outside the U.S. These rules have been reviewed, but originally the key was limited to an effective size of 56 bits. The RC2 and RC4 algorithms achieved this by using a key in which all but 56 bits are set to a fixed value. International (export) versions of software products had this hobbled security built into them. SSL checks for mismatches between the export and nonexport versions in the negotiation phase of the handshake. For example, if a U.S. browser tries to connect with SSL to an export server, they will agree on export-strength encryption. See

21.2.7, "Export/import restrictions on cryptography" on page 677 for more information on recent changes of U.S. export regulations of cryptographic material.

21.9 Transport Layer Security (TLS)

The Transport Layer Security 1.0 protocol is based on SSL. The TLS 1.0 protocol is documented in RFC 2246. Two applications (without knowing each other's code) may use TLS to communicate securely. There are no significant differences between SSL 3.0 and TLS 1.0. They can interoperate with some modifications on the message formats. A TLS 1.0 application can back down to an SSL 3.0 connection.

21.10 Secure Multipurpose Internet Mail Extension (S-MIME)

Secure Multipurpose Internet Mail Extension (S-MIME) can be thought of as a very specific SSL-like protocol. S-MIME is an application-level security construct, but its use is limited to protecting e-mail via encryption and digital signatures. It relies on public key technology, and uses X.509 certificates to establish the identities of the communicating parties. S-MIME can be implemented in the communicating end systems; it is not used by intermediate routers or firewalls.

21.11 Virtual private networks (VPN) overview

The Internet has become a popular, low-cost backbone infrastructure. Its universal reach has led many companies to consider constructing a secure virtual private network (VPN) over the public Internet. The challenge in designing a VPN for today's global business environment will be to exploit the public Internet backbone for both intra-company and inter-company communication while still providing the security of the traditional private, self-administered corporate network.

In this chapter, we begin by defining a virtual private network (VPN) and explaining the benefits that customers can achieve from its implementation. After discussing the security considerations and planning aspects, we then describe the VPN solutions available in the market today.

21.11.1 VPN Introduction and benefits

With the explosive growth of the Internet, companies are beginning to ask: "How can we best exploit the Internet for our business?" Initially, companies were using the Internet to promote their company's image, products, and services by providing World Wide Web access to corporate Web sites. Today, however, the Internet potential is limitless, and the focus has shifted to e-business, using the global reach of the Internet for easy access to key business applications and data that reside in traditional IT systems. Companies can now securely, and cost-effectively, extend the reach of their applications and data across the world through the implementation of secure virtual private network (VPN) solutions.

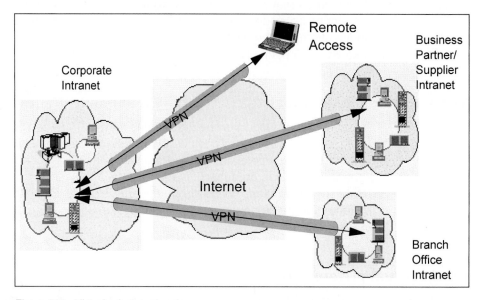

Figure 310. Virtual private networks

A virtual private network (VPN) is an extension of an enterprise's private intranet across a public network such as the Internet, creating a secure private connection, essentially through a private *tunnel*. VPNs securely convey information across the Internet connecting remote users, branch offices, and business partners into an extended corporate network, as shown in Figure 310. Internet service providers (ISPs) offer cost-effective access to the Internet (via direct lines or local telephone numbers), enabling companies to eliminate their current, expensive leased lines, long-distance calls, and toll-free telephone numbers.

A 1997 VPN Research Report, by Infonetics Research, Inc., estimates savings from 20% to 47% of wide area network (WAN) costs by replacing leased lines to remote sites with VPNs. And, for remote access VPNs, savings can be 60% to 80% of corporate remote access dial-up costs.

Additionally, Internet access is available worldwide where other connectivity alternatives may not be available.

The technology to implement these virtual private networks, however, is just becoming standardized. Some networking vendors today are offering non-standards-based VPN solutions that make it difficult for a company to incorporate all its employees and/or business partners/suppliers into an extended corporate network. However, VPN solutions based on Internet Engineering Task Force (IETF) standards will provide support for the full range of VPN scenarios with more interoperability and expansion capabilities.

The key to maximizing the value of a VPN is the ability for companies to evolve their VPNs as their business needs change and to easily upgrade to future TCP/IP technology. Vendors who support a broad range of hardware and software VPN products provide the flexibility to meet these requirements. VPN solutions today run mainly in the IPv4 environment, but it is important that they have the capability of being upgraded to IPv6 to remain interoperable with your business partner's and/or supplier's VPN solutions. Perhaps equally critical is the ability to work with a vendor who understands the issues of deploying a VPN. The implementation of a successful VPN involves more than technology. The vendor's networking experience plays heavily into this equation.

21.12 Kerberos authentication and authorization system

The Kerberos Network Authentication Service Version 5 is a *proposed standard protocol*. It's status is *elective* and described in RFC 1510.

According to *The Enlarged Devil's Dictionary,* by Ambrose Bierce, Kerberos is "the watchdog of Hades, whose duty it was to guard the entrance against whom or what does not clearly appear; Kerberos is known to have had three heads".

A Kerberos service is normally run on it's own system, in a secure area. Users have to validate themselves to Kerberos, before they are allowed to connect to other servers on the network. The server's identities can also be checked against Kerberos.

The Kerberos Authentication and Authorization System is an encryption-based security system that provides mutual authentication between the users and the servers in a network environment. The assumed goals for this system are:

- Authentication to prevent fraudulent requests/responses between users and servers that must be confidential and between groups of at least one user and one service.

- Authorization can be implemented independently from the authentication by each service that wants to provide its own authorization system. The authorization system can assume that the authentication of a user/client is reliable.

- Permits the implementation of an accounting system that is integrated, secure and reliable, with modular attachment and support for "chargebacks" or billing purposes.

The Kerberos system is mainly used for authentication purposes, but it also provides the flexibility to add authorization information.

21.12.1 Assumptions

Kerberos assumes the following:

- The environment using this security system will include public and private workstations that can be located in areas with minimal physical security, a campus network without link encryption that can be composed of dispersed local networks connected by backbones or gateways, centrally operated servers in locked rooms with moderate physical security and centrally operated servers with considerable physical security.

- Confidential data or high-risk operations such as a bank transaction may not be part of this environment without additional security, because once you have a workstation as a terminal you can emulate certain conditions and normal data will be flowing without any encryption protection.

- One of the cryptosystems used is the Data Encryption Standard (DES), which has been developed to be modular and replaceable by the Kerberos designers.

- Kerberos assumes a loosely synchronized clock in the whole system so the workstation has to have a synchronization tool such as the time server provided.

21.12.2 Naming

A *principal identifier* is the name that identifies a client or a service for the Kerberos system.

In Version 4, the identifier consists of three components:

- The *principal* name is unique for each client and service assigned by the Kerberos Manager.

- The *instance* name used for distinct authentication is an added label for clients and services which exist in several forms. For users, an instance can provide different identifiers for different privileges. For services, an instance usually specifies the host name of the machine that provides this service.

- The *realm* name used to allow independently administered Kerberos sites. The principal name and the instance are qualified by the realm to which they belong, and are unique only within that realm. The realm is commonly the domain name.

In Version 4, each of the three components has a limit of 39 characters long. Due to conventions, the period (.) is not an acceptable character.

In Version 5, the identifier consists of two parts only, the *realm* and the *remainder*, which is a sequence of however many components are needed to name the principal. Both the realm and each component of the remainder are defined as ASN.1 (Abstract Syntax Notation One, ISO standard 8824) GeneralStrings. This puts few restrictions on the characters available for principal identifiers.

21.12.3 Kerberos authentication process

In the Kerberos system, a client that wants to contact a server for its service, first has to ask for a *ticket* from a mutually trusted third party, the Kerberos Authentication Server (KAS). This ticket is obtained as a function where one of the components is a private key known only by the service and the Kerberos Authentication Server, so that the service can be confident that the information on the ticket originates from Kerberos. The client is known to the KAS as a principal name (c). The private key (K_c) is the authentication key known only to the user and the Kerberos Authentication Server (KAS).

In this chapter, the symbol {X,Y} indicates a message containing information (or data) X and Y. {X,Y}K_z indicates that a message that contains the data X and Y, has been enciphered using the key K_z.

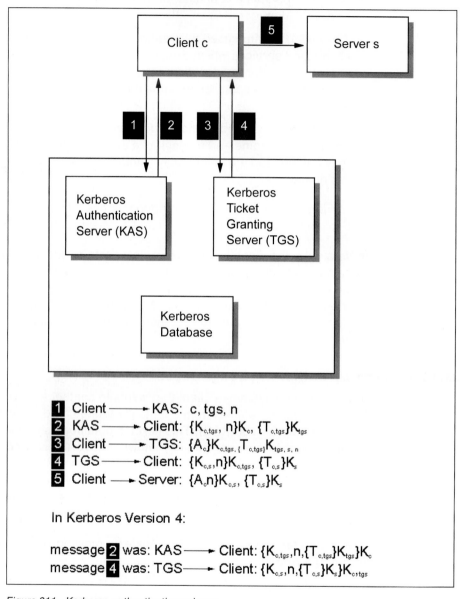

Figure 311. Kerberos authentication scheme

The authentication process consists of exchanging five messages (see Figure 311):

1 Client -> KAS

The client sends a message {c, tgs, n}, to the KAS, containing its identity (c), a nonce (a timestamp or other means to identify this request), and requests for a ticket for use with the ticket-granting server (TGS).

2 KAS -> Client

The authentication server looks up the client name (c) and the service name (the ticket-granting server, tgs) in the Kerberos database, and obtains an encryption key for each (K_c and K_{tgs}).

The KAS then forms a response to send back to the client. This response contains an initial ticket $T_{c,tgs}$, which grants the client access to the requested server (the ticket-granting server). $T_{c,tgs}$ contains $K_{c,tgs}$, c, tgs, nonce, lifetime and some other information. The KAS also generates a random encryption key $K_{c,tgs}$, called the session key. It then encrypts this ticket using the encryption key of the ticket-granting server (K_{tgs}). This produces what is called a *sealed ticket* $\{T_{c,tgs}\}K_{tgs}$. A message is then formed consisting of the sealed ticket and the TGS session key $K_{c,tgs}$.

Note:

In Kerberos Version 4, the message is:

$\{K_{c,tgs}, n, \{T_{c,tgs}\}K_{tgs}\}K_c$

While in Kerberos Version 5, the message is of a simpler form:

$\{K_{c,tgs}, n\}K_c, \{T_{c,tgs}\}K_{tgs}$

This simplifies the (unnecessary) double encryption of the ticket.

---

3 Client -> TGS

Upon receiving the message, the client decrypts it using its secret key K_c, which is only known to it and the KAS. It checks to see if the nonce (n) matches the specific request, and then caches the session key $K_{c,tgs}$ for future communications with the TGS.

The client then sends a message to the TGS. This message contains the initial ticket $\{T_{c,tgs}\}K_{tgs}$, the server name (s), a nonce, and a new authenticator A_c containing a timestamp. A_c is {c, nonce}. The message is:

$\{A_c\}K_{c,tgs}, \{T_{c,tgs}\}K_{tgs}, s, n$

4 TGS -> Client

The ticket-granting server (TGS) receives the above message from the client (c), and first deciphers the sealed ticket using its TGS encryption key. (This ticket was originally sealed by the Kerberos authentication server in step 2 using the same key.) From the deciphered ticket, the TGS obtains the TGS-session-key. It uses this TGS session key to decipher the sealed authenticator. (Validity is checked by comparing the client name both in the ticket and in the authenticator, the TGS server name in the ticket, the network address that must be equal in the ticket, in the authenticator, and in the received message.)

Finally, it checks the current time in the authenticator to make certain the message is recent. This requires that all the clients and servers maintain their clocks within some prescribed tolerance. The TGS now looks up the server name from the message in the Kerberos database, and obtains the encryption key (K_s) for the specified service.

The TGS forms a new random session key $K_{c,s}$ for the benefit of the client (c) and the server (s), and then creates a new ticket $T_{c,s}$ containing:

```
K_{c,s}, n, nonce, lifetime,
```

It then assembles and sends a message to the client.

Note:

In Kerberos Version 4, the message is:

$$\{K_{c,s}, n, \{T_{c,s}\}K_s\}K_{c,tgs}$$

While in Kerberos Version 5, the message is of a simpler form:

$$\{K_{c,s}, n\}K_{c,tgs}, \{T_{c,s}\}K_s$$

This simplifies the (unnecessary) double encryption of the ticket.

---

5 Client -> Server

The client receives this message and deciphers it using the TGS session key that only it and the TGS share. From this message it obtains a new session key $K_{c,s}$ that it shares with the server(s) and a sealed ticket that it cannot decipher because it is enciphered using the server's secret key K_s.

The client builds an authenticator and seals it using the new session key $K_{c,s}$. At last, it sends a message containing the sealed ticket and the authenticator to the server (s) to request its service.

The server (s) receives this message and first deciphers the sealed ticket using its encryption key, which only it and KAS know. It then uses the new session key contained in the ticket to decipher the authenticator and does the same validation process that was described in step 4.

Once the server has validated a client, an option exists for the client to validate the server. This prevents an intruder from impersonating the server. The client requires then that the server sends back a message containing the timestamp (from the client's authenticator, with one added to the timestamp value). This message is enciphered using the session key that was passed from the client to the server.

Let us summarize some of the central points in this scheme:

- In order for the workstation to use any end server, a ticket is required. All tickets, other than the first ticket (also called the *initial ticket*) are obtained from the TGS. The first ticket is special; it is a ticket for the TGS itself and is obtained from the Kerberos authentication server.

- Every ticket is associated with a session key that is assigned every time a ticket is allocated.

- Tickets are reusable. Every ticket has a lifetime, typically eight hours. After a ticket has expired, you have to identify yourself to Kerberos again, entering your login name and password.

- Unlike a ticket, which can be reused, a new authenticator is required every time the client initiates a new connection with a server. The authenticator carries a timestamp within it, and the authenticator expires a few minutes after it is issued. (This is the reason why clocks must be synchronized between clients and servers.)

- A server should maintain a history of previous client requests for which the timestamp in the authenticator is still valid. This way a server can reject duplicate requests that could arise from a stolen ticket and authenticator.

21.12.4 Kerberos database management

Kerberos needs a record of each user and service in its realm and each record keeps only the needed information, as follows:

- Principal identifier (c,s)
- Private key for this principal (K_c, K_s)
- Date of expiration for this identity
- Date of the last modification in this record
- Identity of the principal who last modified this record (c,s)
- Maximum lifetime of tickets to be given to this principal (Lifetime)

- Attributes (unused)
- Implementation data (not visible externally)

The private key field is enciphered using a master key so that removing the database will not cause any problem as the master key is not in it.

The entity responsible for managing this database is the Kerberos Database Manager (KDBM). There is only one KDBM in a realm, but it is possible to have more than one Kerberos Key Distribution Server (KKDS), each one having a copy of the Kerberos database. This is done to improve availability and performance so that the user can choose one in a group of KKDSs to send its request to. The KKDS performs read-only operations, leaving the actualization to the KDBM, which copies the entire database a few times a day. This is done to simplify the operation using a Kerberos protected protocol. This protocol is basically a mutual authentication between KDBM and KKDS before a file transfer operation with checkpoints and checksum.

21.12.5 Kerberos Authorization Model

The Kerberos Authentication Model permits only the service to verify the identity of the requester but it gives no information on whether the requester can use the service or not. The Kerberos Authorization Model is based on the principle that each service knows the user so that each one can maintain its own authorization information. However, the Kerberos Authentication System could be extended by information and algorithms that could be used for authorization purposes. (This is made easier in Version 5, as shown in 21.12.6, "Kerberos Version 5 enhancements" on page 764.) The Kerberos could then check if a user/client is allowed to use a certain service.

Obviously, both the client and the server applications must be able to handle the Kerberos authentication process. That is, both the client and the server must be *kerberized*.

21.12.6 Kerberos Version 5 enhancements

Kerberos Version 5 has a number of enhancements over Version 4. Some of the important ones are:

- Use of encryption has been separated into distinct program modules which allows for supporting multiple encryption systems.

- Network addresses that appear in protocol messages are now tagged with a type and length field. This allows support of multiple network protocols.

- Message encoding is now described using the ASN.1 (Abstract Syntax Notation 1) syntax in accordance with ISO standards 8824 and 8825.

- The Kerberos Version 5 ticket has an expanded format to support new features (for example, the inter-realm cooperation).

- As mentioned in 21.12.2, "Naming" on page 758, the principal identifier naming has changed.

- Inter-realm support has been enhanced.

- Authorization and accounting information can now be encrypted and transmitted inside a ticket in the authorization data field. This facilitates the extension of the authentication scheme to include an authorization scheme as well.

- A binding is provided for the Generic Security Service API (GSSAPI) to the Kerberos Version 5 implementation.

21.13 Remote access authentication protocols

Remote dial-in to the corporate intranet and to the Internet has made the remote access server a very vital part of today's internetworking services. More and more mobile users are requiring access not only to central-site resources, but to information sources on the Internet. The widespread use of the Internet and the corporate intranet has fueled the growth of remote access services and devices. There is an increasing demand for simplified connection to corporate network resources from mobile computing devices such as a notebook computer, or a palmtop device for e-mail access.

The emergence of remote access has caused significant development work in the area of security. The AAA (triple A) security model has evolved in the industry to address the issues of remote access security. Authentication, authorization and accounting answers the questions who, what, and when respectively. A brief description of each of the three As in the AAA security model is listed below:

Authentication   This is the action of determining who a user (or entity) is. Authentication can take many forms. Traditional authentication utilizes a name and a fixed password. Most computers work this way, However, fixed passwords have limitations, mainly in the area of security. Many modern authentication mechanisms utilize one-time passwords or a challenge-response query. Authentication generally takes place when the user first logs in to a machine or requests a service of it.

Authorization   This is the action of determining what a user is allowed to do. Generally, authentication precedes authorization, but again, this is not required. An authorization request may indicate that the user is not authenticated. (we don't know who they are.) In this case it is up to the authorization agent to determine if an unauthenticated user is allowed the services in question. In current remote authentication protocols authorization does not merely provide yes or no answers, but it may also customize the service for the particular user.

Accounting   This is typically the third action after authentication and authorization. But again, neither authentication or authorization are required. Accounting is the action of recording what a user is doing, and/or has done.

In the distributed client/server security database model, a number of communications servers, or clients, authenticate a dial-in user's identity through a single, central database, or authentication server. The authentication server stores all information about users, their passwords and access privileges. Distributed security provides a central location for authentication data that is more secure than scattering the user information on different devices throughout a network. A single authentication server can support hundreds of communications servers, serving up to tens of thousand of users. Communications servers can access an authentication server locally or remotely over WAN connections.

Several remote access vendors and the Internet Engineering Task Force (IETF) have been in the forefront of this remote access security effort, and the means whereby such security measures are standardized. Remote Authentication Dial In User Service (RADIUS) and Terminal Access Controller Access Control System (TACACS) are two such cooperative ventures that have evolved out of the Internet standardizing body and remote access vendors.

Remote Authentication Dial-In User Service (RADIUS) is a distributed security system developed by Livingston Enterprises. RADIUS was designed based on a previous recommendation from the IETF's Network Access Server Working Requirements Group. An IETF Working Group for RADIUS was formed in January 1996 to address the standardization of RADIUS protocol; RADIUS is now an IETF-recognized dial-in security solution (RFC 2058 and RFC 2138).

Similar to RADIUS, Terminal Access Controller Access Control System (TACACS) is an industry standard protocol specification, RFC 1492. Similar to RADIUS, TACACS receives authentication request from a NAS client and forwards the user name and password information to a centralized security server. The centralized server can either be a TACACS database or an external security database. Extended TACACS (XTACACS) is a version of TACACS with extensions that Cisco added to the basic TACACS protocol to support advanced features. TACACS+ is another Cisco extension that allows a separate access server (the TACACS+ server) to provide independent authentication, authorization, and accounting services.

Although RADIUS and TACACS Authentication Servers can be set up in a variety of ways, depending upon the security scheme of the network they are serving, the basic process for authenticating a user is essentially the same. Using a modem, a remote dial-in user connects to a remote access server, (also called the network access server or NAS) with a built-in analog or digital modem. Once the modem connection is made, the NAS prompts the user for a name and password. The NAS then creates the so-called authentication request from the supplied data packet, which consists of information identifying the specific NAS device sending the authentication request, the port that is being used for the modem connection, and the user name and password.

For protection against eavesdropping by hackers, the NAS, acting as the RADIUS or TACACS client, encrypts the password before it sends it to the authentication server. If the primary security server cannot be reached, the security client or NAS device can route the request to an alternate server. When an authentication request is received, the authentication server validates the request and then decrypts the data packet to access the user name and password information. If the user name and password are correct, the server sends an Authentication Acknowledgment packet. This acknowledgement packet may include additional filters, such as information on the user's network resource requirements and authorization levels. The security server may, for instance, inform the NAS that a user needs TCP/IP and/or IPX using PPP, or that the user needs SLIP to connect to the network. It may include information on the specific network resource that the user is allowed to access.

To circumvent snooping on the network, the security server sends an authentication key, or signature, identifying itself to the security client. Once the NAS receives this information, it enables the necessary configuration to allow the user the necessary access rights to network services and resources. If at any point in this log-in process all necessary authentication conditions are not met, the security database server sends an authentication reject message to the NAS device and the user is denied access to the network.

21.14 Layer 2 Tunneling Protocol (L2TP)

L2TP permits the tunneling of PPP. Any protocol supported by PPP can be tunneled. This protocol extends the span of a PPP connection. Instead of beginning at the remote host and ending at a local ISP's point of presence (PoP), the *virtual PPP* link now extends from the remote host all the way back to the corporate gateway. L2TP tunneling is currently supported over IP/UDP. The specification can be found in RFC 2661.

L2TP is a consensus standard that came from the merging of two earlier tunneling protocols: Point-to-Point Tunneling Protocol (PPTP) and Layer 2 Forwarding (L2F; described in RFC 2341). These earlier protocols did not provide as complete a solution as the L2TP protocol; one addresses tunnels created by ISPs and the other addresses tunnels created by remote hosts. L2TP supports both host-created and ISP-created tunnels.

L2TP adds the ability to create a virtual private network where multiple protocols and privately addressed IP, IPX, and AT (AppleTalk) are allowed. In addition, L2TP will give remote users the ability to connect to a local ISP and tunnel through the internet to a home network, avoiding long distance charges. It will also provide a mechanism on which to solve the multiple box PPP multilink problem. (Calls connecting to different physical routers that are destined for the same MP bundle can be tunneled to the same endpoint where MP can be terminated for all links.)

21.14.1 Terminology

Before describing the protocol, a definition of some L2TP terminology is provided.

L2TP access concentrator (LAC) A device attached to one or more public service telephone network (PSTN) or integrated services digital network (ISDN) lines capable of handling both the PPP operation and L2TP protocol. The LAC implements the media over which L2TP operates. L2TP passes the traffic to one or more L2TP servers (LNS).

L2TP network server (LNS) An LNS operates on any platform that can be a PPP endstation. The LNS handles the server side of the L2TP protocol. Because L2TP relies only on the single media over which L2TP

	tunnels arrive, the LNS can have only a single LAN or WAN interface, yet is still able to terminate calls arriving from any PPP interfaces supported by an LAC, such as async, synchronous, ISDN, V.120, etc.
Network access servers (NAS)	A device providing temporary, on-demand network access to users. This access is point-to-point using PSTN or ISDN lines.
Session (Call)	L2TP creates a session when an end-to-end PPP connection is attempted between a dial-in user and the LNS, or when an outbound call is initiated. The datagrams for the session are sent over the tunnel between the LAC and the LNS. The LNS and LAC maintain the state information for each user attached to a LAC.
Tunnel	A tunnel is defined by an LNS-LAC pair. The tunnel carries PPP datagrams between the LAC and the LNS. A single tunnel can multiplex many sessions. A control connection operating over the same tunnel controls the establishment, release, and maintenance of all sessions and of the tunnel itself.
Attribute value air (AVP)	A uniform method of encoding message types and bodies. This method maximizes the extensibility while permitting interpretability of L2TP.

21.14.2 Protocol overview

Since the host and the gateway share the same PPP connection, they can take advantage of PPP's ability to transport protocols other than just IP. For example, L2TP tunnels can be used to support remote LAN access as well as remote IP access. Figure 312 outlines a basic L2TP configuration:

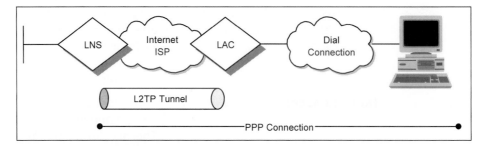

Figure 312. Layer 2 Tunnel Protocol (L2TP) scenario

Referring to Figure 312, the following occurs:

1. The remote user initiates a PPP connection.
2. The NAS accepts the call.
3. The NAS identifies the remote user using an authorization server.
4. If the authorization is OK, the NAS/LAC initiates an L2TP tunnel to the desired LNS at the entry to the enterprise.
5. The LNS authenticates the remote user through its authentication server and accepts the tunnel.
6. The LNS confirms acceptance of the call and the L2TP tunnel.
7. The NAS logs the acceptance.
8. The LNS exchanges PPP negotiation with the remote user.
9. End-to-end data is now tunneled between the remote user and the LNS.

L2TP is actually another variation of an IP encapsulation protocol. As shown in Figure 313, an L2TP tunnel is created by encapsulating an L2TP frame inside a UDP packet, which in turn is encapsulated inside an IP packet whose source and destination addresses define the tunnel's endpoints. Since the outer encapsulating protocol is IP, clearly IPsec protocols can be applied to this composite IP packet, thus protecting the data that flows within the L2TP tunnel. AH, ESP, and ISAKMP/Oakley protocols can all be applied in a straightforward way.

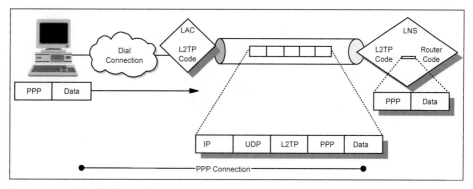

Figure 313. L2TP Packet Changes during Transit

L2TP can operate over UDP/IP and support the following functions:

- Tunneling of single user dial-in clients
- Tunneling of small routers, for example a router with a single static route to set up based on an authenticated user's profile
- Incoming calls to an LNS from an LAC
- Multiple calls per tunnel
- Proxy authentication for PAP and CHAP
- Proxy LCP
- LCP restart in the event that proxy LCP is not used at the LAC
- Tunnel endpoint authentication
- Hidden AVP for transmitting a proxy PAP password
- Tunneling using a local realm (that is, user@realm) lookup table
- Tunneling using the PPP user name lookup in the AAA subsystem (see 21.13, "Remote access authentication protocols" on page 765)

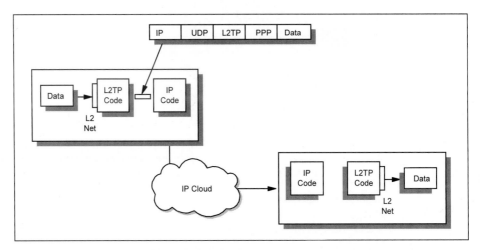

Figure 314. L2TP packet flow through any IP cloud

21.14.3 L2TP security issues

Although L2TP provides cost-effective access, multiprotocol transport, and remote LAN access, it does not provide cryptographically robust security features. For example:

- Authentication is provided only for the identity of tunnel endpoints, but not for each individual packet that flows inside the tunnel. This can expose the tunnel to man-in-the-middle and spoofing attacks.

- Without per-packet integrity, it is possible to mount denial-of-service attacks by generating bogus control messages that can terminate either the L2TP tunnel or the underlying PPP connection.

- L2TP itself provides no facility to encrypt user data traffic. This can lead to embarrassing exposures when data confidentiality is an issue.

- While the payload of the PPP packets can be encrypted, the PPP protocol suite does not provide mechanisms for automatic key generation or for automatic key refresh. This can lead to someone listening in on the wire to finally break that key and gain access to the data being transmitted.

Realizing these shortcomings, the PPP Extensions Working Group of the IETF considered how to remedy these shortfalls. Rather than duplicate work done elsewhere, it was decided to recommend using IPsec within L2TP. This is described in RFC 2888.

In summary, layer 2 tunnel protocols are an excellent way of providing cost-effective remote access. And when used in conjunction with IPsec, they are an excellent technique for providing secure remote access. However, without complementary use of IPsec, an L2TP tunnel alone does not furnish adequate security.

21.15 Secure electronic transactions (SET)

SET is the outcome of an agreement by MasterCard International and Visa International to cooperate on the creation of a single electronic credit card system. Prior to SET, each organization had proposed its own protocol and each had received support from a number of networking and computing companies. Now, most of the major players are behind the SET specification (for example, IBM, Microsoft, Netscape and GTE).

The following sections describes at a high level the components and processes that make up the specification. Please refer to MasterCard and Visa home pages for more information about SET.

21.15.1 SET roles

The SET specification defines several roles involved in the payment process:

The merchant
This is any seller of goods, services or information.

The acquirer
This is the organization that provides the credit card service and keeps the money flowing. The most widely known acquirers are MasterCard and Visa.

The issuer
This is the organization that issued the card to the purchaser in the first place. Usually this is a bank or some other financial institution who should know better.

The cardholder
This is the Web surfer, who has been given a credit card by the issuer and now wants to exercise his or her purchasing power on the Web.

The acquirer payment gateway
This provides an interface between the merchant and the bankcard network used by the acquirer and the issuer. It is important to remember that the bankcard network already exists. The acquirer payment gateway provides a well-defined,

secure interface to that established network from the Internet. Acquirer payment gateways will be operated on behalf of the acquirers, but they may be provided by third-party organizations, such as Internet services providers (ISPs).

The certificate authority

SET processing uses public key cryptography, so each element of the system need one or more public key certificates. Several layers of CA are described in the specification. (SET certificates are discussed in 21.15.3, "The SET certificate scheme" on page 777.)

21.15.2 SET transactions

The SET specification describes a number of transaction flows for purchasing, authentication, payment reversal, etc. Figure 315 shows the transactions involved in a typical online purchase.

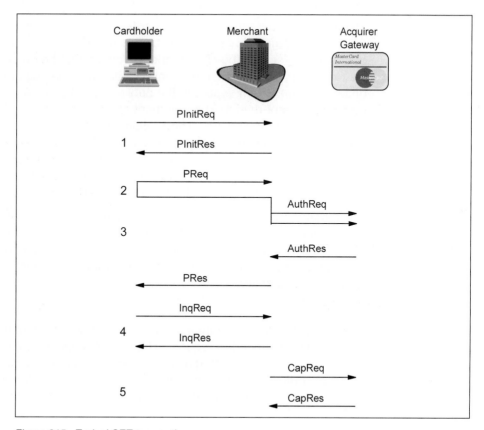

Figure 315. Typical SET transaction sequence

The diagram shows the following transactions (each transaction consists of a request/response pair):

1. PInit

This initializes the system, including details such as the brand of card being used and the certificates held by the cardholder. SET does not insist that cardholders have signing certificates, but it does recommend them. A cardholder certificate binds the credit card account number to the owner of a public key. If the acquirer receives a request for a given card number signed with the cardholder's public key, it knows that the request came from the real cardholder. To be precise, it knows that the request came from a computer where the cardholder's keyring was installed and available. It *could* still be a thief who had stolen the computer and cracked the keyring password.

2. Purchase order

This is the actual request from the cardholder to buy something. The request message is in fact two messages combined, the order instruction (OI), which is sent in the clear to the merchant and the purchase instruction (PI), which the merchant passes on to the acquirer payment gateway. The PI is encrypted in the public key of the acquirer, so the merchant cannot read it. The merchant stores the message for later transmission to the acquirer. The PI also includes a hash of the OI, so the two messages can only be handled as a pair. Note that the card number is only placed in the PI portion of the request. This means that the merchant never has access to it, thereby preventing a fraudulent user from setting up a false store front to collect credit card information.

The purchase order has a response, which is usually sent (as shown here) after acquirer approval has been granted. However, the merchant can complete the transaction with the cardholder before authorization, in which case the cardholder would see a message that the request was accepted pending authorization.

3. Authorization

In this request the merchant asks the acquirer, via the acquirer payment gateway, to authorize the request. The message includes a description of the purchase and the cost. It also includes the PI from the purchase order that the cardholder sent. In this way the acquirer knows that the merchant and the cardholder both agree on what is being purchased and the amount.

When the acquirer receives the request it uses the existing bank card network to authorize the request and sends back an appropriate response.

4. Inquiry

The cardholder may want to know how his or her request is getting on. The SET specification provides an inquiry transaction for that purpose.

5. Capture

Up to this point, no money has changed hands. The capture request from the merchant tells the acquirer to transfer the previously authorized amount to its account.

In fact, capture can be incorporated as part of the authorization request/response (see above). However there are situations in which the merchant may want to capture the funds later. For example, most mail order operations do not debit the credit card account until the goods have actually been shipped.

There are several other transactions within the SET specification, but the summary above shows the principles on which it is based.

21.15.3 The SET certificate scheme

The SET specification envisions hundreds of thousands of participants worldwide. Potentially, each of these would have at least one public key certificate. In fact the protocol calls for an entity to have multiple certificates in some cases. For example, the acquirer payment gateways need one for signing messages and another for encryption purposes.

Key management on such a large scale requires something beyond a simple, flat certification structure. The organization of certifying authorities proposed for SET is shown in Figure 316.

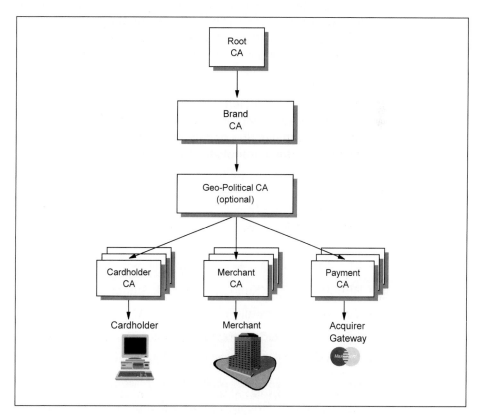

Figure 316. SET certifying authorities

At the top of the certificate chain, the root certifying authority is to be kept offline under extremely tight arrangements. It will only be accessed when a new credit card brand joins the SET consortium. At the next level in the hierarchy, the brand level CAs are also very secure. They are administered independently by each credit card brand.

There is some flexibility permitted under each brand for different operating policies. It would be possible to set up CAs based on region or country, for example. At the base of the CA hierarchy are the CAs that provide certificates for merchants, cardholders and acquirer payment gateways. The SET specification provides protocols for merchants and cardholders to request certificates online. It is important to have a simple process because SET aims to encourage cardholders to have their own certificates. It envisions the cardholder surfing to the CA Web site, choosing a Request Certificate option to invoke the certificate request application on the browser and then filling in a form to send and receive the certificate request.

Of course, if the system allows certificates to be created easily, it must also be able to revoke them easily, in the event of a theft or other security breach. The SET specification includes some certificate update and revocation protocols for this purpose. Although the mechanism for requesting a certificate may be simple, there is still a need for user education. For example, it is obvious that a cardholder should notify the credit card company if his or her wallet is stolen, but less obvious that he or she should also notify them if his or her computer is stolen. However, if the computer includes his keyring file containing the private key and certificate, it could allow the thief to go shopping at the cardholder's expense.

21.16 References

The following RFCs provide detailed information on the TCP/IP security solutions presented in this chapter:

- RFC 1492 – An Access Control Protocol, Sometimes Called TACACS
- RFC 1510 – The Kerberos Network Authentication Service (V5)
- RFC 1579 – Firewall-Friendly FTP
- RFC 1928 – SOCKS Protocol Version 5
- RFC 1929 – Username/Password Authentication for SOCKS V5
- RFC 1961 – GSS-API Authentication Method for SOCKS Version 5
- RFC 2003 – IP Encapsulation within IP
- RFC 2104 – HMAC: Keyed-Hashing for Message Authentication
- RFC 2138 – Remote Authentication Dial In User Service (RADIUS)
- RFC 2246 – The TLS Protocol Version 1.0

- RFC 2313 – PKCS 1: RSA Encryption Version 1-5
- RFC 2314 – PKCS 10: Certification Request Syntax Version 1-5
- RFC 2315 – PKCS 7: Cryptographic Message Syntax Version 1-5
- RFC 2401 – Security Architecture for the Internet Protocol
- RFC 2402 – IP Authentication Header
- RFC 2403 – The Use of HMAC-MD5-96 within ESP and AH
- RFC 2404 – The Use of HMAC-SHA-1-96 within ESP and AH
- RFC 2405 – The ESP DES-CBC Cipher Algorithm With Explicit IV
- RFC 2406 – IP Encapsulating Security Payload (ESP)
- RFC 2407 – The Internet IP Security Domain of Interpretation for ISAKMP
- RFC 2408 – Internet Security Association and Key Management Protocol
- RFC 2409 – The Internet Key Exchange (IKE)
- RFC 2410 – The NULL Encryption Algorithm and Its Use With IPsec
- RFC 2411 – IP Security Document Roadmap
- RFC 2412 – The OAKLEY Key Determination Protocol
- RFC 2661 – Layer Two Tunneling Protocol "L2TP"
- RFC 2888 – Secure Remote Access with L2TP
- RFC 3022 – The IP Network Address Translator (NAT)

Chapter 22. Quality of Service

With the increased use of the IP based networks, including the Internet, there has been a large focus on providing necessary network resources to certain applications. That is, it has become better understood that some applications are more 'important' than others, thereby demanding preferential treatment throughout an internetwork. Additionally, applications have different demands, such as real-time requirements of low latency and high bandwidth.

This chapter discusses the topic of traffic prioritization, or Quality of Service (QoS). It explains why QoS may be desirable in an intranet as well as in the Internet, and presents the two main approaches to implementing QoS in TCP/IP networks:

- Integrated Services
- Differentiated Services

22.1 Why QoS?

In the Internet and intranets of today, bandwidth is an important subject. More and more people are using the Internet for private and business purposes. The amount of data that is being transmitted through the Internet is increasing exponentially. Multimedia applications, such as IP telephony and video conferencing systems, need a lot more bandwidth than the applications that were used in the early years of the Internet. Whereas traditional Internet applications, such as WWW, FTP or TELNET, cannot tolerate packet loss but are less sensitive to variable delays, most real-time applications show just the opposite behavior, meaning they can compensate for a reasonable amount of packet loss but are usually very critical towards high variable delays.

This means that without any bandwidth control, the quality of these real-time streams depends on the bandwidth that is currently available. Low or unstable bandwidth causes bad quality in real-time transmissions by leading to, for example, dropouts and hangs. Even the quality of a transmission using the real-time protocol (RTP) depends on the utilization of the underlying IP delivery service.

Therefore, certain concepts are necessary to guarantee a specific Quality of Service (QoS) for real-time applications in the Internet. A QoS can be described as a set of parameters that describe the quality (for example, bandwidth, buffer usage, priority, CPU usage, and so on) of a specific stream of data. The basic IP protocol stack provides only one QoS, which is called *best-effort*. Packets are transmitted from point to point without any guarantee for a special bandwidth or minimum time delay. With the best-effort traffic model, Internet requests are handled with the *first come, first serve* strategy. This means that all requests have the same priority and are handled one after the other. There is no possibility to make bandwidth reservations for specific connections or to raise the priority for special requests. Therefore, new strategies were developed to provide predictable services for the Internet.

Today, there are two main rudiments to bring QoS to the Internet and IP based internetworks: Integrated Services and Differentiated Services.

Integrated Services

Integrated Services bring enhancements to the IP network model to support real-time transmissions and guaranteed bandwidth for specific flows. In this case, we define a *flow* as a distinguishable stream of related datagrams from a unique sender to a unique receiver that results from a single user activity and requires the same QoS.

For example, a flow might consist of one video stream between a given host pair. To establish the video connection in both directions, two flows are necessary. Each application that initiates data flows can specify which QoS are required for this flow. If the video conferencing tool needs a minimum bandwidth of 128 kbps and a minimum packet delay of 100 ms to assure a continuous video display, such a QoS can be reserved for this connection.

Differentiated Services

Differentiated Services mechanisms do not use per-flow signaling, and as a result, do not consume per-flow state within the routing infrastructure. Different service levels can be allocated to different groups of users, which means that all traffic is distributed into groups or classes with different QoS parameters. This reduces the maintenance overhead in comparison to Integrated Services.

22.2 Integrated Services

The Integrated Services (IS) model was defined by an IETF working group to be the keystone of the planned IS Internet. This Internet architecture model includes the currently used best-effort service and the new real-time service that provides functions to reserve bandwidth on the Internet and internetworks.

IS was developed to optimize network and resource utilization for new applications, such as real-time multimedia, which requires QoS guarantees. Because of routing delays and congestion losses, real-time applications do not work very well on the current best-effort Internet. Video conferencing, video broadcast, and audio conferencing software need guaranteed bandwidth to provide video and audio of acceptable quality. Integrated Services makes it possible to divide the Internet traffic into the standard best-effort traffic for traditional uses and application data flows with guaranteed QoS.

To support the Integrated Services model, an Internet router must be able to provide an appropriate QoS for each flow, in accordance with the service model. The router function that provides different qualities of service is called *traffic control*. It consists of the following components:

Packet scheduler   The packet scheduler manages the forwarding of different packet streams in hosts and routers, based on their service class, using queue management and various scheduling algorithms. The packet scheduler must ensure that the packet delivery corresponds to the QoS parameter for each flow. A scheduler can also police or shape the traffic to conform to a certain level of service. The packet scheduler must be implemented at the point where packets are queued. This is typically the output driver level of an operating system and corresponds to the link layer protocol.

Packet classifier   The packet classifier identifies packets of an IP flow in hosts and routers that will receive a certain level of service. To realize effective traffic control, each incoming packet is mapped by the classifier into a specific class. All packets that are classified in the same class get the same treatment from the packet scheduler. The choice of a class is based upon the source and destination IP address and port number in the existing packet header or an additional classification number, which must be added to each packet. A class can correspond to a broad category of flows.

For example, all video flows from a video conference with several participants can belong to one service class. But it is also possible that only one flow belongs to a specific service class.

Admission control   The admission control contains the decision algorithm that a router uses to determine if there are enough routing resources to accept the requested QoS for a new flow. If there are not enough free routing resources, accepting a new flow would impact earlier guarantees and the new flow must be rejected. If the new flow is accepted, the reservation instance in the router assigns the packet classifier and the packet scheduler to reserve the requested QoS for this flow. Admission control is invoked at each router along a reservation path, to make a local accept/reject decision at the time a host requests a real-time service. The admission control algorithm must be consistent with the service model.

Admission control is sometimes confused with policy control, which is a packet-by-packet function, processed by the packet scheduler. It ensures that a host does not violate its promised traffic characteristics. Nevertheless, to ensure that QoS guarantees are honored, the admission control will be concerned with enforcing administrative policies on resource reservations. Some policies will be used to check the user authentication for a requested reservation. Unauthorized reservation requests can be rejected. As a result, admission control can play an important role in accounting costs for Internet resources in the future.

Figure 317 shows the operation of the Integrated Service model within a host and a router.

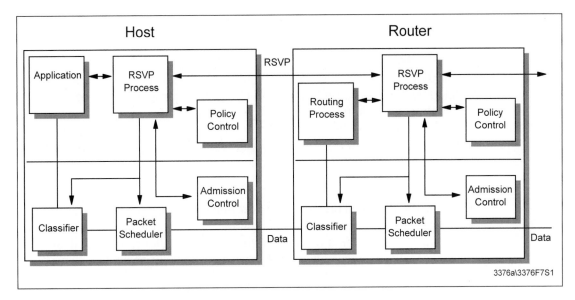

Figure 317. Integrated Services model

Integrated Services use the Resource Reservation Protocol (RSVP) for the signalling of the reservation messages. The IS instances communicate via RSVP to create and maintain flow-specific states in the endpoint hosts and in routers along the path of a flow. Please see 22.2.2, "The Resource Reservation Protocol (RSVP)" on page 790 for a detailed description of the RSVP protocol.

As shown in Figure 317, the application that wants to send data packets in a reserved flow communicates with the reservation instance RSVP. The RSVP protocol tries to set up a flow reservation with the requested QoS, which will be accepted if the application fulfilled the policy restrictions and the routers can handle the requested QoS. RSVP advises the packet classifier and packet scheduler in each node to process the packets for this flow adequately. If the application now delivers the data packets to the classifier in the first node, which has mapped this flow into a specific service class complying the requested QoS, the flow is recognized with the sender IP address and is transmitted to the packet scheduler. The packet scheduler forwards the packets, dependent on their service class, to the next router or, finally, to the receiving host.

Because RSVP is a simplex protocol, QoS reservations are only made in one direction, from the sending node to the receiving node. If the application in our example wants to cancel the reservation for the data flow, it sends a message to the reservation instance, which frees the reserved QoS resources in all routers along the path. The resources can then be used for other flows. The IS specifications are defined in RFC 1633.

22.2.1 Service classes

The Integrated Services model uses different classes of service that are defined by the Integrated Services IETF working group. Depending on the application, those service classes provide tighter or looser bounds on QoS controls. The current IS model includes the *Guaranteed Service*, which is defined in RFC 2212, and the *Controlled Load Service*, which is defined in RFC 2211. To understand these service classes, some terms need to be explained.

Because the IS model provides per-flow reservations, each flow is assigned a flow descriptor. The flow descriptor defines the traffic and QoS characteristics for a specific flow of data packets. In the IS specifications, the flow descriptor consist of a filter specification (filterspec) and a flow specification (flowspec), as illustrated in Figure 318.

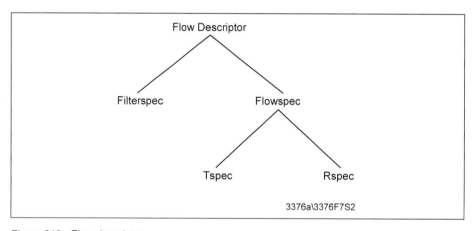

Figure 318. Flow descriptor

The filterspec is used to identify the packets that belong to a specific flow with the sender IP address and source port. The information from the filterspec is used in the packet classifier. The flowspec contains a set of parameters that are called the *invocation information*. It is possible to assort the invocation information into two groups:

- Traffic Specification (Tspec)
- Service Request Specification (Rspec)

The Tspec describes the traffic characteristics of the requested service. In the IS model, this Tspec is represented with a *token bucket filter*. This principle defines a data-flow control mechanism that adds characters (token) in periodical time intervals into a buffer (bucket) and allows a data packet to leave the sender only if there are at least as many tokens in the bucket as the packet length of the data packet. This strategy allows a precise control of the time interval between two data packets on the network. The token bucket system is specified by two parameters: the *token rate r*, which represents the rate at which tokens are placed into the bucket, and the *bucket capacity* b. Both r and b must be positive. Figure 319 illustrates the token bucket model.

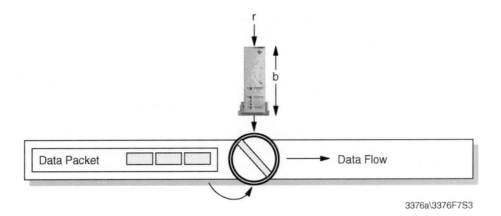

3376a\3376F7S3

Figure 319. Token bucket filter

The parameter r specifies the long term data rate and is measured in bytes of IP datagrams per second. The value of this parameter can range from 1 byte per second to 40 terabytes per second. The parameter b specifies the burst data rate allowed by the system and is measured in bytes. The value of this parameter can range from 1 byte to 250 gigabytes. The range of values allowed for these parameters is intentionally large, in order to be prepared for future network technologies. The network elements are not expected to support the full range of the values. Traffic that passes the token bucket filter must obey the rule that over all time periods T (seconds), the amount of data sent does not exceed rT+b, where r and b are the token bucket parameters.

Two other token bucket parameters are also part of the Tspec. The *minimum policed unit* m and the *maximum packet size* M. The parameter m specifies the minimum IP datagram size in bytes. Smaller packets are counted against the token bucket filter as being of size m. The parameter M specifies the maximum packet size in bytes that conforms to the Tspec. Network elements must reject a service request if the requested maximum packet size is larger than the MTU size of the link. Summarizing, the token bucket filter is a policing function that isolates the packets that conform to the traffic specifications from the ones that do not conform.

The Service Request Specification (Rspec) specifies the Quality of Service the application wants to request for a specific flow. This information depends on the type of service and the needs of the QoS requesting application. It may consist of a specific bandwidth, a maximum packet delay, or a maximum packet loss rate. In the IS implementation, the information from Tspec and Rspec is used in the packet scheduler.

22.2.1.1 Controlled Load Service

The Controlled Load Service is intended to support the class of applications that are highly sensitive to overloaded conditions in the Internet, such as real-time applications. These applications work well on underloaded networks, but degrade quickly under overloaded conditions. If an application uses the Controlled Load Service, the performance of a specific data flow does not degrade if the network load increases.

The Controlled Load Service offers only one service level, which is intentionally minimal. There are no optional features or capabilities in the specification. The service offers only a single function. It approximates best-effort service over lightly loaded networks. This means that applications that make QoS reservations using Controlled Load Services are provided with service closely equivalent to the service provided to uncontrolled (best-effort) traffic under lightly loaded conditions. In this context, *lightly loaded conditions* means that a very high percentage of transmitted packets will be successfully delivered to the destination, and the transit delay for a very high percentage of the delivered packets will not greatly exceed the minimum transit delay.

Each router in a network that accepts requests for Controlled Load Services must ensure that adequate bandwidth and packet processing resources are available to handle QoS reservation requests. This can be realized with active admission control. Before a router accepts a new QoS reservation, represented by the Tspec, it must consider all important resources, such as link bandwidth, router or switch port buffer space and computational capacity of the packet forwarding.

The Controlled Load Service class does not accept or make use of specific target values for control parameters, such as bandwidth, delay, or loss. Applications that use Controlled Load Services must guard against small amounts of packet loss and packet delays.

QoS reservations using Controlled Load Services need to provide a Tspec that consists of the token bucket parameters r and b, as well as the minimum policed unit m and the maximum packet size M. An Rspec is not necessary, because Controlled Load Services does not provide functions to reserve a fixed bandwidth or guarantee minimum packet delays. Controlled Load Service provides QoS control only for traffic that conforms to the Tspec that was provided at setup time. This means that the service guarantees only apply for packets that respect the token bucket rule that over all time periods T, the amount of data sent cannot exceed rT+b.

Controlled Load Service is designed for applications that can tolerate reasonable amount of packet loss and delay, such as audio and video conferencing software.

22.2.1.2 Guaranteed Service

The Guaranteed Service model provides functions that assure that datagrams will arrive within a guaranteed delivery time. This means that every packet of a flow that conforms to the traffic specifications will arrive at least at the maximum delay time that is specified in the flow descriptor. Guaranteed Service is used for applications that need a guarantee that a datagram will arrive at the receiver not later than a certain time after it was transmitted by its source.

For example, real-time multimedia applications, such as video and audio broadcasting systems that use streaming technologies, cannot use datagrams that arrive after their proper play-back time. Applications that have hard real-time requirements, such as real-time distribution of financial data (share prices), will also require guaranteed service. Guaranteed Service does not minimize jitter (the difference between the minimal and maximal datagram delays), but it controls the maximum queueing delay.

The Guaranteed Service model represents the extreme end of delay control for networks. Other service models providing delay control have much weaker delay restrictions. Therefore, Guaranteed Service is only useful if it is provided by every router along the reservation path.

Guaranteed Service gives applications considerable control over their delay. It is important to understand that the delay in an IP network has two parts: a fixed transmission delay and a variable queueing delay. The fixed delay depends on the chosen path, which is determined not by guaranteed service but by the setup mechanism. All data packets in an IP network have a minimum delay that is limited by the speed of light and the turnaround time of the data packets in all routers on the routing path. The queueing delay is determined by Guaranteed Service and it is controlled by two parameters: the token bucket (in particular, the bucket size b) and the bandwidth R that is requested for the reservation. These parameters are used to construct the *fluid model* for the end-to-end behavior of a flow that uses Guaranteed Services.

The fluid model specifies the service that would be provided by a dedicated link between sender and receiver that provides the bandwidth R. In the fluid model, the flow's service is completely independent from the service for other flows. The definition of Guaranteed Service relies on the result that the fluid delay of a flow obeying a token bucket (r,b) and being served by a line with bandwidth R is bounded by b/R as long as R is not less than r. Guaranteed Service approximates this behavior with the service rate R, where R is now a share of bandwidth through the routing path and not the bandwidth of a dedicated line.

In the Guaranteed Service model, Tspec and Rspec are used to set up a flow reservation. The Tspec is represented by the token bucket parameters. The Rspec contains the parameter R, which specifies the bandwidth for the flow reservation. The Guaranteed Service model is defined in RFC 2212.

22.2.2 The Resource Reservation Protocol (RSVP)

The Integrated Services model uses the Resource Reservation Protocol (RSVP) to set up and control QoS reservations. RSVP is defined in RFC 2205 and has the status of a proposed standard. Because RSVP is an Internet control protocol and not a routing protocol, it requires an existing routing protocol to operate. The RSVP protocol runs on top of IP and UDP and must be implemented in all routers on the reservation path. The key concepts of RSVP are flows and reservations.

An RSVP reservation applies for a specific flow of data packets on a specific path through the routers. As described in 22.1, "Why QoS?" on page 781, a flow is defined as a distinguishable stream of related datagrams from a unique sender to a unique receiver. If the receiver is a multicast address, a flow can reach multiple receivers. RSVP provides the same service for unicast and multicast flows. Each flow is identified from RSVP by its destination IP address and destination port. All flows have dedicated a flow descriptor, which contains the QoS that a specific flow requires. The RSVP protocol does not understand the contents of the flow descriptor. It is carried as an opaque object by RSVP and is delivered to the router's traffic control functions (packet classifier and scheduler) for processing.

Because RSVP is a simplex protocol, reservations are only done in one direction. For duplex connections, such as video and audio conferences, where each sender is also a receiver, it is necessary to set up two RSVP sessions for each station.

The RSVP protocol is receiver-initiated. Using RSVP signalling messages, the sender provides a specific QoS to the receiver, which sends an RSVP reservation message back, with the QoS that should be reserved for the flow, from the sender to the receiver. This behavior considers the different QoS requirements for heterogeneous receivers in large multicast groups. The sender does not need to know the characteristics of all possible receivers to structure the reservations.

To establish a reservation with RSVP, the receivers send reservation requests to the senders, depending on their system capabilities. For example, a fast workstation and a slow PC want to receive a high-quality MPEG video stream with 30 frames per second, which has a data rate of 1.5 Mbps. The workstation has enough CPU performance to decode the video stream, but the PC can only decode 10 frames per second. If the video server sends the messages to the two receivers that it can provide the 1.5 Mbps video stream, the workstation can return a reservation request for the full 1.5 Mbps. But the PC does not need the full bandwidth for its flow because it cannot decode all frames. So the PC may send a reservation request for a flow with 10 frames per second and 500 kbps.

22.2.2.1 RSVP operation

A basic part of a resource reservation is the path. The path is the way of a packet flow through the different routers from the sender to the receiver. All packets that belong to a specific flow will use the same path. The path gets determined if a sender generates messages that travel in the same direction as the flow. Each sender host periodically sends a path message for each data flow it originates. The path message contains traffic information that describes the QoS for a specific flow. Because RSVP does not handle routing by itself, it uses the information from the routing tables in each router to forward the RSVP messages.

If the path message reaches the first RSVP router, the router stores the IP address from the *last hop* field in the message, which is the address of the sender. Then the router inserts its own IP address into the last hop field, sends the path message to the next router, and the process repeats until the message has reached the receiver. At the end of this process, each router will know the address from the previous router and the path can be accessed backwards. Figure 320 shows the process of the path definition.

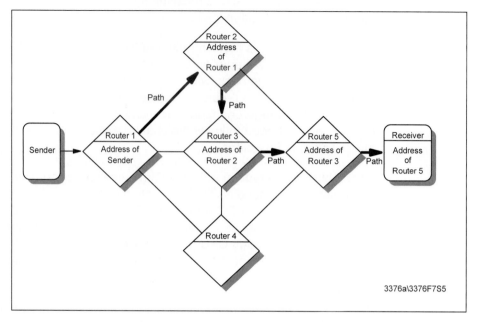

Figure 320. RSVP path definition process

Routers that have received a path message are prepared to process resource reservations for a flow. All packets that belongs to this flow will take the same way through the routers (the way that was defined with the path messages).

The status in a system after sending the path messages is as follows: All receivers know that a sender can provide a special QoS for a flow and all routers know about the possible resource reservation for this flow.

Now if a receiver wants to reserve QoS for this flow, it sends a reservation (resv) message. The reservation message contains the QoS requested from this receiver for a specific flow and is represented by the filterspec and flowspec that form the flow descriptor. The receiver sends the resv message to the last router in the path with the address it received from the path message. Because every RSVP-capable device knows the address of the previous device on the path, reservation messages travel the path in reverse direction towards the sender and establish the resource reservation in every router. Figure 321 shows the flow of the reservation messages trough the routers.

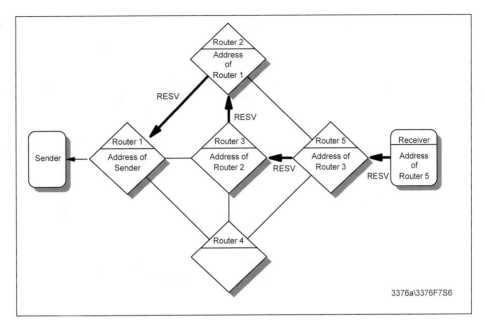

Figure 321. RSVP resv messages flow

At each node, a reservation request initiates two actions:

1. QoS reservation on this link

   The RSVP process passes the request to the admission control and policy control instance on the node. The admission control checks if the router has the necessary resources to establish the new QoS reservation, and the policy control checks if the application has the authorization to make QoS requests. If one of these tests fails, the reservation is rejected and the RSVP process returns a *ResvErr* error message to the appropriate receiver. If both checks succeed, the node uses the filterspec information in the resv message to set the packet classifier and the flowspec information to set the packet scheduler. After this, the packet classifier will recognize the packets that belong to this flow, and the packet scheduler will obtain the desired QoS defined by the flowspec.

   Figure 322 shows the reservation process in an RSVP router.

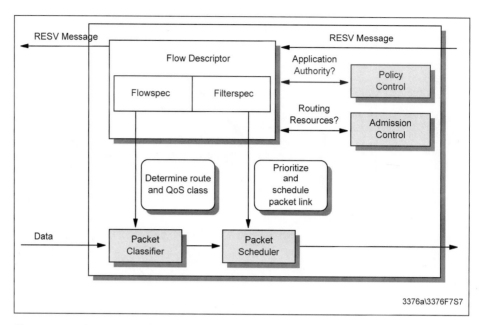

Figure 322. RSVP reservation process

2. Forwarding of the reservation request

After a successful admission and policy check, a reservation request is propagated upstream towards the sender. In a multicast environment, a receiver can get data from multiple senders. The set of sender hosts to which a given reservation request is propagated is called the *scope* of that request. The reservation request that is forwarded by a node after a successful reservation can differ from the request that was received from the previous hop downstream. One possible reason for this is that the traffic control mechanism may modify the flowspec hop-by-hop. Another more important reason is that in a multicast environment, reservations from different downstream branches, but for the same sender, are *merged* together as they travel across the upstream path. This merging is necessary to conserve resources in the routers.

A successful reservation request propagates upstream along the multicast tree until it reaches a point where an existing reservation is equal or greater than that being requested. At this point, the arriving request is merged with the reservation in place and need not be forwarded further.

Figure 323 shows the reservation merging for a multicast flow.

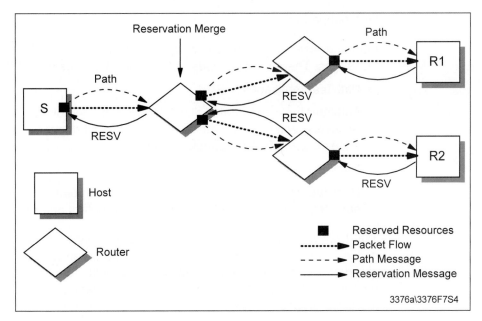

Figure 323. RSVP reservation merging for multicast flows

If the reservation request reaches the sender, the QoS reservation was established in every router on the path and the application can start to send packets downstream to the receivers. The packet classifier and the packet scheduler in each router make sure that the packets are forwarded according to the requested QoS.

This type of reservation is only reasonable if all routers on the path support RSVP. If only one router does not support resource reservation, the service cannot be guaranteed for the whole path because of the "best effort" characteristics of normal routers. A router on the path that does not support RSVP would be a bottleneck for the flow.

A receiver that originates a reservation request can also request a confirmation message that indicates that the request was installed in the network. The receiver includes a confirmation request in the Resv message and gets a ResvConf message if the reservation was established successfully.

RSVP resource reservations maintain soft-state in routers and hosts, which means that a reservation is canceled if RSVP does not send refresh messages along the path for an existing reservation. This allows route changes without resulting in protocol overhead. Path messages must also be present because the path state fields in the routers will be reset after a time-out period.

Path and reservation states can also be deleted with RSVP *teardown* messages. There are two types of teardown messages:

- PathTear messages

   PathTear messages travel downstream from the point of initiation to all receivers, deleting the path state as well as all dependent reservation states in each RSVP-capable device.

- ResvTear messages

   ResvTear messages travel upstream from the point of initiation to all senders, deleting reservation states in all routers and hosts.

Teardown request can be initiated by senders, receivers, or routers that notice a state timeout. Because of the soft-state principle of RSVP reservations, it is not really necessary to explicitly tear down an old reservation. Nevertheless, it is recommended that all end hosts send a teardown request if a consisting reservation is no longer needed.

22.2.2.2 RSVP reservation styles

Users of multicast multimedia applications often receive flows from different senders. In the reservation process described in 22.2.2.1, "RSVP operation" on page 791, a receiver must initiate a separate reservation request for each flow it wants to receive. But RSVP provides a more flexible way to reserve QoS for flows from different senders. A reservation request includes a set of options that are called the *reservation style*. One of these options deals with the treatment of reservations for different senders within the same session. The receiver can establish a *distinct* reservation for each sender or make a single *shared* reservation for all packets from the senders in one session.

Another option defines how the senders for a reservation request are selected. It is possible to specify an *explicit* list or a *wildcard* that selects the senders belonging to one session. In an explicit sender-selection reservation, a filterspec must identify exactly one sender. In a wildcard sender-selection the filterspec is not needed. Figure 324 shows the reservation styles that are defined with this reservation option.

Sender Selection	Distinct Reservation	Shared Reservation
Explicit	Fixed-Filter (FF) Style	Shared-Explicit (SE) Style
Wildcard	(Not Defined)	Wildcard-Filter (WF) Style

Figure 324. RSVP reservation styles

Where:

Wildcard-Filter (WF)   The Wildcard-Filter style uses the options shared reservation and wildcard sender selection. This reservation style establishes a single reservation for all senders in a session. Reservations from different senders are merged together along the path so that only the biggest reservation request reaches the senders.

A wildcard reservation is forwarded upstream to all sender hosts. If new senders appear in the session, for example, new members enter a video conferencing, the reservation is extended to these new senders.

Fixed-Filter (FF)   The Fixed-Filter style uses the option's distinct reservations and explicit sender selection. This means that a distinct reservation is created for data packets from a particular sender. Packets from different senders that are in the same session do not share reservations.

Shared-Explicit (SE)   The Shared-Explicit style uses the option's shared reservation and explicit sender selection. This means that a single reservation covers flows from a specified subset of senders. Therefore, a sender list must be included into the reservation request from the receiver.

Reservations established in shared style (WF and SE) are mostly used for multicast applications. For this type of application, it is unlikely that several data sources transmits data simultaneously, so it is not necessary to reserve QoS for each sender.

For example, in an audio conference that consists of five participants, every station sends a data stream with 64 kbps. With a Fixed-Filter style reservation, all members of the conference must establish four separate 64 kbps reservations for the flows from the other senders. But in an audio conference, usually only one or two people speak at the same time. Therefore, it would be sufficient to reserve a bandwidth of 128 kbps for all senders, because most audio conferencing software uses silence suppression, which means that if a person does not speak, no packets are sent. This can be realized if every receiver makes one shared reservation of 128 kbps for all senders.

Using the Shared-Explicit style, all receivers must explicitly identify all other senders in the conference. With Wildcard-Filter style, the reservation counts for every sender that matches the reservation specifications. If, for example the audio conferencing tool sends the data packets to a special TCP/IP port, the receivers can make a Wildcard-Filter reservation for all packets with this destination port.

22.2.2.3 RSVP message format

An RSVP message basically consists of a common header, followed by a body consisting of a variable number of *objects*. The number and the content of these objects depends on the message type. The message objects contain the information that is necessary to realize resource reservations, for example, the flow descriptor or the reservation style. In most cases, the order of the objects in an RSVP message makes no logical difference. RFC 2205 recommends that an RSVP implementation should use the object order defined in the RFC, but accepts the objects in any permissible order. Figure 325 shows the common header of a RSVP message.

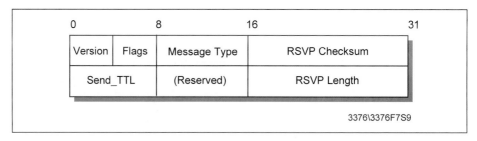

Figure 325. RSVP common header

Where:

Version   4-bit RSVP protocol number. The current version is 1.

Flags	4-bit field that is reserved for flags. No flags are defined yet.
Message type	8-bit field that specifies the message type:

- Path
- Resv
- PathErr
- ResvErr
- PathTear
- ResvTear
- ResvConf

RSVP vhecksum	16-bit field. The Checksum can be used by receivers of an RSVP message to detect errors in the transmission of this message.
Send_TTL	8-bit field, which contains the IP TTL value the message was sent with.
RSVP length	16-bit field that contains the total length of the RSVP message including the common header and all objects that follow. The length is counted in bytes.

The RSVP objects that follow the common header consist of a 32-bit header and one or more 32-bit words. Figure 326 shows the RSVP object header.

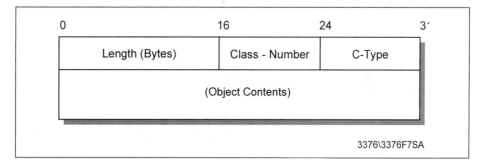

Figure 326. RSVP object header

Where:

Length	16-bit field that contains the object length in bytes. This must be a multiple of 4. The minimum length is 4 bytes.

Class-Number   Identifies the object class. The following classes are defined:

- Null

  The NULL object has a Class-Number of zero. The length of this object must be at least 4, but can be any multiple of 4. The NULL object can appear anywhere in the object sequence of an RSVP message. The content is ignored by the receiver.

- Session

  The session object contains the IP destination address, the IP protocol ID, and the destination port, to define a specific session for the other objects that follow. The session object is required in every RSVP message.

- RSVP_HOP

  The RSVP_HOP object contains the IP address of the node that sent this message and a logical outgoing interface handle. For downstream messages (for example, path messages), the RSVP_HOP object represents a PHOP (previous hop) object, and for upstream messages (for example, resv messages), it represents an NHOP (next hop) object.

- Time_Values

  The Time_Values object contains the refresh period for path and reservation messages. If these messages are not refreshed within the specified time period, the path or reservation state is canceled.

- Style

  The style object defines the reservation style and some style-specific information that is not in Flowspec or Filterspec. The style object is required in every resv message.

- Flowspec

  This object specifies the required QoS in reservation messages.

- Filterspec

   The Filterspec object defines which data packets receive the QoS specified in the Flowspec.

- Sender_Template

   This object contains the sender IP address and additional demultiplexing information, which is used to identify a sender. The Sender_Template is required in every Path message.

- Sender_Tspec

   This object defines the traffic characteristics of a data flow from a sender. The Sender_Tspec is required in all path messages.

- Adspec

   The adspec object is used to provide advertising information to the traffic control modules in the RSVP nodes along the path.

- Error_Spec

   This object specifies an error in a PathErr, ResvErr, or a confirmation in a ResvConf message.

- Policy_Data

   This object contains information that allows a policy module to decide whether an associated reservation is administratively permitted or not. It can be used in Path, Resv, PathErr, or ResvErr messages.

- Integrity

   The integrity object contains cryptographic data to authenticate the originating node and to verify the contents of an RSVP message.

- Scope

   The Scope object contains an explicit list of sender hosts to which the information in the message are sent. The object can appear in a Resv, ResvErr, or ResvTear messages.

- Resv_Confirm

This object contains the IP address of a receiver that requests confirmation for its reservation. It can be used in a Resv or ResvConf message.

C-Type   The C-Type specifies the object type within the class number. Different object types are used for IPv4 and IPv6.

Object contents The object content depends on the object type and has a maximum length of 65528 bytes.

All RSVP messages are built of a variable number of objects. The recommended object order for the most important RSVP messages, the path and the resv message, are shown in Figure 327, which gives an overview about the format of the RSVP path message. Objects that can appear in a path message, but that are not required, are parenthesized.

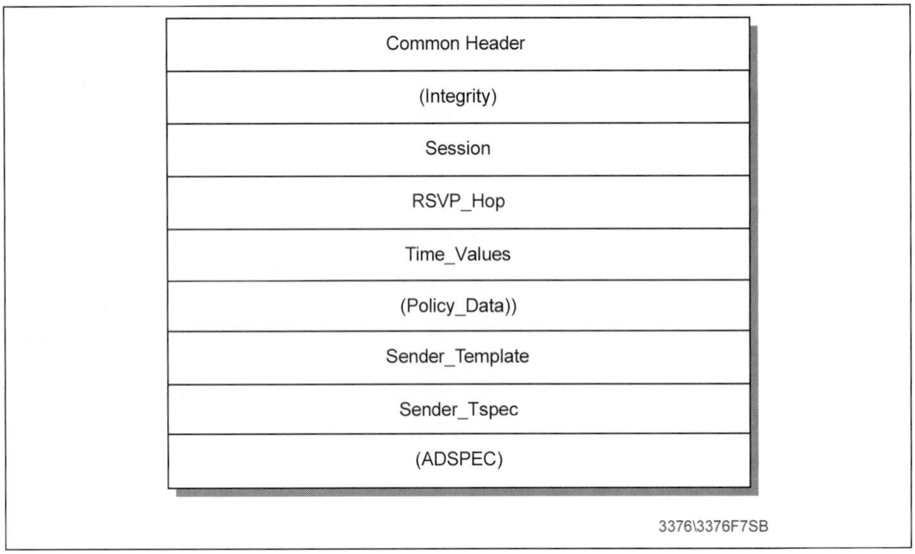

Common Header
(Integrity)
Session
RSVP_Hop
Time_Values
(Policy_Data))
Sender_Template
Sender_Tspec
(ADSPEC)

3376\3376F7SB

Figure 327. RSVP path message format

If the Integrity object is used in the path message, it must immediately follow the common header. The order of the other objects may differ in different RSVP implementations, but the one shown in Figure 327 is recommended by the RFC.

The RSVP Resv messages looks similar to the path message. Figure 328 shows the objects used for reservation messages.

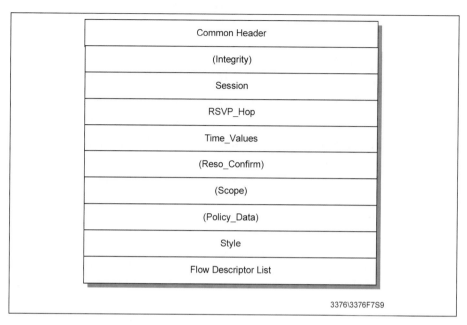

Common Header
(Integrity)
Session
RSVP_Hop
Time_Values
(Reso_Confirm)
(Scope)
(Policy_Data)
Style
Flow Descriptor List

3376\3376F7S9

Figure 328. RSVP resv message format

As in the path message, the Integrity object must follow the common header if it is used. Another restriction applies for the Style object and the following flow descriptor list. They must occur at the end of the message. The order of the other objects follows the recommendation from the RFC.

For a detailed description of the RSVP message structure and the handling of the different reservation styles in reservation messages, please consult RFC 2205.

22.2.3 Integrated Services outlook

Integrated Services is designed to provide end-to-end Quality of Service (QoS) to applications over heterogeneous networks. This means that Integrated Services has to be supported by several different network types and devices. It also means that elements within the network, such as routers, need information to provide the requested service for an end-to-end QoS flow. This information setup in routers is done by the Resource Reservation Protocol (RSVP). RSVP is a signaling protocol that may carry Integrated Services information.

While RSVP may be used to request resources from the network, Integrated Services defines the needed service types, quantifying resource requirements and determining the availability of the requested resource.

There are some factors that have prevented the deployment of RSVP and, thus, Integrated Services in the Internet. These include:

- Only a small number of hosts currently generate RSVP signalling. Although the number is expected to grow in the near future, many applications may not generate RSVP signalling.
- Integrated Services is based on flow-state and flow-processing. If flow-processing rises dramatically, it could become a scalabiltiy concern for large networks.
- The necessary policy control mechanisms, such as access control authentication and accounting, have only recently become available.

The requirements of the market will determine if Integrated Services with RSVP will inspire service providers to use these protocols. But this would require that network devices (for example, routers) need the required software support.

Another aspect may also needs to be considered. Support of Integrated Services running over Differentiated Services networks is a possibility. This solution provides:

- End-to-end QoS for applications, such as IP telephony, and video on-demand.
- Intserv enables hosts to request per-flow, quantify able resources, along the end-to-end path, including feedback about admission to the resources.
- Diffserv eliminates the need for per-flow state and per-flow processing, and therefore enables the scalability across large networks.

The solution is described under 22.3.2, "Integrated Services (Intserv) over Diffserv networks" on page 815

22.3 Differentiated Services

The Differentiated Services (DS) concept is currently under development at the IETF DS working group. The DS specifications are defined in some IETF Internet drafts and there is no RFC available yet. This section gives an overview about the rudiments and ideas to provide service differentiation in the Internet. Because the concept is still under development, some of the specifications mentioned in this book may be changed in the final definition of differentiated services.

The goal of the DS development is to provide differentiated classes of service for Internet traffic, to support various types of applications, and meet specific business requirements. DS offers predictable performance (delay, throughput, packet loss, and so on) for a given load at a given time. The difference between Integrated Services, described in 22.2, "Integrated Services" on page 782, and Differentiated Services is that DS provides scalable service discrimination in the Internet without the need for per-flow state and signaling at every hop. It is not necessary to perform a unique QoS reservation for each flow. With DS, the Internet traffic is split into different classes with different QoS requirements.

A central component of DS is the Service Level Agreement (SLA). The SLA is a service contract between a customer and a service provider that specifies the details of the traffic classifying and the corresponding forwarding service a customer should receive. A customer may be a user organization or another DS domain. The service provider must assure that the traffic of a customer, with whom it has an SLA, gets the contracted QoS. Therefore, the service provider's network administration must set up the appropriate service policies and measure the network performance to guarantee the agreed traffic performance.

To distinguish the data packets from different customers in DS-capable network devices, the IP packets are modified in a specific field. A small bit-pattern, called the *DS field*, in each IP packet is used to mark the packets that receive a particular forwarding treatment at each network node. The DS field uses the space of the former TOS octet in the IPv4 IP header (see 3.1.8.1, "IP datagram format" on page 90) and the traffic class octet in the IPv6 header. All network traffic inside of a domain receives a service that depends on the traffic class that is specified in the DS field.

To provide SLA conform services, the following mechanisms must be combined in a network:

- Setting bits in the DS field (TOS octet) at network edges and administrative boundaries.

- Using those bits to determine how packets are treated by the routers inside the network.

- Conditioning the marked packets at network boundaries in accordance with the QoS requirements of each service.

The currently defined DS architecture only provides service differentiation in one direction and is therefore asymmetric. Development of a complementary symmetric architecture is a topic of current research. The following section describes the DS architecture in more detail.

22.3.1 Differentiated Services architecture

Unlike Integrated Services, QoS guarantees made with Differentiated Services are static and stay long-term in routers. This means that applications using DS do not need to set up QoS reservations for specific data packets. All traffic that passes DS-capable networks can receive a specific QoS. The data packets must be marked with the DS field that is interpreted by the routers in the network.

22.3.1.1 Per-hop behavior (PHB)

The DS field uses six bits to determine the Differentiated Services Code Point (DSCP). This code point will be used by each node in the net to select the PHB. A two-bit currently unused (CU) field is reserved. The value of the CU bits are ignored by differentiated services-compliant nodes, when PHP is used for received packets. Figure 329 shows the structure of the defined DS field.

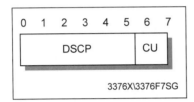

Figure 329. DS field

Each DS-capable network device must have information on how packets with different DS field should be handled. In the DS specifications, this information is called the *per-hop behavior* (PHB). It is a description of the forwarding treatment a packet receives at a given network node. The DSCP value in the DS field is used to select the PHB a packet experiences at each node. To provide predictable services, per-hop behaviors need to be available in all routers in a Differentiated Services-capable network. The PHB can be described as a set of parameters inside of a router that can be used to control how packets are scheduled onto an output interface. This can be a number of separate queues with priorities that can be set, parameters for queue lengths, or drop algorithms and drop preference weights for packets.

DS requires routers that support queue scheduling and management to prioritize outbound packets and control the queue depth to minimize congestion on the network. The traditional FIFO queuing in common Internet routers provides no service differentiation and can lead to network performance problems. The packet treatment inside of a router depends on the router's capabilities and its particular configuration, and it is selected by the DS field in the IP packet. For example, if a IP packet reaches a router with eight different queues that all have different priorities, the DS field can be used to select which queue is liable for the routing of this packet. The scale reaches from zero, for lowest priority, to seven for highest priority.

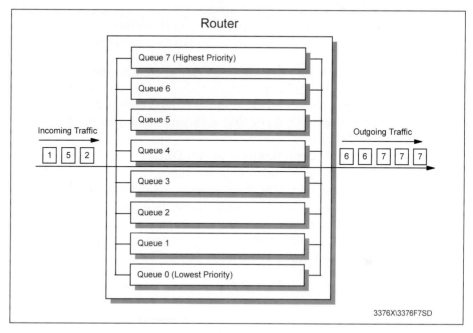

Figure 330. DS routing example

Another example is a router that has a single queue with multiple drop priorities for data packets. It uses the DS field to select the drop preference for the packets in the queue. A value of zero means "it is most likely to drop this packet," and seven means "it is least likely to drop this packet." Another possible constellation is four queues with two levels of drop preference in each.

To make sure that the per-hop behaviors in each router are functionally equivalent, certain common PHBs must be defined in future DS specifications to avoid having the same DS field value causing different forwarding behaviors in different routers of one DS domain. This means that in future DS specifications, some unique PHB values must be defined that represent specific service classes. All routers in one DS domain must know which service a packet with a specific PHB should receive. The DiffServ Working Group will propose PHBs that should be used to provide differentiated services. Some of these proposed PHBs will be standardized, others may have widespread use, and still others may remain experimental.

PHBs will be defined in groups. A PHB group is a a set of one or more PHBs that can only be specified and implemented simultaneously, because of queue servicing or queue management policies that apply to all PHBs in one group. A default PHB must be available in all DS-compliant nodes. It represents the standard best-effort forwarding behavior available in existing routers. When no other agreements are in place, it is assumed that packets belong to this service level. The IETF working group recommends you use the DSCP value 000000 in the DS field to define the default PHB.

Another PHB that is proposed for standardization is the *Expedited Forwarding* (EF) PHB. It is a high priority behavior that is typically used for network control traffic, such as routing updates. The value 101100 in the DSCP field of the DS field is recommended for the EF PHB.

22.3.1.2 Organization of the DSCP

There are some IANA considerations concerning the DSCP. The codepoint space for the DSCP distinguishes between 64 codepoint values. The proposal is to divide the space into tree pools. Pool1 could be used for standard actions. The other pools may be used for experimental local usage, where one of the two pools is provided for experimental local use in the near future (see Table 27 on page 808).

The proposal is, to divide the space into three pools:

Table 27. DSCP pools

Pool	Codepoint space	Assignment
1	xxxxx0	standard action
2	xxxx11	experimental/local use
3	xxxx01	future exp./local use

22.3.1.3 Differentiated Services domains

The setup of QoS guarantees is not made for specific end-to-end connections but for well-defined Differentiated Services domains. The IETF working group defines a Differentiated Services domain as a contiguous portion of the Internet over which a consistent set of Differentiated Services policies are administered in a coordinated fashion. It can represent different administrative domains or autonomous systems, different trust regions, different network technologies, such as cell or frame-based techniques, hosts, and routers. A DS domain consists of boundary components that are used to connect different DS domains to each other and interior components that are only used inside of the domains. Figure 331 shows the use of boundary and interior components for two DS domains.

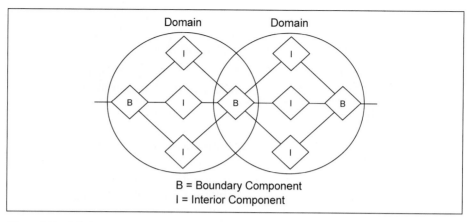

Figure 331. DS domain

A DS domain normally consists of one or more networks under the same administration. This can be, for example, a corporate intranet or an Internet Service Provider (ISP). The administration of the DS domain is responsible for ensuring that adequate resources are provisioned and reserved to support the SLAs offered by the domain. Network administrators must use appropriate measurement techniques to monitor if the network resources in a DS domain are sufficient to satisfy all authorized QoS requests.

22.3.1.4 DS boundary nodes

All data packets that travel from one DS domain to another must pass a boundary node, which can be a router, a host, or a firewall. A DS boundary node that handles traffic leaving a DS domain is called an *egress node* and a boundary node that handles traffic entering a DS domain is called an *ingress node*. Normally, DS boundary nodes act both as ingress node and egress node, depending on the traffic direction. The ingress node must make sure, that the packets entering a domain receives the same QoS as in the domain the packets traveled before. A DS egress node performs conditioning functions on traffic that is forwarded to a directly connected peering domain. The traffic conditioning is done inside of a boundary node by a *traffic conditioner*. It classifies, marks, and possibly conditions packets that enter or leave the DS domain. A traffic conditioner consists of the following components:

Classifier A classifier selects packets based on their packet header and forwards the packets that match the classifier rules for further processing. The DS model specifies two types of packet classifiers:

- Multi-field (MF) classifiers, which can classify on the DS field as well as on any other IP header field, for example, the IP address and the port number, like an RSVP classifier.

- Behavior Aggregate (BA) classifiers, which only classify on the bits in the DS field.

Meter   Traffic meters measure if the forwarding of the packets that are selected by the classifier correspond to the traffic profile that describes the QoS for the SLA between customer and service provider. A meter passes state information to other conditioning functions to trigger a particular action for each packet, which either does or does not comply with the requested QoS requirements.

Marker   DS markers set the DS field of the incoming IP packets to a particular bit pattern. The PHB is set in the first 6 bits of the DS field so that the marked packets are forwarded inside of the DS domain according to the SLA between service provider and customer.

Shaper/dropper   Packet shapers and droppers cause conformance to some configured traffic properties, for example, a token bucket filter, as described in 22.2.1, "Service classes" on page 786. They use different methods to bring the stream into compliance with a traffic profile. Shapers delay some or all of the packets. A shaper usually has a finite-size buffer, and packets may be discarded if there is not sufficient buffer space to hold the delayed packets. Droppers discard some or all of the packets. This process is know as *policing* the stream. A dropper can be implemented as a special case of a shaper by setting the shaper buffer size to zero packets.

The traffic conditioner is mainly used in DS boundary components, but it can also be implemented in an interior component. Figure 332 shows the cooperation of the traffic conditioner components.

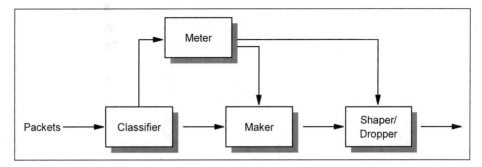

Figure 332. DS traffic conditioner

The traffic conditioner in a boundary component makes sure that packets that transit the domain are correctly marked to select a PHB from one of the PHB groups supported within the domain. This is necessary because different DS domains can have different groups of PHBs, which means that the same entry in the DS field can be interpreted variably in different domains.

For example, in the first domain a packet traverses, all routers have four queues with different queue priorities (0-3). Packets with a PHB value of three are routed with the highest priority. But in the next domain the packet travels through, all routers have eight different queues and all packets with the PHB value of seven are routed with the highest priority. The packet that was forwarded in the first domain with high priority has only medium priority in the second domain. This may violate the SLA contract between customer and service provider. Therefore, the traffic conditioner in the boundary router that connects the two domains must assure that the PHB value is remarked from three to seven if the packet travels from the first to the second domain. Figure 333 shows an example for the remarking of data packets that travel trough two different domains.

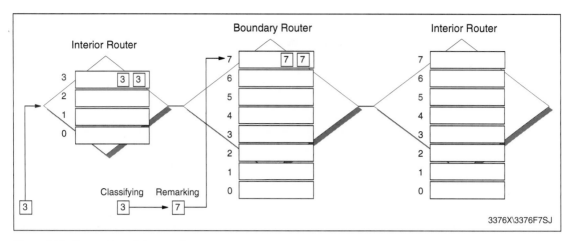

Figure 333. Remarking of data packets

If a data packet travels through multiple domains, the DS field can be remarked at every boundary component to guarantee the QoS that was contracted in the SLA. The SLA contains the details of the *Traffic Conditioning Agreement (TCA)* that specifies classifier rules and temporal properties of a traffic stream. The TCA contains information on how metering, marking, discarding, and shaping of packets must be done in the traffic conditioner to fulfill the SLA. The TCA information must be available in all boundary components of a DS network to guarantee that packets passing through different DS domains receives the same service in each domain.

22.3.1.5 DS interior components

The interior components inside of a DS domain select the forwarding behavior for packets based on their DS field. The interior component is usually a router that contains a traffic prioritization algorithm. Because the value of the DS field normally does not change inside of a DS domain, all interior routers must use the same traffic forwarding policies to comply with the QoS agreement. Data packets with different PHB values in the DS field receive different QoSs according to the QoS definitions for this PHB. Because all interior routers in a domain use the same policy functions for incoming traffic, the traffic conditioning inside of an interior node is done only by a packet classifier. It selects packets based on their PHB value or other IP header fields and forwards the packets to the queue management and scheduling instance of the node. Figure 334 shows the traffic conditioning in an interior node.

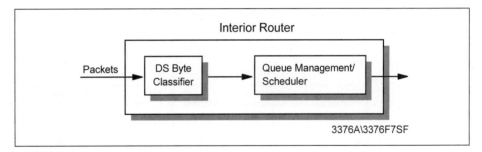

Figure 334. DS interior component

Traffic classifying and prioritized routing is done in every interior component of a DS domain. After a data packet has crossed a domain, it reaches the boundary router of the next domain and gets possibly remarked to cross this domain with the requested QoS.

22.3.1.6 Source domains

The IETF DS working group defines a source domain as the domain that contains one or more nodes which originate the traffic that receives a particular service. Traffic sources and intermediate nodes within a source domain can perform traffic classification and conditioning functions. The traffic that is sent from a source domain may be marked by the traffic sources directly or by intermediate nodes before leaving the source domain.

In this context, it is important to understand that the first PHB marking of the data packets is not done by the sending application itself. Applications do not notice the availability of Differentiated Services in a network. Therefore, applications using DS networks must not be rewritten to support DS. This is an important difference to Integrated Services, where most applications support the RSVP protocol directly when some code changes are necessary.

The first PHB marking of packets that are sent from an application can be done in the source host or the first router the packet passes. The packets are identified with their IP address and source port. For example, a customer has an SLA with a service provider that guarantees a higher priority for the packets sent by an audio application. The audio application sends the data packets through a specific port and can be recognized in multi-field classifiers. This classifier type recognizes the IP address and port number of a packet and can distinguish the packets from different applications. If the host contains a traffic conditioner with an MF classifier, the IP packet can be marked with the appropriate PHB value and consequently receives the QoSs that are requested by the customer. If the host does not contain a traffic conditioner, the initial marking of the packets is done by the first router in the source domain that supports traffic conditioning. Figure 335 shows the initial marking of a packet inside of a host and a router.

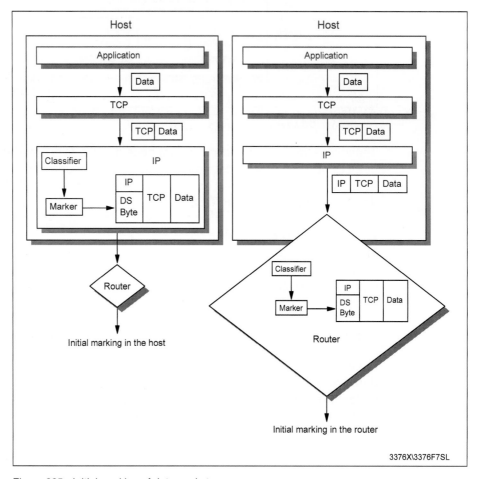

Figure 335. Initial marking of data packets

In our example, the DS network has the policy that the packets from the audio application should have higher priority than other packets. The sender host can mark the DS field of all outgoing packets with a DS codepoint that indicates higher priority. Alternatively, the first-hop router directly connected to the sender's host may classify the traffic and mark the packets with the correct DS codepoint. The source DS domain is responsible for ensuring that the aggregated traffic towards its provider DS domain conforms to the SLA between customer and service provider. The boundary node of the source domain should also monitor that the provided service conforms to the requested service and may police, shape, or re-mark packets as necessary.

22.3.2 Integrated Services (Intserv) over Diffserv networks

The basic idea is to use both architectures to provide an end-to-end, quantitative QoS, which will also allow scalability. This will be achieved by applying the Intserv model end-to-end across a network containing one or more Diffserv regions.

Intserv views the Diffserv regions as virtual links connecting Intserv capable routers or hosts running Intserv. Within the Diffserv regions, the routers are implemented with specific PHB definitions to provide aggregate traffic control. The total amount of traffic that is admitted into the Diffserv region may be limited by a determined policy at the edges of the Diffserv network. The Intserv traffic has to be adapted to the limits of the Diffserv region.

There are two possible approaches for connecting Intserv networks with Diffserv networks:

1. Resources within the Diffserv network or region include RSVP aware devices, which participate in RSVP signalling

2. Resources within the Diffserv region include no RSVP signalling

In our sample (Figure 336), we will describe the second configuration, because it is assumed to become the most current approach to be used.

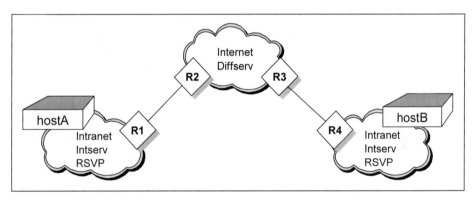

Figure 336. Integrated Services and RSVP using Differentiated Services

This configuration consists of two RSVP-capable intranets that are connected to Diffserv regions. Within the intranets, there are hosts using RSVP to communicate the quantitative QoS requirements with a partner host in another intranet running QoS aware applications.

The intranets contain edge routers R1 and R4, which are adjacent to the Diffserv region interface. They are connected with the border routers R2 and R3, which are located within the Diffserv region.

The RSVP signalling process is initiated by the service requesting application in the host (for example, hostA). Traffic control in the host may mark the DSCP in the transmitted packets, and shape transmitted traffic to the requirements of the Intserv services in use.

The RSVP end-to-end signaling messages are exchanged between the hosts in the intranets. Thus, the RSVP/Intserv resource reservation is accomplished outside the Diffserv region.

The edge routers act as admission control agents of the Diffserv network. They process the signaling messages from the hosts in both intranets, and apply admission control. Admission control is based on resources available within the Diffserv region. It is also defined in a company's policy for the intranets.

Since the border routers in our sample (R2 and R3) are not aware of RSVP, they act as pure Diffserv routers. These routers control and submit packets based on the specified DSCP and the agreement for the host's aggregate traffic control.

The Diffserv network or region supports aggregate traffic control, and is assumed to be not capable of MF classification. Therefore, any RSVP messages will pass transparently with negligible performance impact through a Diffserv network region.

The next aspect to be considered is the mapping of the Intserv service type and the set of quantitative parameters, known as flowspec. Because Diffserv networks use PHB or a set of PHBs, a mapping of the Intserv flowspec has to be defined accordingly. The mapping value is a bit combination in the DSCP. However, this mapping has to viewed under bandwidth management considerations for the Diffserv network.

The DSCP value has been made known to all routers in the Diffserv network. The question arises how the DSCP will be propagated to these routers.

There are two choices:

1. DSCPs may be marked at the entrance of the Diffserv region (at the boundary routers). In this case, they can be also remarked at the exit of the Diffserv region (at the other boundary router).

2. DSCP marking may occur in a host or in a router of the intranet. In this case, the appropriate mapping needs to be communicated to the marking device. This can be provided by RSVP.

The following sequence shows how an application obtains end-to-end QoS support.

1. HostA, attached to an intranet, requests a service from hostB, attached to another intranet. Both intranets are connected via a Diffserv network (see Figure 336 on page 815).

2. HostA generates a RSVP PATH message, which describes the traffic offered by the sending application.

3. The PATH message is sent over the intranet to router R1. Standard RSVP/Intserv processing is done by the network devices within the intranet.

4. The PATH state is defined in the router R1, and is forwarded to the Router R2 in the Diffserv network.

5. The PATH message is ignored in the Diffserv network, at R2 and R3. It is sent to R4 in the intranet, and to hostB.

6. When the PATH message is received by hostB, a RSVP RESV message is built, indicating the offered traffic of a specific Intserv service type.

7. The RESV message is sent to the Diffserv network.

8. The Diffserv network will transparently transmit the message to router R1.

9. In R1, the RESV message triggers admission control processing. This means requested resources in the initial RSVP/Intserv request are compared to the resources available in the Diffserv network at the corresponding Diffserv service level. The corresponding service level is determined by the Intserv to Diffserv mapping function. The availability of resources is determined by the capacity defined in the SLA.

10. If R1 approves the request, the RESV message is admitted and is allowed to be sent to the sender, hostA. R1 updates its tables with reduced capacity available at the admitted service level on this particular transmit interface.

11. If the RESV message is not rejected by any RSVP node in the intranet, it will be received at hostA. The QoS process interprets the receipt of the message as indication that the specified message flow has been admitted for the specified Intserv service type. It also learns the DSCP marking, which will be used for subsequent packets to be sent for this flow.

22.3.3 Configuration and administration of DS with LDAP

In a differentiated services network, the service level information must be provided to all network elements to ensure correct administrative control of bandwidth, delay, or dropping preferences for a given customer flow. All DS boundary components must have the same policy information for the defined service levels. This makes sure that the packets marked with the DS field receive the same service in all DS domains. If only one domain in the DS network has different policy information, it is possible that the data packets passing this domain will not receive the service that was contracted in the SLA between customer and service provider.

Network administrators can define different service levels for different customers and manually provide this information to all boundary components. This policy information remains statically in the network components until the next manual change.

But in dynamic network environments, it is necessary to enable flexible definitions of class-based packet handling behaviors and class-based policy control. Administrative policies can change in a running environment, so it is necessary to store the policies in a directory-based repository. The policy information from the directory can be distributed across multiple physical servers, but the administration is done for a a single entity by the network administrator. The directory information must be propagated on all network elements, such as hosts, proxies, and routers, that use the policy information for traffic conditioning in the DS network.

In today's heterogeneous environments, it is likely that network devices and administrative tools are developed by different vendors. Therefore, it is necessary to use a standardized format to store the administrative policies in the directory server function and a standardized mechanism to provide the directory information to the DS boundary components, which act as directory clients. These functions are provided by the *Lightweight Directory Access Protocol (LDAP)* which is a commonly used industry standard for directory accessing (see 8.4, "Lightweight Directory Access Protocol (LDAP)" on page 316). LDAP is a widely deployed and simple protocol for directory access. Policy rules for different service levels are stored in directories as LDAP schema and can be downloaded to devices that implement the policies, such as hosts, routers, policy servers, or proxies. Figure 337 shows the cooperation of the DS network elements with the LDAP server.

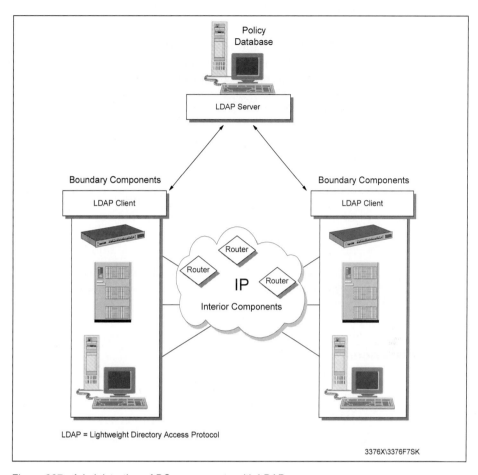

Figure 337. Administration of DS components with LDAP

22.3.4 Using Differentiated Services with IPSec

The IPsec protocol that is described in 21.5, "The IP security architecture (IPsec)" on page 698 does not use the DS field in an IP header for its cryptographic calculations. Therefore, modification of the DS field by a network node has no effect on IPsec's end-to-end security, because it cannot cause any IPsec integrity check to fail. This makes it possible to use IPsec-secured packets in DS networks.

IPsec's tunnel mode provides security for the encapsulated IP header's DS field. A tunnel mode IPsec packet contains an outer header that is supplied by the tunnel start point, and an encapsulated inner header that is supplied by the host that has originally sent the packet.

Processing of the DS field in the presence of IPSec tunnels would then work as follows:

1. The node where the IPsec tunnel begins encapsulates the incoming IP packets with an outer IP header and sets the DS field of the outer header accordingly to the SLA in the local DS domain.

2. The secured packet travels through the DS network, and intermediate nodes modify the DS field in the outer IP header, as appropriate.

3. If a packet reaches the end of an IPSec tunnel, the outer IP header is stripped off by the tunnel end node and the packet is forwarded using the information contained in the inner (original) IP header.

4. If the DS domain of the original datagram is different from the DS domain where the IPSec tunnel ends, the tunnel end node must modify the DS field of the inner header to match the SLA in its domain. The tunnel end node would then effectively act as a DS ingress node.

5. As the packet travels onwards in the DS network on the other side of the IPSec tunnel, intermediate nodes use the original IP header to modify the DS field.

22.4 References

Please refer to the following RFCs for more information on QoS in the Internet:

- RFC 1349 – Type of Service in the Internet Protocol Suite
- RFC 1633 – Integrated Services in the Internet Architecture: An Overview
- RFC 2205 – Resource Reservation Protocol (RSVP) – Version 1 Functional Specification
- RFC 2206 – RSVP Management Information Base Using SMIv2
- RFC 2207 – RSVP Extensions for IPSEC Data Flows
- RFC 2208 – Resource Reservation Protocol (RSVP) – Version 1 Applicability Statement
- RFC 2209 – Resource Reservation Protocol (RSVP) – Version 1 Message Processing Rules
- RFC 2210 – The Use of RSVP with IETF Integrated Services
- RFC 2211 – Specification of the Controlled Load Network Element Service
- RFC 2212 – Specification of Guaranteed Quality of Service
- RFC 2474 – Definition of the Differentiated Services Field (DS Field)

- RFC 2988 – A Framework for Integrated Services (Intserv) Operation over Diffserv Networks).

Chapter 23. Availability, scalability, and load balancing

The Internet business has grown so rapidly that continuous availability of mission-critical data and applications residing on servers is a most important requirement for enterprises. The Internet challenges companies to develop new strategies for increasing revenue and/or providing detailed product and delivery information. The result should raise customer and business partner satisfaction. Also, the management of enterprises' internal business processes that are accessed through the Internet by the workforce should be better optimized.

Increasing demands from customers, business partners, and employees for access to applications and data are challenges for the development of new server and networking strategies and services. Three main aspects should be considered:

- How can availability to an enterprise's information be made available 24 hours a day and 7 days a week?

- How can these services also be guaranteed even if the number of transactions increases very rapidly, for example, because of a spike in customer or business partner inquiries?

- How can the access to server applications and data be shared among parallel installed servers?

The answers are availability, scalability, and load balancing. In this chapter we discuss techniques that can be employed to achieve availability, scalability, and load balancing. Because these solutions are not standardized, we primarily limit our discussion to functions available in Cisco routers and IBM OS/390 (z/OS), yet the techniques employed by these platforms can, and in some cases, are applied by other platforms.

23.1 Availability

Application instances, network interfaces, and machines may fail (planned for maintenance or unplanned due to application or system error). In these cases, end users should not lose their service. Recovering from application instance failure is fairly straightforward in that the application is simply restarted. Network interface failures can also be tolerated by making use of Virtual IP Address (VIPA), which is not tied to any particular physical interface and hence will never fail.

Machine failure, however, is a bit more complex. Users should be able to immediately reconnect to the service without knowing that they now are using an alternate image of the application on another system. Users also should not be aware that the path to the other system has been automatically changed.

In order to provide the referenced availability requirement, another system organization has to be applied. This leads to running multiple application instances on multiple machines, including TCP/IP stacks with parallel connections to the TCP/IP network. This solution, called the clustering technique in general terms, is used for load balancing purposes but is also valid for solving high availability requirements.

The clustering technique dispatches connections to target servers, excluding failed servers, from a list of target servers that can receive connections. In this way, the dispatching function avoids routing connections to a server that is not capable of satisfying such a request.

The clustering technique requires the implementation of equal application instances running on different machines. If the application, the operating system with TCP/IP stack, or the machine fails, the dispatching technique immediately provides a backup.

A user requesting service from a particular server would no longer address an application in a particular server. Now he addresses a group of servers. The connection request is now sent to the dispatcher, who decides to which available application server it is forwarded. Thus, the user is not aware to which application server (within the group) he is connected to.

The clustering technique requires addresses that refer to groups of applications. This could be solved through virtual IP addresses. A virtual IP address (VIPA) is the IP address of a group of application servers, for example, a Telnet server. This VIPA is used for a connection request. The dispatcher is the receiver of the connection request from the user. It selects from a list of available servers a real server, and forwards the request to this server.

The process of selecting an available application server may be extended by the dispatcher using different kind distribution rules. The distribution of connection requests will be discussed in the load balancing section.

Another aspect of availability to consider is when the dispatcher fails. In this case, a backup dispatcher has to be implemented with the same IP address, so that users may send their connection requests to the backup dispatcher. A backup dispatcher will also propagate its IP address to the network. Thus, routers will use the new path that directs the user's connection requests to the backup dispatcher.

If dispatchers maintain client-server connections, the backup dispatcher has to take over the currently running connections. A takeback process should be implemented to return running connections to the primary dispatcher.

An example of a non-disruptive takeback process after recovery of the primary distribution manager is explained in 23.4.6, "Takeover/takeback of DVIPA addresses" on page 830.

23.2 Scalability

Scalability means to provide a solution for a growing business that requires additional system capacity. When workload capacity becomes smaller due to many more new connection requests from customers or business partners, a non-disruptive growth of the current system environment must be made available.

In a traditional single system environment (no clustered systems), a non-disruptive upgrade of systems is relatively limited. In order to raise capacity, these systems have to be taken down to install new features. Thus, they are not available for a certain time.

The implementation of clustered systems would be a better approach. Adding a new system to the cluster running equal applications instances would not impact the other systems in the cluster. This solution would add seamless capacity for a growing business. Compared to traditional systems, the user is not bound to a given system in a clustered server environment. Thus, the management of user connections to servers is more flexible. When a new system comes online, new connections are directed to that machine taking over a new workload.

23.3 Load balancing

Assigning applications with user connections to a specific system may overload this system's capacity, while other systems with fewer connection requests to other applications may waste free capacity.

To reach the goal for an equal level of load of all systems, these systems should be organized in a clustered system group. All systems in this cluster can provide information about their workload to the dispatcher (also called the distribution manager). This manager will now be responsible for distributing connection requests from users to the systems of the application servers, based on workload information.

Users are not aware of such clusters. They try to connect to a service, assuming it is running in the machine of the distribution manager. The distribution manager forwards the connection request to the real service provider based on the current workload of all systems in the cluster. The information about the state of the workload could be provided by a function, such as a workload manager residing in every target system.

In case there is no workload information from target systems, the distribution manager, may use distribution rules, such as:

- A simple round-robin distribution
- Number of distributed connections

23.4 Terms used in this chapter

There are some terms used in this chapter that have to be explained before we describe the solutions. These are:

- Sysplex
- Workload Manager (WLM)
- Virtual IP address (VIPA)

23.4.1 Sysplex

In the context of this chapter, we use the term *sysplex* to refer to a group of loosely coupled S/390 or z/Series (OS/390 or z/OS) images. For example, a sysplex could be multiple logical partitions (LPARs) and/or physical hosts connected via channels and S/390 Coupling Facility technology. These OS/390 or z/Series hosts, in a sysplex, are able to cooperate with each other to share DASD, provide backup capabilities, and distribute workload. The term sysplex is also used for a cluster of systems or LPARs.

See *The OS/390 V2R10.0 Parallel Sysplex Overview*, GC28-1860, for more details.

23.4.2 Workload Manager (WLM)

WLM is a component of OS/390 used for the control of work scheduling, load balancing, and performance management. TCP/IP for OS/390 V2R10 uses its own interface to WLM, which provides the Sysplex Distributor with information that allows it to load balance. Periodic updates received from

WLM tell the Sysplex Distributor which hosts in the sysplex have the most processing resources available.

See *OS/390 V2R10.0 MVS Planning: Workload Management*, GC28-1761, for more details.

23.4.3 Virtual IP-address (VIPA)

Actually, a VIPA address is a application group address. This address will be used by users to send a connection request to a dispatcher or distribution manager. The distribution manager forwards the request to a target server based on load balancing rules.

Within the IBM OS/390 or z/OS TCP/IP environment, the VIPA address is used differently. There are three types of VIPA addresses:

- Static VIPA
- Dynamic VIPA (DVIPA)
- Distributed DVIPA

23.4.3.1 Static VIPA address

The IP address is the ISO/OSI network layer address, representing a logical connection point to the network layer. The IP address maps the hardware adapter address, such as the LAN MAC address, on the data link layer that represents the physical address.

The virtual IP address (VIPA) is a network layer address also, but this address does not map to a hardware adapter. Hardware may fail, so the connection to the system via the failed adapter is not possible. Since a VIPA address does not map a hardware adapter, it is always available as a connection end-point on the path from the OS/390 TCP/IP stack to the Internet or an intranet. In case of a hardware adapter failure, a secondary path over another adapter to the VIPA address is automatically selected by router software.

VIPA addresses are defined in an OS/390 TCP/IP profile. They are called static VIPA addresses, because they belong, with their subsequent definitions, to the TCP/IP stack.

23.4.3.2 Dynamic virtual IP address (DVIPA)

In contrast to the static VIPA defined for only one TCP/IP stack, the dynamic VIPA (DVIPA) can be moved to another TCP/IP stack if the primary TCP/IP stack fails. Thus, applications accessed via this DVIPA may be reached (if they are brought up) in another system with the same DVIPA address. If the user reconnects to the application, he is not aware of the change.

For most of the application servers with well-known port numbers the network administrator only defines DVIPAs for primary use in the TCP/IP stack. The administrator also defines backup DVIPAs, which may be taken over from other TCP/IP stacks in case of system failures (see 23.4.5, "Dynamic IP addressing in a sysplex" on page 828 for an example).

If more than one TCP/IP stack is planned for the takeover of DVIPAs, the rank number, defined for the DVIPA in the backup stack, decides which stack has to take over the DVIPA first.

Basically, all VIPAs are designed to use routing daemons. OS/390 TCP/IP provides the routing daemons OMPROUTE or ROUTED to establish routes to the IP network.

23.4.3.3 Distributed Virtual IP Address
A distributed DVIPA is a special type of DVIPA. It can distribute connections within a sysplex to another TCP/IP stack on the same or another operating system image. It is used by the Sysplex Distributor to forward connections to selected target systems where application servers are located. The Sysplex Distributor works as the dispatcher or distribution manager mentioned earlier in this chapter.

23.4.4 Dynamic XCF

Dynamic XCF means "dynamic communication over the cross system coupling facility." This function allows the cross communication facility to dynamically generate connections to other TCP/IP stacks within the same sysplex using the attachments of the cross system coupling facility. When system partners detect a new IP-stack, definitions for connecting to the new-comer are automatically made. If DYNAMICXCF is used with a routing program like OMPROUTE or OROUTED, the configuration data and routing tables are automatically created as well.

23.4.5 Dynamic IP addressing in a sysplex

Figure 338 on page 829 shows three IP-stacks, each in one system. A system may be on different hardware, or just a logical partition (LPAR), within one or more systems. The administrator has defined DVIPA addresses that may be taken over by other TCP/IP stacks. There are also defined DVIPA BACKUP addresses which the stack may take over from other stacks. If an equal multiple DVIPA addresses appear in different systems, then the system with a defined higher rank will take over the DVIPA address. DVIPA addresses may be associated with an application instance.

In our example (see Figure 338 on page 829), the DVIPA addresses 10.1.1.1 and 10.1.1.2 are defined to be used primarily in system TCP1. If TCP1 fails, system2 gets information over the cross coupling facility about the failure. It knows that is has to activate the backup addresses 10.1.1.1 and 10.1.1.2 to provide the application services. In TCP3, the backup for 10.1.1.1 will not be activated, because the defined rank for this backup is lower than in TCP2.

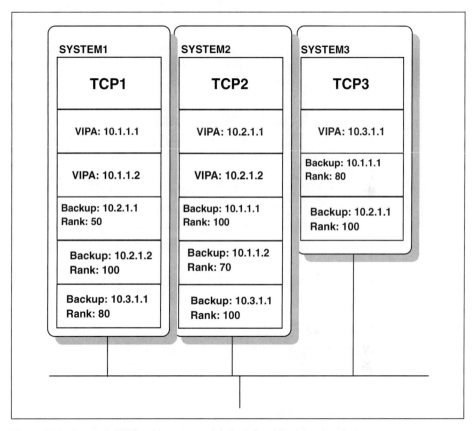

Figure 338. Dynamic VIPA addresses and their defined backups in other systems

Activation of DVIPA means that the backup systems have to automatically create definitions in the TCP/IP profile and delete these definitions when the backup is no longer required. The only task of the administrator is to define which system should be the backup for the dynamic DVIPA addresses.

23.4.6 Takeover/takeback of DVIPA addresses

Takeover (No. 1 in Figure 339): In case of a TCP/IP stack or system failure, the takeover of a DVIPA to another TCP/IP stack is automatically executed if a backup is defined for this DVIPA on that stack. Multiple backup systems may be defined for the same DVIPA. A specified rank determines which system has to take over the DVIPA: first, second, and so on.

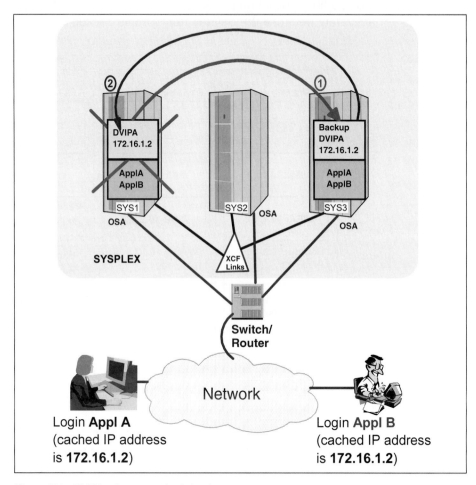

Figure 339. DVIPA takeover and takeback

In Figure 339, three systems belong to a sysplex cluster. All systems are connected through links via the cross coupling facility. On SYS1, two applications (ApplA and ApplB) are running. Both map the DVIPA 172.16.1.2. In case of a system failure, SYS3 should take over the DVIPA 172.16.1.2.

Now, a TCP/IP stack or a system failure occurs. SYS3 automatically takes over the DVIPA 172.16.1.2 based on the backup and rank definitions. Applications ApplA and ApplB initiate the activation of the DVIPA by dynamically updating profile definitions in the TCP/IP stack of SYS3. The stack informs the routing protocol of the new DVIPA, which updates its routing table. The routing protocol informs other router neighbors of the takeover of the DVIPA. Clients may now reconnect to the application. They are not aware that the application is now running on another system.

Takeback (No. 2 in Figure 339): The takeback procedure is more complex. First, the failed system has to be brought up again. All other systems in the sysplex cluster receive information about the restart of the previously failed system. This information is sent over the cross coupling facility links. The dynamic XCF function dynamically defines the IP paths between the systems within the sysplex (in our case, from SYS2 to SYS1 and SYS3 to SYS1 and reverse). The DVIPA 172.16.1.2 in SYS1is also available, but not active.

Now, a decision has to be made about how the takeback should be organized. The problem is to transfer workload back to SYS1, but without disrupting current connections. In previous OS/390 solutions, there was only the chance to direct workload for new VIPA addresses in SYS1. But this would mean that clients had to log on to VIPA addresses rather than using application names (like ApplA,) because the name server maps to one VIPA address, the old one only.

OS/390 Version 2.10 TCP/IP offers the possibility of duplicate DVIPAs. When the SYS1 TCP/IP stack is restarted, there are two choices, based on DVIPA definitions:

1. Should the DVIPA move immediately and non disruptively?

2. Should the DVIPA move when the backup stack has no longer previously taken over connections, or should the takeback process be disruptively?

The first case provides the following capabilities:

- This stack is the owner of the DVIPA 172.16.1.2. It is propagated to router daemons in the IP-net. Thus, new connection requests are routed to SYS1.

- Current connections remain on the backup stack (in our sample, on SYS3), but will administered by the stack on SYS1. Clients work non-disruptively with their application servers (ApplA or ApplB).

In the second case, the DVIPA will be transferred back to SYS1 only if there are no connections running with this DVIPA as end-point on SYS3. That is, when the DVIPA has the state *idle,* or when it is the desire of the administrator to take back the DVIPA to SYS1, but in a disruptive manner

23.5 Introduction of available solutions

There are still some questions remaining. For example:

- What kind of dispatcher or distribution manager hardware and software is available to handle client-server connection requests under the referenced circumstances?

- At which location should the dispatcher or distribution manager be installed? Within a cluster, or on machines in the IP-network or in routers (in a primary and secondary) controlling the cluster?

The following section describes several proprietary solutions of IBM and Cisco. Our description starts with dispatchers implemented outside the cluster. These are:

- Network Dispatcher (part of the WebSphere Edge Server)

- Cisco Local Director

We continue in our description with the complete cluster-internal solution, the IBM OS/390 Sysplex Distributor. Then, we compare internal and external functions provided by Cisco MultiNode Load Balancing (MNLB).

There is also a joint solution from both companies, based on cooperative research and development projects, that provides the best method to benefit from the advantages of both hardware and software offerings with additional improved coding. This solution consists of the IBM Sysplex Distributor CASA Manager and Cisco Forwarding Agent.

Finally, some other solutions using traditional software offerings will be explained. These are:

- TCP/IP for OS/390 Domain Name Server using Workload Manager (DNS/WLM)

- Virtual Router Redundancy Protocol (VRRP)

- Round Robin DNS

- NAT-based techniques

23.6 Network Dispatcher

Network Dispatcher, formerly known as Network Dispatcher (ND), is a fundamentally new approach to load balancing. It is described and compared to other solutions in the following sections.

23.6.1 Network Dispatcher components

Network Dispatcher has been developed to address these limitations and provide customers with advanced functions to meet their site's scaleability and availability needs. It consists of two components:

Interactive Session Support Can address the above limitations of round-robin DNS while still providing the same DNS interface as before for the clients. It provides a least-disruptive migration path for applications that are already deployed using round-robin DNS.

Dispatcher Provides an advanced IP level load balancing mechanism that can be installed instead of round-robin DNS. Once installed, the Dispatcher remains completely invisible to clients, but can deliver superior load balancing, management, and availability function.

These two components can be deployed separately or together in various configurations to suit a wide variety of customer application requirements.

23.6.1.1 Interactive Session Support

Interactive Session Support (ISS) is the DNS-based component. It provides a load-monitoring daemon that can be installed on each of the servers that form part of your installation. This group of daemons is referred to as a cell. One of the members of the cell becomes the "spokesman" for the load-monitoring service.

Standard memory or processor utilization figures can be used to measure load with the ISS daemon, or, alternatively, a custom set of criteria can be provided, for example, with an application-aware executable module or a simple shell script, and tell ISS how to use it. This is referred to as a custom metric.

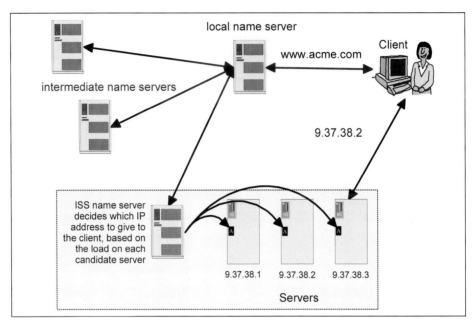

local name server

www.acme.com

Client

intermediate name servers

9.37.38.2

ISS name server
decides which IP
address to give to
the client, based on
the load on each
candidate server

9.37.38.1   9.37.38.2   9.37.38.3

Servers

Figure 340. Interactive Session Support

ISS provides an *observer* interface to enable other applications to use the load-monitoring service. Observers watch the cell and initiate actions based on the load. The observer applications provided in Network Dispatcher are of two kinds: name server observer and dispatcher observer.

1. As shown in Figure 340, the name server observer allows the load monitoring service to provide an intelligent DNS name resolution service that returns IP addresses to your clients (in response to a gethostbyname() call) based on feedback from the ISS daemons running on each server machine, rather than the strict rotation of round-robin. Also, if a server is down, its IP address will not be returned.

2. The dispatcher observer is used in conjunction with the Dispatcher component, and is described later.

ISS can also be configured in *ping triangulation* mode, where the ISS daemons respond based on the ping time from each of them to the client. This allows load balancing based on network topology.

23.6.1.2 The Dispatcher

The Dispatcher is an IP-level load balancer. It uses a fundamentally different approach to load balancing based on patented technology from IBM's Research Division. Dispatcher does not use DNS in any way, although normal static DNS will still usually be used in front of the Dispatcher. Once installed and configured, the Dispatcher actually becomes the site IP address to which clients send all packets. This externally advertised address is referred to as the cluster address. As many cluster addresses as needed can be defined. The ports that should be supported inside each cluster can be configured, and then the actual servers that will provide the service on each of those ports. Optionally, the real IP addresses of the servers in the cluster can be concealed from the clients by filtering them at the gateway router. This object-oriented cluster-port-server structure provides a simple configuration interface that can be created and modified dynamically, permitting true 24 x 7 operation. See Figure 341 for details.

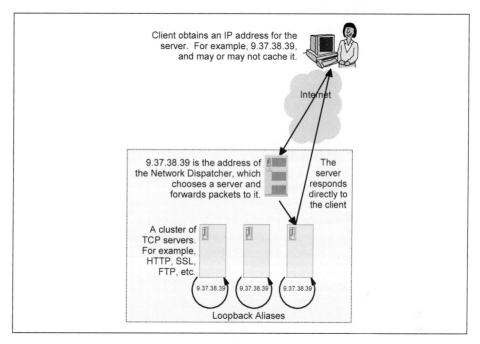

Figure 341. Dispatcher

The core function of the Dispatcher is the Executor. It is a kernel-level function (or device driver) that examines only the header of each packet and decides whether the packet belongs to an existing connection, or represents a new connection request. It uses a simple connection table stored in memory to achieve this. Note that the connection is never actually set up on the Dispatcher machine (it is between the client and the server, just as it would be if the Dispatcher were not installed) but the connection table records its existence and the address of the server to which the connection was sent.

If the connection already exists, which means it has an existing entry in the in-memory connection table, then the packet is rapidly forwarded to the same server chosen on the initial connection request without further processing. Since most of the packets that flow are of this type, the overhead of the whole load balancing process is kept to a minimum. This is one of the reasons why the Dispatcher is so superior to its competition in performance and scaleability.

If the packet is a new connection request, the Executor will look at the configuration to see which servers can support a request on the port requested by the client on the requested cluster address. Then it uses stored weights for each such server to determine the right server to which the connection will be forwarded. An entry mentioning this server is made in the connection table, ensuring that subsequent packets for this connection are correctly forwarded to the chosen server.

Note that the right server is not always the best server, since it is desirable for all eligible servers to process their share of the load. Even the worst server needs to shoulder some of the burden. If traffic is only ever forwarded to the best server, it can be guaranteed that it will rapidly cease to be the best. As a result, load allocation experiences swings that prevent optimal balance from being achieved. Dispatcher's patented algorithm for choosing the right server and its advanced smoothing techniques achieve optimal balance in the shortest possible time.

The Executor does not modify the client's IP packet when forwarding it. Because the Dispatcher is on the same subnet as its clustered servers, it simply forwards the packet explicitly to the IP address of the chosen server, just like any ordinary IP packet. The Dispatcher's TCP/IP stack modifies only the packet's MAC address in the operating system approved manner and sends the packet to the chosen server.

To allow the TCP/IP stack on that server to accept the unmodified packet from the Dispatcher and pass it to the chosen port for normal application processing, the IP address of the Dispatcher machine is also installed as a non-advertising alias on each of the clustered servers. This is achieved by configuring the alias on the loopback adapter.

The server's TCP then establishes the server-to-client half of the connection according to standard TCP semantics, by simply swapping the source and target addresses as supplied by the client, rather than determining them from its own basic configuration. This means that it replies to the client with the IP address of the Dispatcher. As a direct result, the balancing function is invisible both to the client and the clustered servers. This invisibility means that the Dispatcher is not dependent upon server platforms, provided they implement standard TCP/IP protocols.

Another key performance and scaleability benefit of the Dispatcher is that the application server returns the response to the client's request directly to the client without passing back through the Dispatcher. Indeed, there is no need even to return using the original physical path; a separate high-bandwidth connection can be used. In many cases, the volume of outbound server-to-client traffic is substantially greater than the inbound traffic. For example, Web page HTML and imbedded images sent from the server are typically at least 10 times the size of the client URLs that request them. This capability was important to address the scaling requirements of the Web site for the 1998 Nagano Winter Olympic Games.

Because the Dispatcher is a truly generic TCP/IP application, its functions can be applied not only to HTTP or FTP traffic, but also to other standards-compliant types of TCP and UDP traffic.

23.6.2 Load balancing with weights

The Dispatcher has a Manager function, which sets the weights that the Executor obeys (see Figure 342). The Manager uses four metrics to set these weights:

- Active connection counts for each server on each port. This count is held inside the Executor.

- New connection counts for each server on each port. This count is held inside the Executor.

- A check that each server is up-and-running. The Advisor performs this function.

- A check that each server has *displaceable capacity*, which means that it can realistically process the work. The ISS Load Monitor performs this function.

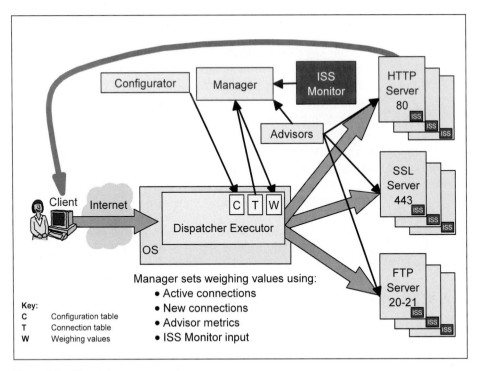

Figure 342. Dispatcher components

The Advisor is a lightweight client that runs as part of the Dispatcher, but actually passes real commands to each application server. It only executes a trivial command, but it needs to be more than a ping, which will only verify that the TCP/IP protocol stack is up. If this request is successful, the server is deemed to be up. If it fails, the Advisor informs the Manager, and the Manager sets the weight of that server to zero, until the server responds again.

If the application server has the ISS Load Monitor daemon installed (with or without a custom metric), periodic load reports can be passed to the Dispatcher via the Dispatcher observer. The results of these reports can be factored into the process of setting the individual server weights for the Dispatcher.

23.6.3 High availability

The Dispatcher already provides high availability, because one of its basic functions is to avoid choosing a failed server clustered behind it. The Dispatcher can also be configured to eliminate the load balancer itself as a single point of failure, as part of a comprehensive hardware and software implementation of high availability.

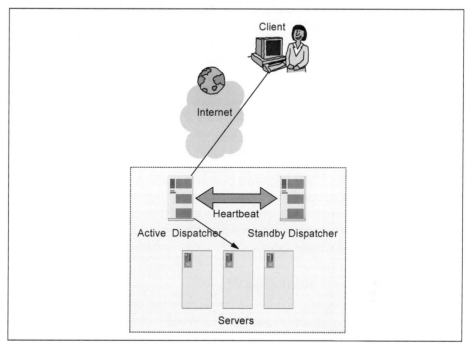

Figure 343. High availability

As shown in Figure 343, the Dispatcher can optionally be configured with a secondary/standby machine on the same subnet that synchronizes its state, including that of its connection table, with that of the primary/active machine, and listens for a heartbeat from the primary/active machine.

Various additional customer-defined *reachability* criteria can also be specified, such as access to gateway routers across duplicated adapters and networks, and so on. If the heartbeat fails, or defined reachability criteria are not met, the primary machine is deemed to be down, and the standby machine takes over the role of forwarding packets. Typically, the failover process will take less than five seconds, minimizing the number of connection failures that might occur. Other failover approaches that rely on the age-out of ARP entries can take as much as a minute to complete.

In the event of a failure, the connection table on the standby machine is closely synchronized with that of the now failed primary machine, so the great majority of the existing connections in flight will survive the failure. The newly active machine still knows where to send all packets that it receives, and TCP automatically resends any individual packets that were lost during the actual failover. The most likely connections to fail are those that are just in the process of either opening or closing. In the case of opening requests, the client TCP/IP stack or the application may be able to retry and be successful without the client being aware of the failure. In the case of closing requests, it is likely that there will be no loss of data.

23.6.4 Server affinity

This function is sometimes referred to as the *sticky* option. It is provided to allow load balancing for those applications which preserve some kind of persistent state in between connections on behalf of clients, without losing the state when the client reconnects.

When a client originally contacts the site, it is associated with a chosen server in the normal way. When the sticky option is configured, the difference is that any subsequent connections sent in by the client will be dispatched to the same server until a configurable time-out value expires. The Dispatcher allows configuration of this sticky capability on a per-port basis.

23.6.5 Rules-based balancing

Rules-based balancing introduces the concept of rules and a set of servers among which to load balance if the rule is obeyed. The following rules are available:

- Client IP address
- Client port
- Time of day
- Connections per second for a port
- Active connections for a port

This allows the site to take account of its traffic and the identity of the clients that access it when setting up the load balancing policy. A range can be specified where required, so for example all client IP addresses in a particular subnet can be forwarded to a particular set of servers, or "between the hours of 8 a.m. to 5 p.m., use this set of ten servers, otherwise use that set of five servers." This provides a simple method of implementing quality of service for individuals, groups of clients, or time-of-day, without imposing unique or proprietary additional semantics or protocols on the client/server relationship.

23.6.6 Wide Area Network Dispatcher

Previous releases of the Dispatcher required that all clustered servers be on the same subnet as the Dispatcher. With Version 2 of the Dispatcher, there is no distance limitation to remote servers, either inside a private network or even across the Internet, to provide a site that is geographically distributed over a few miles or across the globe. Another Dispatcher must be installed at the remote location.

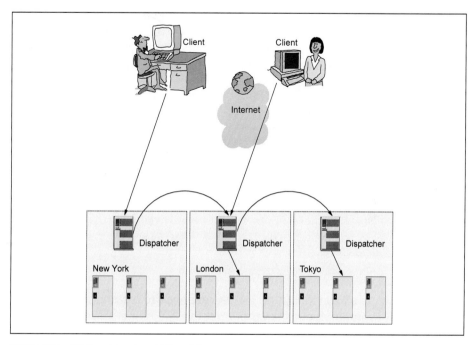

Figure 344. Wide area network dispatcher

As shown in Figure 344, when using this option, a truly distributed wide area network site can be configured. Any client data can be forwarded to any of the configured servers at any location. The choice can be based on server load, rules, or a combination of the two. The choice of which site should receive the client's packets first can be achieved in several ways, including the "which site is closest" mode provided by ISS running in ping triangulation mode (see 23.6.7, "Combining ISS and Dispatcher" on page 842).

The transmission of packets to remote sites is achieved by encapsulating the unmodified client packets at the originating Dispatcher, and then un-encapsulating them at the receiving Dispatcher. The server to client data flow goes direct, as it does with the local area network Dispatcher, thus keeping the overhead to a minimum.

23.6.7 Combining ISS and Dispatcher

The two components of the Network Dispatcher product can be usefully deployed together to support a geographically distributed site.

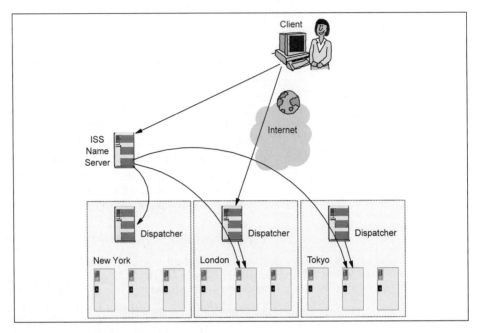

Figure 345. ISS and Dispatcher together

As shown in Figure 345, in response to a standard name resolution request from an application program, the ISS name server returns to the client the IP address of the chosen site, based on feedback from the ISS daemons running on the Dispatcher machines running at the individual sites. The ISS daemons can be configured to return results in one of two ways:

1. Based on system load, which will direct the client to the least loaded site. The ISS daemon can use a custom metric, if needed.

2. Based on ping triangulation, which will direct the client to the closest site from a network topology point of view.

The client then sends its connection request to the selected Dispatcher machine at the chosen location, which will in turn select the individual server from the cluster at that site, based on its own set of weights. Note that this configuration can also include the wide area network Dispatcher support described above.

23.6.8 Advisors and custom advisors

The Dispatcher supplies standard advisors for HTTP, HTTPS (SSL), FTP, NNTP, SMTP, POP3, and Telnet. A customer may wish to use other standard or private protocols with the Dispatcher or to implement specific extensions to the standard advisors. For this purpose, a Custom Advisor facility has been provided, with well-documented sample source code. Custom advisors must be written in Java at Release 1.1.2 or higher of the Java Development Kit, which is not provided with Dispatcher.

This powerful extension capability can be coupled with custom code written to run on the application server machine to provide a high degree of synergy between the Dispatcher and the applications it balances. One example of this use would be a link between a custom advisor and a Java servlet running inside a Web server. The servlet could be coded to extract in-depth performance data from each server and return it to the Dispatcher, thus allowing the Dispatcher to benefit from results more precisely tailored to the customer's real application environment.

23.6.9 SNMP support

A simple network management protocol (SNMP) management information base (MIB) for Dispatcher data is provided. This MIB contains a comprehensive set of values associated with the state and current performance of the Dispatcher. An SNMP-enabled management tool, such as Tivoli NetView or any other similarly equipped tool, can access this MIB. In addition, SNMP traps are also generated if a clustered server fails or if the Dispatcher itself fails over to its standby.

23.6.10 Co-location option

If a company is starting from a small site, but has plans to grow rapidly, it has some simple options to keep costs down in the early stages of its growth, while still benefiting from the high availability and scaleability options of Network Dispatcher, and positioning itself for that growth when it occurs.

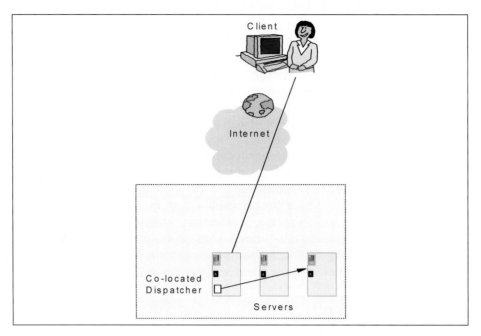

Figure 346. Co-location option

As shown in Figure 346, as the site's load increases to the point where it needs more than one server to handle the traffic, the company can add the Dispatcher to its existing network infrastructure with a minimum of hardware and software investment by installing the Dispatcher software on one of the machines where the application servers reside. It will not have to change its existing network configuration in any way. In the simplest case, all that needs to be done is configuring the Dispatcher and either replicating the application server content on to another server, or sharing it with a shared file system.

The co-location option of the Dispatcher lets a company start quickly with minimum cost and evolve to a stand-alone Dispatcher or to a high-availability configuration when the volume of traffic requires it. Even when a dedicated Dispatcher has been deployed, one can still choose to co-locate a standby Dispatcher with one of the application servers.

23.6.11 ISP configuration

Internet service providers (ISPs) with a large backbone network, or hosting a busy search engine, can address their scaling and availability requirements by coupling Network Dispatcher in high availability mode with high-capacity caching proxy servers and an enterprise shared file system. These components have been combined into the IBM WebSphere Edge Server, as shown in Figure 347.

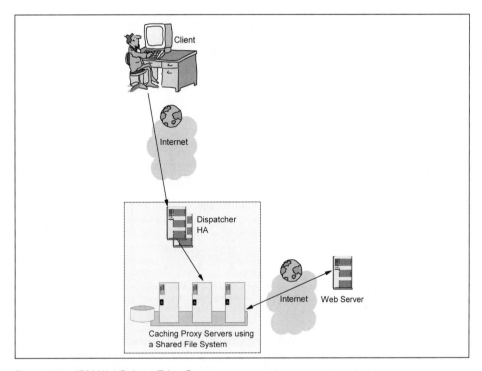

Figure 347. IBM WebSphere Edge Server

An efficiently managed cache can significantly reduce backbone network congestion, which provides delivery of faster response times to the clients and better customer service while reducing traffic costs.

23.6.12 OS/390 Parallel Sysplex support

Companies with enterprise application servers on the OS/390 parallel sysplex can use information from OS/390's Workload Manager (WLM) as input to the load balancing process of the Dispatcher feature.

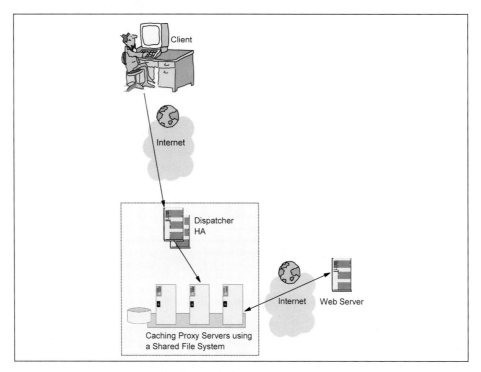

Figure 348. Dispatcher and OS/390 Parallel Sysplex

These versions of the Dispatcher have an additional advisor called the WLM Advisor. As shown in Figure 348, it interacts with the OS/390 Workload Manager and feeds tailored results to the Dispatcher's Manager in the same format as the ISS Dispatcher observer. The WLM Advisor metric measures the following for each configured server:

- The server is available.

- The server has displaceable capacity.

- The server is currently doing work deemed less important.

- The speed of the processor.

- No shortage conditions exist.

Please refer to 23.4.2, "Workload Manager (WLM)" on page 826 for more information on WLM.

23.7 Cisco LocalDirector

This section describes, in a brief overview, the functionality and explains the client connection and data flow of LocalDirector.

23.7.1 Overview

The LocalDirector is a special network unit designed for building highly redundant and fault-tolerant server farms. It works like a transparent learning bridge, which forwards incoming data packets from the IP network (Internet or intranet) to a selected application server within the server farm. The LocalDirector uses load balancing methods for directing IP datagrams containing TCP or UDP content.

Figure 349 shows the location of the LocalDirector in the IP network.

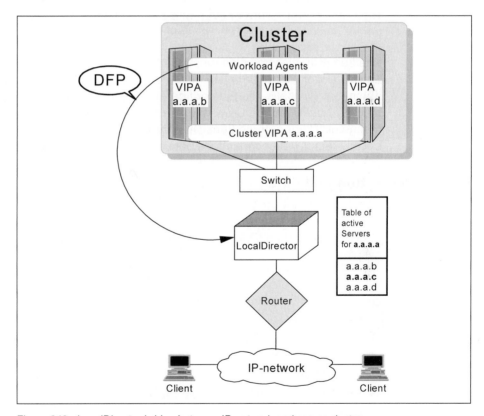

Figure 349. LocalDirector bridge between IP-network and server cluster

All servers appear as one virtual server. Therefore, only one IP address (for example, a.a.a.a) and a single Uniform Resource Locator (URL) is required for all members of the server cluster.

The LocalDirector communicates with the servers within the cluster to get information such as state of the application server, current workload of the server, and so on. This information is transferred via the Dynamic Feedback Protocol (DFP) from the servers to the LocalDirector. IBM OS/390 has a Workload Agent that is the DFP partner for the LocalDirector.

DFP will also be used to distribute information about server availability and load to a Cisco Distributed Director (not shown in Figure 349) at remote sites of the network. This facility improves Web site response time for clients.

The LocalDirector is able to redirect Hypertext Transfer Protocol (HTTP) messages, used mainly for Web traffic, to redirect to a different location in case of a server failure or even of a server cluster. If all real servers are no longer available, redirection of clients to another Web site is provided.

The LocalDirector has also functions to prepare a quick fail-over to a standby LocalDirector. Should a failure situation occur, a fail-over mechanism automatically replicates the configuration of the origin LocalDirector to the standby LocalDirector. Current user connections to servers that were maintained by the origin LocalDirector are now maintained by the secondary LocalDirector. The connections between clients and servers are not dropped.

23.7.2 Connection and datagram flow

Clients get access to the server cluster using a single URL which is translated by the domain name sever into a server cluster IP address. This address is also called a virtual IP for the cluster. A static VIPA may be used in an IBM sysplex.

When the IP address of the LocalDirector, which represents the server cluster, is known, a TCP handshake process is started by the client.

Normally, the handshake process consists of:

- Sending a SYN request from the client to a server requesting the first part of the connection
- Sending a SYN ACK response (acknowledgment) from the server to the client
- Sending a SYN request from the server to the client requesting the second part of the connection from the server to the client

- Sending an ACK response from client to the server

Connection setup going through the LocalDirector to server cluster is different.

Because the real server is not known by the client, the server cluster IP address is used. But this address is used only to reach the LocalDirector as a representative of the server cluster. Only the LocalDirector knows if the resources the client requests is available. If it is available, the server cluster IP address will be assigned to the real server IP address.

This procedure requires the interruption of the first SYN request at the LocalDirector. The LocalDirector first has to find out, based on load balancing rules, which real server has to be selected. When the selection process is done, it assigns the real destination IP address and forwards the SYN to the selected server. It also adds the connection to the list of all client-server connections going through this LocalDirector. This information is important in case of a takeover through a secondary LocalDirector.

The TCP handshaking process will now be continued between the real server and the client. Every time a packet flows through the LocalDirector it is aware that the connection is still running, and that the application and the system is working.

23.8 IBM Sysplex Distributor

The following section describes:

- Elements of the Sysplex Distributor
- Start and takeover/takeback tasks
- Load-balancing rules
- Handling connection requests

23.8.1 Sysplex Distributor elements

The sysplex distributor environment consists of several systems/LPARs within a sysplex cluster. All TCP/IP stacks are connected via the cross coupling facility to the other systems and IP-links to LAN-switches/routers over OSA adapters (for example, OSA Express) or channel-attached routers.

Figure 350 on page 853 gives an overview of the components of the sysplex distributor and the data flow from the client to the application server and back to the client.

The sysplex distributor is a TCP/IP function that is defined in the TCP/IP profile. It contains information about DVIPAs and its association to TCP/IP applications. In our sample, it is the DVIPA 172.7.1.1 that is associated with the file transfer daemon (FTP) accessed via port 20 and 21. The sysplex distributor has information on which target systems this DVIPA may be distributed to. In our sample, the DVIPA for FTP is distributed to systems A, B, and C. These target systems have equal DVIPAs, such as 172.7.1.1 for FTP. The DVIPAs on the target systems are hidden DVIPAs, which can be addressed by the sysplex distributor only. They are not propagated to the network for routing purpose.

IP-addresses of the network 172.16.0.0 belong to the cross coupling links. In order not to overload the figure, the IP-addresses for the connections to the switch/router are not shown.

23.8.2 Sysplex Distributor initialization and takeover/takeback

When the sysplex distributor (in our sample SYS1) is started, it contacts all defined target stacks about its dynamic XCF address of the cross coupling link and about the distribution DVIPAs (see 23.4.3.3, "Distributed Virtual IP Address" on page 828).

Target stacks add the distributed DVIPAs to their own TCP/IP profile as non-routeable DVIPAs. These distributed DVIPAs will not be propagated to the network. The target stacks inform the distribution stack about the state of the server application mapping the distributed DVIPA. This state and some other information are used by the sysplex distributor to forward connection requests to the target system.

In case of a system or a TCP/IP failure, a backup sysplex distributor (in our sample, SYS2) will takeover all activities of SYS1. This is done as described in 23.4.6, "Takeover/takeback of DVIPA addresses" on page 830.

In order to shorten the time for a takeover, the primary sysplex distributor (in our sample, SYS1) informs the backup sysplex distributor (SYS2) about the distribution DVIPAs of the target stacks. Thus, the backup sysplex distibutor is always aware of the current connections that the primary is servicing. In the event of a primary failure, these connections must be maintained.

Maintenance means:

- The sysplex distributor has to create and update a destination port table for active DVIPAs associated with ports to reach the applications on target stacks.

- There is also a "current" routing table to be maintained for distributing connection requests. The content of these tables is used for operator displays showing, for example:
    - Which DVIPA target stacks and ports are currently available with applications ready to receive workload
    - Over which dynamic XCF IP-address can this target stack be reached
    - How many connections are routed to the DVIPA and port target stacks
    - What WLM weights and QoS values are currently valid for the DVIPA and port target stack

23.8.3 Sysplex Distributor load balancing rules

There are different load balancing rules for the incoming connection requests. Distribution may be done based on:

- Workload manager (WLM) information of the target systems and application state

- WLM information and quality of service (QoS) information supplied by the policy agent, an additional TCP/IP application

- "Round robin," a sequential load balancing

23.8.4 Handling connection requests

When the Sysplex Distributor receives a connection request (see No 1 in Figure 350 on page 853) from the client via the Internet or intranet, it looks at tables to find out what target systems have the desired application with the requested distributed DVIPA. Based on the load balancing rules, it selects the appropriate target system. In our sample, the sysplex distributor selected the target system C for the FTP-connection. The connection-request is now forwarded (see No 2 in Figure 350 on page 853) to the distributed DVIPA using the link via the cross coupling facility.

The application server starts the connection establishment process, sending the first SYN-request to the client. The way back to the client (see No. 3 in Figure 350 on page 853) does not traverse the sysplex distributor. It goes directly (in our sample, via the OSA adapter) to the network, to a switch, or to a router.

23.8.5 Data path after connection establishment

The subsequent data flow for this connection has its path from the client to the application server always via the Sysplex Distributor and cross coupling links. From the application server to the client, there is again a direct path via the OSA adapter to the switch/router.

The sysplex distributor may cause, for the inbound traffic, a certain bottleneck. But because the outbound traffic uses another path to the network, it might not be regarded as significant. In most connections, like Web server traffic, the amount of inbound data is much smaller than the amount of outbound data.

The advantage of this solution is that all functions are located internally within the sysplex cluster. No function is on external systems or router.

System definitions and/or changes are handled by the OS/390 administration only.

23.8.6 Takeover/takeback

23.8.6.1 Takeover
If the primary sysplex distribution stack fails, all backup distribution stacks get information about this failure via the cross coupling facility. The backup distribution stack with the highest rank activates all distributed DVIPAs learned from the primary distribution stack when this stack was started.

The new distribution stack (the backup stack) informs all target stacks that it is, from now on, the distribution stack for all "hidden" DVIPAs. Again, the target stacks inform the backup distribution stack about the state of the DVIPAs and the ports representing the application servers and the current connections.

The backup distribution stack creates the destination port table and the current routing table for the operating support. Finally, it propagates its taken over distributed DVIPAs to the network. This enables routers to update their routing table and their path to the new entry point into the sysplex cluster. The new entry point is the IP-address of (in our sample, the OSA adapter of SYS2) the backup distribution stack.

23.8.6.2 Takeback
The primary sysplex distribution stack is restarted. All defined distributed DVIPAs are activated. The primary sysplex distribution stack informs the backup distribution stack and all defined target stacks that it is ready to take back connections. The target stacks inform the primary distribution stack about the state of their "hidden" DVIPAs and ports.

The backup distribution stack transfers the content of the current routing table with all connections to the primary distribution stack. It also updates the distribution routing table by deleting the returned DVIPAs. But this is done only if these DVIPAs are predefined as "moveable immediately."

Finally, the primary distribution stack propagates its distributed DVIPAs to the network. Routers will update their routing tables and paths to reach again the primary sysplex distribution stack.

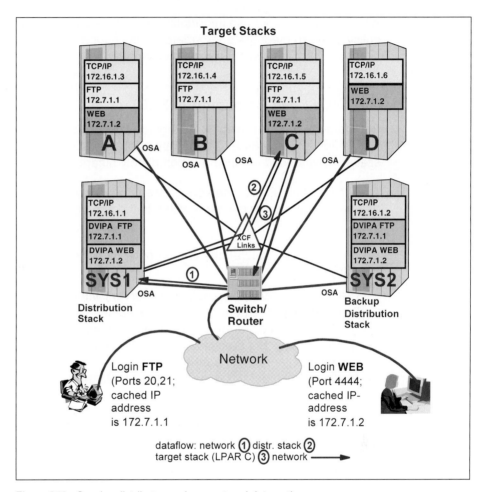

Figure 350. Sysplex distributor environment and data path

23.8.7 Attaining availability, scalability, and load balancing

Application availability is provided by implementing multiple target stacks on systems/LPARs with parallel running equal application instances. If one system/LPAR or application fails, the end user may reconnect very quickly using the same application name. This application name points to the same "hidden" DVIPA, however, in another system/LPAR.

Permanent access to the sysplex distributor stack is also provided through one or multiple backup sysplex distributor stacks. Takeover and takeback of connections running through defined backup distributor stack(s) and primary distribution stack are automatically handled without reconnection.

All distribution stacks use information from the workload manager and/or policy agent to meet the appropriate decision for a selection of the currently best target address within the sysplex cluster.

23.9 Cisco MultiNode Load Balancing (MNLB)

Compared to the IBM Sysplex Distributor solution (see 23.8, "IBM Sysplex Distributor" on page 849), Cisco's approach to reach the goals of availability, scalability, and load balancing is completely different.

Availability of application servers is seen from the view of the network attached to the server cluster. Access to the server cluster is reached via switches or routers.

Beyond the server cluster, the entire control is done externally for the following:

- The access to available application servers within the server cluster
- The scalability of extending the access to the server cluster
- The administration of the workload of each server within the server cluster
- The load balancing process to select the currently best machine for the requested client-server connection
- The forwarding of this connection request to the selected server target

This requires that information in the servers within the cluster have to be transferred to special service applications implemented in machines (switches, routers, or other server) attached to the intranet.

These service applications are called MNLB components. There are four available components:

- Service manager
- Forwarding agent
- Workload agent
- Backup service manager

Figure 351 on page 855 shows the location of the MNLB components.

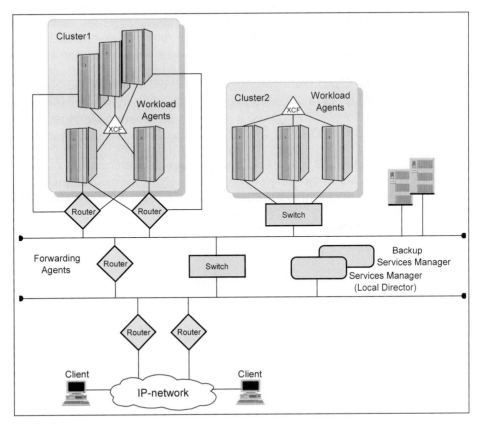

Figure 351. MNLB components

23.9.1 Overview of the MultiNode Load Balancing functions

MNLB is designed as a server load balancing solution for new e-commerce and e-business applications. MNLB consists of software running in Cisco routers and switches, Cisco LocalDirector, and application server platforms. It distributes TCP connection requests and IP-datagrams based on load balancing information across any number of routers with the highest level of availability, scalability, and performance for server applications, also located within the IBM sysplex environment.

A *Service Manager*, located in the Cisco LocalDirector, is responsible for the the distribution of connection requests. This is done using information about application availability, server processor capacity, and load balancing algorithms, like round robin, least connections, or information received through Dynamic Feed Back Protocol (FDP). This protocol, for example, carries information of the IBM OS/390 Workload Manager (WLM).

A *Workload Agent* provides the information the Service Manager needs to calculate an optimum load balancing result for the server selection. The Workload Agent is software which runs on server platforms, or machines that manage server farms or clustered server environments.

The Cisco Workload Agent for OS/390 uses IBM OS/390 Workload Manager (WLM) data. It converts these data into a common used Dynamic Feed Back Protocol (DFP) before it is sent to the Service Manager. The Cisco Workload Agent for OS/390 optimizes load balancing in an IBM Sysplex environment.

A *Forwarding Agent* is used as a packet redirector that forwards packets based on the Service Manager's instructions. The Forwarding Agent is software running in Cisco routers or route switches modules.

A *Backup Service Manager* is responsible for providing connection establishment when the primary Service Manager fails.

23.9.2 Connection establishment and subsequent data flow

The steps for establishing a connecting and subsequent data flow are:

1. The client starts a connection sending the connection request to an application server.

2. A name server resolves the domain name into a virtual IP address. It is also called Cluster IP Address, Cluster VIPA, or distributed VIPA. It is a generic IP address that addresses an application running in a clustered environment. This address has to be assigned to a real IP address after the load balancing process.

3. When a Forwarding Agent receives this connection request, the request is forwarded to the Service Manager. The connection request is discovered by the Forwarding Agent through checking the TCP header with the SYN flag on.

4. The Service Manager meets its load balancing decision based on periodic information provided by the Workload Agents. The optimal application server is selected out of a cluster of servers.

5. The Service Manager sends the connection request, containing the IP address of the optimal application server, back to the Forwarding Agent.

6. Thus the Forwarding Agent learned the destination of the specific connection request. It forwards the connection request to the application server.

7. The server receives the connection request, it tries to establish the connection sending the acknowledgment for the received SYN request. It also sends a SYN request to the client.

8. When the client accepts the SYN request it also acknowledges the received SYN and sends the first data directly to the application server using the IP address provided by the Service Manager.

The Service Manager is no longer contacted during the existing connection.

The following figure shows previously discussed connection flow:

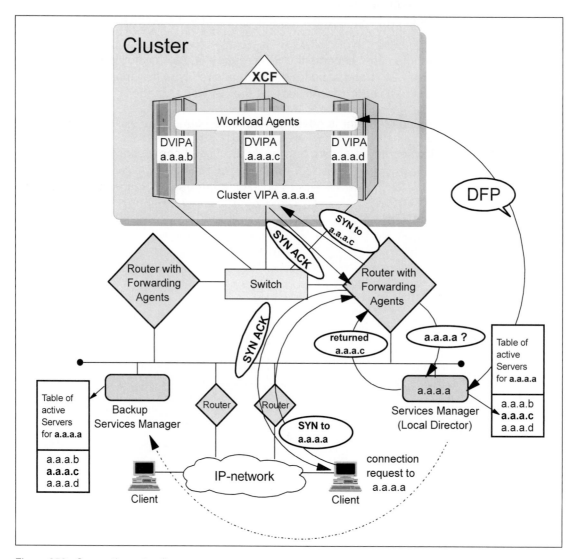

Figure 352. Connection setup flow

> **Note:**
>
> Clients do not use the host IP address for the application, but use the
> cluster VIPA address instead, which is a group address only for all hosts
> within the cluster. The real host IP address for the application is determined
> by the Service Manager based on Workload Management information.

23.9.3 Client-server connection restart

If a system/LPAR, TCP/IP stack, or application fails, the end user may reconnect very quickly to another application instance on a different TCP/IP stack within the same cluster VIPA address. The end user will again use the known application domain name, which will be translated by the domain name server into the cluster VIPA address.

The Forwarding Agent within the router again discovers the SYN request and asks the Service Manager for the real host VIPA.

The Service Manager has received the information of the failing system/LPAR, TCP/IP stack, or application through DFP message exchange from the Workload Manager, including the state of the currently running applications. It instructs the Forwarding Agent to use a new host VIPA address for the desired application, based on load balancing policies.

The rest of the connection establishment process is done as described under 23.9.2, "Connection establishment and subsequent data flow" on page 856.

23.9.4 Attaining availability, scalability, and load balancing

The analysis is divided into two parts:

- The first part views the clustered application server within the sysplex environment and the connection via the OSA adapter to the switch.
- The second part views components of the intranet, such as the Service Managers, the Forwarding Agent, and routers.

23.9.4.1 Sysplex environment

The Cisco solution does not necessarily require dynamic VIPA. Applications may also be members of static VIPAs defined for each host. Multiple application instances are started on the other systems/LPARs within the same cluster VIPA. DVIPAs have the advantage that they may be moved to another TCP/IP stack if the origin stack fails.

Which of the DVIPA/VIPA address will finally be used for the client-server connection depends on the result of the Service Manager's load balancing decision.

Thus, the control of using the application resources is done externally from the sysplex environment by the Service Manager, in cooperation with the internal function of the Workload Agent residing in each system/LPAR.

Application server availability is determined by the load of the machines within the sysplex and the amount of running application instances. Static VIPA do not provide automatic takeover or takeback. This is not necessary, because the external Service Manager is responsible for the distribution of the connections. Thus, the Service Manager determines the workload of the components within the sysplex.

Connections from the sysplex to the intranet may have several backups to provide alternative paths.

Availability and load balancing will be treated well by the components within the sysplex and the external Service Manager.

Should the business grow, an easy scalability solution should be taken into consideration. This could be, for example, installing additional servers within the sysplex without interrupting current connections. This can be achieved through adding new systems, using dynamic XCF for all systems within the sysplex. New DVIPAs/VIPAs have to be added to the existing cluster DVIPA/VIPA and propagated to the Service Manager.

23.9.4.2 Components of the intranet

The components of the intranet are as follows:

Service Managers

The most important component is the Service Manager, located in the LocalDirector's machine. The Service Manager is the address for all client connections requests. When this component fails or it is not reachable due to failed hardware (for example, adapter or line), then no connection request could be handled from any client to applications, for example, running in the sysplex.

Therefore, a backup Service Manager should be installed. In case of a failed primary Service Manager, a quick switch to the backup Service Manager has to occur. A prerequisite for the fast switch over is that the backup Service Manager must have the same knowledge that the primary Service Manager has about the states of the components of the sysplex. This means that the primary Service Manager has to exchange data such as workload data, information about the states of application servers, and so on, with the backup Service Manager.

Service Managers broadcast the IP address and cluster DVIPAs/VIPAs that they are responsible for. These addresses are used by Forwarding Agents to determine to which Service Manager a connection request has to be sent for assigning the applications DVIPA/VIPA.

Implementation of only one Service Manager might be crucial, because it can become a bottleneck, especially when Web services are requested. Web services use Hypertext Transmission Protocol (HTTP), which uses many TCP connections during Web surfing. Thus, the availability of the external Service Managers may become crucial for quick client access to application servers. Caching of repeating connection requests and their associated DVIPAs/VIPAs in the Forwarding Agent might reduce the load of the Service Manager.

If scalability is needed, additional machines with Service Manager functions may be installed in the intranet. Consequently, Service Manager should not be responsible for too many cluster VIPAs.

Forwarding Agents

Since Forwarding Agents discover connection requests, they are as important as Service Managers. A failure of the Forwarding Agent may be solved through a backup solution within the intranet. In this situation, another Forwarding Agent on the path to the desired cluster VIPA would discover the connection request. It would send the request to the Service Manager's IP address, which is responsible for the addressed cluster VIPA.

The availability of the external Forwarding Agent is also crucial for quick client access to application servers.

Scalability is easily achieved by installing additional routers with Forwarding Agents in the intranet. This would have no impact on currently running connections. A question to resolve is how to implement parallel paths from clients to Forwarding Agents in order to avoid overloading the path to the Forwarding Agent. This path will also be used by the current datagram traffic. This question is a hint only. It is not subject of the book.

23.10 IBM Sysplex Distributor and Cisco MNLB

Because of the explosive growth and forecasts in the near future for IP applications and leveraging access to traditional OS/390 and z/OS controlled transactions and databases, IBM and Cisco in cooperation, researched a "High Availability Web Services" solution, which is expected to be made available in z/OS V1R2. This solution provides an extended and adapted package of hardware and software cooperation between the IBM sysplex server site with all its dynamic functions and Cisco's MultiNode Load Balancing (MNLB) functions.

The advantages of this solution include:

- Avoids inbound traffic flow through the Sysplex Distributor
- No delays in learning load balancing information
- Use policy or quality of service (QoS) information for the selection of the "best" server
- No need for installation of the LocalDirector for the sysplex traffic

23.10.1 What does this mean?

IBM Sysplex Distributor provides the load balancing. Cisco MNLB provides the routing.

- The Sysplex Distributor receives functions of the Cisco Services Manager for the Cisco MNLB.
  - It selects the "best" appropriate server based on each system's WLM information, Quality of Service (QoS) data, or policy information provided by the Policy Agent (PAGENT). Since the Sysplex Distributor does the load balancing based on the data the WLMs within the cluster provide, the usage of the Dynamic Feedback Protocol (DFP) will no longer be necessary.
  - It provides connection information to the switch's (such as Cisco CAT 6500) MNLB function, the Forwarding Agent. This information is transferred via a proprietary Cisco protocol known as CASA (Cisco Appliance Services Architecture).
- The switch (or router) uses this information to forward subsequent client-server data directly to the selected server within the sysplex, thus avoiding all inbound traffic going through a single point, such as the LocalDirector or the Sysplex Distributor.
  - Existing MNLB Forwarding Agents will be used. The path for inbound traffic via the Sysplex Distributor and over cross coupling links is no longer used. The switch uses the direct way to the server, for example, via the OSA Express adapter. Sharing of the OSA Express adapter will be discussed later.

Note:

The Sysplex Distributor may be used concurrently, as designed for OS/390 V2.10, and for the new functions. This means that there are DVIPAs for use with Cisco Services Manager functions, and DVIPAs for use of the previous V2.10 workload distribution solution may be defined in the TCP/IP profile.

23.10.2 Overview of IBM Sysplex Distributor with Service Manager

In the Cisco proprietary MNLB configuration, the Service Manager provides the load balancing algorithm for the distribution. In order to get workload data for the load balancing process, the Services Manager communicates with the Cisco Workload Agent in each server, which is an address space under OS/390. This program retrieves information from the OS/390 WLM. The Services Manager uses the Dynamic Feedback Protocol (DFP) to communicate with the Workload Agent.

The Services Manager selects, after the load balancing process, the appropriate application server from a server cluster. Finally, it instructs the Forwarding Agent to which real server IP address the connection request has to be forwarded. The exchange of this information between the Services Manager and the Forwarding Agent is done via the Cisco Appliance Services Architecture (CASA) protocol.

In the IBM Cisco solution, the Sysplex Distributor now has functions of the Cisco Services Manager. The Sysplex Distributor uses the same technology as in the previous release. This means it uses a distributed DVIPA as a cluster address. It also does the selection of the "best" application server based on OS/390 Workload Manager (WLM) weighted information. But this selection is extended by using further information about QoS and policies defined in the policy agent's data base, such as the LDAP server or a private data base.

The Sysplex Distributor communicates with the external Forwarding Agent in a switch or router using also the CASA protocol to exchange data with the Forwarding Agent. The Sysplex Distributor instructs the Forwarding Agent what real IP address is valid for the application server in the connection request (see 23.10.5, "Connection establishment process" on page 864).

In order to let the Forwarding Agent know which cluster server IP addresses and ports are maintained by the Sysplex Distributor, a device activation process has to be started prior to resolving the first connection request. This is done by sending a CASA packet with information to the Forwarding Agent, such as:

- The DVIPA for Destination IP address and port, which defines the cluster address

- Interest address, which is a Dynamic XCF IP address and port that defines the address to be used by the Forwarding Agent for CASA packets.

This information causes the Forwarding Agent to watch for packets containing the destination DVIPA with the specified port and, if it is a connection request, gets the real server IP address from the Sysplex Distributor for the specified Dynamic XCF IP address cluster address.

23.10.3 Cisco Forwarding Agent: overview and functions

The Forwarding Agent works as described in 23.9.1, "Overview of the MultiNode Load Balancing functions" on page 855.

It is responsible for detecting all incoming connection requests, requesting the real server's IP address from the Sysplex Distributor, and routing the connection requests and all subsequent datagrams directly to the real server.

The Forwarding Agent creates an affinity record for all connections, which is updated when the Services Manager returns the real server IP address.

23.10.4 Cisco Workload Agent

The Workload Agent resides in the system of the application server. It provides feedback to the Services Manager concerning workload and availability. The Workload Agent uses the DFP protocol to provide the Services Manager with workload information. The Cisco OS/390 Workload Agent is an implementation of the Workload Agent. It is a program running in an OS/390 address space, which retrieves workload information from the IBM OS/390 Workload Manager (WLM).

In a sysplex configuration, the Sysplex Distributor communicates directly with the IBM Workload Managers of each system/LPAR. Therefore, the Cisco OS/390 Workload Agent is not required.

23.10.5 Connection establishment process

The following description gives an overview of a TCP connection establishment process. Figure 353 on page 866 shows the graphical relationship.

1. The client starts a TCP connection request by logging into a server (for example, TN3270E server, FTP server, Web server, and so on). The client selects, as host name, not a real application server but a server group or cluster name within the sysplex cluster. The host name is translated by a domain name server into an IP address for the sysplex cluster.

2. The connection request is transmitted to the IP net. It is a TCP SYN request. The first router (the default router for the client) finds, in its routing table, the IP address of the sysplex cluster, which is defined as virtual IP address in a table of a Forwarding Agent responsible for the requested sysplex cluster. We will later explain how this sysplex cluster IP

address (a dynamic virtual IP address (DVIPA)) is registered in the Forwarding Agent's table and propagated to the network.

3. When the Forwarding Agent receives IP packets, it explores the contents of these packets. If a connection request was received (this is marked by a SYN-bit in the TCP header), it sends a CASA request to the Services Manager (in the IBM Sysplex Distributor), requesting the real IP address of a application server within the sysplex.

4. The Forwarding Agent creates, for this first part of the connection establishment process, a source IP address/port - destination IP address/port transport protocol affinity, which is an entry in a cache table for the requested connection. The purpose of this affinity cache will be explained later.

5. The Services Manager in the Sysplex Distributor uses the WLM, QoS, or Policy Agent information to select the "best" application server within the sysplex and returns, in a CASA response, the real IP address for the client-server connection.

   This real IP address is a dynamically created IP address. It is built when the TCP/IP stack comes up and starts connections to other TCP/IP stacks within the sysplex. The Services Manager also creates the previous mentioned source-destination affinity to control the TCP connection, for example, to provide information for console displays, such as showing the connection routing table.

6. After receiving the CASA response, the Forwarding Agent updates its affinity cache with the real server address and forwards the connection request packet to the TCP/IP stack of the application server.

7. The TCP/IP stack on the application server system/LPAR checks if the IP and TCP header are valid. If all is OK, TCP returns an acknowledgement (ACK) for the received SYN request and also sends a SYN request to the client to establish a full duplex connection.

8. When the Forwarding Agent detects that the SYN/ACK for the previous connection request is on its way to the client, then the affinity record is updated with the information of a running connection. The affinity cache is recorded for multicasting to other Forwarding Agents. Other Forwarding Agents may also be used on the path from the client to the server and vice-versa.

   If another Forwarding Agent receives an IP packet for the referenced application server, it checks its affinity table for an existing source-destination affinity. If a matching record is found, the client packet is pointed to the real server IP address to which it is already connected, but now using a parallel path via another Forwarding Agent.

9. The Forwarding Agent that received the SYN/ACK also informs the Services Manager in the Sysplex Distributor about the source-destination connection information. This is also the source for z/OS console displays, such as the connection routing table.

10. When the SYN/ACK is received by the client, the connection establishment process is finished, and the first application data may be sent.

The described connection establishment process intentionally did not touch upon protocols for security, in order to keep this overview simple.

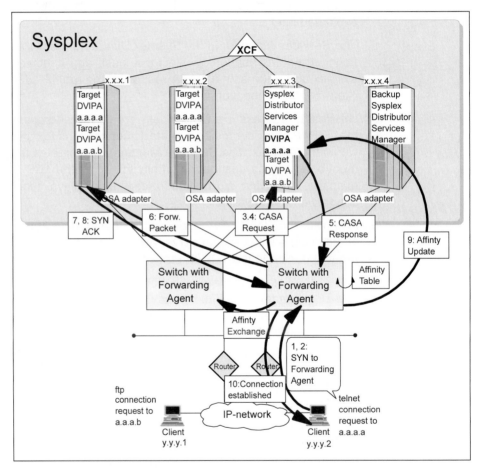

Figure 353. Establishment for a telnet connection

Figure 353 shows a telnet connection from a client to a telnet server group a.a.a.a. The Sysplex Distributor selected for this connection has the real server IP address x.x.x2. Another client connection may be routed to x.x.x.1, based on the load balancing process.

The other client has a connection to the real server x.x.x.1.

23.10.6 Stack, Server, or LPAR failure

If the application server, the TCP/IP stack, or the system/LPAR fails, there is no real IP address available and the client connection will be lost. The sysplex distributor knows about this failure through WLM information. The client may immediately start a new reconnection with the same cluster address (for example, a.a.a.a for telnet). The Forwarding Agent will setup a new CASA request to the Sysplex Distributor. The Sysplex Distributor will look for an alternative running application instance on another TCP/IP stack and returns another real IP address to the Forwarding Agent (for example, x.x.x.1). The connection establishment process continues as described before.

23.10.7 Failure of the Sysplex Distributor

If the Sysplex Distributor fails the Backup Sysplex Distributor will takeover all responsibilities of the primary Sysplex Distributor. The Backup Sysplex Distributor gets the Information via the cross coupling facility via the WLM of the failing application, or TCP/IP stack. In case the whole system is down, then the WLMPOLL of the Backup Sysplex Distributor will time out. This is the signal for the takeover process. Please see detailed information about the takeover and takeback process in 23.4.6, "Takeover/takeback of DVIPA addresses" on page 830.

23.10.8 Routing packets

Routing of inbound packets is done through the Forwarding Agent (installed in Cisco switch). Inbound packets have cluster IP address of the application server. The Forwarding Agent looks at the content of the packet, compares the information with its affinity cache. If it finds a matching entry, it knows that there is a running connection. It routes the packet to the associated real IP address of the application server.

Outbound packets are sent via the switch or router to the intranet. OSPF load balancing mechanism may be used to distribute the load over parallel equal cost paths.

The information in the affinity cache consists of source IP address/port, destination IP address/port, protocol, and real IP address

Figure 354 shows the content of the affinity cache based on the previous connection sample.

```
                                                            internal connection
                                                            information
Affinity Table
Source Address  Port    Dest. Address  Port    Prot       real server
y.y.y.2         4213    a.a.a.a        23      TCP        y.y.y.2
a.a.a.a         23      y.y.y.2        4213    TCP        y.y.y.2
y.y.y.1         4178    a.a.a.b        20      TCP        y.y.y.1
y.y.y.1         4178    a.a.a.b        21      TCP        y.y.y.1
a.a.a.b         20      y.y.y.1        4178    TCP        y.y.y.1
a.a.a.b         21      y.y.y.1        4178    TCP        y.y.y.1
```

Figure 354. Affinity table cache

23.10.9 Additional tasks of the MNLB components

23.10.9.1 Services Manager

The Services Manager is configured with DVIPAs specifying the cluster address that map to a real server address.

The Services Manager uses multicast addresses to send its mapping information to Forwarding Agents via CASA protocol using Internet Group Management Protocol (IGMP) IP address and port.

This initial multicast contains wild card information to offer services for the cluster addresses (in our sample a.a.a.a and a.a.a.b). The information creates the following wildcard cache entries for the inbound and outbound traffic to be observed by the Forwarding Agent.

The Sysplex Distributor offers the TCP protocol.

```
Source Address  Source Mask       Port  Dest Address  Dest Mask          Port Prot
0.0.0.0         0.0.0.0           0     a.a.a.a       255.255.255.255 23      TCP
0.0.0.0         0.0.0.0           0     a.a.a.b       255.255.255.255 20      TCP
0.0.0.0         0.0.0.0           0     a.a.a.b       255.255.255.255 21      TCP
a.a.a.a         255.255.255.255 23    0.0.0.0       0.0.0.0            0       TCP
a.a.a.b         255.255.255.255 20    0.0.0.0       0.0.0.0            0       TCP
a.a.a.b         255.255.255.255 21    0.0.0.0       0.0.0.0            0       TCP
```

Figure 355. Wildcard cache

The first three lines in Figure 355 on page 868 determine that the Forwarding Agent accepts incoming client packets from any IP address with any source port for the cluster addresses with the defined destination and port address (for example, a.a.a.a, 23).

Lines four to six describe the allowed outbound address combinations.

All information will be used by the Forwarding Agent for content checking of all IP packets.

23.10.9.2 Backup Services Manager

The entire CASA architecture is dependent of the Services Manager. If the Services Manager fails, no client request for connection setup can be executed. Therefore, the implementation of one or more Backup Services Managers is very important.

The Backup Services Manager periodically registers flow information via wildcard affinities with the Forwarding Agents. In case the Services Manager fails, the Forwarding Agent automatically chooses, out of a precedence selection, the Backup Services Manager with the next highest backup precedence flow.

23.10.9.3 Forwarding Agent

The Forwarding Agent is responsible for the routing of IP packets. Routing is done based on the information of the Services Manager. It learns, via wildcards received from the Services Manager, which functions to perform. This means that the Forwarding Agent has to look at IP packets for source and destination IP addresses, and for ports that the Services Manager has, via received wildcards, notified the Forwarding Agent about.

Therefore, the Forwarding Agent checks all IP headers of the inbound and outbound traffic to see if a new connection request comes in or if a registration already has occurred. A registration is an entry in the a affinity cache. If there is no registration, the Services Manager is contacted to provide the IP address of the "best" target server. If it matches the information of one affinity entry in the cache, a connection already exists.

The Forwarding Agent is able to receive wildcard information via the same multicast IGMP address and port as the Services Manager. Thus, the Sysplex Distributor running the CASA protocol has to be configured with the same multicast IGMP address and port as the Forwarding Agent.

23.11 OS/390 DNS/WLM

In addition to the highly sophisticated Sysplex Distributor/MNLB solution, there is a simple way to use the OS/390 Domain Name Server (DNS) for workload balanced connection distribution to several application server instances in a sysplex environment. This will be achieved with OS/390 BIND Domain Name System (DNS) running in a sysplex[1]. It cooperates with the OS/390 Workload Manager (WLM). In this case, WLM has to run in goal mode, which provides weighted values for the state of the workload in a system/LPAR.

For more information about the BIND DNS see Chapter 8, "Directory and naming protocols" on page 279.

23.11.1 DNS in a sysplex environment

23.11.1.1 Reasons
Domain names consist of a hierarchical names space structure. For example:

```
mvs1.itso.raleigh.ibm.com
```

This domain name points to an LPAR called *mvs1,* located in the *ITSO,* a department of *IBM* in *Raleigh*, with its high-level qualifier *com.*

If a client wants to imitate a telnet 3270 connection with the mvs1 machine, the client would type at his PC:

```
tn3270 mvs1
```

For the name resolution the resolver of the PC adds the domain itso.raleigh.ibm.com and sends the resolver request to the domain name server getting the IP address for the following address:

```
tn3270 mvs1.itso.raleigh.ibm.com
```

If the application is not available, or mvs1 is down, the client would have no chance to access the desired service. The client might try to search for the application tn3270 on another machine by using for example tn3270 mvs2. However, this could be a frustrating method if you have to search many systems for the one that is working.

An alternative is to use a cluster address and let the domain name server search for a running application instance on machines defined for the cluster address tn3270.

---

[1] OS/390 Berkeley Internet Name Domain (BIND) Domain Name System (DNS) is the UNIX name server.

23.11.1.2 Solution

If the domain name server is intelligent enough to select the first server in a cluster, and also to look at the load of the machine, then the name server could return to the client the IP address of the desired server with the lowest load. This would satisfy the client with better response times during the TCP connection to tn3270. This approach is achieved with the DNS/WLM solution.

However, two new terms have to be considered:

1. A new term *cluster address* has to be implemented. For example tn3270grp. This group contains all applications in one sysplex running the same application program (for example, tn3270 server).

2. The cluster address belongs to a new *sysplex sub-domain*. For example tn3270grp.mvsplex

The client uses a fully qualified domain name to access the name server. For example, to access any tn3270 server of the group tn3270grp in the sysplex, called mvsplex, he types:

```
tn3270 tn3270grp.mvsplex.itso.raleigh.ibm.com
```

This determines the application tn3270 out of a cluster of machines running in the specified sysplex, called *mvsplex*, which belongs to the itso.raleigh.ibm.com domain.

23.11.1.3 Configuration sample

The following figure shows that there are three TCP/IP stacks running on three systems/LPARs. The stack TCP1 and TCP3 runs the TN3270 server. Both applications belong to the cluster TN3270GRP. There is also a FTPGRP, which is a cluster for FTP servers. WLM provides workload information to the DNS.

Two DNSs are installed: A primary name server and a secondary name server as backup. Both are able to communicate with the Workload Managers to get weighted information for load balancing decisions.

Load balancing decisions are made at TCP connection establishment only. If the connection setup is done, the client/server connection remains until the client quits the connection.

If the connection fails due to the failure of the application server, or TCP/IP stack, or because of a system abend, the client may reconnect via the name server by getting the application on another system. If the primary name server fails, the secondary name server will provide the load balanced new IP address of the desired application.

It is very important that the DNS/WLM name servers (primary and secondary) are installed on OS/390 systems, because they only have the capability to run the DNS/WLM code.

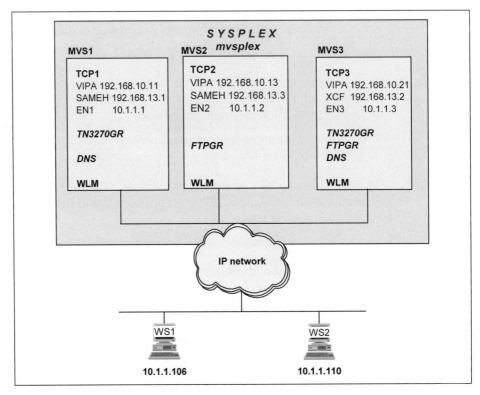

Figure 356. DNS/WLM solution

23.11.1.4 Process of application registration with the name server

To register an application with the name server, follow these steps:

1. When an application is started, it is registered at the WLM. This enables the WLM to control application's life, state, and load.

   After registration, the WLM knows:

   - Group name, server name, host name, IP address

   - CPU load, available storage, I/O rates, etc.

2. WLMs exchange this information via the cross coupling links with other systems.

3. Each WLM has an image of the resources and load of all systems within the sysplex.

4. Depending on the definition, every 1 to 5 minutes the DNS will receive an update of weighted figures of all WLMs DNS is connected to (via one TCP/IP stack). It now knows which applications are active with which DNS server name and IP address. It defines dynamically entries its forwarding tables. See Figure 359 on page 875.

5. This updated, weighted information is the base for the load balancing process to select the "best" IP address for an incoming TCP connection request.

6. The client resolver request arrives at the DNS with a fully qualified domain name including the group name. The DNS selects the "best" application server based on the last update received from the WLM and returns the IP address for this server to the client.

7. The client sends the TCP connection request directly to the returned IP address and the connection setup continues.

Figure 357 shows the flow described above.

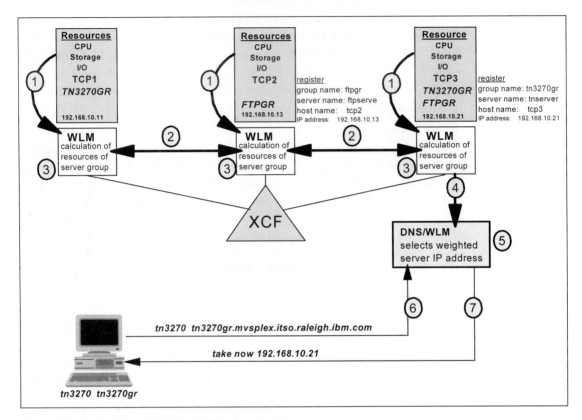

Figure 357. Application registration and resolver request.

23.11.2 DNS/WLM with remote name server

If a decision is made for a DNS/WLM implementation, this OS/390 name server system has to be integrated into existing name server systems based on UNIX installations. This is easy to do. In the remote name server, an entry to the server group in the sysplex has to be added that points to the primary DNS/WLM. If the connection to the primary DNS/WLM fails, a second entry has to point to the secondary name server. See Figure 358 on page 874 for an example.

```
mvsplex   NS   tcp1.mvsplex.itso.raleigh.ibm.com

mvsplex   NS   tcp3.mvsplex.itso.raleigh.ibm.com
```

Figure 358. New entries at the remote name server

If a resolver request arrives at the remote name server, this server recognizes the new subdomain *mvsplex.* Since it does not posses the responsibility to solve the name (missing $origin for this sub-domain entry) it points the request to tcp1.mvsplex.itso.ibm.com, another name server for resolution of the name. If tcp1 fails, then the secondary name server, tcp3, will be contacted.

For both systems, tcp1 and tcp3, host entries are also required to point to these IP address in DNS/WLM name servers.

The primary and secondary name server need entries for the cluster names which are associated to the mvsplex and according IP addresses. See the sample in Figure 359.

CNAMEs are canonical names to associate to the subdomain. Host entries (A entries) are also required for the cluster names. These are created dynamically when the register process takes place.

```
$ORIGIN mvsplex.itso.raleigh.ibm.com

                IN   NS   tcp1
                IN   NS   tcp3

tcp1            IN   A    192.168.10.11
tcp3            IN   A    192.168.10.21

tn3270gr        IN   cname tn3270gr.mvsplex.itso.raleigh.ibm.com
ftpgr           IN   cname ftpgr.mvsplex.itso.raleigh.ibm.com

----------- dynamically created entries by the -----------
----------- name server after WLM registration -----------

tn3270          IN   A    192.168.10.11
                IN   A    192.168.10.21
ftpgr           IN   A    192.168.10.13
                IN   A    192.168.10.21
```

Figure 359. Cluster entries of the dynamically created hosts

23.12 Virtual Router Redundancy Protocol (VRRP)

Virtual Router Redundancy Protocol (VRRP) was issued to the IETF by IBM, Ascend Communications, Microsoft, and Digital Equipment Corporation in April 1998 and is documented in RFC number 2338. Its status is a proposed standard.

23.12.1 Introduction

The use of a statically configured default route is quite popular for host IP configurations. It minimizes configuration and processing overhead on the end host and is supported by virtually every IP implementation. This mode of operation is likely where dynamic host configuration protocols such as DHCP (see 3.7, "Dynamic Host Configuration Protocol (DHCP)" on page 126) are deployed, which typically provide configuration for an end-host IP address and default gateway. However, this creates a single point of failure. Loss of the default router results in a catastrophic event, isolating all end hosts that are unable to detect any alternate path that may be available.

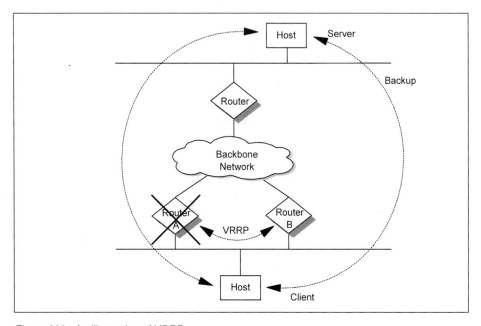

Figure 360. An illustration of VRRP

VRRP is designed to eliminate the single point of failure inherent in the static default routed environment. VRRP specifies an election protocol that dynamically assigns responsibility for a virtual router to one of the VRRP routers on a LAN. The VRRP router controlling the IP address(es) associated with a virtual router is called the master, and forwards packets sent to these IP addresses. The election process provides dynamic fail-over in the forwarding responsibility should the master become unavailable. Any of the virtual router's IP addresses on a LAN can then be used as the default first hop router by end hosts. The advantage gained from using VRRP is a higher availability default path without requiring configuration of dynamic routing or router discovery protocols on every end host (see router discovery protocols in 3.2, "Internet Control Message Protocol (ICMP)" on page 102).

23.12.2 VRRP Definitions

Some terms used in VRRP are:

VRRP router	A router running the Virtual Router Redundancy Protocol. It may participate in one or more virtual routers.
Virtual router	An abstract object managed by VRRP that acts as a default router for hosts on a shared LAN. It consists of a virtual router identifier and a set of associated IP address(es) depending on the definition, across a common LAN. A VRRP Router may back up one or more virtual routers.
IP address owner	The VRRP router that has the virtual router's IP address(es) as real interface address(es). This is the router that, when up, will respond to packets addressed to one of these IP addresses for ICMP pings, TCP connections, etc.
Primary IP address	An IP address selected from the set of real interface addresses. One possible selection algorithm is to always select the first address. VRRP advertisements are always sent using the primary IP address as the source of the IP packet.
Virtual router master	The VRRP router that is assuming the responsibility of forwarding packets sent to the IP address(es) associated with the virtual router and answering ARP requests for these IP addresses. Note that if the IP address owner is available, then it will always become the master.
Virtual router backup	The set of VRRP routers available to assume forwarding responsibility for a virtual router should the current master fail.

23.12.3 VRRP overview

VRRP specifies an election protocol to provide the virtual router function described earlier. All protocol messaging is performed using IP multicast datagrams (see Chapter 6, "IP multicast" on page 229), thus the protocol can operate over a variety of multiaccess LAN technologies supporting an IP multicast. Each VRRP virtual router has a single well-known MAC address allocated to it. The virtual router MAC address is used as the source in all periodic VRRP messages sent by the master router to enable bridge learning in an extended LAN.

A virtual router is defined by its virtual router identifier (VRID) and a set of IP addresses. A VRRP router can associate a virtual router with its real addresses on an interface and can also be configured with additional virtual router mappings and priority for virtual routers it is willing to back up. The mapping between VRID and addresses must be coordinated among all VRRP routers on a LAN. However, there is no restriction against reusing a VRID with a different address mapping on different LANs.

The scope of each virtual router is restricted to a single LAN. To minimize network traffic, only the master for each virtual router sends periodic VRRP advertisement messages. A backup router will not attempt to preempt the master unless it has higher priority. This eliminates service disruption unless a more preferred path becomes available. It's also possible to administratively prohibit all preemption attempts. The only exception is that a VRRP router will always become master of any virtual router associated with addresses it owns. If the master becomes unavailable then the highest priority backup will transition to master after a short delay, providing a controlled transition of the virtual router responsibility with minimal service interruption.

The VRRP protocol design provides rapid transition from master to backup to minimize service interruption, and incorporates optimizations that reduce protocol complexity while guaranteeing controlled master transition for typical operational scenarios. The optimizations result in an election protocol with minimal runtime state requirements, minimal active protocol states, and a single message type and sender. The typical operational scenarios are defined to be two redundant routers and/or distinct path preferences among each router. A side effect when these assumptions are violated (for example, more than two redundant paths all with equal preference) is that duplicate packets can be forwarded for a brief period during master election. However, the typical scenario assumptions are likely to cover the vast majority of deployments, loss of the master router is infrequent, and the expected duration in master election convergence is quite small (< 1 second). Thus the VRRP optimizations represent significant simplifications in the protocol design while incurring an insignificant probability of brief network degradation.

23.12.4 Sample configuration

Figure 361 shows a simple example network with two VRRP routers implementing one virtual router.

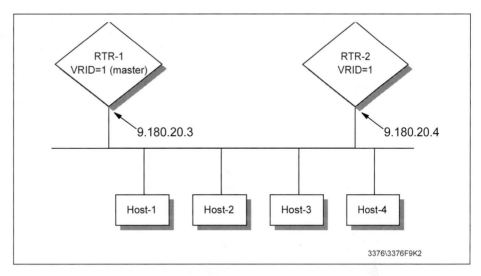

Figure 361. VRRP simple configuration example

The above configuration shows a very simple VRRP scenario. In this configuration, the end hosts install a default route to the IP address of virtual router #1 (IP address 9.180.20.3) and both routers run VRRP. The router on the left becomes the master for virtual router #1 (VRID=1) and the router on the right is the backup for virtual router #1. If the router on the left should fail, the other router will take over virtual router #1 and its IP addresses, and provide uninterrupted service for the hosts. Note that in this example, IP address 9.180.20.4 is not backed up by the router on the left. IP address 9.180.20.4 is only used by the router on the right as its interface address. In order to back up IP address 9.180.20.4, a second virtual router would have to be configured. This is shown in Figure 362.

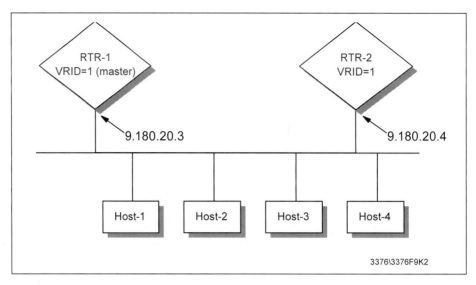

Figure 362. VRRP simple load-splitting configuration example

Figure 362 shows a configuration with two virtual routers with the hosts splitting their traffic between them. This example is expected to be very common in actual practice. In the above configuration, half of the hosts install a default route to virtual router #1's (IP address of 9.180.20.3), and the other half of the hosts install a default route to virtual router #2's (IP address o f9.180.20.4). This has the effect of load balancing the traffic from the hosts through the routers, while also providing full redundancy.

23.12.5 VRRP packet format

The purpose of the VRRP packet is to communicate to all VRRP routers the priority and the state of the master router associated with the virtual router ID. VRRP packets are sent encapsulated in IP packets. They are sent to the IPv4 multicast address assigned to VRRP. The IP address, as assigned by the IANA for VRRP, is 224.0.0.18. This is a link local scope multicast address. Routers must not forward a datagram with this destination address regardless of its TTL (see 3.1, "Internet Protocol (IP)" on page 65). The TTL must be set to 255. A VRRP router receiving a packet with the TTL not equal to 255 must discard the packet.

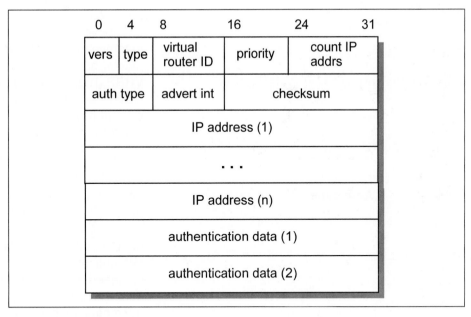

0	4	8	16	24	31

vers	type	virtual router ID	priority	count IP addrs
auth type	advert int		checksum	
IP address (1)				
. . .				
IP address (n)				
authentication data (1)				
authentication data (2)				

Figure 363. VRRP packet format

The fields of the VRRP header are defined as follows:

Version
The version field specifies the VRRP protocol version of this packet. (In RFC 2338 the version is 2.)

Type
The type field specifies the type of this VRRP packet. The only packet type defined in this version of the protocol is 1.

Virtual Router ID (VRID)
The virtual router identifier (VRID) field identifies the virtual router this packet is reporting the status for.

Priority
The priority field specifies the sending VRRP router's priority for the virtual router. Higher values equal higher priority. The priority value for the VRRP router that owns the IP address(es) associated with the virtual router must be 255. VRRP routers backing up a virtual router must use priority values between 1-254. The

default priority value for VRRP routers backing up a virtual router is 100. The priority value zero (0) has special meaning indicating that the current master has stopped participating in VRRP. This is used to trigger backup routers to quickly transition to master without having to wait for the current master to time out.

Count IP Addrs

The number of IP addresses contained in this VRRP advertisement.

Auth Type

The authentication type field identifies the authentication method being utilized. Authentication type is unique on a per interface basis. The authentication type field is an 8-bit unsigned integer. A packet with unknown authentication type or that does not match the locally configured authentication method must be discarded. The authentication methods currently defined are:

0 - No Authentication

1 - Simple text password

2 - IP Authentication Header

Advertisement Interval (Adver Int)
The default is 1 second. This field may be used for troubleshooting misconfigured routers.

Checksum

It is used to detect data corruption in the VRRP message.

IP address(es)

One or more IP addresses that are associated with the virtual router.

Authentication data

The authentication string is currently only utilized for simple text authentication.

23.13 Round-robin DNS

Early solutions to address load balancing were often located at the point where host names are translated into actual IP addresses: The Domain Name System (see 8.1, "Domain Name System (DNS)" on page 279). By rotating through a table of alternate IP addresses for a specific service, some degree of load balancing is achieved. This approach is often called round-robin DNS (see Figure 364). The advantages of this approach are that it is protocol-compliant and transparent both to the client and the destination host. Also, it is performed only once at the start of the transaction.

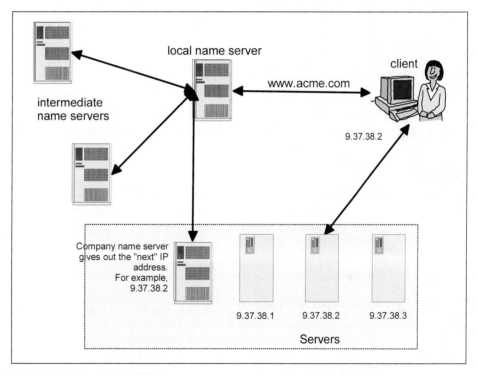

Figure 364. Round-robin DNS

Unfortunately, this approach is sometimes defeated by the fact that intermediate name servers and client software (including some of the most popular browsers) cache the IP address returned by the DNS service and ignore an expressly specified time-to-live (TTL) value (see 3.1, "Internet Protocol (IP)" on page 65), particularly if the TTL is short or zero. As a result, the balancing function provided by the DNS is bypassed, because the client continues to use a cached IP address instead of resolving it again. Even if a client does not cache the IP address, basic round-robin DNS still has limitations:

- It does not provide the ability to differentiate by port.
- It has no awareness of the availability of the servers.
- It does not take into account the workload on the servers.

23.14 Alternative solutions to load balancing

There are many vendors currently offering load balancing hardware or software products. The techniques used vary widely and have advantages and disadvantages. What follows is a consideration of some of these alternative approaches in comparison to the approach used by Network Dispatcher.

23.14.1 Network address translation

Network Address Translation (NAT) works by modifying the source and target IP addresses in the inbound client-to-server packets and restoring the IP address to the original values in the outbound server-to-client packets. (Please refer to 21.4, "Network Address Translation (NAT)" on page 694 for more details on NAT.)

Note that if NAT is to be transparent to the server, eliminating the need for specialized agent code on the server, then all packets sent back to the client must pass back through the load balancer in order to restore the IP addresses originally used by the client, as shown in Figure 365. This is a significant overhead, which will have a varying impact on the load balancer and the servers whose resources it manages

This added overhead and latency can mean network delay, and queuing delay in the load balancer itself. This drastically limits the potential scaleability of NAT solutions. To overcome such delays, the capacity of the load balancer must not only be sufficient to handle both inbound and outbound packets, but also be able to cope with the disproportionately higher volume of outbound traffic.

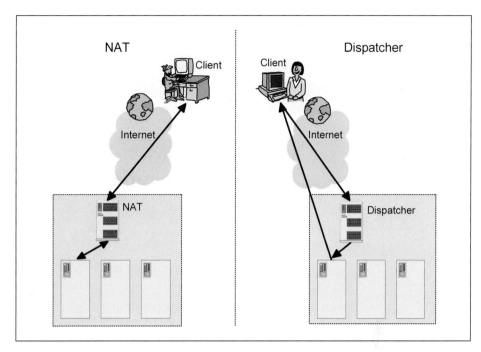

Figure 365. Network Address Translation versus Network Dispatcher - 1

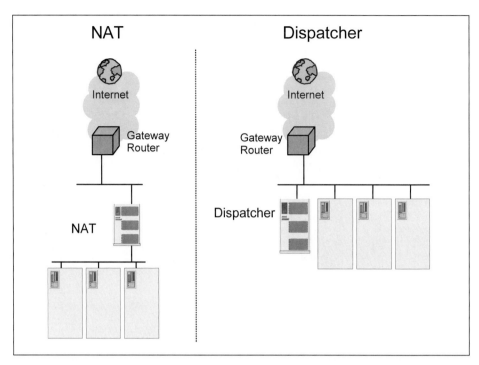

Figure 366. Network Address Translation versus Network Dispatcher - 2

As shown in Figure 366, NAT offerings sometimes enforce the need to see both inbound and outbound requests by obliging the NAT device to be installed as a bridge (without permitting bridges of any other kind), thus forcing the servers on to what is essentially a private segment. This can complicate installation, since it requires a significant physical change to existing networks. All traffic for those servers must pass through the load balancer whether the traffic is to be load balanced or not.

Conversely, the Dispatcher can be quickly and easily installed without disruption to the existing network infrastructure. Also, the flexibility of configuration offered by the Dispatcher allows an asymmetric network to be configured to handle very high bandwidth.

The one advantage of NAT as originally conceived (the ability to forward packets to remote destinations across a wide area network) cannot be usefully deployed since the wide area network connection is behind the bridge and, therefore, can only be within the site's private network. Additionally, the same NAT device must still be the only exit from the wide area network link. Dispatcher's wide area network support does not suffer from this limitation.

To attempt to overcome these limitations, some NAT solutions add to the overhead that is fundamental to NAT by providing unnecessary add-ons. For example, the capability to map one port address to another. This is implicitly at odds with the standards for well-known ports. This is often touted as an advantage for NAT-based solutions, but the so-called advantages of port mapping are of marginal value, and the same functionality can be deployed in other ways that are more standards-compliant.

To check if a server is up, NAT-based load balancing solutions need to sacrifice an actual client request, and so a server outage is typically perceived only as a result of a timeout of one of these real client requests. Dispatcher's use of specialized advisors is less disruptive and reacts more quickly to a failure.

NAT Devices often only map affinity or *stickiness* based on the client's IP address, and not at the port level. This means that once a client has contacted a server, then all traffic from that client that is intended for other applications is forwarded to the same server. This drastically restricts configuration flexibility, in many cases rendering the sticky capability unusable in the real world.

23.14.2 Encapsulation

Other approaches to load balancing are proxies that encapsulate packets rather than modifying them, and then pass them to the server. This approach has some merit, particularly since it permits the load balancer to forward traffic across a wide area network, unlike the bridging NAT solutions. But other implementations use encapsulation for all traffic and this requires an agent of the load balancer to be installed on each server. This agent reverses the encapsulation process. As a result, the choice of server platform is, by definition, restricted to the platforms for which the server agent is available. Also, like NAT, it entails further processing of the packet, which increases the likelihood that it will not be scalable to the levels required for major sites.

Dispatcher, on the other hand, does not require any code to be installed on the servers clustered behind it. Indeed, it has no knowledge of the hardware or operating system platform on which the servers are running.

Appendix A. Platform implementations

IBM operating systems have been equipped with TCP/IP functionality for many years and have constantly increased and improved their coverage of TCP/IP. This chapter presents a sample of the main TCP/IP functions and protocols that can be found on some IBM operating systems and hardware platforms. It is by no means intended to be an exhaustive survey, either in terms of platforms nor in terms of functionality, but rather a highlight of the different TCP/IP stack functionality available from IBM.

A.1 IBM Communications Server for OS/390 V2R10

IBM enterprise servers running OS/390 provide customers with the necessary power, scalability, security, and availability to help them run their mission-critical workloads. It is beyond the scope of this redbook to detail the vast, rich functionality of CS for OS/390, which includes QoS, RSVP, and advanced security mechanisms. In this section, we highlight some of power and flexibility of this implementation. For a more complete description, please refer to *IBM Communications Server for OS/390 TCP/IP Implementation Guide Volume 1: Configuration and Routing,* SG24-5227.

IBM Communications Server for OS/390 IP is the second phase of an OS/390 TCP/IP evolution towards using OS/390 UNIX System Services. Today's CS for OS/390 IP enjoys improved performance due to a redesigned stack, one that takes advantage of Communications Storage Management (CSM) and of VTAM's Multi-Path Channel (MPC) and Queued Direct I/O (QDIO) capabilities. This tight coupling with VTAM provides enhanced performance and serviceability. In CS for OS/390 IP, two worlds converge, providing access to OS/390 UNIX System Services and the traditional MVS environment via network attachments both old and new.

A.1.1 Supported connectivity protocols and devices

DLCs can be classified into two categories: TCP exclusive DLCs and shared DLCs. TCP exclusive DLCs are those only available for the CS for OS/390 IP stack and cannot be shared between multiple instances of CS for OS/390 IP. The TCP exclusive DLCs supported by CS for OS/390 IP include the following channel protocols:

- Channel Data Link Control (CDLC)

   This protocol supports a native IP connection between CS for OS/390 IP and an IP router coded within a 374x running Network Control Program (NCP) or within a 9x0 channel-attached router.

- Common Link Access to Workstation (CLAW)

  This protocol is used to connect the CS for OS/390 IP to a 3172 running ICCP, an RS/6000, and Cisco routers supporting this interface.

- Channel-to-Channel (CTC)

  This protocol is supported between two CS for OS/390 IP systems and uses one read/write channel pair. Both parallel and ESCON channels are supported.

- Hyperchannel

  This protocol is used to connect via the NSC A220 Hyperchannel Adapter and its descendants.

- LAN Channel Station (LCS)

  This protocol is used by OSA, the 3172 running ICP, the 2216, and the 3746-9x0 MAE.

In addition, one more protocol TCP exclusive DLC protocol exists, although it does not make use of S/390 channels. Not to be confused with PTP Samehost, the SAMEHOST DLC enables communication between CS for OS/390 IP and other servers running on the same MVS image. In the past, this communication was provided by IUCV. Currently, three such servers exploit the SAMEHOST DLC:

- SNALINK LU0

  This server provides connectivity through SNA networks using LU0 traffic. It acts as an application to OS/390 VTAM.

- SNALINK LU6.2

  This sever provides connectivity through SNA networks using LU6.2 traffic. It also acts as an application to OS/390 VTAM.

- X.25

  This server provides connectivity to X.25 networks by using the NCP packet switching interface (NPSI).

Shared DLCs are those that can be simultaneously used by multiple instances of multiple protocol stacks. For example, a shared DLC may be used by one or more instances of CS for OS/390 IP and one or more instances of OS/390 VTAM. These shared DLCs include:

- Multipath Channel+ (MPC+)

  MPC+ is an enhanced version of the Multipath Channel (MPC) protocol. It allows for the efficient use of multiple read and write channels. High

Performance Data Transfer (HPDT) uses MPC+ together with Communication Storage Manager (CSM) to decrease the number of data copies required to transmit data. This type of connection can be used in two ways.

The first of these is called MPCPTP, in which CS for OS/390 IP is connected to a peer IP stack in a point-to-point fashion. In this way, CS for OS/390 IP can be connected to each of the following:

- Another CS for OS/390 IP stack

- 2216

- RS/6000

- 3746-9x0 MAE

- Cisco routers via the Cisco Channel Interface Processor (CIP) or the Cisco Channel Port Adapter (CPA)

The second way to use MPC+ is to connect to an Open Systems Adapter (OSA). In this configuration, OSA acts as an extension of the CS for OS/390 IP stack and not as a peer IP stack, as in MPCPTP. The following are supported in this manner:

- OSA-2 native ATM (RFC1577)

- OSA-2 Fast Ethernet and FDDI (MPCOSA)

- OSA-Express QDIO uses MPC+ for the exchange of control signals between CS for OS/390 IP and the OSA-Express

• MPCIPA (QDIO)

The OSA-Express provides a new mechanism for communication called Queued Direct I/O (QDIO). Although it uses the MPC+ protocol for its control signals, the QDIO interface is quite different from channel protocols. It uses Direct Memory Access (DMA) to avoid the overhead associated with channel programs. Originally, the OSA-Express and CS for OS/390 IP only supported the Gigabit Ethernet attachment. CS for OS/390 V2R10 IP provides QDIO support for Fast Ethernet and ATM LAN emulation as well.

A partnership between CS for OS/390 IP and the OSA-Express Adapter provides offload of compute-intensive functions from the S/390 to the adapter. This interface is called IP Assist (IPA). Offloading reduces S/390 cycles required for network interfaces and provides an overall improvement in the OS/390 OSA-Express environment, compared to existing OSA-2 interfaces.

- XCF

  The XCF DLC allows communication between multiple CS for OS/390 IP stacks within a Parallel Sysplex via the Cross-System Coupling Facility (XCF). The XCF DLC can be defined, as with traditional DLCs, but it also supports XCF Dynamics, in which the XCF links are automatically brought up.

- PTP Samehost

  Sometimes referred to as IUTSAMEH, this connection type is used to connect two or more CS for OS/390 IP stacks running on the same MVS image. In addition, it can be used to connect these CS for OS/390 IP stacks to OS/390 VTAM for the use of Enterprise Extender.

A.1.2 Supported routing applications

CS for OS/390 IP ships two routing applications, ORouteD and OMPROUTE. OMPROUTE and ORouteD cannot run on the same TCP/IP stack concurrently. These applications add, delete, and change routing entries in the routing table and can be used as an alternative to static routes created via GATEWAY or BEGINROUTES definitions in the CS for OS/390 IP profile.

A.1.2.1 ORouteD

ORouteD is the CS for OS/390 IP implementation of the Routing Information Protocol (RIP) Version 1 (RFC 1058) and RIP Version 2 (RFC 1723). A much older application than OMPROUTE, ORouteD has limitations. ORouteD does not support zero subnets. In addition, ORouteD does not support equal-cost multipath routes to a destination network or host. As a result, OMPROUTE is the recommended routing application (also called routing daemon).

A.1.2.2 OMPROUTE

In OS/390 V2R6 IP and later, OMPROUTE implements the Open Shortest Path First (OSPF) protocol described in RFC 1583 (OSPF Version 2), as well as the RIPv1 and RIPv2. When configured properly, the OS/390 host running with OMPROUTE becomes an active OSPF and/or RIP router in a TCP/IP network. Either (or both) of these two routing protocols can be used to dynamically maintain the host routing table. Additionally, OS/390 V2R7 IP provides a new OMPROUTE subagent that implements the OSPF MIB variable containing OSPF protocol and state information. This MIB variable is defined in RFC 1850.

A.1.3 Enterprise Extender

OS/390 V2R6 and later supports Enterprise Extender (also known as HPR/IP). Enterprise Extender provides the traditional advantages of APPN (advanced peer-to-peer networking), such as class of service and transmission priority, in an IP network. With Enterprise Extender, you can configure layer-3 networks with the following characteristics:

- A private IP-backbone network
- Stable and reliable service for mission-critical SNA applications
- Cost-effective network provisioning

Enterprise Extender uses User Datagram Protocol (UDP) to access the IP network.

A.1.4 Virtual IP Addressing (VIPA)

The original purpose of (static) Virtual IP Addressing (VIPA) was to eliminate a host application's dependence on a particular network attachment. A client connecting to a server would normally select one of several network interfaces (IP addresses) to reach the server. If the chosen interface goes down, the connection also goes down and has to be reestablished over another interface. Additionally, while the interface is down, new connections to the failed interface (and IP address) cannot be established.

With VIPA, you define a virtual IP address that does not correspond to any physical attachment or interface. CS for OS/390 IP then makes it appear to the IP network that the VIPA address is on a separate subnetwork, and that CS for OS/390 itself is the gateway to that subnetwork. A client selecting the VIPA address to contact its server will have packets routed to the VIPA via any one of the available real host interfaces. If that interface fails, the packets will be rerouted nondisruptively to the VIPA address using another active interface.

CS for OS/390 V2R8 IP extended the availability coverage of the VIPA concept to allow for the recovery of failed system images or entire TCP/IP stacks. In particular, it introduced two enhancements to VIPA:

- The automatic VIPA takeover function allows you to define the same VIPA address on multiple TCP/IP stacks in a sysplex. One stack is defined as the primary or owning stack and the others are defined as secondary or backup stacks for the VIPA. Only the primary one is made known to the IP network. If the owning stack fails, then one of the secondary stacks takes its place and assumes ownership of the VIPA. The network simply sees a change in the routing tables. In this case, applications associated with these DVIPAs are active on the backup systems, thereby providing a *hot standby* for the services.

- Dynamic VIPA (for an application instance) allows an application to register to the TCP/IP stack with its own VIPA address. This lets the application server move around the sysplex images without affecting the clients that know it by name or address; the name and address stay constant, although the physical location of the single application instance may move. In this way, the application can dynamically activate the VIPA on the system image it wishes to host the application. Because the application instance is only active on one image in the sysplex at a time, the other images provide a *cold standby* of the service.

These VIPA enhancements were enabled by the use of XCF to communicate between the TCP/IP stacks. That is, XCF has become the basis for communication regarding VIPAs within the sysplex. Because of the ease of configuration provided by XCF dynamics, many of the newer VIPA functions in turn exhibit facilitated configuration.

A.1.5 Sysplex Distributor

Sysplex Distributor is the state of the art in connection dispatching technology among S/390 IP servers. Essentially, Sysplex Distributor extends the notion of Dynamic VIPA and Automatic VIPA Takeover to allow for load distribution among target servers within the sysplex. It combines technology used with Network Dispatcher for the distribution of incoming connections with that of Dynamic VIPAs to ensure high availability of a particular service within the sysplex.

In Sysplex Distributor, one IP entity advertises ownership of some IP address by which a particular service is known. In this fashion, the single system image of Sysplex Distributor is also that of a special IP address. This IP address is called the *distributed DVIPA*. Further, in Sysplex Distributor, the IP entity advertising the distributed VIPA and dispatching connections destined for it is itself a system image within the sysplex, referred to as the *distributing stack*.

Sysplex Distributor makes use of workload manager (WLM) and its ability to gauge server load. In this paradigm, WLM informs the distributing stacks of this server load so that the distributing stack may make the most intelligent decision regarding where to send incoming connection requests. Additionally, Sysplex Distributor has the ability to specify certain policies within the policy agent so that it may use QoS information from target stacks in addition to

WLM server load. Further, these policies can specify which target stacks are candidates for clients in particular subnetworks.

Connection requests are directed to the distributed stack of Sysplex Distributor. The stack selects which target server is the best candidate to receive an individual request and routes the request to it. It maintains state so that it can forward data packets associated with this connection to the correct stack. Additionally, data sent from servers within the sysplex need not travel through the distributing stack.

Sysplex Distributor also enhances the Dynamic VIPA and Automatic VIPA Takeover functions introduced in SecureWay Communications Server for OS/390 V2R8 IP. The enhancements allow a VIPA to move *non-disruptively* to another stack. That is, in the past, a VIPA was only allowed to be active on one single stack in the sysplex. This led to potential disruptions in service when connections existed on one stack, yet the intent was to move the VIPA to another stack. With Sysplex Distributor, the movement of VIPAs can now occur without disrupting existing connections on the original VIPA owning stack.

In summary, Sysplex Distributor offers the following advantages:

- Ease of configuration

  Sysplex Distributor takes ease of configuration to another level. The initial configuration of a distribution is made extremely easy. Additionally, servers can be added to a distribution without the need for any configuration.

- More accurate measure of server load

  Sysplex Distributor makes use of WLM-provided server load information. But it can also use QoS performance metrics from target servers to guide the selection of target servers on incoming connections. Additionally, the set of potential target stacks can be different depending on which client is requesting the connection. This allows for the reservation of particular stacks to some subset of clients in a straightforward manner.

- The ultimate in availability

  Sysplex Distributor can function with Automatic VIPA Takeover to ensure that the distribution of connections associated with a particular service is made available. Because every stack in the sysplex distribution can be a back-up distributing stack, the survival of just one system image ensures the availability of the service. In this way, target servers can become backup stacks for the distribution of incoming connections.

- Easy integration

  The end users are not aware of the distribution being performed by Sysplex Distributor; they just connect to a new server IP address (or host name).

- Independence from DNS

  Sysplex Distributor does not depend on host name resolution for load balancing.

- No additional hardware required

  Because all of the Sysplex Distributor function is contained within the sysplex, no additional hardware is necessary to take advantage of this function.

- Performance

  Because Sysplex Distributor is contained within the sysplex, CS for OS/390 IP can take advantage of the homogeneity within the cluster. That is, forwarding connection and data through the distributing stack is done extremely fast. Additionally, extra communication occurs between the stacks in the sysplex, allowing for fast recognition of VIPA failure and enhanced backup functions.

A.1.6 Quality of Service (QoS)

The OS/390 UNIX service policy agent (PAGENT) is a server responsible for reading the service level policies from a configuration file and installing them in the TCP/IP stack.

Network administrators can use PAGENT to define service level policies for their users' benefits of the service level policies:

- Control of TCP throughput.

- Admission control for connection requests from clients.

- Blocking of unwanted datagrams.

- Activation of specification of policies depending on date and time.

- Prioritization of all IP traffic both within CS for OS/390 and IP routers that use TOS settings for priority queuing and selective discards.

- From OS/390 V2R8 IP, policy agent provides limits for RSVP reservation parameters requested by RSVP applications, and limiting total active RSVP traffic flows.

- With CS for OS/390 V2R10 IP, the policy agent supports Traffic Regulation and Sysplex Distributor policies.

The policy agent retrieves service policy rules and statements from a policy configuration file or from the LDAP server and installs them in the CS for OS/390 stack (across all MVS images).

PAGENT sets the TOS value of outgoing IP packets, and it can be used to flush out existing policies in the stack or update them as necessary. PAGENT also logs information and error messages into a HFS file. The policy agent also monitors the local file and LDAP server dynamically for updated policies maintained in the TCP/IP stack.

A.2 IBM OS/400 V5R1

IBM @server iSeries and AS/400 servers are renowned for their reliability in the midrange market. For many years, this server's hardware and software has been built on 64-bit architecture. Following several OS/400 versions and releases, this server platform has been enhanced to become the e-business server of choice. IBM @server iSeries servers come with a complete and robust suite of TCP/IP protocols, servers and services.

The TCP/IP communication protocol function, along with related administration and configuration functions, are built into and packaged with OS/400. TCP/IP applications, such as TELNET, Simple Mail Transfer Protocol (SMTP), File Transfer Protocol (FTP), Routing Information Protocol 1 and 2 (RIP), and LPR/LPD (remote print support) remain part of the TCP/IP utilities along with the Pascal-based API. These TCP/IP utilities are automatically shipped to all customers that order OS/400.

TCP/IP is fundamental to the network computing paradigm. Much of the new IBM @server iSeries e-business infrastructure runs exclusively on TCP/IP, including Lotus Domino, Java, WebSphere, Web serving and IBM Network Stations. Recent TCP/IP enhancements make the IBM @server iSeries an even more powerful e-business server.

This section provides a sample of some of the features included with OS/400 V5R1. This is not intended to be an exhaustive list of features.

A.2.1 GUI configuration support

The entire IBM @server iSeries TCP/IP configuration can be managed through the graphical user interfaces provided by the IBM @server iSeries Operations Navigator. Included is a graphical wizard that provides simplified step-by-step guidance for configuring TCP/IP. Other configuration wizards are available to support you setting up various server configurations. IBM @server iSeries server network administration has never been easier.

A.2.2 TCP/IP Connectivity Utilities for IBM @server iSeries

TCP/IP Connectivity Utilities for IBM @server iSeries has a rich suite of servers and services including:

- GUI configuration support
- File Transfer Protocol (FTP) client and server
- Simple Mail Transfer Protocol (SMTP)
- Post Office Protocol (POP) Version 3 server
- Web-based Administration server
- Network File System (NFS) client and server
- Domain Name System (DNS) server
- Dynamic Domain Name System (DDNS) server
- Dynamic Host Configuration Protocol (DHCP) server
- IP Printing
- Line printer requester (LPR) and line printer daemon (LPD)
- 5250/HTML Workstation Gateway (WSG) server
- Telnet client and server
- Remote EXECution (REXEC) client and server
- Remote IPL support
- BOOTP server
- TFTP server

The IBM @server iSeries servers support a wide range of physical interfaces, including:

- IBM Token-Ring LAN
- Ethernet LAN
- Ethernet 100 Mb LAN
- 1 Gbps Ethernet
- Frame relay
- Wireless (LAN)
- Integrated PC Server LAN
- Asynchronous support
- Synchronous support
- Integrated Services Digital Network (ISDN)
- ATM (LAN emulation)

A.2.3 Dynamic IP routing (RIP and RIP2)

Routing Information Protocol (RIP) is a dynamic IP routing protocol that communicates with adjacent routers, informing each other of their respective network connections. Dynamic routing protocols make network maintenance easier and improves network performance and reliability. IBM @server iSeries includes both RIP version 1 and RIP version 2. Version 2 of RIP adds security and efficiency features.

A.2.4 Advanced functions

The AS/400 platform includes a number of advanced TCP/IP functions, some of which are described here.

A.2.4.1 Simple Network Management Protocol (SNMP)

Simple Network Management Protocol (SNMP) provides a means for managing an Internet environment. SNMP is used in each node of a TCP/IP network that is monitored or managed by an SNMP manager. An IBM @server iSeries SNMP agent provides support for the exchange of network management messages and information among hosts. OS/400 supports Management Information Base II (MIB-II). The features included in SNMP for IBM @server iSeries are:

- SNMP APIs for managing applications have the ability to manipulate management data via local or remote SNMP agents. Using AnyNet/400 support, information can be retrieved from systems on SNA or TCP/IP networks, which makes it easier to discover and manage potential problems anywhere within the network.

- SNMP agents are extendable, and APIs are provided that allow the dynamic addition of sub-agents to show additional information needed to make good management decisions. OS/400 also supports a Host Resources Management Information Base (MIB) for hardware and software inventory of an IBM @server iSeries server. Independent Software Vendors (ISVs) can use the SNMP APIs to write IBM @server iSeries management applications to collect inventory data, monitor, and change resources in the network and a variety of other tasks. They can also write sub-agents that allow access to additional IBM @server iSeries management information from management applications running on other platforms.

- The SNMP management function is split between two kinds of entities, named the "manager" and the "agent." The SNMP agent function runs on the IBM @server iSeries server and allows it to be managed by network management stations that have implemented the SNMP manager function. The OS/400 SNMP agent provides configuration, performance, and problem management data concerning TCP/IP to an SNMP manager. Management Information Bases supported include:

  - MIB-II

  - Transmission Groups

- APPN

- Private

- Placing printers in a TCP/IP network on a LAN is common practice today. SNMP management gives you the option to send print files to those printers and manage responses from those printers in this network. This option is configured in the OS/400 printer device description and is based on the industry-standard Simple Network Management Protocol (SNMP). It supports SNMP printers that support the printer message information block.

- Prior to V4R5, either the current Printer Job Language (PJL) driver or Line Print Requestor (LPR) is used to print to ASCII printers with the output from the Host Print Transform. The new SNMP driver allows more printers to be accessed from an IBM @server iSeries server with the same capabilities seen with direct attached printers or those using the Printer Job Language (PJL) driver.

A.2.4.2 Network Quality of Service (QoS)

In V5R1, IBM @server iSeries provides the ability to control and manage TCP/IP traffic in the network and take advantage of the leading-edge networking Quality of Service (QoS) functions contained in routers and switches. The IBM @server iSeries QoS functions for managing TCP/IP traffic provide the ability to drop, mark, and shape TCP/IP traffic based on the QoS policy being applied. In addition, QoS admission control capability is provided for controlling bandwidth management requests. The QoS functions supported are:

- Resource Reservation Protocol (RSVP), including an IBM @server iSeries RSVP agent

- RSVP APIs (X/Open standard APIs) for applications

- Differentiated Services (DiffServ)

- QoS policies based on the TCP/IP 5-tuple (Source IP address, Destination IP address, Source Port, Destination Port, and Protocol), address ranges, and wild-cards. This support includes a policy agent, and a wizard-based GUI in Operations Navigator for configuring the QoS policies.

- QoS monitoring APIs and a GUI for monitoring the effectiveness of your QoS policies.

A.2.5 Proxy Address Resolution Protocol (Proxy ARP)

Proxy ARP is an IP networking technique that allows one machine, the proxy agent, to answer ARP request on behalf of another machine. It is useful for

SLIP, PPP, and twinax connections. This is because it can make devices appear to be all logically on the same local LAN subnet and therefore avoid the need to implement either dynamic routing protocols or static route definition. Proxy ARP is also used for transparent subnetting in Frame Relay networks or for virtual LAN communications between LPAR partitions.

A.2.6 Point-to-Point Protocol (PPP)

Point-to-Point Protocol (PPP) is an open protocol for wide area network TCP/IP connectivity that can support both dial and leased lines. It can be used to extend an enterprise intranet across multiple locations. It is also the *de facto* standard for connecting to the Internet through an Internet Service Provider (ISP). PPP is a more robust alternative to SLIP (Serial Line Internet Protocol) when used as a dial-up protocol. PPP's IDSN support enables IBM @server iSeries to attach to ISDN switched networks. Using PPP, the IBM @server iSeries provides an excellent integrated solution for remote LAN access and as a remote office gateway into an organization's intranet. Filtering based on authenticated users or responder connection profiles allow controlled access to resources within or behind the IBM @server iSeries server. The IBM @server iSeries also supports multi-link connections allowing you to bundle multiple lines to reduce latency and dynamically add or removes lines depending or bandwidth needs.

A.2.7 Security features

The AS/400 addresses security with a number of features, some of which are outlined here.

A.2.7.1 TCP/IP packet security

TCP/IP packet security, also referred to as filtering or packet rules, selectively limits, or journals, network access to applications and services. This security enables additional protection for IBM @server iSeries servers that run sensitive applications or act as Web servers. TCP/IP packet security helps protect an entire subnetwork when the IBM @server iSeries acts as a casual router. When implementing network security in layers, you can also implement TCP/IP Packet Security as a second level of defense.

A.2.7.2 Virtual Private Networks

IBM @server iSeries virtual private networking support is based on industry standards that include:

- IP Security Protocol (IPSec)
- Internet Key Exchange (IKE)
- Layer 2 Tunneling Protocol (L2TP)

IBM @server iSeries VPN (Virtual Private Networking) support, introduced in V4R4 and enhanced in V5R1, provides additional security, greater reliability, improved performance, and is easier to use. Operations Navigator has been redesigned to intuitively navigate VPN configurations, and you can use the VPN wizard to set up and implement your network security policy. Digital certificates provide a scalable and secure mechanism for cryptographic operations. Now in V5R1, you can use them in your VPN configurations to authenticate the identities of the VPN endpoints. IKE negotiations can be performed using main or aggressive mode with pre-shared secrets or RSA signatures. OS/400 VPN also provides a platform unique VPN Network Address Translation (VPN NAT) that overcomes the typical NAT restrictions when using the IPSec protocols AH or ESP. Normal NAT applied within a VPN connection breaks the authentication with AH, does not work with ESP in tunnel mode, and also cannot be used with ESP in transport mode due to the Security Association (SA) setup. An integral part of IBM @server iSeries VPN is IP Packet Filtering. In V5R1, this component is enhanced to allow filter activation and deactivation on a per-interface basis.

A.2.7.3 Layer 2 Tunneling Protocol (L2TP)

Layer 2 Tunneling Protocol (L2TP) is an enhanced link protocol that provides a multi-hop virtual circuit through the Internet. L2TP is also known as "Virtual PPP," because it creates a virtual circuit at a link layer and then utilizes Point-to-Point Protocol (PPP) to complete the connection at the network layer. L2TP is typically used in conjunction with Virtual Private Networks (VPN) to provide a secure connection over the Internet.

The following modes are supported for Layer 2 Tunneling Protocol:

- Remote dial-on-demand (compulsory tunnel): This mode type is to set up an L2TP tunnel between an ISP and your IBM @server iSeries server. The remote user would be unaware that any tunneling was occurring. Compulsory tunnels are ideal, but the ISP of your choice must support this L2TP mode.

- Initiator-on-demand (voluntary tunnel): This mode is to enable the IBM @server iSeries to automatically connect to a remote system over an L2TP tunnel. When outbound IP traffic needs to be routed to a remote system, this IBM @server iSeries server would automatically initiate a tunnel to connect to the remote system, which would act as the L2TP Network Server (LNS).

- Multi-hop: This mode type enables the IBM @server iSeries server to redirect L2TP traffic on behalf of client L2TP Access Concentrators (LACs) and L2TP Network Servers (LNSs). To establish an L2TP Multi-hop connection, this IBM @server iSeries server would act as both an LNS to one or more LACs at the same time as acting as a LAC to a given LNS.

A.2.7.4 Network address translation (NAT)

When the TCP/IP addressing schemes of networks conflict, or you need to hide all or part of the network topology, network address translation (NAT) capabilities provide a solution. In addition, TCP/IP address hiding allows all the computers on one network to access servers on another network by sharing a single TCP/IP address. Masquerading is particularly useful when connecting to another network, such as the Internet, using a dial-up link.

A.2.8 Virtual IP Addressing (VIPA)

Virtual IP Addressing creates a virtual TCP/IP address that is not associated with a physical network interface on the IBM @server iSeries. This virtual address on the IBM @server iSeries server can be reached from the network through all installed physical interfaces. This allows the use of a single IP address with load balancing over multiple physical interfaces and can dramatically increase network performance for high-volume IBM @server iSeries e-business servers. VIPA also improves fault tolerance for IBM @server iSeries clusters or in backup system environments.

A.2.9 Application programming interfaces (APIs)

Many times an enterprise has unique interoperability requirements for its private networks. The enterprise must provide its own applications to fulfill these unique requirements. IBM @server iSeries provides programming interfaces to accomplish this. The Sockets API allows distributed applications to exchange data locally and over networks. Both connection-oriented and connectionless communications are supported by the Sockets API. In addition to IP, you use the Sockets API to write applications that communicate over Internetwork Packet Exchange (IPX) protocols directly.

A.2.9.1 RPC

The Remote Program Call (RPC) interface is also available to distributed application developers. This approach essentially views remote applications as callable programs. In addition, both Java and Lotus Domino provide various programming options for implementing distributed applications over TCP/IP networks.

A.2.9.2 Sockets and SSL support

Sockets programming uses the socket application program interface (API) to establish communication links between remote and local processes. The sockets API is located in the communications model between the application and the transport layers. The sockets API allows applications to interface with the transport or networking layers on the typical communications model. It is shipped as part of OS/400. The sockets API is part of the open environment on the IBM @server iSeries server. The sockets API, along with the integrated file system, eases the effort that is required to move UNIX applications to IBM @server iSeries servers. Secure Sockets Layer (SSL) is a security protocol that provides privacy over an open communications network (for example, the Internet). SSL protocol allows client/server applications to communicate in a way that is designed to prevent eavesdropping, tampering, and message forgery. Many applications on the IBM @server iSeries servers are SSL enabled in V4R4, including Telnet, HTTP server, CA/400 host servers, systems management, and LDAP. Also, OS/400 SSL support includes a set of APIs, which, when used in addition to the existing OS/400 sockets APIs, provide the functions required for applications to establish secure communications. Sockets application can be written to secure the connection by using the SSL APIs or the new Global Secure ToolKit (GSKit) APIs.

A.2.9.3 Async IOCP

TCP/IP includes support for Asynchronous I/O Completion Ports (Async IOCP) as part of the OS/400 sockets APIs implementation. These new socket APIs provide a scalable, efficient, and powerful method for multi-threaded Internet and e-business server applications to process client data.

Internet, e-business, and other network server applications utilizing Asynchronous I/O Completion Ports design models and APIs should allow a much smaller pool of threads to process work from clients when compared to other design models and APIs. In the typical threaded server application design model, there is usually one thread per client connection. Each thread, especially in applications where there is intermittent data flow being exchanged, such as an interactive application like Telnet, spends much of its time waiting for data. This means each thread expends CPU cycles going to sleep when no data is available or waking up when data finally becomes available.

Applications using Async IOCP designs and APIs should allow any of the applications threads to service any client. This means fewer threads are needed per server application, and each thread is constantly kept busy. Therefore, little or no system resource is consumed by the server application's threads either waiting for data, going to sleep, or waking up. This means that for many Internet or e-business applications designed and written to use Async IOCP APIs, there can be a drastic and dramatic reduction in CPU utilization rates. In general, less system CPU resource, less paging resource, less system memory, and less system storage is needed by Async IOPCP-enabled applications.

Sockets on the system are based on and are compatible with Berkeley Software Distributions (BSD) 4.3 sockets. Application programs written in the Integrated Language Environment (ILE), for example, C/400 or ILE RPG, can use the sockets API.

A.2.9.4 TLS and SSL support

Most OS/400 TCP/IP server applications are enabled for SSL. In releases prior to V4R5, SSL V2.0 and SSL V3.0 was supported. Now, the SSL support has been enhanced to include the TLS protocol. Support for TLS is the latest protocol and the industry-standard definition of Secure Sockets Layer (SSL) support. The TLS protocol is an evolutionary upgrade of the SSL Version 3.0 protocol. TLS Version 1 and SSL Version 3 share the same basic record construction and line flows. TLS provides the same function as SSL and is compatible with SSL, but includes new features and clarifications for protocol flows. TLS helps standardize the SSL definition and implementation, making the SSL protocol more secure, and the specification of the protocol is more concise and complete.

TLS support on the IBM @server iSeries server allows customers and business partners continued access to take advantage of the latest technology implementation of Internet application security enablement in the industry. TLS support is automatically part of any SSL-enabled application, like HTTP, FTP, and Telnet servers. Parameter values on the SSL and GSKit APIs enable SSL and TLS for business partner and customer-provided SSL applications. The HTTP server (Original) and (powered by Apache) both support server directives to control the cipher suites and protocols accepted for client connections.

SSL/TSL support on the IBM @server iSeries requires one of the Cryptographic Access Provider products (5722-AC2 or 5722-AC3) to be installed (to enable cryptographic functions). In OS/400 V5R1, you can also install an IBM 4758-023 Cryptograhpic Coprocessor card to improve SSL handshake performance.

A.2.10 Supported applications

This section provides a brief introduction into some of the applications provided on the AS/400 platform.

A.2.10.1 LDAP

OS/400 provides an LDAP-accessible directory server and corresponding APIs that communicate with other LDAP directory servers. APIs are provided for both OS/400 and Windows applications written in Java, C, and C++. LDAP-enabled applications, such as Internet mail clients, can access, update, and manage the IBM @server iSeries directory.

You can develop OS/400 applications to use LDAP for managing distributed information across the Internet and intranets using LDAP directories for both IBM and non-IBM platforms. IBM @server iSeries user information, such as e-mail addresses, is accessible to mail clients and other LDAP applications.

Directory Services implements SecureWay Directory for OS/400. This provides support for LDAP V3. LDAP V3 includes support for internal characters (UTF-8), which supports national language data, and is a mixed, multibyte codepage. LDAP V3 also provides support for dynamic schema, where the schema is stored in the directory and is managed by the LDAP server. The schemas can be updated using the new Directory Management Tool, importing from an Lightweight Directory Access Protocol Data Interchange Format (LDIF) file, or from LDAP command line utilities.

The OS/400 V5R1 LDAP support allows information about IBM @server iSeries printers and NetServer print shares to be published into LDAP directories. This allows the user to write applications that query the LDAP directory for IBM @server iSeries printer information, such as a printer's location or capabilities. It also allows the user to configure IBM @server iSeries printers directly on their Windows 2000 desktop by using the Add Printer wizard available in Windows 2000 and specifying that the information necessary to publish the printer be obtained from the Windows 2000 Active Directory.

A.2.10.2 NFS

The IBM @server iSeries Integrated File System includes support for the Network File System, a popular protocol used in UNIX-based client/server computing environments. The NFS server and NFS client communicate using Remote Program Calls. The NFS client provides seamless access to remote files for local applications. The remote files could be on a remote UNIX machine, Linux, or any machine that is running an NFS server. Other systems that support the NFS client can mount IBM @server iSeries directories exported via the IBM @server iSeries NFS server.

A.2.10.3 Simple Mail Transfer Protocol (SMTP)

Simple Mail Transfer Protocol is used to send or receive electronic mail. For consistency with other IBM @server iSeries mail functions, SMTP interoperates with Systems Network Architecture (SNA) Distribution Services (SNADS) through AnyMail/400. SNADS and AnyMail/400 are part of OS/400.

SMTP supports mail objects up to 2 GB of SMTP distribution, MIME, optional automatic enrollment of senders of incoming mail, in the system distribution directory and alias tables, OfficeVision for AS/400 notes, messages, and attachments. You can tune SMTP depending on the mail load on your system, therefore enabling greater scalability.

A.2.10.4 POP3 server

The Post Office Protocol (POP) Server is the IBM @server iSeries implementation of the POP3 mail server. This server enables the IBM @server iSeries to act as a POP server for any client that supports the POP mail protocol, including major e-mail clients, such as Netscape and Eudora, running in Windows, OS/2, AIX, and Macintosh. The POP server allows users to exchange mail, including Multipurpose Internet Mail Extensions (MIME) mail, between OfficeVision for AS/400 and POP clients through the AnyMail/400 mail server framework, which is part of OS/400.

A.2.10.5 DNS and DDNS

OS/400 includes a full-function DNS server. It can be configured for primary, secondary, and caching roles. DNS configuration data from other platforms can easily be migrated to the IBM @server iSeries DNS server. In addition, a migration utility that moves existing IBM @server iSeries host table information into the DNS configuration databases is provided.

OS/400 DNS (Domain Name System) services are enhanced significantly in V5R1. The DNS services are based on the widely used industry-standard DNS reference implementation. Topping the list of enhancements are the new dynamic update capabilities, which have transformed the DNS into a Dynamic DNS (DDNS).

Combined with enhancements made to IBM @server iSeries Dynamic Host Configuration Protocol (DHCP) server that allow it to be configured to send dynamic DNS update transactions, IBM @server iSeries now supports an integrated Dynamic IP solution that automatically manages TCP/IP addresses and their associated DNS host names on your networks.

With OS/400 V5R1, you have the choice of running a DNS server based on the BIND Version 4.9.3 or BIND Version 8.2.3. With V5R1, the DNS server (BIND 8.2.3) runs as a UNIX application under the Portable Application

Solutions Environment (PASE). PASE provides a run-time environment for UNIX applications, switching the IBM @server iSeries main processor from OS/400 RISC mode to UNIX RISC mode. By using this implementation, newer BIND versions can be implemented in OS/400 as soon as they become available.

A.2.10.6 DHCP

Deploying DHCP to centrally control all TCP/IP workstation configuration tasks can dramatically reduce the cost of managing a TCP/IP network. DHCP is a standard protocol supported natively by most popular workstations, including Windows 95/NT, UNIX, and IBM Network Station. Using DHCP, all IP configuration data (IP addresses, subnet masks, default routers, and so on) is dynamically assigned when new workstations are added to the network.   Furthermore, DHCP can automatically recover and recycle network resources when workstations are removed from the network. These capabilities eliminate the time-consuming and error-prone task of manual workstation configuration.

OS/400 includes a full-function DHCP server with an intuitive GUI administrative interface. OS/400 also comes with a DHCP relay agent (also called a BOOTP relay agent), which can be deployed to route DHCP requests from multiple subnetworks to one or more central DHCP servers.

A.2.10.7 Telnet client and server

The Telnet protocol allows a system (the Telnet client) to access and use the resources of a remote system (the Telnet server) as if the Telnet client's workstation were locally connected to the remote system. IBM @server iSeries Telnet provides both the Telnet client and the Telnet server functions. The Telnet protocol provides a mechanism for the client and server to negotiate options that control the operating characteristics of a Telnet connection. Among other things, these negotiations involve determining the best terminal type supported by both the client and server.

Depending on the terminal type negotiated, the IBM @server iSeries Telnet client operates in one of the following full-screen modes: 3270, 5250, VT100 or VT220. The IBM @server iSeries Telnet server operates in ASCII line mode or in one of the following full-screen modes: 3270, 5250 or VT100. The functions available in a Telnet session depend on the operating mode. Security and automation features are included in the IBM @server iSeries Telnet 5250 server.

Registered Telnet server exits for both session initialization and session termination. These exits require only that a customer-written user exit program be registered at the proper exit point. No changes are needed for the connecting Telnet client emulator, so existing clients can immediately benefit from this feature.

Virtual Device selection by the attaching client (or a registered Telnet server exit program) provides for more traditional job-routing to preferred subsystems and allows for associated work management tuning. With Virtual Device selection, preferred code page, character set, and keyboard attributes can be established on a per session basis, thereby offering greater flexibility in national language support.

Printer Passthru support consists of two new terminal (IBM 3812-1 and IBM 5553-B01) which provide additional printer support for the TCP/IP environment. This support allows the Telnet server to provide the client with the flexibility to dynamically create and/or select a virtual printer device through enhanced negotiation, or via assignment by the initialization exit program.

Telnet server supports secure Telnet sessions via SSL. The Telnet server supports server authentication only or both server and client authentication through digital certificates.

A.3 Linux

The Linux operating system is available on a large range of platforms, from small and not so small Intel systems to large-scale zSeries servers. The popularity of Linux is largely attributable to its openness, both in terms of availability and its embracing of open protocols and standards. As a result, developers from around the world contribute to the source of the basic kernel which in turn feeds into the many distributions of Linux that exist today.

This type of development environment allows Linux to offer the latest in TCP/IP standards. Often times, implementations of protocols are first done in Linux as a way of proving the protocol's viability. One of the most interesting functions provided by Linux is the Linux firewall, which also provides NAT support.

A.3.1 Linux firewall

The Linux kernel has support for IP masquerading. This allows a modem connection to the Internet to be shared between several other computers. An extension of this is VPN masquerading, which adds IPsec based and PPTP based support.

The kernel keeps track of which connection goes where. This is known as `ipchains` support. The Linux firewall is thus mainly in the Linux kernel. The ipchains command may be used to allow/deny/masquerade normal or VPN connections based on their IP address and direction.

For more information, see the VPN Masquerade howto file at:

`http://www.redhat.com/mirrors/LDP/HOWTO/VPN-Masquerade-HOWTO-3.html`

A.4 The network computer

An alternative approach to solving the problem of a mobile workforce is not to try and cope with the addressing issues of users' machines being moved around the organization, but to provide fixed workstations around the organization that allow any user to access their own data and applications from anywhere. This is the principle of the *network computer*.

In general terms, a network computer is usually a microprocessor-based system with:

- Local memory (NVRAM)
- No disk (neither hard drive nor diskette)
- Some form of network connection
- Terminal emulation capabilities
- IP-based protocols, such as:
    - TCP
    - FTP
    - Telnet
    - NFS
- A Web browser
- A Java Virtual Machine

In short, a network computer can be thought of as a smart terminal.

All of the software required by a network computer, including the operating system, is stored on a server in the network and downloaded on demand when the network computer is powered on or when the user activates new functions.

The network computer stores only sufficient code in its own local NVRAM (the boot monitor program) to be able to make a BOOTP or DHCP connection to a server, in order to be able to download its operating system kernel. Download of the remainder of the operating system is then carried out using TFTP or NFS, depending upon implementation and configuration.

Typically, having powered on a network computer, a user is presented with a logon panel. On completion of a successful logon, the user is presented with a personalized desktop with his or her own set of application icons. Selection of any of those icons causes an application to be downloaded from a server. (Several different servers may be accessed.)

The network computer relies on TCP/IP protocols for all of its connectivity. As well as using NFS or TFTP to download applications, the applications themselves, if they require communication, will use TCP/IP. SNA emulators, for example, use TN3270 or TN5250 as appropriate.

Although the network computer is not, typically, based on an Intel processor, it is able to access Windows applications on a Windows Terminal Server or Citrix Systems Metaframe, by loading an ICA (independent console architecture) client. In this case, processing of the Windows application is carried out on the NT server itself and only screen changes are delivered to the client. The network computer may run applications remotely on a UNIX-based system, in a similar manner, by downloading an X Window server.

Having all the network computer software stored on a server allows for centralized management and simplified updates of operating system and application code.

IBM's implementation of the network computer, the IBM Network Station, may be booted, and managed from, Windows NT, AIX, OS/400, OS/390, and OS/2 servers. For further information on the IBM Network Station, please refer to the IBM Network Station home page at:

http://www.pc.ibm.com/us/netvista/thinclient.html

Appendix B. Special notices

This publication is intended to help networking specialists understand the TCP/IP protocol suite. The information in this publication is not intended as the specification of any programming interfaces that are provided by any TCP/IP products.

References in this publication to IBM products, programs or services do not imply that IBM intends to make these available in all countries in which IBM operates. Any reference to an IBM product, program, or service is not intended to state or imply that only IBM's product, program, or service may be used. Any functionally equivalent program that does not infringe any of IBM's intellectual property rights may be used instead of the IBM product, program or service.

Information in this book was developed in conjunction with use of the equipment specified, and is limited in application to those specific hardware and software products and levels.

IBM may have patents or pending patent applications covering subject matter in this document. The furnishing of this document does not give you any license to these patents. You can send license inquiries, in writing, to the IBM Director of Licensing, IBM Corporation, North Castle Drive, Armonk, NY 10504-1785.

Licensees of this program who wish to have information about it for the purpose of enabling: (i) the exchange of information between independently created programs and other programs (including this one) and (ii) the mutual use of the information which has been exchanged, should contact IBM Corporation, Dept. 600A, Mail Drop 1329, Somers, NY 10589 USA.

Such information may be available, subject to appropriate terms and conditions, including in some cases, payment of a fee.

The information contained in this document has not been submitted to any formal IBM test and is distributed AS IS. The use of this information or the implementation of any of these techniques is a customer responsibility and depends on the customer's ability to evaluate and integrate them into the customer's operational environment. While each item may have been reviewed by IBM for accuracy in a specific situation, there is no guarantee that the same or similar results will be obtained elsewhere. Customers attempting to adapt these techniques to their own environments do so at their own risk.

Any pointers in this publication to external Web sites are provided for convenience only and do not in any manner serve as an endorsement of these Web sites.

The following terms are trademarks of the International Business Machines Corporation in the United States and/or other countries:

AIX	AnyNet
Application System/400	APPN
AS/400	AT
C/400	CICS
C/370	CT
Current	DB2
Domino	DPI
e (logo)® @	ESCON
IBM ®	IBM.COM
IBM Global Network	Integrated Language Environment
IPDS	Language Environment
Lotus	Lotus Notes
MVS/ESA	Netfinity
Network Station	Notes
Redbooks	Redbooks Logo
OfficeVision	Operating System/2
OS/2	OS/390
OS/400	PAL
Parallel Sysplex	Presentation Manager
RACF	RISC System/6000
RS/6000	SAA
S/390	SecureWay
SPVTAM	System/390
Wave	WebSphere
XT	

The following terms are trademarks of other companies:

Tivoli, Manage. Anything. Anywhere.,The Power To Manage., Anything. Anywhere.,TME, NetView, Cross-Site, Tivoli Ready, Tivoli Certified, Planet Tivoli, and Tivoli Enterprise are trademarks or registered trademarks of Tivoli Systems Inc., an IBM company, in the United States, other countries, or both. In Denmark, Tivoli is a trademark licensed from Kjøbenhavns Sommer - Tivoli A/S.

C-bus is a trademark of Corollary, Inc. in the United States and/or other countries.

Java and all Java-based trademarks and logos are trademarks or registered trademarks of Sun Microsystems, Inc. in the United States and/or other countries.

Microsoft, Windows, Windows NT, and the Windows logo are trademarks of Microsoft Corporation in the United States and/or other countries.

PC Direct is a trademark of Ziff Communications Company in the United States and/or other countries and is used by IBM Corporation under license.

ActionMedia, LANDesk, MMX, Pentium and ProShare are trademarks of Intel Corporation in the United States and/or other countries.

UNIX is a registered trademark in the United States and other countries licensed exclusively through The Open Group.

SET, SET Secure Electronic Transaction, and the SET Logo are trademarks owned by SET Secure Electronic Transaction LLC.

Other company, product, and service names may be trademarks or service marks of others.

Appendix C. Related publications

The publications listed in this section are considered particularly suitable for a more detailed discussion of the topics covered in this redbook.

C.1 IBM Redbooks

For information on ordering these publications see "How to get IBM Redbooks" on page 921.

- *Administering DCE and DFS 2.1 for AIX (and OS/2 Clients)*, SG24-4714
- *AS/400 Mail: Multiple SMTP Domains Behind a Firewall*, SG24-5643
- *AS/400 TCP/IP Autoconfiguration: DNS and DHCP Support*, SG24-5147
- *Beyond DHCP - Work Your TCP/IP Internetwork with Dynamic IP*, SG24-5280
- *A Comprehensive Guide to Virtual Private Networks, Volume I: IBM Firewall, Server and Client Solutions*, SG24-5201
- *Data Sharing: Using the OS/390 Network File System*, SG24-5262
- *DCE Cell Design Considerations*, SG24-4746
- *IBM Communications Server for OS/390 TCP/IP Implementation Guide, Volume 1,* SG24-5227
- *IBM Communications Server for OS/390 V2R10 TCP/IP Implementation Guide, Volume 2*, SG24-5228
- *IBM Router Interoperability and Migration Examples*, SG24-5865
- *IP Network Design Guide,* SG24-2580
- *Internetworking over ATM: An Introduction*, SG24-4699
- *Local Area Network Concepts and Products: Routers and Gateways*, SG24-4755
- *Load-Balancing Internet Servers*, SG24-4993
- *Managing OS/390 TCP/IP with SNMP*, SG24-5866
- *Migrating Subarea Networks to an IP Infrastructure Using Enterprise Extender*, SG24-5957
- *MPTN Architecture Tutorial and Product Implementations*, SG24-4170
- *OS/390 eNetwork Communications Server V2R7 TCP/IP Implementation Guide, Volume 3*, SG24-5229

- *OSA-Express Implementation Guide*, SG24-5948

- *Secure e-business in TCP/IP Networks on OS/390 and z/OS*, SG24-5383

- *Security on the Web Using DCE Technology*, SG24-4949

- *The Technical Side of Being an Internet Service Provider*, SG24-2133

- *TCP/IP in a Sysplex*, SG24-5235

- *Understanding LDAP*, SG24-4986

- *Understanding OSF DCE 1.1 for AIX and OS/2*, SG24-4616

- *Understanding Optical Communications*, SG24-5230

C.2 IBM Redbooks collections

Redbooks are also available on the following CD-ROMs. Click the CD-ROMs button at ibm.com/redbooks for information about all the CD-ROMs offered, updates and formats.

CD-ROM Title	Collection Kit Number
IBM System/390 Redbooks Collection	SK2T-2177
IBM Networking Redbooks Collection	SK2T-6022
IBM Transaction Processing and Data Management Redbooks Collection	SK2T-8038
IBM Lotus Redbooks Collection	SK2T-8039
Tivoli Redbooks Collection	SK2T-8044
IBM AS/400 Redbooks Collection	SK2T-2849
IBM Netfinity Hardware and Software Redbooks Collection	SK2T-8046
IBM RS/6000 Redbooks Collection	SK2T-8043
IBM Application Development Redbooks Collection	SK2T-8037
IBM Enterprise Storage and Systems Management Solutions	SK3T-3694

C.3 Other resources

These publications are also relevant as further information sources:

- *iSeries Handbook*, GA19-5486

- *LAN Technical Reference: 802.2 and NetBIOS Application Program Interfaces*, SC30-3587

- *Network and e-business Products Reference*, GX28-8002

- Albitz, et al., *DNS and BIND, Fourth Edition*, O'Reilly & Associates, Inc., 2001, ISBN 0-596-00158-4

- Bates, *Broadband Telecommunications Handbook*, McGraw-Hill Professional Publishing, 1999, ISBN 0-0713-46481

- Black, *IP Routing Protocols: RIP, OSPF, BGP, PNNI and Cisco Routing Protocols*, Prentice Hall, 2000, ISBN 0-130-14248-4

- Comer, *Internetworking with TCP/IP, Volume I, Principles, Protocols and Architecture, Fourth Edition*, Prentice-Hall, Inc., 2000, ISBN 0-13-018380-6

- Comer, et al., *Internetworking with TCP/IP, Volume II, Design, Implementation, and Internals, Third Edition*, Prentice-Hall, Inc., 1998, ISBN 0-13-973843-6

- Comer et al., *Internetworking with TCP/IP, Volume III, Client Server Programming and Applications, Windows Sockets Version*, Prentice-Hall, Inc., 1997, ISBN 0-13-848714-6

- Costales, et al., *sendmail, Second Edition*, O'Reilly & Associates, Inc., 1997, ISBN 1-56592-222-0

- Cypser, *Communications for Cooperating Systems - OSI, SNA and TCP/IP*, Addison-Wesley, Publishing Company, Inc., 1992, ISBN 0-201-50775-7

- December, et al., *HTML 3.2 & CGI Unleashed*, Sams.net Publishing, 1996, ISBN 1-57521-177-7

- Halabi, et al., *Internet Routing Architectures, Second Edition*, Cisco Press, 2000, ISBN 1-57870-233-X

- Huitema, *IPv6: The New Internet Protocol, Second Edition*, Prentice-Hall, Inc., 1998, ISBN 0-13-850505-5

- Hunt, et al., *TCP/IP Network Administration, Second Edition*, O'Reilly & Associates, Inc., 1995, ISBN 1-56592-322-7

- Schneier, *Applied Cryptography: Protocols, Algorithms, and Source Code in C*, second edition, John Wiley & Sons, Inc., 1995, ISBN 0-471-11709-9

- Stevens, *TCP/IP Illustrated, Volume I, The Protocols*, Addison Wesley, 1994, ISBN 0-201-63346-9

- Stevens, et al., *TCP/IP Illustrated, Volume II, The Implementation*, Addison Wesley, 1995, ISBN 0-201-63354-X

- Stevens, et al., *TCP/IP Illustrated, Volume III, TCP for Transactions, HTTP, NNTP, and the UNIX Domain Protocols*, Addison Wesley, 1996, ISBN 0-201-63495-3

- Thomas, *IPng and the TCP/IP Protocols*, John Wiley & Sons, Inc., 1996, ISBN 0-471-13088-5

- Wireless Application Protocol Forum Ltd, *Official Wireless Application Protocol: The Complete Standard with Searchable CD-ROM*, John Wiley & Sons, 1999, ISBN 0-471-32755-7

- Zwicky, et al., *Building Internet Firewalls, Second Edition*, O'Reilly & Associates, Inc., 2000, ISBN 1-565-92871-7

C.4 Referenced Web sites

These Web sites are also relevant as further information sources:

- http://www.ietf.org/
- http://www.iana.org/
- http://www.irtf.org/
- http://www.isoc.org/
- http://www.iab.org/

How to get IBM Redbooks

This section explains how both customers and IBM employees can find out about IBM Redbooks, redpieces, and CD-ROMs. A form for ordering books and CD-ROMs by fax or e-mail is also provided.

- **Redbooks Web Site** ibm.com/redbooks

  Search for, view, download, or order hardcopy/CD-ROM Redbooks from the Redbooks Web site. Also read redpieces and download additional materials (code samples or diskette/CD-ROM images) from this Redbooks site.

  Redpieces are Redbooks in progress; not all Redbooks become redpieces and sometimes just a few chapters will be published this way. The intent is to get the information out much quicker than the formal publishing process allows.

- **E-mail Orders**

  Send orders by e-mail including information from the IBM Redbooks fax order form to:

	e-mail address
In United States or Canada	pubscan@us.ibm.com
Outside North America	Contact information is in the "How to Order" section at this site: http://www.elink.ibmlink.ibm.com/pbl/pbl

- **Telephone Orders**

United States (toll free)	1-800-879-2755
Canada (toll free)	1-800-IBM-4YOU
Outside North America	Country coordinator phone number is in the "How to Order" section at this site: http://www.elink.ibmlink.ibm.com/pbl/pbl

- **Fax Orders**

United States (toll free)	1-800-445-9269
Canada	1-403-267-4455
Outside North America	Fax phone number is in the "How to Order" section at this site: http://www.elink.ibmlink.ibm.com/pbl/pbl

This information was current at the time of publication, but is continually subject to change. The latest information may be found at the Redbooks Web site.

IBM Intranet for Employees

IBM employees may register for information on workshops, residencies, and Redbooks by accessing the IBM Intranet Web site at http://w3.itso.ibm.com/ and clicking the ITSO Mailing List button. Look in the Materials repository for workshops, presentations, papers, and Web pages developed and written by the ITSO technical professionals; click the Additional Materials button. Employees may access MyNews at http://w3.ibm.com/ for redbook, residency, and workshop announcements.

IBM Redbooks fax order form

Please send me the following:

Title	Order Number	Quantity

First name _____ Last name _____

Company _____

Address _____

City _____ Postal code _____ Country _____

Telephone number _____ Telefax number _____ VAT number _____

☐ Invoice to customer number _____

☐ Credit card number _____

Credit card expiration date _____ Card issued to _____ Signature _____

We accept American Express, Diners, Eurocard, Master Card, and Visa. Payment by credit card not available in all countries. Signature mandatory for credit card payment.

Abbreviations and acronyms

IAAA	Authentication, Authorization and Accounting
AAL	ATM Adaptation Layer
AFS	Andrews File System
AH	Authentication Header
AIX	Advanced Interactive Executive Operating System
API	Application Programming Interface
APPN	Advanced Peer-to-Peer Networking
ARP	Address Resolution Protocol
ARPA	Advanced Research Projects Agency
AS	Autonomous System
ASCII	American Standard Code for Information Interchange
ASN.1	Abstract Syntax Notation 1
AS/400	Application System/400
ATM	Asynchronous Transfer Mode
BGP	Border Gateway Protocol
BIND	Berkeley Internet Name Domain
BNF	Backus-Naur Form
BRI	Basic Rate Interface
BSD	Berkeley Software Distribution
CA	Certification Authority
CBC	Cipher Block Chaining
CCITT	Comité Consultatif International Télégraphique et Téléphonique (now ITU-T)
CDMF	Commercial Data Masking Facility
CERN	Conseil Européen pour la Recherche Nucléaire
CGI	Common Gateway Interface
CHAP	Challenge Handshake Authentication Protocol
CICS	Customer Information Control System
CIDR	Classless Inter-Domain Routing
CIX	Commercial Internet Exchange
CLNP	Connectionless Network Protocol
CORBA	Common Object Request Broker Architecture
COS	Class of Service
CPCS	Common Part Convergence Sublayer
CPU	Central Processing Unit
CSMA/CD	Carrier Sense Multiple Access with Collision Detection
DARPA	Defense Advanced Research Projects Agency
DCE	Distributed Computing Environment
DCE	Data Circuit-terminating Equipment
DDN	Defense Data Network

DDNS	Dynamic Domain Name System	**DTP**	Data Transfer Process
DEN	Directory-Enabled Networking	**DVMRP**	Distance Vector Multicast Routing Protocol
DES	Digital Encryption Standard	**EBCDIC**	Extended Binary Communication Data Interchange Code
DFS	Distributed File Service		
DHCP	Dynamic Host Configuration Protocol	**EGP**	Exterior Gateway Protocol
DLC	Data Link Control	**ESCON**	Enterprise Systems Connection
DLCI	Data Link Connection Identifier	**ESP**	Encapsulating Security Payload
DLL	Dynamic Link Library	**FDDI**	Fiber Distributed Data Interface
DLSw	Data Link Switching		
DLUR	Dependent LU Requester	**FQDN**	Fully Qualified Domain Name
DLUS	Dependent LU Server	**FR**	Frame Relay
DME	Distributed Management Environment	**FTP**	File Transfer Protocol
		GGP	Gateway-to-Gateway Protocol
DMI	Desktop Management Interface	**GMT**	Greenwich Mean Time
DMTF	Desktop Management Task Force	**GSM**	Group Special Mobile
		GUI	Graphical User Interface
DMZ	Demilitarized Zone	**HDLC**	High-level Data Link Control
DNS	Domain Name Server		
DOD	U.S. Department of Defense	**HMAC**	Hashed Message Authentication Code
DOI	Domain of Interpretation	**HPR**	High Performance Routing
DOS	Disk Operating System	**HTML**	Hypertext Markup Language
DSA	Digital Signature Algorithm		
DSAP	Destination Service Access Point	**HTTP**	Hypertext Transfer Protocol
DSS	Digital Signature Standard	**IAB**	Internet Activities Board
DTE	Data Terminal Equipment	**IAC**	Interpret As Command

IANA	Internet Assigned Numbers Authority	**IPv4**	Internet Protocol Version 4
IBM	International Business Machines Corporation	**IPv6**	Internet Protocol Version 6
ICMP	Internet Control Message Protocol	**IPX**	Internetwork Packet Exchange
ICSS	Internet Connection Secure Server	**IRFT**	Internet Research Task Force
ICV	Integrity Check Value	**ISAKMP**	Internet Security Association and Key Management Protocol
IDEA	International Data Encryption Algorithm		
IDLC	Integrated Data Link Control	**ISDN**	Integrated Services Digital Network
IDRP	Inter-Domain Routing Protocol	**ISO**	International Organization for Standardization
IEEE	Institute of Electrical and Electronics Engineers	**ISP**	Internet Service Provider
IESG	Internet Engineering Steering Group	**ITSO**	International Technical Support Organization
IETF	Internet Engineering Task Force	**ITU-T**	International Telecommunication Union - Telecommunication Standardization Sector (was CCITT)
IGMP	Internet Group Management Protocol		
IGN	IBM Global Network		
IGP	Interior Gateway Protocol	**IV**	Initialization Vector
IIOP	Internet Inter-ORB Protocol	**JDBC**	Java Database Connectivity
IKE	Internet Key Exchange	**JDK**	Java Development Toolkit
IMAP	Internet Message Access Protocol	**JES**	Job Entry System
		JIT	Java Just-in-Time Compiler
IMS	Information Management System	**JMAPI**	Java Management API
IP	Internet Protocol	**JVM**	Java Virtual Machine
IPC	Interprocess Communication	**JPEG**	Joint Photographic Experts Group
IPSec	IP Security Architecture	**LAC**	L2TP Access Concentrator

LAN	Local Area Network	**MPTN**	Multiprotocol Transport Network
LAPB	Link Access Protocol Balanced	**MS-CHAP**	Microsoft Challenge Handshake Authentication Protocol
LCP	Link Control Protocol		
LDAP	Lightweight Directory Access Protocol	**MTA**	Message Transfer Agent
LE	LAN Emulation (ATM)	**MTU**	Maximum Transmission Unit
LLC	Logical Link Layer	**MVS**	Multiple Virtual Storage Operating System
LNS	L2TP Network Server		
LPD	Line Printer Daemon	**NAT**	Network Address Translation
LPR	Line Printer Requester		
LSAP	Link Service Access Point	**NBDD**	NetBIOS Datagram Distributor
L2F	Layer 2 Forwarding	**NBNS**	NetBIOS Name Server
L2TP	Layer 2 Tunneling Protocol	**NCF**	Network Computing Framework
MAC	Message Authentication Code	**NCP**	Network Control Protocol
MAC	Medium Access Control	**NCSA**	National Computer Security Association
MD2	RSA Message Digest 2 Algorithm	**NDIS**	Network Driver Interface Specification
MD5	RSA Message Digest 5 Algorithm	**NetBIOS**	Network Basic Input/Output System
MIB	Management Information Base	**NFS**	Network File System
MILNET	Military Network	**NIC**	Network Information Center
MIME	Multipurpose Internet Mail Extensions	**NIS**	Network Information Systems
MLD	Multicast Listener Discovery	**NIST**	National Institute of Standards and Technology
MOSPF	Multicast Open Shortest Path First	**NMS**	Network Management Station
MPC	Multi-Path Channel		
MPEG	Moving Pictures Experts Group	**NNTP**	Network News Transfer Protocol
MPLS	Multiprotocol Label Switching	**NRZ**	Non-Return-to-Zero
MPOA	Multiprotocol over ATM		

NRZI	Non-Return-to-Zero Inverted	**PIM**	Protocol Independent Multicast
NSA	National Security Agency	**PKCS**	Public Key Cryptosystem
NSAP	Network Service Access Point	**PKI**	Public Key Infrastructure
NSF	National Science Foundation	**PNNI**	Private Network-to-Network Interface
NTP	Network Time Protocol		
NVT	Network Virtual Terminal	**POP**	Post Office Protocol
		POP	Point-of-Presence
ODBC	Open Database Connectivity	**PPP**	Point-to-Point Protocol
ODI	Open Datalink Interface	**PPTP**	Point-to-Point Tunneling Protocol
OEM	Original Equipment Manufacturer	**PRI**	Primary Rate Interface
		PSDN	Packet Switching Data Network
ONC	Open Network Computing		
ORB	Object Request Broker	**PSTN**	Public Switched Telephone Network
OSA	Open Systems Adapter	**PVC**	Permanent Virtual Circuit
OSI	Open Systems Interconnect		
OSF	Open Software Foundation	**QLLC**	Qualified Logical Link Control
OSPF	Open Shortest Path First	**QoS**	Quality of Service
		RACF	Resource Access Control Facility
OS/2	Operating System/2	**RADIUS**	Remote Authentication Dial-In User Service
OS/390	Operating System for the System/390 platform		
		RAM	Random Access Memory
OS/400	Operating System for the AS/400 platform	**RARP**	Reverse Address Resolution Protocol
PAD	Packet Assembler/ Disassembler	**RAS**	Remote Access Service
		RC2	RSA Rivest Cipher 2 Algorithm
PAP	Password Authentication Protocol	**RC4**	RSA Rivest Cipher 4 Algorithm
PDU	Protocol Data Unit		
PGP	Pretty Good Privacy	**REXEC**	Remote Execution Command Protocol
PI	Protocol Interpreter		

RFC	Request for Comments	**SMTP**	Simple Mail Transfer Protocol
RIP	Routing Information Protocol	**SNA**	System Network Architecture
RIPE	Réseaux IP Européens	**SNAP**	Subnetwork Access Protocol
RISC	Reduced Instruction-Set Computer	**SNG**	Secured Network Gateway (former product name of the IBM eNetwork Firewall)
ROM	Read-only Memory		
RPC	Remote Procedure Call		
RSH	Remote Shell	**SNMP**	Simple Network Management Protocol
RSVP	Resource Reservation Protocol	**SOA**	Start of Authority
RS/6000	IBM RISC System/6000	**SONET**	Synchronous Optical Network
RTCP	Realtime Control Protocol	**SOCKS**	SOCK-et-S (An internal NEC development name that remained after release)
RTP	Realtime Protocol		
SA	Security Association		
SAP	Service Access Point	**SPI**	Security Parameter Index
SDH	Synchronous Digital Hierarchy	**SSL**	Secure Sockets Layer
SDLC	Synchronous Data Link Control	**SSAP**	Source Service Access Point
SET	Secure Electronic Transaction	**SSP**	Switch-to-Switch Protocol
SGML	Standard Generalized Markup Language	**SSRC**	Synchronization Source
		SVC	Switched Virtual Circuit
SHA	Secure Hash Algorithm	**TACACS**	Terminal Access Controller Access Control System
S-HTTP	Secure Hypertext Transfer Protocol		
SLA	Service Level Agreement	**TCP**	Transmission Control Protocol
SLIP	Serial Line Internet Protocol	**TCP/IP**	Transmission Control Protocol/Internet Protocol
SMI	Structure of Management Information		
		TFTP	Trivial File Transfer Protocol
S-MIME	Secure Multipurpose Internet Mail Extension	**TLPB**	Transport-Layer Protocol Boundary

TLS	Transport Layer Security	*X11*	X Window System Version 11
TOS	Type of Service	*X.25*	CCITT Packet Switching Standard
TRD	Transit Routing Domain		
TTL	Time to Live	*X.400*	CCITT and ISO Message-handling Service Standard
UDP	User Datagram Protocol		
UID	Unique Identifier	*X.500*	ITU and ISO Directory Service Standard
URI	Uniform Resource Identifier	*X.509*	ITU and ISO Digital Certificate Standard
URL	Uniform Resource Locator	*3DES*	Triple Digital Encryption Standard
UT	Universal Time		
VC	Virtual Circuit		
VM	Virtual Machine Operating System		
VPN	Virtual Private Network		
VRML	Virtual Reality Modeling Language		
VRRP	Virtual Router Redundancy Protocol		
VTAM	Virtual Telecommunications Access Method		
WAE	Wireless Application Environment		
WAP	Wireless Application Protocol		
WSP	Wireless Session Protocol		
WTP	Wireless Transaction Protocol		
WAN	Wide Area Network		
WWW	World Wide Web		
XDR	External Data Representation		
XML	Extensible Markup Language		

Index

Numerics

2210   642
2210/2216 Router
    Bandwidth Reservation System (BRS)   642
    Enterprise Extender   641
    High Performance Routing (HPR)   641
2216   642
6Bone   612

A

A5 algorithm   664
AAA security model   765
abbreviations   923
Abstract Syntax Notation One (ASN.1)   526
accounting   766
acronyms   923
address allocation   127
Address Resolution (ATMARP and InATMARP)   45
Address Resolution Protocol (ARP)
    algorithm   118
    BOOTP   122
    cache   114
    Ethernet   30, 115
    Frame Relay   42
    gratuitous ARP   639
    IEEE 802.2 standard   30
    IEEE 802.x standards   115
    IPv6   581
    Mobile IP   639
    packet   115, 120
    proxy ARP   639
    Proxy-ARP   118
    reply   114
    request   114
Agent Solicitation message   630
AIX   299
algorithm
    block   663
    Diffie-Hellman   668
    Digital Signature   674, 730
    key-exchange   667
    public-key   665, 666, 667
    RSA   667
    stream   663
    symmetric   663, 664

    TCP congestion control   221
Andrew File System (AFS)   361
    access control list (ACL)   384
    authentication   383
    cell   383
    client cache   383
    Kerberos   383
    management utilities   384
    name space   383
    remote procedure call (RPC)   383
    replication   384
Anonymous FTP   371
anycast   82
Apache   429, 447
application layer   6
application level gateway   680
application programming interface (API)
    sockets   202
    TCP   220
    UDP   206
application protocols   8
architecture   3
    application   6
    architectural model   6, 8
    internetwork   7
    layers   5
    network interface   7
    transport   6
arithmetic, modular   667
ARPANET   13
    Network Working Group   12
ASN.1   526
Assigned Numbers RFC   703
Asynchronous Transfer Mode   44
athentication   684
ATM   44, 49, 51, 52, 54, 56
atm   48
ATM LAN Emulation   54
ATMARP   45
ATM-Attached Host Functional Group (AHFG)   61
attacks   656
audio   430
Authentication   656
authentication   35, 329, 352, 383, 419, 640, 660, 662, 665, 670, 671, 741, 747, 765, 774, 882
    IP Control Protocol (IPCP)   36
    IPCP   36

931

Authentication Header (AH)
  Authentication Data   705
  Authentication Data field   672
  combinations with ESP   715
  Flags field   702
  Fragment Offset   702
  header checksum   702
  header format   702
  HMAC-MD5-96   705
  HMAC-SHA-1-96   705
  Integrity Check Value (ICV)   705
  IP fragment   702
  IPv6 environment   707
  Keyed MD5   705
  mutable fields   702, 706
  Next Header field   703
  Payload Length   703
  replay protection   704
  Reserved field   703
  Security Parameter Index (SPI)   703
  Sequence Number   704
  Time To Live (TTL)   702
  transform   698
  transport mode   705, 716
  tunnel mode   705, 716
  Type of Service (TOS)   702
authentication method   726
authorization   329, 352, 656, 765, 793
  Simple Authentication and Security Layer
  (SASL)   330
autoconfiguration   591
automatic VIPA takeover   893
Autonomous systems   138
availability   843, 884

B

Backus-Naur Form (BNF)   390
balancing   833, 883
Bandwidth Reservation System (BRS)   642
base-64   438
Berkeley Internet Name Domain (BIND)   304
Berkeley Software Distribution (BSD)   13
BGMP   253
BGP   180
  aggregation   193
  confederations   194
  Multiprotocol extensions   253
  protocol description   185

  route reflectors   196
  synchronization   191
block algorithm   663
Bluetooth   27
BNF   390
BOOTP forwarding   125, 526
BOOTP relay agent   526
BOOTP server   121
Bootstrap Protocol (BOOTP)   121
  ARP   122
  BOOTPREQUEST message   125
  BOOTREPLY message   124
  DHCP interoperability   136
  forwarding   81, 125
  message format   123
  Network Computer   911
  TFTP   122
Border Gateway Multicast Protocol   253
Border Gateway Protocol   180
Border Gateway Protocol (BGP)
  protocol description   185
  Version 4 (BGP-4)   89
bridge   10
broadcast
  description   81
  reverse path forwarding algorithm   82
brute-force attack   655, 663
bulk encryption   667

C

cache   361, 383, 884
  ARP cache   114
  HTTP caching   433, 439
  ICMPv6 neighbor cache   584
care-of address   629
CBC   663
CCITT   12
CDMF   359, 664
Cell   49
Center Based tree algorithm   237
CERN   429
certificate   656, 724, 753
certificate authority   730, 774
certification authority (CA)   675
Channel Data Link Control (CDLC)
  description   889
Channel Protocols   889
Channel-to-Channel (CTC)   890

checksum
    IPv6   564
        TCP datagram   214
        UDP datagram   205
chicken and egg problem   122
CICS   277
CICS Socket Interface   277
cipher   661
    restricted   661
Cipher Block Chaining (CBC)   663
ciphertext   666
circuit level gateway   680
Cisco
    Local Director   832
Classical IP over ATM   48, 59
classless inter-domain routing (CIDR)
    IP prefix   88
    transit routing domains (TRDs)   88
cleartext   661
client/server model   9, 261
CLNP   38, 40
codebook   663
collision-resistant   669
combined tunnel   718
Commercial Data Masking Facility (CDMF)   664
Commercial Internet Exchange (CIX)   17
Common Gateway Interface (CGI)   442
Common information Model (CIM)   335
Common Link Access to Workstation (CLAW)   890
Common Object Request Broker Architecture (CORBA)   445
Communication Storage Manager (CSM)   891
Connections
    ATM   44
    DLSW   642
    FDDI   32
    Frame Relay   40
    ISDN   36
    MPC+   44
    MPOA   58
    PPP   34
    SLIP   33
    SONET   43
    X.25   38
Convergence   148
counting to infinity   148
Cross-System Coupling Facility (XCF)   892
cryptanalysis   656, 661
cryptanalyst   677

crypto couple   662
cryptographic algorithm   661
cryptography   660, 669
    strong   661
cryptography, strong   661
cryptosystem   667, 676
CSNET
    mail gateway service   390
Customer Information Control System (CICS)   277

D

DARPA   12
Data Encryption Standard (DES)   663, 758
Data Link Connection Identifier (DLCI)   40
Data Link Switching
    Switch-to-Switch Protocol   642
        IEEE 802.2 LLC Type 2   643
        NetBIOS   642
        SDLC   643
data-link layer   7
DCA   13
DDN Network Information Center   279
DDNS   299
decryption   660, 661
Default Forwarder Function Group (DFFG)   61
default router   62, 876
Defense Advanced Research Projects Agency (DARPA)   12
Defense Communication Agency (DCA)   13
Demilitarized Zone (DMZ)   693
denial-of-service attack   655, 656, 702, 722, 772
Department of Defense (DoD)   13
DES   359, 663, 667, 676, 758
destination options extension header   707, 714
DHCPv6   598
dictionary attack   655
Differentiated Services
    Behavior Aggregate (BA) classifier   810
    boundary node   814
    byte, DS   812
    class of service   805
    classifier   809, 813
    directory client   818
    directory information   818
    directory server   818
    DS boundary node   809
    DS byte   805, 810, 812, 818, 820
    DS domain   805, 808, 812, 818

DS marker 810
egress node 809
Expedited Forwarding (EF) PHB 808
ingress node 809, 820
interior component 812
IPsec 819
LDAP 818
multi-field (MF) classifier 810
packet dropper 810
packet shaper 810
Per-Hop Behavior (PHB) 806
PHB 806
policing 810
policy information 818
predictable performance 805
QoS 805, 808, 812
scalable service discrimination 805
security 819
Service Level Agreement (SLA) 805
SLA 809, 812, 818
source domain 813
token bucket filter 810
TOS octet 805
traffic class octet 805
traffic conditioner 810, 813
Traffic Conditioning Agreement (TCA) 812
traffic meter 810
traffic prioritization algorithm 812
traffic profile 810
Diffie-Hellman 667, 668, 676, 727, 728, 732, 733, 735, 736, 738
dig 299
digital certificate 675
digital envelope 671
digital signature 304, 665, 671, 731
Digital Signature Standard 672, 723
Direct Memory Access (DMA) 891
Directory Access Protocol (DAP) 317
disconnected use model 421
discrete logarithms 667, 669
diskless host 121
Distance Vector Multicast Routing Protocol 238
distance vector protocol 145
Distance vector routing 142
Distributed Computing Environment (DCE) 327
    Access Control List Facility 353
    Application Program Interfaces 349
    Architectural Components 349
    authentication 352

Authentication Service 353, 354
authorization 352
Backup Courier Time Server 360
cache manager 361
CDS namespace 351
cell 332, 350, 361
Cell Directory Service (CDS) 332, 350
Courier Time Server 360
DCE architecture 316
DFS administrative domains 361
Directory Service 316, 349
Distributed File Service 349
Distributed Time Service 349
Episode File System 362
Extended Privilege Attribute Certificate (EPAC) 355
File Naming 362
Fileset Location Database (FLDB) 351
Global Directory Agent (GDA) 332, 350
Global Directory Service (GDS) 350
Global Time Server 360
Interface Definition Language (IDL) 359
Internet Domain Name Services (DNS) 352
Kerberos 353
Local File System (LFS) 362
Local Time Server 360
Login Facility 354
Master Replica 350
NFS interoperability 361
Privilege Service 353
Privilege Ticket Granting Ticket (PTGT) 356
Public Key Support 357
Read-only Replica 350
registry 353
Registry Service 353
Remote Procedure Call 349
Security Service 349
Threads 349
Ticket Granting Ticket (TGT) 355
Transport Services 349
X.500 333, 352
X/Open Directory Service (XDS) 333
distributed DVIPA 894
DIXIE 317
DLSW 642
DNS
    client authentication 299
    DNS security 299
    domain name resolution 284

dynamic DNS   299
hierarchical namespace   281
name resolver   282
name server   282
top-level domains   281
transport   285
DOI   725, 727
Domain Internet Groper   299
Domain Name System (DNS)   24, 332
    applications   299
        dig   299
        host   299
        nslookup   299
    authoritative answer   286
    Berkeley Internet Name Domain (BIND)   304
    cache   285, 287, 884
    country domains   282
    DDNS extensions   300
    distributed namespace   283
    example   294
    fully qualified domain name   281
        example   297
    generic domains   281
    gethostbyaddr()   285
    gethostbyname()   285
    hierarchical namespace   280
    IPv6   602
    IPv6 extensions   595
    IPv6 inverse lookups   595
    iterative query   286
    message compression   294
    message format   301
    messages   290
        description   290, 294
    name resolver   284
        full resolver   285
        operation   286
        stub resolver   285
    name server   284
        caching-only   287
        operation   287
        primary   287
        secondary   287
    network object   288
    non-authoritative answer   286
    non-recursive query   286
    Pointer Queries   283
    print='the .in-addr.arpa domain'.in-addr.arpa
    282

recursive query   286
resource record (RR)
    description   288, 289
    format   288, 308, 595
resource record for IPv6   595
root name server   283
round-robin DNS   883
time-to-live (TTL)   287, 289
transport   298
TTL   883
zone   283
zone data   297
zone of authority   283
zone transfer   287
Domain of Interpretation (DOI)   725, 727
DSA   674
DSS   672, 674
DUAL algorithm   177
DVMRP   238
Dynamic DNS   299
Dynamic Domain Name System (DDNS)   629
    A record update   313
    Berkeley Internet Name Domain (BIND)   304
    DDNS client   304
    DHCP option 81   314
    DHCP server   304
    digital signature   304
    DNS extensions   300
    DNS update message   301
    Dynamic Presecured Mode   306
    dynamic secured mode   306
    IBM DDNS UPDATE message format   312
    IBM Dynamic IP   308
    IBM implementation   311
    KEY resource record   308
    KEY resource record format   308
    MD5   308
    mechanism   304
    mixed environment   315
    proxy A record update   313
    PTR record update   313
    public key   308
    resource record format   308
    RSA   308
    RSA public-key   304
    security   306
    SIG resource record   309
    SIG resource record format   309
    TTL   310

Dynamic Host Configuration Protocol (DHCP) 121,
126, 314, 629
    address allocation 127
    BOOTP forwarding 125
    BOOTP interoperability 136
    BOUND state 133
    client/server interaction 130, 133, 134
    DHCPACK message 130
    DHCPDECLINE message 130
    DHCPDISCOVER message 130
    DHCPINFORM message 130
    DHCPNACK message 130
    DHCPRELEASE message 130
    DHCPREQUEST message 130
    DHCPv6
        DHCP Advertise 600
        DHCP Reconfigure 600
        DHCP Release 600
        DHCP Reply 600
        DHCP Request 600
        DHCP Solicit 599
    IBM implementation 311
    ICMPv6 591
    INIT state 131
    lease time 133
    message format 128
    Message Types 129
    Network Computer 911
    option 81 314
    proxy A record update 313
    PTR record update 313
    REBINDING state 133
    RENEWING state 133
    timer 133
Dynamic routing
        140
Dynamic VIPA 894

E
EBGP 183
EBONE 3
e-business 756
ECB 663
Edge Device Functional Group (EDFG) 60
EGP 139, 180
EIGRP 145, 174
EJB 445
Electronic Codebook Mode (ECB) 663

Electronic Mail 387
electronic mail models 421
e-mail 387
Encapsulating Security Payload (ESP)
    authentication 708, 716
    Authentication Data 712
    CDMF 711
    combinations with AH 715
    DES-CBC transform 711
    encryption 708, 711
    ESP authentication data 709
    ESP header 709
    ESP trailer 709
    HMAC-MD5 712
    HMAC-SHA-1 712
    integrity check 708
    Integrity Check Value (ICV) 712
    IP fragment 708
    IPv6 environment 714
    Next Header field 711
    Pad Length 711
    Padding 711
    Payload Data 711
    replay protection 711
    Security Parameter Index (SPI) 709
    Sequence Number 710
    transform 698
    transport mode 712, 716
    tunnel mode 712, 716
encapsulation 700
encryption 320, 329, 660, 661, 671, 741
        656
encryption algorithm 677, 726
encryption key 661
Enhanced Interior Gateway Routing Protocol 174
Enterprise Extender 641, 893
Enterprise JavaBean 445
Entity 536
Entity EJBs 446
ephemeral port 10, 202
Ethernet
    802.2 Logical Link Control (LLC) 30
    ARP 30, 115
    DIX 29, 115
    DSAP 30
    frame formats 29
    header fields 29
    IEEE 802.3 standard 29, 31
    IEEE 802.4 standard 31

IEEE 802.5 standard   31
IEEE 802.x standards   123
IPv6   581
LSAP   30
protocol-type number   29
SNAP   30
SSAP   30
Sub-Network Access Protocol (SNAP)   30
Extended TACACS   767
Extensible Markup Language (XML)   441
Exterior Gateway Protocol   180
Exterior Gateway Protocols   139

F

factoring   666
FDDI   32
Feasible Successor   175
File Transfer Protocol (FTP)   6, 365, 837
   Anonymous FTP   371
   end the transfer session   369
   login   367
   Network Computer   910
   normal mode   685
   operations   366
   passive mode   368, 685
   proxy   368
   proxy server   684, 685
   reply codes   369
   scenario   370
   subcommands
      cd   367
      close   369
      dir   367
      get   368
      lcd   367
      ls   367
      mode   367
      open   367
      pass   367
      put   368
      quit   369
      site   367
      type   367
      user   367
finger   554
fingerprint   670
firewall   11, 659, 699, 720
   advanced filtering   682

application level gateway   691
application-level gateway   741
athentication   684
bastion host   691, 693
circuit level gateway   687
circuit-level gateway   739
demilitarized zone   693
DMZ   693
dual-homed gateway   690
filter rules   681
FTP normal mode   685
FTP passive mode   685
FTP proxy   684, 685
HTTP proxy   684
IBM Firewall   684
inbound connections   688
introduction   11
logging   684
Network Address Translation (NAT)   694
non-secure network   679
outbound connections   688
packet filtering firewall   689
packet filtering router   693
packet-filtering   680
packet-filtering rules   681
policy   659, 681
proxy   683, 688, 690
screened host firewall   691
screened subnet firewall   693
secure network   679
security ID cards   684
service level filtering   681
SOCKS   688
source/destination level filtering   682
TELNET proxy   685
Flags field   702
flat namespace   279
   geographical domains   282
   organizational domains   281
For Your Information document (FYI)   25
foreign agent   630
forwarding capacity   59
Fragment Offset   702
fragmentation   96
fragmentation extension header   707, 714
Frame Relay
   ARP   42
   Data Link Connection Identifier (DLCI)   40
   Network Level Protocol ID (NLPID)   40

protocol data unit (PDU)   40
Subnetwork Access Protocol (SNAP)   40
virtual circuit   40

G
gated   199
gateway   10, 11, 121
gateway address   121
GetBulkRequest   537
GIF   409
Gigabit Ethernet   891
Graphical User Interface (GUI)   547
gratuitous ARP   639
GUI   547

H
hacker   656, 660
hash function   669, 670, 673, 733
hash value   669, 672, 673
Hashed Message Authentication Code (HMAC)
673
header checksum   702
High Performance Data Transfer (HPDT)   44, 890
High Performance Routing (HPR)   641
HMAC   673
home agent   629
hop limit   563
hop-by-hop extension header   707, 714
host (program)   299
HTML   430, 441, 442
HTTP
  authentication   438
  basic authentication   438
  caching   433, 439
  communication   430
  cookie   431
  digest authentication   438
  entity   435
  expiration mechanism   439
  message format   434
  methods   436
  negotiation   438
  privacy exposure   431
  protocol parameters   433
  proxy   432, 684
  request message   435
  response message   435
  Secure Sockets Layer (SSL)   431

status code definitions   436
transaction   430
Uniform Resource Identifier (URI)   433
Uniform Resource Locator (URL)   433
Uniform Resource Name (URN)   433
validation mechanism   440
Web browser   430
Hybrid routing   144
hypertext document   430
Hypertext Markup Language (HTML)   427, 430, 441
Hypertext Transfer Protocol (HTTP)   430, 837

I
IAB   22
IASG Coordination Functional Group (ICFG)   61
IBGP   183
IBM Dynamic IP   308
IBM HTTP Server   429
IBM Web Application Servers   446
ICMP
  Destination Unreachable   198
  Redirect   198
  Source Quench   199
  Time Exceeded   199
ICMPv6   579
IDEA   664
IEEE 802.11   27
IEEE 802.x standards   30
IESG   21
IGMP   232
  local group database   234
IGP   139
IIOP   445
images   430
impersonation   655
IMS Socket Interface   277
InATMARP   45
InformRequest   539
initialization vector   676
initialization vector (IV)   663
Integrated Services
  admission control   783
  bucket capacity   787
  Controlled Load Service   786, 788
  filterspec   786
  flow   782, 784, 785, 789, 790

flow descriptor   786
flowspec   786
fluid model   790
guaranteed bandwidth   782
Guaranteed Service   786, 789
maximum packet size   787
minimum policed unit   787
packet classifier   783, 785
packet scheduler   783, 785
QoS   785
real-time service   784
real-time transmissions   782
reservation   790
resource reservation   784
Resource Reservation Protocol (RSVP)   785
Rspec   786, 788, 789, 790
service classes   786
service rate   790
token bucket filter   787, 790
token rate   787
traffic control   783
Tspec   787, 788, 790
videoconferencing   782
Integrated Services (IS)   782
integrity check   662, 670
integrity checking   656
Interior Gateway Protocols   139
International Data Encryption Algorithm (IDEA)   664
Internet   3, 12
internet   3, 4
Internet Architecture Board (IAB)   21, 22
Internet Assigned Numbers Authority (IANA)   21, 25, 84, 229, 402, 410, 703
Internet Control Message Protocol (ICMP)   102
  Address Mask Reply   112
  Address Mask Request   112
  Destination Unreachable   105
  Echo   104
  Echo Reply   104
  Information Reply   111
  Information Request   111
  Parameter Problem   110
  Path MTU Discovery   102
  Ping   112
  Redirect   107
  Router Advertisement   107
  Router Discovery   102
  router discovery protocol   108
  Router Solicitation   107
    Source Quench   106
    Time Exceeded   109
    Timestamp Reply   110
    Timestamp Request   110
Internet Control Message Protocol (ICMPv6)   598
  address resolution   581
  autoconfiguration   591
  DHCP server   591
  message format   579
  MTU   586
  multicast group   592
  Multicast Listener Discovery (MLD)   592
  multicast listener done message   595
  multicast listener report   594
  neighbor advertisement message   583
  neighbor cache   584
  neighbor discovery   581
  neighbor solicitation message   581, 591
  neighbor unreachability detection (NUD)   590
  prefix discovery   584
  redirect message   588
  router advertisement message   584, 591
  router discovery   584
  router solicitation message   587, 591
  stateful autoconfiguration   591, 598, 602
  stateless autoconfiguration   591, 598
  tentative address   591
Internet Engineering Steering Group (IESG)   21
Internet Engineering Task Force (IETF)   21, 22, 757
internet gateway   10
Internet Group Management Protocol   232
Internet Group Management Protocol (IGMP)   114, 232, 579
  Multicast Listener Discovery (MLD)   592
Internet Inter-ORB Protocol   445
internet layer   7
Internet Message Access Protocol Version 4 (IMAP4)   420
Internet Network Information Center (InterNIC)   66
Internet Protocol (IP)   7, 127
  care-of address   629
  datagram   90
  datagram header   90
  fragmentation   96
  High Performance Routing (HPR)   641
  IP prefix   88
  Loose Source Routing option   97
  Mobile IP   629

Mobile IP operation   631
Mobile IP Registration   634
MTU   96
private IP address   694
Record Route option   99
routing options   97
Strict Source Routing option   99
timestamp   100
TTL   93
tunneling   637
Internet protocol suite   3
Internet Service Providers (ISPs)   17
Internet Society (ISOC)   21
Internet2
    participants   18
Internet2 mission   18
internetwork   3
Internetwork Address Sub-Group (IASG)   60
internetwork layer protocol   58
internetworking   3, 12
IP   48
    protocol stack   121
    the Next Generation (IPng)   612
IP address   5
    exhaustion   83, 559
    host number   5
    network number   5
IP address exhaustion   559
IP Assist   891
IP datagram   90
    introduction   7
    TOS octet   805
IP datagram header   90
IP gateway   10
IP prefix   88
IP router   5
IP Security Architecture (IPSec)
    combinations of AH and ESP   715
    combined tunnel   718
    concepts   698
    cryptographic concepts   660
    differentiated services   819
    Diffie-Hellman algorithm   668
    Diffie-Hellman key exchange   669
    Digital Signature Algorithm   674
    encapsulation   700
    Hashed Message Authentication Code (HMAC)
    673
    HMAC   673

integrity check   819
IPSec module   700
iterated tunneling   715
modulus   667, 669
nested tunneling   715
private exponent   668
private key   668
processing sequence   716
public exponent   668
public key   668
RSA algorithm   667
SA bundle   699, 715
Security Association (SA)   699
Security Association Database (SAD)   700
Security Parameter Index (SPI)   699
Security Policy Database (SPD)   700
transform   698
transport adjacency   715, 718
tunnel mode   819
tunneling   700
IP stack   121
IP Version 6 (IPv6)   579, 581, 584, 591
    6Bone   612
    address space   572
    anycast address   578
    automatic tunneling   603
    configured tunneling   608
    datagram   561
    DNC extensions   595
    Domain Name Service   595
    dual stack   602
    extension headers   565
        authentication   571
        destination options   572
        ESP   572
        fragment   571
        hop-by-hop   567
        redid=ipv6ext.type-length-value (TLV) op-
        tion format   565
        routing   569
        type-length-value (TLV) option format   567
    flow   579
    flow labels   579
    format prefix   573
    fragment header   571
    header checksum   564
    header translation   610
    Hop-by-Hop header   567
    host   561

inverse DNS lookups   595
IPv4-compatible address   574
IPv4-mapped address   574
IPv6 addresses   572
link-local unicast address   574
mobility support   600
node   561
options   564
packet   561
   header format   561
packet sizes   564
router   561
site-local unicast address   574
solicited node multicast address   578
traffic class octet   805
transition from IPv4   601
tunneling   567, 603
   automatic   603
   configured   608
tunneling over IPv4 networks   603
VPN   757
IP6.INT domain   595
IPA   891
IP-FDDI   32
IPv6   757
IPX   701
ISAKMP/Oakley
   application-layer security   732
   authentication   667, 732, 733
   authentication key   729
   authentication mechanism   723, 732
   authentication method   726
   certificate   724, 730, 739
   certificate authority   730
   Certificate Payload   731
   certificate payload   730
   Certificate Request message   730
   certificates   733
   composite value   728
   cryptographic key   723
   cryptographic keys   727, 729, 733
   denial-of-service   722
   destination port   725
   Diffie-Hellman   724, 727, 728, 731, 732, 733,
   735, 738
   Diffie-Hellman algorithm   668
   Digital Signature   731
   digital signature   731
   Digital Signature Algorithm   674, 730

Digital Signature Standard   723
DOI   725, 727
Domain of Interpretation (DOI)   725, 727, 735
encryption   732
encryption algorithm   726
Encryption Bit   730
Encryption Flag   734
encryption key   729
exponent   727
Flags field   730
hash function   733
Hash Payload   734, 736, 737
identity   727
Identity Payload   731
identity payload   730
Identity Protect exchange   724
Initiator Cookie   725, 726, 728
Integrity Check Value (ICV)   737
ISAKMP Header   725, 726, 732, 734, 737
ISAKMP header   730
Key Exchange attribute   733
Key Exchange field   728, 733
Key Exchange Payload   735, 736
KEY_OAKLEY   726, 727
keying material   722, 729, 736, 738
LDAP   730
man-in-the-middle   722
master key   724
master secret   723
Message 1   724, 733, 738
Message 2   726, 736, 738
Message 3   727, 737
Message 4   728
Message 5   730
Message 6   731
Message ID   725, 726, 736, 737
Message ID field   732
Message-ID   734
nonce   727, 728, 733, 735, 736, 738
Nonce field   728
Nonce Payload   736
Oakley Main Mode   724, 732
Oakley Quick Mode   732, 733
Perfect Forward Secrecy (PFS)   722, 733
permanent identifier   723, 739
PFS   722, 733
Phase 1   723
Phase 2   723
pre-shared keys   723

private value   727, 728
Proposal Payload   725, 727, 735
protection suite   738
Protection Suites   725
PROTO_ISAKMP   725, 727
protocol code point   736
proxy negotiator   733
pseudo-random function   726, 734
public key   723, 724
public value   727, 728, 731, 732, 733, 735, 736,
738
remote access   738
remote host   723, 738
Responder Cookie   725, 726, 728
revised RSA public key authentication   728
RSA algorithm   667
RSA public key authentication   727
RSA public key encryption   723
secure DNS server   730
secure local cache   730
Security Association   727, 732
security association   723, 724
Security Association field   725, 727
Security Association Payload   735, 738
Security Payload   736
security protection suite   723
signature payload   730
SKEYID   724, 729, 731, 736
SKEYID_a   729, 734
SKEYID_d   729
SKEYID_e   729
SPI   731, 736, 738, 739
Transform Payload   726, 727, 735
ISDN
    Basic Rate Interface (BRI)   36
    B-channel   36
    D-channel   36
    Maximum-Transmission-Unit (MTU)   37
    NRZ encoding   37
    PPP encapsulation   36
    Primary Rate Interface (PRI)   36
ISO   12
ISO 3166   282
    print='the .arpa domain'.arpa   282
ISO 8859   404
ISP   720
iterated tunneling   715
ITU-T   12
IV   663

J
Java
    applet   442
    Java Server Pages (JSP)   443
    JavaScript   442
    Network Computer   443, 910
    servlet   443
    signed applets   442
Java Server Pages (JSP)   443
JavaBean   444
JavaScript   442
jitter   789
JPEG   409

K
KAS   760
KDBM   764
Kerberos Authentication Server (KAS)   760
Kerberos Database Manager (KDBM)   764
Kerberos Key Distribution Server (KKDS)   764
Kerberos System   331, 353, 383
    assumed goals
        accounting   758
        authentication   757
        authorization   758
    assumptions   758
    authentication process   759, 763
    authorization model   764
    database management   763
    naming   758
        instance name   759
        principal name   758
        realm name   759
key length   666
key management   664, 741, 777
key refresh   656
keyed algorithm   661
key-exchange   664
key-exchange algorithm   667
keying material   722, 729, 736, 738
keyspace   661
KKDS   764

L
LAN Channel Station (LCS) protocol   890
LAN emulation (LANE)   59
LAN Emulation Server   56
LAN replacement   48

LAN segment   121
LANE
   layer   60
latency   59
Layer 2 Forwarding (L2F)   768
Layer 2 Tunneling Protocol (L2TP)   768
   Access Concentrator   768
   LAC   768
   LNS   768
   NAS   769
   Network Access Server   769
   Network Server   768
   security features   772
   session   769
   tunnel   769
layers   5
LDAP   730
Lightweight Directory Access Protocol (LDAP)
   access rights   320
   authentication   329
   authorization   329
   binding   320
   communication protocol   319
   differentiated services   818
   directory   319
   Directory Access Protocol (DAP)   317
   directory entry   321
   Directory Information Tree (DIT)   321, 325
   distinguished name (DN)   321, 324
   encryption   320, 329
   functional model   327
   gateway process   319
   information model   322
   Kerberos   331
   LDAP client   319
   LDAP server   319, 326, 332
   Name Service Interface (NSI)   333
   naming model   324
   relative distinguished name (RDN)   321, 324
   schema   323
   schema-checking   323
   search   327
   search filter   321, 328
   security   329
   security methods   320
   Simple Authentication and Security Layer (SASL)   330
   syntax   322
   X.500   317, 333

   X/Open Directory Service (XDS)   333
link layer   7
link state   143
link state database   143
Link state routing   143
LIS   46
LocalDirector   832, 847
logical connection   204
Logical IP Subnetwork (LIS)   51
long-term key   674
Loose Source Routing   97
Lotus Domino   447
Lotus Notes   676
LSAP   30

M
MA   532
MAC   670, 673
mailbox   391
Management   535
Management Agent (MA)   532
Management Information Base
   IBM-specific part   531
   MIB-II group definition   528
   object definition example   527
   overview   528
Management Information Base (MIB)   527
man-in-the-middle   722
man-in-the-middle attack   675, 772
master key   754
master secret   723
Maximum Transmission Unit (MTU)   33, 96
   ICMPv6   586
   ISDN   37
   Path MTU Discovery   564
MD5   301, 308, 640, 672, 673
message authentication code   656
Message Authentication Code (MAC)   670, 754
message sequence number (IMAP4)   423
Metropolian Fiber Systems (MFS)   17
Metropolitan Area Ethernet (MAE)   17
MIB   527
Microsoft Internet Explorer   428
MILNET   13
Mobile IP   629, 701
   agent advertisement   632
   broadcast datagram   638
   registration   634

tunneling 637
Mobile IP operation 631
modular arithmetic 667
Mosaic 427
MOSPF 242
MOTIF 547
MOUNT command 376
MPC+ 891
MPEG 409
MPOA 58, 59, 62
    benefits 58
    client 59
    functional components 59
    functional group layer 60
    logical components 59
    operation 62
    server 59
MPTN 645
mrouted 238
MSDP 251
multicast 82
    addresses 229
    All hosts group 234
    DVMRP 238
    host group 82, 229
    Interconnecting multicast domains 251
    Multicast Backbone (MBONE) 254
    multicast group 592
    Multicast Listener Discovery (MLD) 592
    multicast listener done message 595
    multicast listener report 594
    RSVP 790
    server (MCS) 61
    TTL value 231
    VRRP 880
multicast address resolution server (MARS) 61
Multicast Backbone (MBONE) 254
Multicast delivery tree 235
Multicast OSPF 242
Multicast Source Discovery Protocol 251
multi-homed 74, 88, 89, 234
multi-homing 66
Multimedia 449
MultiNode Load Balancing (MNLB) 832, 854
    and Sysplex Distributor 861
MultiNode Load Balancing (MNLB)Forwarding
Agent 856
MultiNode Load Balancing (MNLB)Service Manager
855

MultiNode Load Balancing (MNLB)Workload Agent
856
Multi-Path Channel+ (MPC+) 44
Multiprotocol Encapsulation 52
Multiprotocol Transport Network Architecture
(MPTN)
    address mapping server node 648
    function compensation 646
    higher level functions 646
    MPTN gateway 648
    multicast server node 648
    Naming and addressing functions 646
    transport functions 646
    transport-layer protocol boundary (TLPB) 647
Multi-Purpose Internet Mail Extensions (MIME)
    Addressing mailboxes 397
    character sets 417
        ISO-8859 404
        US-ASCII 404
    Content Types 403
    encoded words 417
    encoding 410
    header fields 403
    overview 399
    Registering new MIME field values 402
    relationship to SMTP 388
mutable fields 702

N

name server
    delegation of authority 283
    zone data example 297
NAS 767
National Institute of Standards and Technology
(NIST) 672
National Science Foundation (NSF) 14
National Science Founfation Network (NFSNET)
14
National Security Agency (NSA) 672
NCF
    Lotus Domino 447
    WebSpere Application Server 446
    WebSphere Performance Pack 447
NCSA httpd 429
NE 532
neighbor discovery 581
nested tunneling 715
NetBIOS 701

Data Link Switching
    Switch-to-Switch Protocol   642
    datagram distributor (NBDD)   652
    end node   651
    name server (NBNS)   652
    scope   651
    service   650
Netscape Navigator   428
NETSTAT   554
Network Access Points (NAPs)   17
network access server   767
Network Address Translation (NAT)
    address pool   695
    FTP packet   696
    IP network design   696
    IPSec   698
    load balancer   884
    non-secure network   695
    private IP address   694
    secure network   695
    TCP packet   696
    timeout value   697
    translation mechanism   695
Network Computer   443, 910
Network Control Program (NCP)   12
Network Dispatcher   832
    Advisor   838, 843
    balancing   840
    cluster   835
    Dispatcher   833, 834, 841
    Executor   835, 837
    high availability   838
    Interactive Session Support   833
    load balancing   833
    load-monitoring service   833
    Manager   837
    metric   842
    metrics   837
    observer   834
    performance   837
    ping triangulation   842
    remote servers   841
    rules   840
    standby machine   839
    sticky option   840
    weights   842
        837
    Workload Manager (WLM)   845
Network Element (NE)   532

Network File System (NFS)
    Cache File System   381
    concept   375
    file system   380
    Lock Manager Protocol   380
    MOUNT command   376
        options   377
    Mount protocol   376
    Network Computer   910
    NFS protocol   379
    NFS URL   382
    Remote Procedure Call   375
Network Information System (NIS)   315
network interface layer   7
network layer   7
Network layer reachability information   182
network management
    object identifier   531
    SGMP   526
    Structure and Identification of Management In-
    formation   526
Network Management Application (NMA)   532
Network Management Station (NMS)   532
Network News Transfer Protocol   553
network object   288
Network Virtual Terminal (NVT)   338
news agent   554
news groups   553
NewsReader/2   554
Next Generation Internet (NGI) initiative   18
NIS   315
NIST   672
NLRI   182
NMA   532
NMS   532
NNTP   553
nonce   727, 728, 733, 735, 736, 738
non-repudiation   656, 662, 666
Not-So-Stubby area   172
NSA   672
NSFNET   3
nslookup   299
NVT   338

O

Oakley Main Mode   732
Oakley Quick Mode   732, 733
Object Management Group (OMG)   445

Object Request Broker (ORB)   444
offline model   421
OMPROUTE   892
one-time password   656
one-way function   669
online model   421
OPEN
    active/passive   219, 220
Open Look   547
Open Shortest Path First   158, 892
Open Software Foundation (OSF)   547
Open System Interconnection (OSI)   5
OS/2 Warp Server   299
OS/390   299
    Sysplex   826
    Workload Manager (WLM)   845
OSA-Express   891
OSF   547
OSI   526
OSI protocol stack   317
OSPF   229, 892
OSPF areas   159
OSPF virtual links   169
overlapping fragment attack   702
over-the-air protocol (OTA)   491

P

packet-filtering   680
packet-filtering router   680
Party   536
Path attributes   188
Path MTU Discovery   102
Perfect Forward Secrecy (PFS)   722, 733
per-session key   674
PFS   722, 733
PGP   664
physical layer   60
PIM   245
PIM dense mode   246
PIM sparse mode   247
PIM-DM   246
PIM-SM   247
Ping   112
point of presence   768
Pointer Queries   283
Point-to-Point Protocol (PPP)   767
    authentication   35
    IP Control Protocol (IPCP)   36

IPCP   36
L2TP tunnel   769
LCP   34
Link Control Protocol (LCP)   34
NCP   35
Network Control Protocol (NCP)   35
Synchronous Digital Hierarchy (SDH)   43
Synchronous Optical Network (SONET)   43
Synchronous Payload Envelope (SPE)   43
Van Jacobson header compression   36
Point-to-Point Tunneling Protocol (PPTP)   768
poison reverse   240
policy agent   894, 896
port   201
    ephemeral   202
    well-known   201
Portmap   379
Post Office Protocol   418
PostScript   387, 401, 409
prefix discovery   584
Pretty Good Privacy (PGP)   664
prime factor   674
prime number   666
principal identifier   758
private IP address   701
private key   664, 674
Project Athena   547
Protocol Independent Multicast   245
protocol number
    in an IPv6 header   562
protocol stack   5
protocol virtual LAN (PVLAN)   58
proxy   368, 680
proxy server   739
ProxyArec   314
    ProxyArec   314
proxy-ARP   79, 639
    Concept   118
pseudo-header
    IPv6   564
    TCP checksum   214
    UDP checksum   205
pseudo-random function   726
pseudorandom generator   677
public key   308, 664, 674, 675, 723, 754
public-key algorithm   666, 667
public-key algorithms   665
pull technology   489
push technology   489

PVC   46

Q

QoS
   best-effort   781
Quality of Service (QoS)   781
Queued Direct I/O   891
Queued Direct I/O (QDIO)   891

R

RADIUS   766
random function   676
random-number generator   676
RC2   678
RC4   678
Real-Time Transport Protocol   449
Reconfigure, DHCP   600
Record Route   99
refresh keys   733
Reliable transport protocol   176
remote access   738
remote access server (RAS)   659
Remote Authentication Dial In User Service   766
remote dial-in   765
Remote Exec Daemon (REXECD)   347
   principle   387
   REXEC command   348
   REXECD   348
Remote Forwarder Functional Group (RFFG)   62
remote host   721, 723
Remote Method Invocation (RMI)   445
Remote Printing (LPR/LPD)   547
Remote Procedure Call (RPC)   266
   Call Message   268
   concept   267
   Portmap   270
   Reply Message   269
   transport   268
Remote Shell Protocol (RSH)   347
rendezvous   247
rendezvous point (RP)   247
replay attack   655
replay protection   704
Request for Comments (RFC)
   Internet Standards Track   22
   purpose   22
   RFC 0768   204, 206
   RFC 0791   65

RFC 0792   102, 103
RFC 0793   206, 220
RFC 0821   387, 390, 398, 399
RFC 0822   387, 390, 398, 400, 407
RFC 0826   45, 49, 63, 114, 115
RFC 0854   347, 374
RFC 0855   347
RFC 0877   38
RFC 0894   30, 63
RFC 0903   120
RFC 0904   180
RFC 0906   122, 125
RFC 0919   65
RFC 0922   65, 82
RFC 0925   118
RFC 0934   401
RFC 0948   31, 32
RFC 0950   65, 102, 103
RFC 0951   22, 121, 124
RFC 0959   365
RFC 0974   387, 397, 398
RFC 0977   554
RFC 1001   650
RFC 1002   650
RFC 1010   31
RFC 1013   553
RFC 1027   118
RFC 1028   526
RFC 1032   299
RFC 1033   299
RFC 1034   24, 279, 289, 299
RFC 1035   24, 279, 289, 299
RFC 1042   31, 32, 52, 63
RFC 1049   387, 398, 401
RFC 1052   525, 544
RFC 1055   33, 63
RFC 1057   270
RFC 1058   145, 151, 152, 892
RFC 1075   238
RFC 1085   544
RFC 1101   299
RFC 1112   113
RFC 1122   25, 54
RFC 1123   25, 373, 388, 448
RFC 1138   448
RFC 1144   34, 36, 63
RFC 1148   448
RFC 1149   22
RFC 1155   526, 544

RFC 1156 526, 528
RFC 1157 526, 532, 533, 534, 544
RFC 1166 66, 67
RFC 1179 547
RFC 1183 300
RFC 1188 63
RFC 1191 102, 564, 612
RFC 1202 317
RFC 1206 25
RFC 1213 526, 528, 544
RFC 1215 544
RFC 1228 544
RFC 1239 544
RFC 1249 317
RFC 1256 102, 107
RFC 1288 554
RFC 1293 45
RFC 1325 25
RFC 1327 448
RFC 1349 65, 92, 820
RFC 1350 371, 373, 374
RFC 1351 544
RFC 1352 544
RFC 1356 38, 63
RFC 1390 32
RFC 1408 341
RFC 1437 22
RFC 1441 535, 544
RFC 1466 86
RFC 1480 282, 300
RFC 1483 52, 63
RFC 1487 317, 335
RFC 1492 766, 778
RFC 1494 400
RFC 1496 400
RFC 1510 757, 778
RFC 1518 87, 88
RFC 1518 - 1520 87
RFC 1519 87
RFC 1520 87, 89
RFC 1542 22, 121
RFC 1577 45, 59
RFC 1579 686, 778
RFC 1583 892
RFC 1584 242
RFC 1591 300
RFC 1592 273, 544
RFC 1594 25
RFC 1618 36, 63

RFC 1619 43, 63
RFC 1631 779
RFC 1633 786, 820
RFC 1652 388, 398
RFC 1661 34, 63
RFC 1662 34, 63
RFC 1700 25, 35, 38, 46, 63, 229
RFC 1706 289, 300
RFC 1723 153, 892
RFC 1733 421
RFC 1734 419
RFC 1748 544
RFC 1752 560, 612
RFC 1755 54, 63
RFC 1771 180, 185
RFC 1777 317, 335
RFC 1778 318, 335
RFC 1779 318, 335
RFC 1795 63, 642
RFC 1809 579
RFC 1812 25, 158
RFC 1813 375, 383
RFC 1823 318, 335
RFC 1825 707
RFC 1826 705
RFC 1827 709, 710, 712
RFC 1869 388, 392
RFC 1870 389
RFC 1883 560, 612
RFC 1886 595, 596, 612
RFC 1889 449
RFC 1890 449
RFC 1901 536, 545
RFC 1904 545
RFC 1905 535, 537, 545
RFC 1906 535, 545
RFC 1907 536, 545
RFC 1909 536, 545
RFC 1910 536, 545
RFC 1918 86
RFC 1928 740, 741, 778
RFC 1929 740, 778
RFC 1939 418
RFC 1945 429, 447
RFC 1959 318, 335
RFC 1960 318, 335
RFC 1961 740, 778
RFC 1970 580
RFC 1995 300, 301

RFC 1996	300, 301		RFC 2251	318, 320, 335
RFC 2002	629, 634, 636, 637, 640		RFC 2252	318, 335
RFC 2003	701, 778		RFC 2253	318, 335
RFC 2011	528, 545		RFC 2254	318, 335
RFC 2012	528, 545		RFC 2255	318, 331, 335
RFC 2013	528, 545		RFC 2256	318, 336
RFC 2026	21		RFC 2283	253
RFC 2045	388, 400, 418		RFC 2313	779
RFC 2046	388, 400, 418		RFC 2314	779
RFC 2047	388, 400, 416, 418		RFC 2315	779
RFC 2048	388, 400, 402, 410, 418		RFC 2328	158, 163
RFC 2049	388, 400, 418		RFC 2338	875, 881
RFC 2050	86		RFC 2341	768
RFC 2054	383		RFC 2347	371, 373
RFC 2055	383		RFC 2355	346, 347
RFC 2058	766		RFC 2362	246
RFC 2060	420		RFC 2373	572, 578, 612
RFC 2065	311		RFC 2374	574, 612
RFC 2080	155		RFC 2375	578, 612
RFC 2090	375		RFC 2390	45, 63
RFC 2104	778		RFC 2396	433, 447
RFC 2109	447		RFC 240	779
RFC 2131	126		RFC 2400	25, 48, 63
RFC 2132	121, 125, 126, 129, 133		RFC 2401	779
RFC 2136	299, 300, 301, 310, 312		RFC 2402	702, 707
RFC 2137	311		RFC 2403	779
RFC 2138	766, 778		RFC 2404	779
RFC 2156	400, 418, 448		RFC 2405	779
RFC 2159	418		RFC 2406	709, 714, 779
RFC 2181	25		RFC 2407	779
RFC 2183	418		RFC 2408	779
RFC 2185	601, 612		RFC 2409	779
RFC 2203	381, 383		RFC 2410	779
RFC 2205	790, 798, 803, 820		RFC 2411	779
RFC 2206	820		RFC 2412	779
RFC 2207	820		RFC 2427	40, 63
RFC 2208	820		RFC 2460	560, 579, 612
RFC 2209	820		RFC 2461	579, 580, 590, 612
RFC 2210	820		RFC 2462	591, 592, 612
RFC 2211	786, 820		RFC 2463	579, 580, 612
RFC 2212	786, 790, 820		RFC 2474	820
RFC 2222	330, 335		RFC 2535	300
RFC 2223	22		RFC 2570	542, 545
RFC 2224	382, 383		RFC 2571	542, 545
RFC 2225	45, 48, 52, 63		RFC 2572	542, 545
RFC 2228	365		RFC 2573	542, 545
RFC 2231	418		RFC 2574	542, 545
RFC 2236	113, 231		RFC 2575	542, 545
RFC 2246	755		RFC 2578	535, 545

RFC 2579   535, 545
RFC 2580   536, 545
RFC 2616   429, 431, 433, 434, 435, 440, 448
RFC 2617   438, 448
RFC 2661   768, 779
RFC 2664   25
RFC 2742   545
RFC 2800   25
RFC 2822   433, 448
RFC 2845   311
RFC 2888   772, 779
RFC 2893   601, 612
RFC 2909   253
RFC 2988   821
RFC 3007   299, 300, 301
RFC 3010   375, 383
RFC 3022   694, 779
RFC 922   82
state   23
    draft standard   23
    experimental   23
    historic   23
    informational   23
    proposed standard   23
    standard   23
status   24
    elective   24
    limited use   24
    not recommended   24
    recommended   24
    required   24
Réseaux IP Européens (RIPE)   83
Resource Reservation Protocol (RSVP)   579, 785, 790
    authorization   793
    common header   798
    distinct reservation   796
    Filterspec   801
    filterspec   792, 796
    Fixed-Filter style   797
    flow   790, 791
    flow descriptor   792
    Flowspec   800
    flowspec   792
    message objects   798
    multicast address   790
    path   791
    path definition   791
    path message   792

PathTear message   796
policy control   793
QoS   790, 792, 797
QoS reservation   793, 795
receiver   791
reservation   790
reservation message   792
reservation request   795
reservation style   796
ResvTear message   796
router   791
routing table   791
sender   791
shared reservation   796
Shared-Explicit style   797
soft-state   795
teardown request   796
Tspec   801
Wildcard-Filter style   797
restricted cipher   661
Reverse Address Resolution Protocol (RARP)
    operation code field   120
    packet format   120
    reply   120
    request   120
Reverse path forwarding algorithm   236
REXX Sockets   278
RIP   145, 892
    packet format   146
RIP Version 1   152
RIP Version 2   153
RIPng for IPv6   155
route redistribution   170
Route Server Functional Group (RSFG)   61
route summarization   173
routed   199
router   5, 10, 526
    default router   876
    router discovery protocol   108
    RSVP   791, 795
    soft-state   795
    virtual router   876, 878
Router Discovery   102
router discovery   584
router discovery protocol   108
routing   74
    direct   75
    indirect   75
    partial routing information   74

routing extension header   707, 714
Routing Information Protocol   145
Routing Protocols   137
routing table   76
    RSVP   791
routing table explosion   87
RPC
    External Data Representation (XDR)   267
RPCGEN   271
RSA   301, 308, 666, 667
RSA algorithm   667
RSH   347
RTCP   449
RTE   156
RTP   449
    Control Protocol   449
    header format   451

S

SA bundle   699, 718
secret, shared   667
secure DNS server   730
Secure Electronic Tranactions (SET)   671
    acquirer   773
    cardholder   773
    certificate authority   774
    issuer   773
    key management   777
    merchant   773
    payment gateway   773
    transactions   774
Secure Hash Algorithm 1 (SHA-1)   672
secure local cache   730
Secure Sockets Layer (SSL)   747
    certificate   753
    change cipher spec protocol   751
    compability   749
    connection state   751
    generate encryption key   753
    handshake phase   749
    Handshake Protocol   748, 751
    HTTP   431
    master key   754
    Message Authentication Code (MAC)   754
    public key   754
    Record Layer   751
    Record Protocol   748, 754
    security issues   749

session   750
session state   750
states   750
symmetric-key   754
TCP port 443   749
Security Association Database (SAD)   700
security exposures   656
security ID cards   684
Security Parameter Index (SPI)   699, 703, 709
security policy   659
Security Policy Database (SPD)   700
security solutions   656, 658
Serial Line IP (SLIP)   767
    addressing
        33
    implementations   34
    overview   33
    Van Jacobson header compression   34
server, LDAP   326
server-side includes   443
Service Level Agreement (SLA)   805
servlet   443
Session EJBs   446
SET   676
SGMP   526
SHA-1   672
shared keys   666
shared secret   667, 669, 672, 673
Shortest-Path First algorithm   143
Simple Gateway Monitoring Protocol (SGMP)   526
Simple Internet Transition (SIT)   601
Simple Mail Transfer Protocol (SMTP)
    destination address   394
    Domain Name System   387, 396
        MX Resource Records   397
    mail exchange protocol   392
    mail header format   390
        MIME extensions   403
        using non-ASCII characters   416
    mailbox   391
    mailbox address   394
    National Language Support   387
    non-textual data   387
    overview   387
    scenario   395
Simple Network Management Protocol (SNMP)
    community name   534
    components   533
    MA   532

Management Agent (MA) 532
message format 535
NE 532
Network Element (NE) 532
Network Management Application (NMA) 532
Network Management Station (NMS) 532
NMA 532
NMS 532
protocol data unit 534
SKEYID 729, 736
SKEYID_a 729, 734
SKEYID_d 729
SKEYID_e 729
SMI 526
SMTP Service Extensions 388, 392
SNA 642
    LCP 34
    Link Control Protocol (LCP) 34
    NCP 35
    Network Control Protocol (NCP) 35
SNMP 535
SNMPv2 535
SNMPv2 Entity 536
SNMPv2 Party 536
socket
    address 203
    association 203
    CICS Socket Interface 277
    conversation 203
    datagram type 263, 266
    definition 202
    half-association 203
    IMS Socket Interface 277
    interface 202
    raw type 263, 266
    REXX Sockets 278
    stream type 263, 266
    system call 265
    transport address 203
SOCKS
    authentication methods 741
    circuit-level gateway 739
    encapsulation method 743
    encryption standards 741
    firewall 688, 739
    key management systems 741
    method options 742
    request detail message 744
    SOCKS server 739

SOCKSified client 740
SOCKSified TCP/IP stack 740
SOCKSv4 740
SOCKSv5 740
TCP connection 742
tunneling protocols 741
UDP connection 746
UDP port 746
UDP relay server 746
UDP support 741
version identifier 742
source-routing bridges 526
SPF algorithm 159
Split horizon 150
Split horizon with poison reverse 151
spoofing attack 772
Standard Protocol Numbers (STD) 24
    STD 01 25, 34
    STD 02 25, 93, 344, 402
    STD 03 25, 298
    STD 04 25
    STD 05 65, 102
    STD 06 204
    STD 07 206
    STD 08 337
    STD 09 365
    STD 10 387, 399
    STD 11 387
    STD 13 279, 418
    STD 14 387
    STD 33 371
    STD 51 34
Static routing 140
stream algorithm 663
Strict Source Routing 99
strong cryptography 715
Structure and Identification of Management Information (SMI) 526
stub areas 172
subagent 274
subnet mask 70
    determining 74
subnet number 70
subnets 69
subnetting
    static 71
    variable length 71
Sub-Network Access Protocol (SNAP) 30
Subnetwork Access Protocol (SNAP) 38, 40

Sun HotJava browser   428
supernetting   87
SVC   46
symmetric algorithm   663, 664
symmetric-key   754
Synchronous Digital Hierarchy (SDH)   43
Synchronous Optical Network (SONET)   43
Synchronous Payload Envelope (SPE)   43
Sysplex   826
Sysplex Distributor   832, 849, 894
    advantages   895
    and Cisco MNLB   861
    distributing stack   894
    load balancing rules   851
    using QoS information   894
Systems Network Architecture (SNA)   5

T

TACACS   766
TACACS+   767
tapping the wire   655
TCP
    SOCKSified stack   740
TCP/IP
    layers   5
TCP/IP protocol suite   3
TELNET   337
    basic commands   344
    command structure   342
    full-screen capability   341
    Network Computer   910
    Network Virtual Terminal   338
    Network Virtual Terminal (NVT)   338
    NVT   338
    NVT printer   339
    option negotiation   343
    principle of operation   337
    proxy server   685
Telnet   6
Terminal Access Controller Access Control System   766
TGS   761
The Internet   13
    Acceptable Use Policy (AUP)   16
    Advance Network and Services (ANS)   16
    ANS CO+RE   16
    bridged segments   526
    Commercial Internet Exchange (CIX)   16

    Commercial use of   16
    source-routing   526
Ticket-Granting Server (TGS)   761
timestamp   666
time-to-live
    DDNS   310
    IP   93
    IPSec Authentication Header (AH)   702
    IPv6 hop limit   563
    NetBIOS name   653
    RSVP   799
TN3270   344
Token-Ring LAN   32
topology database   163
transform   698
Transmission Control Protocol (TCP)   837
    acknowledgment   217
    application programming interface   220
    characteristics   207
    checksum   214
    congestion avoidance   223
    congestion control algorithm   221
    connection establishment   219
    definition   206
    fast retransmit   225
    flow control   208
    full duplex   208
    half-association   204
    logical connection   208
    multiplexing   208
    push   208
    reliability   208
    retransmission   217
    segment   207, 212
        format   213
        mapped on IP datagrams   220
        options   215
    slow start   222
    socket   203
    stream data transfer   207
    three-way handshake   220
    variable timeout interval   219
    window   211
Transmission Control Protocol/Internet Protocol (TCP/IP)   3
transparent subnetting   118
transport adjacency   715, 718
transport layer   6
transport-layer protocol boundary (TLPB)   647

Triggered updates   152
triple-DES   663, 677
Trivial File Transfer Protocol (TFTP)
    BOOTP   122
    data modes   374
    NetASCII   374
    Network Computer   911
    overview   371
    packet types   373
    protocol   372
    Sorcerer's Apprentice Syndrome   373
    TFTP RFCs   372
trust chain   676
tunnel   769
    tunnel mode   819
tunneling   603, 700, 741
two-way random number handshake   656
Type of Service (TOS)   702
type-length-value (TLV)   567

U

UMOUNT command   378
unicast
    address   80
Uniform Resource Identifier (URI)   433
Uniform Resource Locator (URL)   433
Uniform Resource Name (URN)   433
University Corporation for Advanced Internet Development (UCAID)   19
Usenet News   553
User Datagram Protocol (UDP)   204, 837
    application programming interface   206
    checksum   205
    datagram format   205
    port   205

V

value, hash   672
Version 2 of the Simple Network Management Protocol (SNMPv2)   535
video   430
VIPA
    cold standby   894
    Dynamic VIPA   894
    hot standby   894
    overview   893
    takeover   893
Virtual Connection VC   49

virtual reality   430
virtual router   876, 878
Virtual Router Redundancy Protocol (VRRP)
    authentication   882
    default router   876
    election protocol   877
    IP Address Owner   877
    multicast address   880
    Primary IP Address   877
    priority   881
    Virtual Router   877, 878
    Virtual Router Backup   877
    Virtual Router Identifier   877
    Virtual Router Master   877
    VRRP Router   877
virus   655
VRML   430

W

Web browser   427
Web server   429
WebSpere Application Server   446
WebSphere Edge Server   447
well-known port   10, 201
well-known services   270, 397
window
    applied to TCP   211
    principle   208, 211
Windows Internet Name Service   653
WINS   653
Winsock interface   263
Wireless application environment (WAE)   496
Wireless Application Protocol (WAP)   27, 479
Wireless Session Protocol (WSP)   498
Wireless Telephony Application (WTA)   496, 498
Wireless Transaction Protocol (WTP)   511
WLM   894
World Wide Web
    Apache   429
    CERN   429
    client/server processing model   428
    Common Gateway Interface (CGI)   442
    FTP client   427
    HTML interpreter   427
    HTTP client   427
    IBM Web Application Servers   446
    Java Server Pages (JSP)   443
    Lotus Domino   447

Microsoft Internet Information Server API (ISA-PI)   443
Mosaic   427
NCSA httpd   429
Netscape Navigator   428
Netscape Server API (NSAPI)   443
Network News Transfer Protocol   553
NNTP   553
NNTP client   427
POP client   427
server-side includes   443
servlet   443
SMTP client   427
Sun HotJava browser   428
Uniform Resource Identifier (URI)   433
Uniform Resource Locator (URL)   433
Uniform Resource Name (URN)   433
Web browser   427, 430
Web server   429
WebSpere Application Server   446
WebSphere Performance Pack   447
World Wide Web (WWW)   3, 427
WWW   427

X.500   317, 333, 352
X.509   676
X.509 certificates   755
XCF   894
XML   441
XNS   145
XTACACS   767

X

X Window   547
concept   548
Mosaic   427
Network Computer   911
protocol   553
used TCP ports   553
widget   551
X Client   549
X Protocol   550
X Server   549
X Toolkit   550
X Window Manager   550
Xlib   550
X.25
Call Request packet   38
Call User Data (CUD)   38
Network Layer Protocol Identifier (NLPID)   38
Organizationally Unique Identifier (OUI)   40
Protocol Data Unit (PDU)   38
Protocol Identifier (PID)   40
Subnetwork Access Protocol (SNAP)   38
Subsequent Protocol Identifier (SPI)   38
virtual circuits   38

IBM Redbooks review

Your feedback is valued by the Redbook authors. In particular we are interested in situations where a Redbook "made the difference" in a task or problem you encountered. Using one of the following methods, **please review the Redbook, addressing value, subject matter, structure, depth and quality as appropriate.**

- Use the online **Contact us** review redbook form found at ibm.com/redbooks
- Fax this form to: USA International Access Code + 1 845 432 8264
- Send your comments in an Internet note to redbook@us.ibm.com

Document Number **Redbook Title**	GG24-3376-06 TCP/IP Tutorial and Technical Overview
Review	
What other subjects would you like to see IBM Redbooks address?	
Please rate your overall satisfaction:	O Very Good O Good O Average O Poor
Please identify yourself as belonging to one of the following groups:	O Customer O Business Partner O Solution Developer O IBM, Lotus or Tivoli Employee O None of the above
Your email address: The data you provide here may be used to provide you with information from IBM or our business partners about our products, services or activities.	O Please do not use the information collected here for future marketing or promotional contacts or other communications beyond the scope of this transaction.
Questions about IBM's privacy policy?	The following link explains how we protect your personal information. ibm.com/privacy/yourprivacy/

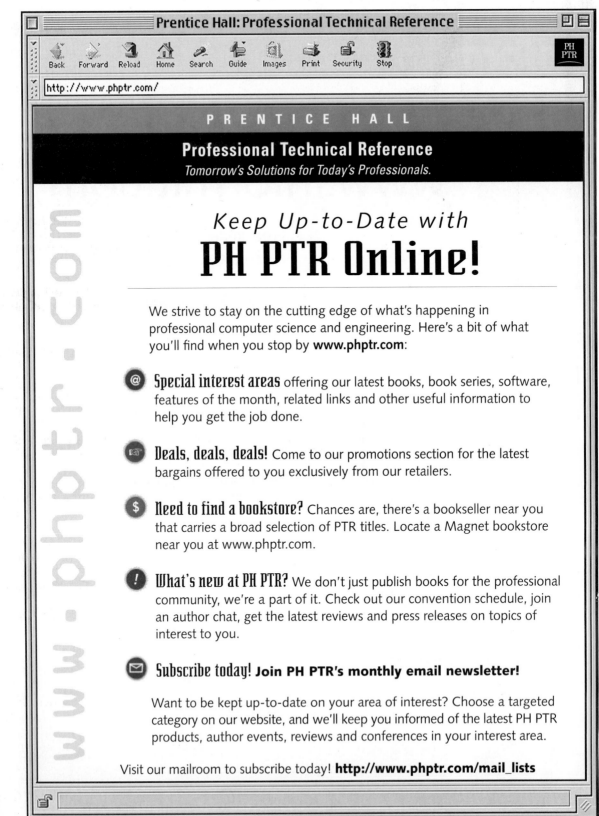